WORLD MINERAL TRENDS
AND U.S. SUPPLY PROBLEMS

Research Paper R-20

WORLD MINERAL TRENDS AND U.S. SUPPLY PROBLEMS

Leonard L. Fischman
Project Director

RESOURCES FOR THE FUTURE / WASHINGTON, D.C.

Resources for the Future is a nonprofit organization for research and education in the development, conservation, and use of natural resources and the improvement of the quality of the environment. It was established in 1952 with the cooperation of the Ford Foundation. Grants for research are accepted from government and private sources only if they meet the conditions of a policy established by the Board of Directors of Resources for the Future. The policy states that RFF shall be solely responsible for the conduct of the research and free to make the research results available to the public. Part of the work of Resources for the Future is carried out by its resident staff; part is supported by grants to universities and other nonprofit organizations. Unless otherwise stated, interpretations and conclusions in RFF publications are those of the authors; the organization takes responsibility for the selection of significant subjects for study, the competence of the researchers, and their freedom of inquiry.

Research Papers are studies and conference reports published by Resources for the Future from the authors' typescripts. The accuracy of the material is the responsibility of the authors and the material is not given the usual editorial review by RFF. The Research Paper series is intended to provide inexpensive and prompt distribution of research that is likely to have a shorter shelf life or to reach a smaller audience than RFF books.

Library of Congress Catalog Card Number 80-8025

ISBN 0-8018-2491-5

Copyright © 1980 by Resources for the Future, Inc.

Distributed by The Johns Hopkins University Press,
  Baltimore, Maryland 21218

Manufactured in the United States of America

Published December 1980. $15.00.

v

TABLE OF CONTENTS

TABLES

Page

Page

Page

Page

FIGURES

Page

FOREWORD

Considerations of mineral supply have played only a small role in U.S. foreign policy since World War II, despite substantial reliance on imports for a number of minerals. It was implicitly assumed that investment in mining capacity would be sufficient to meet world demand and that U.S. industry would be able to compete freely for mineral output.

The presumed validity of these assumptions began to fade as one country after another nationalized minerals properties and revised the terms of mining concessions in the late 1960s. The actions of the Organization of Petroleum Exporting Countries in the early 1970s lengthened the shadow over mineral supplies, raising as it did the possibility of similar actions on the part of nonfuel mineral suppliers. While, indeed, the bauxite and copper industries have seen such attempts, this fear has remained largely unrealized. It has, however, precipitated new interest in the adequacy of mineral supplies for U.S. consumers and a certain amount of concern.

Resources for the Future has a history of research in nonfuel minerals that goes back to the early 1960s and the work of Orris Herfindahl. It has supported and published such widely accessible works as Minerals and Men (2nd ed., 1974) by James McDivitt and Gerald Manners, and a major review of the copper industry (Raymond F. Mikesell, The World Copper Industry, 1979) as well as reports on materials substitutability and the economics of various mineral industries.

This work, then, follows in a long line of minerals studies by RFF. The authors have brought together a vast amount of material on seven major nonfuel minerals and present it in a form that can be used by a wide range of analysts. They identify long-term potential supply and price problems--information that will be highly useful in evaluating policy on stockpiles, tariffs, or mineral substitution--and suggest areas in which short-term supply problems may arise.

Their analysis of expected supplies, demand, and prices will be of interest to anyone concerned with mineral commodities--government planners in the United States and abroad, commodities dealers, producers, and industrial consumers. The identification of potential trouble spots and of the implications of supply disruptions in major producing countries will be particularly useful for those engaged in public or private strategic planning.

The authors depart from the usual approach for such studies and present data for each of the main feedstock forms of the minerals studied, allowing a clearer view of an industry as a whole. And it is in assembling the whole picture that a major virtue of this work lies.

This book puts the current concerns about mineral supplies into perspective. In doing so, the authors make a substantial contribution to the kind of understanding of U.S. mineral supply problems that is necessary for intelligent policy decisions.

November 1980   Milton Russell
                                                 Director
                                                 Center for Energy
                                                 Policy Research

PREFACE

In December 1977, at the direction of the President, an interagency
review of federal nonfuel minerals policy was initiated under the direction
of a Policy Coordinating Committee (PCC) chaired by the secretary of the
interior. A project management plan divided the review into two principal
phases: Phase I was to identify, within nine areas, those problems requiring policy attention; Phase II would identify the principal issues. A
certain amount of overlap was provided among the nine problem areas, each
of which was to be explored under the guidance of a particular agency.

The study from which this report is taken was performed by Resources
for the Future under contract with the Office of Science and Technology in
the Executive Office of the President, which served as the channel for
making the findings available to the PCC staff.[*] The study addresses
itself to the first area, "major mineral supply problems," which is the
broadest in scope and thus has the greatest amount of overlap with the
other areas. This same subject was addressed within the federal government
by a Mineral Review Committee, chaired by the then associate director of
the U.S. Bureau of Mines; the RFF effort was intended to provide an additional, and outside, viewpoint.

It would have been impossible to complete the original study in the
limited time available without the assistance of several other senior
contributors--John E. Tilton, of The Pennsylvania State University;
Jacob J. Kaplan, consulting economist; and John J. Schanz, Jr., at
Resources for the Future. I apologize for any misguided alterations or
reinterpretations I may have made of their original drafts. The work
also depended critically on the efforts of a number of contract and staff

---

[*]The full study, under the title, Major Mineral Supply Problems, is
available from the National Technical Information Service as document
PB 80-117674.

research personnel, of whom John E. Jankowski, Jr., made the largest
and most continuing contribution, particularly to this version.

For this research report, principal credit lies with Ruth Haas,
RFF staff editor, who did most of the work necessary to produce a ration-
ally reorganized, condensed, and improved version of the original document.
Careful reviews by Milton Russell, Emery N. Castle, Kent Price, and
Ronald G. Ridker led to further critical improvements. To all of these
helpers, both named and unnamed, I wish to express my appreciation.

October 1980   Leonard L. Fischman

WORLD MINERAL TRENDS
AND U.S. SUPPLY PROBLEMS

INTRODUCTION

Concern over availability of raw materials in the United States is a recurring issue, as a wealth of literature testifies. This work had its genesis in this concern and an attempt of the federal government to identify major mineral supply problems. The question is, of course, what constitutes "major" and what is a "problem." And, if one wants to anticipate problems, there is also the question of how far ahead one can predict with any degree of confidence. Within the limits of the specifications set for the study, we have used long-range projections both to identify long-range supply problems and to provide a framework for evaluating shorter term contingencies. The study considers seven metals--manganese, chromium, cobalt, aluminum, copper, lead, and zinc--in each of their major forms of use.

A by-product of this approach was the generation of the world mineral trend series that are included here for their reference value. This approach also generated certain conceptualizations and interpretations that occasionally depart from the conventional. Moreover, it was our conclusion that prior projections of world mineral consumption have been almost uniformly too high--principally because of overestimation of long-term growth rates in gross economic output of the principal consuming countries.

The discussion that follows indicates the methodology used, its rationale, and some of the findings that evolved. The principal conclusion is that the United States faces only one type of "major mineral supply problem": an undue vulnerability, for some minerals, to contingencies that might either seriously disrupt supplies or cause a sharp upward movement of prices, with serious economic impacts. Among the minerals studied, this is particularly true for chromium, in the form in which it is consumed by the steel industry (principally ferrochromium). The degree of seriousness is less clear for the other minerals, either because there is a limited likelihood of a contingency or because the damage that would result is limited.

This is not meant to imply that minor problems should be dismissed: they deserve attention and study even if no action is warranted. This also applies to situations that on analysis turn out to be nonproblems, since it may be important to avoid ill-conceived action.

Trends

It is in the industrialized countries that the bulk of industrial consumption of metals takes place. World demand and supply projections for the commodity forms of the minerals studied here were derived from individual projections for these countries and from the supply potential among their principal suppliers. Price projections were based on demand and supply prospects in the groups of countries accounting for the bulk of each commodity's world trade.

The long-range supply problems that were of interest were not expected to take the form of mineral exhaustion within the period under consideration (up to the year 2000). What was more important was the possibility that demand and supply would not grow in tandem--more specifically, that past and prospective periods of overinvestment or underinvestment would lead to surpluses or shortages of mining or processing capacity. Thus, in terms of physical flows, or price, or both, problems would be created either for the producers of mineral commodities or for their consumers. Data and projections appropriate to this kind of evaluation need to avoid year-to-year sensitivity (they must smooth out business cycle fluctuations), but must reflect intermediate-term variations in demand and capacity variations (long cycles). Five-year moving-average trends were calculated for historical data periods, reflecting typical business-cycle periodicity, and a conceptually analogous smoothing was aimed at for the projections. More elaborate statistical "filtering" methods were rejected as infeasible and straight-line trends were rejected as inappropriate.

Demand

Among the commodities studied, cobalt metal is the least directly related to gross economic output. We expect its consumption in the United

States to increase by about 70 percent between 1975 and 2000 and in the world as a whole by about 60 percent. We project U.S. consumption of chromite to decline, although at a lesser rate than in the recent past, while world consumption will increase by about 70 percent. Ferrochromium consumption is expected to increase by about 60 percent in the United States, but more than double in Japan and more than quadruple in the Soviet Union. Ferromanganese consumption in the United States is projected to increase only slightly over the quarter century, while world consumption will double. U.S. consumption of manganese ore is projected to decline until about 1990, then rise again slightly. All of these projections refer to trend values for five-year intervals over 1975-2000.

Among the nonferrous metals, aluminum will remain the fastest growing, although its expected tripling over 1975-2000 contrasts with the mere fifteen-year period which the last tripling required. This refers to the world as a whole; for the United States, we foresee less than a doubling between 1975 and 2000. An increasing proportion of U.S. aluminum consumption is projected to come from imports and from scrap; an increasing proportion of U.S. alumina feed will also come from imports rather than from domestic refining of imported and domestic bauxite.

U.S. consumption of copper metal is projected to rise somewhat from its recent plateau, while world consumption doubles, but the United States will remain by far the world's largest copper consumer. An increasing proportion of U.S. copper will probably be imported in refined form, thus dampening the increase in consumption of blister copper which will also tend to be held down by increased resort to electrowinning. Lead consumption is projected to increase in the United States at the rate of about 1.7 percent per year and in the world as a whole only slightly more rapidly. An increasing proportion of the world's lead supply will probably come from scrap rather than ore, but in the United States we expect the scrap proportion to decline for a while before starting to climb again. World zinc consumption is projected to increase by nearly 90 percent, but U.S. consumption by only about 35 percent. The USSR alone among industrialized countries seems likely to have large gains in zinc consumption and will probably soon surpass the United States as the world's leading consumer.

Supply

There is hardly any question at all about the adequacy of world
cobalt resources, but actual supply depends upon uncertain by-product
relationships and the timely construction of processing capacity; we
have assumed that the desired amounts (at recent price levels) will be
forthcoming. Chromium also presents no basic resource problem, and it
looks as if present tightness in mining capacity will diminish over the
balance of the century. There may be some difficulties, however, in
maintaining an adequate supply of refractory-type ore, owing to concentration in the Philippines. Ferrochromium capacity is likely to become
increasingly concentrated in southern Africa. There are differences of
opinion with regard to manganese ore, though the world supply potential
seems to us ample. World ferromanganese capacity, on the other hand,
seems to be moving toward an untenably small reserve margin.

The prospect--especially nearer term--is for tight supplies of bauxite
on the world market. An even tighter world situation appears to be developing for alumina, but, owing to intracompany and bilateral relationships,
relatively little of the impact from such a shortfall seems likely to
fall upon the United States and other leading Western consumers. Aluminum
smelting capacity also promises to be tight in relation to demand, but
less so than alumina capacity.

Copper mining capacity in market-oriented countries appears to be
sufficient to maintain a thin margin over ore consumption among the leading
consumers. It is our feeling that the United States will maintain more
copper smelting capacity than is generally expected and by the end of the
century will thus be importing ore out of necessity, rather than for cost
advantage. The United States is likely still to be the world's leading
copper refiner at the end of the century, and over most of the intervening
period world refining capacity is likely to remain ample.

Because both metals occur largely in complex ores, lead and zinc
mining (including concentrating) capacity is hard to define. In relation
to consumption, however, supplies of zinc concentrates are likely to be
much more ample than those of lead--in fact in relative surplus. On a
world-total basis, refined lead capacity seems likely to fall short of
desired growth in consumption; among current trading countries, on the

other hand, the prospect is for an adequate capacity margin in the aggregate, though the United States will probably find it increasingly necessary
(rather than merely economically desirable) to resort to refined lead
imports. World zinc smelting capacity promises to be in fairly good
balance with requirements. The United States will have to import at least
a third of its refined zinc, but this represents a stabilization of proportions, in contrast with the decline of recent years.

Prices

Since it is feedstock for U.S. industry that is important--from the
point of view of both the industrial consumer and the competitive U.S.
producer--a special effort was made to determine the extent of correspondence between "market" prices and the delivered costs of the particular
mineral commodity to U.S. industrial consumers as well as the unit sales
value realized by competitive U.S. producers. It was also necessary to
consider whether the price of a metallic mineral at only one stage of
processing was essentially the sum of mining and processing costs up to
that stage or the price left after further processing costs were subtracted
from the independently determined price of the next most advanced form.
The answer is rarely clear and seems to vary from commodity to commodity,
from place to place, and from time to time.

No attempt was made to conduct the evaluation in terms of "real"
prices. In part this is because of the dichotomy of concern between
producers and consumers: what is real to the former may be irrelevant
to the latter. More important, however, while mineral prices are necessarily influenced by changes in the general price level, as well as by
international exchange rates, they appear to be far more an independent
function of comparative changes in mineral demand and mineral production
capacity. Even if it is assumed that long-run mineral prices may be
related in some way to costs, it is impossible to identify any one price
series than can adequately reflect changing monetary influences on a
changing mix of factor costs and world suppliers. We have concluded,
therefore, that the task of mineral price projection is not much aided
by utilizing real prices. Conceptually, the price forecasts in this

study are in terms of current dollars and may be subjected to whatever deflation is appropriate to the particular analytical application.

The art of long-term mineral price forecasting is just that--an art-- with little consensus on how to go about it. Even the relationship of long-term to short-term prices is in doubt: is the former an abstraction, to be merely distilled from the latter, or do short-term changes fluctuate around a path that long-term influences independently determine? We have made the latter assumption. This leaves us with the abstraction of a long-term market--an anomaly both in theory and in practice. How this is worked out is discussed in part III of this study. Part III also contains further discussion of the price deflation question.

We found that cobalt prices have reflected the monopolistic nature of the supply structure; we believe that the sharp increases in 1978-79 pushed the price about as high as is currently feasible and that there may be some future mild declines. Chromite prices have recently softened, after a sharp rise in 1975, but we still expect them to double over the 1975-2000 period. Ferrochromium prices seem likely to rise less rapidly than those of chromite and end up at near stability. Both for manganese ore and for ferromanganese, fluctuating trends seem to be in store, with the ferroalloy even experiencing a slight price decline before the end of the 1980s, after having had an accelerated rise in the immediate future. Late-century prices for both cobalt and manganese could be substantially (but not necessarily) lowered as the result of ocean-nodule mining.

Aluminum prices have been rising quite rapidly and, at least until about 1985, promise to continue doing so. Costs of alumina to U.S. smelters seem likely to quadruple over the 1975-2000 period, but bauxite costs should cease their rapid increases after the mid-1980s. London Metal Exchange copper prices will probably continue a firm (but not steep) upward trend; the cost of copper ore should rise slightly more rapidly. A combination of decreasing excess capacity for refined lead, relative stringency in ore supply, and relatively declining scrap contribution in key countries seems likely to bring about steeply rising lead prices for the balance of the century. Future rates of price increase for zinc should be much milder.

Possible Problems

The study discusses both the kinds of problems associated with persistent conditions, or trends, and those arising out of large deviations from trend or other transitory occurrences. For convenience, the former are referred to as "long-term problems" and the latter as "short-term contingencies."

Long-term Problems

Possible types of persistent, or trend, problems are (1) monopolistic control of prices, (2) long-term exposure to short-term supply contingencies, (3) declining U.S. processing capacity, (4) steep price rises, (5) depressed prices, (6) price instability, and (7) physical supply stringency.

Cobalt is typical of minerals for which monopoly control can persist, in that its sources are geographically concentrated, it is used in relatively small quantities, and it is relatively price inelastic, owing to a combination of high utility in its applications and small cost in relation to the end products in which it is employed. Even a commodity with such characteristics is not totally devoid of price elasticity, however, and it appears that recent cobalt price increases have been large enough and abrupt enough to have stimulated a significant amount of movement toward conservation and substitution. Between this and the stimulation of probable new production (in the United States, for example), prices have probably found at least an interim ceiling.

Chromium exemplifies the problem of long-term exposure to supply contingencies, which occurs when there is physical concentration of supply in areas (in these cases, South Africa) that are unusually subject to politically motivated supply interruptions. Because of the continuing possibility of an international embargo, the risk in the case of chromium (and probably platinum as well) is great enough, for a critical enough mineral, that the problem may be termed "major." For manganese, it is probably less than major, since there is a broader choice of supply sources.

Absolute or relative <u>declines in U.S. processing capacity</u> (examples
are zinc, alumina, ferrochromium) may be a problem because of increasing
supply vulnerability, because of the loss of domestic income and employment, or some combination thereof, but are not likely to constitute a
major problem. They may, in fact, be part of a solution to another kind
of problem, namely, environmental pollution. In many cases, maintenance
of current processing capacity would only transform the nature of the
problem to one of adequate ore feedstock. So far as income and employment
are concerned, the real problem may be the lack of adequate regional and
national adjustment mechanisms.

Aluminum and lead look as if they are about to exemplify the problem
of <u>persistent steep price rises</u>. That such price changes are a real
problem is evidenced by the amount of defensive activity, in the form of
conservation and substitution, they usually engender. To qualify as a
major problem, however, they would have to imply significant curtailment
of real income, either through real increases in underlying costs or
through the draining off of national income to pay for higher priced
imports. However, none of the metals covered (in fact even all of them
together) is a large enough component of national output to have a significant overall income effect.

<u>Flat price trends</u> for ferromanganese and ferrochromium could be a
problem for U.S. ferroalloy producers, especially as the costs of the
relevant ores will probably continue rising. Yet in both cases much
more of the cost of production appears to be in the smelting than in the
raw material, so that energy and foreign competition rather than ore
costs would be the critical factors. We have assumed that U.S. ferrochromium capacity will be further reduced and that ferromanganese capacity
will be no more than maintained. A competitive problem for the ferroalloy
industry does not equate to a major problem for the country as a whole,
however, since employment in ferroalloy manufacture is fairly low and
since the weak price trends are a corresponding benefit to ferroalloy
consumers.

<u>Persistent price instability</u> has been a characteristic of copper,
lead, and zinc, and there is a chance it might also come to characterize
aluminum. This instability has such costs attached to it as are associated

with (1) ill-timed decisions to expand capacity and (2) frequent start-up
and close-down of operations or parts of operations. These costs are
significant enough that instability may qualify at times as a major problem.

Protracted periods of physical supply stringency could occur for some
of the mineral commodities, but in no case are such persistent shortages
likely to be large enough to constitute a major national problem.

Short-term Contingencies

Most supply contingencies fall within the bounds of normal business
risks, not requiring governmental attention. Of the kind that may have
policy significance, four varieties may be distinguished: (1) actions
by foreign governments or other entities intended to disrupt supplies or
raise prices, (2) actions or events that might incidentally disrupt supplies, (3) generalized demand surges, and (4) natural disasters.

Cobalt is subject to contingencies of both the first and the second
variety: there is enough monopoly power in the industry to manipulate
prices, and there is a significant chance that further events in Zaire
or surrounding countries might substantially interrupt either cobalt
production or its transportation. Our judgment is that the possibility
of a short-term concerted run-up in prices continues but will become
increasingly constrained. On the other hand, civil or military conflict
in the producing areas is judged to have a rather high possibility of
reoccurring, with the effect of interrupting a fifth or more of the total
cobalt supply for a number of months and a smaller proportion for even
longer. The resultant impact would be serious, but probably not major.

Chromium is also subject to contingencies of both varieties, the
first deriving from a possible UN embargo against South Africa in which
there is U.S. cooperation, and the second deriving from political and
racial conflicts in South Africa or Namibia. It is to ferrochromium
rather than chromite supply that the important contingent risks attach,
since there are ample reserve stocks of the ore in the United States, but
little of the ferroalloy, and reserve smelting capacity outside of southern
Africa is quite limited. The potential supply interruption and consequent

impact are significant enough that this contingency seems to qualify as a major problem.

It is also to the ferroalloy rather than the ore that significant contingency risks for manganese apply. The most serious contingency is that of U.S. participation in a UN embargo against South Africa, which, directly or indirectly, could deprive the United States for a time of as much as a third of its ferromanganese supply. Unless the embargo were imposed, however, during a period of already high economic activity, there is enough possibility for supply adaptation that the impact would be less than major.

For aluminum, copper, lead, and zinc, the largest risk in each case is the possibility of a concerted world economic boom, which would probably cause a surge in demand for the metals that would exceed processing capacity. For all of the metals except zinc, the shortage could be significant and could persist over a fairly extended period. National impact, however, would probably not be of major proportions.

Measurement of Mineral Commodities

Conventionally, a country's consumption of a metallic mineral is measured in terms of the amount of metal entering into "end use." The measurement may be either inclusive or exclusive of recycled "new," or industrial, scrap, but either way tends to be a more or less abstract aggregation of metal entering into end use through a variety of routes (e.g., chemical as well as metallic uses, remelted as well as re-refined scrap). The conventional approach tends to be particularly abstract in terms of its treatment of sources of supply, identifying a particular country, for example, as a source of the U.S. supply of a metal regardless of whether it ships the metal to the United States in refined form, in intermediate form, or as the content of concentrate or ore. This is a useful kind of accounting for many purposes, including, to some extent, an evaluation of U.S. supply problems. It is reasoned here, however, that a supply problem has to do with the availability and price of a specific feedstock for U.S. industry. It was decided, therefore, that the study should investigate the demand and supply situation for each

important form of the metallic minerals under study. In all, nineteen
forms of the seven minerals were differentiated, and as far as possible,
separate historical series and projections were arrived at for each.

It was necessary also to establish a cutoff point. Metallic minerals
enter into the U.S. supply stream, not only as ore and smelted and refined
metal, but as fabricated metal and in end products. A full consumption
accounting would consider all these forms, including the additional amounts
of metal not entering into final consumption but dissipated as non-
recoverable waste somewhere along the process stream. Since this is a
"mineral" supply study, however, the decision was taken not to go beyond
each mineral's metallic stage or equivalent, on the grounds that beyond
this "fully extracted" form, it was no longer a mineral.

The choice of a dividing line involves cutting rather arbitrarily
through some technological and institutional inconveniences. Only to
a limited extent do metals emerge from the minerals industry, as we have
defined it, in an actually pure form. Much of the aluminum, copper, lead,
and zinc, for example, leaves the "refining" industry deliberately alloyed,
and so does almost all of the chromium and manganese intended for use
in steelmaking. Metallic scrap, which seems like a post-minerals item,
can be used as an alternative for virgin material in both smelting and
refining. And much of the very same kinds of scrap that go to metal
refineries are also used directly by foundries, mills, and other fabricators for the same kinds of applications for which they purchase "refined"
metal. In this study, we have generally considered the smelters, refiners,
and remelters of secondary aluminum and lead to be part of the minerals
industry, on the ground that the material they turn out is generally
either indistinguishable from or competitive with the primary "refined"
product. We have made a contrary decision for copper remelt (mostly
brass and bronze ingot) plants and zinc remelt plants, partly on statistical grounds and partly on the basis that such plants serve a limited
segment of industrial consumers, some of whom (or many of the competitors
of whom) maintain similar recovery facilities within their own establish-
ments. The scrap itself, however, is counted as a mineral commodity no
matter who consumes it.

In general, the forms of each of the seven minerals which have been separately evaluated in this study are as follows:

Cobalt: Metal only (shot, granules, cathodes, powder).

Chromium: (1) Ores formerly classified either as metallurgical or as chemical grades;

(2) Refractory-grade ores;

(3) Ferrochromium (whether high- or low-carbon).

Manganese: (1) Ores classified either as manganese ore (35%+ Mn) or as ferruginous manganese ore (10-35% Mn);

(2) Ferromanganese, whether high-, medium-, or low-carbon.

Aluminum: (1) Guianan-type, or trihydrate, bauxite (gibbsite);

(2) Caribbean-type, or mixed, bauxite;

(3) Alumina (calcined);

(4) Aluminum metal (ingot or equivalent), primary or secondary;

(5) Aluminum-base scrap.

Copper: (1) Ores, concentrates, precipitates;

(2) Blister copper, both primary and secondary;

(3) Refined (including fire-refined), both primary and secondary, but excluding remelt;

(4) Copper-base scrap.

Lead: (1) Ores and concentrates;

(2) Refined, both primary and secondary; including lead recovered as contents of alloys;

(3) Lead-base scrap.

Zinc: (1) Ores and concentrates;

(2) Metal, both primary and secondary, but excluding remelt.

For convenience, ores, concentrates, precipitates, and even leach liquids are generally collectively referred to in the report simply as "ores."

Cobalt

We confined the analysis to cobalt metal because of the limited interest in other forms of cobalt consumption in the United States at

present. This may not hold in the future. Since 1977, there has been
a domestic cobalt refinery operating on imported copper-nickel and nickel
matte, and a second one has been under development; hence cobalt-bearing
matte may become an important feedstock. There is also the possibility
of a significant revival of domestic ore production, as well as increased
recovery of cobalt from scrap, thus adding cobalt-bearing concentrates
and scrap as feedstocks worth considering.

U.S. firms may also recover large quantities of cobalt from deep-sea
nodules. The recovery, however, would presumably be as metal, and such
a potential supply source for metal is taken into account in connection
with the long-term outlook.

Chromium

Although chromium is found in various minerals, the ore known as
chromite is the sole commercial source. Historically, chromite has been
classified into three general grades: metallurgical, chemical, and refractory. During the past decade, however, technological advance has
led to considerable interchangeability among the various grades, particularly in respect to the chemical grade, which can be used in all three
consuming industries. The principal substitution has been of chemical
for metallurgical, however, and we therefore drop the distinction between
these two. Refractory (high aluminum) ore has tended to remain paramount
in its specialized market.

Chromium enters into steelmaking, its major application, in the
form of an alloy with iron, ferrochromium. There are three significant
types of this ferroalloy: "high carbon," "low carbon," and ferrochromium
silicon. Owing to the almost complete adoption by now of the AOD (argon-
oxygen decarburization) process for alloy steelmaking, the previous
requirement for large amounts of low-carbon ferrochromium has given way
to one of a quarter or less of the total demand. Looking to the future,
it is now reasonable to consider all forms of ferrochromium, for the
bulk of its uses, as substantially one commodity, valued essentially for
its chromium content. Other specifications, such as accompanying carbon
and silicon, may be treated as subsidiary characteristics, reflected in
price differentials.

Thus, the preferred form for measuring the consumption and supply of ferrochromium seems to be the chromium content, regardless of proportions of accompanying carbon. Similarly, for chromite, the preferred measurement seems to be the chromic acid (or chromium--the two are in exact ratio) content.

As a practical matter, it is necessary, in particular contexts, to deviate from this standard. World data do not permit a breakdown of ore consumption by types; all chromium ores are therefore combined in our world statistics and projections. Price series, on the other hand, are specific to particular types, so the report considers both specific series as well as a composite comparable to the supply and consumption data. Where it is separable, the consumption of ferrochromium silicon is omitted from consideration, as a distinct item that is of small importance.

Manganese

For its domestic statistics, the U.S. Bureau of Mines has for many years classified those ores with a natural manganese content of 35 percent or over as manganese ores, those with 10 to 35 percent manganese as ferruginous manganese ores, and those below 10 percent as iron ores. However, nearly all manganese ores are upgraded before shipment, thus obscuring the significance of the natural-content measure. Moreover, different countries use different cutoff points, and for statistical purposes the Bureau is generally constrained to accept whatever cutoff point each country designates. U.S. import statistics adhere to a cutoff point of 35 percent, but this presumably refers to upgraded ore as delivered.

The analysis in this report must also make do with the kinds of statistics that are available. In general, the aim has been to combine, in terms of manganese content, the data for manganese ore as such and ferruginous manganese ore. Both of these are potential feed for the ferroalloy industry, thus providing alternative modes of eventually introducing manganese into steelmaking furnaces.

As a practical matter, nearly all the manganese consumed for metallurgical purposes is now via ferromanganese as such. The lower grade (ferruginous) manganese ores may be converted into spiegeleisen--a highly manganiferous pig iron--but this once-important form has fallen into

relative insignificance. A more important current form of manganese ore
conversion is silicomanganese. Its use in steelmaking is functionally
distinguishable, but since this form provides only about 10 percent of
the total manganese and is not significantly imported, we have omitted
considering it. Though there are three distinguishable grades of ferromanganese—high-, medium-, and low-carbon—the choice of type for use
in steelmaking appears to be determined as much by cost as by technical
considerations. Thus, in this study we have treated the three grades
in combination.

Aluminum

Our analyses for aluminum generally attempt to distinguish among
three different types of aluminum ores, an intermediate extraction product
(alumina), refined aluminum metal, and aluminum-base scrap. Each of
these has a fairly distinct industrial market, while subvariants of each
are relatively interchangeable.

Although the element aluminum is one of the most ubiquitous in the
earth's crust, and is present in many forms, an earthy substance known as
bauxite promises to continue for some time as the near-exclusive commercial
source. Owing to the difficulty of finding separate data on the non-
metallurgical grades of bauxite and to their small proportion in total
consumption, we do not, for the most part, attempt to distinguish them
in the analysis. We do, on the other hand, divide bauxite in general into
three types, each of which requires a relatively specialized variant of
the prevailing (Bayer) process for "refining" bauxite into alumina. The
types are gibbsite, or trihydrate; boehmite, or monohydrate; and "mixed";
but only the first and last of these are significant as U.S. industrial
feedstock.

In contrast with bauxite, alumina is predominantly a standard material, usable in any aluminum "smelter" (in the aluminum industry, the
operation that transforms alumina to aluminum metal). The type of alumina
used for this purpose is referred to as "calcined." Other types serve as
raw material principally for abrasives or for refractories; it is not
usually possible to separate them statistically from the prevailing,
metallurgical type, but their amounts are relatively small.

The variants of aluminum metal also are not worth distinguishing. Usually produced first as almost pure aluminum (molten or pig) and then sold to consumers in one or another standard alloy, the output mix is easily adjusted to the current market. Even the fact of primary (virgin) versus secondary origin is mostly irrelevant, primary and secondary product frequently coming jointly out of the same aluminum smelters.

Aluminum scrap per se is a different commodity, since it has its own set of consumers. Among these are both "primary" and secondary aluminum smelters and aluminum remelters. Aluminum scrap is also consumed directly by foundries and other aluminum fabricators, bur except for a few measurements for a few countries, these amounts are either not separable or are omitted; where we have a choice we include them. Also, there is a sufficient amount of substitutability between new and old (postconsumption) aluminum scrap that the two are considered here as a single commodity, even in the rare cases where statistical data permit the distinction. A melted, but otherwise unprocessed, form of scrap known as "sweated pig" is sometimes also included in the aluminum scrap statistics.

Copper

The important forms of copper feedstock for U.S. industry comprise: (1) what is fed into smelters, (2) what is fed into copper refineries, and (3) what is fed into "brass mills," foundries, and other processers or fabricators of copper metal. There is nothing very uniform about any of these three categories. Even the one presumed common denominator--the element copper--is sometimes estimated on a total-content basis, sometimes on a recoverable-content basis, and sometimes inclusive of incidental alloying elements. Once again, it is necessary to find a reasonable compromise between concept and available statistics.

What goes into a copper smelter is usually referred to as "copper ore," but is more likely actually to be a copper concentrate, the result of a preliminary beneficiating operation conducted at a copper "mill." It may also be a "precipitate" (sometimes called "cement copper"), obtained by the deposition of copper onto "tin" cans or other ferrous scrap, after acid leaching of newly mined ore, of mine waste, or of in situ deposits.

There are other variants as well, and the practical connotation is that
an "ore" is almost anything that gets shipped to smelters from a mining
location. In fact, U.S. statistics on mine output even include the copper
content of the small amounts of materials that bypass copper smelters
altogether. The latter ends up mostly as "electrowon" copper. The relative amount of such copper is growing, but it was not considered important
enough as yet to warrant adjusting the ore statistics in this report.

Smelting copper is ordinarily a two-stage operation, resulting in
the output of copper "matte" (30 to 45 percent copper) at the first stage
and "blister" copper (98+ percent) at the second. There have been some
imports as well as domestic flows of matte, but on the whole, smelting
operations are integrated and the amounts of matte therefore too small
in the total copper picture to warrant separate treatment. Blister copper,
on the other hand, is an important article of commerce and serves as the
feed for both electrolytic and fire refining. Some of it is made from
scrap, and from the standpoint of refinery feed, there is no need to
identify these quantities. However, secondary blister is less than fully
accounted for in the total blister series.

Refined copper may come either out of an electrolytic or a fire-
refining facility; the two types of copper are sufficiently interchangeable
that they may be considered a single commodity. It is of little consequence whether the refined copper has a virgin- or secondary-material
origin. Prices differ for various qualities or forms of refined copper,
but they tend to adjust to one another. So-called "remelt" copper is
not included in the "refined" category for purposes of this report, since
it represents scrap recovery mostly in the form of alloys, in which refined
copper may be an alternative input. All copper scrap, on the other hand,
has been considered as a single commodity, whether new or old and whether
pure copper or copper-base alloy, though it is measured uniformly, to
the extent possible, in terms of copper content.

Lead

As with copper, any lead-rich material shipped from mine site to
smelter qualifies as a lead "ore," whether it comes directly from the
mine or from a concentrator and whether the origin is a lead or lead-zinc

ore or some other kind of mineral. "Base bullion" is the smelted lead product ready for refining, but since, unlike blister copper, very little of it figures as nonintegrated feedstock, this report omits considering it and jumps to refined lead. There are various grades of the latter, with differentiations that are important to some users. However, the various types appear to constitute part of a single market, the more specialized varieties being characterized by price differentials. The really important definitional question has to do with antimonial lead, which is of secondary origin and has long been the type predominantly used in storage batteries. This material has been directly competitive with newly refined lead and is still competitive enough that it is treated here as a variant of the same commodity, even though changing battery specifications are beginning to undermine the rationale for such aggregation. Lead scrap, since it consists predominantly of antimonial (old-battery) lead, is subject to the same qualification, though it, too, is handled in this report as if all varieties were still essentially a single commodity.

Zinc

Zinc also comes from a variety of ores, its mine production being measured by the zinc content of what is shipped to smelters. As with lead, the intermediate products of smelting are unimportant as articles of commerce, so the analysis here jumps from ore to refined. The various grades of refined zinc largely represent differences in purity and are all regarded here as variants of a single commodity. As with copper, "remelt" zinc is usually an alloy, suitable only for part of the zinc market, and is therefore not included in the refined zinc total. Zinc-based scrap accounts only for about 10 percent of the U.S. zinc supply and is therefore also omitted from consideration. Something like half the secondary zinc is actually recovered in the United States as part of remelt copper alloy.

Structure of this Report

This report extracts four kinds of information from the original, more detailed, study: consumption, supply, prices, and problems. The consumption section gives historical details on a country-by-country basis, followed by trend projections. The supply section first seeks to establish which international flows are significant for world market purposes, as well as which supply sources (including domestic and secondary) have been most significant for the United States; it then projects world and trading world supply, largely on the basis of the evidence offered by publicized expansion plans. The price section seeks to judge future price trends from the juxtaposition of the consumption and supply projections; the conclusions reached, however, rest more upon changes in the degree of surplus or tightness over time than on static balances. Finally, the problem section uses the price conclusions, particularly, to derive qualitative conclusions about long-run problems. It also identifies supply situations which in the nearer term future predispose toward contingency risks.

PART I: WORLD CONSUMPTION

Chapter 1

HISTORICAL PATTERNS 1950-77

General Characteristics

This chapter gives historical world consumption patterns for most of the commodity variants identified in the introduction over a period ranging from the 1950s to 1977. In general, what is shown is apparent consumption, which is obtained by using data on domestic production in conjunction with that on stock changes and foreign trade. Not all of this information is available in all cases, or when it is, is not equally comprehensive. Series on apparent consumption tend to be more accurate than those on "actual" or surveyed consumption because consumption surveys tend to fall short of complete coverage. The principal world consumers listed for each commodity include the centrally planned economies wherever relevant and possible, but in some cases the data had to be confined to the market economy countries.[1]

---

[1]A detailed discussion of the sources used, the problems encountered, and the solutions devised in organizing and presenting these data can be found in the larger report from which this work was drawn: Leonard L. Fischman, Jacob J. Kaplan, John J. Schanz, Jr., John E. Tilton, John E. Jankowski, Jr., and Barry Silverman, "Major Mineral Supply Problems," a study prepared for the Office of Science and Technology Policy, Executive Office of the President, September 1979, Chapter 6, appendix. Available from the National Technical Information Service, Springfield, Va., PB No. 80-117674.

Rates of Growth

Growth patterns for individual country/commodity combinations are discussed later in this chapter. Here we examine the commodities on a global basis.

Aluminum, as is well known, is the fastest growing commodity, with a growth rate in world consumption since the mid-1950s of something over 8 percent per year. Less well known is the fact that consumption of ferro-chromium, though subject to considerable fluctuation, has been growing since 1960 at an average rate of nearly 7 percent. Cobalt, also subject to considerable fluctuation, is not far behind at an average rate of about 6 percent.

Lead has had one of the slowest growth rates—about 2 1/2 percent per year since the mid-1950s. Ferromanganese, reflecting both the relative maturity and the relative instability of the world's steel industry, has had a greatly fluctuating growth rate, which has surpassed that of lead by very little on average. Zinc and copper have both been expanding fairly evenly, at about 4 1/2 percent. All of these latter rates are below the estimated world real economic growth rate over a similar period of about 5 percent.

The rate of world growth for each of the seven metals and the consistency with which that rate is maintained may be seen in figures 1-1 through 1-7. Each figure shows both annual apparent consumption estimates and a trend line, arrived at as a five-year moving average. All of the figures have been drawn on roughly proportional scales in order to provide a reliable impression of comparative growth rates.

Aside from the differences in growth rates, perhaps the most striking phenomenon is the relative persistence of trend for most of the metals, though there is also a noticeable tendency toward slowdown in the mid-1970s. Also quite noticeable are the generally severe fluctuations that occurred in just about every case throughout the 1970s, which are clearly connected with the large general fluctuations in the economies of the principal industrial countries. There was also considerable fluctuation in the late 1950s and early 1960s.

The comparative susceptibility of each of the metals to short-term fluctuations shows up in figures 1-8 through 1-14, which portray the percentage deviations around the moving-average trend. These also have been plotted on comparable scales and reveal the relatively greater volatility of the ferroalloying metals than of the nonferrous metals. Contrary to the impression that might be conveyed by their price behavior, copper and lead have had particularly stable consumption patterns; zinc also was rather stable until recently, and aluminum was stable over most of the period covered. One cannot avoid drawing at least the tentative inference that it is speculation on the commodity exchanges, rather than fluctuations in demand, that mostly accounts for short-term price volatility, since it is the traded metals (copper, lead, zinc) that experience such volatility despite their more closely channeled demand patterns. Intermittent shortage and surplus may still be the basic generator of price changes for such metals, but commodity trading magnifies them.

It is probably also true that the largest-volume metals have the firmest base of continuing demand—particularly on a worldwide basis—and thus are the more resistant to large percentage fluctuations. This hypothesis finds some confirmation in the fact that, among the ferroalloying elements, ferromanganese, which is intimately bound up with basic steel output, is more stable in its consumption pattern than either ferrochromium or cobalt.

The similarity of annual deviation patterns for the various metals confirms the pervasive importance of business cycles in short-term fluctuations. Figures 1-8 through 1-14 also reveal interesting differences among the metals. For example, all of them exhibit a dip in the early 1970s and a boom in 1973-74, but the nonferrous metals all had their low point in 1971 and the ferroalloying elements a year later. Similarly, the nonferrous metals hit their high in 1973 and the steel-related metals in 1974.

On a world basis, one may expect fair consistency—at least in trend—between the consumption of refined metals and the consumption of the ores and intermediates (alumina and blister copper) required for their output. Timing differences may make for discrepancies in the deviations from trend, and there will be other differences for some metals, owing to the role of scrap. The most important discrepancies between metal consumption and ore and intermediate consumption, however, relate to the differing geographical locations of the successive mineral stages. Some general aspects of the shifting processing geography are mentioned in the section that follows.

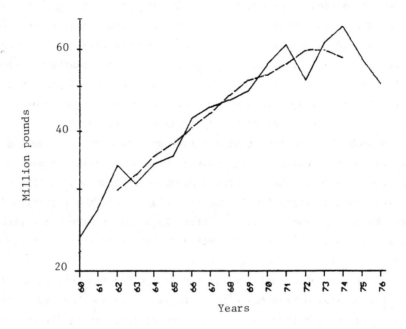

Figure 1-1. World Apparent Consumption of Cobalt Metal, 1960–1976, Annually and Five-Year Moving-Average Trend

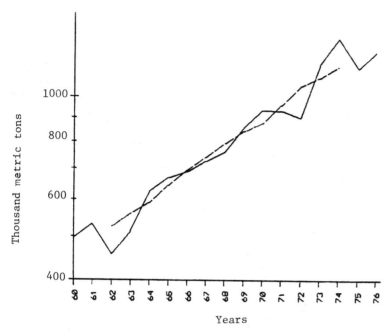

Figure 1-2.   World Apparent Consumption of Ferrochromium, 1960–1976,
Annually and Five-Year Moving-Average Trend

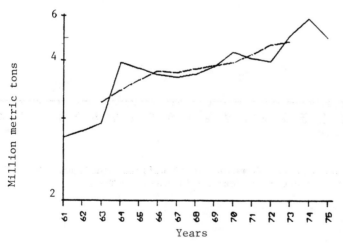

Figure 1-3.   World Apparent Consumption of Ferromanganese, 1961–1975,
Annually and Five-Year Moving-Average Trend

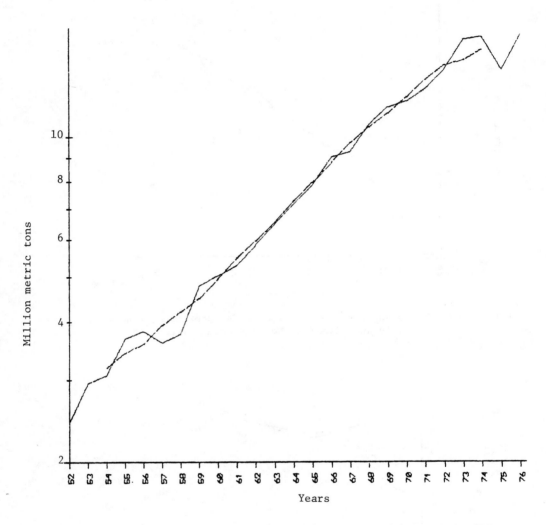

Figure 1-4. World Apparent Consumption of Refined Aluminum, 1952-1976, Annually and Five-Year Moving-Average Trend

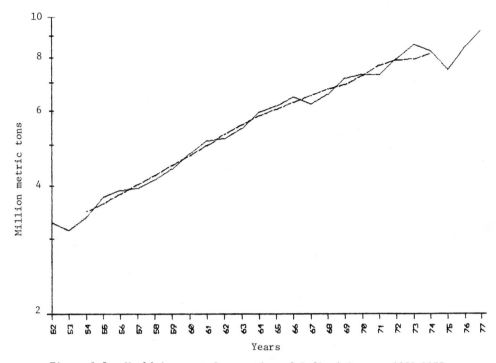

Figure 1-5. World Apparent Consumption of Refined Copper, 1952–1977,
           Annually and Five-Year Moving-Average Trend

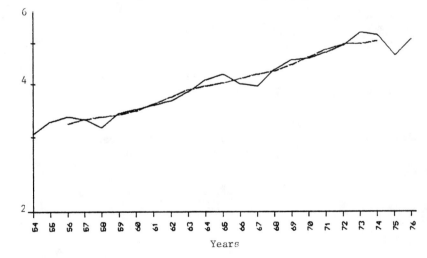

Figure 1-6. World Apparent Consumption of Lead Metal, 1954–1976,
           Annually and Five-Year Moving-Average Trend

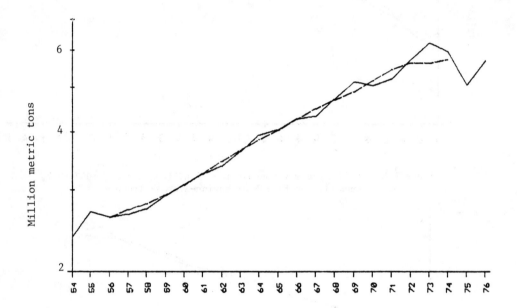

Figure 1-7.   World Apparent Consumption of Refined Zinc, 1954-1976,
Annually and Five-Year Moving-Average Trend

31

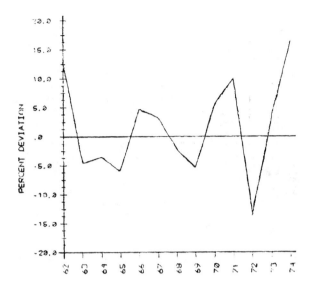

Figure 1-8. Annual Fluctuations Around Five-Year Moving-Average
Trend in World Consumption of Cobalt, 1962-1974

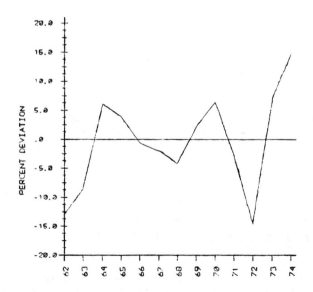

Figure 1-9. Annual Fluctuations Around Five-Year Moving-Average
Trend in World Consumption of Ferrochromium, 1962-1974

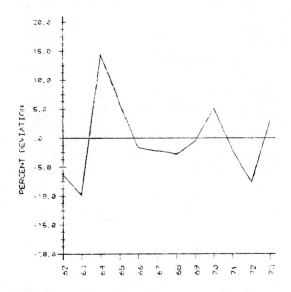

Figure 1-10.　Annual Fluctuations Around Five-Year Moving Average
Trend in World Consumption of Ferromanganese, 1962-1973

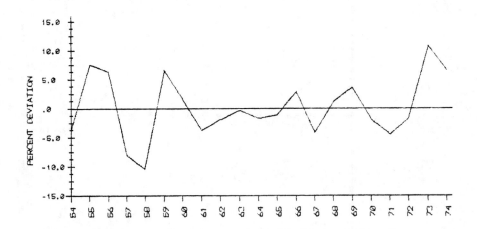

Figure 1-11.　Annual Fluctuations Around Five-Year Moving-Average
Trend in World Consumption of Refined Aluminum,
1954-1974

33

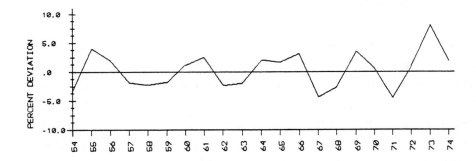

Figure 1-12.   Annual Fluctuations Around Five-Year Moving-Average
Trend in World Consumption of Refined Copper, 1954-1974

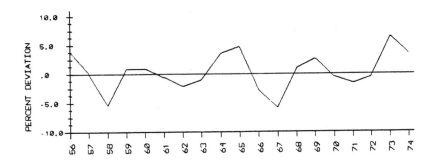

Figure 1-13.   Annual Fluctuations Around Five-Year Moving-Average
Trend in World Consumption of Lead Metal, 1956-1974

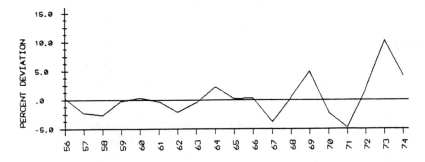

Figure 1-14.   Annual Fluctuations Around Five-Year Moving-Average
Trend in World Consumption of Refined Zinc, 1956-1974

Degree of Concentration

The spread of world industrialization is reflected in the decreasing concentration of world metal consumption. In 1952, for example, almost three-fourths of the world's refined aluminum consumption was in three countries--the United States, the USSR, and the United Kingdom. By 1976, these countries' proportion was less than half; soaring Japanese consumption accounted for a large part of the change, but not as much as that accounted for by all other countries. The same "big three" were also the leading copper consumers in the early 1950s, accounting for about two-thirds of the world's total consumption of refined copper. Their share in this commodity declined to little more than 40 percent by the mid-1970s, with Japan's expansion again accounting for only a minor portion of the difference. For both aluminum and copper, however, Japan's growth was enough that it displaced the United Kingdom from a leading position. The new "big three" accounted for a little more than half the world's refined aluminum consumption in 1977 and slightly under half its copper consumption.

Both lead and zinc consumption were more diffuse to begin with, the United States, USSR, and United Kingdom together accounting for about 55 percent of the world's consumption of each of these metals in the mid-1950s. By the same token, the decrease in concentration was less marked, the "big three" of 1977 accounting for about 40 percent of the world's total in both cases. By this time, Japan had displaced the United Kingdom as a leading zinc consumer. In the case of lead, for reasons obviously connected with their automobile industries, Germany, Japan, and Italy had all pulled abreast of the United Kingdom as a world consumers.

The situation with regard to concentration of the ferroalloying metals differs principally in the composition of the original big three. Reflecting the distribution of the world's steel industry, the 1960[2] leaders for both ferromanganese and ferrochromium were the United States, the USSR,

---

[2]Series for the ferroalloying metals were readily compilable only from this year. The difference in composition of the "big three" remains, however, since there had been no change as of that date in the leadership positions for the nonferrous metals.

and Germany; they accounted at that time for two-thirds of the ferromanganese consumption, but less than 60 percent of ferrochromium. This
reflection of a wider dispersion of stainless than of carbon steel production has since been reversed, since the "big three" concentration in ferrochromium remains at close to 60 percent, while that for ferromanganese has
declined to about 50 percent. However, Japan has displaced Germany as a
leading ferromanganese consumer and has surpassed the USSR in its consumption of ferrochromium: in fact, at a quarter of the world's consumption
of the latter, its share now exceeds that of the United States.

In the case of cobalt, the United Kingdom, rather than the USSR, was
among the "big three" in 1960, and the trio as a whole accounted for about
70 percent of the world's cobalt metal consumption in that year. By 1972,
however, both Germany and the United Kingdom had been displaced from the
leading positions and the new "big three"--consisting of the United States,
Japan, and the USSR--became responsible for a fluctuating share which
seems to gravitate around 60 percent (though it was closer in 1973 to the
original 70).

The widespread presumption that there is increasing decentralization
of mineral processing, especially into the developing world, is not necessarily borne out by the data on concentration of metallic ore consumption. In the case of copper, for example, the four leading ore processors
of the mid-1950s--the United States, USSR, Chile, and Zambia--who accounted
for about two-thirds of the consumption at that time, were down to around
55 percent in the mid-1970s. Their relative displacement, however, was
not by another ore-producing country, but by Japan. With the inclusion
of Japan's share of consumption, that of the now "big five" hovered around
two-thirds of the world total for the entire two decades.

The bauxite record is almost as equivocal. The record, unfortunately,
starts only in 1965, at which time the United States and the Soviet Union
accounted for 54 percent of world consumption, with lesser participation
by Jamaica, Japan, France, Germany, and Canada. This duo is now down to
a 33-percent share, but the more dramatic change between 1965 and 1976 was
the rapid expansion of alumina production in Australia. Australia's 1977
bauxite consumption was actually greater than that of the United States,
the three leaders accounting for 53 percent of world consumption.

In the case of lead ores, the four consumers who accounted for 54 percent of world consumption in 1954 (the United States, USSR, Australia, and Mexico) accounted for 53 percent twenty years later, 51 percent in 1975 and 1976, and 50 percent in 1977; of other significant consumers, only Japan increased very much in relative importance over the period. It took the combined consumption of the United States, the USSR, Belgium, and Germany to account for more than half of zinc ore consumption in 1954; it took five countries (the United States, USSR, Japan, Germany, and Canada) to achieve a similar proportion in 1976, at which time both the USSR and Japan were more important consumers than the United States.

The consumption of both chromium and manganese ores also became more dispersed between 1960 and 1976, but not much and not among developing countries. The three countries that accounted for a little over half the chromite consumption in 1960--the United States, USSR, and Germany--were down to a one-third share in 1976. The four leading countries of the latter year--the United States, USSR, Japan, and South Africa--accounted for just over half the ore conversion. It took only two countries--the United States and the Soviet Union--to account for more than half the consumption of manganese ore (around 55 percent) in the early 1960s, and the share of these two was down to little more than a third in 1976. By that time, however, both South Africa and Japan had become more important consumers than the United States and together with the USSR accounted for more than half the world total.

U.S. Shares

The most consistent phenomenon of the world consumption picture is that the United States, which some fifteen or twenty years ago was the leading consumer of at least the refined form of each of the seven metals under review, has had usually the most pronounced relative decline in share and in at least one instance has ceased to be the leading consumer of the world's supply.[3] Its share of aluminum consumption, for example,

---

[3]Ferrochromium, whose leading consumer, as noted above, is now Japan. The United States may also be yielding first place--to the USSR--with respect to consumption of zinc.

declined from just over half the world total in the early 1950s to less than a third in the mid-1970s. It consumed close to 40 percent of the world's copper in the mid-1950s, but only around 20 percent in the mid-1970s. The U.S. lead share, in the same period, went from something over one-third to a little over one-quarter. The zinc share was also a bit over one-third in the mid-1950s, but in this case the decline was to under 20 percent.

The bulk of these various declines had taken place by 1960, and since we do not have comparable data for the ferroalloying metals, it is not known whether their behavior was similar. Since the early 1960s, however, the U.S. share of world ferrochromium consumption has dropped from the neighborhood of 30 percent to around 20 percent. The record on ferromanganese is similar. Only in the case of cobalt--for reasons presumably having to do mostly with the aerospace industry--has the U.S. share more or less held its own, though the fluctuations have been considerable, ranging cyclically from more than 45 percent to well under 30.[4]

Consumption of Individual Commodities

Cobalt

Cobalt is an exception among the commodities considered in this report, in that we have not attempted to deal with its ore and intermediate forms. In part this is because of the elusiveness of the relevant data; in part it is because in the United States there has been only limited and intermittent consumption of the intermediate forms, so that the supply-demand situation for such intermediates is of interest only as it indirectly affects refined metal supplies.[5]

---

[4]Given the inadequacy of data by which to adjust for inventories, some of this statistical fluctuation undoubtedly represents purchases for stock rather than actual consumption.

[5]The situation is beginning to change: see footnote 2 in chapter 5.

Even for cobalt metal, as will be seen in table 1-1, the apparent consumption accounting is rather poor, with as much as a fifth of the total apparent supply in particular years remaining unassignable to specific consuming countries. Part of the problem clearly has to do with the incompleteness of data on stocks--particularly dealer stocks.[6] There is also the special problem of Zairian cobalt passing through Belgium, the volume of which cannot be specifically identified as to timing and destination.

Given the mix of principal consuming countries, it may be presumed that the main ingredients in the rapid, though erratic, growth of world cobalt consumption have to do with the manufacture of jet aircraft engines ("superalloys"), precision electronics (high efficiency permanent magnets), and high-speed machine tools for the engineering industries. If the estimates are correct, the USSR is consuming an increasing portion of the world total, but with no significant impact on the trading world, since Soviet supplies originate in domestic (and perhaps Cuban) mines.[7] Still, about three-fourths of the world supply moves in trade among market countries, half or more of that, in turn, being consumed by the United States. It is the United States, too, that is by far the principal factor in demand growth, although Japan has also been contributing significantly. Figure 1-15 shows the growth of cobalt consumption in these two countries and underlines its relative unpredictability--especially for Japan--even in terms of trend. Inevitably, that same relative unpredictability carries through to the relationship of cobalt consumption to any macroeconomic indicator, such as GNP.[8]

---

[6]This is a general problem in commodity consumption accounting.

[7]The USSR, however, purchased quantities of cobalt metal on Western markets during 1978.

[8]One may note that in the United States, cobalt demand in the recent past does seem to have followed the general economy--rising in the period of escalation of war in Vietnam, then again in the boom of 1973-74, plunging during the recession of 1975, and then rising again.

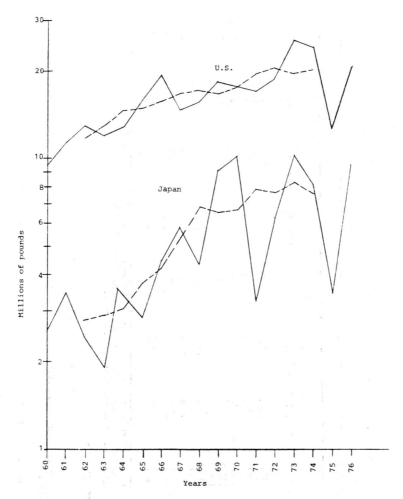

Figure 1-15. Apparent Consumption of Cobalt Metal in the
United States and Japan, 1960-1976, Annually
and Five-Year Moving-Average Trends

TABLE 1-1. WORLD APPARENT CONSUMPTION OF COBALT METAL, 1960-1977, BY COUNTRY

(THOUSAND POUNDS)

| YEAR | PRINCIPAL INTERNATIONAL TRADERS | | | | | | OTHER COUNTRIES | | UNDETER-MINED[b] | WORLD TOTAL[a] |
	UNITED STATES	GERMANY (F.R.)	FRANCE	UNITED KINGDOM	JAPAN	TOTAL	USSR	OTHER		
1960	9488	3517	1366	3649	2531	20551	1320	4162	-2450	23580
1961	11355	3425	1050	3102	3463	22395	1620	3621	-390	27240
1962	13000	2662	806	2686	2448	21602	2310	2978	6830	33730
1963	11985	2399	1244	601	1911	18140	3200	2618	6730	30680
1964	12886	2941	896	3221	3591	23535	3700	3122	3600	33960
1965	15864	3324	1219	3687	2845	26939	4110	2436	1760	35250
1966	19443	3073	1482	3053	4491	31542	4340	3240	3470	42590
1967	14802	2781	1816	2772	5833	28004	5080	3240	8770	45090
1968	15718	3755	1073	2925	4332	27803	5800	3633	9370	46600
1969	18507	4805	1870	2545	9204	36931	6700	3757	1270	48660
1970	17661	4666	2229	3973	10225	38754	6800	5773	4280	55610
1971	17113	3006	1863	3779	3243	29004	6900	4500	21000	61400
1972	18945	3146	1583	2015	6506	32197	7000	4612	7420	51230
1973	25670	4070	2179	3168	10267	45354	7300	3274	6000	61940
1974	24131	4461	2908	5565	8192	45257	7400	3518	10960	67130
1975	12713	3519	2636	3521	3483	25872	7500	3500	20320	57190
1976	20847	4249	1749	2167	9588	38595	7500	3425	880	50400
1977	16419	4542	N.P.	N.A.	6646	--	N.A.	--	--	N.A.

SOURCE: U.K. INSTITUTE OF GEOLOGICAL SCIENCES STATISTICAL SUMMARY OF THE MINERAL INDUSTRY AND WORLD MINERAL STATISTICS 1970-1974 AND 1972-1976; U.S. BUREAU OF MINES, MINERALS YEARBOOK AND UNPUBLISHED COMPILATIONS; DEUTSCHES INSTITUTE FUR WIRTSCHAFTFORSCHUNG, KOBALT.

N.A. - NOT AVAILABLE

NOTE: DETAIL MAY NOT ADD TO TOTALS, OWING TO ROUNDING.

[a] ACTUALLY, TOTAL KNOWN METAL SUPPLY, THAT IS, METAL PRODUCTION PLUS U.S. GOVERNMENT/CONSUMER STOCKPILE CHANGES.

[b] THE DIFFERENCE BETWEEN 'WORLD TOTAL' AND KNOWN APPARENT CONSUMPTION.

Chromium

Though an increasing proportion of an expanding need for ferrochromium in the United States—used mostly in, and essential for, stainless steel production—is being met by imports, the greater part of U.S. supply remains a product of the domestic ferroalloys industry. Competitive supply and consumption both of ferrochromium and of the relevant grades of chromium ore (chromite) are thus of continuing interest.

The relevant ore types, given present-day practice, are aluminiferous chromite, used for refractory purposes, and other ores that have reasonably high chromium content and chromium-iron ratios, which are used as input into ferroalloys. Data to differentiate these two general types are available only for the United States. The data on chromium ore given in table 1-2, therefore, are for all types combined.

With the USSR, a leading consumer, being also counted among leading world traders (as exporter), the portion of chromite consumption that affects world prices tends toward nearly three-fourths the world total. Besides the United States and the USSR, both Japan and the Union of South Africa are leading consumers—Japan with an eye to ultimate use in steel production and South Africa with an eye mostly to ferrochromium exports. Next in importance are West Germany and Rhodesia (Zimbabwe), with an analogous contrast in objectives.[9] Consumption patterns for these half-dozen countries are shown in figures 1-16 through 1-18.

One may assume a close relationship between chromite consumption in any given country and ferrochromium production. Ferrochromium production, in turn, is related—though in a gradually changing way—to ferrochromium consumption in the same country or, in the case of ferrochromium exporters, either world consumption or the consumption of principal trading partners. The historical record (which in some cases is based on estimated underlying data) for the relevant ratios is shown in table 1-3. Actual quantities of ferrochromium consumed are given in table 1-4. Figure 1-19 shows how the once outstanding consumer, the United States, has been overtaken by the new top consumer, Japan.

---

[9]This work was already in production when the new nation of Zimbabwe was recognized. Therefore, historical and table references are to Rhodesia and current references are to Zimbabwe.

For any individual country there are fairly smooth trends in the input-output ratios for chromite into ferrochrome (the former measured as chromic oxide and the latter in terms of chromium content). Fluctuations are probably due in part to incomplete corrections for inventory change. The differences among countries, on the other hand, as well as most of the variation over time within individual countries, are presumably due to the utilization of some chromite for refractory purposes, more than to efficiency of conversion.[10]

Part B of table 1-3 clearly shows up the net importers and the net exporters, as well as the changes in status that have taken place over the years (among them the continuing decline in U.S. self-sufficiency). Part C of the table is designed to explore, for principal consuming countries, the practicality of working directly with ratios between chromite consumption and ferrochromium consumption.

The entry for the "world" in part B of table 1-3 implies an increasing rate of stock buildup from what, in the earlier years, must have been a general deficiency in working inventories. Such a phenomenon would be consistent with an accelerating rate of increase in world consumption--which, however, does not appear to be the case (see figure 1-2). It would be consistent with increasing dispersion of production in relation to consumption (or vice versa), necessitating increasing relative amounts of material in transportation pipelines. This may be the case, but another possible explanation is an increasing buildup of contingency stocks in an unsettled supply environment.

For the two countries--Rhodesia and South Africa--whose output of ferrochromium is primarily for export, it is the ferrochromium consumption of trading partners which is particularly relevant. These trading partners are--or have been, depending upon what period and information source is chosen for Rhodesia--the principal industrialized countries of the Western world ("principal international traders," in table 1-4). The steadily

_____

[10]Rhodesia, in the few years of record, came closest to the theoretical conversion possibility, chromite to chromium alloy, of just under 1.5 to 1, although data limitation may be partially responsible for the indicated technical-efficiency ratio.

increasing role of Rhodesian and South African ore processing in meeting
the ferroalloy needs of these industrialized countries is clear. One may
infer from the data shown that, by around 1973, nearly 20 percent of the
Western world's need for ferrochromium was being satisfied by the conversion of chromite into ferroalloy within these two countries.[11] Close to
another 50 percent seems to have been taken care of by the direct export
of chromite from these two countries for conversion in the recipient
countries. The United States appears to be on the high side of both these
general averages.

Though it is used somewhat more ubiquitously than cobalt, ferrochromium is only moderately more systematic in the consumption relationships to either gross national output (GNP) or steel output. While the
bulk of it does go into the making of stainless and other alloy steel,
a significant proportion also goes into non-steel alloys, and that part
which does go into steel involves only a relatively small segment of total
steel output. Still, given the impracticability, within this study, of
carrying out more detailed analysis, the relationships of ferrochromium
consumption both to GNP and to steel production are of potential interest
as a base for projections and are given in tables 1-5 and 1-6.

The relationships to GNP (or gross domestic product) are in terms of
individual country currencies and provide time trends. A notion of inter-
country differences may be obtained by converting to U.S. dollars. Using
the average New York buying rates for 1975 as reported in the Federal
Reserve Bulletin, the utilization of chromium in ferrochromium around that
same year, per million dollars of GNP, was 16 kilos in the United States,
30 kilos in Germany, 23 in France, 12 in the United Kingdom, 61 in Japan,
and 25 in Italy. Because of the extensive use of chromium-bearing steel
and other alloys in important categories of capital equipment, the relative
rates of capital investment in the various countries probably go a long
way toward explaining the differences. The Japanese rate is presumably

---

[11]Combined ratios of Rhodesia and South Africa in part D of the
table (0.636), divided by the input-output ratio for South Africa in part A
of the table--the latter with some downward shading to allow for the
presumably lower ratio for Rhodesia.

also sustained in part by automobile production (chromium-bearing steel is needed particularly in emission-control equipment), and the U.S. rate might be lower were it not for chromium's important role in automobiles.

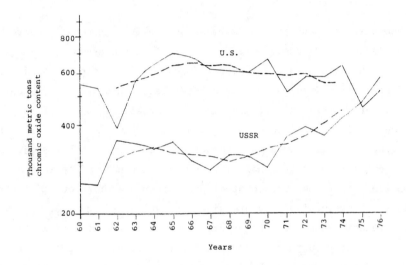

Figure 1-16.   Apparent Consumption of Chromite in the United States and the USSR, 1960-1976, Annually and Five-Year Moving-Average Trends

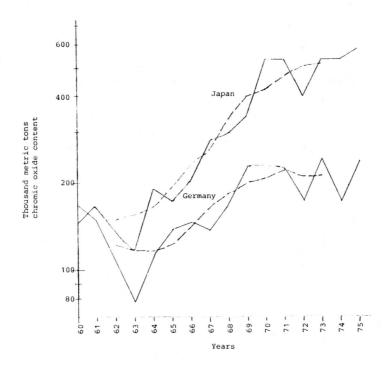

Figure 1-17.   Apparent Consumption of Chromite in Japan
and Germany, 1960-1975, Annually and
Five-Year Moving-Average Trends

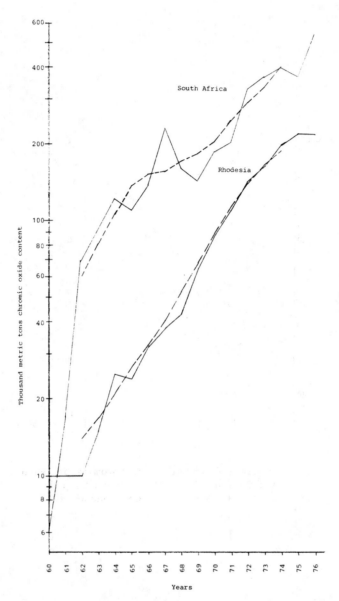

Figure 1-18.   Apparent Consumption of Chromite in
South Africa and Rhodesia, 1960-1976,
Annually and Five-Year Moving-Average Trends

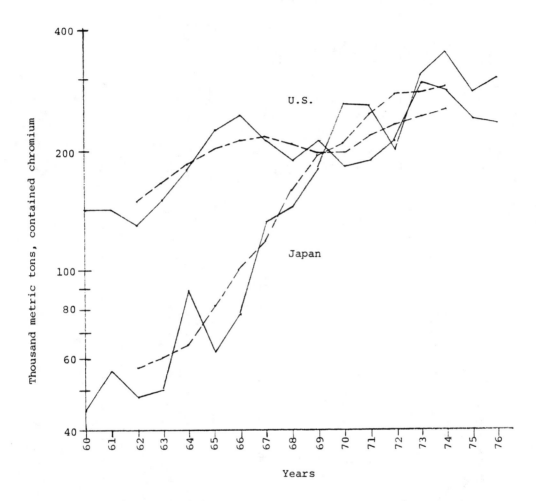

Figure 1-19. Apparent Consumption of Ferrochromium in the United States and Japan, 1960-1976, Annually and Five-Year Moving-Average Trends.

TABLE 1-2. WORLD APPARENT CONSUMPTION OF CHROMIUM ORE,[a] 1960-1977, BY COUNTRY

(THOUSAND METRIC TONS, CHROMIC OXIDE CONTENT)[b]

| YEAR | PRINCIPAL INTERNATIONAL TRADERS | | | | | | | | | OTHER COUNTRIES | WORLD TOTAL[c] |
	UNITED STATES	JAPAN	FRANCE	GERMANY (F.R.)	SWEDEN	RHODESIA	SOUTH AFRICA	USSR	TOTAL		
1960	552	145	92	166	69	10	6	253	1293	551	1844
1961	538	166	96	149	52	10	17	251	1279	475	1754
1962	392	133	78	107	52	10	70	354	1196	457	1653
1963	566	115	74	78	56	15	90	345	1339	444	1783
1964	648	189	94	112	74	25	121	333	1596	543	2139
1965	705	171	110	139	69	24	110	349	1677	603	2280
1966	679	204	116	146	78	32	137	301	1693	475	2168
1967	622	279	121	138	69	38	230	282	1779	481	2260
1968	613	295	127	170	73	43	160	314	1795	610	2405
1969	608	337	159	229	90	65	142	311	1941	656	2597
1970	668	528	204	229	97	87	185	286	2284	755	3039
1971	513	528	158	224	92	108	200	361	2184	759	2943
1972	585	392	133	174	72	141	329	390	2216	710	2926
1973	587	525	162	243	123	162	365	366	2533	838	3371
1974	639	548	173	172	131	196	394	421	2654	851	3505
1975	459	576	166	239	164	217	364	472	2657	1012	3669
1976	524	540	165	254	152	217	536	578	2960	735	3800
1977	499	428	N.A.	N.A.	N.A.	N.A.	N.A.	613	--	--	N.A.

SOURCE: CANADA DEPARTMENT OF ENERGY, MINES AND RESOURCES, CANADIAN MINERALS YEARBOOK; DEUTSCHES INSTITUT FUR WIRTSCHAFTSFORSCHUNG, CHROM; JAPANESE MINISTRY OF FINANCE, EXPORTS AND IMPORTS; ORGANIZATION FOR ECONOMIC COOPERATION AND DEVELOPMENT, FOREIGN TRADE STATISTICS, SERIES C; U.K. INSTITUTE OF GEOLOGICAL SCIENCES, STATISTICAL SUMMARY OF THE MINERAL INDUSTRY AND WORLD MINERAL STATISTICS, 1970-1974 AND 1972-1976; U.S. BUREAU OF MINES, MINERALS YEARBOOK AND UNPUBLISHED COMPILATIONS; UNITED NATIONS STATISTICAL OFFICE, WORLD TRADE ANNUAL.

N.A. – NOT AVAILABLE

[a]INCLUDES ALL TYPES OF CHROMITE: HIGH-CHROMITE, HIGH-IRON, AND HIGH-ALUMINUM.

[b]CHROMIUM CONTENT MAY BE OBTAINED BY MULTIPLYING THE FIGURES SHOWN BY .6842.

[c]EXCLUDES ESTIMATES FOR CHINA (P.R.).

Table 1-3. Ratios of Chromite Consumption to Ferrochromium Production and Consumption, for the World and Leading Chromite Consumers 1960-1976[a]

A. Chromite (Cr_2O_3) Consumption/Ferrochrome Production

	1962	1963	1964	1965	1966	1967	1968	1969	1970	1971	1972	1973	1974
United States	4.14	3.93	3.76	3.67	3.55	3.44	3.47	3.44	3.60	3.45	3.49	3.52	3.72
Japan	2.31	2.22	2.16	2.12	2.09	2.05	2.06	2.02	1.98	1.92	1.79	1.79	1.72
France	2.05	2.06	2.04	2.00	1.97	1.98	2.13	2.23	2.19	2.24	2.26	2.37	N.A.
Germany (F.R.)	1.78	1.73	1.73	1.76	1.89	2.03	2.08	2.17	2.25	2.30	2.13	2.19	"
Sweden	1.86	1.73	1.85	1.86	1.85	1.86	1.95	1.97	1.96	2.06	1.99	2.08	"
Rhodesia	1.61	1.60	1.59	(b)	(b)	(b)	(b)	(b)	(b)	(b)	(b)	(b)	(b)
South Africa	1.78	2.06	2.37	2.69	2.71	2.48	2.60	2.68	2.84	3.17	3.57	3.60	N.A.
USSR	3.36	3.46	3.60	3.52	3.58	3.85	3.95	4.31	4.51	4.34	4.00	3.77	3.63
World	3.52	3.46	3.41	3.30	3.24	3.16	3.12	3.12	3.15	3.06	2.99	2.97	N.A.

B. Ferrochromium Production to Consumption

	1962	1963	1964	1965	1966	1967	1968	1969	1970	1971	1972	1973	1974
United States	.873	.878	.857	.871	.879	.872	.890	.900	.847	.791	.742	.652	.598
Japan	1.129	1.143	1.147	1.101	1.076	1.054	1.002	1.002	1.008	1.000	1.016	1.054	1.044
France	1.356	1.344	1.354	1.316	1.282	1.208	1.142	1.106	1.053	1.003	.963	.911	N.A.
Germany (F.R.)	.920	.874	.853	.826	.816	.822	.841	.848	.845	.848	.853	.821	"
Sweden	1.366	1.282	1.240	1.205	1.130	1.041	1.069	1.041	.989	.935	.949	.936	"
USSR	1.148	1.150	1.167	1.205	1.260	1.356	1.461	1.547	1.609	1.612	1.517	1.406	1.354
World	.996	.995	.997	1.000	1.001	1.000	1.009	1.011	1.009	1.005	1.004	1.010	1.009

49

(continued on next page)

Table 1-3. (cont.)

C. Chromite (Cr_2O_3) Consumption/Ferrochrome Consumption

	1962	1963	1964	1965	1966	1967	1968	1969	1970	1971	1972	1973	1974
United States	3.62	3.45	3.22	3.19	3.12	3.00	3.08	3.09	3.05	2.73	2.59	2.30	2.23
Japan	2.61	2.54	2.48	2.33	2.25	2.16	2.07	2.02	2.00	1.92	1.82	1.83	1.79
France	2.78	2.77	2.76	2.63	2.52	2.39	2.43	2.46	2.31	2.25	2.18	2.16	N.A.
Germany (F.R.)	1.63	1.51	1.47	1.45	1.54	1.67	1.75	1.84	1.90	1.95	1.82	1.80	"
Sweden	2.55	2.22	2.29	2.25	2.09	1.93	2.09	2.05	1.94	1.93	1.89	1.95	"
USSR	3.86	3.98	4.15	4.24	4.51	5.22	5.77	6.67	7.26	7.00	6.06	5.32	4.92
World	3.50	3.44	3.40	3.30	3.25	3.17	3.15	3.15	3.18	3.11	3.00	3.00	N.A.

D. Chromite (Cr_2O_3) Consumption/Ferrochromium Consumption by Principal World Traders[c]

	1962	1963	1964	1965	1966	1967	1968	1969	1970	1971	1972	1973	1974
Rhodesia	.039	.044	.052	.058	.064	.073	.089	.108	.136	.157	.181	.212	N.A.
South Africa	.171	.214	.257	.299	.300	.283	.286	.290	.312	.342	.384	.424	"

N.A. - Not available.

[a] Ratios are based on five-year moving average trends, centered on years shown.

[b] Not applicable, since Rhodesian chromite production for 1967 on was estimated by applying a content-plus-loss factor to ferrochrome production.

[c] Includes United States, Japan, France, Germany, Italy, and United Kingdom. All of these are important gross importers.

50

TABLE 1-4. WORLD APPARENT CONSUMPTION OF FERROCHROMIUM,[a] 1960-77, BY COUNTRY

(THOUSAND METRIC TONS, CONTAINED CHROMIUM)

YEAR	PRINCIPAL INTERNATIONAL TRADERS							OTHER COUNTRIES			WORLD TOTAL[d]
	UNITED STATES	JAPAN	FRANCE	GERMANY (F.R.)	ITALY	UNITED KINGDOM[c]	TOTAL	USSR	OTHER	UNDETERMINED	
1960	143	44	30	80	19	33	349	62	54	31	496
1961	142	56	36	79	14	30	356	69	60	46	531
1962	130	48	30	60	12	17	297	83	65	11	456
1963	150	50	27	71	12	25	334	90	69	18	511
1964	180	89	33	84	19	34	439	94	68	25	626
1965	224	62	37	94	20	40	478	74	86	31	668
1966	243	78	44	86	25	33	509	64	74	40	688
1967	211	132	55	87	28	29	542	58	75	50	725
1968	189	144	56	107	32	32	559	60	87	53	759
1969	210	180	73	119	34	44	661	42	113	44	859
1970	181	260	71	121	39	46	718	35	100	79	932
1971	188	258	57	104	34	35	677	38	127	87	929
1972	212	198	81	89	39	20	638	54	101	105	898
1973	293	307	81	130	42	29	881	76	147	67	1172
1974	281	351	91	130	48	25	926	98	195	113	1332
1975	237	277	57	132	41	28	772	112	170	93	1146
1976[b]	232	301	85	134	50	31	833	113	--	--	1244
1977	246	N.A.	N.A.	N.A.	N.A.	N.A.	--	N.A.	--	--	N.A.

SOURCE: CANADA DEPARTMENT OF ENERGY, MINES AND RESOURCES, CANADIAN MINERALS YEARBOOK; DEUTSCHES INSTITUT FUR WIRTSCHAFTSFORSCHUNG, CHROM; JAPANESE MINISTRY OF FINANCE, EXPORTS AND IMPORTS; ORGANIZATION FOR ECONOMIC COOPERATION AND DEVELOPMENT, FOREIGN TRADE STATISTICS, SERIES C; U.K. INSTITUTE OF GEOLOGICAL SCIENCES, STATISTICAL SUMMARY OF THE MINERAL INDUSTRY AND WORLD MINERAL STATISTICS, 1970-1974; U.S. BUREAU OF MINES, MINERALS YEARBOOK AND UNPUBLISHED COMPILATIONS, AND MINERAL TRADE NOTES (VOLUME 74, NUMBER 10); UNITED NATIONS STATISTICAL OFFICE, WORLD TRADE ANNUAL.

N.A. - NOT AVAILABLE.

[a] INCLUDES BOTH HIGH-CARBON AND LOW-CARBON FERROCHROMIUM.

[b] AMOUNTS SHOWN FOR 1976 ARE GENERALLY PRELIMINARY FIGURES.

[c] ESTIMATES BASED ON NET TRADE ONLY: PRODUCTION IS NOT KNOWN.

[d] ACTUALLY WORLD PRODUCTION OF FERROCHROMIUM PLUS ADJUSTMENTS FOR CHANGES IN U.S. STOCKS EXCLUDES ESTIMATES FOR CHINA (P.R.), POLAND, CZECHOSLOVAKIA, GERMAN DEMOCRATIC REPUBLIC, AND THE UNITED KINGDOM.

Table 1-5. Ratios of Ferrochromium Consumption to GNP/GDP, for Leading Ferrochromium Consumers, 1960-77[a]

(metric tons chromium content)

Denominator	U.S. $ million	Japan Y billion	France Fr billion	Germany (F.R.) DM million	Italy L billion	U.K. L million	USSR Index[b]
1962	.147	1.13	40.9	.116	.224	.364	1.20
1963	.155	1.10	40.4	.114	.217	.370	1.18
1964	.165	1.07	40.0	.111	.237	.367	1.11
1965	.172	1.22	43.5	.115	.267	.384	.99
1966	.170	1.35	47.4	.120	.302	.389	.86
1967	.168	1.43	52.8	.124	.321	.403	.70
1968	.157	1.70	56.3	.125	.344	.407	.57
1969	.145	1.88	55.6	.123	.347	.401	.49
1970	.141	1.82	56.8	.117	.355	.373	.46
1971	.150	1.93	57.6	.117	.359	.355	.47
1972	.156	2.06	57.6	.115	.370	.308	.55
1973	.161	1.99	53.5	.115	.365	.268	.67
1974	.162	1.94	55.4	.118	.381	.255	.78
1975	.162	2.04	c 53.6	c .123	c .386	c .276	c .85

a Ratios, in metric tons per denominator shown at head of column, are based on five-year moving-average trends, centered on year shown.

b GNP index, 1970 = 100 (see chapter 2). Ratios are per index point.

c Underlying consumption average includes an estimated figure for 1977.

Table 1-6. Ratios of Ferrochromium Consumption to Steel Production, for the World and for Leading Ferrochromium Consumers, 1960-77[a]

(kilos of chromium in ferrochromium, per metric ton of steel)

	U.S.	Japan	France	Germany (F.R.)	Italy	U.K.	USSR	World
1962	1.54	1.85	1.74	2.21	1.60	1.18	1.05	1.40
1963	1.61	1.75	1.78	2.16	1.50	1.21	1.02	1.41
1964	1.70	1.69	1.83	2.18	1.57	1.22	.94	1.40
1965	1.76	1.85	2.04	2.27	1.68	1.28	.83	1.44
1966	1.77	1.96	2.27	2.34	1.80	1.30	.73	1.45
1967	1.78	1.99	2.60	2.42	1.84	1.37	.59	1.46
1968	1.71	2.25	2.82	2.56	1.98	1.41	.44	1.49
1969	1.66	2.48	2.85	2.58	1.99	1.44	.41	1.52
1970	1.64	2.43	2.98	2.51	2.03	1.36	.42	1.51
1971	1.76	2.58	3.06	2.51	2.05	1.33	.41	1.56
1972	1.87	2.67	3.10	2.47	2.04	1.23	.48	1.64
1973	2.00	2.65	3.03	2.58	1.96	1.16	.58	1.68
1974	2.05	2.63	3.26	2.68	2.00	1.20	.67	1.72
1975	2.13	2.86	[b]3.31	[b]2.92	[b]2.02	[b]1.31	[b].73	N.A.

[a] Ratios are based on five-year moving-average trends, centered on year shown.

[b] Underlying consumption average includes an estimated figure for 1977.

53

Manganese

Though used in far larger quantities, both in the United States and around the world, manganese is much like chrome in the manner of its use and in the world's substantial dependence on southern Africa. The dispersion both in ore sources and in locale of processing is greater, however. Thus, it takes more countries to account for the bulk of manganese ore consumption. Significant ferromanganese consumption, because of its being intimately bound up with ordinary (carbon) steel production, may be found in any of the countries with a large steel output. Thus, in addition to the leading industrialized countries, Spain, India, and China are already important ferromanganese (as well as manganese ore) consumers, and countries like Brazil, Mexico, Venezuela, Australia, and South Korea may soon be added to the leading-consumer list.

Not all these countries have, or will have, important influence on the internatinal market, however. Only Brazil, South Africa, and Australia figure both among leading world suppliers of manganese ore and leading consumers. Brazil, moreover, may follow in the footsteps of India, which has already sharply limited its ore exports in favor of domestic processing into ferroalloy, mostly for its own steel industry. The USSR is utilizing the large bulk of its manganese ore for its own consumption (and that of other Comecon countries), only occasionally providing significant quantities to the international marketplace. Among those depending for feedstock upon their own mineral resources, South Africa is the only important international provider of ferromanganese; but France (and to a lesser extent, Japan), besides being a leading consumer of ferroalloy made from imported ore, is also a leading international ferromanganese supplier, while Norway turns imported manganese ore into ferromanganese almost wholly for the international marketplace.

Historical data on the consumption of manganese ore are given in table 1-7 and on ferromanganese in table 1-8. Four countries--the United States, the USSR, Japan, and South Africa--stand out as ore consumers, and two countries--the United States and the USSR--as ferromanganese consumers: trends for these countries are shown in figures 1-20 through 1-22. The rise, then fall, in manganese ore consumption in the United States may be compared with the hesitant, but now clearly rising trend in the Soviet Union. Both may be compared with the steeply rising trends in Japan and South Africa. The former of these has been under way for some twenty-five years and is beginning to slacken off; the latter is just getting started and perhaps cannot be sustained for long. Except for South Africa, the ultimate disposition of the manganese consumed in these countries is essentially in domestic steelmaking, while South Africa largely exports it as ferroalloy.

The considerable spread in relationships between manganese ore inputs and ferromanganese production in these and other principal manganese-ore consumers is shown in part A of table 1-9. If manganese ore were used only in the manufacture of ferromanganese and there were little or no loss in processing, the ratio would be in the neighborhood of 80 percent.[12] It may be seen that almost that low a ratio was achieved in Germany, on the average, in the first half of the 1960s.[13] But manganese ore also has other uses--principally in dry cell batteries--as well as in steelmaking; it is introduced not only as ferromanganese but directly as ore, as silico-manganese, as manganiferous pig iron, and as pure manganese metal.[14] These alternative modes of application--and undoubtedly large processing losses in some instances--are reflected in large ore to ferromanganese ratios. The importance of alternative forms of input into steel at least partly explains the once very high ratios in Brazil and the increasingly high ratios in Australia; this tends to be confirmed by the compensating trends in ferromanganese ratios shown in part E of table 1-9.[15] Interestingly, however, the substantial substitution of silicomanganese for

---

[12]The ore data used here are in terms of manganese content.

[13]It is to be remembered that the table shows values for ratios between moving-average trends.

[14]None of these other forms of consumption is included in the ferromanganese series.

[15]There is also the possibility of statistical inaccuracy, including inaccuracy in the estimation of manganese content of ore, but in Brazil's case, at least, a cross-check among sources suggests that this is not a likely source of significant error.

separate ferromanganese and ferrosilicon steel inputs in Japan appears to be counterbalanced by other factors in determining the ore to ferromanganese ratio.

The progressively higher ratios of ore per unit of ferromanganese in India may be largely a consequence of the increased conversion losses that accompany use of lower grades of ore. A similar phenomenon may be helping to sustain high ratios in the USSR, though other applications of manganese are undoubtedly also important. The increasing consumption ratio in the United States reflects mostly the relative increase in importance of nonferroalloy applications as the output of ferromanganese decreases. A reverse phenomenon has probably occurred in Norway. The tendency toward increasing ratios in the world as a whole presumably reflects in part the need for larger inventories in pipeline as total world consumption of manganese continues to expand, as well as the increasing use of ore for silicomanganese.

Part B of table 1-9 provides an indirect reading on each country's net position in international trade in ferromanganese. Declining self-sufficiency in the United States and Germany is clearly evident, as is the increasing net export contribution of Japan, France, Brazil, and the USSR (trends which will not necessarily persist). The declining trend for the world as a whole may represent a declining need for inventory expansion, accompanying some slowdown in rate of increase in world consumption (see figure 1-3).

Parts C and D of the table are designed to facilitate projections by directly relating manganese ore consumption to the relevant consumption of ferromanganese. Domestic consumption is given for countries producing the ferroalloy mostly for home use, and total trading world consumption is given for those countries producing ferromanganese mostly for export. France is near the borderline in terms of classification, but is primarily a net exporter; one may note, too, that France's own consumption is included in the total for the trading world.

As a base for projecting ferromanganese consumption, part E of the table relates this series, for the world and for principal consumers, to raw steel production. Other than statistical inaccuracy, which is not believed to be that important, it is difficult to find an explanation

for the high ratios in India, other than large processing losses. The
low ratios for Japan are largely explainable by the substitution of silicomanganese, already noted. Use of substitute forms of manganese in steel
probably explains the declining ratios for the world as a whole, although
some tendency to increased efficiency of use is probably also at work.

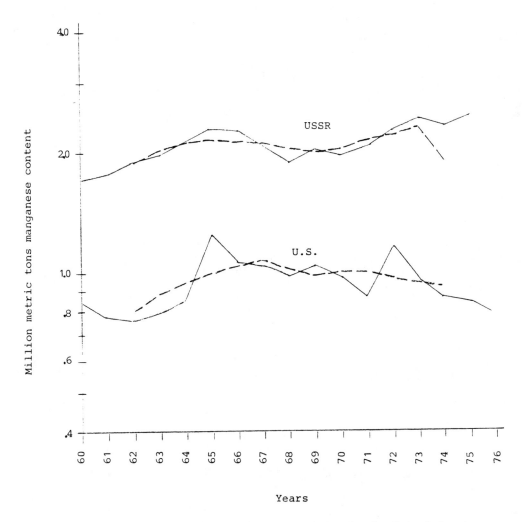

Figure 1-20. Apparent Consumption of Manganese Ore in the United States
and the USSR, 1960-1976, Annually and Five-Year Moving-
Average Trends

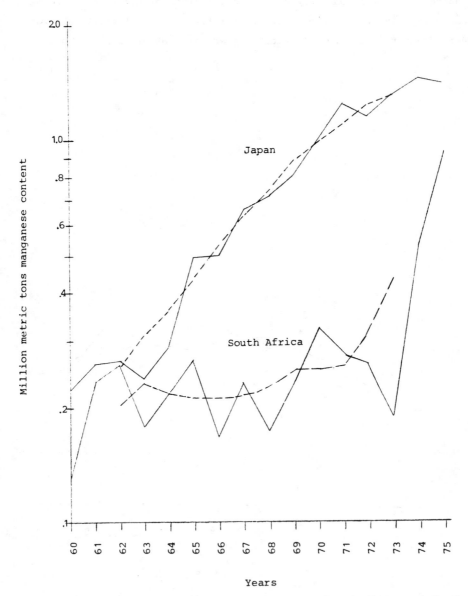

Figure 1-21. Apparent Consumption of Manganese Ore in Japan and South
Africa, 1960–1975, Annually and Five-Year Moving-Average
Trends

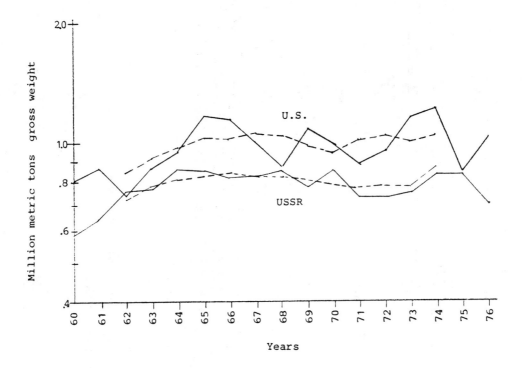

Figure 1-22. Apparent Consumption of Ferromanganese in the United States
and the USSR, 1960–1976, Annually and Five-Year Moving-
Average Trends.

TABLE 1-7. WORLD APPARENT CONSUMPTION OF MANGANESE ORE, 1960-77, BY COUNTRY[a]

(THOUSAND METRIC TONS, MANGANESE CONTENT)

YEAR	PRINCIPAL INTERNATIONAL TRADERS									OTHER COUNTRIES			WORLD TOTAL[b]
	UNITED STATES	JAPAN	FRANCE	GERMANY (F.R.)	NORWAY	AUSTRALIA	BRAZIL	SOUTH AFRICA	TOTAL	USSR	INDIA	OTHER	
1960	844	224	332	135	139	4	46	129	1913	1716	27	844	4500
1961	773	260	302	230	98	20	65	232	1980	1776	141	854	4751
1962	760	265	301	223	124	0	184	259	2116	1904	221	768	5007
1963	790	238	309	312	105	32	187	176	2149	1987	109	824	5069
1964	851	289	347	305	159	40	234	220	2445	2141	c110	979	5675
1965	1251	493	378	293	229	58	147	267	3116	2295	197	941	6549
1966	1057	496	367	342	220	134	223	167	3006	2271	285	996	6558
1967	1046	650	304	269	243	150	369	232	3263	2073	313	989	6638
1968	985	705	396	370	298	168	436	173	3531	1894	230	1083	6738
1969	1038	801	436	259	282	143	517	232	3708	2026	378	1176	7288
1970	975	995	494	276	247	51	202	323	3563	1974	491	1236	7264
1971	869	1235	485	327	338	168	362	272	4056	2072	445	1298	7871
1972	1170	1145	505	181	334	192	397	259	4183	2282	333	1227	8025
1973	962	1291	645	296	376	328	372	189	4459	2431	376	1451	8717
1974	870	1430	623	333	485	327	133	525	4726	2335	324	1473	8858
1975	844	1398	503	238	483	285	291	931	4973	2470	396	1342	9181
1976	785	840	459	266	439	406	471	915	4585	2505	d480	1455	9025
1977	1011	d561	N.A.	N.A.	N.A.	N.A.	N.A.	N.A.	N.A.	2430	N.A.	--	N.A.

SOURCE: CANADA DEPARTMENT OF ENERGY, MINES AND RESOURCES, CANADIAN MINERALS YEARBOOK; DEUTSCHES INSTITUT FUR WIRTSCHAFTSFORSCHUNG, MANGAN; JAPANESE MINISTRY OF FINANCE, JAPAN EXPORTS AND IMPORTS; ORGANIZATION FOR ECONOMIC COOPERATION AND DEVELOPMENT, FOREIGN TRADE STATISTICS, SERIES C; U.K. INSTITUTE OF GEOLOGICAL SCIENCES, STATISTICAL SUMMARY OF THE MINERAL INDUSTRY AND WORLD MINERAL STATISTICS 1970-1974 AND 1972-1976; U.S. BUREAU OF MINES, MINERALS YEARBOOK, MINERAL TRADE NOTES (VARIOUS ISSUES), AND UNPUBLISHED DATA; UNITED NATIONS STATISTICAL OFFICE, WORLD TRADE ANNUAL.

NOTE: DETAIL MAY NOT ADD TO TOTALS OWING TO ROUNDING.

N.A. - NOT AVAILABLE.

[a] INCLUDES ORES OF 10 PERCENT OR GREATER CONTENT.

[b] EXCLUDES ESTIMATES FOR THE PEOPLES' REPUBLIC OF CHINA AND ROMANIA.

[c] ESTIMATE BASED ON FERROMANGANESE PRODUCTION.

[d] PRELIMINARY.

TABLE 1-8. WORLD APPARENT CONSUMPTION OF FERROMANGANESE, 1960-77, BY COUNTRY[a]

(THOUSAND METRIC TONS, GROSS WEIGHT[b])

YEAR	UNITED STATES	PRINCIPAL INTERNATIONAL TRADERS							OTHER COUNTRIES			WORLD TOTAL[d]
		JAPAN	BELGIUM[c]	FRANCE	GERMANY (F.R.)	ITALY	UNITED KINGDOM	TOTAL	USSR	INDIA	OTHER	
1960	800	115	115	146	331	55	217	1780	592	33	183	2588
1961	864	172	114	150	327	61	173	1861	647	46	181	2735
1962	736	146	115	154	324	69	192	1736	756	99	223	2814
1963	860	152	93	145	295	82	157	1784	764	96	284	2928
1964	941	202	135	165	315	71	207	2036	856	38	521	3451
1965	1164	205	110	163	312	91	244	2289	849	93	609	3840
1966	1139	222	110	161	293	93	208	2226	815	93	552	3720
1967	1000	307	115	144	287	104	205	2162	824	127	593	3686
1968	868	339	133	137	364	102	204	2147	845	76	664	3732
1969	1081	396	112	180	337	138	246	2490	773	40	572	3875
1970	989	464	150	181	373	131	233	2541	850	88	683	4162
1971	881	517	160	207	298	135	214	2412	731	146	748	4037
1972	946	503	164	154	339	120	233	2459	730	85	710	3984
1973	1159	613	166	199	382	187	224	2930	745	114	744	4533
1974	1214	586	195	168	408	222	206	2999	831	126	968	4924
1975	839	522	130	173	332	191	180	2367	829	128	1126	4450
1976	1032	512	115	130	348	193	240	2570	701	146	950	4367
1977	807	492	N.A.	N.A.	N.A.	N.A.	N.A.	--	N.A.	N.A.	--	N.A.

SOURCE: CANADA DEPARTMENT OF ENERGY, MINES AND RESOURCES, CANADIAN MINERALS YEARBOOK; DEUTSCHES INSTITUT FUR WIRTSCHAFTSFORSCHUNG, MANGAN; JAPANESE MINISTRY OF FINANCE, JAPAN EXPORTS AND IMPORTS; ORGANIZATION FOR ECONOMIC COOPERATION AND DEVELOPMENT, FOREIGN TRADE STATISTICS, SERIES C; U.K. INSTITUTE OF GEOLOGICAL SCIENCES, STATISTICAL SUMMARY OF THE MINERAL INDUSTRY AND WORLD MINERAL STATISTICS 1970-1974 AND 1972-1976; U.S. BUREAU OF MINES, MINERALS YEARBOOK, MINERAL TRADE NOTES (VOLUME 74, NUMBER 10) AND UNPUBLISHED DATA; UNCTAD SECRETARIAT, CONSIDERATION OF INTERNATIONAL MEASURES OF MANGANESE; UNITED NATIONS STATISTICAL OFFICE, WORLD TRADE ANNUAL.

N.A. - NOT AVAILABLE.

[a] INCLUDES HIGH-CARBON, MEDIUM-CARBON, AND LOW-CARBON FERROMANGANESE.

[b] AN ESTIMATE OF ACTUAL MANGANESE CONTENT CAN BE OBTAINED BY MULTIPLYING THE FIGURES SHOWN BY 78 PERCENT.

[c] ACTUALLY, BELGIUM AND LUXEMBOURG.

[d] EXCLUDES ESTIMATES FOR THE PEOPLES REPUBLIC OF CHINA.

61

Table 1-9. Ratios of Manganese Ore Consumption to Ferromanganese Production and Consumption, for the World and Leading Manganese Ore Consumers, 1960-76[a]

A. Manganese Ore (Mn content) Consumption/Ferromanganese Production

	1962	1963	1964	1965	1966	1967	1968	1969	1970	1971	1972	1973	1974
United States	1.10	1.12	1.14	1.17	1.18	1.24	1.26	1.27	1.34	1.41	1.47	1.54	1.65
Japan	1.44	1.63	1.78	1.91	2.00	2.12	2.13	1.77	1.79	1.82	1.88	1.88	1.72
France	1.05	1.03	1.05	1.06	1.08	1.11	1.12	1.13	1.15	1.15	1.16	1.18	N.A.
Germany (F.R.)	.90	.97	1.03	1.08	1.09	1.10	1.11	1.17	1.14	1.16	1.14	1.14	"
Norway	2.15	1.97	1.97	1.90	1.88	1.71	1.65	1.58	1.53	1.50	1.51	1.48	"
Australia	1.04	1.19	1.54	1.96	2.57	2.84	2.78	3.01	3.19	3.85	4.80	5.75	"
Brazil	7.02	7.71	8.41	9.35	10.28	10.92	10.04	8.65	7.36	6.15	4.27	4.00	"
So. Africa	1.80	1.68	1.38	1.22	1.15	1.15	1.28	1.28	1.23	1.12	1.20	1.42	"
USSR	2.45	2.43	2.43	2.41	2.33	2.32	2.23	2.20	2.27	2.43	2.46	2.57	"
India	1.13	1.28	1.44	1.52	1.64	1.94	2.26	2.39	2.34	2.54	2.51	2.49	"
World	1.57	1.61	1.60	1.62	1.63	1.70	1.73	1.76	1.79	1.86	1.87	1.93	"

B. Ferromanganese Production/Consumption

	1962	1963	1964	1965	1966	1967	1968	1969	1970	1971	1972	1973	1974
United States	.87	.86	.85	.84	.86	.82	.80	.80	.79	.71	.63	.61	.54
Japan	1.12	1.08	1.08	1.05	1.03	1.01	.98	1.21	1.09	1.20	1.20	1.25	1.29
France	1.99	2.05	2.06	2.08	2.15	2.16	2.23	2.21	2.35	2.42	2.60	2.59	N.A.
Germany (F.R.)	.88	.89	.93	.94	.92	.88	.83	.77	.72	.67	.69	.68	"
Norway[b]													
Australia	.48	.61	.77	.78	.78	.80	.81	.81	.83	.86	.83	.84	N.A.
Brazil	1.00	1.07	1.07	1.07	1.06	1.05	1.04	1.05	1.15	1.16	1.15	1.15	"
So. Africa[b]													
USSR	1.08	1.08	1.08	1.09	1.10	1.11	1.12	1.13	1.15	1.16	1.16	1.16	1.17
India	1.73	1.63	1.42	1.44	1.57	1.67	1.71	1.70	1.84	1.68	1.41	1.26	1.27
World	1.09	1.06	1.07	1.06	1.06	1.06	1.04	1.05	1.05	1.02	1.01	1.01	N.A.

Table 1-9 (cont'd)

	1962	1963	1964	1965	1966	1967	1968	1969	1970	1971	1972	1973	1974
C. Manganese Ore (Mn content) Consumption/Ferromanganese Consumption													
United States	.96	.97	.97	.98	1.02	1.02	1.00	1.02	1.06	.99	.93	.94	.89
Japan	1.62	1.76	1.92	1.99	2.07	2.14	2.09	2.15	2.18	2.18	2.26	2.36	2.22
Germany (F.R.)	.79	.87	.96	1.01	1.01	.96	.92	.90	.83	.77	.78	.78	.73
Australia	.50	.73	1.18	1.53	2.01	2.26	2.24	2.44	2.66	3.30	4.01	4.83	N.A.
Brazil	7.02	8.25	9.03	10.00	10.92	11.51	10.40	9.11	8.47	7.12	4.94	4.60	4.65
USSR	2.63	2.61	2.62	2.62	2.55	2.57	2.49	2.50	2.61	2.82	2.85	3.00	3.10
India	1.95	2.09	2.04	2.20	2.57	3.17	3.87	4.06	4.31	4.28	3.52	3.13	3.19
World	1.71	1.71	1.72	1.72	1.74	1.79	1.80	1.84	1.88	1.90	1.88	1.94	N.A.
D. Manganese Ore (Mn content) Consumption/Ferromanganese Consumption by Principal Int'l Traders[c]													
France	.173	.169	.169	.162	.165	.166	.173	.180	.192	.200	.206	.210	.205
Norway	.068	.074	.083	.091	.106	.112	.112	.120	.124	.123	.133	.153	.159
South Africa	.110	.119	.108	.101	.098	.095	.097	.105	.104	.099	.118	.165	.210
E. Ferromanganese Consumption (kilos)/Steel Production (metric tons)													
United States	8.71	8.92	8.89	8.94	8.65	8.70	8.41	8.15	7.98	8.23	8.39	8.33	8.49
Japan	5.08	5.03	4.78	4.89	4.94	4.90	4.96	5.20	5.23	5.24	5.12	5.12	5.12
Belgium	9.78	9.26	8.94	8.53	8.49	7.63	7.75	7.93	7.95	6.11	5.44	4.52	N.A.
France	8.49	8.49	8.43	8.10	7.78	7.70	7.58	7.75	7.25	7.77	7.39	7.45	"
Germany (F.R.)	9.42	8.74	8.48	8.08	8.04	7.83	8.13	7.96	7.94	7.72	7.76	7.75	"
Italy	7.12	7.26	7.33	7.11	6.68	6.99	7.10	7.26	7.15	7.77	8.03	8.22	"

(continued on next page)

63

Table 1-9 (cont'd)

	1962	1963	1964	1965	1966	1967	1968	1969	1970	1971	1972	1973	1974
United Kingdom	8.05	8.07	8.23	8.10	8.25	8.56	8.43	8.51	8.66	8.78	8.77	8.92	N.A.
USSR	9.58	9.60	9.41	9.02	8.70	8.10	7.72	7.24	6.78	6.33	6.17	5.90	5.64
India	12.73	13.53	15.10	14.63	13.78	13.84	13.69	14.51	13.59	17.20	18.15	17.36	N.A.
Brazil	7.85	7.07	7.20	7.03	7.17	7.54	7.64	8.45	8.22	8.67	9.14	9.49	"
Australia	8.93	8.72	8.75	9.82	9.25	9.17	8.86	8.33	8.09	7.63	7.49	7.27	"
World	7.74	7.94	7.97	7.86	7.72	7.46	7.20	7.03	6.82	6.70	6.74	6.72	"

N.A. - Not available.

a
Ratios are based on five-year moving-average trends, centered on years shown.

b
Usable consumption series not available; country is a substantial net exporter.

c
Includes the United States, Japan, Belgium, France, Germany, Italy, and the United Kingdom. All except France and Japan are important gross importers of ferromanganese.

Aluminum

Aluminum has been the fastest growing of the principal nonferrous metals (see figure 1-4), and its consumption, both as metal and in crude and intermediate forms (bauxite and alumina) is increasingly dispersed. Nonetheless, three countries--the United States, the USSR, and Japan-- account for more than half the world's consumption both of aluminum and alumina. It also takes only three countries to account for more than half the world's consumption of bauxite, but in this case, Australia substitutes for Japan. Consumption trends for these countries, plus a number of runner-up consumers, are shown in figures 1-23 through 1-27. The numerical data for all leading consumers are shown in tables 1-10 through 1-12.

Figure 1-27 confirms the very rapid growth of aluminum consumption in Japan, eclipsing even the rapid growth in Germany in the past quarter- century. Germany, in turn, has increased its aluminum consumption at a faster pace than that of the United States or the Soviet Union, which (figure 1-26) has settled into a pattern of rather similar growth trends, though consumption in the United States exhibits considerably more year- to-year fluctuation.

Comparative trends for alumina (figure 1-25) reflect changes in the degree of smelting self-sufficiency. Japan has remained rather steady in this respect, while the United States has tended to become slightly more of an aluminum importer and the USSR more of an exporter. Canada converts alumina into aluminum mostly for export, the quantities tending to trend slightly upward. The sharp drop in consumption in 1976 reflects strikes in the refining and smelting industries; there was a subsequent recovery in 1977 to near-1974 levels.

The most striking thing about bauxite consumption is the steep rise in Japan, exceeded only by the meteoric rise in Australia (figure 1-24). Japan had already had a rise comparable to Australia's; its consumption in 1954 was lower than that in Australia a decade later. The difference, besides timing, is that Japan's rise in bauxite consumption reflects the rate of increase in its domestic metal consumption; in Australia it is the substantial shift from crude to refined bauxite in the service of other countries' metal consumption. A similar (though less extensive) shift in Jamaica results in a steep rise in bauxite consumption in that country as well (figure 1-23), though one which is more vulnerable to business cycles and to the state of Jamaica's relations with alumina-consuming customers. Since the shift into bauxite refining in both Australia and Jamaica has been largely at the expense of such refining in the United States, the trend in U.S. consumption of bauxite shows up as relatively flat.

Three countries stand out in their use of aluminum scrap--the United States, Japan, and Germany. Their consumption is shown in figure 1-28 and, along with that of other important consumers, presented numerically in table 1-13. As may be seen, Japan's use has grown from almost nothing at the start of the 1950s to a point where it now exceeds Germany's. The explanation, of course, is the equally steep rise in aluminum consumption, which, with a lag, generates scrap to match. Figures 1-29 through 31 compare the consumption of scrap with the consumption of refined aluminum in each of the three countries. The lag between the two curves is limited by the fact that part of the scrap consumption accounted for is prompt industrial scrap. Other discrepancies in movement arise out of the fact that there is a difference between obsolete scrap generation (discards) and the amounts actually reclaimed, since the latter amounts are in part responsive to current demand and price realization. Hence, the trends in scrap consumption tend to match concurrent trends in refined aluminum consumption as much as they do the lagged trends.

It is useful to examine the consumption ratios for bauxite in making alumina and for alumina in making aluminum metal. This is done in tables 1-14 and 1-15. Since the bauxite consumption data are in terms of estimated aluminum content and the alumina data in terms of gross weight, technical perfection should result in a ratio between the two (part A of table 1-14) of approximately 0.53. The fact that the ratios for both Australia and Canada have dipped below that mark may be due to statistical inadequacies or to impurities. The much lower ratios for Surinam, on the other hand, appear to be due to a serious data incompatibility between aluminum content of bauxite production and bauxite exports, as estimated

by our data source, UNCTAD.[16] The higher ratios for the United States
and the other industrialized consuming countries are presumably due to
the diversion of some amounts of bauxite to the production of abrasives,
refractories, and various chemicals, as well as to losses in processing.

Part B of table 1-14 reveals trends in alumina self-sufficiency.
This has been declining both for the United States and Japan, but Japan
appears to have been able to slow down the rate of increasing dependence
on foreign sources. Germany has moved from being more than self-sufficient
to being a net importer, though its position in this regard appears to
have stabilized. France is increasingly a net exporter, shipping mostly
to other countries in Western Europe.

Part of C of the table relates bauxite consumption directly to alumina
consumption for those countries (including France) that consume the bulk
of their alumina domestically. In the case of Australia, Jamaica, and
Surinam, the more useful relationship is to total alumina consumption in
the "trading world" (part D). The latter includes both important ultimate
consumers of aluminum and those--specifically Canada and Norway--that turn
the alumina into aluminum mostly for others. Taking into account the
bauxite (aluminum content) to alumina conversion ratio, it may be seen that
Australia has grown to be a supplier of more than a fifth of the trading
world's alumina requirements. Jamaica and Surinam are also increasingly
refining bauxite into alumina for others and between them account for
roughly another fifth of the total trading-world requirement.

Coefficients relating alumina consumption to aluminum production,
for most of the countries given in part A of table 1-15, are well below
technical input-ouput levels, which would approximate 1.9 if there were
no processing losses. The reason is the inclusion in the denominator of
secondary aluminum (refined and remelted only), which is important for
all the countries shown except Canada and Norway. Norway's ratios, it
may be noted, have come close to the technical limits; Canada's seem to
be steadily receding therefrom, for reasons that could conceivably have
to do either with impurity (including hydration) of the alumina, or processing losses, or both. In actuality, the true input-output ratios

[16]See footnote b in table 1-14.

(aluminum to primary aluminum) in Norway are slightly higher than those shown in part A (for example, 1.99 in 1974), since there is some secondary utilization, but the trends remain. The same may be said of Canada. In fact, in terms of purely primary aluminum output, only Germany, in recent years, has had poorer alumina input ratios than Canada, though the German trend is toward improvement. On this same basis, both France and the United States have done better than Norway—the former declining from a 2.08 ratio in 1969 to 1.91 in 1974 and the latter from 2.00 in 1969 to 1.97 in 1974.[17]

Trends in relative self-sufficiency are visible in part B of table 1-15. Both the United States and France have had declining self-sufficiency; Germany, though still a net importer, has been increasing in self-sufficiency. The USSR, it will be noted, was already a significant net exporter of aluminum in 1968 (other Comecon countries are presumably the principal recipients) and has been slowly increasing its net export position.

The combination ratios in part C of the table reflect the joint effect of scrap utilization, foreign trade, and conversion efficiency. They are designed as shortcut routes to alumina projection. Since Canada and Norway primarily supply others with aluminum rather than themselves, their alumina consumption ratios are related to aluminum consumption in the whole Western trading world.

Comparative long-term trends in the relative use of scrap, shown in table 1-16, include some surprises—notably that all the leading consumers have higher percentages than the United States. Germany's has been declining, and this has much to do with the rising alumina/aluminum ratios shown in table 1-15. Japan's scrap use has been rising at a rate that is remarkable for a country that is also increasing its aluminum consumption so rapidly, since a rapid rate of consumption growth automatically depresses the percentage of obsolete scrap available. One may hypothesize that there is a fairly high ratio of current scrap generation in Japanese aluminum fabrication, presumably because of the kinds of products made.

---

[17] It is to be remembered that all these ratios refer to five-year moving averages centered on the years mentioned.

Moreover, there is not a direct technical relationship between scrap consumption and refined metal consumption, as here compiled, because the former includes quantities of purchased scrap which are reused directly by foundries and fabricators rather than being sent back through refining or remelting into marketed aluminum.[18] Finally, Japan (as Germany) is a significant aluminum scrap importer, though not to the extent that this would wholly explain the high scrap-use ratios. The fact that the United Kingdom has maintained one of the highest of the scrap ratios is consistent with its having one of the slowest rates of growth in aluminum consumption.

Aluminum/macroeconomic relationships are given in table 1-17. Because the denominators are in different currency units, it takes a set of currency conversion assumptions to compare "intensities of use"[19] among countries. However, over the twenty-five-year period for which moving-average relationships are shown in table 1-17, it may be seen directly that all of the principal consumers have increased their aluminum consumption intensities, with the highest rates of increase being exhibited by Japan and the lowest by the United Kingdom (which may have passed its intensity peak). As will be seen in similar tabulations for the other nonferrous metals covered here, the rapid increases exhibited in table 1-17 are not generally characteristic of metals use in the advanced industrial countries. Declining, rather than rising ratios per unit of gross product seem to be typically the case for metals (and materials generally) in the aggregate. The exceptional trends for aluminum reflect its substitution for other metals, notably copper, zinc, and steel.

If 1975 international exchange rates are applied to the average ratios centered on 1974, it leads to the conclusion that Japan's rapid increase in aluminum use has brought it almost abreast of the U.S. intensity level of 3 1/2 tons per million dollars of GNP. Germany and the United Kingdom are lower, at 2 1/2 tons, and France trails, at less than 2 tons. These rates

---

[18]For an analysis of the percentage contribution of scrap in the United States to the refined aluminum supply as such, see table 4-9.

[19]A phrase which seems to have been introduced by Professor Wilfred Malenbaum of the University of Pennsylvania, originally in projection studies done in 1972 for the National Commission on Materials Policy.

of usage relative to the United States are unusual. For metals other than aluminum (and for metals generally), Germany and Japan both tend to have higher rates of consumption per unit of GNP, while the United Kingdom tends to be on a par with the United States; data for France have not yet been calculated. The implication is that the upward trend in intensity of use in Germany and Japan, at least, has not yet run its course, even if that in the United States conforms to the recent indications that it has probably peaked out.

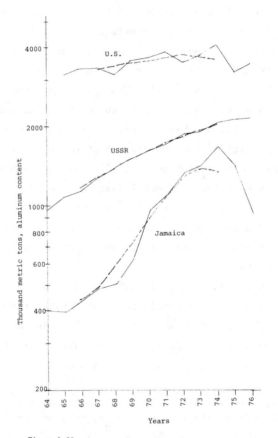

Figure 1-23. Apparent Consumption of Bauxite in the United States, USSR, and Jamaica, 1964-1976, Annually and Five-Year Moving-Average Trends

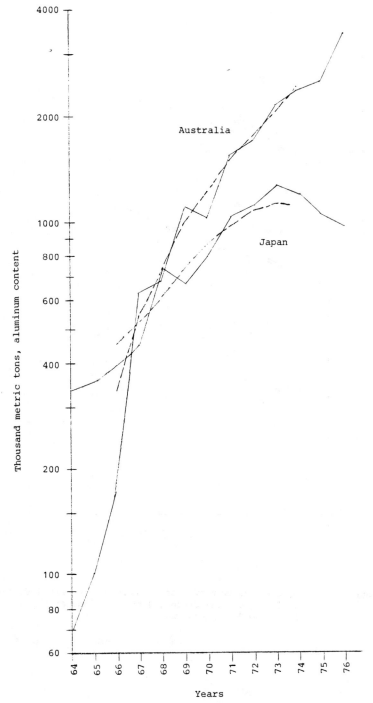

Figure 1-24. Apparent Consumption of Bauxite in Japan and Australia, 1964-1976, Annually and Five-Year Moving-Average Trends

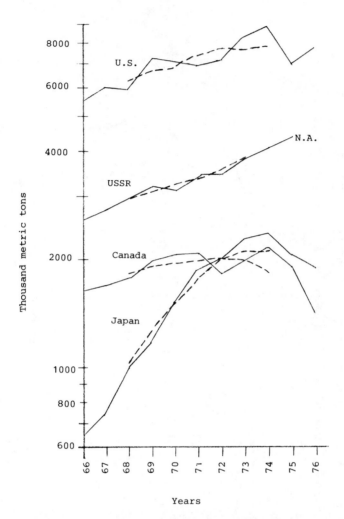

Figure 1-25. Apparent Consumption of Alumina in the United States, USSR, Japan, and Canada, 1966–1976, Annually and Five-Year Moving-Average Trends

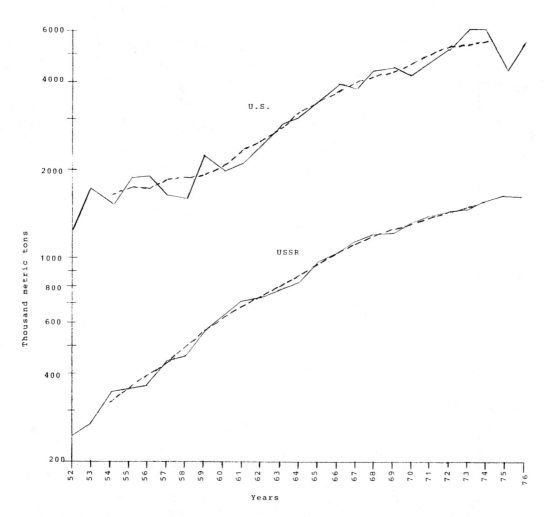

Figure 1-26.   Apparent Consumption of Refined Aluminum in the United
                States and the USSR, 1952-1976, Annually and Five-Year
                Moving-Average Trends

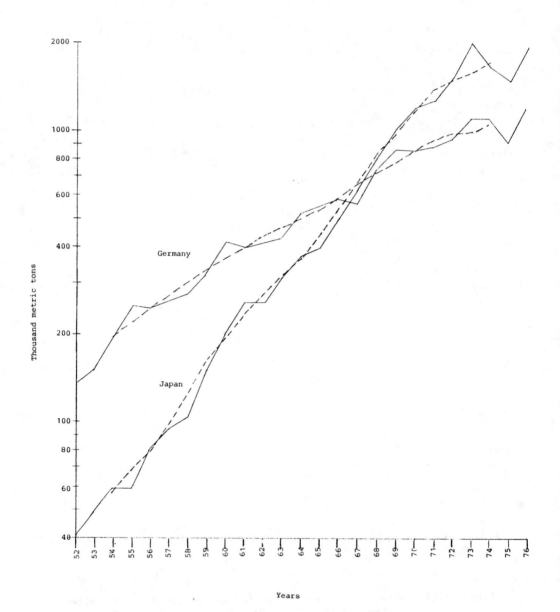

Figure 1-27.   Apparent Consumption of Refined Aluminum in Germany and
Japan, 1952-1976, Annually and Five-Year Moving-Average
Trends

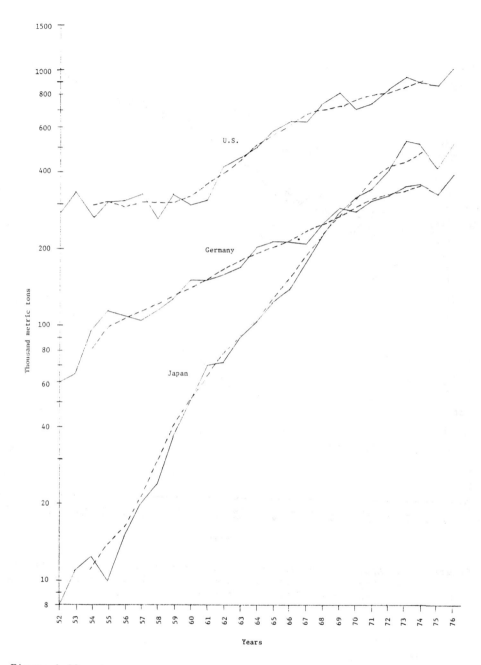

Figure 1-28. Apparent Consumption of Aluminum Scrap in the United States, Japan, and Germany, 1952–1976, Annually and Five-Year Moving-Average Trends

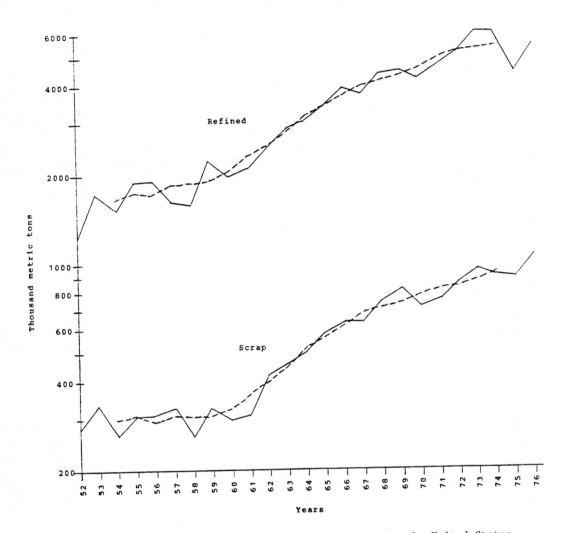

Figure 1-29. Apparent Consumption of Aluminum Scrap in the United States
Compared With Apparent Consumption of Refined Aluminum,
Annually and Five-Year Moving-Average Trends

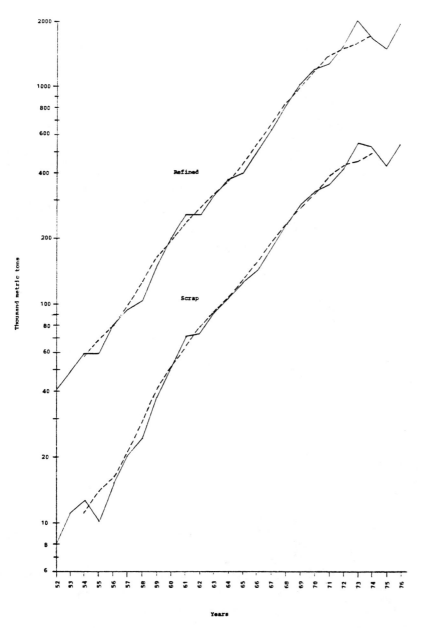

Figure 1-30. Apparent Consumption of Aluminum Scrap in Japan
Compared With Apparent Consumption of Refined
Aluminum, Annually and Five-Year Moving-Average
Trends

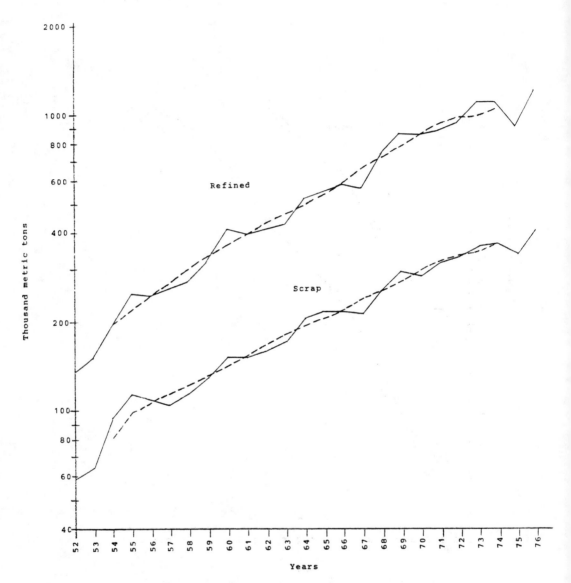

Figure 1-31. Apparent Consumption of Aluminum Scrap in Germany Compared
With Apparent Consumption of Refined Aluminum, Annually
and Five-Year Moving-Average Trends

TABLE 1-10. WORLD APPARENT CONSUMPTION OF BAUXITE,[a] 1964-77, BY COUNTRY[a]

(THOUSAND METRIC TONS, ALUMINUM CONTENT)

| YEAR | UNITED STATES[b] | AUSTRALIA | USSR | PRINCIPAL INTERNATIONAL TRADERS | | | | | | | OTHER COUNTRIES | WORLD TOTAL[c] |
				JAMAICA	JAPAN	FRANCE	GERMANY (F.R.)	CANADA	SURINAM	TOTAL		
1964	N.A.	70	960	405	341	448	389	365	0	--	3712	6690
1965	3142	100	1080	403	362	488	393	434	0	6402	1438	7840
1966	3300	178	1140	443	401	503	451	527	58	7001	1269	8270
1967	3320	633	1290	491	459	546	433	535	204	7911	1189	9100
1968	3146	680	1390	508	759	555	475	524	261	8298	1102	9400
1969	3545	1103	1520	637	687	607	485	520	401	9505	1495	11000
1970	3621	1032	1630	966	831	659	626	576	418	10359	2561	12920
1971	3792	1545	1720	1108	1071	698	676	568	516	11694	2696	14390
1972	3501	1702	1863	1339	1154	747	567	594	685	12152	4028	16180
1973	3690	2151	1920	1427	1306	688	663	596	539	12980	3070	16050
1974	4043	2381	2050	1683	1232	775	1074	615	394	14247	3753	18000
1975	3196	2515	2120	1399	1078	823	1027	581	433	13172	3328	16500
1976	3447	3464	2150	924	1001	933	973	581	485	13672	3528	17200
1977	3437	3796	N.A.	[d]1060	1170	857	982	295	530	--	--	17720

SOURCE: METALLGESELLSCHAFT AG, METAL STATISTICS; U.K. INSTITUTE OF GEOLOGICAL SCIENCES, WORLD MINERAL STATISTICS; UNCTAD SECRETARIAT, CONSIDERATION OF INTERNATIONAL MEASURES ON BAUXITE; U.S. BUREAU OF MINES, MINERALS YEARBOOK AND UNPUBLISHED DATA.

NOTE: DETAIL MAY NOT ADD TO TOTALS, OWING TO ROUNDING.

N.A. - NOT AVAILABLE.

[a] INCLUDES ALL TYPES OF BAUXITE: GIBBSITE, BOEHMITE, AND MIXED.

[b] INCLUDES THE VIRGIN ISLANDS.

[c] ACTUALLY, PRODUCTION OF BAUXITE AS ESTIMATED BY METALLGESELLSCHAFT AG, MULTIPLIED BY UNCTAD METAL CONTENT PERCENTAGE ESTIMATES. ADJUSTED FOR U.S. GOVERNMENT STOCK CHANGES.

[d] PRELIMINARY.

TABLE 1-11. WORLD APPARENT CONSUMPTION OF ALUMINA, 1966-77, BY COUNTRY[a]

(THOUSAND METRIC TONS)[a]

YEAR	PRINCIPAL INTERNATIONAL TRADERS								OTHER COUNTRIES	WORLD TOTAL[b]
	UNITED STATES	USSR	JAPAN	CANADA	FRANCE	GERMANY (F.R.)	NORWAY	TOTAL		
1966	5460	2600	652	1633	721	562	609	12232	2543	14780
1967	5949	2766	754	1690	740	585	985	13469	2971	16440
1968	5904	2988	993	1772	776	613	944	13989	3481	17470
1969	7127	3196	1195	1969	742	656	994	15879	3871	17750
1970	7092	3118	1535	2048	809	781	997	16380	4620	21200
1971	6982	3405	1886	2066	810	1034	1128	17311	5469	22780
1972	7217	3448	2015	1821	738	1020	1010	17269	6341	23610
1973	8224	3803	2294	1986	735	1186	1226	19454	2346	26600
1974	8746	4066	2368	2148	731	1556	1258	20874	7856	28730
1975	6923	4329	2069	1894	733	1483	1240	18671	7769	26440
1976	7638	4350	1915	1398	720	1480	1314	18815	8725	27540
1977	8211	N.A.	2521	1883	778	1632	1268	--	--	30050

SOURCE: METALLGESELLSCHAFT AG, METAL STATISTICS; U.S. BUREAU OF MINES, MINERALS YEARBOOK, AND UNPUBLISHED DATA.

NOTE: DETAIL MAY NOT ADD TO TOTALS, OWING TO ROUNDING.

N.A. - NOT AVAILABLE.

[a] AN ESTIMATE OF METAL CONTENT MAY BE OBTAINED BY MULTIPLYING THE FIGURES SHOWN BY 50 PERCENT.

[b] ACTUALLY, PRODUCTION OF ALUMINA AS ESTIMATED BY METALLGESELLSCHAFT AG.

TABLE 1-12. WORLD APPARENT CONSUMPTION OF REFINED ALUMINUM,[a] 1952-77, BY COUNTRY

(THOUSAND METRIC TONS)

YEAR	PRINCIPAL INTERNATIONAL TRADERS						OTHER COUNTRIES		WORLD TOTAL[b]
	UNITED STATES	GERMANY (F.R.)	FRANCE	UNITED KINGDOM	USSR	TOTAL	JAPAN	OTHER	
1952	1238	137	111	298	250	2034	41	345	2420
1953	1735	152	98	265	275	2526	49	385	2960
1954	1537	194	126	314	350	2520	59	481	3060
1955	1863	249	140	388	358	3017	59	603	3680
1956	1913	246	167	378	370	3074	80	655	3810
1957	1637	260	190	316	445	2847	95	669	3610
1958	1593	274	184	337	465	2853	104	803	3760
1959	2429	322	212	403	553	3719	150	922	4790
1960	1978	412	257	471	632	3249	200	1071	5020
1961	2098	397	250	396	714	3855	255	1170	5280
1962	2447	410	282	412	734	4286	256	1308	5850
1963	2611	428	292	459	778	4768	312	1430	6510
1964	3019	521	300	524	825	5189	370	1602	7160
1965	3394	548	299	517	971	5729	398	1743	7870
1966	3895	578	358	523	1044	6398	500	2142	9040
1967	3739	561	357	517	1147	6320	630	2311	9260
1968	4333	730	367	563	1212	7204	807	2598	10610
1969	4467	859	455	581	1230	7593	1021	2977	11590
1970	4186	857	501	583	1331	7758	1178	3264	11900
1971	4659	882	475	489	1394	7899	1255	3506	12660
1972	5140	936	510	577	1445	8608	1515	3847	13970
1973	5994	1099	584	664	1482	9823	1975	4402	16200
1974	5941	1101	597	655	1571	9865	1649	4867	16380
1975	4370	905	513	534	1648	8070	1480	4430	13880
1976	5397	1208	630	585	1640	9460	1921	5199	16580
1977	5695	1180	672	558	1760	9865	1802	5527	17190

SOURCE: METALLGESELLSCHAFT AG, METAL STATISTICS AND U.S. BUREAU OF MINES, MINERALS YEARBOOK.

NOTE: DETAIL MAY NOT ADD TO TOTALS, OWING TO ROUNDING.

N.A. - NOT AVAILABLE.

[a] INCLUDES REMELTED ALUMINUM, BUT EXCLUDES SCRAP USED DIRECTLY. (FOR THE U.S., EXCLUDES ONLY THE ALUMINUM RECOVERED OTHER THAN AS ALUMINUM METAL OR ALUMINUM-BASE ALLOY.)

[b] TOTAL CONSUMPTION OF ALUMINUM AS ESTIMATED BY METALLGESELLSCHAFT, MINUS KNOWN DIRECT USE OF SCRAP.

TABLE 1-13. WORLD APPARENT CONSUMPTION OF ALUMINUM (AND ALUMINUM ALLOY) SCRAP, 1952-77, COUNTRY[a]

(THOUSAND METRIC TONS, ALUMINUM CONTENT)

| YEAR | UNITED STATES | PRINCIPAL INTERNATIONAL TRADERS | | | | | | OTHER COUNTRIES | WORLD TOTAL[b] |
		JAPAN	GERMANY (F.R.)	UNITED KINGDOM	ITALY	FRANCE	TOTAL		
1952	276	8	59	86	17	21	467	39	506
1953	334	11	64	93	20	23	545	43	588
1954	265	12	91	96	24	27	515	49	564
1955	305	10	114	109	23	32	592	60	652
1956	308	15	109	109	22	32	595	60	655
1957	328	20	105	111	23	37	623	69	692
1958	263	24	115	115	27	41	583	81	664
1959	327	37	128	124	30	45	690	87	777
1960	299	50	151	129	42	44	714	95	809
1961	309	70	151	131	45	43	748	63	811
1962	419	72	159	141	56	47	893	71	964
1963	459	91	171	159	65	50	994	83	1077
1964	501	104	203	182	58	50	1099	97	1196
1965	581	124	214	190	61	50	1219	109	1328
1966	629	141	214	200	85	60	1327	144	1471
1967	633	181	212	174	102	63	1365	172	1537
1968	741	227	251	190	102	74	1584	187	1771
1969	817	281	290	209	178	88	1863	162	2025
1970	709	322	283	199	154	87	1754	223	1977
1971	741	349	312	188	150	98	1837	231	2068
1972	858	412	327	200	164	112	2072	245	2317
1973	943	537	361	200	192	124	2355	319	2674
1974	901	517	369	188	209	128	2311	355	2666
1975	689	424	338	173	151	107	2081	326	2407
1976	1048	526	400	173	198	142	2487	398	2885
1977	1153	575	462	171	225	153	2739	415	3154

SOURCE: METALLGESELLSCHAFT AG, METAL STATISTICS.

NOTE: DETAIL MAY NOT ADD TO TOTALS, OWING TO ROUNDING.

[a]DATA ACTUALLY RELATE TO DIRECT AND IMPLICIT ALUMINUM RECOVERY FROM ALL TYPES OF SCRAP AND WASTE, HOWEVER, ONLY A NEGLIGIBLE PROPORTION, USUALLY, IS OTHER THAN ALUMINUM-BASE SCRAP.

[b]EXCLUDES USSR, CHINA, AND EASTERN EUROPE. ACTUALLY, ALUMINUM RECOVERED FROM SCRAP AS ESTIMATED BY METALLGESELLSCHAFT, PLUS DIRECT USE OF SCRAP BY MANUFACTURERS WHERE AVAILABLE (GERMANY, UNITED KINGDOM, AND UNITED STATES).

82

Table 1-14. Ratios of Bauxite Consumption to Alumina
Production and Consumption, for the World and
Leading Bauxite Consumers, 1965-76[a]

	1967	1968	1969	1970	1971	1972	1973	1974
A. Bauxite (Al content) Consumption/Alumina Production (gross weight)								
United States	.59	.59	.62	.60	.60	.62	.63	.63
Australia	.59	.55	.56	.54	.54	.52	.52	.52
USSR	N.A.	.54	.58	.62	.64	.65	.65	N.A.
Jamaica	N.A.	.55	.56	.58	.58	.59	.61	.60
Japan	.69	.69	.69	.70	.67	.67	.68	.69
France	.60	.61	.62	.64	.67	.69	.71	.76
Germany (F.R.)	.72	.74	.76	.74	.73	.76	.77	.75
Canada	N.A.	.54	.52	.52	.52	.51	.51	.52
Surinam[b]	(c)	.33	.37	.41	.42	.41	.40	.41
World	N.A.	.57	.58	.61	.62	.63	.63	.63
B. Alumina Production/Consumption[d]								
United States	.94	91	.86	.86	.82	.79	.76	.73
USSR	N.A.	.89	.84	.82	.80	.79	.78	N.A.
Japan	.93	.89	.86	.84	.85	.82	.81	.79
France	1.22	1.24	1.27	1.32	1.32	1.36	1.41	1.43
Germany (F.R.)	1.06	1.04	.97	.94	.88	.85	.83	.85
Canada	N.A.	.55	.55	.56	.56	.57	.59	.56

(continued on next page)

Table 1-14 (cont'd.)

	1967	1968	1969	1970	1971	1972	1973	1974	1975
C. Bauxite (Al content) Consumption/Alumina Consumption									
United States	.56	.54	.53	.51	.50	.49	.48	.46	.45
USSR	.56	.48	.49	.50	.51	.51	.51	.50	N.A.
Japan	.64	.61	.60	.59	.57	.55	.55	.54	.52
France	.74	.76	.79	.84	.89	.93	1.00	1.08	1.10
Germany (F.R.)	.76	.77	.73	.69	.65	.65	.64	.64	.64
Canada	N.A.	.29	.29	.29	.29	.29	.30	.30	.29
World[e]	N.A.	.57	.58	.61	.62	.63	.63	.63	N.A.
D. Bauxite (Al content) Consumption/Alumina Cons. by Prin. Int'l Traders									
Australia	N.A.	.050	.065	.075	.087	.097	.110	N.A.	N.A.
Jamaica	N.A.	.042	.048	.056	.063	.071	.074	"	"
Surinam	N.A.	.019	.023	.028	.030	.028	.027	"	"

N.A. - Not available.

[a] Ratios are based on five-year moving-average trends, centered on years shown.

[b] The Surinam data are prima facie invalid, since the technical content of aluminum in alumina (Al_2O_3) is around 53 percent. The bauxite data--which were derived by UNCTAD in terms of aluminum content from gross data from other sources--are the series believed at fault. UNCTAD estimates ascribed a higher aluminium content to exported bauxite than to bauxite consumed locally, thereby probably underestimating local consumption.

[c] There was no alumina production in Surinam in 1965 (at least according to some sources), thereby making a five-year moving-average centered on 1967 misleading.

[d] Bauxite consumers not shown exported all, or nearly all, their alumina production. The ratio for the world is 1.00, since world production had to be taken as the measure of world consumption.

[e] Same as ratio in part A, for reason given in preceding footnote.

Table 1-15. Ratios of Alumina Consumption to Aluminum
Production and Consumption, for the World
and Leading Alumina Consumers, 1966-77[a]

	1968	1969	1970	1971	1972	1973	1974	1975
A. Alumina Consumption/Aluminum Production								
United States	1.65	1.65	1.63	1.63	1.63	1.62	1.62	N.A.
USSR	1.97	1.95	1.91	1.90	1.88	1.91	N.A.	"
Japan	1.41	1.45	1.45	1.44	1.45	1.44	1.41	"
Canada	1.95	1.96	1.97	2.00	2.02	2.03	2.05	"
France	1.70	1.70	1.64	1.59	1.55	1.51	1.45	"
Germany (F.R.)	1.29	1.34	1.35	1.37	1.43	1.47	1.45	"
Norway	2.05	2.10	1.95	1.94	1.93	1.97	1.97	"
World[b]	1.71	1.74	1.73	1.72	1.73	1.76	1.73	"
B. Aluminum Production/Consumption								
United States	.93	.94	.92	.92	.91	.90	.90	"
USSR	1.25	1.26	1.28	1.30	1.31	1.32	1.33	"
Japan	.88	.90	.91	.89	.92	.94	.89	"
France	1.09	1.06	1.02	.95	.92	.93	.89	"
Germany (F.R.)	.69	.70	.71	.74	.80	.87	.88	"
C. Alumina Consumption/Aluminum Consumption								
United States	1.53	1.55	1.51	1.50	1.48	1.46	1.44	1.45
USSR	2.46	2.45	2.44	2.47	2.47	2.53	N.A.	N.A.
Japan	1.24	1.30	1.32	1.29	1.33	1.35	1.25	1.27
France	1.86	1.80	1.68	1.52	1.43	1.40	1.29	1.23
Germany (F.R.)	.89	.94	.96	1.01	1.14	1.28	1.28	1.34
World	1.71	1.74	1.73	1.72	1.73	1.76	1.73	N.A.

(continued on next page)

Table 1-15 (cont'd.)

	1968	1969	1970	1971	1972	1973	1974	1975
D. Alumina Consumption/Aluminum Cons. by Prin. Int'l Traders								
Canada	.314	.316	.301	.287	.276	.271	.244	.239
Norway	.156	.167	.158	.155	.154	.160	.159	.162

N.A. - Not available.

[a] Ratios are based on five-year moving-average trends, centered on year shown. Aluminum production and consumption refer to refined aluminum, primary and secondary (see table 1-13).

[b] Actually, ratio to refined aluminum consumption. It was not possible to arrive at a comparable series for world production, owing to the inadequacy of data on refined aluminum recovery from scrap.

Table 1-16. Ratios of Aluminum Scrap Consumption to
Aluminum Consumption, for the World and Leading
Aluminum Consumers, 1957-1975

Year	U.S.	Germany (F.R.)	Italy	France	U.K.	Japan	World
1954	.179	447	.265	.210	.300	.194	.186
1955	.177	.439	.266	.209	.312	.199	.184
1956	.172	.437	.270	.209	.312	.204	.180
1957	.165	.423	.266	.209	.312	.217	.175
1958	.163	.402	.260	.197	.309	.232	.171
1959	.160	.390	.273	.192	.317	.250	.167
1960	.156	.388	.290	.186	.317	.262	.163
1961	.157	.386	.301	.177	.319	.273	.162
1962	.161	.385	.310	.169	.328	.278	.163
1963	.165	.390	.313	.169	.348	.290	.165
1964	.166	.387	.322	.168	.358	.290	.166
1965	.166	.385	.332	.170	.356	.290	.166
1966	.168	.372	.325	.177	.354	.287	.166
1967	.172	.361	.362	.182	.357	.284	.168
1968	.171	349	.367	.183	.351	.279	.168
1969	.170	347	.371	.190	.351	.278	.167
1970	.170	.343	.368	.199	.353	.275	.167
1971	.166	.340	.374	.202	.344	.274	.167
1972	.160	.339	.358	.206	.329	.282	.165
1973	.166	.347	.353	.212	.325	.284	.166
1974	.173	.342	.349	.216	.309	.283	.168
1975	.180	.351	.351	.218	.302	.292	N.A.

N.A. - Not available

[a]Excludes USSR, for which scrap data are not available.
Ratios are based on five-year moving-average trends, centered on years
shown. In lieu of data on aluminum scrap as such, consumption data
actually are for direct and indirect aluminum recovery from scrap.

Table 1-17. Ratios of Refined Aluminum Consumption to GNP/GDP, for Leading Aluminum Consumers, 1952-76[a]

(metric tons)

Denominator	U.S. $ million	Germany (F.R.) DM million	France Fr million	U.K. £ million	Japan Y million	USSR Index[b]
1954	2.07	N.A.	.255	5.40	2.3	7.5
1955	2.11	.51	.273	5.29	2.5	7.9
1956	2.04	.53	.292	5.40	2.7	8.2
1957	2.14	.55	.308	5.55	3.1	8.4
1958	2.11	.58	.331	5.65	3.7	9.0
1959	2.10	.60	.340	5.54	4.3	9.7
1960	2.20	.62	.350	5.67	4.7	10.1
1961	2.37	.64	.360	5.81	5.2	10.8
1962	2.43	.67	.362	5.92	5.5	11.1
1963	2.59	.68	.352	5.85	5.7	11.6
1964	2.78	.70	.358	6.00	6.0	11.9
1965	2.87	.72	.356	6.06	6.6	12.4
1966	2.99	.77	.354	6.12	7.2	12.8
1967	3.09	.82	.366	6.11	8.1	13.1
1968	3.12	.86	.384	6.12	8.9	13.2
1969	3.16	.89	.384	5.90	9.5	13.3
1970	3.27	.93	.388	5.88	10.1	13.4
1971	3.39	.96	.400	5.90	11.1	13.3
1972	3.51	.97	.403	5.90	11.3	13.3
1973	3.46	.96	.390	5.70	11.3	13.4
1974	3.46	1.00	.398	5.79	11.6	13.3

a Ratios, in metric tons per denominator shown at head of column, are based on five-year moving-average trends, centered on year shown. Currencies are all in constant (1975) currencies.

b GNP index, 1970 = 100 (see chapter 2). Ratios are per index point.

Copper

All three of the world's leading consumers of copper--the United States, Japan, and the USSR--have highly integrated supply systems. Even in Japan, which alone among the three countries depends principally on imported ore, refined copper is very largely the end product of domestic smelting and refining. Thus all three countries figure among the leading consumers of ore and blister copper, as well as refined copper and scrap.

In the consumption both of ore[20] and of blister copper, however, these leaders have important competitors (tables 1-18 and 1-19). Both Chile and Canada process large amounts of ore domestically and export ore directly, while Zambia and Zaire smelt nearly all of their ore before export. Canada and Zambia further process most or all of the smelted (blister) copper into refined; Chile has been refining progressively more and exporting progressively less; but Zaire still exports the bulk of its blister copper to Belgium for refining. The result is that Chile, Zambia, and Canada were until recently only moderately behind Japan as blister copper consumers. Runners-up in the consumption of refined copper (table 1-20) are Germany, the United Kingdom, France, and Italy.

At all stages Japan has had much the highest growth rates (figures 1-32 to 1-34). USSR growth rates have also been higher than those of the United States, and a lot steadier (at least according to available data). The large dips in U.S. ore and blister consumption in 1959 and 1967 are not due to cyclical fluctuations, however, but to prolonged strikes in each of those years. Consumption of refined copper was only mildly affected by these strikes, since supplies could be made up by imports and stock drawdowns.

Another copper feedstock scrap is only partly coordinated with the consumption of refined copper. So much copper scrap, both new and old, is directly consumed by foundries, fabricators, and other processors that the consumption of scrap in Japan in the early 1950s actually exceeded the amount of refined copper (primary and secondary) produced. Since then,

---

[20]Throughout, "ore" actually is meant to include the metal content of ores and concentrates.

scrap use in Japan (see table 1-21) has tended toward the average world relationship of scrap to refined copper (see table 1-24). Despite the implied slower growth rate of its scrap/refined ratio, Japan's absolute use of scrap nonetheless places it among the fastest growing of any of the principal consumers, being approached only by Italy. Figures 1-35 and 1-36 show the relative trends.

Analogously with aluminum, ore consumption may be related to blister copper consumption, and blister to refined copper. This is done for all of the principal consumers in tables 1-22 and 1-23, which also indicate production/consumption, or self-sufficiency, relationships. The fact that the United States, Japan, and Canada all show input-output ore to blister relationships of less than one (table 1-22) is presumably due mostly to the inclusion of some scrap copper in the smelter feed.[21] For a number of the consuming countries, ore consumption as such was not available and had to be taken as equal to blister copper production.

The increasing degree of blister self-sufficiency in the United States, and the downward-upward swings in Japan and Canada are evident in part B of table 1-22.[22] The series for Chile and for Zambia confirm the progressive tendency in those countries (now almost complete in the latter) to put the blister copper through refining before export. Zaire has an equivocal record, but seems to be moving toward greater dependence on refining in Belgium (and elsewhere) in place of the 50-50 split between domestic and foreign refining which appeared to hold for a number of years.[23]

---

[21]In the case of the United States, at least, smelting losses are washed out statistically by the U.S. practice of estimating copper content or ores on a "recoverable" basis. Since blister copper has a copper content of less than 100 (96-99) percent, the U.S. input-output ratio for smelting would have to be less than one, since the blister is measured in gross weight. As a countervailing factor, however, not all ore goes through smelting.

[22]The Canadian (as well as the USSR) series should not be interpreted too precisely, however. Blister copper consumption had to be estimated in both these cases as being the same as refined copper production, whereas it could actually have been either higher (refining losses, other uses) or lower (scrap or copper-bearing liquors going directly to refineries).

[23]The 1973-77 average production/consumption ratio rose to 2.44 from the 2.13 ratio for 1972-76 shown in the last column of the table.

Part C of table 1-22 reflects both the use of scrap as part of the
smelter feed and the net import or export of blister copper; it is intended
as a combination ratio for making projections. Since domestic refining of
the blister now predominates in all ore-consuming countries except Zaire,
the consumption of ore has been related, with this one exception, to domestic consumption of blister. In Zaire's case, the salient position of
Belgium as the further processor suggested that Zairian smelting (ore consumption) should be related to Belgian refining (consumption of blister).
This arrangement may conceivably change, but if the change takes the likely
form of a simple bypassing of Belgium in the service of Belgium's usual
refined copper markets, use of the ratio series shown would still be valid
for projection of Zambia's copper ore consumption.

Ratios of less than one in part A of table 1-23 presumably reflect
mostly the concurrent input of scrap,[24] which is apparently most extensive
in Germany and Belgium, though it is significant also in the United States.
The increasingly higher ratios in Japan presumably reflect an increasing
(though modest) diversion of blister copper to uses other than the production of refined. The ratios for Chile and Zambia seem too close to unity
to be precisely valid, but the error, if any, would be too small to matter.

From part B of the table it may be seen that the United States has
settled down into near balance between production and consumption of
refined copper, with a tendency toward net importation replacing a previous
tendency toward net exportation. Japan and Germany are both net importers,
but Japan has been increasing its self-sufficiency while Germany has not.
Both Canada and Belgium export as much or more refined copper than they
consume domestically, while the USSR is a modest net exporter. Chile and
Zambia are both so overwhelmingly committed to production for export that
the ratios are too high to be worth showing.

Combination ratios suitable as a base for projection are shown in
part C of table 1-23 for the countries whose refined copper production is
essentially for home consumption. Given both the use of scrap and the

---

[24]See footnote 22.

importation of a significant part of its refined copper, the relative input of blister is particularly low in Germany. From the ratios given in part D of the table, it may be inferred that the four countries named in that part jointly account for some 40 percent of the trading world's refined copper supply.[25] Zambia has maintained a steady share of about 13 percent and Canada 10 to 11 percent. Chile, with its substitution of refined for less process forms, has increased its share from little more than 7 percent in 1960-64 to nearly 12 percent in 1973-77, while the Belgian share has declined. Belgium's customers are scattered throughout Western Europe, while those of the other three world suppliers include Japan and the United States as well.

All of the leading consumers of refined copper are also leading consumers of copper scrap.[26] As noted above, only a minor portion of this scrap consumption tends to show up as input into refined copper; the major portion finds a more direct route back into industrial production via brass, etc. ingot makers and the remelt furnaces of copper mills and foundries. This "direct use" of scrap serves to dilute the parallelism one would expect to find between copper scrap consumption and refined copper consumption owing to the combined influence on current scrap recovery of both past copper production and current copper demand. The relationships that actually obtain are shown in table 1-24.

The principal surprise in this table is that already noted--an apparent direct use of scrap in Japan in the early 1950s that is large enough to cause total copper scrap consumption in that country to exceed refined copper consumption. There has been a general tendency for the scrap ratios in the leading industrial countries to decrease--even in the United States, where there has been considerable stability. In general, however, the trends are perhaps smoother than might have been expected, given that the relationship between scrap consumption and refined copper consumption is

---

[25]They account for some two-thirds of the refined copper mining in international trade.

[26]This must be surmised for the Soviet Union, since estimates of USSR scrap consumption are not available.

governed less by technical factors than by a set of institutional arrangements which somewhat fortuitously determine which portion of scrap reclamation will or will not be statistically counted as scrap consumption. To the extent that the general tendency toward decline (the U.K. and Italy being apparent exceptions) does reflect underlying technological change, an appropriate hypothesis would have to do with changes in fabrication techniques and product mixes that have the effect of reducing the extent of new scrap generation. In the United States, such scrap generated in current industrial processing accounts for some two-thirds of the total copper scrap supply, and there are indications that it is a high proportion in other countries as well.

As a base for projecting the consumption of refined copper itself, the macro relationships shown in table 1-25 are relevant. The declining intensity-of-use record for copper, it may be seen, is the opposite of that for aluminum for all the industrialized countries, except perhaps the USSR. This decline in intensity has held for the United States over the entire twenty-year period, whereas it set in for the other countries after peaks reached anywhere from the mid-1950s to around 1970, Japan's being the most recent. Work in progress at RFF suggests that the intensity of use of metals is closely associated, among other determinants, with relative emphasis on investment as part of gross output; such an emphasis has been particularly high in Germany and Japan, but in both countries is now easing. It is interesting that, even within the relatively stable relationship found in the USSR, there was an upward tendency toward a mild peak in the mid-1960s, followed by a slight decline.

By around 1975, if official international exchange rates are used as a means of comparison, France's decline in intensity of use had brought it slightly below the United States in intensity of refined copper consumption--1.09 metric tons per million dollars of gross product for France compared with the 1.18 for the United States. The other industrialized countries (excluding the USSR, which cannot readily be compared) were all either moderately or much higher, with Italy at 1.7 tons, Japan at 2.0, the U.K. at 2.1, and Germany at 2.8. All these ratios refer to 1973-77 averages.

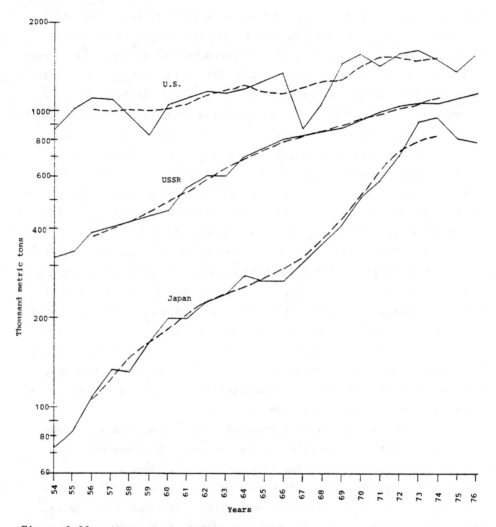

Figure 1-32.   Apparent Consumption of Copper Ore and Concentrate in the
United States, Japan, and the USSR, 1954-1956, Annually and
Five-Year Moving-Average Trends

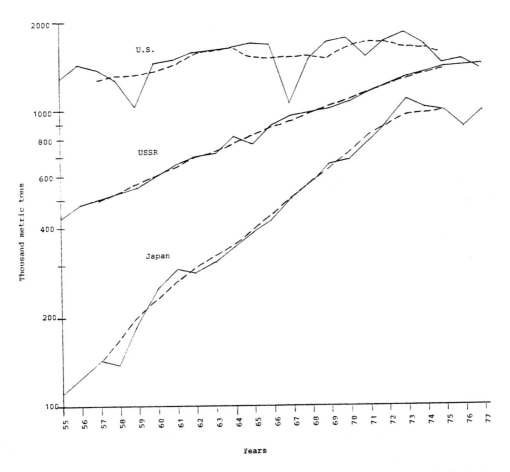

Figure 1-33.   Apparent Consumption of Blister Copper in the United States,
Japan, and the USSR, 1955-1977, Annually and Five-Year
Moving-Average Trends

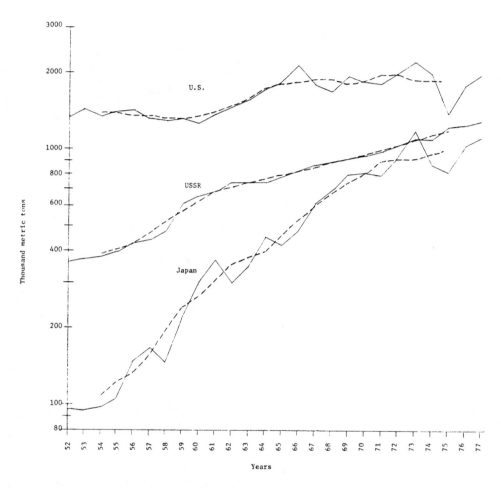

Figure 1-34. Apparent Consumption of Refined Copper in the United States, Japan, and the USSR, 1952-1977, Annually and Five-Year Moving-Average Trends

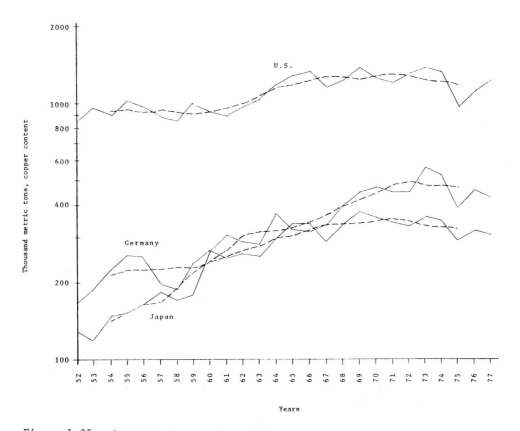

Figure 1-35.   Apparent Consumption of Copper Scrap in the United States,
Japan, and Germany, 1952-1975, Annually and Five-Year Moving-
Average Trends

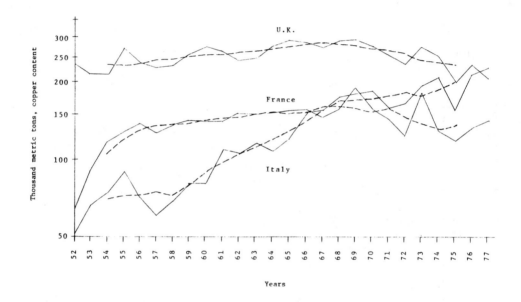

Figure 1-36. Apparent Consumption of Copper Scrap in the U.K., Italy, and France, 1952-1975, Annually and Five-Year Moving-Average Trends

TABLE 1-18. WORLD APPARENT CONSUMPTION OF COPPER ORES AND CONCENTRATES, 1954-77, BY COUNTRY

(THOUSAND METRIC TONS, COPPER CONTENT)

YEAR	PRINCIPAL INTERNATIONAL TRADERS					OTHER COUNTRIES				WORLD TOTAL[a]
	UNITED STATES	JAPAN	CHILE	CANADA	TOTAL	ZAMBIA	ZAIRE	USSR	OTHER	
1954	863	73	334	232	1502	385	221	320	403	2830
1955	1008	83	405	258	1755	348	232	335	410	3080
1956	1100	109	462	285	1957	395	249	390	450	3440
1957	1085	134	450	284	1952	427	241	405	474	3500
1958	962	132	438	286	1817	387	237	420	559	3420
1959	820	165	517	330	1831	539	281	440	509	3600
1960	1043	199	505	355	2102	576	302	460	861	4300
1961	1096	199	525	359	2179	569	294	550	768	4360
1962	1152	227	557	334	2270	554	295	600	851	4570
1963	1143	241	557	326	2267	578	271	600	914	4630
1964	1173	278	587	347	2384	639	277	700	900	4900
1965	1250	267	558	382	2456	696	289	750	909	5100
1966	1335	267	606	373	2581	596	317	800	807	5100
1967	860	309	630	439	2238	633	321	825	883	4900
1968	1058	355	623	428	2464	664	326	850	1196	5500
1969	1435	413	648	377	2873	704	364	875	1165	5930
1970	1534	511	647	448	3139	683	386	925	1167	6300
1971	1401	582	629	450	3063	644	401	990	1272	6370
1972	1542	715	642	449	3349	697	428	1030	1506	7010
1973	1576	924	626	478	3603	683	461	1060	1483	7290
1974	1479	955	746	478	3657	710	468	1060	1656	7550
1975	1338	808	725	410	3309	648	463	1100	1751	7270
1976	1526	786	849	438	3599	706	408	1130	1827	7670
1977	1396	758	885	501	3540	651	452	1100	2047	7790

SOURCE: COMMODITIES RESEARCH UNIT (DATA SERVICE; METALLGESELLSCHAFT AG, METAL STATISTICS; U.K. INSTITUTE OF GEOLOGICAL SCIENCES, STATISTICAL SUMMARY OF THE MINERAL INDUSTRY; U.S. BUREAU OF MINES, MINERALS YEARBOOK AND UNPUBLISHED DATA.

NOTE: DETAIL MAY NOT ADD TO TOTALS, OWING TO ROUNDING.

a ACTUALLY, SMELTER PRODUCTION OF COPPER AS ESTIMATED BY METALLGESELLSCHAFT AG.

TABLE 1-19. WORLD APPARENT CONSUMPTION OF BLISTER COPPER, 1952-77, BY COUNTRY

(THOUSAND METRIC TONS)

YEAR	PRINCIPAL INTERNATIONAL TRADERS						OTHER COUNTRIES				WORLD TOTAL[b]
	UNITED STATES	JAPAN	CHILE	GERMANY (F.R.)	BELGIUM[a]	TOTAL	ZAMBIA	CANADA	USSR	OTHER	
1952	N.A.	N.A.	311	89[c]	N.A.	--	84	178	365	--	2790
1953	1262	N.A.	208	100	N.A.	--	137	215	380	--	2960
1954	1158	N.A.	182	103	N.A.	--	176	230	400	--	2980
1955	1286	110	230	108	N.A.	--	172	262	430	--	3260
1956	1444	124	249	121	N.A.	--	240	298	480	--	3630
1957	1392	141	218	146	N.A.	--	253	299	500	--	3660
1958	1276	137	188	167	N.A.	--	247	332	525	--	3590
1959	1034	190	261	166	N.A.	--	375	378	550	--	3780
1960	1460	247	232	159	N.A.	--	422	369	610	--	4510
1961	1499	290	223	177	N.A.	--	411	347	660	--	4650
1962	1578	282	264	177	N.A.	--	420	344	700	--	4830
1963	1600	304	262	197	N.A.	--	431	370	720	--	4920
1964	1640	342	277	241	243	2743	485	394	820	852	5270
1965	1693	385	283	248	255	2864	543	394	770	939	5510
1966	1681	426	371	274	286	3038	510	454	900	819	5660
1967	1048	502	390	332	296	2568	554	476	960	815	5350
1968	1480	564	399	327	276	3046	568	408	960	941	6020
1969	1703	650	459	327	213	3352	597	493	990	1064	6440
1970	1747	743	457	331	249	3527	579	478	1020	1135	6810
1971	1526	777	449	312	267	3331	545	478	1075	1316	6820
1972	1721	897	481	291	263	3653	545	496	1150	1516	7500
1973	1826	1081	430	347	288	3972	610	498	1225	1610	8020
1974	1678	1071	510	267	274	3800	678	559	1300	1834	8220
1975	1433	989	545	211	253	3431	629	529	1350	1751	7740
1976	1478	889	625	291	301	3584	685	511	1400	2011	8210
1977	1372	1020	672	269	320	3653	642	509	1420	2056	8300

SOURCE: COMMODITIES RESEARCH UNIT (DATA SERVICE); METALLGESELLSCHAFT AG, METAL STATISTICS; U.S. BUREAU OF MINES, MINERALS YEARBOOK. AMERICAN BUREAU OF METAL STATISTICS, INC., YEARBOOK AND NON-FERROUS METAL DATA.

NOTE: DETAIL MAY NOT ADD TO TOTALS, OWING TO ROUNDING.

[a] EXCLUDES SEMI-REFINED (LEACHED) COPPER CATHODES FROM ZAIRE.

[b] ACTUALLY, ESTIMATED WORLD PRODUCTION.

[c] ESTIMATED BY RFF.

TABLE 1-20. WORLD APPARENT CONSUMPTION OF REFINED COPPER, 1952-77, BY COUNTRY

(THOUSAND METRIC TONS)

| YEAR | PRINCIPAL INTERNATIONAL TRADERS | | | | | | | OTHER COUNTRIES | | WORLD TOTAL |
	UNITED STATES	JAPAN	GERMANY (F.R.)	UNITED KINGDOM	FRANCE	ITALY	TOTAL	USSR	OTHER	
1952	1326	96	174	429	161	73	2260	360	650	3270
1953	1425	95	221	328	98	79	2246	370	524	3140
1954	1343	98	310	455	177	111	2494	380	496	3370
1955	1399	105	354	504	194	114	2670	395	705	3770
1956	1419	147	349	510	188	130	2742	428	730	3900
1957	1316	168	397	516	212	135	2743	440	767	3950
1958	1297	147	431	543	225	127	2770	475	885	4130
1959	1319	219	447	487	196	140	2807	607	966	4380
1960	1272	304	516	560	237	185	3074	652	1034	4760
1961	1379	372	562	529	244	202	3287	682	1121	5090
1962	1472	301	501	526	244	214	3257	735	1168	5160
1963	1574	352	494	553	250	228	3456	736	1258	5450
1964	1727	457	561	633	292	202	3872	740	1338	5950
1965	1844	427	536	650	287	192	3937	783	1430	6150
1966	2156	482	459	593	291	195	4175	817	1468	6460
1967	1798	616	501	514	271	222	3923	867	1430	6220
1968	1704	695	609	539	293	226	4066	890	1594	6550
1969	1951	806	656	547	335	238	4532	913	1695	7140
1970	1860	820	698	554	331	274	4536	950	1804	7290
1971	1834	805	631	517	344	270	4400	985	1905	7290
1972	2031	951	672	535	390	290	4869	1030	2051	7950
1973	2224	1201	727	541	408	295	5396	1100	2054	8550
1974	2004	880	731	497	414	308	4834	1100	2366	8300
1975	1395	827	635	458	365	299	3971	1220	2269	7460
1976	1812	1050	745	458	367	322	4753	1250	2534	8540
1977	1995	1127	725	512	326	326	5011	1290	2709	9010

SOURCE: METALLGESELLSCHAFT AG, _METAL STATISTICS._

NOTE: DETAIL MAY NOT ADD TO TOTALS, OWING TO ROUNDING.

TABLE 1-21. WORLD APPARENT CONSUMPTION OF COPPER (AND COPPER ALLOY) SCRAP, 1952-77, BY COUNTRY[a]

(THOUSAND METRIC TONS, COPPER CONTENT)

YEAR	UNITED STATES	PRINCIPAL INTERNATIONAL TRADERS						OTHER COUNTRIES	WORLD TOTAL[b]
		JAPAN	GERMANY (F.R.)	UNITED KINGDOM	ITALY	FRANCE	TOTAL		
1952	849	129	166	232	51	63	1489	154	1643
1953	963	119	187	217	67	90	1643	146	1789
1954	898	148	222	217	74	117	1675	168	1843
1955	1018	152	255	269	89	128	1911	192	2103
1956	973	164	251	238	71	137	1833	179	2012
1957	886	183	197	227	61	127	1681	183	1864
1958	855	171	188	232	68	136	1648	193	1841
1959	995	179	237	255	81	142	1889	211	2100
1960	920	261	266	274	81	141	1941	221	2162
1961	892	304	249	241	109	141	1957	264	2221
1962	962	288	252	262	106	151	2007	292	2299
1963	1028	283	296	247	116	150	2076	325	2401
1964	1173	369	339	276	108	151	2372	394	2766
1965	1261	320	339	290	141	155	2485	522	3007
1966	1327	314	339	286	151	157	2574	489	3063
1967	1145	334	334	272	156	146	2342	498	2840
1968	1215	394	334	289	174	157	2563	566	3129
1969	1370	449	376	293	181	190	2858	602	3460
1970	1245	464	356	277	185	157	2683	611	3294
1971	1196	455	342	256	159	144	2551	588	3139
1972	1296	458	330	236	167	124	2610	635	3245
1973	1360	555	357	272	195	183	2922	709	3631
1974	1317	521	348	254	209	129	2778	749	3527
1975	964	389	290	199	157	119	2119	592	2711
1976	1099	457	318	233	215	133	2455	679	3134
1977	1207	427	305	207	228	143	2517	693	3210

SOURCE: METALLGESELLSCHAFT AG, METAL STATISTICS.

NOTE: DETAIL MAY NOT ADD TO TOTALS, OWING TO ROUNDING.

[a] DATA ACTUALLY RELATE TO DIRECT AND IMPLICIT COPPER RECOVERY FROM ALL TYPES OF SCRAP AND WASTE, HOWEVER, ONLY A VERY SMALL PROPORTION, USUALLY, IS OTHER THAN COPPER-BASE SCRAP.

[b] EXCLUDES USSR, CHINA, AND EASTERN EUROPE.

Table 1-22. Ratios of Copper Ore Consumption to Blister Copper Consumption, for Leading Copper Ore Consumers, 1960-76[a]

	1962	1963	1964	1965	1966	1967	1968	1969	1970	1971	1972	1973	1974	1975
A. Copper Ore (Cu Content) Consumption/Blister Copper Production														
United States	.91	.91	.92	.94	.93	.94	.96	.96	.95	.97	.97	.97	.99	N.A.
Japan	.76	.78	.79	.79	.79	.80	.81	.84	.86	.89	.91	.93	.94	"
Chile	1.00	1.00	1.00	1.00	1.01	1.00	1.02	1.03	1.03	1.05	1.05	1.04	1.04	"
Canada	.99	.99	.98	.99	.99	.99	.98	.99	.98	.99	.99	.96	.94	"
B. Blister Copper Production/Consumption														
United States	.80	.80	.80	.80	.81	.83	.85	.87	.89	.91	.91	.92	.93	N.A.
Japan	1.00	.93	.88	.84	.80	.80	.80	.80	.82	.85	.89	.91	.91	"
Chile	2.17	2.13	1.97	1.85	1.73	1.61	1.50	1.44	1.38	1.34	1.34	1.34	1.33	"
Canada	.96	.97	.97	.96	.95	.95	.94	.94	.94	.93	.92	.93	.95	"
Zambia	1.34	1.33	1.28	1.24	1.21	1.19	1.17	1.17	1.17	1.15	1.12	1.09	1.06	"
Zaire	1.80	1.99	2.01	1.98	1.96	1.97	1.98	2.00	2.00	1.98	1.92	1.94	2.13	"
USSR	.84	.87	.88	.88	.88	.88	.86	.86	.86	.85	.83	.82	.80	"
C. Copper Ore (Cu Content) Consumption/Blister Copper Consumption														
United States	.72	.73	.74	.75	.75	.78	.81	.84	.85	.88	.89	.90	.92	.94
Japan	.78	.76	.74	.70	.67	.64	.66	.68	.72	.77	.83	.84	.86	.84
Chile	2.17	2.13	1.97	1.86	1.75	1.61	1.52	1.47	1.42	1.40	1.41	1.39	1.38	1.38
Canada	.95	.96	.95	.95	.94	.94	.93	.93	.92	.93	.91	.88	.87	.88
Zambia	1.34	1.33	1.28	1.25	1.21	1.19	1.17	1.17	1.17	1.15	1.12	1.09	1.07	1.04
USSR	.83	.87	.88	.88	.88	.88	.85	.86	.86	.85	.83	.82	.80	.79
D. Copper Ore (Cu Content) Consumption/Blister Copper Consumption in Belgium[c]														
Zaire	N.A.	N.A.	N.A.	N.A.	1.13	1.22	1.30	1.38	1.50	1.59	1.60	1.65	1.64	1.54

[a]Ratios are based on five-year moving average trends, centered on years shown.

[b]Zambia, Zaire, and USSR omitted, although leading ore consumers, since ore consumption in these countries had to be estimated as equal to blister copper production. Similarly for world consumption.

[c]Belgium takes nearly all of Zaire's blister and semi-refined (leached) copper exports.

N.A. = Not available.

Table 1-23. Ratios of Blister Copper Consumption to Refined Copper Production and Consumption, for Leading Blister Copper Consumers, 1960-77[a]

	1962	1963	1964	1965	1966	1967	1968	1969	1970	1971	1972	1973	1974	1975
A. Blister Copper Consumption/Refined Copper Production[b]														
United States	.92	.91	.90	.87	.86	.85	.84	.85	.86	.86	.86	.86	.86	.86
Japan	1.02	1.04	1.04	1.04	1.04	1.04	1.05	1.05	1.07	1.09	1.09	1.10	1.11	1.11
Chile	1.00	1.00	1.01	1.01	1.01	1.01	1.01	1.00	1.00	1.01	.99	1.00	1.00	.99
Germany (F.R.)	.59	.64	.69	.76	.80	.81	.83	.83	.79	.80	.76	.70	.67	.65
Belgium	N.A.	N.A.	N.A.	N.A.	.90	.87	.85	.83	.80	.79	.78	.79	.76	N.A.
Zambia	.99	.99	1.00	1.02	1.02	1.02	1.01	1.01	1.01	1.00	1.00	1.00	1.00	1.00
B. Refined Copper Production/Consumption[c]														
United States	1.14	1.10	1.04	.97	.95	.95	.96	.97	1.02	1.01	.99	1.00	.99	.96
Japan	.80	.81	.83	.81	.80	.80	.81	.82	.84	.83	.90	.92	.90	.90
Germany (F.R.)	.61	.61	.65	.66	.67	.67	.66	.64	.62	.60	.59	.61	.60	.60
Belgium	2.42	2.47	2.56	2.69	2.66	2.57	2.52	2.42	2.24	2.17	2.18	2.08	2.02	1.98
Canada	2.51	2.21	1.96	1.94	1.92	1.91	1.96	2.09	2.09	2.11	2.20	2.31	2.37	2.39
USSR	.99	1.00	1.03	1.06	1.08	1.09	1.11	1.13	1.15	1.16	1.18	1.18	1.17	1.16
C. Blister Copper Consumption/Refined Copper Consumption														
United States	1.05	1.00	.93	.84	.82	.80	.81	.82	.87	.86	.85	.86	.86	.83
Japan	.82	.84	.86	.84	.83	.84	.82	.85	.87	.89	.95	1.02	.99	.97
Germany (F.R.)	.36	.39	.45	.51	.53	.55	.54	.53	.49	.48	.45	.42	.40	.39
USSR[d]	.99	1.00	1.03	1.06	1.08	1.09	1.11	1.13	1.15	1.16	1.18	1.18	1.17	1.16
D. Blister Copper Consumption/Refined Copper Cons. by Principal Int'l Traders														
Chile	.074	.074	.078	.082	.086	.092	.098	.100	.100	.096	.097	.103	.109	.116
Belgium	N.A.	N.A.	N.A.	N.A.	.068	.064	.062	.061	.057	.054	.056	.057	.058	.06
Zambia	.128	.129	.128	.130	.133	.134	.132	.132	.129	.125	.127	.132	.136	.137
Canada	.107	.102	.099	.101	.105	.103	.105	.108	.105	.100	.105	.109	.109	.109

[a] Ratios are based on five-year moving-average trends, centered on years shown.

[b] Canada and USSR omitted, although leading blister copper consumers, since blister copper consumption in these countries had to be estimated as equal to refined copper consumption. Similarly for world consumption.

[c] Chile and Zambia omitted, since the ratios are quite high. Nearly all (Zambia) or the overwhelming bulk (Chile) of refined copper production has been for export.

[d] Ratios same as for production/consumption, since refined copper production had to be taken as the measure of blister consumption.

Table 1-24. Ratios of Copper Scrap Consumption to Refined Copper
Consumption, for the World and Leading Copper Consumers,
1952-1977[a]

Year	U.S.	Japan	Germany (F.R.)	U.K.	Italy	France	World
1954	.680	1.316	.768	.527	.694	.654	.538
1955	.686	1.250	.682	.505	.636	.689	.530
1956	.684	1.230	.605	.468	.588	.648	.505
1957	.700	1.080	.570	.477	.573	.660	.493
1958	.699	.973	.532	.469	.505	.646	.472
1959	.691	.907	.483	.475	.507	.617	.457
1960	.686	.896	.488	.478	.513	.620	.452
1961	.684	.849	.501	.481	.509	.619	.450
1962	.670	.843	.502	.463	.504	.579	.449
1963	.665	.819	.526	.454	.540	.568	.457
1964	.656	.780	.582	.453	.584	.560	.464
1965	.652	.694	.594	.465	.628	.546	.466
1966	.663	.647	.599	.482	.685	.534	.473
1967	.668	.598	.607	.503	.730	.545	.477
1968	.666	.572	.580	.516	.733	.531	.469
1969	.675	.560	.548	.519	.695	.504	.460
1970	.674	.545	.532	.502	.667	.456	.449
1971	.653	.520	.520	.495	.649	.441	.439
1972	.644	.527	.501	.490	.637	.391	.428
1973	.646	.510	.491	.479	.607	.364	.411
1974	.638	.485	.468	.481	.623	.354	.398
1975	.631	.462	.454	.474	.648	.376	.387

[a]Excludes USSR, for which scrap data are not available. Ratios are
based on five-year moving-average trends, centered on years shown. In lieu
of data on copper scrap as such, consumption data actually are for direct
and implicit copper recovery from scrap.

Table 1-25. Ratios of Refined Copper Consumption to GNP/GDP, for Leading Copper Consumers, 1952-77[a]

(metric tons)

Year	U.S. $ million	Japan Y billion	Germany (F.R.) DM million	U.K. £ million	France Fr million	Italy £ billion	USSR Index[b]
1954	1.72	4.28	N.A.	7.31	.325	N.A.	9.1
1955	1.68	4.53	.758	7.37	.329	"	8.9
1956	1.62	4.59	.802	7.88	.360	"	8.7
1957	1.56	5.05	.808	7.80	.350	"	9.0
1958	1.49	5.82	.822	7.76	.347	"	9.5
1959	1.45	6.48	.854	7.59	.347	"	9.8
1960	1.44	6.54	.844	7.42	.338	"	10.3
1961	1.44	6.81	.821	7.22	.326	"	10.8
1962	1.46	7.04	.814	7.34	.332	3.04	10.7
1963	1.50	6.86	.782	7.34	.326	2.92	10.6
1964	1.56	6.63	.720	7.29	.319	2.77	10.5
1965	1.55	6.94	.696	7.03	.309	2.66	10.3
1966	1.50	7.15	.699	6.78	.302	2.53	10.1
1967	1.47	7.27	.693	6.43	.294	2.48	10.0
1968	1.43	7.32	.701	6.07	.286	2.52	9.8
1969	1.35	7.23	.709	5.76	.280	2.55	9.7
1970	1.35	7.15	.710	5.67	.284	2.59	9.7
1971	1.37	7.34	.700	5.49	.287	2.61	9.6
1972	1.35	6.98	.691	5.25	.285	2.63	9.5
1973	1.26	6.67	.666	4.96	.280	2.61	9.7
1974	1.22	6.67	.671	4.76	.273	2.62	9.8
1975	1.18	6.62	.666	4.66	.256	2.61	9.8

N.A. - Not available.

a
Ratios, in metric tons per denominator shown at head of column, are based on five-year moving-average trends, centered on year shown. Currencies are all in constant (1975) prices.

b
GNP index, 1970 = 100 (see chapter 2). Ratios are per index point.

Lead

Because lead production and consumption are even more completely integrated than that for copper, only three significantly traded lead commodities have been identified--ore, refined lead, and scrap. In this case we have defined "refined" to include the antimonial lead and other alloys in the form of which such a large portion of secondary lead is recovered, so long as this recovery is not directly affected by battery makers and other lead consumers. This definition materially affects the need for newly mined lead in relation to refined metal production and consumption. Yet all but two of the leading refined lead consumers do consume important quantities of lead ores. And the two exceptions--the United Kingdom and Italy--consume substantial quantities of virgin lead indirectly, obtaining it as refined-lead imports.

Tables 1-26 and 1-27 give the basic consumption series. As may be seen, the United States is far and away the largest refined-lead consumer, but its greater dependence on imports of refined metal, as well as use of scrap, puts it roughly on a par with the USSR as an ore consumer.[27]

In general, trends in lead consumption are relatively flat. Figure 1-37 compares U.S. and Soviet consumption of ore, while figure 1-38 does the same for their consumption of refined lead. Once again, the relative stability of the USSR series contrasts with the considerable fluctuations in the United States.

Differences in trend show up among the principal smelters of lead ore for export--Australia, Canada, and Mexico--whose ore consumption is compared in figure 1-39. Because of the closeness of level, each of these countries had to be shown against its own axis, but the proportions are comparable. Australian smelting (ore consumption) has exhibited slow but steady growth, while the fluctuating and somewhat inversely related fortunes of Canada and Mexico suggest a certain amount of competition for market.

---

[27]More precisely, not much above USSR levels. Owing to the lack of direct data, the USSR's lead ore consumption (measured as lead content) was taken as equal to refined lead production, without allowance for use of scrap. The series is thus an overstatement, though scrap use in the Soviet Union is probably small compared with that in the United States.

Disregarding the Soviet Union, because of the lack of data, the United States is far and away the world's largest lead scrap consumer--a reflection, undoubtedly, of its large motor vehicle population and consequent turnover of lead in batteries. The data are shown in table 1-28 along with those for half a dozen lesser scrap consumers. The United Kingdom led the lesser consumers in the 1960s, but its scrap consumption has since declined to levels lower than that of several other industrialized countries. Germany and Japan are now distant runners-up to the United States, both having increased their scrap consumption materially over the past couple of decades.

The relationship of ore to refined lead production and consumption, for principal ore consumers, is given in table 1-29. Since the ore data are given in terms of lead content (in some cases estimated as recoverable lead content), the technical relationship between ore and refined lead production, barring inputs other than ore and outputs other than refined lead, ought, as in the case of Mexico, to be close to unity. It is much lower for all the industrialized countries because of the re-refining of lead from scrap. The significantly higher figure for Australia reflects that country's direct export of an intermediate product, lead bullion, for refining elsewhere--overwhelmingly in the United Kingdom.

Degrees of self-sufficiency in refined lead are evident from part B of the table. All of the non-Communist industrialized countries have been net importers and all have been moving toward greater self-sufficiency, but only Germany has achieved it; in fact, unless the explanation of Germany's recent ratios is a build-up of stocks, it has become a modest net exporter. The USSR is also a modest net exporter, but to an apparently declining degree.

The combined result of scrap use and refined lead importation is shown in part C of the table for the industrialized consuming countries. The result is remarkably similar for all such countries except the USSR; because of a lack of data on scrap consumption in the Soviet Union, that country's true ore consumption ratio is unknown, and the one given in the table is undoubtedly overstated. The ratios in the United States and Japan reflect both increasing self-sufficiency in lead refining and increasing relative use of virgin metal. World ratios also reflect increasing relative use of virgin metal. The somewhat equivocal results for Germany and France reflect increasing self-sufficiency, on the one hand, and increasing relative use of scrap, on the other.

Australia, Canada, and Mexico had all been producing refined lead primarily for foreign consumption, but in all three cases, the proportions domestically consumed have been increasing--to the extent that Canada has lately been consuming more than it exports (part B of table 1-29) and Mexico seems to have arrived at a 50-50 distribution. Still, it seems more valid to gauge future demand for ore from these three countries by total trading world than by domestic lead consumption. The reference consumers, on this basis, are all the principal industrialized countries, including the USSR. As implied by part D of table 1-29, Australia in the early 1960s had been meeting some 11 percent of this group's refined lead needs, but its contribution has shown a slight tendency to decline. Canada and Mexico jointly had been meeting about 12 percent of the group's requirements, but have faded to about 9 percent. These declines are the counterpart of the industrialized countries' increasing self-sufficiency.

One would expect the generally increasing ore ratios shown in table 1-29 to be associated with generally decreasing scrap ratios. This is true enough so far as the production totals include remelt lead. Since refined lead consumption also includes refined lead imports, however, the overall relation of scrap to lead consumption (table 1-30) can be considerably altered from the underlying input-output ratio. Or it may be that it is relative scrap availability in relation to refined lead demand that is important in helping determine the extent of lead imports. In the United States, for example, since 1962, there has been decreasing use of scrap per unit of refined product, but an increasing self-sufficiency, resulting in approximately unchanged total amounts of scrap in relation to lead consumption. In Japan, on the other hand, lead consumption has grown so rapidly that a decreasing proportion of scrap per unit of refined lead production has been accompanied by decreases in proportion of scrap per unit of lead consumption as well, despite increasing self-sufficiency.

Table 1-30 also makes it clear that the trends since 1962 are not necessarily extensions of longer term movements. Over the longer term, the United States has had a net increase in scrap use per unit of lead consumption, Germany and Italy have both had a downward and an upward swing, and France has had an upward, then a downward, swing. Japan's recent decline in relative scrap use, however, is in fact part of a longer term trend.

Intensities of refined lead use per unit of gross product are shown in table 1-30. Generally, the industrialized consumers shown have had declining intensities over time. Exceptions are the USSR, which has maintained a relatively unchanged intensity, and the People's Republic of China, whose intensity of lead use has also reached an approximately unchanging level after an earlier rise. Italy alone has had a continously upward intensity trend, at least for the shorter period for which data on this country are available.

If comparisons are made on the basis of officially quoted (FRB) foreign exchange rates, there are some wide differences among countries. The United Kingdom had long been the most intensive lead user, and even with the decline in intensity remains so: its 1.41 tons per dollar of gross output is more than double the 1972-76 average intensity for either France (0.69) or Japan (0.61). Italy's intensity increase, however, has brought it more than abreast of the U.K., at 1.45 tons per dollar of gross output. The United States is now down to 0.92 ton per dollar and Germany to 0.75 ton.

The high lead use in the United Kingdom was principally ascribable, a couple of decades ago, to cable covering, but this use has now declined and been surpassed by growing lead consumption in storage batteries. There is no salient consumption category which explains Italy's growth, though batteries, again, have been a leading item. The declines in intensity in both the United States and Japan have occurred despite important growth in battery use of lead in both places and, additionally, in use of tetraethyl lead in the United States.

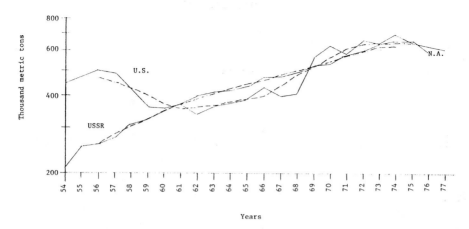

Figure 1-37.   Apparent Consumption of Lead Ore in the United States and the
USSR, 1954-1977, Annually and Five-Year Moving-Average Trends

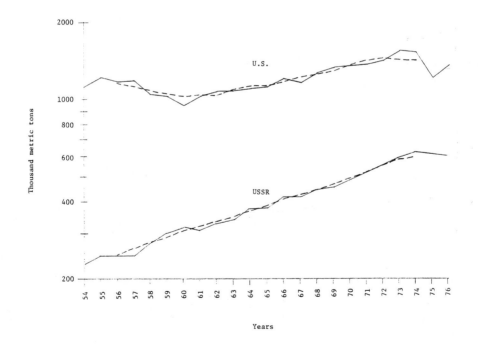

Figure 1-38.   Apparent Consumption of Refined Lead in the United States
and the USSR, 1954-1976, Annually and Five-Year Moving-
Average Trends

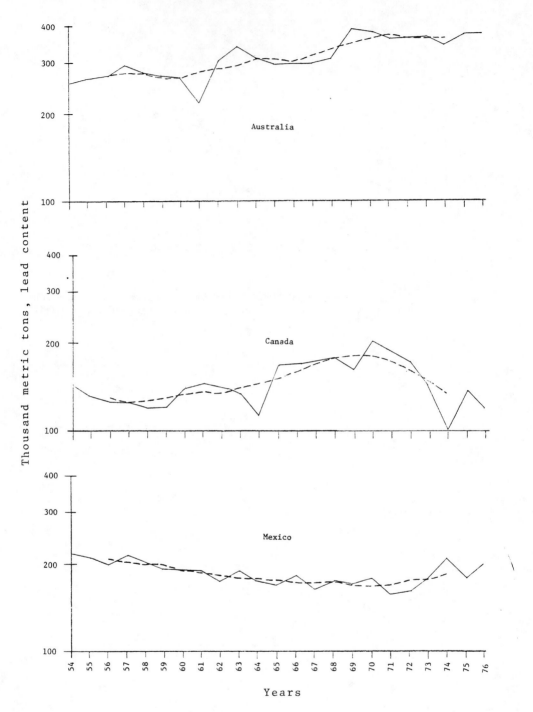

Figure 1-39. Apparent Consumption of Lead Ore in Australia, Canada, and Mexico, 1954-1976, Annually and Five-Year Moving-Average Trends

TABLE 1-26. WORLD APPARENT CONSUMPTION OF LEAD ORES AND CONCENTRATES, 1954-77, BY COUNTRY

(THOUSAND METRIC TONS, LEAD CONTENT)

YEAR	PRINCIPAL INTERNATIONAL TRADERS								OTHER COUNTRIES		WORLD TOTAL[b]
	UNITED STATES	USSR	GERMANY (F.R.)	JAPAN	AUSTRALIA	CANADA	FRANCE	TOTAL	MEXICO	OTHER	
1954	442	210	120	32	253	144	71	1270	215	595	2080
1955	468	255	115	41	262	131	85	1357	209	614	2180
1956	498	260	120	43	266	126	84	1397	198	645	2240
1957	467	275	129	62	291	125	81	1449	212	679	2340
1958	425	310	141	52	275	120	87	1410	201	699	2310
1959	358	325	140	57	268	121	86	1354	190	756	2300
1960	355	350	143	63	263	140	76	1389	189	802	2380
1961	367	375	138	84	215	145	78	1402	188	830	2420
1962	338	400	138	75	302	141	79	1473	173	894	2540
1963	360	415	112	90	334	134	101	1546	188	826	2560
1964	371	425	111	78	307	112	113	1518	173	899	2590
1965	385	440	125	94	293	168	106	1610	168	992	2770
1966	423	475	160	108	294	170	110	1745	181	974	2900
1967	400	480	183	141	294	174	114	1785	163	952	2900
1968	407	500	191	141	305	178	114	1836	173	991	3000
1969	562	530	169	183	384	162	114	2104	170	986	3260
1970	621	540	201	201	377	203	124	2266	176	978	3420
1971	585	580	166	214	357	187	134	2223	156	1061	3440
1972	654	600	152	191	360	173	139	2268	160	1062	3490
1973	640	640	127	202	360	140	130	2239	177	1144	3560
1974	638	660	132	189	339	100	140	2249	208	1103	3560
1975	643	660	149	173	367	137	107	2236	178	1186	3600
1976	622	600	140	171	370	118	91	2112	199	1209	3520
1977	609	625	139	162	[a]384	[a]146	101	2166	[a]164	1260	3590

SOURCE: METALLGESELLSCHAFT AG, METAL STATISTICS; COMMODITIES RESEARCH UNIT (DATA SERVICES).

NOTE: DETAIL MAY NOT ADD TO TOTALS, OWING TO ROUNDING.

[a] PRELIMINARY FIGURES.

[b] ACTUALLY, LEAD ORE PRODUCTION AS ESTIMATED BY METALLGESELLSCHAFT.

TABLE 1-27. WORLD APPARENT CONSUMPTION OF REFINED LEAD, 1954-77, BY COUNTRY[a]

(THOUSAND METRIC TONS)

YEAR	PRINCIPAL INTERNATIONAL TRADERS								OTHER COUNTRIES		WORLD TOTAL[b]
	UNITED STATES	USSR	UNITED KINGDOM	GERMANY (F.R.)	JAPAN	FRANCE	ITALY	TOTAL	CHINA (P.R.)	OTHER	
1954	1124	230	341	188	89	169	88	2229	15	806	3050
1955	1213	246	378	210	96	192	90	2414	18	828	3260
1956	1180	246	363	195	133	202	91	2411	26	913	3350
1957	1189	248	355	198	140	210	90	2429	45	826	3300
1958	1051	278	342	208	103	204	86	2271	60	829	3160
1959	1038	305	351	228	124	192	97	2335	75	1010	3420
1960	956	320	385	256	162	196	108	2382	70	1038	3490
1961	1032	312	374	256	183	204	111	2471	85	1014	3570
1962	1072	332	385	265	180	202	111	2547	85	1018	3650
1963	1074	344	393	268	197	207	118	2601	90	1139	3830
1964	1106	379	427	287	228	211	117	2754	100	1246	4100
1965	1124	385	435	302	210	205	118	2779	100	1331	4210
1966	1203	420	410	284	205	219	130	2870	100	1030	4000
1967	1165	425	393	283	214	222	147	2850	100	1010	3960
1968	1273	450	384	321	241	224	155	3047	150	1133	4330
1969	1340	460	367	361	255	232	164	3179	185	1186	4550
1970	1352	490	350	359	281	232	190	3254	160	1186	4600
1971	1373	530	346	336	288	223	208	3305	170	1265	4740
1972	1434	560	355	325	309	229	226	3437	170	1313	4920
1973	1555	600	364	350	348	240	259	3716	170	1394	5280
1974	1527	630	325	327	291	229	261	3590	175	1445	5210
1975	1233	620	293	284	261	216	242	3143	185	1323	4660
1976	1363	610	301	303	310	237	286	3410	190	1490	5090
1977	1224	620	290	348	334	224	272	3312	200	1808	5320

SOURCE: COMMODITIES RESEARCH UNIT (DATA SERVICE); METALLGESELLSCHAFT AG, METAL STATISTICS.

NOTE: DETAIL MAY NOT ADD TO TOTALS, OWING TO ROUNDING.

[a] INCLUDES PRIMARY AND SECONDARY REFINED LEAD.

[b] ACTUALLY, WORLD CONSUMPTION OF PRIMARY REFINED LEAD, PLUS LEAD RECOVERED FROM SCRAP, MINUS KNOWN DIRECT USE OF SCRAP, ALL AS ESTIMATED BY METALLGESELLSCHAFT.

114

TABLE 1-28. WORLD APPARENT CONSUMPTION OF LEAD (AND LEAD ALLOY) SCRAP 1952-77, BY COUNTRY[a]

(THOUSAND METRIC TONS, LEAD CONTENT)

YEAR	PRINCIPAL INTERNATIONAL TRADERS							OTHER COUNTRIES		WORLD TOTAL[b]
	UNITED STATES	GERMANY (F.R.)	ITALY	UNITED KINGDOM	CANADA	FRANCE	TOTAL	JAPAN	OTHER	
1952	428	32	23	99	31	34	647	23	23	693
1953	442	35	25	84	30	35	650	38	26	714
1954	436	42	34	79	22	37	650	42	23	705
1955	456	46	34	93	26	44	697	41	16	755
1956	460	53	30	103	26	46	717	62	5	784
1957	444	41	24	98	24	52	682	53	22	757
1958	365	40	27	90	23	57	602	42	21	665
1959	410	39	34	89	25	37	634	45	17	695
1960	426	38	30	94	22	35	645	63	18	726
1961	411	45	25	94	24	43	643	57	12	712
1962	403	44	20	107	29	45	648	63	9	720
1963	448	41	26	107	30	37	686	66	16	770
1964	491	41	28	120	32	38	750	63	19	833
1965	522	41	26	123	38	61	811	62	21	894
1966	520	39	25	117	29	51	780	57	24	861
1967	502	35	24	117	30	58	767	51	19	837
1968	500	45	22	108	32	40	745	60	32	837
1969	548	62	19	92	38	34	792	67	46	906
1970	542	59	26	89	32	40	787	70	55	912
1971	541	73	41	70	33	35	792	79	67	938
1972	559	67	47	77	44	27	820	78	76	974
1973	594	73	65	82	49	26	889	81	89	1059
1974	634	78	68	59	54	30	923	73	89	1085
1975	597	73	57	55	45	36	863	71	86	1020
1976	659	89	65	55	50	30	948	80	102	1130
1977	673	91	64	49	52	34	963	88	109	1160

SOURCE: METALLGESELLSCHAFT AG, METAL STATISTICS.

NOTE: DETAIL MAY NOT ADD TO TOTALS, OWING TO ROUNDING.

[a]DATA ACTUALLY RELATE TO DIRECT AND IMPLICIT LEAD RECOVERY FROM ALL TYPES OF SCRAP AND WASTE. HOWEVER, ONLY A SMALL PROPORTION, USUALLY, IS OTHER THAN LEAD-BASE SCRAP.

[b]EXCLUDES USSR, CHINA, AND EASTERN EUROPE. ACTUALLY, LEAD RECOVERED FROM SCRAP AS ESTIMATED BY METALLGESELLSCHAFT, PLUS SCRAP INCLUDED IN FIGURES FOR PRIMARY REFINED PRODUCTION WHERE AVAILABLE (U.S. AND JAPAN).

Table 1-29. Ratios of Lead Ore Consumption to Refined Lead Production and Consumption, for the World and Leading Lead Ore Consumers, 1960 - 76[a]

	1962	1963	1964	1965	1966	1967	1968	1969	1970	1971	1972	1973	1974
A. Lead Ore (Pb content) Consumption/Refined Lead Production[b]													
United States	.436	.429	.434	.441	.438	.457	.482	.491	.509	.524	.536	.538	.534
Germany (F.R.)	.540	.514	.510	.515	.554	.557	.569	.543	.522	.466	.439	.417	.407
Japan	.506	.522	.527	.573	.586	.636	.677	.701	.697	.702	.689	.683	.649
Australia	1.33	1.35	1.37	1.35	1.37	1.49	1.53	1.63	1.71	1.74	1.69	1.72	1.69
Canada	.789	.782	.797	.800	.804	.821	.847	.862	.842	.790	.756	.690	.618
France	.742	.760	.756	.757	.735	.718	.706	.719	.714	.696	.700	.695	.640
Mexico	1.02	.99	1.00	.99	.97	.96	.97	.96	.97	.97	1.00	1.04	1.07
World[c]	.670	.665	.675	.683	.687	.705	.722	.722	.718	.713	.706	.711	.705
B. Refined Lead Production/Consumption[d]													
United States	.78	.78	.78	.78	.77	.78	.79	.81	.82	.83	.82	.84	.85
USSR	1.16	1.17	1.16	1.14	1.13	1.13	1.12	1.12	1.10	1.09	1.07	1.06	1.05
Germany (F.R.)	.89	.88	.90	.94	.94	.96	.99	1.01	.99	1.01	1.05	1.07	1.08
Japan	.81	.81	.83	.84	.87	.93	.96	.97	.97	.95	.95	.95	.94
Australia	4.10	3.98	3.91	3.69	3.46	3.35	3.29	3.25	3.22	3.15	3.16	3.01	2.99
Canada	2.27	2.32	2.22	2.13	2.21	2.20	2.27	2.39	2.31	2.19	2.07	1.95	1.87
France	.59	.61	.65	.67	.70	.71	.72	.74	.77	.80	.82	.83	.83
Mexico	3.79	3.25	2.90	2.63	2.44	2.20	2.10	1.94	1.85	1.81	1.90	1.95	2.05

Table 1-29(cont'd)

	1962	1963	1964	1965	1966	1967	1968	1969	1970	1971	1972	1973	1974	1975
C. Lead Ore (Pb content) Consumption/Refined Lead Consumption														
United States	.342	.337	.337	.343	.339	.357	.382	.396	.418	.434	.440	.451	.457	.464
USSR[e]	1.16	1.17	1.16	1.14	1.13	1.13	1.12	1.12	1.10	1.09	1.07	1.06	1.05	1.03
Germany	.482	.453	.459	.485	.521	.534	.562	.548	.516	.471	.458	.448	.441	.426
Japan	.411	.422	.436	.485	.512	.593	.647	.688	.677	.669	.657	.647	.610	.578
France	.438	.464	.488	.511	.515	.506	.510	.530	.548	.555	.578	.575	.530	.499
World[f]	.670	.665	.675	.683	.687	.705	.722	.722	.718	.713	.706	.711	.705	.698
D. Lead Ore (Pb content) Consumption/Refined Lead Cons. by Principal Int's Traders														
Australia	.111	.110	.113	.110	.104	.107	.109	.110	.110	.109	.104	.104	.104	.106
Canada	.053	.053	.054	.055	.056	.058	.058	.058	.056	.051	.046	.043	.039	.037
Mexico	.071	.068	.065	.063	.060	.058	.057	.054	.051	.050	.051	.051	.053	.054

[a]
Ratios are based on five-year moving-average trends, centered on years shown.

[b]USSR omitted, since ore consumption (Pb content) was taken as equal to refined lead production.

[c]Actually, ratio of world mine production to total refined lead consumption. Data to adjust for production/consumption (stock-change) differences were not available.

[d]
World ratio omitted, since separate production and consumption estimates could not be made (see footnote c).

[e]
Same as production/consumption ratios, for reason given in footnote b.

[f]
Same as consumption/production ratios, for reason given in footnote c.

117

Table 1-30. Ratios of Lead Scrap Consumption to Refined Lead Consumption, for the World and Leading Lead Consumers, 1954-74[a]

	U.S.	Germany (F.R.)	Italy	U.K.	Canada	France	Japan	World
1956	.375	.222	.335	.260	.341	.153	.436	.227
1957	.376	.211	.328	.264	.344	.175	.415	.222
1958	.389	.194	.307	.264	.333	.199	.400	.217
1959	.390	.177	.285	.257	.328	.223	.365	.210
1960	.391	.170	.265	.258	.357	.217	.359	.203
1961	.406	.163	.248	.260	.361	.197	.348	.202
1962	.416	.157	.228	.266	.365	.194	.328	.202
1963	.420	.154	.217	.274	.397	.218	.312	.203
1964	.427	.146	.210	.280	.385	.222	.305	.206
1965	.438	.138	.205	.284	.357	.230	.284	.209
1966	.432	.136	.187	.286	.358	.229	.267	.207
1967	.425	.143	.162	.280	.355	.221	.264	.206
1968	.412	.149	.148	.275	.350	.198	.255	.203
1969	.405	.165	.153	.259	.375	.183	.256	.200
1970	.397	.180	.164	.242	.385	.154	.258	.197
1971	.395	.193	.189	.230	.392	.140	.253	.199
1972	.396	.206	.216	.217	.412	.137	.251	.201
1973	.411	.224	.232	.204	.413	.136	.255	.205
1974	.422	.239	.237	.200	.425	.130	.252	.209
1975	.457	.251	.242	.191	.485	.137	.255	.213

[a]Excludes USSR, for which scrap data are not available. Ratios are based on five-year moving-average trends, centered on years shown. In lieu of data on lead scrap as such, consumption data actually are for direct and implicit lead recovery from scrap.

Table 1-31. Ratios of Refined Lead Consumption to GNP/GDP, for Leading Lead Consumers, 1954- 76[a]

(metric tons)

Denominator	U.S. $ million	USSR Index[b]	U.K. L million	Germany (F.R.) DM million	Japan Y billion	France Fr million	Italy L billion	China (P.R.)[b] Index
1956	1.37	5.15	5.55	.435	3.81	.353	N.A.	.342
1957	1.31	5.10	5.45	.424	3.76	.345	"	.437
1958	1.22	5.08	5.33	.417	3.91	.329	"	.515
1959	1.16	5.04	5.21	.416	3.81	.313	"	.633
1960	1.10	5.06	5.16	.417	3.66	.295	"	.714
1961	1.06	5.10	5.12	.415	3.72	.279	"	.787
1962	1.03	5.10	5.14	.412	3.74	.267	1.67	.821
1963	1.02	5.05	5.10	.406	3.58	.255	1.62	.837
1964	.99	5.10	5.05	.397	3.35	.244	1.60	.772
1965	.97	5.09	4.91	.389	3.14	.236	1.61	.737
1966	.95	5.05	4.74	.387	2.93	.228	1.63	.782
1967	.95	5.00	4.50	.389	2.70	.220	1.65	.852
1968	.96	4.98	4.21	.386	2.56	.213	1.71	.870
1969	.96	4.98	3.97	.380	2.47	.202	1.79	.900
1970	.97	5.04	3.79	.370	2.41	.192	1.88	.911
1971	.98	5.10	3.63	.358	2.37	.183	2.00	.847
1972	.98	5.18	3.46	.339	2.27	.174	2.09	.772
1973	.94	5.26	3.29	.318	2.14	.165	2.14	.743
1974	.92	5.17	3.14	.304	2.07	.161	2.21	.722

N.A. - Not available.

a

Ratios, in metric tons per denominator shown at head of column, are based on five-year moving-average trends, centered on year shown. Currencies are all in constant (1975) prices.

b

GNP index, 1970=100 (see chapter 2), Ratios are per index point.

Zinc

Only two commodity forms have been defined for zinc: ore and refined metal. Not only is the smelting and refining process essentially integrated, with little commercial exchange of intermediates, but only a small portion of refined zinc--at least in the past--has been reclaimed from scrap.[28]

The United States and the Soviet Union are the world's largest zinc consumers, though the USSR has come to this point only as the result of large increases in consumption over the past couple of decades, while the United States has been at high levels of zinc consumption for some time. The other big difference between the two countries is that the USSR is essentially self-sufficient all the way through, whereas the United States has become increasingly dependent upon imported zinc, already refined. The contrasting trends in consumption of ore and refined metal, respectively, in the two countries are shown in figures 1-40 and 1-41.

The only close competitor for the leading zinc consumer niche is Japan, whose rate of increase has been even more rapid than that of the Soviet Union. At its peak, in 1973-74, Japanese zinc consumption was eight times what it had been twenty years earlier, and its ore consumption had increased to match (tables 1-32 and 1-33). Intensity of zinc use in Japan is falling, however (see table 1-35), and the rate of increase in its aggregate consumption is decidedly slowing down.

As evident from table 1-32, world zinc smelting activity is quite dispersed. In those cases where data on ore consumption are available, the relationship between ore input and refined zinc output (table 1-34) tends to be close to unity, owing to the measurement of ore consumption in

---

[28]A more significant amount of zinc is reclaimed in the form of copper-base (brass) alloy from corresponding copper-base scrap. This and other secondary recovery in other than re-refined form is excluded from our refined-zinc consumption series.

terms of zinc content and the limited reliance on scrap.[29] For the Communist countries, for which data are not available, the relationship is assumed to be unity. On the other hand, considerable disparity in degrees of self-sufficiency in refined zinc, as exemplified by the contrast between the United States and the USSR and shown in part B of table 1-34, results in widely varying ore consumption/metal consumption relationships (part C). Those relationships are shown only for countries whose smelting is primarily for domestic consumption; for those whose metal production is primarily for export (Australia and Canada), ore consumption is related to the refined zinc consumption of the entire "trading world" (of which both Canada and Australia are a part). Because Belgium is also an important supplier to the trading world, even though most of its refined zinc output is consumed domestically, its ore input ratios are shown relative to both domestic and trading-world consumption, the latter providing a slightly smoother progression.

Table 1-35, which evaluates zinc consumption per unit of GNP or GDP, reveals for most countries the same downward trend in intensity of use that characterizes copper and lead. China and the USSR are conspicuous exceptions, while the Japanese trend has been first upward, then downward, over the period shown. One may guess that these exceptional trends have mostly to do with the use of galvanized iron in construction, although in Japan there has also been significant use of galvanized sheeting in the automobile industry.

The importance of zinc's use as a coating for iron and steel suggests the possibility of close relationships between zinc consumption and iron and steel production. That such relationships do in fact exist is confirmed by

---

[29]Ratios of greater than unity (e.g., Italy) presumably reflect mostly the diversion of some ore into direct processing for chemical use, a phenomenon which in some other countries is outweighed by the extent of scrap utilization. In Australia's case, the high ratios in the early years presumably reflect the export of an intermediate product for refining elsewhere. Although processing losses are also involved, they are made irrelevant in some countries--e.g., the United States--by the estimation of zinc content of ore on a "recoverable" basis. The Canadian ratios are understated because apparent consumption has been calculated from production on a recoverable content basis and exports apparently on as assay content basis.

table 1-36, which makes the comparison for the world and for the leading industrialized countries. There has been some tendency for the relationship to weaken, although again the USSR, exceptionally, exhibits the opposite tendency. The United Kingdom is also an exception, in the sense that the relationship tends to be maintained, and in other countries, save for Japan, the downward tendency is rather mild. Only Japan has deviated very far from the apparent norm of 8 to 10 kilograms of zinc per ton of crude steel, and the upward trend in the Soviet Union may be viewed as a movement toward that norm.

If foreign exchange rates are used for currency coversion, it appears that as of 1974 or 1975 Japan had the highest intensity of zinc use among the five leading non-Communist consumers, at about 1.4 metric tons per million dollars of gross product, and the United States the lowest intensity, at about 0.7 tons per million dollars. The United Kingdom is roughly in the middle, at some 1.1 tons, and France and Germany a bit below the middle, at around 0.8 tons. Japan's high intensity may be presumed to be connected both with the high rates of investment in that country--and consequent high rates of construction activity--and the importance of automotive output in its economy.

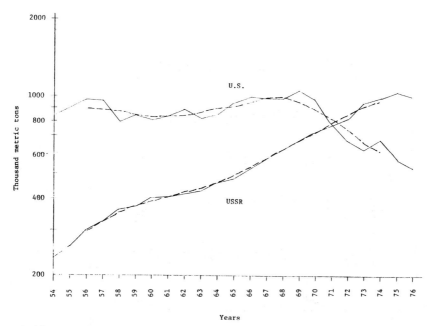

Figure 1-40. Apparent Consumption of Zinc Ore in the United States and the
USSR, 1954-1976, Annually and Five-Year Moving-Average Trends

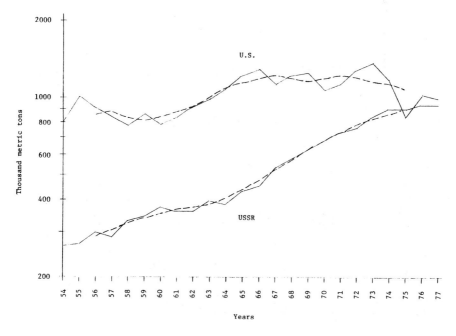

Figure 1-41. Apparent Consumption of Refined Zinc in the United States and
the USSR, 1954-1977, Annually and Five-Year Moving-Average
Trends

TABLE 1-32. WORLD APPARENT CONSUMPTION OF ZINC ORES AND CONCENTRATES, 1954-77, BY COUNTRY

(THOUSAND METRIC TONS, ZINC CONTENT)

| YEAR | PRINCIPAL INTERNATIONAL TRADERS | | | | | | | | OTHER COUNTRIES | | | | WORLD TOTAL[a] |
	GERMANY (F.R.)	BELGIUM	FRANCE	ITALY	AUSTRALIA	JAPAN	CANADA	TOTAL	UNITED STATES	USSR	POLAND	OTHER	
1954	145	194	150	74	103	111	178	955	843	235	142	575	2750
1955	158	216	186	88	150	114	220	1141	901	260	156	512	2970
1956	177	222	180	89	128	141	203	1138	969	300	153	580	3140
1957	201	212	193	89	134	164	206	1174	960	325	154	608	3220
1958	168	185	219	93	138	152	188	1176	793	360	163	639	3130
1959	185	213	155	84	125	171	195	1112	839	370	168	671	3360
1960	181	228	172	98	184	208	236	1311	809	400	176	665	3360
1961	172	196	191	93	138	257	221	1278	836	405	182	730	3430
1962	154	168	186	95	196	201	237	1255	885	415	181	804	3540
1963	161	169	181	91	201	268	258	1321	818	425	181	865	3610
1964	146	195	230	90	232	360	255	1523	845	460	187	954	3970
1965	163	231	214	99	250	386	303	1627	941	475	190	997	4230
1966	144	244	227	96	257	485	338	1809	992	520	193	955	4470
1967	176	228	218	124	255	538	341	1847	983	570	196	1195	4790
1968	267	245	222	127	258	674	275	1977	976	620	203	1205	4980
1969	282	225	256	144	319	704	365	2280	1048	670	208	1134	5340
1970	278	118	255	161	241	737	326	2120	962	725	209	1454	5470
1971	345	246	238	161	268	772	325	2288	767	770	220	1425	5470
1972	387	207	264	184	364	790	433	2587	665	820	228	1360	5660
1973	392	261	276	204	257	843	370	2598	615	940	235	1502	5890
1974	354	223	301	243	245	893	260	2556	671	980	233	1480	5920
1975	366	253	237	186	323	712	350	2415	560	1030	243	1663	5910
1976	N.A.	224	264	210	231	736	395	2426	521	1000	237	1806	5990
1977	N.A.	N.A.	N.A.	N.A.	N.A.	N.A.	N.A.	—	567	1020	228	N.A.	6290

SOURCE: COMMODITIES RESEARCH UNIT (DATA SERVICE); METALLGESELLSCHAFT AG, METAL STATISTICS.

NOTE: DETAIL MAY NOT ADD TO TOTALS, OWING TO ROUNDING.

[a] ACTUALLY, MINE PRODUCTION OF ZINC AS ESTIMATED BY METALLGESELLSCHAFT AG.

N.A. = NOT AVAILABLE

124

TABLE 1-33. WORLD APPARENT CONSUMPTION OF REFINED ZINC, 1954-77, BY COUNTRY [a]

(THOUSAND METRIC TONS)

YEAR	PRINCIPAL INTERNATIONAL TRADERS					OTHER COUNTRIES				WORLD TOTAL
	UNITED STATES	GERMANY (F.R.)	UNITED KINGDOM	USSR	TOTAL	JAPAN	FRANCE	CHINA (P.R.)	OTHER	
1954	799	203	246	265	1513	103	143	13	599	2370
1955	1013	240	257	269	1759	108	155	15	653	2690
1956	911	215	233	297	1656	115	156	18	676	2620
1957	843	225	236	285	1589	129	168	37	737	2660
1958	780	233	227	330	1570	136	178	41	804	2730
1959	863	266	251	343	1723	155	171	60	811	2920
1960	790	297	276	371	1733	189	172	70	915	3080
1961	838	306	259	359	1762	234	189	90	965	3240
1962	929	291	246	359	1825	243	186	90	1036	3380
1963	996	280	262	393	1931	305	181	90	1124	3630
1964	1089	321	288	382	2079	364	204	100	1193	3940
1965	1221	330	282	430	2263	330	186	100	1171	4050
1966	1285	310	273	450	2318	389	197	120	1247	4270
1967	1130	303	259	530	2221	462	203	120	1315	4320
1968	1221	362	281	580	2443	523	202	120	1422	4710
1969	1252	398	289	630	2569	600	239	135	1507	5120
1970	1074	396	278	680	2428	623	220	150	1619	5040
1971	1137	388	274	730	2528	628	225	170	1649	5200
1972	1286	413	279	760	2738	717	264	170	1841	5730
1973	1364	438	305	840	2947	815	290	190	1998	6240
1974	1168	389	268	900	2725	695	306	200	2064	5990
1975	839	297	207	900	2243	541	223	220	1823	5050
1976	1028	331	243	935	2537	699	265	220	2010	5730
1977	1000	330	245	937	2512	667	258	225	2088	5750

SOURCE: METALLGESELLSCHAFT AG, METAL STATISTICS.

NOTE: DETAIL MAY NOT ADD TO TOTALS, OWING TO ROUNDING.

[a] EXCLUDES REMELTED ZINC.

Table 1-34. Ratios of Zinc Ore Consumption to Refined Zinc Production and Consumption, for the World and Leading Zinc Ore Consumers, 1960-76a

	1962	1963	1964	1965	1966	1967	1968	1969	1970	1971	1972	1973	1974
A. Zinc Ore (Zn content) Consumption/Refined Zinc Production b													
Germany (F.R.)	.95	.92	.88	.86	.84	.85	.88	.93	.96	.98	.98	1.00	1.06
Belgium	.85	.86	.90	.93	.97	.96	.87	.90	.86	.85	.83	.95	.92
France	1.15	1.14	1.14	1.15	1.14	1.10	1.11	1.06	1.06	1.07	1.09	1.11	1.11
Italy	1.15	1.17	1.21	1.25	1.23	1.20	1.18	1.16	1.14	1.14	1.17	1.15	1.13
Australia	1.20	1.17	1.23	1.26	1.28	1.29	1.21	1.16	1.15	1.07	.99	1.10	1.09
Japan	1.02	1.00	1.00	1.04	1.07	1.04	1.06	1.06	1.04	1.02	1.03	1.02	1.01
Canada	.93	.92	.93	.93	.87	.88	.85	.83	.83	.82	.77	.78	.78
United States	.99	.97	.97	.97	.98	1.01	1.03	1.04	1.03	1.04	1.07	1.08	1.09
World c	1.03	1.03	1.03	1.05	1.05	1.05	1.05	1.05	1.04	1.03	1.03	1.03	1.02
B. Refined Zinc Production/Consumption													
Germany (F.R.)	.60	.58	.59	.58	.58	.62	.67	.66	.72	.78	.85	.89	.94
Belgium	1.88	1.80	1.84	1.92	2.00	2.00	1.99	1.85	1.81	1.69	1.63	1.67	1.73
France	.90	.93	.95	.96	.98	1.01	1.00	1.03	1.01	.98	.94	.91	.89
Italy	.81	.75	.69	.67	.67	.70	.72	.76	.78	.80	.84	.90	.93
Australia	1.77	1.93	2.23	1.95	1.97	2.05	2.13	2.20	2.39	2.51	2.56	2.60	2.68
Japan	.96	.99	1.04	1.06	1.10	1.16	1.15	1.14	1.14	1.11	1.12	1.15	1.14
Canada	3.87	3.64	3.53	3.50	3.46	3.53	3.62	3.55	3.52	3.54	3.40	3.21	3.20
United States	.92	.87	.84	.82	.81	.80	.80	.78	.72	.64	.57	.52	.49
USSR	1.13	1.15	1.15	1.13	1.13	1.10	1.08	1.07	1.07	1.08	1.08	1.10	1.10
Poland	1.68	1.65	1.61	1.60	1.59	1.60	1.59	1.59	1.60	1.60	1.60	1.60	1.59
World	1.01	1.00	1.00	.99	1.00	1.01	1.02	1.02	1.01	.99	.98	.99	1.00

Table 1-34 (cont'd)

	1962	1963	1964	1965	1966	1967	1968	1969	1970	1971	1972	1973	1974	1975
C. Zinc Ore (Zn content) Consumption/Refined Zinc Consumption														
Germany (F.R.)	.57	.53	.52	.50	.49	.53	.58	.62	.69	.77	.83	.91	.99	1.05
Belgium	1.59	1.55	1.65	1.79	1.94	1.92	1.74	1.67	1.57	1.45	1.36	1.59	1.59	N.A.
France	1.03	1.06	1.09	1.10	1.12	1.11	1.11	1.09	1.07	1.04	1.02	1.01	1.00	1.00
Italy	.93	.89	.83	.83	.83	.84	.85	.88	.89	.91	.98	1.04	1.05	N.A.
Japan	.97	1.00	1.04	1.10	1.18	1.21	1.21	1.19	1.14	1.16	1.18	1.18	1.15	1.16
United States	.90	.85	.81	.80	.80	.81	.83	.81	.74	.66	.61	.57	.53	.53
USSR	1.13	1.13	1.14	1.12	1.12	1.09	1.08	1.07	1.07	1.08	1.08	1.10	1.10	1.10
Poland	1.68	1.65	1.61	1.60	1.59	1.60	1.59	1.59	1.60	1.60	1.60	1.60	1.59	1.60
World	1.04	1.03	1.03	1.04	1.05	1.06	1.07	1.07	1.04	1.02	1.01	1.02	1.03	N.A.
D. Zinc Ore (Zn content) Consumption/Refined Zinc Cons. by Principal Int'l Traders														
Belgium	.102	.097	.097	.099	.101	.099	.088	.087	.082	.080	.079	.090	.089	.092
Australia	.102	.103	.109	.111	.111	.113	.111	.110	.114	.110	.103	.111	.108	.100
Canada	.129	.129	.134	.138	.134	.137	.137	.134	.136	.138	.128	.132	.137	.139

a
Ratios are based on five-year moving-average trends, centered on years shown.

b
USSR, Poland, and People's Republic of China omitted, since data on ore consumption not directly available and assumed equal to refined zinc production.

c
Mine production used in lieu of ore consumption.

127

Table 1-35. Ratios of Refined Zinc Consumption to GNP/GDP, for Leading Zinc Consumers, 1954-77[a]

(metric tons)

Denominator	U.S. $ million	Germany (F.R.) DM million	U.K. L million	USSR[b] Index	Japan Y billion	France Fr million	China (P.R.)[b] Index
1956	1.04	.478	3.74	5.96	4.08	.289	.258
1957	1.02	.473	3.67	5.87	4.13	.286	.333
1958	.94	.475	3.63	5.92	4.28	.277	.422
1959	.91	.481	3.60	5.81	4.51	.273	.563
1960	.89	.479	3.53	5.77	4.66	.264	.668
1961	.90	.469	3.51	5.77	4.95	.250	.777
1962	.91	.462	3.48	5.64	5.26	.244	.840
1963	.95	.450	3.39	5.54	5.30	.234	.891
1964	.98	.432	3.33	5.52	5.36	.223	.813
1965	.97	.421	3.25	5.70	5.50	.215	.798
1966	.97	.426	3.20	5.82	5.53	.209	.796
1967	.95	.427	3.13	6.13	5.54	.205	.799
1968	.90	.424	3.05	6.37	5.56	.200	.807
1969	.86	.423	2.98	6.66	5.48	.194	.818
1970	.86	.425	2.95	6.84	5.42	.193	.813
1971	.85	.421	2.90	7.04	5.42	.196	.808
1972	.82	.405	2.79	7.21	5.21	.197	.804
1973	.77	.377	2.60	7.34	4.85	.191	.812
1974	.73	.357	2.50	7.43	4.71	.189	.811
1975	.68	.334	2.40	7.43	4.45	.183	.805

[a]Ratios, in metric tons per denominator shown at head of column, are based on five-year moving-average trends, centered on year shown. Currencies are all in constant (1975) prices.

[b]GNP index, 1970 = 100 (see chapter 2). Ratios are per index point.

Table 1-36. Ratios of Refined Zinc Consumption to Raw Steel Production,
for the World and for Leading Steel Producers, 1960-77[a]

(Kilos of zinc per metric ton of steel)

	U.S.	USSR	Japan	Germany	France	U.K.	World
1962	9.6	4.9	8.6	8.8	10.4	11.3	9.2
1963	9.9	4.8	8.5	8.5	10.3	11.1	9.2
1964	10.1	4.7	8.4	8.4	10.2	11.0	9.2
1965	10.0	4.8	8.3	8.3	10.1	10.8	9.0
1966	10.1	4.9	8.0	8.3	10.0	10.7	8.9
1967	10.1	5.2	7.7	8.4	10.1	10.7	8.9
1968	9.9	5.4	7.4	8.7	10.0	10.6	8.8
1969	9.8	5.7	7.2	8.9	9.9	10.7	8.8
1970	10.0	5.8	7.2	9.1	10.1	10.7	8.9
1971	9.9	6.0	7.2	9.1	10.4	10.9	8.9
1972	9.7	6.2	6.8	8.7	10.6	11.1	8.7
1973	9.6	6.3	6.5	8.5	10.8	11.2	8.6
1974	9.3	6.4	6.4	8.1	11.1	11.1	8.5
1975	8.9	6.4	6.2	8.0	11.3	11.3	8.4

[a]Ratios are based on five-year moving-average trends, centered on year
shown.

Comparative Trends

Because there are numerous applications in which one nonferrous metal
is substitutable for another, the trends in use intensity for individual
metals are frequently more understandable if they are mutually compared.
This is done for the leading industrialized countries in table 1-37. It
would have been additionally instructive to have extended the comparison
to iron and steel, since there are important applications where steel (or
zinc-coated steel) is an alternative to copper or aluminum, but it did not
seem cost effective to compile the requisite iron and steel consumption
series for this one purpose.

In all six of the countries compared, it may be seen, aluminum is now
the dominant nonferrous metal.[30] This has been true in the United States
and France since before 1960, whereas it was not until 1962 that aluminum
surpassed copper in the USSR; in Germany, 1965; in Japan, 1966; and the
United Kingdom, 1968.

In most of the countries, zinc has been a more important metal than
lead, but not so in the United States, where refined lead consumption has
exceeded refined zinc consumption in most of the past fifteen years, or in
the United Kingdom, where refined lead consumption has exceeded refined
zinc consumption by a larger margin. This is true not only in terms of
weight, but for the most part in terms of value as well, since lead and
zinc prices tend to run close to each other per pound. It must be borne
in mind, however, that relatively more zinc than lead is consumed in a
form which bypasses the need for what we have defined as refined metal.

For every country, it will be seen, rising aluminum trends are accompanied by declining copper intensities. Taken together, intensity of consumption of the two metals tends to rise in every country but France and
Great Britain, the former exhibiting a mild decline and the latter a

---

[30]Actually, it is even more dominant than comparison on a strictly
weight basis indicates, since it generally takes fewer pounds of aluminum
than of substitute metals to accomplish the same purpose.

stronger one. Though aluminum also competes importantly with zinc
(through die castings and galvanized iron), and declining zinc trends
are in fact to be found in most of the countries as noted, there is the
exact opposite of a compensating decline in zinc use in the USSR and a
rather equivocal record in Japan, though decline now seems to have set in.

The joint intensity of aluminum, copper, and zinc rises over time in
all of the countries--in Japan markedly so. If weight is a proper criterion, therefore, and if steel is omitted, there would seem to be a continuation of increasing intensities of metal use in the industrialized
world. However, market value, it might be argued, is a more appropriate
criterion than weight for aggregating different kinds of metals, since
unit value should have some relationship to the "indifference point" of
consumption of the various commodities at the margin--or, in other words,
to their marginal equivalence in actual use. The price of aluminum, in
fact, has been below the price of its nearest competitor, copper, over
most of the period covered by table 1-37, and this could depress aluminum's
weight in the total metal mix sufficiently to alter the composite upward
intensity trend. Recently, however, the price of aluminum has been trend-
ing upward more steeply than that of copper, and, in general, there is not
enough difference among prices of the various nonferrous metals to alter
significantly the results of aggregation purely on a weight basis. More
serious for the validity of finding increasing aggregate intensity in
metals use is the omission of steel, whose consumption has exhibited
generally downward intensity trends and whose volume and value, both, could
be great enough to offset the picture presented by nonferrous metals alone.

Table 1-37. Comparative Consumption of Four of the Six Leading Industrial Countries, 1958-76[a]

(metric tons per specified unit of GNP/GDP)

	1960	1961	1962	1963	1964	1965	1966	1967	1968	1969	1970	1971	1972	1973	1974
United States ($ million)															
Aluminum	2.20	2.37	2.43	2.59	2.78	2.87	2.99	3.09	3.12	3.16	3.27	3.39	3.51	3.46	3.46
Copper	1.44	1.44	1.46	1.50	1.56	1.55	1.50	1.47	1.43	1.35	1.35	1.37	1.35	1.26	1.22
Lead	1.10	1.06	1.03	1.02	1.03	.99	.97	.95	.95	.96	.97	.98	.98	.94	.92
Zinc	.89	.90	.91	.95	.98	.97	.97	.95	.90	.86	.86	.85	.82	.77	.73
USSR (GNP index, 1970 = 100)															
Aluminum	10.1	10.8	11.1	11.6	11.9	12.4	12.8	13.1	13.2	13.3	13.4	13.3	13.3	13.4	13.3
Copper	10.3	10.8	10.7	10.6	10.5	10.3	10.1	10.0	9.8	9.7	9.7	9.6	9.5	9.7	9.8
Lead	5.1	5.1	5.1	5.1	5.1	5.1	5.0	5.0	5.0	5.0	5.0	5.1	5.2	5.3	5.2
Zinc	5.8	5.8	5.6	5.5	5.5	5.7	5.8	6.1	6.4	6.7	6.8	7.0	7.2	7.3	7.4
Japan (Y billion)															
Aluminum	4.7	5.2	5.5	5.7	6.0	6.6	7.2	8.1	8.9	9.5	10.1	11.1	11.3	11.3	11.6
Copper	6.5	6.8	7.0	6.9	6.6	6.9	7.1	7.3	7.3	7.2	7.2	7.3	7.0	6.7	6.7
Lead	3.7	3.7	3.7	3.6	3.4	3.1	2.9	2.7	2.6	2.5	2.4	2.4	2.3	2.4	2.1
Zinc	4.7	5.0	5.3	5.3	5.4	5.5	5.5	5.5	5.6	5.5	5.4	5.4	5.2	4.9	4.7
Germany (DM million)															
Aluminum	.62	.64	.67	.68	.70	.72	.77	.82	.86	.89	.93	.96	.97	.96	1.00
Copper	.84	.82	.81	.78	.72	.70	.70	.69	.70	.71	.71	.70	.69	.67	.67
Lead	.42	.42	.41	.41	.40	.39	.39	.39	.39	.38	.37	.36	.34	.32	.30
Zinc	.48	.47	.46	.45	.43	.42	.43	.43	.42	.42	.42	.42	.40	.38	.36

132

Table 1-37 (cont'd)

	1960	1961	1962	1963	1964	1965	1966	1967	1968	1969	1970	1971	1972	1973	1974
France (Fr million)															
Aluminum	.350	.360	.362	.352	.358	.356	.354	.366	.384	.384	.388	.400	.403	.390	.398
Copper	.338	.326	.332	.326	.319	.309	.302	.294	.286	.280	.284	.287	.285	.280	.273
Lead	.295	.279	.267	.255	.244	.236	.228	.220	.213	.202	.192	.183	.174	.165	.161
Zinc	.264	.250	.244	.234	.223	.215	.209	.205	.200	.194	.193	.196	.197	.191	.189
United Kingdom (L million)															
Aluminum	5.67	5.81	5.92	5.85	6.00	6.06	6.12	6.11	6.12	5.90	5.88	5.90	5.90	5.70	5.79
Copper	7.42	7.22	7.34	7.34	7.29	7.03	6.78	6.43	6.07	5.76	5.67	5.49	5.25	4.96	4.76
Lead	5.16	5.12	5.14	5.10	5.05	4.91	4.74	4.50	4.21	3.97	3.79	3.63	3.46	3.29	3.14
Zinc	3.53	3.51	3.48	3.39	3.33	3.25	3.20	3.13	3.05	2.98	2.95	2.90	2.79	2.60	2.50

a
Ratios are based on five-year moving-average trends, centered on year shown.

Chapter 2

PROJECTED PATTERNS

Introduction

We have taken as our outlook period the years between the late 1970s and the year 2000. The projections in this chapter are for five-year intervals, being stated as consumption in the years 1980, 1985, 1990, 1995, and 2000. In no case, however, is there any intention to provide anything but a trend value. There is no attempt, even for near-future years, to take account of either cyclical or other kinds of deviations. The projections are not straight-line ones, however, either arithmetic or geometric, but extensions of the five-year moving-average trends which formed the basis for much of the presentation in chapter 1. The figure for any given projection year, therefore, is to be read as an average for that year and surrounding years. Similarly, the 1975 "base year" values used in this chapter are not actual 1975 values, but averages for the period 1973-77.

The projections are not intended to be anything more than a crude means for judging the potential emergence of mineral supply problems. There are too many unpredictables for even in-depth analysis and modeling to provide projections of very high reliability for any significant distance into the future. It is virtually certain that any attempt to predict deviations from trend is doomed to high inaccuracy, even for an immediately ensuing 12-month period, let alone something more extended. Thus, we do not attempt to fix on expected actual values. One cannot effectively consider short-term supply contingencies without giving at least qualitative attention to expectable deviations from trend, however, and this is done in chapter 9. The figures in chapter 1 show how much relative deviation there might be from trend performance for the commodities discussed.

Why, if accuracy is so hard to achieve, do we even bother with a new set of projections, rather than relying upon some of those which already exist? One of the reasons is that none of the known projections adheres to quite the same definitions of mineral commodities or of "consumption" that we have selected as being most pertinent to U.S. mineral supply problems. Another reason is that the known existing projections do not provide aggregates for the "trading world" totals that we have presumed are particularly pertinent to price determination. Still another is that the existing projections are based on varying sets of demographic and macroeconomic assumptions (or projections, depending upon the methodology).[1]

In our projections, the word "consumption" is used deliberately to avoid any implication that we are dealing with demand in any classical economic sense--that is, either as a demand schedule or as the result of market equilibrium at a predicted price. Rather--and this is true even when we occasionally substitute the word "demand"--what we have in mind is the commodity consumption consequences of some generalized assumptions as to economic growth and controlling prices, with no supply constraints.

As noted above, our commodity projections are tied to our own demographic and macroeconomic assumptions. It is the difference between our macro assumptions and those of others that should be taken as our expression of how we judge the future will unfold, more than the specific figures presented. The seeming precision of these figures, in terms of significant digits, is ordinarily greater (in order to facilitate further calculations) than the degree of accuracy we mean to attribute to them.

Perhaps the single greatest difference between the approach taken in our projections and that taken in other sets of world commodity-consumption projections is the method used for arriving at world totals. The Bureau of Mines goes to world totals directly, and the other studies generally

---

[1]For a detailed comparison of four projections currently in use, see Leonard L. Fischman, et al., "Major Mineral Supply Problems," available from National Technical Information Service, Springfield, Va. (PB80-117674) chapter 9.

group countries into aggregates of interest (e.g., OECD, developing, advanced developing); here, instead, we have based world totals on the selected individual countries which account for the bulk of each commodity's utilization. By and large, these are the leading industrial countries for the refined metals, and a combination of industrial countries and other mineral-rich countries for the cruder forms of metals. It takes projections of the macroeconomies of only about a dozen countries, all told, to provide the base for projecting the bulk of the consumption of all eighteen commodity forms covered, plus crude steel, as an important intermediate variable. The aggregate consumption of the leading consumers of each form, though gradually declining in relation to world totals as new consumers enter the picture, may, it is hypothesized, reasonably accurately be "blown up" to a world total for any given future year by extrapolating their declining share--or, similarly, may be blown up to the "trading world" total which in this study is of particular interest.

For projection purposes, two classes of mineral commodities have been distinguished: the refined metals, whose consumption may be linked to macroeconomic variables, and the inputs into metal refining, whose consumption may be linked to the consumption of refined metals.[2] In the latter case, however, the projected parameter must not fail to take into account the changing degree to which refined metal supply in any given country is likely to be domestically produced or imported.

A special case arises in the case of countries whose consumption of, for example, an ore is linked, not to their own requirements for an intermediate or refined metal, but primarily to the requirements of those countries that import intermediate or refined metals from them. In such cases, our projection method has been to utilize the parameters between (a) the input of ore in the world-supplying countries in which the ore is consumed and (b) the consumption of intermediate or refined metal in the principal consuming countries that depend on international trade (including the exporting country itself if it happens also to be a principal consumer

---

[2] For the purpose of projecting ferromanganese, in this chapter we classify steel production as a sort of macroeconomic variable.

of the more advanced form). In discussing these parameters in the text, we frequently treat them as a measure of the proportion of total advanced-form supply available to the principal trader-consumers that is accounted for by the particular processing country. This is roughly valid, but it must be realized that there are likely also to be other consumers of such supply, including the supplying country itself in cases where it is not explicitly included among the tabulated leading consumers.

Macro Projections

Whenever long-term commodity projections are based directly or indirectly on long-term projections of gross economic output, the commodity-projection accuracy tends to depend more upon the accuracy of the gross national or domestic product (GNP or GDP) projections than upon the parameters that join GNP/GDP to individual commodities. Another probable truth is that when long-term GNP/GDP projections err, the error is likely to be mostly the consequence of failing to take into account the interrelationships between GNP growth and population.

In all countries, growth in GDP increases with the population, but the nature of the relationship differs for developed and developing countries. In developed countries, higher rates of population growth, with their attendant pressure for housing and consumer goods tend to increase labor force participation and thus GDP. In developing countries, on the other hand, the demands of meeting the basic needs of the current population impose constraints on capital investment and consequently on newer and higher productivity jobs, and any increases in population tend to increase the constraints.

Gross Economic Product

In projecting GNP/GDP for the various countries of interest, we have chosen to be rather simplistic. The reason is that there is considerable tendency for compensation among the factors that go to make up a country's gross economic output: labor force participation, annual hours, hourly productivity, and the further elements of each of these (e.g., hours per week and weeks per year). Thus, projecting each such factor or element individually and then multiplying them one by the other is a more hazardous forecasting technique than projecting them in the composite. On these grounds, since detailed behavioral modeling was out of the question for the present study, an aggregative approach was the happy choice.

Even in aggregation, however, there has to be some means of bringing qualitative judgment to bear. This is quite difficult if the simplistic approach is carried to the extreme of simply projecting GNP/GDP growth rates. At the very least, it takes a separation of the two major components, population and output per capita, in order to judge the net effect of the population age distribution, incentives to work, and other determinants of per capita productivity. While it might have been somewhat better also to have taken explicitly into account the likely trends in labor force participation (in relation to working-age population), this would have required an excursion into demographics that did not seem cost and time effective within study constraints.

Unavoidably, in converting qualitative judgments into actual numbers, the point of departure has to be historical trend, and reliance upon this trend has to be more or less strong as there is less or more basis for assuming future deviations from it. In general, the actual trend for developed countries has been one of declines in rate of growth of per capita productivity, and we have assumed a continuation of this phenomenon, softened only by such periodic stimulation as might be expected to result from the generational effects of the population surges that occurred in a number of countries soon after the end of World War II. For the developing countries, our assumptions of per capita productivity have depended on where the countries now stand, in comparison with our feelings as to their long-run potential. The conclusions are set forth in table 2-1, which shows both the projected GNP/GDP growth rates and their components of population growth and per capita productivity growth for five-year intervals to the year 2000. The table also provides historical comparisons. The historical rates of change are calculated from moving-average values, and the projections, too, refer to trend values of similar concept.

In all cases, save for China,[3] gross product was derived by applying per capita productivity changes, although initial judgments as to rate of productivity gain were in some instances rethought in the light of the resultant calculation of GNP growth. The final projections are shown in table 2-2.

Aside from the general considerations mentioned above, the projected rates of gain in per capita GNP for individual countries took into account the following elements:

United States: The projected 2.2 percent growth rate for 1975 to 1980 compares with an approximately 2.6 percent rate of gain from the 1975 base to 1978, but there has been a progressive slowing in rates of productivity gain since 1976.[4] This slowing is assumed to be part of a persistent long-term trend, but one may expect the deceleration to be temporarily halted around the early 1990s, owing to a consumption surge as the children of the 1950s baby-boom generation reach adulthood. The growth-rate projections depart from a trend benchmark rather than the actual growth rate for 1968-72 to 1973-77 (shown in the table as 1970-75), since the 1975-centered average for U.S. per capita GNP seemed aberrationally low.

Japan: The 5.0 percent rate assumed for 1975-80 is well beyond the 2.83 percent registered for 1975-77, but there was a sharp upturn of economic activity in Japan in 1978, which is expected by the OECD to continue at least partway through 1979.[5] The 4.84 percent rate of productivity gain registered for 1970-75 is

---

[3] For lack of a reasonable basis for making independent projections for China, its rate of GNP growth was taken as a constant 3.75 percent per annum—the rate suggested by "Global 2000."

[4] This and the various other current-period changes referred to in the immediately following text (e.g., changes from 1975 to 1977) relate the 1975-centered five-year average to a subsequent single latest year for which information is readily available.

[5] References to the OECD in this section relate to their Economic Outlook No. 24, December 1978.

also considered to be below trend and thus not inconsistent
with the higher value chosen for the current quinquennium. For
the longer run, however, it seems reasonable to assume a sharply declining rate of per capita gain as Japan moves out of its
extremely high savings-investment stance, diminishing stimulus
is provided by population growth, and there is progressively
less margin for shifting labor force from lower productivity
to higher productivity employment.

United Kingdom: The 1.9 percent rate of gain assumed for 1975-
80 is well beyond the 0.59 percent recorded for 1975-77, but starting late in 1977 the United Kingdom had a decided pickup in economic activity that was at least partly ascribable to North Sea
oil exploitation. For the further future, however, there seems
no reason not to expect resumption of the earlier downward trend
in rates of productivity growth, except for such arresting of the
decline as is likely to occur near century's end for demographic
reasons.

Federal Republic of Germany: Like Japan, the FRG is assumed to
have passed its peak as a high-investment, low-labor-compensa-
tion economy, but, having attained less of a peak, not to be
subject to as sharp a fall. The productivity growth rate of 2.8
percent assumed for 1975-80 is a shade higher than the 2.68 percent registered for 1975-77, but yields GDP growth which is somewhat lower than that suggested by OECD estimates and expectations
for 1978 and 1979. The latter difference may be explained, at
least in part, by post-1979 expectations, which need to be reflected in a 1975-80 moving average trend.

France: Productivity trends assumed for France are similar to
those for Germany, though France's 1975-80 rate implies a slightly better recovery for the balance of the quinquennium, since it
takes off from a slightly lower average rate for 1975-77. The
resultant 1975-80 GNP growth rate is closely consistent with
OECD expectations for the immediate future. For a time, France's
larger proportion of labor force still engaged in agricultural

pursuits (over 14 percent, compared with Germany's less than 9 percent) provides opportunity for occasionally greater rates of per capita output gain, but this differential stimulus will have faded later in the century.

Italy: A still heavily underutilized labor force, especially in Italy's south, provides considerable potential for rapid growth, but a persistence of political and other institutional difficulties is assumed to have a more than counterbalancing effect.[6] The growth rate of 2.0 percent assumed for 1975-80 is somewhat higher than the average rate of 1.46 percent registered for 1975-77, but yields rates of GNP gain which are on the low side in relation to OECD expectations for the current period.

Belgium: With its economy chiefly dependent upon in-transit processing and other manufacturing for export, the rapidly declining rates of population growth in Belgium over the past decade or so have resulted in high, rather than low, rates of growth in per capita output. Population growth is now down to the lowest rates in Western Europe, however, and further declines are expected to be modest, at the same time as Belgium will probably have to yield some of its minerals-processing and other manufacturing functions to developing countries. Thus, per capita growth rates, while still relatively high for a developed country, are projected to be considerably lower than in the immediate past, though comparable with those of the late 1950s. The rate assumed for the current (1975-80) period is somewhat higher than that actually registered in 1975 to 1977, but implies a GNP growth roughly the same as that being estimated by OECD for current years.

USSR: Per capita GNP growth in the Soviet Union is projected on the basis that, as a mature economy with sharply declining

---

[6]At some 19 percent of total labor force, Italy's present commitment to agriculture is higher than that of either France or Germany. It may be assumed that a good deal of such agricultural employment involves unnecessarily liberal use of labor. Percentage derived from the UN International Labor Office, Yearbook of Labor Statistics, 1976.

Table 2-1. Projected Population and Real Gross Product Growth Rates, 1975-2000, for Principal
Minerals Consuming Countries, with 1950-75 Comparisons[a]

(percent growth per annum)

	Historical					Projected				
	1950-1955	1955-1960	1960-1965	1965-1970	1970-1975	1975-1980	1980-1985	1985-1990	1990-1995	1995-2000
United States										
Population	1.73	1.74	1.49	1.08	.86	.93	1.01	.91	.75	.65
Per capita GNP	2.06	.89	3.05	2.39	1.80	2.2	2.0	1.9	1.9	1.8
Gross national product	3.81	2.64	4.59	3.49	3.30	3.2	3.0	2.8	2.7	2.5
Japan										
Population	1.28	1.10	1.00	1.08	1.25	1.03	.70	.56	.52	.51
Per capita GNP	N.A.	7.52	9.27	9.95	4.84	5.0	3.0	2.5	2.2	2.1
Gross national product	"	8.70	10.36	11.14	6.14	6.1	3.7	3.1	2.7	2.6
United Kingdom										
Population	.24	.52	.76	.30	.33	.24	.29	.32	.31	.30
Per capita GDP	N.A.	2.05	2.52	2.22	1.94	1.9	1.7	1.5	1.3	1.3
Gross domestic product	"	2.58	3.30	2.53	2.14	2.1	2.0	1.8	1.6	1.6
Germany (F.R.)										
Population	.48	1.59	1.27	.57	.36	.11	.27	.42	.36	.27
Per capita GDP	N.A.	4.57	3.39	4.08	2.68	2.8	2.5	2.2	2.2	2.2
Gross domestic product	"	6.24	4.71	4.66	3.05	2.9	2.8	2.6	2.6	2.5
France										
Population	.73	1.09	1.32	.81	.78	.75	.64	.55	.47	.40
Per capita GDP	N.A.	3.98	4.50	4.87	3.50	2.8	2.5	2.3	2.1	2.1
Gross domestic product	"	5.11	5.88	5.71	4.31	3.6	3.2	2.9	2.6	2.5

142

Italy

Population	.53	.67	.77	.79	.79	.51	.49	.48	.47	.46
Per capita GDP	N.A.	N.A.	3.23	4.34	2.63	2.0	1.8	1.6	1.5	1.4
Gross domestic product	"	"	4.02	5.17	3.43	2.5	2.3	2.1	2.0	1.9

Belgium

Population	.57	.58	.67	.42	.29	.24	.19	.21	.21	.19
Per capita GNP	N.A.	2.27	4.12	4.41	4.19	2.4	2.4	2.3	2.2	2.1
Gross domestic product	"	2.91	4.81	4.83	4.49	2.6	2.6	2.5	2.4	2.3

USSR

Population	2.14	1.36	1.48	1.04	.94	.94	.87	.72	.58	.52
Per capita GNP	N.A.	4.74	3.12	4.11	3.26	3.0	2.7	2.4	2.2	2.0
Gross national product	"	6.17	4.65	5.19	4.23	4.0	3.6	3.1	2.8	2.5

Brazil

Population	N.A.	N.A.	2.97	2.77	2.98	2.98	3.02	3.01	2.98	2.96
Per capita GDP	"	"	N.A.	6.60	7.15	7.0	7.0	6.8	6.4	6.0
Gross domestic product	"	"	"	9.55	10.34	10.2	10.2	10.0	9.6	9.1

India

Population	1.22	2.54	2.38	2.07	2.10	2.27	2.05	1.92	1.61	1.39
Per capita GDP	N.A.	N.A.	1.82	1.58	1.78	1.4	1.6	2.0	2.2	2.5
Gross domestic product	"	"	4.24	3.67	3.92	3.7	3.7	4.0	3.8	3.9

China (P.R.)

Gross domestic product[b]	N.A.	3.75	4.81	6.64	7.42	3.75	3.75	3.75	3.75	3.75

N.A. - Not available.

[a] GNP/GDP figures refer to changes between five-year averages centered on years specified. Population changes based on actual population in the single year specified.

[b] As an exception, the "Global 2000" medium assumption was adopted for GDP growth in China.

rates of population gain, it will also have declining rates of
gain in per capita output, converging toward those characterizing
the United States.

Brazil: This country is assumed to have passed its peak in rates
of per capita output growth, though it still maintains much higher
rates than in the more developed countries and higher as well than
in developing countries with less success in internal management
and attraction of external capital.

India: In contrast with Brazil, India is assumed to be well short
of its eventual peak. A gradual, though uneven, acceleration in
growth rates of per capita output is projected for the balance of
the century, modulated by the lagged impact of demographic waves
on investment capability. The initial decline to a low in the
1975-80 period reflects the particular difficulties that India
has had in recent years as a result of crop failures, rising oil
prices, and political instability--the combination of which produced actual declines in per capita output in the 1975-77 period.
The projections were guided in large measure by a special study
on India done as part of another RFF project.

Steel Production

For the special purposes of this study, steel production has to be
added as a macro indicator: it clearly determines ferromanganese consumption; it is at least as good an indicator for ferrochromium consumption as
GNP; and it is a useful indicator for zinc. It is important to note that
it is production, not consumption, of steel that is being projected, since
we are concerned in this study, not with where the steel and its contained
manganese or chromium end up but where these metals go in.

The projection technique for steel production, however, is similar
to that used in this study to project consumption of the various other
refined metals--that is, steel production is related to the respective
countries' GNP/GDP. The rationale is that steel production, like the
consumption of principal industrial commodities, bears a somewhat predictable relationship to gross economic output, tending to keep up with

Table 2-2. Historical and Projected GNP/GDP Trends, 1950-2000, for Leading Industrial Consumers of Refined Metals

	U.S.	USSR	Japan	Germany	France	China	U.K.	Italy	Brazil	India	Belgium
	($ trillion)	(Index, 1970=100)	(Y trillion)	(DM trillion)	(Fr trillion)	(Index 1957=100)	(L billion)	(Lire trillion)	(Cr$ trillion)	(Rs billion)	(Fr trillion)
Historical Values[a]											
1954	.80	42	25	N.A.	.50	82	60.9	N.A.	N.A.	N.A.	N.A.
1955	.82	45	27	.43	.53	87	62.8	..	..	..	1.04
1956	.84	49	29	.46	.55	96	64.2	..	..	..	1.07
1957	.87	52	31	.49	.58	103	65.7	..	..	..	1.09
1958	.89	55	34	.52	.61	107	67.4	..	..	..	1.12
1959	.91	58	37	.55	.64	106	69.4	..	..	..	1.16
1960	.94	61	41	.58	.68	105	71.3	..	..	..	1.20
1961	.98	63	45	.61	.72	103	73.7	..	..	..	1.26
1962	1.02	66	51	.65	.76	105	76.4	68	..	468	1.32
1963	1.06	69	56	.68	.81	110	78.9	71	..	481	1.39
1964	1.12	73	61	.71	.85	123	81.2	74	..	492	1.46
1965	1.18	77	67	.73	.90	133	83.8	78	..	509	1.52
1966	1.23	81	75	.76	.95	141	86.4	82	.39	524	1.58
1967	1.29	86	83	.80	1.03	149	88.4	87	.43	540	1.65
1968	1.32	90	93	.83	1.06	160	90.4	92	.47	566	1.73
1969	1.35	95	103	.87	1.12	170	92.7	96	.51	592	1.82
1970	1.39	99	114	.92	1.19	183	95.0	100	.56	610	1.92
1971	1.44	103	125	.97	1.26	202	98.1	105	.62	630	2.03
1972	1.48	108	133	1.00	1.32	219	100.7	109	.70	646	2.15
1973	1.51	113	140	1.02	1.37	234	102.4	112	.78	666	2.23
1974	1.55	117	147	1.05	1.43	247	104.2	115	.86	686	2.32
1975	1.59	122	154	1.07	1.47	262	105.6	119	.94	b706	2.39
1975, in $ (U.S.) billion[c]	1537	649	513	416	320	290	216	162	107	82	64
Projections[d]											
1980	1.86	148	207	1.23	1.75	315	117.2	134	1.65	823	2.72
1985	2.16	176	248	1.42	2.05	379	129.4	151	2.69	987	3.09
1990	2.48	206	288	1.61	2.37	455	141.4	167	4.33	1201	3.50
1995	2.83	236	330	1.83	2.69	548	153.1	185	6.84	1447	3.94
2000	3.21	266	375	2.07	3.05	659	165.8	203	10.57	1752	4.42

N.A. - Not available.

Source: Historical data, except for USSR and China (P.R.), calculated from International Monetary Fund computerized data bank, as updated through 1977. USSR from U.S. Congress, Joint Economic Committee, Soviet Economy in a New Perspective: A Compendium of Papers (Joint Committee Print, October 14, 1976), pp. 269-300; later years from CIA unpublished data. China from U.S. Congress, Joint Economic Committee, Chinese Economy Post-Mao: A Compendium of Papers (Joint Committee Print, November 9, 1978), pp. 204-238.

[a] Five-year moving-average trend values, centered on years shown.

[b] Partly estimated.

[c] Estimates given in 1978 World Bank Atlas.

[d] Trend values.

or outpace the growth of GNP in newly industrializing countries and to
lag progressively behind the growth of GNP in mature industrial societies.
Moreover, the relationship is by now fairly independent of the geographical
distribution of resources for steelmaking, owing to the decreasing relative
importance of transportation in total steel costs, the expanding role of
"mini-mills" and direct reduction, and the importance attached to steel
production as a core activity in development programs.

Given the method of deriving future steel production, any of the
commodities whose consumption is later related to steel production could
in theory have been related instead directly to GNP/GDP, without any
difference in result. To have done so, however, would have foreclosed
an important opportunity for separate judgment as to the course of steel
production, a subject that has been widely thought about and discussed.

Table 2-3 presents historical data on the ratios between moving
averages of steel production and of GNP/GDP in the countries of interest
here, and table 2-4 gives the corresponding projections. The historical
data confirm the general decline of steel/GNP ratios in the mature industrial countries. Italy may be counted either as an exception or as a
country still industrializing; and in some cases--Japan and the USSR--
the decline in ratio has only recently set in. Both Brazil and India
seem to have settled down to rates of gain in steel production which pace
those in gross economic output, but probably for different reasons and
with implications--especially for India--which are less than clear. In
Brazil's case, the rapidity of population and economic growth suggests
that steel production cannot easily grow any faster; in India's case,
there was a deliberate rapid expansion of steel capacity under earlier
five-year plans, which, if efficiently utilized, will take some time
to absorb. A need for additional capacity could develop before the end
of the century, however, and in that case, the choice of a constant
steel production/GNP ratio for India may be an understatement for the
final part of the projection period. Further notes on the larger steel
producing countries follow:

United States: Both because of the generally decreasing materials
intensity of the U.S. economy and further modest growth in net

steel imports, a continuing decline in steel output/per unit of GNP is to be expected. The ratios chosen for projection are a rough geometric extension of the historical rate of decline (decreasing arithmetic changes) and imply a still slowly growing absolute volume of U.S. steel output.

USSR: The ratios used are an arithmetic extension of the modestly declining historical trend, but result in a level of steel output in the Soviet Union that is more than twice as high as that in the United States by the end of the century. It is likely that the USSR will be a net steel exporter in coming decades--especially if account is taken of the steel contained in exported machinery and other finished products.

Japan: The declining ratios of steel to GNP continue the apparent geometric trend that set in after Japan's intensity peak in 1972. They are nevertheless high enough to imply Japan's early displacement of the United States as the world's second largest steel producer.

Federal Republic of Germany: Germany's declining steel production intensity is assumed to continue an existing geometric trend (from about 1967) which is almost as steep as that of the United States. The ratio trend implies still increasing aggregate steel output, but at a declining rate of gain as output approaches a probable peak soon after the year 2000.

Italy: A large expansion in its steel industry after World War II brought Italy to a peak in steel production intensity around 1968; a further expansion in the 1970s brought it to a second high in 1974 and 1975. It is assumed that there is henceforth likely to be a decreasing intensity of Italian steel output with relation to GNP, relatively rapid at first and much slower in later years. Without the slowdown part of the assumption, the implied size of Italy's steel industry would be inconsistent with the presumed continuing importance of machinery, automobile, and ship production in the economy.

France: A continuation of the geometric declining trend in steel production intensity is assumed. Implied steel production reaches a peak in the 1990s and then eases off slightly.

United Kingdom: Steel production intensity in the U.K. is assumed to fall off rapidly at first, consistent with apparent recent trends, but to stop falling by 1995 and then even to recover slightly. The resultant steel output would reach a low in the late 1980s and then recover sharply, but without quite regaining 1960s' levels within the present century. Though the U.K. steel industry is beset with competitive problems, the basic importance of steel and steel-containing products in both export trade and domestic consumption (including the new requirements for petroleum production and transportation) are presumed to put a floor under the industry's decline.

Belgium-Luxembourg: Luxembourg currently adds more than a third to Belgium's level of steel output, but the two countries are closely linked, and the American Iron and Steel Institute (AISI) source used for historical statistics did not separate their production. Jointly, they depend heavily on export markets; thus, given the increasing decentralization of the world's steel industry, the Belgium-Luxembourg output must decrease considerably in relation to their own GNPs.[7] The decline in ratio is assumed to be steep at first, consistent with the trend that seems to have been established since a peak at 1970, but to become increasingly milder as time goes on. The implied result is a fairly stable level of actual steel production through the 1980s, followed by the resumption of a growth trend.

China, it may be noted, is not included in the tables, even though it is already a larger steel producer than Italy and will probably take over Germany's fourth-place position by 2000. The reason for the omission

---

[7] Actually Belgium's GNP alone is used for the calculations, but the addition of Luxembourg would increase the GNP total only by about 3 percent.

Table 2-3. Ratios of Steel Production to GNP/GDP, for Leading Steel Producers, 1960-77[a]

(metric tons)

Denominator	U.S. $ million	USSR Index[c]	Japan Y billion	Germany (F.R.) DM million	Italy L billion	France Fr million	U.K. L million	Belgium-Lux.[b] Fr million	Brazil Cr $ million	India Rs million
1962	95.0	1,142	611	52.2	140	23.4	307	8.84	N.A.	10.5
1963	96.2	1,162	627	53.0	145	22.7	305	8.77	"	11.4
1964	97.1	1,178	637	51.2	151	21.9	302	8.66	"	12.2
1965	97.3	1,189	662	50.8	159	21.3	301	8.70	8.37	12.4
1966	96.0	1,182	690	51.2	168	20.9	300	8.97	8.39	12.2
1967	94.1	1,179	721	51.0	174	20.3	293	9.20	8.26	11.9
1968	91.4	1,181	754	48.8	174	20.0	287	9.23	8.63	11.3
1969	87.4	1,174	760	47.7	174	19.5	279	9.28	8.75	10.6
1970	85.6	1,173	751	46.8	174	19.1	275	9.42	8.84	10.5
1971	85.3	1,169	748	46.4	175	18.8	267	9.39	8.63	10.3
1972	83.8	1,162	772	46.4	181	18.6	251	9.31	8.39	10.2
1973	80.1	1,165	749	44.5	186	17.6	231	8.80	8.29	10.4
1974	78.9	1,165	738	43.9	191	17.0	225	8.36	8.30	11.1
1975	76.0	1,154	714	42.0	191	16.2	212	7.60	8.55	N.A.
1975, per $(U.S.) mil-lion[d]	76.0	216	212	103	125	69.4	95.5	279	64.2	89.1[e]

N.A. - Not available.

[a] Ratios, in metric tons per denominator shown at head of column, are based on five-year moving-average trends, centered on year shown. Currencies are all in constant (1975) prices.

[b] Combined steel production of Belgium and Luxembourg is related to Belgian GNP only; separate production data not available in the source used, and GNP data for Luxembourg not tabulated. Inclusion of Luxembourg GNP in the denominator would have reduced the ratio by about 3 percent.

[c] GNP index, 1970=100; see table 2-2.

[d] Using FRB buying-rate exchange conversions, or World Bank U.S. dollar GNP estimates for countries (Brazil and USSR) for which the exchange rate is not quoted.

[e] 1974.

149

Table 2-4. Projected Ratios of Steel Production to GNP/GDP, 1980-2000, and
Derived Raw Steel Output, for the World and Leading Steel Producers,
with 1965-75 Comparisons

(million metric tons)

	Historical[a]			Projected[b]				
	1965	1970	1975	1980	1985	1990	1995	2000
Ratios to GNP/GDP[c]								
United States	97.3	85.6	76.0	67	59	52	47	42
USSR	1,189	1,173	1,154	1,136	1,118	1,100	1,082	1,064
Japan	662	751	714	635	565	505	450	400
Germany (F.R.)	50.8	46.8	42.0	37.5	34.0	30.5	27.5	24.5
Italy	159	174	191	180	160	152	150	148
France	21.3	19.1	16.2	14.7	13.0	12.0	10.2	9.0
United Kingdom	301	275	212	175	157	144	140	145
Belgium-Luxembourg	8.70	9.42	7.60	6.5	5.9	5.5	5.2	4.9
Brazil	8.37	8.84	8.55	8.5	8.5	8.5	8.5	8.5
India	12.4	10.5	[d]11.2	11.1	11.1	11.1	11.1	11.1
Steel prod. (million M.T.)								
United States	114	119	121	125	127	129	133	135
USSR	91	116	140	168	197	226	255	284
Japan	45	86	110	131	140	146	148	150
Germany (F.R.)	37	43	45	46	48	49	50	51
Italy	12	18	23	24	24	25	28	30
France	19	23	24	26	27	28	28	27
United Kingdom	25	26	22	21	20	20	22	24
Belgium-Luxembourg	13	18	18	18	18	19	20	22
Brazil	3	6	9	14	23	37	58	90
India	6	6	8	9	11	13	16	20
Total	365	461	520	582	635	692	758	833
Percent of world	81.5	79.3	76.4	72.8	68.7	64.1	59.2	54.0
World total	448	581	681	799	924	1080	1280	1543

[a]Five-year averages, centered on year shown.

[b]Trend values.

[c]For denominators, see table 2-3.

[d]Partly estimated.

150

is that we have no direct need for a projection of Chinese steel production since we have no historical base from which to project Chinese ferroalloy consumption. The probable Chinese expansion, however, is part of
what lies behind the declining proportion of world production assumed to
be accounted for by the ten steel-producing countries listed. Among these
ten countries, it may be seen from the last line of table 2-3, the Belgium-
Luxembourg combination currently has the highest relationship of steel
output to GNP, followed by the USSR and Japan. Brazil, France, and the
United States are at the opposite extreme. Basically, the countries with
the higher intensities are net steel exporters, though in the USSR case
the export margin appears to be in the form of steel-containing products
rather than steel as such. The lower intensity countries are more nearly
in steel-trade balance.

Cobalt

Of all the metals specifically covered in this study, cobalt has the
least relevant relationship to such a macroeconomic indicator as GNP.
Though the highest-GNP countries are also among the largest cobalt consumers, neither their past nor their prospective cobalt consumption may
be expected to have any smoothly changing relationship to gross economic
output. Rather, it is the growth of the particular specialized applications in which cobalt is used that is determining; and, for the future,
another important determinant will be the outcome of the flurry of inquiry
into potential substitution that has been induced by cobalt's recent
excursions into shockingly higher price ranges. Predictions are not
helped either by the fact that in those applications where substitution
is least seriously contemplated--cutting tools and jet engines--demand
for such items is itself one of the less predictable kinds of demand for
metal in an advanced economy.[8]

The basic reference used here for cobalt projection is the historical
record of past consumption. The extrapolation for each country builds

---

[8]"Success in Hunt for Cobalt Substitutes Could Turn Current Crisis
Into Surplus," American Metal Market, May 4, 1979.

upon either the whole of this past record or the most recent part of it, and in each case is heavily influenced by judgment. Of necessity, this judgment is affected by the demand implications of present high price levels. If the present price itself connotes a "problem," then some of the problem in cobalt supply has been begged. Mostly, however, the trade reports make out present pricing to be only a limited annoyance, less important per se than as a stimulant to concern about the future.

Table 2-5 presents this study's projections, both for leading cobalt-metal consumers and for the world as a whole. Some of the specific considerations, country by country, are as follows:

United States: The immediate prospect is for rapid increase in the consumption of cobalt, despite the higher price levels, owing to the substantial volume of orders on hand for jet aircraft. As this influence wears off, however, and initiatives toward substitution take hold in some of cobalt's uses, future growth in consumption is likely to take place at a progressively slower pace.

West Germany: A preponderance of cobalt in Germany appears to be used in construction, machine tools, and other capital equipment and thus to be related to the pace of investment in the economy.[9] Thus, a slowdown in use is assumed for the current quinquennium, consistent with the slowdown in the German economy, followed by slightly larger constant arithmetic increases (equivalent to declining percentage rates of increase) but still reflecting an assumed smaller role of investment in the future than in the earlier post-World War II decades.

France: Cobalt consumption in France is also heavily associated with industrial investment, but has been increasing more rapidly than in Germany, possibly because of the amounts also used in

---

[9]Reference for much of the information on end-use consumption is Bundesanstalt fur Geowissenschaften and Rohstoffe (BGR), Hanover, and Deutsches Institut fur Wirtschaftsforschung (DIW), Berlin, Kobalt (Oct. 1978), pp. 127 ff. (Authors hereinafter cited as BGR/DIW.)

France for superalloys for jet engines. The rate of increase has been decreasing, however, and it was this kind of trend that was assumed to continue.

United Kingdom: Cobalt consumption in Great Britain has fluctuated considerably over the years, mostly in response to changing needs for high-temperature alloys for aircraft engines. Permanent magnets have tended to be the second most important, and more stable, application, though miscellaneous alloying applications have at times been the greater user. Partly on the assumption of continued long-term (even if not year-to-year) preeminence (along with the United States) in jet engine manufacture, a trend rate of increase in cobalt consumption has been projected which is similar to that selected for Germany.

Japan: In most of the recent years, more than half of Japan's consumption of cobalt has been for permanent magnets, principally for use in its radio and electronics industry. Much of the rest has been directly or indirectly connected with its heavy volume of industrial investment. Since the latter, in particular, is slowing down, our projection of cobalt consumption for Japan is at roughly the average rates of the 1970s, rather than at the steeper rates of increase that characterized earlier years, when investment was very high and the electronics industry was in rapid expansion. Nonetheless, the projected increases are more rapid than those assumed for any other of the Western industrialized countries.

USSR: There is little to go on with respect to future consumption in the Soviet Union, but our assumption is that investment rates will continue high and that there is potential for future burgeoning of consumer electronics. The projected rate of increase is thus comparable to that assumed for Japan; it is also consistent with actual rates of increase since 1971 and less rapid than those of earlier years.

Table 2-5. Trends in the Consumption of Cobalt Metal, 1965-2000, for the World and Principal Consuming Countries[a]

(million pounds)

	Historical			Projected				
	1965	1970	1975	1980	1985	1990	1995	2000
Principal world traders:								
United States	15.0	17.6	20.0	24.5	27.0	29.5	32.0	33.5
West Germany (F.R.)	2.9	3.9	4.2	4.3	4.5	4.8	5.1	5.4
France	1.3	1.7	b2.3	2.8	3.2	3.5	3.8	4.1
United Kingdom	2.7	3.0	b3.5	3.8	4.0	4.2	4.5	4.8
Japan	3.7	6.7	7.6	8.2	8.9	9.6	10.4	11.3
Total	25.6	32.9	b37.6	43.6	47.6	51.6	55.8	59.1
USSR	4.1	6.6	b7.4	8.2	8.8	9.4	9.8	10.2
All principal consumers	29.7	39.6	b45.0	51.8	56.4	61.0	65.6	69.3
Percent of world consumption	79.2	75.1	76.1	76	75	74	73	72
World consumption	37.5	52.7	b59.1	68	75	82	90	96

Note: Historical detail may not add to totals, owing to rounding.

[a]Projections refer to points on a trend line. Data through 1975 are actual or estimated moving averages for the five-year period centered on the year shown.

[b]Estimated.

Because cobalt is so predominantly a "high technology" metal, one may expect future dispersion of its consumption outside of the leading industrial countries to be relatively limited. This is reflected in the percentages shown in the next-to-last line of table 2-5. On this basis, world consumption by the year 2000 is projected to increase by about 60 percent over the 1973-77 (shown in the table as "1975") average.

The proportion of the world's cobalt metal consumed by the leading international purchasers was about 68 percent around 1965 and subsequently declined to about 63 percent. If our projections are correct, there would be a slight future loss of relative position--to some 61 percent by the year 2000.

Chromium

The general procedure for making the mineral commodity projections in this study was, first, to relate consumption of the refined metal to the appropriate macro indicator, then, to derive the ore or semirefined input into the refined metal. Thus, we first project the consumption of ferrochromium, then consider its raw mineral, chromite.

Ferrochromium

In chapter 1 we laid the basis for relating the consumption of ferrochromium either to gross economic output or to the production of steel. Neither relationship has a clear superiority over the other in terms of either constancy of parameter or smoothness of its trend. There seems to be a slight mechanical advantage in using the ferrochromium/steel relationship, however, and this is the one we have chosen--at the same time checking for plausibility the relationship of ferrochromium to GNP/GDP which the ferrochromium/steel relationship implies. A primary reliance on the relationship to steel is also favored by the fact that nearly all ferrochromium goes into steelmaking and the fact that such a comparison may be made wholly in terms of weight (kilos of chromium per ton of steel output), thus permitting direct judgments regarding trends in future proportions of stainless and other corrosion-resistant steels.

From table 2-6 it may be inferred that we have judged the use of
such corrosion-resistant steel to be a continually higher proportion of
all steel use, yet, like most other industrial materials, to exhibit a
generally declining relationship to GNP. This is true at least for the
industrialized countries; for the world as a whole, the implicit ratios
of ferrochromium to steel also eventually decline, since carbon rather
than alloy steel is the principal stuff of rapid industrialization. Even
in the industrialized countries, however, the quantities of alloying
elements are small: an average of about 2 kilograms of chromium (content
of ferrochromium) per ton of steel, or about 0.2 percent. This is not
because the amount of alloying element in alloy steels is small (the
chromium content of stainless steel is typically in excess of 10 percent),
but because only a modest amount of stainless and other anticorrosion
steel is used in the typical industrial society.

In the United States, at present, stainless steel goes mostly into
construction, into automobiles (especially into catalytic converters),
and into machinery and equipment (especially for chemical and food processing). It has not been possible to assemble information on end use
applications in other countries. It is assumed, however, that the rapid
rise of ferrochromium consumption in Japan is due largely to its automotive output, though it is also sustained by other uses (e.g., ship
fittings and industrial equipment). Thus, the form of emission control
to be used in future automobiles is an important question for Japan, as
it also is in the United States, Germany, and France. Should automotive
emission control take a form which does not impose the same heavy stainless steel requirement as do the present catalytic converters, our projections may be overstated.

Though the rate of gain in Japan's chromium use that is shown in
table 2-6 is steep, and leads to an end-century intensity of use in
relation to steel which is well beyond that of most of the countries
listed, it actually represents a continuing deceleration of the trend
which has obtained in Japan since the early 1960s.[10] It also connotes,

---

[10]Note that the ferrochromium measurement in this study is in terms
of chromium content.

Table 2-6. Projections of Ferrochromium Consumption, 1980-2000, for the World and
Leading Ferrochromium Consumers, with 1965-75 Comparisons

	Historical[a]			Projected[b]				
	1965	1970	1975	1980	1985	1990	1995	2000
Ratios to steel production[c]								
Principal world traders:								
United States	1.76	1.64	2.13	2.35	2.55	2.75	2.90	3.05
Japan	1.85	2.43	2.86	3.35	3.70	4.05	4.30	4.50
Germany (F.R.)	2.27	2.51	[d]2.92	2.95	3.15	3.30	3.45	3.55
France	2.04	2.98	[d]3.31	3.55	3.8	4.0	4.2	4.3
United Kingdom	1.28	1.36	[d]1.31	1.36	1.40	1.46	1.54	1.64
Italy	1.68	2.03	[d]2.02	2.20	2.25	2.35	2.45	2.50
Total[e]	1.83	2.07	2.48	2.79	2.89	3.30	3.56	3.60
USSR	.83	.42	[d].73	.95	1.13	1.30	1.45	1.57
All principal consumers[e]	1.56	1.62	1.98	2.22	2.30	2.57	2.69	2.77
World total[e]	1.44	1.51	1.83	1.99	1.96	2.05	1.96	1.81
Aggregate consumption[f]								
Principal world traders:								
United States	202	196	258	293	325	355	386	410
Japan	82	208	[d]314	439	518	590	638	675
Germany (F.R.)	84	108	[d]131	137	151	162	174	180
France	39	68	[d]79	92	101	112	116	118
United Kingdom	32	35	[d]29	28	28	30	34	40
Italy	21	36	[d]46	53	54	60	68	75
Total	460	651	857	1042	1117	1309	1416	1500
USSR	76	46	[d]103	160	223	294	370	445
All principal consumers	536	697	960	1202	1340	1603	1786	1945
Percent of world cons.	83.2	79.7	77.1	75.6	74.0	72.6	71.2	69.8
World consumption[g]	644	875	[d]1245	1590	1810	2210	2510	2790
Implicit ratios to GNP/GDP[h]								
United States	.172	.141	.162	.158	.150	.143	.136	.128
Japan	1.22	1.82	2.04	2.12	2.09	2.05	1.93	1.09
Germany (F.R.)	.115	.117	[d].123	.111	.106	.101	.095	.087
France	.044	.057	[d].054	.053	.049	.047	.043	.039
United Kingdom	.384	.373	[d].276	.239	.216	.212	.222	.241
Italy	.267	.355	[d].386	.396	.358	.359	.368	.369
USSR	.99	.46	[d].85	1.08	1.27	1.43	1.57	1.67

[a]Five-year averages, centered on year shown, or calculated from five-year averages.

[b]Trend values.

[c]Kilos of chromium in ferrochromium, per metric ton of steel.

[d]Partly estimated.

[e]Projected ratios are those implied by the added or calculated totals for aggregate consumption (see second section of table).

[f]Thousand metric tons of chromium content. Calculations were made from unrounded figures for steel production and therefore will not always reconcile precisely.

[g]Projections are rounded from actually calculated values. For want of historical data the table conceptually omits any self-supplied consumption in Eastern Europe (other than the USSR), China (P.R.), and the United Kingdom.

[h]Metric tons of chromium content, per denominator shown in table 2-3.

as may be seen, decreasing intensity in relation to GNP. France, which currently has the highest intensity of chromium use in relation to steel, is projected to end up moderately behind Japan; in part, this may be explained by the slowness of introduction of argon-oxygen decarburization (AOD) processing in France, and thus of its attendant chromium conservation. Up to now, the French have also had an even more steeply rising use of chromium in steel than have the Japanese, and, as in the Japanese case, the ultimate high use is despite an assumed continuing deceleration in trend.

By far the most rapid increase in use of chromium in steel is that assumed for the Soviet Union. It is presumed that there are few, if any, catalytic converters currently manufactured in the USSR, and that there is probably little use of stainless steel in the architectural and household applications common in the Western countries, but that this should progressively change. In addition, it is assumed that a continually growing need for chemical food-processing as well as other heat and corrosion resistant equipment will impose further requirements for stainless steel and other chromium-bearing materials.

Chromium Ore (Chromite)

In any one country, two principal elements go into the relationship between the consumption of chromite and the consumption of ferrochromium: chromite consumption per unit of ferrochromium produced, and net foreign trade in ferrochromium. In chapter 1, we worked out not only these two individual parameters, but also the joint relationship, and the latter is the one we use here for projecting chromite consumption. However, our projected trends in this joint relationship take each of the two components into account, as detailed in the country summaries below.

As a general matter, projections of the parameter for chromite consumption/ferrochromium production can be guided by technical constraints on the relationship: with perfect conversion, which there has been a tendency to approach with the spread of the AOD process, it would take nearly 1.5 units of chromic oxide (the unit in which we have measured chromite) to provide 1 unit of chromium (the content unit in which we have measured

ferrochromium). Chromite is also devoted to other uses, however--
refractories and chemicals--and an increasing amount is finding its way
into steel via ferrosilicon alloys; along with unavoidable losses, all
these things serve to increase the minimum ratio. For the world as whole,
since foreign trade is netted out and stock changes, on a trend basis,
are of minimal importance, the plausibility of the implied input-output
ratio can be readily checked.

Another constraint which is important for chromite consumption is
the joint position of Zimbabwe and South Africa. It is easy to extra-
polate trends for these countries that would quickly imply a questionably
large share of the world's total ferrochromium production, leaving insufficient room for the minimum degrees of self-sufficiency in ferrochromium
production which the steelmaking countries of the world--advanced and
advancing--are likely to go to considerable lengths to try to preserve.

It would have been possible, of course, to have jumped ahead to the
analysis in chapter 5, "Potential Future Capacity," and to have used any
readily available intelligence on prospective ferrochromium capacity to
determine the likely future geographical distribution of the world's
chromite consumption. One difficulty with such an alternative approach
is that there is a high degree of convertibility of manufacturing facilities from one ferroalloy to another (or even to pig iron). The most
important consideration, however, is that it is the aim of this study--
especially for the United States--to look into the demand for chromite
(production of ferrochromium and other chromite uses) that is implied by
current policies and trends. The trends indicate a continuing decline
in ferrochromium self-sufficiency, but there has clearly been a national
disposition--reflected for example, in tariff changes--to try to slow
that decline. Both of these considerations enter into our "independently
projected" U.S. demand level. Later, in chapter 5, an independent ap-
praisal of the supply potential will suggest whether or not there may be
conditions on the chromite supply side that will interfere with achieve-
ment of the projected degree of ferrochromium self-sufficiency.

The chromite consumption projections are given in table 2-7. Specific
country considerations follow:

United States: It is assumed that the United States will continue to decline in ferrochromium self-sufficiency, but by the end
of this century not below 40 percent. Allowing for nonferrochrome
uses--especially ferrosilicon-chromium, chromium metal, and re-
fractories--a plausible asymptote for the declining parameter
(part A of the table) would be around 0.75, but a reasonable curvilinear extension of trend begins to approach that asymptote
only around century's end.

Japan: On the assumption that it would maintain a higher resistance
to lowered domestic processing, Japan's minimum self-sufficiency
is assumed to be around 60 percent. In Japan, also, there is assumed to be relatively small use of chromite other than in ferrochromium, so that the asymptote for the combined parameter would
be around 1.0. Japan's actual rate of decline in the parameter,
though rapid, has been less rapid than for the United States;
still, a reasonable extension of trend has the parameter reaching
its asymptote by century's end.

France and Germany: It is assumed that both of these countries
would strongly resist falling below 50-percent self-sufficiency
in ferrochrome and that their uses of chromite for other purposes
would be intermediate between that of Japan and that of the United
States; hence, an asymptote of around 0.9. The input parameter for
France has had a rather steady downward geometric trend, almost
as sharp as that in Japan, and we have assumed a continuation of
that geometric trend almost without change until near the end of
the century. In Germany, past behavior of the parameter has been
more ambivalent, but it now appears to be on a midly declining
trend which we have extended, at lessening rates of decline, to
the year 2000. At that point, the chromite/ferrochrome consumption ratio is not far from that of France.

Sweden: Owing to its traditional advantages in electric power, it is surprising that Sweden has had to yield any ground at all in ferrochromium self-sufficiency, but it has in fact done so, and it is assumed that it will continue to do so, though at lessening rates of decline, down to a limit of about 70 percent. Assuming, also, intermediate usage of chromite for other purposes, Sweden just about reaches its asymptote of approximately 1.3 by century's end.

USSR: The Soviet Union is currently a net exporter of ferrochromium and is expected to remain more than self-sufficient at least for the balance of the century. However, since 1970 it has been on a clear downward trend in its utilization of chromite per unit of chromium content of ferrochromium--partly because of a declining net export position and partly, it is presumed, because of improving conversion technology. This decline is assumed to continue through the rest of the century, although at a progressively slower rate.

South Africa and Zimbabwe: Both of these countries--especially Zimbabwe--are considered capable of a much more rapid expansion in their ferrochromium output (chromite consumption) than table 2-7 actually assumes. A sharper rise in the parameters (part B of the table) would have been inconsistent, however, with the self-sufficiency levels assumed for the leading industrial countries--even with allowance for the probably increasing role of southern Africa as supplier to other than the current "principal international traders." Zimbabwe and South Africa's future processing competitiveness, their record of dependability, their willingness to ship unprocessed chromite, the emergence of other low-cost chromite sources, and various political factors will in the end be more important than industrial consumers' processing preferences in determining the world's future distribution of chromite consumption.

Table 2-7.   Projections of Chromite (Chromium Ore) Consumption, 1980-2000, for the
World and Leading Chromite Consumers, with 1965-75 Comparisons

	Historical[a]			Projected[b]				
	1965	1970	1975[c]	1980	1985	1990	1995	2000
A. Ratios to Domestic Ferrochromium Consumption[d]								
United States	3.19	3.05	2.10	1.60	1.26	1.08	.97	.89
Japan	2.33	2.00	1.66	1.42	1.25	1.14	1.05	.98
France	2.63	2.31	2.10	1.82	1.62	1.43	1.25	1.13
Germany (F.R.)	1.45	1.90	1.75	1.53	1.37	1.25	1.16	1.07
Sweden	2.23	1.94	1.85	1.68	1.58	1.50	1.44	1.39
USSR	4.24	7.26	4.76	3.95	3.45	3.10	2.80	2.60
World[e]	3.30	3.18	2.96	2.70	2.65	2.50	2.44	2.39
B. Ratios to Ferrochromium Consumption by Principal International Traders[f]								
Rhodesia	.06	.14	.23	.25	.29	.33	.36	.39
South Africa	.30	.31	.51	.61	.72	.80	.87	.93
C. Aggregate Consumption[g]								
Principal International Traders								
United States	.64	.60	.54	.47	.41	.38	.37	.36
Japan	.19	.42	.52	.62	.65	.67	.67	.66
France	.10	.16	.17	.17	.16	.16	.15	.13
Germany (F.R.)	.12	.21	.23	.21	.21	.20	.20	.19
Sweden	.07	.09	.14	.14	.15	.15	.15	.15
Rhodesia	.03	.09	.20	.26	.32	.43	.51	.59
South Africa	.14	.20	.43	.64	.80	1.05	1.23	1.40
USSR	.32	.33	.49	.63	.77	.91	1.04	1.16
Total	1.62	2.08	2.73	3.14	3.47	3.95	4.32	4.64
Percent of world cons.	76.1	74.9	74.2	73.2	72.3	71.4	70.5	69.6
World consumption	2.13	2.78	3.68	4.29	4.80	5.53	6.13	6.67

[a]Five-year averages, centered on year shown, or calculated from five-year
averages.

[b]Trend values.

[c]Averages, except for the United States, are partly estimated.

[d]Units of chromic oxide (Cr_2O_3) content of ore, per unit of chromium content
of ferrochrome.

[e]Refer to ratios implied by the added totals for aggregate consumption
(part C of table).

[f]For listing, see table 2-6.

[g]Projections, in million metric tons of chromic oxide (Cr_2O_3) content, derived
by applying ratios in parts A and B to aggregate consumption of ferrochromium, as
shown in table 2-6.   Historical and projected data for Sweden, omitted from table 9D-1
because of its lesser importance for ferrochromium, are as follows:

1965	31	1985	94
1970	44	1990	100
1975	75	1995	105
1980	85	2000	110

It should be noted that, for lack of a statistical base, neither we nor others have attempted separate projections of the world's consumption of chromite for refractory rather than metallurgical input, though there were some implications for the relative amount of refractory use in the rationale we employed to guess at the technical limits of chromite to ferrochromium ratios. Yet differences in the supply, the utilization, and, particularly, the degree of substitutability of the two different kinds of chromite are substantial and, as pointed out at the outset of this study, of considerable significance for the extent of potential supply problems. Eventually, we shall have to estimate what the overall trends in chromite mean for U.S. supply of each of the two kinds of chromite individually.

Manganese

Analogously to chromium, we first consider the future consumption of ferromanganese, then the consumption of its antecedent, manganese ore. Also similarly to chromium, a significant amount of manganese is used in steel in forms other than ferromanganese, and a significant amount of manganese ore is consumed outside of steelmaking (approximately 10 percent of the world ore supply)--notably, in the manufacture of dry-cell batteries. A salient difference, however, is that there is little, if any, steel production which does not make use of substantial quantities of manganese, and there is thus a much stronger technical basis for close relationships between manganese consumption and steel output than there is between chromium and steel output. At the same time, though there has so far been scant need for it, there is somewhat wider scope for substitution in the case of manganese than in the case of chromium. Though manganese is currently considered essential to steelmaking, it is cost, not just technical characteristics, that keeps manganese in this key position.[11]

_____

[11]Something like half the manganese which goes into steelmaking is lost in the slag, having served a role as a "scavenger," or desulfurizing and deoxidizing agent.

Given the importance of cost in the consumption of manganese, future use can be substantially affected--in opposite directions--by two kinds of rather unpredictable developments. Political circumstances could result in price-raising constraints on supply, or ocean mining could develop along lines that would make manganese very cheap. The latter might also change the prevailing form of manganese use from ferromanganese to manganese metal. Since for the time being, however, any of these developments, as a matter of trend, must be judged less than probable, our projections rest on the implicit assumption that trends in manganese costs continue along the lines of the past. This assumption is reviewed when we later consider price prospects.

Ferromanganese

A number of factors affect the amount of ferromanganese used in steelmaking, but two are of particular importance: (1) the ratio of scrap to virgin iron in the steel input mix and (2) the introduction of manganese into steel by other routes. A growing factor is the extent of ironmaking by direct reduction.

Both the amount of scrap use and the use of direct reduction are important because of one of the key uses of manganese in steelmaking--desulfurization. It is through the coke used in blast furnaces that sulfur is introduced into the pig iron that in turn goes into steel furnaces, so to the extent that scrap or directly reduced iron is substituted, the amount of manganese required is reduced. The reduction may be less than proportional, because pig iron itself usually contains some manganese and is one of the sources of manganese in the steel mix. On the other hand, scrap also contains manganese and thereby makes a second kind of contribution to reducing the need for new manganese.

The most important alternative to ferromanganese (or at least to some part of it) these days is silicomanganese, which is considered a separate alloy. Manganese may also be introduced as ore (in limited degree), as spiegeleisen, as ferromanganese silicon, as pure manganese metal (currently expensive, but useful in some circumstances), and, as noted, in pig iron, which is sometimes especially enriched for the purpose. Except for the few instances where data problems made complete

separation impossible, none of the other iron-manganese alloys is included
in our consumption data for ferromanganese, which differs from the other
alloys in its materially higher manganese content (around 78 percent).

Table 2-8 gives our projections of ferromanganese-to-steel ratios
for the leading consumers of ferromanganese, as well as each country's
derived aggregate consumption. For the United States, the ratio is assumed
to remain constant, at 8.4 kilos of contained manganese per metric ton of
steel, on the assumption that neither the scrap input ratio nor the relative use of other forms of manganese input into steel will on balance
change very much. The initial decline in the USSR ratio is an extension
of trend, but a floor is assumed to be reached fairly quickly. Only Japan
has ratios as low as those of the USSR, and this is largely attributable
to its significant substitution of silicomanganese.

One of the more significant projections in table 2-8 is that for
Brazil, which up to now has not been important enough in ferromanganese
consumption to qualify as a "leading consumer." However, if we are correct, it will rank behind only the United States and the USSR in volume
of consumption by the end of the century. The principal reason is that
steel production in that country is expected to expand rapidly (see
table 2-4), but the projected continuation (though at a decelerating rate)
of its trend in ferromanganese use per ton of steel is also a factor.
Because of its very rapid growth rate, steelmaking in Brazil will be
especially highly dependent on virgin metal; this seems a plausible explanation for the current high ferromanganese ratios, along with the difficulty, given rapid growth rates, of achieving maximum technical efficiency.

Ferromanganese consumption is assumed to remain more heavily concentrated in the leading consuming countries than is steel consumption--
partly because of the lessened "scavenger" requirements that go along
with direct reduction and electric furnace "mini-mills," and partly because
of lesser requirements for the amount of manganese alloy needed in the
finished steel. Thus, in total, world consumption of ferromanganese is
expected to fall short of doubling over the 1975-2000 period, even as
world steel output more than doubles.

	Historical[a]			Projected[b]				
	1965	1970	1975	1980	1985	1990	1995	2000
Ratios to steel production[c]								
Principal world traders:								
United States	8.94	7.98	8.36	8.4	8.4	8.4	8.4	8.4
Japan	4.89	5.23	e5.00	4.85	4.8	4.8	4.8	4.8
Belgium[d]	8.53	7.95	e7.98	7.88	7.82	7.76	7.70	7.67
France	8.10	7.25	e6.81	6.8	6.5	6.2	6.0	5.8
Germany (F.R.)	8.08	7.94	e8.02	7.85	7.85	7.85	7.85	7.85
Italy	7.11	7.15	e8.66	8.9	9.15	9.4	9.5	9.5
United Kingdom	8.10	8.66	8.78	9.2	9.5	9.9	10.3	10.6
Total[f]	7.92	7.24	7.25	7.1	7.1	7.1	7.1	7.1
USSR	9.02	6.78	e5.57	5.3	5.1	5.0	5.0	5.0
India	14.63	13.59	e16.00	15.0	15.0	15.0	15.0	15.0
Brazil	7.03	8.22	e9.54	10.2	10.6	10.9	11.1	11.3
All principal consumers[f]	8.32	7.22	6.98	6.8	6.7	6.7	6.9	7.0
World total[f]	7.87	6.81	6.49	6.2	5.9	5.7	5.5	5.3
Aggregate consumption[g]								
Principal world traders:								
United States	1.02	.95	1.01	1.05	1.07	1.08	1.12	1.13
Japan	.22	.45	.55	.64	.67	.70	.71	.72
Belgium[d]	.11	.14	e.15	.14	.14	.15	.16	.17
France	.16	.17	e.16	.17	.17	.18	.17	.16
Germany (F.R.)	.30	.34	e.36	.36	.38	.39	.40	.40
Italy	.09	.13	e.20	.21	.22	.24	.26	.29
United Kingdom	.20	.23	e.21	.19	.19	.20	.22	.25
Total[h]	2.10	2.41	2.63	2.76	2.85	2.93	3.03	3.12
USSR	.82	.79	e.78	.89	1.01	1.13	1.28	1.42
India	.09	.09	e.13	.14	.17	.20	.24	.29
Brazil	.02	.05	e.08	.14	.24	.40	.64	1.02
All principal consumers[h]	3.04	3.33	e3.63	3.94	4.26	4.66	5.20	5.84
Percent of world cons.	86.2	84.1	82.0	80.0	78.0	76.0	74.0	72.0
World consumption[h]	3.52	3.96	e4.42	4.92	5.47	6.14	7.02	8.12

[a] Five-year averages, centered on years shown, or calculated from five-year averages.

[b] Trend values.

[c] Kilos of ferromanganese per metric ton of steel. Steel production data may be found in table 2-4.

[d] Includes Luxembourg.

[e] Partly estimated.

[f] Projected ratios are those implied by the added or calculated totals for aggregate consumption (see second section of table).

[g] Million metric tons, gross weight.

[h] Totals have been calculated from unrounded values and will therefore not always add or multiply precisely.

Manganese Ore

In table 2-9 we project the consumption of manganese ore, both world-wide and by leading consuming country. The projections are based on trends in the ratio of manganese ore (manganese content) to the consumption of ferromanganese. Thus one of the same factors that tends to lower the ratio of ferromanganese to steel--namely, the amount of manganese that enters steel by other routes--works to raise the ratio of manganese ore to ferro-manganese. On the other hand, other factors (such as the substitution of scrap for virgin metal) that depress the need for ferromanganese have no necessary effect on the ore/ferromanganese relationship.

A second relevant element is the amount of manganese used for purposes other than steelmaking. The most important of these in most countries is the manufacture of dry cell batteries, but other chemical uses and other metallurgical applications are also significant.

Perhaps the single most important element affecting the relationship is each country's foreign trade position in ferromanganese. If the country is a net importer, its consumption of ore in relation to consumption of ferromanganese will be correspondingly low. If a net exporter, it will be high. In the case of France, Norway, and South Africa, whose production of ferromanganese is primarily for export, it has seemed best to relate ore consumption to ferromanganese consumption of the leading international traders, rather than domestic ferromanganese consumption alone.

Specific considerations for the more important manganese ore consumers shown in table 2-9 are as follows:

United States: The principal reason for the declining ore consumption ratios (part A of the table) is the assumption of continuing declines in ferromanganese self-sufficiency (though not
nearly as much of a decline as in the case of ferrochromium).
In part, this is due to the likely insistence of one of the
current principal sources of manganese ore--Brazil--on increasing its proportion of preexport processing. There has already
been a decline from nearly 90 percent U.S. self-sufficiency in
ferromanganese in the early 1960s to only about 40 percent in
1977; the impact of this on the ore/ferromanganese ratio has,

over most of the period, been augmented by declining relative use of silicomanganese. The fact that so much of a decline in self-sufficiency in ferromanganese has already taken place is the main reason for our assumption of attenuation in the rate of ore to ferromanganese decline.

Japan: Japan's currently high ratios are explained in part by the fact that it has been an increasing net exporter of ferromanganese, as well as its utilization of increasing proportions of its manganese in the form of silicomanganese. Both trends are likely to be reversed, but the Japanese have made it clear that they will go to considerable lengths to preserve domestic ferromanganese production, thus putting a cushion under any future decline in ore/ferromanganese ratio. Another presumed reason for increasing ratios in the past--a burgeoning of dry-cell battery production--is assumed to be a spent trend, in part because of relative market saturation and in part because of increasing use of materials other than manganese dioxide for dry-cell batteries.

Brazil: The projected ballooning of manganese ore consumption in Brazil is in spite of a declining ore/ferromanganese ratio and reflects essentially the expected rapid growth in Brazil's iron and steel industry. The declining ratio follows, though much more slowly than in the past, a trend which is already in progress and is presumably explainable by a combination of increased efficiency in conversion and the faster growth of ferromanganese consumption than of miscellaneous manganese uses. Most important, however, even with increased export of ferromanganese in place of ore, the rapid growth of domestic consumption of ferromanganese is likely to pull down the production/consumption ratio and the ore/consumption ratio along with it.

South Africa: The projected increases both in ratio (to ferromanganese consumption of world traders) and in gross consumption of ore in this area are a direct result of the assumption that

South Africa will be able to insist on further substitution of ferromanganese for ore exports. The trend toward such substitution is already clearly in progress, but looks as if it will be slowed from time to time by political and capacity problems and, increasingly, by exhaustion of the substitution potential. Assuming world-average input-output ratios, the figures imply that by century's end, South Africa, Norway, and France, among them, will be supplying the world amounts equivalent to around 40 percent of the entire ferromanganese supply of the principal OECD countries.

USSR: Historical ratios for the Soviet Union reflect the fact that it has been an increasing net exporter of ferromangnese, but the expectation is that this trend is due for reversal, owing to progressive exhaustion of higher grade ores. Still, some amount of net export position is likely to persist through the balance of the century, and, given also the probably less efficient recovery of manganese as there is resort to lower grade ores, the consumption ratio is assumed not to decline much below 1970s levels. Coupled with the assumed expanding dominance of the Soviet Union as a world steel producer, its projected manganese (in ore) consumption, now nearly three times that of the United States, would thus be nearly five times that of the United States in the year 2000 , and a third more than that of its nearest competitor, Brazil.

Because of the increase in processing of ores in South Africa and Brazil, along with USSR dominance in steel, only a mild dispersion of manganese ore consumption outside of the countries specifically listed in part C of table 2-9 is expected. On a worldwide basis, our projections imply slightly increased ratios of manganese (in ore) to ferromanganese consumption, but since the latter is at the same time projected as slowly declining in its relationship to steel production, the net result is a rate of growth in world manganese ore consumption that is close to but not quite as rapid as that for steel itself.

Table 2-9. Projections of Manganese Ore Consumption, 1980-2000, for the World and Leading Manganese Ore Consumers, with 1965-75 Comparisons

	Historical[a]			Projected[b]				
	1965	1970	1975	1980	1985	1990	1995	2000

A. Ratios to Domestic Ferromanganese Consumption[c]

	1965	1970	1975	1980	1985	1990	1995	2000
United States	.98	1.06	.87	.83	.80	.78	.77	.76
Japan	1.99	2.18	2.03	1.84	1.78	1.75	1.75	1.74
Germany (F.R.)	1.01	.83	.77	.78	.77	.76	.75	.74
Australia	1.53	2.66	5.00	5.00	5.00	5.00	5.00	5.00
Brazil	10.00	8.47	[d]4.40	3.80	3.60	3.38	3.16	3.00
USSR	2.62	2.61	[d]3.11	3.24	3.24	3.18	3.07	2.93
India	2.20	4.31	[d]3.16	3.14	3.07	2.97	2.86	2.75
World[e]	1.72	1.88	2.04	2.09	2.14	2.13	2.14	2.10

B. Ratios to Ferromanganese Consumption of Principal International Traders[f]

	1965	1970	1975	1980	1985	1990	1995	2000
France	.162	.192	[d].207	.203	.198	.193	.187	.178
Norway	.091	.124	[d].169	.187	.203	.215	.222	.225
South Africa	.101	.104	[d].261	.330	.360	.380	.400	.415

C. Aggregate Consumption[g]

Principal Int'l Traders	1965	1970	1975	1980	1985	1990	1995	2000
United States	1.00	1.01	.90	.87	.86	.84	.86	.86
Japan	.43	.98	1.10	1.17	1.20	1.22	1.25	1.25
Germany (F.R.)	.30	.28	[d].28	.28	.29	.29	.30	.30
France	.31	.46	[d].55	.56	.56	.57	.57	.55
Norway	.19	.30	[d].45	.52	.57	.63	.67	.70
Australia[g]	.08	.14	[d].33	.34	.39	.45	.52	.61
Brazil	.23	.38	[d].35	.55	.87	1.36	2.04	3.05
South Africa	.21	.25	.69	.91	1.02	1.11	1.21	1.29
Total	2.75	3.80	[d]4.66	5.20	5.76	6.47	7.42	8.61
Other Principal Consumers								
India	.20	.38	[d].42	.43	.51	.59	.69	.81
USSR	2.15	2.05	2.43	2.88	3.26	3.59	3.92	4.16
All principal consumers	5.10	6.23	[d]7.51	8.51	9.53	10.65	12.03	13.58
Percent of world cons.	84.3	83.7	83.4	82.5	82.0	81.5	80.0	79.4
World consumption	6.07	7.44	[d]9.00	10.30	11.62	13.07	15.04	17.10

[a]Five-year averages, centered on year shown, or calculated from five-year averages.

[b]Trend values.

[c]Units of manganese in ore, per unit of ferromanganese.

[d]Underlying data partly estimated.

[e]Refers to ratios implied by the added totals for aggregate consumption (part C of table).

[f]Principal international trader-consumers of ferromanganese are: United States, Japan, Belgium, France, Germany, Italy, and United Kingdom.

[g]Million metric tons of manganese in ore. Derived, for individual countries, by applying ratios in parts A and B to ferromanganese consumption shown in table 2-8. Historical data and rough projections for Australia, not shown in that table, are (in thousand metric tons):

1965	52	1985	78
1970	53	1990	90
1975	62	1995	104
1980	66	2000	122

Aluminum

In projecting aluminum, we increase the size of our task by having to
project two prior stages as well as refined aluminum, plus the consumption
of aluminum scrap. Except tangentially, we refrain from complicating our
task by assuming that any appreciable part of the world's aluminum will be
produced, between now and the year 2000, from sources or by methods that
will significantly affect the role of alumina as part of the chain of processing. Principal reasons for this assumption are (1) there will be
sufficient bauxite available to make processing changes unnecessary and
(2) in part owing to electricity-conserving improvements in pot-line
(smelting) technology, there will be little if any advantage to other
economically feasible modes of processing in terms of requirements for
primary energy. The second reason does depend to some extent on the further assumption that aluminum smelting will continue to gravitate, on the
whole, to where electricity is relatively cheaper and more available,
rather than being greatly constrained by considerations of national self-
sufficiency.

Refined Aluminum

In considering our projections, it is important to recall that our
definition of refined aluminum includes both primary and secondary as well
as the "remelt" aluminum that serves similar purposes (but excludes, at
least in principle, the remelted aluminum produced "in-house" by foundries
and fabricators from their own or purchased scrap).[12] Aluminum so defined
should closely track the rates of growth of the element aluminum, but will
generally differ in growth rate from the **consumption of primary aluminum**
because of the changing importance of obsolete scrap.

---

[12]Available statistics did not always permit exclusion in fact. For
example, although a recently initiated series for the United States makes
it possible to distinguish between consumption of purchased remelt aluminum
and in-house remelting, the longer term series actually used appears to
combine both types of secondary aluminum recovery.

Table 2-10 shows both our assumptions as to the changing intensity of use of refined aluminum and the resultant country-by-country trends in aggregate consumption. In general, the very rapid rates of growth in aluminum consumption that in the past were propelled in part by the cost advantages of substituting aluminum for copper or galvanized steel will in the future receive lesser support from such substitution, both because of saturation of the applications where the potential has been greatest and because of readjustment of the relative prices of copper, aluminum, and zinc to where the aluminum advantage is less clear-cut.

Specific country considerations behind the projected ratios in the first part of table 2-10 follow:[13]

United States: Though there is still remaining technical potential, the substitution of aluminum for copper, steel, and zinc has probably gone further in the United States than in any other country.[14] It is assumed, therefore, that the growth of U.S. aluminum consumption in relation to GNP has just about reached its peak and will begin to decline, though less slowly than in the case of other metals and industrial raw materials. There is apparent evidence of such slowdown in the record of the past several years, although one cannot be certain that the slowdown may not have been attributable to the general softness in the U.S. economy.

Germany: West Germany is expected to follow the United States in an eventual slowdown of the aluminum/GDP ratio, but only after a later peak, at rather higher than present utilization

---

[13] For background information on current consumption patterns, principal reliance was on OECD, The Non-Ferrous Metals Industry, 1977 (Paris, 1978) table 21.

[14] Continued high rates of growth for aluminum are still possible in flexible packaging of heat-processed foods and the aluminum can market. In 1977 aluminum claimed 67 percent of the beer can market (up from 60 percent in 1976), but only 28 percent of the soft drink can market (22 percent in 1976) allowing sufficient room for continued growth of aluminum consumption in this market. American Metal Market, Oct. 25, 1977.

Table 2-10. Projections of Refined Aluminum Consumption, 1980-2000, for the World and Leading Aluminum Consumers, with 1955-75 Comparisons

	Historical[a]					Projected[b]				
	1955	1960	1965	1970	1975	1980	1985	1990	1995	2000
Ratios to GNP/GDP[c]										
Principal world traders-consumers:										
United States	2.11	2.20	2.87	3.27	3.44	3.8	3.75	3.65	3.55	3.45
Germany (F.R.)	.51	.62	.72	.93	1.03	1.17	1.25	1.25	1.18	1.16
France	.273	.350	.356	.388	.408	.42	.43	.435	.44	.44
United Kingdom	5.29	5.67	6.06	5.88	5.67	5.5	5.35	5.2	5.1	5.0
Japan	2.5	4.7	6.6	10.1	11.5	12.8	13.4	13.6	13.6	13.3
USSR	7.9	10.1	12.4	13.4	13.3	13.3	13.2	13.1	13.0	12.9
Aggregate consumption[d]										
Principal world traders-consumers:										
United States	1.74	2.07	3.37	4.56	5.48	7.1	8.1	9.0	10.0	11.1
Germany (F.R.)	.22	.36	.53	.85	1.10	1.5	1.8	2.0	2.2	2.4
France	.14	.24	.32	.46	.60	.7	.9	1.0	1.2	1.3
United Kingdom	.33	.40	.51	.56	.60	.6	.7	.7	.8	.8
Japan	.07	.19	.44	1.16	1.76	2.6	3.3	3.9	4.5	5.0
USSR	.36	.62	.95	1.32	1.62	2.0	2.3	2.7	3.1	3.4
All principal consumers[e]	2.87	3.89	6.12	8.91	11.16	14.5	17.1	19.5	21.7	24.0
Percent of world consumption	83.7	78.7	76.8	73.3	69.5	65.5	61.8	58.5	55.2	52.0
World consumption	3.42	4.94	7.97	12.15	16.05	22.2	27.7	33.3	39.3	46.2

[a] Five-year averages, centered on year shown, or calculated from five-year averages.

[b] Trend values.

[c] Metric tons, per denominator shown in table 1-17 (q.v. for fuller historical detail).

[d] Million metric tons. Calculations were made from unrounded figures for GNP/GDP and therefore will not reconcile precisely.

[e] Totals were added from unrounded values and therefore will not always reconcile precisely.

levels. Among other areas of as yet apparently unrealized potential, relative use of aluminum in food and beverage packing in Germany is well behind that in the United States, and there is probably residual potential in construction (including electrical transmission). The growth trend in the aluminum/GDP ratio has been comparable to that of the United States over the past couple of decades, but without a comparable recent slowdown.

France: France also had a comparably rapid increase in aluminum per unit of GDP up to the early 1960s, but the subsequent increase has been at a milder rate. However, France has also had relatively small penetration in food and beverage containers and limited penetration in construction as well (though greater penetration than Germany's in electrical construction). Thus, it is assumed that the French intensity ratio will continue a moderate rate of increase up to an upper limit around the end of the century.

United Kingdom: The United Kingdom is already on a declining trend with regard to the ratio of aluminum consumption to GDP, having reached a peak in the late 1960s. The declining trend has been extended to the end of the century, but at an attenuating rate, since the U.K. appears still to have considerable unexploited potential for increased aluminum use in construction and in packaging. Construction usage has been, and probably will continue to be, held down in part by low population and general economic growth rates.

Japan: A still increasing trend in intensity of alunimum use in Japan is not projected to peak out until the 1990s. Continuing high construction activity, plus an as-yet only moderately exploited potential for use of aluminum in containers and packaging, should help to support such a trend.[15]

---

[15] In 1977 less than 10 percent of Japan's aluminum cans were being recycled in spite of an 86 percent annual growth rate since 1971 in aluminum can production. American Metal Market, July 12, 1977.

USSR: There is little to go on with respect to future aluminum consumption in the Soviet Union, but a mildly declining intensity trend has set in which has been geometrically extended to the end of the century. Soviet aluminum production is expected to be increasingly for export.

It will be noted that despite the assumptions of slowdown in the growth of aluminum intensity in relation to GNP, aggregate consumption is projected to keep growing at a fairly rapid rate (though more slowly than heretofore) in all the leading consuming countries. In the United States, in the near future, the aircraft industry is expected to be an important sustaining influence, along with automotive manufacture; in Japan, auto manufacture and construction; in the USSR, probably, construction and electric power transmission. Consumption of refined aluminum is projected to continue its rapid spread around the world, more or less in consistency with past geometric trends, but not rapidly enough in relation to the now leading consumers to avoid a slowdown in aggregate worldwide rates of growth.

Alumina

Technically, if there were no losses in processing, it would take just under 1.9 units of alumina to produce a unit of aluminum metal. However, some alumina is used other than in the production of aluminum metal, and this, in addition to losses, tends to raise the actual alumina/refined aluminum ratio. More important, on the other side of the balance, a substantial and increasing proportion of refined aluminum production comes from scrap, and this tends to lower the ratio. Thus, for the world as a whole, the overall alumina/aluminum ratio is less than 1.9 and is likely to remain so. For any individual country, however, whatever the consumption to production ratio, the consumption to consumption ratio with which we make our projections will be further, and significantly, influenced by the country's net import or export position in aluminum metal.

Table 2-11 gives our projections of alumina consumption for the leading aluminum producing countries and for the world. The fact that

Table 2-11. Projections of Alumina Consumption, 1980-2000, for the World and
Leading Alumina Consumers, with 1970-75 Comparisons

	Historical[a]		Projected[b]				
	1970	1975	1980	1985	1990	1995	2000
A. Ratios to Domestic Aluminum Consumption[c]							
United States	1.51	1.45	1.40	1.35	1.30	1.26	1.22
USSR	2.44	[d]2.60	2.68	2.76	2.84	2.92	3.00
Japan	1.32	1.27	1.25	1.23	1.20	1.17	1.14
France	1.68	1.23	1.13	1.05	0.99	0.94	0.90
Germany (F.R.)	.96	1.34	1.42	1·.48	1.53	1.57	1.60
World	1.73	1.74	1.79	1.79	1.79	1.78	1.76
B. Ratios to Aluminum Consumption of Principal Int'l Traders[e]							
Canada	.301	.239	.240	.227	.218	.209	.203
Norway	.158	.162	.170	.177	.184	.189	.193
C. Aggregate Consumption[f]							
Principal Int'l Traders-Consumers							
United States	6.9	7.9	9.9	10.9	11.8	12.6	13.5
USSR	3.2	[d]4.2	5.3	6.4	7.7	9.0	10.3
Japan	1.5	2.2	3.3	4.1	4.7	5.2	5.7
France	.8	.7	.8	.9	1.0	1.1	1.2
Germany (F.R.)	.8	1.5	2.1	2.6	3.1	3.4	3.8
Canada	1.9	1.9	2.4	2.6	2.8	2.9	3.1
Norway	1.0	1.3	1.7	2.0	2.3	2.6	3.0
Total	16.1	19.7	25.5	29.5	33.4	36.7	40.5
Percent of world cons.	77.0	70.6	64.0	59.5	56.0	52.5	50.0
World consumption	21.0	27.9	39.8	49.6	59.6	70.0	81.1

[a]Five-year averages, centered on year shown, or calculated from five-year
averages.

[b]Trend values.

[c]Units of Al_2O_3 per unit of refined aluminum.

[d]Underlying data partly estimated.

[e]Principal international trader-consumers are: United States,
Germany (F.R.), France, and the United Kingdom.

[f]Million metric tons of alumina (Al_2O_3).

the world ratio rises slightly before falling back to near current levels
is consistent with the expectation (borne out by the record) of more
frequent problems in the developing countries with maintaining power
supply and optimal pot-line operations. These lead to an increase in
world losses as smelting continues to be decentralized--an effect later
mitigated by lessening rates of growth and counterbalanced by faster
growth in aluminum metal than in other uses for alumina.

Comments on the individual country ratios follow:

United States: The projected decline continues the past geometric
trend. The United States is likely to import increasing proportions of its aluminum supply, because of increasing problems in
obtaining supplies of low-cost electric power. Some of the foreign aluminum supply operations will be under U.S. company control,
or at least will have U.S. company participation.

USSR: The Soviet Union continues to expand its aluminum capacity,
mostly in Siberia, taking advantage of large, still-to-be-exploited
hydroelectric power potential. The intention, which it is assumed
will be successfully implemented, is to continue expanding the USSR
net export position in aluminum. Thus a continuing increase in consumption of alumina is projected in relation to domestic aluminum
consumption. It is assumed that the aluminum will be exported
essentially in unfabricated form, so that a relative lack of scrap
returns will further sustain the rate of increase in the alumina
ratio.

Japan: Because of Japan's increasing reliance on imports for
refined aluminum, it is assumed that there will be continuing
declines in the ratio of alumina to aluminum consumption. Japan's
already high scrap ratio suggests that the decline in the alumina
ratio will not be accentuated to any great degree by increased
proportions of scrap use, but some intensification, stemming from
increased availability of obsolete scrap, seems likely.

France: France's alumina ratio has been declining rapidly, because of an increasing net import position in aluminum. It is
assumed that the decline will continue, but at a decelerating
rate. France's growing export surplus in alumina should predispose it to expand aluminum facilities to the greatest extent
possible.

Germany: Increasing degrees of self-sufficiency have served to
increase West Germany's alumina/aluminum consumption ratio, but
in part the increase in domestic aluminum production has been
made possible by excess capacity, which is now more or less oc-
cupied. Thus, future increases in self-sufficiency and in the
alumina ratio are projected to occur at a slower rate than heretofore. In part, the ratio should also be depressed by a reversal in the recent tendency for declining (although high) relative
use of scrap.

Canada: The ratio here is to the aluminum consumption of principal international traders. The projected decline, therefore,
which represents an attenuation of recent trend, is not because
of any lack of continued expansion of Canadian smelting activity,
but because of the faster expansion of other world aluminum suppliers.

Norway: Another world supplier is Norway, whose contribution to
the world total is projected to continue growing, but at declining
rates, the slowdown occurring because of the progressive saturation of Norway's hydroelectric potential.

The fairly rapid (though attenuating) decline in the proportion of
the world's alumina consumption accounted for by the now leading consumers
(which are the leading aluminum producers) is a reflection of the electric-
power problem and the substantial impetus for locating aluminum production
where there are the lowest hydroelectric and fossil-fuel energy costs,
wherever these may be found.

Bauxite

As with aluminum smelting, facilities for refining bauxite into
alumina continue to be dispersed around the world. While much of this
involves processing in the country of origin of bauxite that might previously have been directly exported, there are also a number of third-
party arrangements in addition to the refining of bauxite in conjunction
with newly established aluminum facilities. Venezuela, for example, was
planning to produce alumina feed for large new smelting facilities from
bauxite supplied from Jamaica (although it may shift to recently discovered
large deposits of its own); in the meanwhile it expected to use alumina
from Surinam and Jamaica. Plans were also being laid for an alumina plant
in Jamaica, jointly owned by the Mexican, Venezuelan, and Jamaican governments, to supply the input for expanded smelting in Mexico, in a plant
owned by the Mexican (majority interest) and Jamaican governments, along
with foreign private participants.[16] Aluminum companies in the United
States, Western Europe, and Japan are combining with local private and
governmental interests in various and shifting enterprises to provide
assurance of international supplies of bauxite for refineries or of
alumina for smelters. Many of these, particularly in Brazil, involve
a variety of ventures in various stages of planning, preliminary development, and execution, with intermittent changes of partners and accelerations or decelerations (though mostly the latter) of schedule.

Country-by-country projections of bauxite consumption, under the
circumstances, are rather hazardous, yet no more so than trying to project
bauxite consumption on a direct global basis. Table 2-12 represents a
balancing of the two approaches: it is based principally on a country-by-
country buildup, but at the same time takes into account such relationships
as that between the implicit supply share of alumina from Australia and
the relative self-sufficiency of principal importers, as well as the implicit global relationship between bauxite consumption and alumina production.

---

[16]At last available report, however, this project was in a state of
indefinite postponement.

If bauxite were the only source of alumina and alumina were its only use, and if both of these were accurately measured in dry, nonhydrated weight, and if there were no processing losses, the input-output relationships would be about 0.53. In actual fact (in any event, according to available data) the world ratio is running at about 0.61 and, under our projections, would fall to about 0.57 before rising again to about 0.60. These swings are not very meaningful, however, measured against an historical swing in trend values from 0.57 to 0.63 just between 1967 and 1972, and could easily be the result of changes in utilization efficiency, statistical error, and the changing weight of various bauxite refineries in the total mix. The immediately projected downward trend is consistent with the rapidly growing relative role of Australia, an apparently very efficient converter (see table 1-14), as well as with some small introduction of bauxite substitutes. In the longer run, we do not expect such substitution to be important (at least, not within the twentieth century), and we expect the continuing dispersion of refining to increase the average amount of world processing loss.

Following are further notes on individual countries:

United States: The historical decline in the bauxite to alumina consumption ratio is projected to continue, although at a decelerating rate. Further decline seems ensured by increasing costs of domestic refining and, more important, by the probable success of both Jamaica and Surinam in substituting alumina exports for bauxite exports. Australia has already accomplished the substitution, so far as the United States is concerned, yet is a growing source of feed for the U.S. smelting industry. Haiti is a continuing source of bauxite, but its production potential is likely to decline.

USSR: The Soviet Union is reported to be "disenchanted," on both technologic and economic grounds, with the use of such other aluminum minerals as alunite and nepheline and to be turning its attention to increasing its supplies of imported bauxite instead.[17] However, like other industrialized countries, it is

---

[17] U.S. Congress, Joint Economic Committee, Soviet Economy in a New Perspective (A Compendium of Papers, October 14, 1976) pp. 661ff.

being forced into increasing imports of alumina, and it is assumed
that this trend will prevail, especially in view of the current
and planned rapid expansion of its aluminum smelting capacity.
Japan: Japan, too, has been having to accept increasingly larger
quantities of alumina in relation to bauxite from its overseas
suppliers. (Japanese firms frequently have an interest in the
supplying operations.) The trend is projected to continue, though,
as for the United States, at a decelerating rate.

France: France's ratio is high because it is a net exporter of
alumina. This net export position, which is assumed to be based
wholly or partly on Pechiney's processing of imported bauxite for
ultimate smelting by another Pechiney plant in the Netherlands,
has been growing and is projected to continue to grow, at declining rates, before reversal around 1990.

Germany: Germany's ratio appears to have settled down at a level
which is assumed to persist over the whole of the projection period.

Canada: Canada, among leading aluminum producers, already has
the lowest degree of self-sufficiency in alumina, and its remaining bauxite imports come mostly from sources (among them, Guinea)
which have so far shown the least inclination to push into alumina
production. The Canadian ratio is therefore assumed to remain
unchanged at approximately the recent average level.

Australia: Although Australia is near its current alumina production capacity, a number of plans and projects are in motion
that should keep the Australian potential growing at a rapid rate.
This is what underlies the ratios projected for Australia in part
B of table 2-12, which relate to Australia's role in meeting the
total alumina requirements of principal importing countries. At
present, a lesser Australian expansion might well result in difficulty in achieving the projected growth in world aluminum output.
The ratio for the year 2000 implies that Australia would at that
time be supplying close to half the total alumina requirements of
the world's principal aluminum producers.

Jamaica: The declining ratios reflect, not a cessation of the

Table 2-12. Projections of Bauxite Consumption, 1980-2000, for the World and
Leading Bauxite Consumers, with 1970-75 Comparisons

	Historical[a]		Projected[b]				
	1970	1975	1980	1985	1990	1995	2000

A. Ratios to Domestic Alumina Consumption[c]

United States	.51	.45	.395	.37	.345	.33	.32
USSR	.50	[d].49	.465	.455	.445	.44	.435
Japan	.59	.52	.47	.43	.40	.375	.355
France	.84	1.10	1.15	1.18	1.20	1.18	1.15
Germany (F.R.)	.69	.64	.64	.64	.64	.64	.64
Canada	.29	.29	.30	.30	.30	.30	.30
World	.61	.61	.57	.57	.58	.59	.60

B. Ratios to Alumina Consumption of Principal International Traders[e]

Australia	.075	.145	.21	.24	.26	.275	.285
Jamaica	.056	.066	.058	.053	.05	.047	.045
Surinam	.028	.024	.021	.019	.018	.017	.016

C. Aggregate Consumption[f]

United States	3.5	3.6	3.9	4.0	4.1	4.2	4.3
USSR	1.6	[d]2.1	2.5	2.9	3.4	4.0	4.5
Japan	.9	1.2	1.6	1.8	1.9	1.9	2.0
France	.7	.8	.9	1.1	1.2	1.3	1.4
Germany (F.R.)	.6	.9	1.3	1.7	2.0	2.2	2.4
Canada	.6	.5	.7	.8	.8	.9	.9
Australia	1.2	2.9	5.4	7.1	8.9	10.1	11.5
Jamaica	.9	1.3	1.5	1.6	1.7	1.7	1.8
Surinam	.5	.5	.5	.6	.6	.6	.6
Total	10.5	13.8	18.3	21.6	24.6	26.9	29.4
Percent of world cons.	82.0	81.0	81.0	77.0	71.0	65.0	60.0
World consumption	12.8	17.0	22.6	28.1	34.7	41.4	49.0

[a]Five-year averages, centered on year shown, or calculated from five-year
averages.

[b]Trend values.

[c]Units of aluminum content of bauxite per unit of alumina.

[d]Underlying data partly estimated.

[e]Principal international trader-consumers of alumina are the United States,
USSR, Japan, Canada, France, West Germany, and Norway.

[f]Million metric tons of aluminum content.

movement toward domestic processing of bauxite into alumina before shipment (for example, Jamaica is to supply alumina to new plants in Mexico and Venezuela), but the relative shift in market share to Australia. The decline is projected to taper off as market shares move closer to their eventual values.

Surinam: The situation for this country is somewhat similar to that for Jamaica, except that Surinam has already exhausted much of its potential for shifting into alumina from bauxite. Thus the projected drop in ratio is somewhat steeper.

Given both the large number of currently important bauxite consumers and the developing role of Australia, it is projected that bauxite consumption (alumina production) outside the countries specifically accounted for will increase less rapidly than was assumed for production of aluminum outside the currently important countries. Unaccounted-for countries like Brazil, Guinea, and Yugoslavia are nevertheless sufficiently important that the concentration ratio for currently important consumers of bauxite is projected to drop more rapidly--at least after 1980, than it has in the past decade. During this recent period, it has been Australia's rapid expansion which has kept the concentration ratio high, and this effect is projected to persist for at least a few years.

Aluminum Scrap

Since scrap is the alternative to alumina in the production of aluminum metal, the scrap ratios projected in table 2-13 are more or less the inverse of the alumina consumption ratios shown in table 2-11. It is all the more appropriate that this be so, given that the data on total output of refined aluminum are not statistically pure and tend to include some amounts of remelt aluminum produced in-house by direct scrap consumers. Theoretically, however, scrap consumption should have a certain independence of alumina consumption because of the direct recovery by foundries and fabricators, which we have defined as being apart from aluminum refining or remelting.

Projections of the scrap ratios (part A of table 2-13) are necessarily crude. It will be recalled that both new and old scrap are included: the former tends to change with the changes in fabrication loss attendant on

Table 2-13. Projections of Aluminum Scrap Consumption, 1980-2000, for the World and for Leading Scrap Consumers, with 1955-75 Comparisons

	Historical[a]					Projected[b]				
	1955	1960	1965	1970	1975	1980	1985	1990	1995	2000

A. Ratios to Refined Aluminum Consumption[c]

	1955	1960	1965	1970	1975	1980	1985	1990	1995	2000
United States	.177	.156	.166	.170	.180	.190	.197	.203	.209	.215
Germany (F.R.)	.439	.388	.385	.343	.351	.340	.335	.330	.327	.325
France	.209	.186	.170	.199	.218	.235	.240	.245	.245	.245
United Kingdom	.312	.317	.356	.353	.302	.293	.284	.277	.273	.270
Italy	.266	.290	.332	.368	.351	.335	.328	.320	.315	.310
Japan	.199	.262	.290	.275	.292	.300	.308	.300	.300	.300
World	.186	.163	.166	.167	.164	.164	.162	.157	.151	.148

B. Aggregate Consumption[d]

Principal Consumers

	1955	1960	1965	1970	1975	1980	1985	1990	1995	2000
United States	.31	.32	.56	.77	.99	1.35	1.60	1.84	2.09	2.38
Germany (F.R.)	.10	.14	.20	.29	.39	.49	.59	.66	.71	.78
France	.03	.04	.05	.09	.13	.17	.21	.25	.29	.33
United Kingdom	.10	.13	.18	.20	.18	.19	.20	.20	.21	.22
Italy	.02	.04	.07	.15	.20	.22	.24	.26	.27	.28
Japan	.01	.05	.13	.32	.50	.79	1.02	1.18	1.34	1.50
Total	.57	.72	1.20	1.82	2.39	3.21	3.86	4.39	4.91	5.49
Percent of world cons.	91.1	90.1	90.8	89.7	90.8	88.0	86.0	84.0	82.5	81.0
World consumption	.63	.81	1.32	2.03	2.64	3.65	4.49	5.23	5.95	6.78

[a]Five-year averages, centered on year shown, or calculated from five-year averages.

[b]Trend values.

[c]For refined aluminum data, see table 9F-1. Estimates and projections for Italy, not shown in table 9F-1, but roughly projected (thousand metric tons): 1955, 75; 1960, 140; 1965, 210; 1970, 410; 1975, 570; 1980, 650; 1985, 725; 1990, 800; 1995, 850; 2000, 900.

[d]Million metric tons of recovered aluminum. Calculations were made from unrounded figures; therefore data shown here will not always reconcile precisely.

184

changing applications of aluminum; the latter varies according to the changing lifetimes of different applications, but is also responsive to prices and governmental regulation.

In general, it has been assumed that the scrap ratios for the leading consuming countries will tend to converge. Germany's has been among the highest and, except for the past few years, has been declining; a mild rate of decline is assumed to continue. The U.S. scrap ratio has been the lowest, but since 1960 has shown some tendency to rise, and a moderate continuation of the rise is projected. Slowing rates of consumption growth should help to support such a rise with increasing relative amounts of obsolete scrap availability; container returns and recovery of aluminum from municipal waste should further augment the flow. Japan's relative use of scrap rose rapidly in the 1950s and the early 1960s, and then, after some hesitancy, seems to have started upward again in the past few years; a further mild rise is projected, with a halt in the 1990s, when a relatively high level will have been reached compared to other countries. Both for these countries and for the more minor consumers of scrap, the precise projection levels have been kept roughly consistent with the con-current consumption of virgin aluminum as part of the total amount of refined aluminum production to be accounted for.

For want of a statistical base, scrap consumption in the USSR, China, and Eastern Europe is omitted from the world totals. In other countries not accounted for, the relative increases in scrap consumption are assumed to be mild, as reflected in the projections (part B), for "percent of world consumption." Except for the principal consuming countries, much secondary recovery of aluminum is rudimentary remelting and does not figure in any statistical accounting. Moreover, the rapid rate of growth of aluminum consumption in various parts of the world will limit the relative amount of obsolete scrap available. The widespread dependence on imports for aluminum metal will interfere with the reconcentration of fabricator scrap for larger scale secondary smelting. As a result of such factors, the implicit scrap ratio in that part of the world which is accounted for is expected, after a pause at the 16 percent level, to decline to under 15 percent by the end of the century.

Copper

In this study, copper, like aluminum, is divided into four parts:
refined metal, intermediate (blister copper), ore, and scrap. Unlike
aluminum, the refined metal definition does not encompass the equivalent
of remelt, since most copper scrap treated by simple remelting is recovered
as alloy that is not directly substitutable for refined copper.

The "red metal" is probably the most studied of the nonferrous metals
and the most frequently projected. This does not necessarily make it
easier to project with accuracy, and it is not difficult to find a variety
of viewpoints on its future. To some extent, the plausible range of
projections is constrained by copper's maturity: it is one of the oldest
metals in widespread use. But it remains vulnerable to relatively unpredictable kinds of substitution, and it finds particular use these days
in the investment sector--one of the more variable parts of national
economies.

Refined Copper

In general, intensity of use of refined copper is declining in the
industrialized countries. For most countries, the decline set in during
the late 1950s; in the United States it started earlier. Japan is still
up around its peak levels, and for the Soviet Union, the data permit
almost any interpretation. Without exception, however, for the principal
consuming countries it is assumed that future copper use per unit of gross
product will decline. Specific considerations for the individual larger
consumers (part A of table 2-14) follow:

United States: Among some erratic fluctuations (even after moving-
average smoothing), there is a clear downward trend. Our projections continue that trend, but at a decelerating rate. Electrical
applications (electrical machinery, electronics, electric power
generation and transmission, etc.) currently account for more than
half of copper consumption in the United States, and a good deal
of the possible substitution has already taken place (aluminum in
long-distance transmission lines being a notable example). Further

Table 2-14. Projections of Refined Copper Consumption, 1980-2000, for the World and Leading Copper Consumers, with 1955-75 Comparisons

	Historical[a]					Projected[b]				
	1955	1960	1965	1970	1975	1980	1985	1990	1995	2000
Ratios to GNP/GDP[c]										
Principal world traders:										
United States	1.68	1.44	1.55	1.35	1.18	1.09	1.05	1.01	.99	.97
Japan	4.53	6.54	6.94	7.15	6.62	6.4	6.0	5.4	4.95	4.55
Germany (F.R.)	.758	.844	.696	.710	.666	.61	.584	.562	.54	.522
United Kingdom	7.37	7.42	7.03	5.67	4.66	4.2	3.95	3.75	3.6	3.5
France	.329	.338	.309	.284	.256	.228	.208	.192	.178	.168
Italy	N.A.	N.A.	2.66	2.59	2.61	2.65	2.58	2.53	2.46	2.37
USSR	8.9	10.3	10.3	9.7	9.8	9.6	9.3	9.0	8.75	8.5
Aggregate consumption[d]										
Principal world traders:										
United States	1.38	1.35	1.82	1.88	1.89	2.0	2.3	2.5	2.8	3.1
Japan	.12	.27	.47	.81	1.02	1.3	1.5	1.6	1.6	1.7
Germany (F.R.)	.33	.49	.51	.65	.71	.8	.8	.9	1.0	1.1
United Kingdom	.46	.53	.59	.54	.49	.5	.5	.5	.5	.6
France	.17	.23	.28	.34	.38	.4	.4	.5	.5	.5
Italy	.11	.17	.21	.26	.31	.4	.4	.4	.5	.5
Total[e]	2.58	3.04	3.87	4.48	4.79	5.4	5.9	6.4	6.9	7.5
USSR	.40	.63	.79	.95	1.19	1.4	1.6	1.8	2.1	2.3
All principal consumers	2.98	3.67	4.66	5.43	5.98	6.8	7.6	8.2	9.0	9.7
Percent of world cons.	82.2	78.0	77.1	75.0	71.5	69.0	66.6	64.3	61.9	59.8
World consumption	3.63	4.70	6.05	7.24	8.37	9.8	11.4	12.8	14.5	16.3

N.A. - Not available.

[a]Five-year averages, centered on year shown, or calculated from five-year averages.

[b]Trend values.

[c]Metric tons, per denominator shown in table 1-25 (q.v. for fuller historical detail).

[d]Million metric tons. Calculations were made from unrounded figures for GNP/GDP and therefore will not always reconcile precisely.

[e]Totals were added from unrounded values and therefore will not always reconcile precisely.

likely declines in unit use of copper derive in part from the
general rise in value added per unit of material input; conservation of copper, in part through miniaturization; further substitution of aluminum (including copper-clad aluminum) in local
power distribution and house wiring; and replacement of copper
use in communications by radio (including satellite) connections,
fiber optics, and other devices. For both technological and institutional reasons, it may be assumed that most of these potential substitutions will be limited and will proceed relatively
slowly.

In nonelectrical aspects of construction, which constitute
the second largest area of U.S. copper use, copper continues to
face competition from aluminum, steel, and plastics. Within such
uses (piping, heating and hot water systems, flashing, etc.),
however, copper not only has technical advantages which help to
maintain its position, but is also frequently favored (e.g., in
piping) by building codes. A significant new application is in
solar heating systems, but the size of this potential tends to
be overestimated. Copper seems less likely than it did a few
years back to yield to much substitution by aluminum in automobile
radiators; if it does, it will be primarily in the interest of
weight reduction. In general, the pace of substitution is likely
to be retarded by what appears to be a reversal of aluminum's
earlier price advantage.

Japan: Up until the early 1960s, the rate of increase in intensity of copper use in Japan was quite steep; and our projection
is for almost as pronounced a future rate of decline. Japan's
refined copper has been going overwhelmingly into wire and cable,
and the bulk of this, in turn, into electrical machinery and ap-
paratus. Conservation of copper through miniaturization, increasing sophistication and thus value-added, and a declining role
for electric power expansion in an otherwise still rapidly growing
GNP should combine to produce the declining ratio.

Germany: Electrical machinery and construction have been by far
the largest application of copper in Germany as well. The projected decline in ratio, which extends the apparent trend, though
at a decelerating rate, is consistent with an assumed generally
decreasing role of investment in the economy and relative saturation by this time in both electric power and communications
infrastructure. There is also some continuing substitution of
aluminum.

USSR: In the absence of any details on copper consumption in the
Soviet Union, it was assumed that the bulk of it has been applied
in electrical construction and associated heavy electrical equipment. Although this kind of activity is assumed to remain very
important for some time to come, it should nevertheless decline
somewhat in relation to gross product. In addition, the extensive
plans for expansion of aluminum production in the USSR suggest a
continuing substitution of aluminum. The projected trend in ratio
assumes that, like other industrialized countries, the USSR has
passed its peak in copper intensity, but that the rate of decline
will be moderate.

Following the general proposition that the rate of growth in materials
consumption will for some time be higher in the developing world than in
the already industrialized nations, the proportion of world copper consumption accounted for by the now leading consumers is projected to continue
its historical decline. Of the various trend extrapolations that might
have been plausible, the one chosen represents a comparatively mild rate
of decrease. Still, consumption in countries other than those now leading
would increase from 2.4 million tons to 6.6 million in the year 2000.
Brazil, India, and China are likely to be important contributors to this
increase.

Blister Copper

On a worldwide basis, there ought to be a ratio of a little under
unity for the consumption of blister copper per unit of refined. Blister
lacks a percentage point or two of being pure copper, thus raising the

ratio. On the other hand, a fair amount of refinery output of copper is from recycled material (scrap) which does not go back through the smelter; this lowers the blister/refined ratio. There is also an increasing amount of direct "electrowinning" of refined copper from leach liquid run through copper ore or mine tailings; this further lowers the ratio. As may be seen in table 2-15, historically the implicit world ratio has tended to be influenced mostly by declining proportions of scrap (see table 2-17), but our projections imply that this trend will be overcome before too long by the counterbalancing factors.

Because the technical ratio is so close to unity, it follows that the blister/refined ratio for any particular country is a close reflection of the country's self-sufficiency. Thus, the declining ratio projected for the United States, which is an extension of recent rather than long-term trend, reflects the assumption that an increasing proportion of U.S. refined copper consumption will be met from refined copper imports. In addition, the United States has for some time recycled a particularly large amount of scrap directly back into refined copper and is in the forefront of the trend toward electrowinning.

Of the other countries whose production of refined copper is primarily for home consumption, the USSR and Japan are of particular importance. The USSR reached a peak as a net exporter in the early 1970s, but has since declined in this regard; the rate of decline is projected to continue, though with some deceleration. In part, this is because of the growing ability of Poland to supply Comecon requirements. Japan, since the early 1960s, has had wide swings in the blister/refined ratio, representing in part swings in refined copper self-sufficiency and in part swings in the scrap alternative. The declining ratio of the past few years is taken as the basis for projecting future declines, though at a decelerating rate, primarily on the assumption of increasing substitution of imported for domestic refined. The decline in self-sufficiency is assumed to be limited by the existence of substantial refining capacity and by Japan's ability to maintain a fairly reliable flow of ore from Canada, the Philippines, and/or Papua-New Guinea.

Table 2-15. Projections of Blister Copper Consumption, 1980-2000, for the World
and Leading Blister Copper Consumers, with 1965-75 Comparisons

	Historical[a]			Projected[b]				
	1965	1970	1975	1980	1985	1990	1995	2000
A. Ratios to Domestic Refined Copper Consumption								
United States	.84	.87	.83	.83	.81	.79	.77	.75
Japan	.84	.87	.97	.90	.85	.82	.79	.77
Germany (F.R.)	.51	.49	.41	.43	.43	.43	.43	.43
USSR	1.06	1.15	1.16	1.10	1.05	1.00	.97	.95
World	N.A.	.93	.97	.97	.98	.98	.97	.96
B. Ratios to Refined Copper Consumption of Principal Int'l Traders[c]								
Chile	.082	.100	.116	.126	.134	.140	.146	.150
Belgium	N.A.	.057	.060	.064	.067	.068	.069	.069
Zambia	.130	.129	.137	.140	.143	.145	.148	.150
Canada	.101	.105	.109	.113	.116	.119	.122	.125
C. Aggregate Consumption[d]								
Principal Int'l Traders								
United States	1.53	1.64	1.56	1.6	1.8	2.0	2.2	2.3
Japan	.39	.73	1.01	1.2	1.3	1.3	1.3	1.3
Germany (F.R.)	.26	.32	.29	.3	.4	.4	.4	.5
Chile	.32	.45	.56	.7	.8	.9	1.0	1.1
Belgium	N.A.	.25	[e].29	.3	.4	.4	.5	.5
Total	N.A.	3.39	3.71	4.2	4.7	5.0	5.4	5.7
Other Principal Consumers								
Zambia	.50	.58	.65	.7	.8	.9	1.0	1.1
Canada	.39	.47	.52	.6	.7	.8	.8	.9
USSR	.83	1.09	1.38	1.6	1.7	1.8	2.0	2.2
All principal consumers	N.A.	5.53	[e]6.26	7.1	7.9	8.5	9.2	9.9
Percent of world cons.	"	82.2	77.0	74.0	71.0	68.0	65.5	63.5
World consumption	"	6.72	[e]8.12	9.6	11.1	12.5	14.1	15.6

N.A. - Not available.

[a]Five-year averages, centered on years shown, or calculated from five-year
averages.

[b]Trend values.

[c]Principal international trader-consumers of refined copper are listed in
table 9G-1.

[d]Million metric tons. Calculations were made from unrounded figures; therefore, data shown here will not always reconcile precisely.

[e]Underlying data partly estimated.

The other largest blister copper consumers are essentially suppliers
of refined copper to the trading world. Those shown in table 2-15 currently account for a quantity of refined copper which is around 43 percent
of the total supply of principal importer consumers (the United States,
Japan, West Germany, the United Kingdom, France, and Italy) and, by the
year 2000, are projected to be supplying closer to half.[18] Chile is
projected as having the greatest rate of substitution of refined for
semirefined (blister) copper, continuing a strong existing trend in that
direction, although at a decelerating rate.

Copper Ore

As noted on earlier occasions, "ore" is used in this study as the
generic equivalent of mine production; the material actually shipped is
more usually concentrate, and, in the case of copper, can also take such
forms as leach liquid or precipitate. Since the measurement in any case
is in terms of contained copper (for some countries, e.g., the United
States, recoverable content), there ought to be--on a worldwide basis at
least--a rough parity between consumption of ore and the consumption of
blister. Table 2-16 shows that this is not quite the case, either historically or in projection. The shortfall from full parity may be attributed to the production of some blister copper from scrap--a proportion
which more than exceeds smelting losses in those countries where total
content is measured--and the diversion of some copper ore to uses other
than blister copper production. The progressive narrowing of the differential may be attributed in large part to the spread of electrowinning
technology, which sends leach liquid directly from mine to refinery.
This development in the United States, in fact, is considered of sufficient
future importance to warrant projecting the ore/blister ratio to rise
above unity. It has been important enough so far to account for part
of the historically increasing trend in the ratio, though more of the
past increase was due to declining imports of blister copper--now less

---

[18]Some part of this output is, of course, destined for countries
other than the six principal importers.

Table 2-16. Projections of Copper Ore Consumption[a], 1980-2000, for the World and Leading Copper Ore Consumers, with 1965-75 Comparisons

	Historical[b]			Projected[c]				
	1965	1970	1975	1980	1985	1990	1995	2000
A. Ratios to Domestic Blister Copper Consumption								
United States	.75	.85	.94	.99	1.01	1.03	1.04	1.05
Japan	.70	.72	.84	.83	.79	.76	.73	.70
Chile	1.86	1.42	1.38	1.35	1.32	1.30	1.28	1.27
Canada	.95	.92	.88	.91	.93	.95	.95	.95
Zambia	1.25	1.17	1.04	1.05	1.05	1.05	1.05	1.05
USSR	.88	.86	.79	.78	.75	.73	.71	.70
World	N.A.	.93	.92	.94	.95	.95	.96	.97
B. Ratios to Blister and Semirefined Copper Consumption in Belgium[d]								
Zaire	1.37	1.50	1.54	1.43	1.38	1.36	1.35	1.35
C. Aggregate Consumption								
Principal International Traders								
United States	1.15	1.39	1.46	1.6	1.9	2.0	2.3	2.5
Japan	.27	.52	.85	1.0	1.0	1.0	.9	.9
Chile	.59	.64	.77	.9	1.0	1.2	1.3	1.4
Canada	.37	.43	.46	.6	.6	.7	.8	.9
Total	2.39	2.98	3.54	4.1	4.5	4.9	5.3	5.7
Other Principal Consumers								
Zambia	.63	.68	.68	.8	.9	1.0	1.1	1.2
Zaire	.30	.38	.45	.5	.6	.6	.6	.7
USSR	.74	.93	1.09	1.2	1.3	1.3	1.4	1.5
All principal consumers	4.06	4.97	5.76	6.6	7.3	7.8	8.4	9.1
Percent of world consumption	82.1	79.8	76.7	72.5	69.0	65.5	62.0	59.5
World consumption	4.93	6.23	7.51	9.0	10.5	11.9	13.6	15.2

[a]Data actually refer to copper content (for some countries recoverable copper content) of mine production, whether delivered in the form of ore, or concentrate, precipitate, leach liquid, or otherwise.

[b]Five-year averages, centered on year shown, or calculated from five-year averages.

[c]Trend values.

[d]Belgium is the preeminent consumer of blister and semirefined copper from Zaire.

than 5 percent. Since U.S. mine production is measured in terms of recoverable content, the ratio is presumably unaffected by any loss factor.

Apart from the United States, the largest potential consumers of ore include the USSR, Chile, and Zambia. Of these, the latter two supply copper for external consumption, but Chile is increasingly exporting refined copper instead of blister, and Zambia already processes nearly all of its ore to the refined stage. Thus the projected ore/blister consumption ratio for Chile continues a declining trend (but also continues the past deceleration in rate of decline), while that for Zambia is assumed to remain at a constant level, representing essentially a loss factor. Projections for the USSR are affected by the fact that, in lieu of more direct estimates, the consumption of ore was taken as being equal to production of blister copper and the consumption of blister copper was taken as being equal to the production of refined. This in-effect production/production ratio has been declining since the mid-1960s, presumably because of increasing recovery of refined copper from scrap. Such a trend is assumed to continue, albeit at a decelerating rate.

Since copper mining continues to be well dispersed around the world, and since there is a clear trend toward increased smelting in the countries of production, it is assumed that the world share held by the now leading copper smelting (ore consuming) countries will continue to decline. The result is that world consumption of copper ore is projected approximately to double between 1975 and the year 2000, even as the consumption of leading users increases by only a little more than half.

Copper Scrap

Projections of world and leading-country consumption of copper scrap are given in table 2-17. Long-term series on the consumption of copper scrap as such are generally not available; the data thus actually refer to the amounts of copper recovered from scrap, copper-base and otherwise. Such data would be a reasonable approximation, however, of the copper content of copper-base scrap alone, since limited losses in the course of recovery would tend to be counterbalanced by the limited amount of

Table 2-17. Projections of Copper Scrap Consumption,[a] 1980-2000, for the World and Leading Copper Scrap Consumers, with 1955-75 Comparisons

	Historical[b]						Projected[c]			
	1955	1960	1965	1970	1975	1980	1985	1990	1995	2000
A. Ratios to Refined Copper Consumption										
United States	.686	.686	.652	.674	.631	.62	.605	.59	.595	.56
Japan	1.250	.896	.694	.545	.462	.42	.395	.38	.37	.36
Germany (F. R.)	.682	.488	.594	.532	.454	.42	.405	.40	.40	.40
United Kingdom	.505	.478	.465	.502	.474	.45	.435	.425	.42	.42
Italy	.636	.513	.628	.667	.648	.675	.695	.705	.71	.71
France	.689	.620	.546	.456	.376	.395	.415	.43	.435	.435
World	.530	.452	.466	.449	.387	.37	.36	.35	.35	.34
B. Aggregate Consumption[d]										
Principal Consumers										
United States	.95	.92	1.19	1.26	1.19	1.26	1.37	1.48	1.61	1.74
Japan	.15	.24	.32	.44	.47	.55	.59	.59	.60	.61
Germany (F. R.)	.22	.24	.30	.35	.32	.32	.34	.36	.40	.43
United Kingdom	.23	.25	.27	.27	.23	.22	.22	.23	.23	.24
Italy	.07	.09	.13	.17	.20	.24	.27	.30	.32	.34
France	.12	.14	.15	.15	.14	.16	.18	.20	.21	.22
Total[e]	1.74	1.88	2.36	2.64	2.55	2.75	2.97	3.16	3.75	3.58
Percent of world consumption	91.0	88.9	84.2	81.6	78.9	75.6	72.8	70.0	67.2	64.6
World consumption[e]	1.92	2.12	2.82	3.25	3.24	3.64	4.08	4.51	5.01	5.54

[a]Owing to the nature of available series, the data refer more nearly to all copper recovered from scrap, either in refined form or as a component of alloys.

[b]Five-year averages, centered on year shown, or calculated from five-year averages.

[c]Trend values.

[d]Million metric tons of recovered copper. Calculations were made from unrounded figures; therefore, data shown here will not always reconcile precisely.

[e]Omits the USSR, for which base data are not available.

195

recovery from sources other than copper-base scrap. It should be noted that the data given here are for both new and old scrap, since both are feed for brass mills, refineries, and other industrial consumers.

Disregarding the Soviet Union, for which data on scrap recovery are not available, the United States is far and away the world's leading copper scrap consumer. Its scrap ratios are high, and would be even higher save for the fact that there are continuing scrap exports. The projected ratios extend an already demonstrated declining trend at the same geometric rate. We assume the decline is due to the progressively larger proportion of copper consumption going into wire and wire products, which generate relatively little new scrap compared with brass mill products, whose market share is decreasing. In addition, a probably increasing proportion of the copper going into electrical products is incorporated into integrated circuits and other applications from which old-scrap recovery is less than in grosser types of uses. We assume that such trends will continue, the relative importance of brass mill products being further diminished, particularly by reduction in the size of automobile radiators (owing to smaller engines), as well as by a continuing substitution of aluminum in this application.

Scrap ratios in most other countries are also projected to have diminishing trends. Historically, Japan has had the steepest long-run drop, owing largely to the unsustainability of the very high ratio (facilitated in significant measure by scrap imports) which obtained in the late 1950s; a further decline is projected, but at a sharply decelerating rate. Italy and France have experienced recent reversals in their falling scrap ratios, and based on this indication it was arbitrarily assumed that there would be a further modest rise before stabilization.

Though a considerable decentralization of scrap recovery is assumed to accompany the increasing decentralization of copper processing around the world, the world ratio of scrap to refined copper nevertheless remains heavily influenced by U.S. consumption. It works out to a mildly declining trend, such that the net drop over the 1975-2000 period is rather insignificant relative to that of the preceding two decades. Relative use of scrap copper at century's end would still be more than double that of aluminum.

Lead

Refined Lead

One after another of the important markets for lead have dwindled:
first, plumbing, then paints and cable covering, and, more recently,
gasoline antiknock additive. Even lead use in solders is threatened by
new kinds of plumbing and electrical connections. The result is that
lead consumption is becoming increasingly bound up with a single applica-
tion--storage batteries. This in turn is intimately bound up with automotive transportation.

By itself, this use has not been enough to cushion the overall decline
of lead-use intensity in relation to gross economic product, even though
aggregate use of lead in storage batteries is generally still on the increase. This includes recycled lead, which we have included in our refined
lead consumption series; and the upward trend is one which is only being
moderated, not basically altered, by the spread of longer life batteries.
The trend toward smaller cars also may be expected only to moderate rather
than reverse the trend toward larger (and therefore higher lead-content)
batteries, since there is a continuing addition of incidental equipment
which car batteries are called upon to power. In the view of some, there
is a good chance that battery use of lead will mushroom over the next
decade or so with the widespread introduction of electric automobiles.
The projections here discount such a likelihood, however, on the assumption
that if electric automobiles are produced in volume, it will most likely
be because something other than the lead-acid storage battery will be
their principal source of energy. We also discount the likelihood that
the larger batteries required to start diesel engines will make a significant difference in the total picture.

Accordingly, the projections of lead intensity in table 2-18 (part A)
extend (though in most cases at a decelerating rate) the declines which
have already manifested themselves for each of the leading lead consumers
other than Italy. Italy's record of increase, ascribable largely to automotive production and to chemicals, has brought lead use intensity in
that country to levels which are considered unsustainable, so that an

Table 2-18. Projections of Refined Lead Consumption, 1980-2000, for the World and Leading Lead Consumers, with 1960-75 Comparisons

	Historical[a]				Projected[b]				
	1960	1965	1970	1975	1980	1985	1990	1995	2000
Ratios to GNP/GDP[c]									
Principal int'l traders:									
United States	1.10	.97	.97	.87	.77	.73	.71	.685	.66
USSR	5.06	5.09	5.04	5.07	5.02	5.00	4.98	4.96	4.94
United Kingdom	5.16	4.91	3.79	2.98	2.65	2.35	2.13	1.92	1.78
Germany (F.R.)	.417	.389	.370	.301	.263	.237	.220	.207	.196
Japan	3.66	3.14	2.41	2.01	1.75	1.59	1.46	1.35	1.25
France	.295	.236	.192	.155	.137	.125	.116	.108	.101
Italy	N.A.	1.61	1.88	2.22	2.2	2.13	2.0	1.86	1.72
China (P.R.)	.714	.737	.911	.702	.67	.64	.625	.61	.60
Aggregate consumption[d]									
Principal int'l traders:									
United States	1.03	1.13	1.35	1.38	1.44	1.58	1.76	1.94	2.11
USSR	.31	.39	.50	.62	.74	.88	1.02	1.17	1.31
United Kingdom	.37	.41	.36	.31	.31	.30	.30	.30	.30
Germany (F.R.)	.24	.29	.34	.32	.32	.34	.35	.38	.40
Japan	.15	.21	.27	.31	.36	.39	.42	.44	.47
France	.20	.21	.23	.23	.24	.26	.28	.29	.31
Italy	.10	.13	.19	.26	.30	.32	.33	.34	.35
Total	2.40	2.77	3.24	3.43	3.71	4.07	4.46	4.86	5.25
China (P.R.)	.08	.10	.17	.18	.24	.28	.33	.39	.46
All principal consumers	2.48	2.87	3.41	3.61	3.95	4.35	4.79	5.25	5.71
Percent of world consumption	71.6	71.4	73.7	70.8	70.6	70.2	69.8	69.5	69.2
World consumption	3.46	4.02	4.63	5.11	5.59	6.19	6.86	7.56	8.25

[a] Five-year averages, centered on year shown, or calculated from five-year averages.

[b] Trend values.

[c] Metric tons, per denominator shown in table 1-31 (q.v. for fuller historical detail).

[d] Million metric tons. Calculations were made from unrounded figures for GNP/GDP and therefore will not always reconcile precisely.

early downturn is projected in Italy's·case as well. The mildest rate
of decline in intensity is that projected for the USSR and is a straight
geometric extension of what appears to be the past log-linear trend. The
Soviet Union appears to have much greater room for expansion of its motor
vehicle fleet over the next decade or so than does any other of the leading
lead consumers, save the People's Republic of China. The PRC is further
away than the USSR, however, from large-scale production of motor vehicles,
so that the steep recent downward trend in its lead use per unit of GNP
has been projected only to attenuate, not reverse itself, before the end
of the century.

In general, the rates of decline in lead intensity that are assumed
for the leading industrial consumers are projected to slow, not only by
reason of battery production, but because limits are being reached for
such declining uses as paints and sheathing. Outside of the United States,
moreover, there is reported to be a more leisurely pace in the elimination
of tetraethyl (and tetramethyl) lead. This affects lead consumption in
the United States and the United Kingdom, since these two countries are
the key international TEL/TML suppliers.

Because of the importance of automotive battery production, there
is more tendency for the consumption of lead than of other metals to
remain concentrated in the leading industrial countries. Some amount
of continuing dispersion is assumed, however, in arriving at world consumption figures which, between 1975 and 2000, increase by some 60 percent.

Lead Ore

The relative importance of automotive batteries is also reflected in
the lead ore/metal consumption ratios given in table 2-19. In the United
States, for example, the ratio of lead in ore to refined lead is less
than 50 percent. This is partly explained by refined-lead imports, but
more important by the fact that some 40 percent of the lead currently
being made available is recovered from scrap. Automobile batteries are
by far the major source of such scrap. The new-lead (ore) proportions
are similarly low in Japan and even lower in Germany and France, though
in these cases sources of lead scrap other than batteries have probably

Table 2-19. Projections of Lead Ore Consumption, 1980-2000, for the World and for Leading Lead Ore Consumers, with 1965-75 Comparisons

	Historical[a]			Projected[b]				
	1965	1970	1975	1980	1985	1990	1995	2000
A. Ratios to Refined Lead Consumption[c]								
United States	.343	.418	.464	.485	.50	.505	.50	.495
USSR[d]	1.14	1.10	1.03	.97	.93	.89	.85	.81
Germany (F.R.)	.485	.516	.426	.39	.37	.355	.345	.335
Japan	.485	.677	.578	.49	.445	.415	.395	.38
France	.511	.548	.499	.43	.395	.37	.35	.335
World	.683	.718	.698	.689	.688	.685	.683	.676
B. Ratios to Refined Lead Consumption of Principal Int'l Traders[e]								
Australia	.110	.110	.106	.103	.101	.099	.097	.095
Canada	.055	.056	.037	.032	.029	.027	.026	.025
Mexico	.063	.051	.054	.056	.057	.058	.058	.059
C. Aggregate Consumption[f]								
Principal int'l traders:								
United States	.39	.57	.64	.70	.79	.89	.97	1.05
USSR	.45	.55	.64	.72	.82	.91	.99	1.06
Germany (F.R.)	.14	.18	.14	.13	.12	.12	.13	.13
Japan	.10	.19	.18	.18	.18	.17	.18	.18
France	.11	.13	.11	.10	.10	.10	.10	.10
Australia	.30	.36	.36	.38	.41	.44	.47	.50
Canada	.15	.18	.13	.12	.12	.12	.13	.13
Total	1.64	2.16	2.20	2.33	2.54	2.75	2.97	3.15
Mexico	.17	.17	.19	.21	.23	.26	.28	.31
Total	1.81	2.33	2.39	2.54	2.77	3.01	3.25	3.46
Percent of world cons.	66.2	69.4	66.9	66.0	65.0	64.0	63.0	62.0
World consumption	2.74	3.32	3.57	3.85	4.26	4.70	5.16	5.58

[a]Five-year averages, centered on year shown, or calculated from five-year averages.

[b]Trend values.

[c]Units of lead (or recoverable lead) content in ore per unit of metallic lead consumed.

[d]Ore consumption was taken as equal to refined lead production.

[e]For list of principal international trader-consumers of refined lead, see table 9H-1.

[f]Million metric tons of lead (or recoverable lead) content. Calculations were made from unrounded figures and therefore, as shown, may not reconcile precisely.

been more significant than in the United States. In France, as in the United States, the ratio is additionally depressed by substantial imports of refined lead. The relatively high ore/metal ratio for the world as a whole, while in part reflecting the lesser importance of automobile batteries outside the principal industrial countries, is also significantly influenced by the USSR ratio, which, as the footnote indicates, is in effect exaggerated, since scrap data are not available and ore consumption had to be taken as equal to refined lead production.[19]

Of the countries which consume lead ore primarily to satisfy domestic refined-lead requirements, the United States and the USSR are of salient importance. The increasing ratio projected for the United States is a curvilinear extension of trend and reflects principally the expected effect of longer lived batteries in reducing current scrap runaround, as well as the difficulty of using recycled lead in maintenance-free batteries. The latter influence would be more noticeable were it not for the phaseout of tetraethyl (and methyl) lead, which, along with the fading out of lead paints, will leave increasing proportions of total lead consumption in uses from which the lead can sooner or later be recycled. For the USSR, we extend, though eventually at a decelerating rate, a clearly declining historical trend. Given the absence of historical information on scrap, the USSR ratio reflects, in essence, only its foreign trade position with respect to lead metal. The Soviet Union has moved to near equilibrium in this respect, from once having been a substantial net exporter. The projections imply that it will cross the self-sufficiency line to become a significant net importer. Even while it is a net exporter--mostly to Eastern Europe--the USSR has been importing refined lead from such countries as Yugoslavia and North Korea, as well as from Western European suppliers.

---

[19]As much as 100,000 of the USSR's 620,000 metric tons of refined lead production in 1977 may have been from scrap rather than from lead ores, per the World Bureau of Metal Statistics.

Collectively, Australia, Canada, and Mexico, which traditionally have refined lead ore into metal primarily for the consumption of others, are comparable with the United States and the USSR as ore consumers. Except for Mexico, however, their relative participation in international supply is projected to undergo continuing decline, as increasing proportions of their lead output are used at home and as other suppliers become more important. Canada is already using more of its lead at home than it is sending abroad, and Mexico, for a while, was doing the same, but has returned to exporting more than half its product. Australia, also, at the end of the century will probably still be exporting more lead than it uses, but far less of a proportion than once was the case.

The assumed relative increase in lead ore smelting in countries not now among the principal ore consumers is reflected in the declining ratios for the latter shown in part C of table 2-19. The derived increase in world lead ore consumption is on the order of 70 percent for the last quarter of the century.

Lead Scrap

The scrap ratios shown in part A of table 2-20 generally trend upward for the reasons discussed under "lead ore." There are some exceptions, however. For the United States, though a generally upward trend was assumed, it was also assumed on the basis of the past record that there are long cycles in the generation of old lead scrap that would continue to make themselves felt.[20] The declining ratio for the United Kingdom follows the trend of the past decade though in decelerating fashion. It is assumed that there is a progressive exhaustion of some formerly important sources of obsolete scrap, such as lead piping and cable covering. In France, there have probably been similar factors at work, but the steeply declining trend in relative scrap recovery has also been

---

[20]Currently, also, there is an incipient swing toward sending lead scrap abroad for processing, because of the pressure of U.S. health and safety regulations. In addition, there are capacity and cost problems involved in rerefining antimonial lead scrap (the prevailing battery scrap) into the purer lead needed for maintenance-free batteries.

Table 2-20. Projections of Lead Scrap Consumption, 1980-2000, for the World and for Leading Lead Scrap Consumers, with 1960-75 Comparisons

	Historical[a]				Projected[b]				
	1960	1965	1970	1975	1980	1985	1990	1995	2000
A. Ratios to Refined Lead Consumption[c]									
United States	.391	.438	.397	.457	.49	.47	.44	.44	.46
Germany (F.R.)	.170	.138	.180	.251	.285	.31	.33	.345	.355
Italy	.265	.205	.164	.242	.260	.280	.290	.30	.305
United Kingdom	.258	.284	.242	.191	.17	.155	.145	.140	.135
Canada	.357	.357	.385	[d].430	.445	.50	.50	.50	.50
France	.217	.230	.154	.137	.130	.128	.126	.125	.125
Japan	.359	.284	.258	.255	.305	.345	.37	.39	.405
World	.203	.209	.197	.213	.225	.228	.224	.226	.239
B. Aggregate Consumption[e]									
United States	.40	.50	.54	.63	.70	.74	.77	.85	.97
Germany (F.R.)	.04	.04	.06	.08	.09	.10	.12	.13	.14
Italy	.03	.03	.03	.06	.08	.09	.10	.10	.11
United Kingdom	.09	.12	.09	.06	.05	.05	.04	.04	.04
Canada[f]	.02	.03	.04	.05	.05	.06	.06	.07	.07
France	.04	.05	.04	.03	.03	.03	.03	.04	.04
Japan	.05	.06	.07	.08	.11	.14	.16	.17	.19
Total	.68	.82	.86	1.00	1.11	1.21	1.28	1.40	1.56
Percent of world consumption	97.8	97.6	94.0	91.3	88.0	85.5	83.0	81.0	79.0
World consumption	.70	.84	.91	1.09	1.26	1.41	1.54	1.73	1.97

[a]Five-year averages, centered on year shown, or calculated from five-year averages.

[b]Trend values.

[c]Units of lead recovered from scrap per unit of refined lead.

[d]Underlying data are in part preliminary.

[e]Million metric tons of recovered lead. Calculations were made from unrounded figures and may therefore not reconcile precisely.

[f]Roughly estimated historical data and projections for refined lead consumption in Canada (not shown in table 2-18):

(thousand metric tons)

1960	56	1980	119
1965	84	1985	123
1970	104	1990	128
1975	116	1995	133
		2000	138

[g]Historical detail will not add precisely to totals, owing to rounding.

connected with an increasing proportion of lead going into chemical
(dissipative) uses--an influence which we assume will sharply level off.

Lead scrap use in those parts of the world not specifically accounted
for is expected to increase substantially more rapidly than total lead use.
A good deal of lead has been dispersed around the world in batteries and
other products from which it is relatively easy to recover.

Zinc

Zinc is one of the most difficult metals to make predictions for
because it faces the most uncertain competition. This applies, for
example, both to its use in die castings, for which both aluminum and
plastics are important direct substitutes, and to its use as the coating
for "galvanized" products, where the threat of substitution is indirect.
Still, even for zinc, there is probably less uncertainty attendant on the
input-output parameters than on the various countries' assumed rates of
economic growth.

Refined Zinc

As in the case of copper, we have defined refined (essentially "slab")
zinc to exclude the zinc implicitly recovered (usually by simple remelting)
as a component of secondary alloys. As a rule, brass, bronze, and other
non-zinc-base alloys are the principal vehicles by means of which used
zinc is recycled. In fact, scrap in general is less important for zinc
than for any of the other principal nonferrous metals, and we have omitted
it from consideration (even in its broader definition) as a separate zinc
commodity.

The projections shown in table 2-21 have all been based, as in the
case of the other nonferrous metals, on the relationship of the metal to
GNP/GDP. Chapter 1 also set forth the results of relating zinc consumption
to steel production--a plausible determinant because of the high proportion
of zinc which is used in conjunction with, if not directly as coating on,
steel products. In the end, however, the relationship to GNP/GDP seemed
to have a small advantage in terms of smoothness of historical trends.

Table 2-21. Projections of Refined Zinc Consumption, 1980-2000, for the World and Leading Zinc Consumers, with 1960-75 Comparisons

	Historical[a]				Projected[b]				
	1960	1965	1970	1975	1980	1985	1990	1995	2000
Ratios to GNP/GDP[c]									
Principal world traders:									
United States	.89	.97	.86	.68	.59	.535	.50	.475	.46
Germany (F.R.)	.479	.421	.425	.334	.264	.234	.220	.213	.208
United Kingdom	3.53	3.25	2.95	2.40	2.18	2.04	1.88	1.76	1.65
USSR	5.77	5.70	6.84	7.43	7.43	7.36	7.25	6.88	6.54
Other principal consumers:									
Japan	4.66	5.50	5.42	4.45	3.8	3.4	3.15	3.05	3.0
France	.264	.215	.193	.183	.170	.158	.149	.144	.141
China (P.R.)	.668	.798	.813	.805	.81	.81	.81	.81	.81
Aggregate consumption[d]									
Principal world traders:									
United States	.84	1.14	1.19	1.08	1.10	1.16	1.24	1.34	1.47
Germany (F.R.)	.28	.31	.39	.36	.33	.33	.36	.39	.43
United Kingdom	.25	.27	.28	.25	.25	.26	.26	.27	.28
USSR	.35	.44	.68	.90	1.10	1.30	1.50	1.63	1.74
Total	1.72	2.16	2.54	2.59	2.78	3.05	3.36	3.63	3.92
Other principal consumers:									
Japan	.19	.37	.62	.68	.78	.84	.91	1.00	1.13
France	.18	.19	.23	.27	.30	.32	.35	.39	.43
China (P.R.)	.07	.11	.15	.21	.26	.31	.37	.44	.53
All principal consumers	2.16	2.83	3.54	3.75	4.12	4.52	4.99	5.46	6.01
Percent of world consumption	70.5	70.1	68.7	65.3	63.4	61.5	59.7	57.8	56.0
World consumption	3.07	4.04	5.16	5.75	6.50	7.36	8.36	9.40	10.73

[a] Five-year averages, centered on years shown, or calculated from five-year averages.

[b] Trend values.

[c] Metric tons, per denominator shown in table 1-35 (q.v. for fuller historical datail).

[d] Million metric tons. Calculations were made from unrounded figures for GNP/GDP and therefore, as shown, may not always reconcile precisely.

If our projections are correct, the United States, USSR, and Japan will remain by far the three leading zinc consumers, with the Soviet Union displacing the United States from top position. As indicated in the first part of table 2-21, this emergence of the USSR takes place despite the assumption of declining use of zinc per unit of GNP--a decline which is consistent with the experience of other developed countries, but which, for the USSR, represents a reversal of trend. The implied use of refined zinc per unit of steel output declines slightly faster, but remains above 6 kilos per metric ton. (The current ratio is about 6 1/2 and rising.) The decline is consistent with a diminishing proportionate role of construction in the GNP and a continuing limited role for automobiles.

For the United States, the rapidly declining trend in zinc intensity that has been exhibited since the mid-1960s has been extended to the end of the century in our projections. The implied use of zinc per metric ton of steel production, after dipping a little further than it has already below the 9-kilo mark, rises again to nearly 11 kilos in the year 2000. An important part of the change is the increasing use of zinc in batteries and in other electrical applications--an increase that is faster than that in the economy's use of steel. Of the decreasing amount of steel which continues to be used in automobiles, a substantial proportion is likely to be galvanized (at least on one side). In addition, because of the push to reduce the total amount of steel in automobiles, the residual zinc use in die-cast parts and in the brass of automobile radiators will bulk proportionately larger.

For Japan, too, we extend at a decelerating rate the sharply declining trend in use of zinc per unit of GNP; and the result in terms of zinc in relation to steel is analogous to that for the United States--a decline to about 6 kilos per metric ton from a present ratio which is slightly higher, and a subsequent recovery to about 7 1/2 kilos per metric ton. The reasons in Japan also have to do both with automobiles and with electrical applications, including batteries. In Japan, compared with the United States, there is apparently somewhat less of a sustaining basic use of galvanized iron and steel in construction.

Global consumption of refined zinc is likely to retain its present degree of concentration more than most of the other principal metals, owing both to the particular connection of zinc with automobiles and the relatively high technology involved in a good deal of zinc's use in galvanizing and in electronics. We project the share of the leading consumers to decline from about 65 percent in 1975 to 56 percent in the year 2000. The resultant increase in world zinc consumption is on the order of 87 percent.

Zinc Ore

Regardless of the relative concentration in refined zinc consumption, its production (zinc smelting) is, as noted in chapter 1, quite dispersed. As also noted in chapter 1, the principal determinant of deviations from unity in the ore/refined consumption ratio is a country's foreign trade position. The United States has been particularly affected by a growing dependence on foreign smelters for its refined zinc supply.

In arriving at the projections, the decline in U.S. smelting self-sufficiency has been assumed to continue, but at a slowing pace, as capacity is progressively reduced to a core group of new and retrofitted smelters that are able to meet both efficiency and environmental standards. Compared with Japan and the USSR, however, the United States is already a relatively minor consumer of zinc ore and, by the end of the century, will have even less consequence for global consumption levels (table 2-22). The USSR seems due for the most rapid increases, assuming it does not curtail its role as a slight net exporter of refined zinc. Japan, too, is assumed to retain a role (at least through 2000) as a net exporter, although decreasingly so, in accordance with an extension of the apparent trend since the late 1960s.

Zinc smelting (ore consumption) in three of the leading consumers is assumed to be governed more by the refined-zinc requirements of their export customers than by their home requirements. The bulk of Canadian refined zinc has traditionally gone into export, and there has been an increasing trend in that direction in Australia. Our assumption is that the Canadian contribution will increase a little as a proportion of the

Table 2-22. Projections of Zinc Ore Consumption, 1980-2000, for the World
and for leading Zinc Ore Consumers, with 1965-75 Comparisons

	Historical[a]			Projected[b]				
	1965	1970	1975	1980	1985	1990	1995	2000

A. Ratios to Refined Zinc Consumption[c]

United States	.80	.74	[d].53	.47	.435	.42	.41	.40
Germany	.50	.69	[d]1.05	1.14	1.16	1.16	1.14	1.12
France	1.10	1.07	[d]1.00	.975	.96	.94	.925	.91
Italy	.83	.89	[d]1.05	1.07	1.08	1.08	1.06	1.04
Japan	1.10	1.19	[d]1.16	1.14	1.11	1.08	1.05	1.03
USSR[e]	1.12	1.07	1.10	1.10	1.10	1.10	1.10	1.10
Poland[e]	1.60	1.60	1.60	1.60	1.60	1.60	1.60	1.60
World	1.04	1.04	1.03	1.Q3	1.04	1.03	1.02	1.01

B. Ratios to Refined Zinc Consumption of Principal International Traders[f]

Belgium	.099	.082	[d].092	.095	.098	.099	.099	.099
Australia	.111	.114	[d].110	.106	.104	.102	.101	.100
Canada	.138	.136	[d].139	.142	.143	.144	.145	.146

C. Aggregate Consumption[g]

Principal international
  traders:

Germany (F.R.)	.15	.27	[d].38	.37	.38	.41	.44	.48
Belgium	.21	.21	[d].24	.26	.30	.33	.36	.39
France	.21	.25	[d].27	.29	.31	.33	.36	.39
Italy	.10	.16	[d].20	.22	.24	.25	.26	.27
Australia	.24	.29	[d].26	.29	.32	.34	.37	.39
Japan	.41	.74	[d].79	.89	.93	.98	1.06	1.16
Canada	.30	.34	[d].36	.39	.44	.48	.53	.57
Total	1.62	2.26	2.50	2.71	2.92	3.12	3.38	3.65

Other Principal
  consumers:

United States	.92	.88	.59	.52	.50	.52	.55	.59
USSR	.49	.72	.99	1.21	1.43	1.65	1.79	1.91
Poland	.19	.21	.24	.25	.26	.27	.28	.28
All principal consumers	3.22	4.07	4.32	4.69	5.11	5.56	6.00	6.43
Percent of world consumption	76.5	75.6	73.0	70.0	67.0	64.5	62.0	59.5
World consumption	4.21	5.38	5.92	6.70	7.63	8.62	9.68	10.81

[a]Five-year averages, centered on year shown, or calculated from five-year averages.

[b]Trend values.

[c]Units of zinc (or recoverable zinc) content in ore per unit of refined zinc consumed.

[d]Underlying data partly estimated.

[e]Ore consumption taken as equal to refined zinc production.

[f]For list of principal international trader consumers of refined zinc, see table 2-21.

[g]Million metric tons of zinc (or recoverable zinc) content. Calculations were made from unrounded figures and therefore, as shown, may not reconcile precisely. Historical data and rough projections of refined zinc consumption in Italy and Poland (not shown in table 2-21):

	1965	1970	1975	1980	1985	1990	1995	2000
Italy	.12	.18	.20	.21	.22	.23	.24	.26
Poland	.12	.13	.15	.16	.16	.17	.17	.18

needs of principal trader-consumers, both because Canada has growing opportunities in the U.S. market and because it now exports considerable quantities of zinc ore, some of which it could divert to domestic smelters. Australia is assumed for the time being to have a declining relative role as a world supplier--largely because of difficulty in enlarging capacity-- but nevertheless to be supplying increasing absolute amounts. Belgium's relative supply role is assumed to enlarge slightly, similarly to Canada's. In the aggregate, the three countries now account for an amount of ore consumption equal to about a third of the total quantity of refined zinc consumed by the leading international traders, and the proportion, on balance, is projected to remain essentially the same.

Though quite a few countries are specifically accounted for in table 2-22, in 1975 they were responsible for only 73 percent of the world's zinc ore consumption. Given some further dispersion in smelting activity, this proportion is expected to decline by the year 2000 to under 60 per-cent. The resultant global projection is roughly an 83-percent increase in world ore consumption, slightly less than the increase for the refined metal. The difference is consistent with small increases in the relative amount of scrap recovery or small decreases in smelting losses or (more likely) some combination of these two factors.

PART II: TRADE AND SUPPLY PATTERNS

Chapter 3

INTERNATIONAL TRADE

Introduction

For many of the mineral commodities under review, there is only a vague semblance of a world market. Cost to the industrial consumer, while influenced by world demand and supply conditions, is more nearly determined by trading arrangements made with particular suppliers, or frequently, the essentially pro forma transfer prices agreed upon between units of the same or affiliated companies. But even for those commodities for which there is a significant international marketplace, the prices set in that marketplace do not reflect the output of all producers or the consumption of all consumers. Countries which produce domestically just about what they consume domestically have little impact on international price trends. Likewise, commodity movements that go on within such blocs as Comecon have little impact on world prices.[1] In short, only as countries contribute to or avail themselves of supplies which are exchanged among the countries of the "trading world" do they have much of an impact on international price developments.

To understand world mineral prices (or whatever transfer-cost series might be a reasonable facsimile thereof), it is necessary to contemplate the roster of principal buyers and sellers. Because this roster is not

---

[1] Comecon includes most of the Communist countries of Eastern Europe, along with Cuba, Mongolia, and Vietnam.

constant, one should consider both trends and fluctuations in its makeup. Within the total roster, it is also necessary to understand the dominant bilateral flows and the changing bilateral relationships, since some flows tend to have significant influence on world prices while others take place under circumstances which insulate them from significant world price impact.

The tables which represent the core of this chapter deal with only two of the three dimensions: they present the matrix of bilateral rela- tionships for the principal trading countries for a single, recent year, while omitting any matrix changes over time. Some reference is made in the text to which of the relationships appear to be persistent and which ephemeral, but systematic analysis in this report is confined to the supply mix for the United States alone, presented separately in chapter 4. All the matrix tables are at the end of this chapter.

For the nonferrous metals particularly, the data for the tables came relatively directly out of the sources cited, although they did require some amount of arbitrary reconciliation of trade as reported from the im- port and export sides, respectively, as well as the execution of the per- centage calculations. In the case of the ferroalloying elements, there were some additional complexities, which are referred to in the text that follows.

Cobalt

Cobalt, unfortunately, lacks even a single-year matrix: the data are simply too difficult to arrive at. The meaning of the trade flows, more- over, is rather ambiguous. U.S. imports have been only of cobalt as metal, and the bulk of the flow is ultimately out of mines in Zaire, but some of the conversion to metal (or perhaps only some of the ultimate refining) takes place in Belgium. Prices of the metal are independent of the supply pathway, however, being set either by a semimonopolistic price leader with essential disregard for actual costs of production and delivery, or by dealers selling in a very thin auction market. (See chapter 6.) The lack of usable trade-flow data is thus in part compensated, in this case, by

their essential irrelevance. It is enough to know that Zaire (with
Belgian intervention), Zambia, Finland, Canada, and Australia are the
principal trading world suppliers, while the United States, Japan, the
United Kingdom, and Germany are the principal purchasers. The USSR is a
major user, but apparently is able to supply itself from domestic resources, with some help from Cuba.[2]

Chromium

The trade pattern for chromium ore (<u>chromite</u>) is shown in table 3-1.
In 1975, the USSR and South Africa, between them, accounted for about
half the world's traded supply, but this has not always been the case and
need not necessarily persist. The USSR has been a sporadic contributor
to the world market, taking advantage of a sort of "dealer's" price opportunity in times of market tightness. It suspended exports to the United
States during the 1950-59 decade, presumably because of the Korean War,
but came back into the U.S. market in a significant way in 1963.[3] Imports
from the USSR have faded since 1975, as the lower priced, higher-iron
South African ore became more widely substitutable.

Rhodesia in the period studied was ostensibly out of the world market,
owing to the UN embargo,[4] but during the period 1972 to early 1977 it was
shipping to the United States under the "Byrd amendment." Moreover, despite the evidence of other countries' compliance in the form of blanks in
official trade statistics, it is likely that additional amounts of Rhodesian chrome reached the industrial world, either as ore or as ferrochrome,

---

[2]The USSR did, however, purchase a significant quantity of cobalt from
Zaire prior to the May 1978 price increase.

[3]John L. Morning, <u>Chromium</u> (U.S. Bureau of Mines, Mineral Commodity
Profiles, 1, Washington, D.C., May 1977) p. 2.

[4]Agreed on in 1966, but taking some time thereafter to become generally effective.

and at least partly through South Africa.[5] South Africa is the current principal recorded producer of chromite, pricing its product with a presumed eye to longer-run market position. The Philippines shipments to the United States shown in table 3-1 are essentially of refractory ore, for which there is more or less a separate market; its exports to Japan and the United Kingdom are understood to include both metallurgical and refractory grades.

One important supplier of chromite, Albania, has diversified its customer list in recent years (originally, outside of Eastern Europe, Yugoslavia was the sole customer, but has lately shown signs of curtailing its participation in the free international market). Turkey's market position may be in jeopardy because of declining ore grades, but so far it appears to remain competitive. Official estimates of Soviet reserves throw into question that country's ability to persist as a leading world supplier--and its exports have, in fact, recently been in decline--but the estimate of its subeconomic and unidentified resources is said to be "probably conservative."[6]

In arriving at table 3-1, it was desirable to place the disparate ores upon a common-denominator basis with regard to chromium content. The measure used was chromic oxide (sometimes called chromic acid) content, which was arrived at by applying a content factor to the gross quantities exported or imported. The factors used were those estimated by U.S. Bureau of Mines' specialists for the average chromic oxide (Cr_2O_3) content of ores produced in the various exporting countries. In general, import rather than export data were used to measure the gross weight of ores being exchanged.

---

[5]For example, the 1974 Canadian Minerals Yearbook points out a 200,000-ton discrepancy between Japan's official imports from South Africa and the official export figures of South Africa to Japan in that year. The difference is believed to have originated in Rhodesia. A significant amount of Rhodesian ore is also believed to have found its way to the world at large via the Soviet Union.

[6]Morning, Chromium, p. 5.

The significant sources feeding ferrochromium into world trade are more numerous than those providing chromite, but at the same time there is more concentration. South Africa, in 1974, provided more than a third of the traded supply (table 3-2), and its proportion of the total continues to increase. With the notable exception of South Africa, Rhodesia, Finland, and Norway, which produce ferrochromium mostly or wholly for world markets, other leading producers are concerned mostly with supporting domestic steel industries. However, there has been an apparent trend toward growing export surpluses in Brazil,[7] France, Japan, Yugoslavia, and the USSR. Canada, Great Britain, Germany, Italy, and Austria seem to be growing net importers, along with the Benelux countries, which depend primarily on Germany.

Determining this roster of leading importers and exporters was actually one of the preliminary steps in compiling table 3-2. Initial indications of the list of trading countries were obtained from tables in the DIW study on Chrom,[8] which covered the period 1963-73. The same publication also gives information on ferrochrome capacity in 1974, for all countries other than those in Eastern Europe;[9] except for the USSR, however, the latter production (apparently in Czechoslovakia, Poland, and the German Democratic Republic) does not enter into free market world trade flows.

The table itself is a synthesis of the various sets of data on international flows of ferrochromium circa 1974, which was the latest year for which it seemed possible to compile a reasonably reliable matrix. The flows coming to the United States, for example, are generally from U.S. import data, as reported in the Minerals Yearbook, but Japanese export

---

[7]The sole Brazilian producer, Ferbassa, in 1976 directed about 40 percent each of its export shipments to the United States and to Europe, 20 percent to Japan. It expected the U.S. reembargo on Southern Rhodesia to result in future higher sales to the United States. (American Metal Market, May 27, 1977.)

[8]Deutsches Institut für Wirtschaftsforschung, Chrom (Berlin, 1975) tables 58 and 59, pp. 130 and 131.

[9]Ibid., table 26, pp. 45-46.

Table 3-1. Estimated Distribution of World Trade in Chromium Ore, 1975[a]
(percentages based on Cr_2O_3/chrome content[b])

Exp. / Imp.	USSR	South Africa	Rhodesia	Philippines	Turkey	Albania	Finland	Iran	Mozambique	Malagasy	India	Other	Total
U.S.	8.2	5.8	3.1	3.3	3.6	1.0	0.2	0.2			0.3		25.7
Japan	2.5	7.5		2.7	2.3	1.3		1.3		1.4	8.3	0.6	27.9
Germany (F.R.)	4.4	3.0		0.3	1.8	0.4	0.1	0.2	1.8				12.0
France	2.5	1.2		0.1	1.0	0.3		0.6	0.1	2.5			8.3
U.K.		2.1		0.9	0.5								3.5
Italy	0.7	0.6		0.2	1.4	0.8							3.7
Neth.		0.5					0.1		0.2				0.8
Spain		0.6		0.1	1.0	0.1	0.1	0.1					2.0
Austria		1.0		0.3	0.5			0.3				0.1	2.2
Norway	0.3				1.4	0.1							1.8
Sweden	4.7			0.2	1.9	0.6	0.8						8.2
Yugoslavia	1.5			0.1		2.3							3.9
Total	24.8	22.3	3.1	8.3	15.5	6.9	1.3	2.7	2.1	3.9	8.6	0.7	[c]100.0

Note: Detail may not add to totals, owing to rounding.

Sources: U.S. Bureau of Mines, Minerals Yearbook; Organization for Economic Cooperation and Development, Foreign Trade Statistics, Series C; Japanese Ministry of Finance, Japan Exports and Imports; Deutsches Institut für Wirtschaftsforschung, Chrom.

[a]Represents 95 percent of ore imports of developed countries (82 percent of world imports).

[b]Actual chrome content of chromite ores is the chromic oxide (Cr_2O_3) content multiplied by 0.684.

[c]Equates to imports of 2,000,000 metric tons Cr_2O_3.

215

Table 3-2. Estimated Distribution of World Trade in Ferrochromium, 1974[a]

(percentages based on chromium content[b])

Imp. \ Exp.	South Africa	Rhodesia	Germany (F.R.)	Finland	USSR	Japan	U.S.	Brazil	Sweden	Italy	Yugo-slavia	Norway	Spain	Turkey	France	Other or Undistributed	Total
U.S.	10.1	6.7	1.6	0.3		1.6		1.9	1.3		4.0	0.8		0.4			28.7
Canada	5.4						0.7	0.8									6.8
Germany (F.R.)	7.0				1.0	1.4	0.2	0.8	0.5	0.7	0.4	0.4	0.7	0.5	0.2	1.8	15.5
France	0.6		2.0		0.2				0.7	0.4	0.2	0.7					5.1
Italy	2.9		1.1	2.4	0.2									0.2	0.7		8.3
Nether-lands			0.5			0.7											
Bel./Lux.	0.6		2.0		0.9											2.3	5.6
U.K.	2.1		0.9	0.7	0.2						0.6	1.0	1.0				6.7
Japan	6.0															[d]1.1	7.0
Austria			0.2						0.9	0.8							2.0
Other			1.1	3.2			0.4		0.4	0.4		2.2			0.5	5.0	13.2
Total	34.5	6.7	9.5	6.6	2.7	3.8	0.4	3.4	3.8	2.3	6.1	5.1	1.7	1.5		9.9	[c]100.0

Note: Detail may not add to totals, owing to rounding.

Source: See accompanying text.

[a] Represents total world trade.

[b] Assumptions as to average chromium content of ferrochromium from each supplier are based on Bureau of Mines estimates as well as on reported data as to actual chromium content of ferrochromium imported in recent years by the United States.

[c] Equates to 313,000 metric tons.

[d] Reported by Japan as imported from the United States, but quite possibly having an origin in Rhodesia, with transshipment via the United States.

statistics were used to bring partially into the picture the then burgeoning flows to the United States from that country which had not yet
shown up in the U.S. import statistics.[10] The Canadian Minerals Yearbook
was used as the source of import data for Canada, and World Mineral Statistics, 1970-74 (U.K. Institute of Geological Sciences) and Chrom as sources
for other countries. For the United Kingdom itself, 1974 total imports
were distributed by the 1973 pattern, since the country breakdown was not
available for the later year. The "other" column represents unaccounted-
for exports, including those which may have gone to Eastern Europe, as
well as anomalous movements reported by Japan as having come from the
United States.

The original data were compiled in gross weight and combine high- and
low-carbon ferrochromium, since the types are distinguished only in U.S.
and Japanese data. These were then adjusted to chromium content on the
basis of factors for each producing country, estimated by specialists at
the U.S. Bureau of Mines or derived from U.S. import data.

Manganese

About one-third of the world's exports of maganese ore in 1975 came
out of South Africa (table 3-3). Japan was South Africa's leading customer, taking about 40 percent of its total exports, and South Africa
furnished a comparable percentage of Japan's imports, but the trade flow
from Australia to Japan, constituting some two-thirds of Australia's
exports, was also of considerable importance. Aside from South Africa,
Gabon was the trading world's largest exporter, supplying about half of
France's imports and a third of those of the United States. Apart from
the countries mentioned, Norway is one of the principal purchasers of the
world's manganese ore, converting it into ferromanganese for export.

---

[10]Since then, Japan has once again receded from the international
market as a supplier and is finding itself in a rapidly increasing net
import position.

Several elements in particular made this 1975 picture different from what it had been in earlier years. One is the shift of the United States, once the world's leading manganese ore consumer, to the position of a substantial purchaser of ferromanganese instead. Another is the imposition by India, starting in 1973, of export restrictions on its higher-grade manganese ores, with the result that most or all of its exports are now of the ferruginous variety. India had once been one of the world's principal suppliers—to the extent that its manganese ores were the standard for world pricing—but has become concerned about conserving limited high-grade ore resources for home consumption. Still another recent development is the withdrawal of the USSR from the free-market trading world. This development seems to be due mainly to an increasing flow of trade from the USSR to the Communist countries of Eastern Europe, but there is also the belief, in some quarters, that the USSR is facing early depletion of its higher grade minable deposits. Brazil may have peaked out as a growing world supplier, given the requirements of its domestic steel industry. Gabon and Australia probably both have further potential for relative growth. Gabon, in particular, has been limited by the capacity of an aerial tramway system connecting to a railroad in the Congo; a straight-through railway to a port in Gabon itself is under construction.

Table 3-3, it should be noted, includes the maganese content both of manganese ores per se and of ferruginous manganese ores. World control totals were taken from a table, in gross weights, compiled by UNCTAD;[11] UNCTAD also compiled data in manganese content terms, but the UNCTAD conversion, on analysis, appears not to have adequately allowed for the lesser manganese content of the ferruginous ores. U.S. and Canadian import data (from the Minerals Yearbook and Canadian Minerals Yearbook, respectively) were available directly in content terms; manganese content for other countries was estimated on the basis of the average content of ores

---

[11] United Nations Conference on Trade and Development, "The world market for manganese: characteristics and trends" (part of series on "Consideration of International Measures on Manganese," UNCTAD Doc. TD/B/IPC/MANGANESE/2, 13 May, 1977).

produced in the source countries, either as estimated by the U.S. Bureau
of Mines or as deduced from gross and content quantities given in the
U.K. Institute of Geological Sciences, World Mineral Statistics 1970-74.

Japan and West Germany are the only two important importers of ferruginous ores, and both countries provide separate data for this type. There
are only two important suppliers, South Africa and India; an average manganese content of 30 percent was estimated for the former, 25 percent for
the latter, as well as any other supplying countries. (The theoretical
range for ferruginous ores is 10-30 percent.)

Gross-weight data for Western European countries were taken from
OECD, Foreign Trade Statistics, Series C. Japanese data are from Japan
Exports and Imports. The ore breakdown (between manganese and ferruginous)
for France and Germany is from DIW's Mangan.[12] Imports in all other cases
were assumed to be wholly of manganese ore (that is, 30 percent plus).

U.S. imports of ferromanganese (table 3-4) have been increasing
despite a declining U.S. share in world ferromanganese consumption. In
1975, the United States accounted for more than a third of the trading
world's international purchases; two-thirds of U.S. imports were from
countries possessing no domestic ores. France and Norway, between them,
accounted for half of the world trade supply; the United States was the
key trading partner for, and leaned heavily upon, the former, while Norway's exports were more diffuse. Another important trade flow, equal in
magnitude to that between France and the United States, was between South
Africa and the United States. Both France and South Africa have benefited
as suppliers by the substantial U.S. shift from manganese ore to ferromanganese imports. More generally, however, France's share of world ferromanganese supply seems to have been declining over time, while that of
South Africa has been increasing. Germany is both an importer and an
exporter of ferromanganese; its second position among market-world importers reflects a growing import requirement. Italy has always depended
on imports, but has a requirement that is growing with its steel industry.
Japan's significant position as a world exporter is of recent origin and
reflects only temporary surpluses.

---

[12]Deutsches Institut für Wirtschaftsforschung, Mangan (Berlin, 1977).

Table 3-3. Estimated Distribution of World Trade in Manganese Ore, 1975[a]

(percentages based on Mn content)[b]

Exp.\Imp.	South Africa	Gabon	Australia	Ghana	Zaire	Morocco	Brazil	Mexico	India	Undistributed or other	Total
U.S.	2.1	5.5	1.9		0.2		7.0	0.5			17.3
Japan	14.0	2.1	7.8	0.5	0.1	0.6	0.2	1.1	4.7	2.2	33.5
Germany (F.R.)	3.7	0.3	1.0			0.1	0.5	0.4		0.3	5.9
France	5.1	6.4				0.3		0.4			12.3
U.K.	0.7	0.7		0.1		0.2	0.9			0.3	2.9
Italy	1.5	1.3					0.4			0.7	4.0
Neth.										0.5	0.5
Bel./Lux.	1.6	0.4	0.1		0.9		0.2			0.5	3.7
Sweden		0.1								0.1	0.3
Spain	1.7	1.4	0.3	0.6			0.6			0.3	4.9
Norway	3.5	3.1	1.2	0.8	0.2		2.8			0.4	12.1
Canada		0.9			0.2		0.4			0.2	1.7
Other										0.7	0.7
Total	33.9	22.3	12.4	2.1	1.6	1.3	13.0	2.1	4.7	6.4	100.0[c]

Note: Detail may not add to totals, owing to rounding.
Source: See accompanying text.

[a]Represents total imports of developed countries (87 percent of total world imports).
[b]Includes ores with 10 percent or greater manganese content.
[c]Equates to imports of 4,003,000 metric tons.

220

Table 3-4. Estimated Distribution of World Trade in Ferromanganese, 1975[a]
(percentages based on gross/net quantities[b]).

Exp. \ Imp.	France	Norway	South Africa	Bel./ Lux.	Germany (F.R.)	Japan	U.S.	Spain	India	Other	Total
U.S.	10.2	2.0	10.7	0.2	0.1	8.3		0.8	0.4	1.5	34.2
Germany (F.R.)	4.5	5.5	0.9	1.1		1.2	0.3			1.3	14.8
Italy	5.6	0.5	3.7	0.4	0.6			0.6		0.5	11.8
Bel./Lux.	4.0	1.6	0.2		1.3	0.4					7.4
France		0.1			0.8						0.9
Neth.	0.7	1.5	0.2		0.3	1.0					3.6
U.K.	0.6	5.2	3.1			0.1				0.3	9.3
Sweden		3.8	0.2				0.3				4.3
Denmark		0.8									0.8
Austria		1.5	0.2		0.2						1.8
Canada	0.2			0.5	0.3	0.3	1.9				3.2
Turkey						0.5			0.7		1.2
Undetermined and other	0.2	2.4	1.2	2.0		1.0					6.8
Total	25.9	24.9	20.4	4.2	3.5	12.7	2.5	1.4	1.1	3.5	[c]100.0

Note: Detail may not add to totals, owing to rounding.

Source: See accompanying text.

[a]Represents total ferromanganese trade of "developed" countries. Includes developed countries' trade to and from "developing" and Eastern European countries, if applicable.

[b]Average manganese content varies only within narrow limits (75 to 78 percent).

[c]Equates to total imports of 1,030,000 metric tons.

The data in table 3-4 are from the same sources as those in table
3-3; since there is little variation in the manganese content of ferromanganese, the percentage distribution of trade could be calculated directly from the gross weights. Among the choices made was to utilize data on
Japanese exports to various countries rather than on those countries' imports from Japan. The principal effect was to include a significantly
larger movement from Japan to both the United States and the Netherlands
than would otherwise have been the case.

Aluminum

Trade patterns in aluminum are heavily influenced by the high degree
of international integration of a limited number of major aluminum companies. This is particularly true of bauxite, which predominantly flows to
consuming plants of the same firm. In fact, as pointed out in the Introduction, the dependence of particular alumina plants upon particular types
or mixes of bauxite provides a techno-economic basis for a substantial
degree of stability in supply patterns, even though the imposition of
large tax increases by producing countries in recent years has stimulated
a quest for diversification.

The largest single international flow of bauxite (see table 3-5) is
to the United States from Jamaica: it accounts for about a sixth of the
world movement and about four-fifths of the world movement of mixed (Jamai-
can-type) bauxite. Bauxite from the Dominican Republic and Haiti, which
went wholly to the United States, accounted in 1975 for the balance of
the U.S. imported mixed-bauxite supply.

Around two-thirds of the world movement of bauxite is trihydrate
bauxite, or gibbsite, headed mostly for the United States, Japan, Germany,
Canada, and Italy. The United States depends mostly on Guinea and Surinam;
Japan, Germany, and Italy on Australia; and Canada on Guinea and Guyana.
Less than 10 percent of the world's international flows of bauxite are of
monohydrate (boehmite); they move from Yugoslavia and Greece, mostly to
the USSR. The USSR also supplements its indigenous resources with bauxite
from Guinea and alumina from Hungary.

Among the principal developments in recent years has been the emergence of Guinea and Australia as world suppliers, the former supplying principally the United States, the USSR, and Canada, and the latter serving as a supplier to Japan and Western Europe. Some minor flows from Australia to the United States have been replaced by movements of alumina. Both Japanese and U.S. interests have taken an active interest in bauxite development in Brazil, but the movement from this country, also, is likely to take primarily the form of alumina rather than crude ore.

In respect to alumina (table 3-6), the United States is Australia's largest customer, accounting, in 1974, for well over half its alumina exports; conversely, Australia was the United States' major alumina supplier, at around 60 percent of the total. Other important movements of alumina, within the market-oriented trading world, were to the United States from Jamaica and Surinam, and to Norway and Great Britain from Jamaica. The United States, which, all told, in 1974 accounted for a third of the trading world's imports, itself sends significant quantities of alumina to Canada and other places for smelting into aluminum. Owing both to pressures from the governments of bauxite-producing countries and to the ocean freight economies that stem from on-the-spot refining of bauxite into alumina, there is likely to be a steadily increasing international trade in alumina. The same factors, along with increasing diversion of alumina movements to places with relatively cheaper electric power, are also likely to result in fairly significant changes in alumina trade patterns. However, these various shifts may have only minor significance for the supply and cost of alumina to U.S. consumers.

In part because of the movement of alumina abroad for smelting and return, the United States is the largest single importer of aluminum metal (table 3-7), but it accounts for only 15 percent (1976) of the trading world total. Trade in metal is considerably more diffuse in general than is that in alumina, but some 30 percent of world exports, nevertheless, is provided by two countries, Norway and Canada. Canadian aluminum moves principally to the United States, while Norway is principally a supplier to Western Europe. Other important suppliers to Western Europe are Germany and the Netherlands. There is a good deal of cross-trade in aluminum,

Table 3-5. Estimated Distribution of World Trade in Bauxite by Type, 1975[a]
(percent of total in all forms)[b]

Imp.	Mixed (Jamaican type)			Trihydrate (Gibbsite)							Monohydrate (Boehmite)		Various types	Total
Exp.	Jamaica	Dominican Republic	Haiti	Australia	Guinea	Guyana	Surinam	Indonesia	Malaysia	Sierra Leone	Yugoslavia	Greece	Other	
U.S.[c]	16.6	2.9	1.5	0.3	8.0	2.1	5.7			0.1		0.1		37.3
Canada					3.5	2.5	0.3			1.0		0.1	0.1	7.3
Japan				8.9		0.1		3.0	1.8				0.1	13.9
Germany (F.R.)				8.4	2.4	0.2	0.2			0.9	0.1	0.2	0.4	12.8
France				1.7	2.0	0.2	0.1					0.3	0.1	4.4
Italy				4.4	0.6	0.1		0.1					0.4	5.4
U.K.												0.1	0.7	0.9
USSR					5.6						2.9	1.9	0.2	10.5
Other[d]				0.5		0.9	0.5		0.2	0.2	0.8	2.3	1.7	7.1
Total	16.6	2.9	1.5	24.1	22.1	6.5	6.8	3.1	2.0	2.0	3.9	4.8	3.7	100.0[e]

Note: Detail may not add to totals owing to rounding.
Source: UNCTAD, Consideration of International Measures on Bauxite; Metallgesellschaft A.G., Metal Statistics.

[a]Ore types are roughly separated according to predominant mineral form in each geographic region. Calcined bauxite used for abrasives and refractories is excluded wherever possible.

[b]Percentages based on dry equivalent weight of ores are not strictly comparable in Al_2O_3.

[c]Includes Virgin Islands.

[d]Includes discrepancies between exports and imports.

[e]Equates to total exports of 33,000,000 metric tons.

Table 3-6. Estimated Distribution of World Trade in Alumina, 1974[a]

(percent of total trade)

Exp. / Imp.	Australia	Jamaica	Surinam	U.S.	Hungary	Guinea	Guyana	France	Italy	Germany (F.R.)	Other	Total
U.S.	18.3	7.5	3.9				0.1	0.1			0.3	30.2
Norway	0.7	5.4	2.7	0.1		0.8	0.3				1.5	11.5
USSR		1.3		0.8	3.0		0.7		0.5		1.8	8.1
Canada	3.5	1.5	0.1	1.9			0.2			0.9		8.1
Japan	5.8			0.1								5.9
U.K.	0.5	4.1	0.2	0.1			0.5				0.1	5.5
Neth.			1.8					1.7		0.3	0.7	4.5
Germany (F.R.)	1.3	0.2	1.3			0.4			1.3		0.1	4.6
Spain		0.7				1.5		0.6			0.9	3.7
Other	2.2	3.0		2.5	2.3	2.4	0.8	0.1	0.4	0.9	3.3	17.9
Total	32.3	23.7	10.0	5.5	5.3	5.1	2.6	2.5	2.2	2.1	8.7	[b]100.00

Source: U.K. Institute of Geological Sciences, World Mineral Statistics; Metallgesellschaft A.G., Metal Statistics.

[a]Alumina hydrate excluded wherever possible.

[b]Equates to total imports of 10,897,600 metric tons.

Table 3-7. Estimated Distribution of World Trade in Aluminum and Aluminum Alloys, 1976[a]
(percent of total trade)

Exp. \ Imp.	Norway	Canada	Neth.	Germany (F.R.)	U.K.	France	Ghana	U.S.	Bahrain	New Zealand	Other	Total
U.S.	0.4	10.4			0.3	0.3	2.2		0.1		1.7	15.4
Japan	0.2	0.3			0.2		0.2	0.6	2.2	3.1	6.0	12.8
Germany (F.R.)	4.9		2.4		0.6	0.7	0.1				3.1	11.8
Belgium	1.3		3.2	1.2	0.6	1.0					0.4	7.7
France	0.6		2.1	1.9	0.1			0.2			2.4	7.3
Italy	0.9		0.3	2.1	0.1	1.0	0.6				2.5	6.9
U.K.	3.4	0.5	0.3	0.2		0.1					1.5	6.6
Neth.	1.5	0.1		1.1	2.0	0.1	0.2		0.2		0.6	5.8
China (P.R.)	0.5	0.7		0.6	0.1			1.1	0.6		0.3	3.9
Brazil	0.3	0.4		0.7	0.1	0.2		0.1			0.4	2.2
Other	2.5	2.5	0.2	0.5	0.6	1.0	1.0	2.0	0.6	0.1	8.6	19.6
Total	16.5	14.9	8.5	8.3	4.7	4.4	4.3	4.0	3.7	3.2	27.5	[b]100.00

Source: World Bureau of Metal Statistics.

[a]Includes secondary metal.

[b]Equates to total exports of 3,409,500 metric tons.

Table 3-8. Estimated Distribution of World Trade in Aluminum (and Aluminum Alloy) Scrap, 1975

(percent of total trade)

Exporters \ Importers	U.S.	Canada	Neth.	Germany (F.R.)	France	Austria	Belgium	U.K.	Other	Total
Germany (F.R.)	4.4	0.6	5.9		1.8	2.6	1.6	2.4	5.8	25.2
Italy	0.7	0.2	0.8	2.6	2.6	2.2		0.1	5.2	14.5
U.S.		7.9		1.6				0.6	3.3	13.5
Japan	5.3	1.0							1.7	7.9
France	0.2	0.1	0.7	2.2			1.9	0.4	1.5	6.8
Neth.	0.5	0.1		3.9	0.5		0.4	0.6	0.7	6.7
Belgium	0.5		1.7	0.4	0.8	0.1		0.2	0.3	4.0
Austria									3.8	3.8
U.K.	0.1		0.1	0.3			0.1		3.2	3.7
Other	4.9	1.7			0.4	3.1	0.9	0.5	2.7	14.1
Total	16.5	11.5	9.2	11.1	6.1	8.0	4.9	4.5	28.2	[a]100.00

Source: UN, Commodity Trade Statistics (Statistical Papers, Series D).

[a]Equates to total imports of 368,200 metric tons.

much of it consisting of secondary metal. As with bauxite and alumina, a large proportion of this movement is explained by intracompany relationships.

Movements of aluminum scrap (table 3-8) reflect in large measure the relative maturity of aluminum use in the various countries. There is a great deal of cross and triangular trade. The United States, for example, is the world's largest exporter of aluminum scrap, but the single largest trade flow, in 1975, was comprised of U.S. imports from Canada. Germany is the single largest importer, but in 1975 its exports were half as large as its imports. Italy is another large importer, depending upon flows from Germany, France, and Austria. Other significant aluminum scrap flows in 1975 were from the Netherlands to Germany and from the United States to Japan. Some of these flows—particularly over the U.S.-Canadian border and within the countries of Western Europe—probably reflect local transportation advantages or the availability of scrap processing facilities.

Copper

Trade patterns in copper ore (table 3-9) are very much subject to current price circumstances and to the sporadic emergence of large new mining projects. Papua New Guinea, for example, was not a factor until just a few years ago, yet in 1976 accounted for 15 percent of the international ore movement; Panama, not now a factor, may be an important ore supplier in the future. Much depends upon national and company decisions with regard to domestic processing. Peru, for example, is an important and growing ore producer, but ships its copper in the blister and refined forms. Chile smelts most of its ore but also ships a substantial portion as ore and concentrate. The USSR is a leading producer, but does not trade with the free-market world.

Not only has the considerable intervention of host governments into copper decision-making in recent decades influenced the extent of ore processing before export, it has, even more fundamentally, influenced the international distribution of investment in copper mining and hence availability of ore for any purpose. Additionally, though the importance of open-pit mining in copper production renders its output relatively sensitive even to shorter-term price changes, production-curtailment responses are more likely in countries (such as Canada, the Philippines, Australia) where companies are under private control than in those (such as Zaire, Chile) where national control is paramount and the need to maintain employment and foreign exchange earnings may ensure a continuation of production and exports, even at a current loss. The data for 1976 (table 3-9) are presumably affected by such slack-year influences.

Table 3-10 shows 1976 trade patterns in smelted, but unrefined, copper (essentially blister). What leaps to view is the preeminent position of Zaire, which smelts most of its copper, maintaining the old link with Belgium for refining. By contrast, Chile, which, because of company ties, might once have sent most of its smelted copper to the United States, now ships it principally to Germany. Trade patterns for Peru and Zambia also seem to have been changed by nationalization. In general, although blister copper is the least important form in which copper moves in international trade (both ores/concentrates and refined copper are more important), it still accounts for about a sixth of the total movement.

Over half the total movement of copper in 1976 international trade was in the refined form (table 3-11). Zambia and Chile, in 1976, were well in the fore as exporters. Imports were more widely distributed, with Germany, the United Kingdom, and the United States all participating significantly. The two most notable flows were from Zambia to the United States and from Zambia to Japan—the Zambia-U.S. connection presumably being a holdover from the days when U.S. firms had an important interest in the now-nationalized Zambian (Northern Rhodesian) mines.

A rather significant amount of copper moves in international trade as scrap (table 3-12). This is exchanged almost exclusively among the more industrialized countries, which have the capacity both to generate it and to use it. The United States tends to be a principal exporter, and in 1976 accounted for a third of the total international supply. Germany, with more than a fifth of the purchases, was the most important single importer. The most important single flow, however, was from the United States to Japan, whose "bidding away" of U.S. metallic scrap in general has sometimes been the subject of complaint by domestic users.

Table 3-9. Estimated Distribution of World Trade in Copper Ores and Concentrates, 1976 (percent of total trade, metal content)[a]

Exp. \ Imp.	Canada	Philip-pines	Papua N.G.	Chile	Indonesia	Aus-tralia	Zaire	Norway	South Africa[b]	Other	Total
Japan	16.6	16.7	7.3	4.8	3.7	3.6	3.0			2.8	58.5
Germany (F.R.)	0.3		7.1	1.9	1.9			1.7	1.3	0.5	14.7
U.S.	3.2	1.2	0.1			0.2			0.3	1.4	6.4
Spain				2.1					0.3	1.6	4.0
Sweden	0.3	0.2						0.4		0.3	1.2
Belgium				0.4						0.8	1.2
USSR	1.0									0.2	1.2
Bulgaria				0.8						0.3	1.1
Other	1.5	1.5	0.4	3.0		0.3		0.1		4.9	11.7
Total	22.9	19.6	14.9	13.0	5.6	4.1	3.0	2.2	1.9	12.8	[c]100.00

Source: World Bureau of Metal Statistics.

[a]Reported Cu content used wherever possible. For other countries Cu content was estimated from gross weights.

[b]Including Namibia (S.W. Africa).

[c]Equates to total exports of 1,204,000 metric tons.

Table 3-10. Estimated Distribution of World Trade in Unrefined Copper, 1976[a]

(percent of total trade)

Exporters / Importers	Zaire	Chile	South Africa[b]	Peru	Germany (F.R.)	Zambia	Other	Total
Belgium	36.8	0.6	2.6	0.2	1.8		1.6	43.6
Germany (F.R.)		10.1	7.7	0.3			1.3	19.4
U.K.		3.6	0.7	0.8	2.8	0.2	0.6	8.7
U.S.		4.3	0.3	0.5		0.1	0.3	5.5
China (P.R.)		2.8		1.9				4.7
Japan		1.1	0.5	1.1		0.2	1.3	4.2
Yugoslavia		0.8				1.9	0.4	3.1
Spain		2.2		0.1			0.4	2.7
Other	1.4	2.5	1.0	0.6	0.1	0.4	2.2	8.1
Total	38.2	28.0	12.8	5.5	4.7	2.6	8.2	[c]100.00

Source: World Bureau of Metal Statistics.

[a]Includes secondary blister copper.

[b]Includes Namibia (S.W. Africa).

[c]Equates to total exports of 825,000 metric tons.

231

Table 3-11. Estimated Distribution of World Trade in Refined Unwrought Copper, 1976 (percent of total trade)

Exp. / Imp.	Zambia	Chile	Canada	Belgium	Peru	U.S.	Australia	Zaire	Germany (F.R.)	Yugoslavia	Other	Total
Germany (F.R.)	2.8	3.0	1.3	1.9	0.1	0.8	0.5				4.1	14.5
U.K.	3.4	2.0	3.1	0.5	1.0	0.6	0.6		0.1		1.9	13.2
U.S.	4.4	2.2	3.0		0.8		0.1	0.1		1.5		12.1
France	1.8	2.0	0.8	3.3		0.7	0.4	0.3	0.3		1.3	10.9
Italy	2.6	2.5	0.5	1.4	0.2	0.5	0.1	1.0	0.4	0.2	0.8	10.2
Japan	4.3	1.1	0.4		0.2	0.2	0.2	0.6			0.2	7.2
Brazil		5.0	0.1		0.1	0.1					0.1	5.4
Belgium	0.6	0.4	0.5		0.7		0.4	0.3	0.2		0.6	3.7
Sweden	0.6	0.4	0.4	0.4		0.2	0.2				0.3	2.5
Neth.		0.2	0.1	0.7	0.2	0.2	0.1		0.2		0.5	2.2
Other	4.4	2.0	0.6	2.5	1.1	0.3	0.1	0.3	1.1	0.1	5.6	18.1
Total	24.9	20.8	11.0	10.7	4.3	3.6	2.7	2.6	2.3	1.8	15.3	[a]100.00

Source: World Bureau of Metal Statistics.

[a]Equates to total exports of 2,781,700 metric tons.

Table 3-12. Estimated Distribution of World Trade in Copper and (Copper Alloy) Scrap, 1975 (percent of total trade)

Exp. \ Imp.	U.S.	France	U.K.	Canada	Germany (F.R.)	Neth.	Belgium	Denmark	Switzer-land	Other	Total
Germany (F.R.)	3.7	4.2	4.1	0.5		3.0	0.6	1.6	0.8	3.6	22.1
Belgium	2.9	5.3	1.7	0.3	1.2	2.3				0.8	14.5
Italy	3.9	2.8	2.3	0.5	2.6	0.6	0.2		0.2	0.7	13.8
Japan	7.0			0.5						2.1	9.6
Korea	5.3			0.5						0.3	6.1
U.S.		0.1		2.8						1.7	4.6
Canada	3.8									0.2	4.0
Spain	2.1	0.5		0.6	0.1		0.1		0.1	0.5	4.0
France	0.6		0.3		0.5	0.3	0.6		0.1	1.1	3.5
Other	3.0	0.9	.3	1.8	2.6		0.5	0.3	0.5	7.9	17.8
Total	32.3	13.8	8.7	7.5	7.0	6.2	2.0	1.9	1.7	18.9	[a]100.00

Source: U.N., Commodity Trade Statistics (Statistical Papers, Series D).

[a]Equates to total imports of 404,460 metric tons.

Other significant importers of copper scrap in 1976 were Belgium and
Italy, both of whom depended upon sources (notably France) elsewhere in
Western Europe.

Lead

Lead is one of the most widely available minerals around the world,
but nevertheless is widely traded. (See tables 3-13 and 3-14.) Australia
is by far the world's largest exporter, its shipments of lead bullion to
the United Kingdom constituting the bulk of the limited international
movement of this intermediate form (between ore and refined metal.) The
more important international movements are of ores and of refined lead.
Canada is the predominant overall supplier, shipping somewhat more ore
than metal; Peru, another important supplier, has the same pattern. Australia's shipments of refined lead (it ships relatively little ore) are
almost equivalent to Peru's ore and metal combined.

Apart from the United Kingdom, the world's leading importers are the
United States, Italy, Japan, and Germany. The first two import mostly
refined metal, the latter two mostly ore. The United States relies for
its ore mostly on Canada and Honduras and for its metal on Canada and
Mexico. Italy taps a variety of sources, including principally Germany
for its refined lead; Germany, in turn, relies significantly on lead ore
from Sweden. Belgium is another important importer of ore for export as
metal. Much the largest single movement of ore is from Canada to Japan;
there is no really salient movement of refined lead. An important triangular trade in lead takes place via the United Kingdom.

All five leading importers also have significant domestic supplies;
in the case of the United Kingdom, however, those supplies are essentially
scrap lead rather than ore. Great Britain is in fact an important exporter
of lead scrap (table 3-15), second in this respect only to the United
States. More than a sixth of the international scrap trade in 1975 was
the return of used lead, from the United States to Canada.

Table 3- 13. Estimated Distribution of World Trade in Lead Ores and Concentrates, 1976 (percent of total trade, metal content)[a]

Exp.\Imp.	Canada	Peru	U.S.	Morocco	Sweden	Irish Rep.	Iran	Australia	Greenland	Greece	Honduras	Other	Total
Japan	11.6	3.5	1.7					0.9				1.8	19.5
Germany (F.R.)	1.5	1.0	1.8	1.3	4.7	1.0						2.9	14.2
Belgium	2.4	4.9				1.8	0.2	1.1		1.0		2.0	13.4
U.S.	4.3	1.3						1.7	1.1		3.1	0.3	11.8
France			0.6	1.3	0.4	1.2		0.2				0.1	6.5
USSR							4.6		2.7			1.5	6.1
Tunisia				2.1	0.2								2.3
Greece				0.3				0.5	0.3			1.0	2.1
Italy		0.3				0.3				0.9		0.5	2.0
Brazil	1.7												1.7
Other	0.3	4.2	3.6	0.9	0.1	0.7	0.2	0.5		1.9		8.0	20.4
Total	21.8	15.2	7.7	5.9	5.4	5.0	5.0	4.9	4.1	3.8	3.1	18.1	[b]100.00

Source: World Bureau of Metal Statistics.

[a]Reported lead content used wherever possible. Content for other countries estimated from gross weights.

[b]Equates to total exports of 645,900 metric tons.

Table 3-14. Estimated Distribution of World Trade in Refined Lead, 1976[a]

(percent of total trade)

Exporters / Importers	Australia	Canada	Mexico	Peru	Belgium	U.K.	Germany (F.R.)	Yugoslavia	Morocco	Tunisia	Other	Total
Italy	2.7	0.7	2.1	2.2	0.4		3.1	0.4	1.1	0.8	3.1	16.6
U.S.	0.5	4.7	4.9	2.2				2.2	0.3			14.8
U.K.	4.5	4.5			0.1							9.1
Netherlands	0.2	0.6	0.2		2.2	1.9					0.3	5.4
India	4.4	0.6	0.1					0.1			0.1	5.2
France		0.1			1.9	0.8	0.9		0.4		0.3	4.5
Japan		0.3	1.4	0.9		1.3					1.5	4.1
Germany (F.R.)		0.1			1.4				0.1		1.0	3.8
USSR			0.9	0.4	1.1		0.9				0.4	3.7
China	0.6	1.0		1.6								3.2
Egypt	1.0							0.1			1.5	2.6
Other	5.3	1.3	0.8	0.8	1.0	3.4	1.4	2.6	1.3	1.6	7.9	27.0
Total	19.2	13.9	10.4	8.1	8.1	7.4	6.3	5.4	3.2	2.4	15.6	[b]100.00

Note: Detail may not add to totals owing to rounding.

Source: World Bureau of Metal Statistics.

[a]Except remelted lead.

[b]Equates to total exports of 823,000 metric tons.

Table 3-15. Estimated Distribution of World Trade in Lead (and Lead Alloy) Scrap, 1975

(percent of total trade)

Exporters / Importers	U.S.	U.K.	Germany (F.R.)	Canada	Nether-lands	Belgium	Switzer-land	France	Other	Total
Canada	17.5									17.5
Netherlands	3.5	2.2	5.1			0.4		0.2	2.4	14.0
Italy		4.0	3.4	0.3	0.5		1.9	2.9	0.3	13.4
France		1.3	1.9		2.9	2.9	0.4		0.5	9.1
Belgium	1.1	0.4	3.0		3.0			0.3	1.1	9.0
Germany (F.R.)	0.4	2.7			1.4	0.7		0.4	1.9	7.4
Denmark	0.7	0.8	0.2		0.2				2.5	4.4
Other	8.2	2.0		8.3	0.5	1.5	1.7		2.9	25.0
Total	32.9	12.2	13.6	8.6	8.4	4.8	4.0	3.9	11.5	[a]100.00

Note: Detail may not add to totals owing to rounding.

Source: United Nations, Commodity Trade Statistics (Statistical Papers, Series D); Metallgesellschaft A.G., Metal Statistics.

[a]Equates to 137,800 metric tons.

237

Zinc

The United States is the world's principal zinc importer (tables 3-16 and 3-17), followed by Japan and Germany. However, while the great bulk of the movement into the United States is in the form of slab (refined) zinc,[13] about 95 percent of Japan's imports and about 70 percent of Germany's, are of zinc in ore. Canada is the principal source of foreign supply of zinc metal and concentrate for the United States, and is the world's largest (one fifth the total in 1976) slab zinc exporter. Japan and Germany get their ores from a variety of sources, although the latter depends heavily on Canada (the world's largest exporter of ores as well as metal), while Japan depends in significant measure on Peru (second largest ore exporter) and Australia (third largest), as well as on Canada. Since Peru exports comparatively little slab zinc, while Australia's offerings are tipped slightly to the refined metal side, the latter is the second largest world exporter overall, but still less than half the world trade factor that Canada is. After Canada, the USSR is the world's largest zinc producer, but does not engage in trade with the West.

The single largest movement of ore appears to be from Canada to Belgium, for conversion into slab zinc and reexport. (Belgium has no mine production.) Other important ore movements are those into Japan, noted above. The salient flow of slab zinc is from Canada to the United States. A number of Canadian mines are controlled by U.S. companies, one of which is in turn controlled by a Canadian government corporation. Zinc scrap does move to some extent in international trade, but it is a relatively small part of total zinc consumption (see chapter 1), and its movement is therefore not tabulated.

---

[13]Refined is used in this report in the broad sense of metal brought to its final commercial point of purification. In the case of zinc, "refined" is sometimes used in the trade to denote only metal brought to a point of particularly high purity.

Table 3-16. Estimated Distribution of World Trade in Zinc Ores and Concentrates, 1976
(percent of total trade, metal content)[a]

Exp. / Imp.	Canada	Peru	Aus-tralia	Sweden	Green-land	Mexico	Iran	Irish Rep.	South Africa	Boli-via	Other	Total
Japan	5.0	8.2	5.3			0.1	0.5			0.5	2.6	22.2
Belgium	11.5	0.2	1.4	1.1	0.3	1.9	0.1	0.7	0.1		3.1	20.4
Germany (F.R.)	5.2	0.5	0.2	1.7	0.7	0.9		0.9	2.2	0.1	1.8	14.2
France		2.6		0.2	0.9			0.7		0.4	3.5	8.3
Neth.	0.8	0.8	3.3	0.2	0.2			0.2			0.5	5.8
Italy	1.6	1.4			0.1						1.4	4.5
U.S.	2.2		0.1			0.8					0.9	4.0
Finland		1.3		0.5	1.5	0.2						3.5
Other	3.5	3.1	0.8	2.3	0.3		2.4	0.4		1.2	3.1	17.1
Total	29.8	18.1	11.1	5.8	4.0	3.9	3.0	2.5	2.3	2.2	16.9	100.0

Source: World Bureau of Metal Statistics.

[a]Includes re-exports. Reported Zn content used wherever possible. For other countries Zn content was estimated from gross weights.

[b]Includes Namibia (SW Africa).

[c]Equates to total exports of 2,149,800 metric tons.

Table 3-17. Estimated Distribution of World Trade in Slab Zinc, 1976

(percent of total trade)

Exporters / Importers	Canada	Belgium	Australia	Mexico	Netherlands	Finland	Germany (F.R.)	Japan	Zaire	Other	Total
U.S.	15.9	1.3	1.7	3.0	0.4	1.2	2.6	0.5	1.7	6.3	34.6
U.K.	2.4	0.5	0.3	0.6	3.9	1.9	0.4			1.4	11.4
Germany (F.R.)	0.1	4.1	0.1	0.3	0.9	0.1			0.1	1.6	7.4
France		2.1	0.1		0.6	0.1	0.2			0.8	3.9
Netherlands		0.3	0.1	0.1		0.3	0.8			1.4	3.0
Brazil				1.9						1.1	3.0
India	0.2		0.8					0.3	0.7	0.9	2.9
Italy		0.8		0.1		0.2	0.4		0.1	1.1	2.7
Sweden		0.1			0.1	0.9				1.3	2.4
Other	1.7	1.7	5.8	1.3	1.2	1.6	1.1	3.6	1.2	14.0	28.7
Total	20.3	10.9	8.9	7.3	7.1	6.3	5.5	4.4	3.8	25.5	[a]100.0

Source: World Bureau of Metal Statistics

[a]Equates to total exports of 1,723,300 metric tons.

Chapter 4

SOURCES OF U.S. SUPPLY

Introduction

The historical record of sources of U.S. supply is pertinent to a
determination of the future impact of world consumption and supply on
prices and supply in the United States. This record is provided in a set
of tables listing the total amounts of each commodity available in each
year, along with percentage distributions of the origins of the supply
and its disposition. On the supply side, the sum of domestic production,
gross imports, and stock drawdowns is equated to 100 percent; on the
disposition side, apparent consumption, exports, and stock increases sum
to 100 percent. Principal geographical sources of imports are listed
separately, as components of the import total.

The quantities indicated as "apparent consumption" in these tables
are generally the same as those listed in the world consumption tables
in chapter 1; where they are not strictly comparable, the differences
are pointed out at the appropriate juncture.[1] After a discussion of the
individual commodity forms there is an overall summary of U.S. supply
sources.

The distributions of supply sources are particularly important with
respect to short-run contingencies, since they bear heavily on the relative
dependability of portions of U.S. supply as well as effects transmitted

---

[1]Generally, the scrap data presented in this chapter are in gross
weight, whereas the world apparent consumption data are in content weight.
Also, there may be slight differences among figures due to rounding differences in conversion from one to another measure of quantity (for example, short to metric tons).

to those countries which import significant supplies from the United States. The distributions also have a particular bearing on the relative extent to which the United States is likely to be affected by foreign price developments and initiatives.

Cobalt

The most striking aspect of table 4-1 is the extreme dependence of U.S. consumers on foreign supplies of cobalt metal. Since the end of 1971, when domestic production of cobalt-bearing pyrite concentrates was discontinued, there has been no domestic mining of cobalt; nor is large-scale mining likely in the future, owing to the availability of only low-grade cobalt-bearing ore in the United States.[2] Domestic production of cobalt metal did begin again in 1975 with the opening of a cobalt refinery in Louisiana supplied with nickel-cobalt and copper-cobalt matte from Botswana, New Caledonia, and South Africa. A substantial amount of this refined metal, however, is apparently being exported to foreign purchasers and is not necessarily available for domestic consumption.

Imports, which for all but three years have accounted for over 60 percent of total metal supply, have come primarily from Zaire and Belgium, the latter of which, in turn, obtains its cobalt from Zairian mines. Consequently, over 50 percent of total U.S. supply during the past eighteen years has been of Zairian origin. This may actually be an understatement, since releases from government stockpiles have contained undetermined quantities of cobalt originally imported from Zaire.

Releases from government stocks played a very important role in the total supply picture during the late 1960s and early to middle 1970s. Stockpile sales of approximately 65 million pounds of cobalt (17 percent of total supply) during this period ended in 1977 with the introduction of new, higher stockpile goals; and apparently domestic consumers are

---

[2]However, there is the distinct possibility that some cobalt mining will be resumed as a result of the escalation in price, e.g., in the Blackbird district of Idaho, and from domestic laterites occurring principally in Southwestern Oregon and northern California.

Table 4-1. Sources and Disposition of U.S. Supply of Cobalt Metal[a]

(percentages, except for total supply)

| Year | Sources | | | | | Stock drawdowns | | Total supply (1,000 pounds) | Disposition | | |
| | Domestic production | Imports | | | | | | | Apparent consumption | Stock increases | |
		All sources	Zaire	Belgium	Zambia	Consumer	Government			Consumer	Government
1960	14.0	86.0	37.7	26.1	2.7	–	–	12,559	75.5	3.6	20.8
1961	9.9	88.4	42.9	15.9	1.7	0.4	1.3	11,355	100.0	–	–
1962	5.5	90.9	38.6	15.2	5.6	2.5	1.1	13,000	100.0	–	–
1963	9.0	86.1	40.4	11.8	–	3.2	1.7	11,985	100.0	–	–
1964	8.9	85.8	39.7	13.2	–	–	5.3	13,207	97.6	2.4	–
1965	7.4	92.6	36.0	24.6	–	–	–	16,034	98.9	1.1	–
1966	6.1	90.0	48.9	21.5	–	–	3.8	19,849	98.0	2.0	–
1967	7.6	52.0	20.9	12.0	–	–	40.3	15,277	96.9	3.1	–
1968	7.5	58.7	16.9	21.7	–	2.1	31.7	15,718	100.0	–	–
1969	2.8	64.9	31.4	16.4	–	–	32.4	18,560	99.7	0.3	–
1970	1.8	67.2	39.2	16.5	–	1.7	29.2	17,661	100.0	–	–
1971	1.8	60.7	24.3	17.0	–	2.8	34.7	17,113	100.0	–	–
1972	0	69.1	26.8	17.7	5.7	1.2	29.8	18,945	100.0	–	–
1973	0	68.2	41.6	15.6	–	–	31.8	26,928	95.3	4.7	–
1974	0	61.3	30.9	17.3	–	1.7	37.0	24,131	100.0	–	–
1975	0.5	47.9	17.6	10.7	–	1.7	49.9	12,713	100.0	–	–
1976	1.6	68.2	30.6	10.9	7.8	–	30.2	22,190	93.9	6.1	–
1977	2.9	96.2	44.1	20.0	11.1	–	0.9	16,977	96.7	3.3	–

Source: Derived from U.S. Bureau of Mines, Minerals Yearbook and unpublished data.

Note: Detail may not add to 100 percent, owing to rounding.

[a]Includes cobalt powder.

beginning to turn to Zambia and Finland (not shown in the table) as alternative sources. In short, the end of government stockpile sales has also
ended domestic consumers' protection against total current reliance on
imports.

Data on exports of cobalt metal are not available,[3] but such exports,
until recently, are believed to have been negligible. Thus, since consumer
stocks have not been subject to large fluctuations, roughly the amount
indicated as supply has usually been domestically consumed in the year
shown in the table. There are exceptions, however, since imports may
occasionally be held for extended periods as "producer" (dealer) stocks
for which systematic information is not available.

Chromium

Chromite

Only for the United States is it possible to account for refractory-
grade chromite separately from metallurgical-grade chromite; the latter
category includes both the old chemical-grade high-iron chromite (40 to
46 percent Cr_2O_3) and the old high-chromium, metallurgical-grade ore
(greater than 46 percent Cr_2O_3). The respective breakdowns of sources and
disposition of supplies are presented in tables 4-2 and 4-3.

Except for a small quantity of chromite mined and exported in 1976,
there has been no domestic production of this ore since 1961, when the
last Defense Production Act contract was phased out. Consequently, as
is the case with cobalt, U.S. consumers rely exclusively on imports,
supplemented by stock drawdowns, for their chromite supply.

U.S. imports of high-aluminum chromite come primarily from the
Philippines, while the bulk of remaining imports has come from South
Africa. As with cobalt, releases from government stockpiles, which have

---

[3]As of January 10, 1979, exporters are required by the Department
of Commerce to report exports of commodities containing 10 percent or
more of cobalt, but will still not have to differentiate cobalt and
cobalt alloys from unwrought waste and scrap. (American Metal Market,
January 4, 1979.)

Table 4-2. Sources and Disposition of U.S. Supply of Refractory-Grade Chromite[a]

(percentages, except for total column)

| | Sources | | | | | Total supply | Disposition | | |
| | Imports[a] | | | Stock drawdown[b] | | | Apparent | Stock increases | |
Year	All Sources	Philippines	South Africa	consumer	government	(1,000 short tons Cr$_2$O$_3$ content)	consumption	consumer	government
1960	96.9	74.1	13.0	3.1	—	162	100.0	—	—
1961	100.0	81.9	15.2	—	—	105	96.2	3.8	—
1962	100.0	80.1	19.2	—	—	125	88.0	12.0	—
1963	82.3	70.1	7.3	17.7	—	96	100.0	—	—
1964	61.4	56.7	4.7	38.6	—	127	"	—	—
1965	76.4	69.3	7.1	23.6	—	127	"	—	—
1966	100.0	91.8	5.7	—	—	122	82.8	17.2	—
1967	65.1	59.4	5.7	34.9	—	106	100.0	—	—
1968	49.2	42.3	6.9	50.8	—	130	"	—	—
1969	97.6	82.0	15.4	2.6	—	78	"	—	—
1970	70.8	69.7	1.1	29.2	—	89	"	—	—
1971	72.2	66.7	5.6	1.4	26.4	72	"	—	—
1972	57.3	52.0	—	38.7	4.0	75	"	—	—
1973	69.6	67.4	2.2	3.3	27.2	92	"	—	—
1974	63.2	60.9	0.8	—	36.8	133	95.5	4.5	—
1975	62.3	57.9	—	5.3	32.5	114	100.0	—	—
1976	52.3	35.6	6.0	4.7	43.0	149	"	—	—
1977	35.9	31.7	4.2	—	64.1	167	92.2	7.8	—

Source: U.S. Bureau of Mines, Minerals Yearbook.

Note: Detail may not add to 100 percent, owing to rounding.

[a]Comprises imports of ores containing less than 40 percent Cr$_2$O$_3$, although excludes such ores imported from Turkey, USSR, and Finland, which are imported primarily for chemical and metallurgical use.

[b]Content calculated by RFF.

245

Table 4-3. Sources and Disposition of U.S. Supply of Metallurgical-Grade Chromite[a]

(percentages, except for total column)

Year	Domestic production	Sources — Imports: All Sources	South Africa	Rhodesia	Turkey[b]	USSR[b]	Finland[b]	Stock drawdown: Consumer	Government	Total supply (1,000 short tons Cr$_2$O$_3$ content)	Disposition: Apparent consumption	Exports	Stock increases: Industry	Gov't
1960	8.4	84.2	40.6	29.1	11.7	0.8	–	7.4	–	488	91.2	0.4	–	8.4
1961	7.1	86.1	51.8	18.4	13.3	1.9	–	6.8	–	533	92.0	0.9	–	7.1
1962	–	100.0	52.8	22.7	17.6	3.5	–	–	–	489	68.3	0.7	2.7	28.8
1963	–	93.7	47.1	22.7	6.6	16.6	–	6.3	–	560	94.3	0.7	–	5.0
1964	–	87.7	28.6	24.8	7.5	23.3	–	12.3	–	644	90.2	0.5	–	0.3
1965	–	90.4	31.1	24.8	11.2	20.5	–	7.0	2.6	653	99.5	0.5	9.0	–
1966	–	100.0	49.2	12.1	11.8	21.6	–	–	–	719	89.7	1.3	–	–
1967	–	85.3	36.1	12.1	8.0	28.2	–	1.4	13.3	585	90.3	0.7	–	–
1968	–	79.3	32.4	–	13.9	32.6	–	9.7	10.9	561	98.9	0.7	–	–
1969	–	70.4	27.2	–	12.3	27.6	–	10.9	18.8	624	96.5	3.5	4.1	–
1970	–	84.1	26.5	–	17.0	36.1	–	–	15.9	684	93.1	2.8	20.5	–
1971	–	84.1	28.9	1.9	23.4	25.6	–	–	15.9	640	77.0	2.5	–	–
1972	–	79.1	20.0	7.5	9.2	39.3	–	7.1	13.7	575	98.4	1.6	–	–
1973	–	61.5	23.7	3.7	10.4	20.3	–	20.8	17.7	566	98.2	1.8	–	–
1974	–	67.9	26.0	5.5	9.6	25.6	–	2.9	29.2	585	98.6	1.4	–	–
1975	W[c]	76.9	21.1	9.6	11.8	27.6	0.6	–	23.1	635	62.5	9.6	27.9	–
1976	W[c]	89.3	33.0	2.0	17.7	15.9	12.7	–	10.7	560	84.1	9.8	6.1	–
1977	–	74.5	45.0	–	8.9	6.4	11.9	–	25.5	596	65.9	13.8	20.3	–

W – Witheld

Source: U.S. Bureau of Mines, Minerals Yearbook.

Note: Detail may not add to 100 percent owing to rounding.

[a] Includes chemical-grade chromite, 40 percent and greater Cr$_2$O$_3$ content.

[b] Includes all imports of chromite from these countries, since their reserves are not high-aluminum chromite (i.e., for refractory use), but rather high-chromium and high-iron chromite respectively, as identified by the U.S. Geological Survey, United States Mineral Resources (Professional Paper 820, 1973).

[c] Small amounts, the majority of which were exported.

ended due to increased stockpile goals, account for most of the remaining U.S. supply for years after 1970. Prior to 1971, stock drawdowns were from industry inventories. The current absence of government stock releases probably portends some substitution of other refractory materials, although the immediate shortfall has been made up by purchases from South Africa. There has been a sharp increase in refractory-grade chromite prices.

Similarly, the United States is very import-dependent for its metallurgical-grade chromite. Imports have in the past come consistently from South Africa, the USSR, Turkey, and, depending on the state of U.S. adherence to the UN embargo, Rhodesia. The actual and relative quantities from the USSR have been declining, in line with the recent Soviet policy of reducing all chromite exports, but there was a pickup in 1978. Finland has also become a main source of supply, since the argon-oxygen-decarburization (AOD) process[4] has rendered the Finnish high-iron ores suitable for the U.S. ferrochrome producer. There are indications that Finnish ores are being used to make up for the loss of Soviet and Turkish supplies.[5]

As with the refractory grade, government stock drawdown of metallurgical/chemical-grade chromite has been important to the supply picture in recent years. However, expanded stockpile goals will cut off this source. If one may judge by the increased exports and consumer stock buildups from 1975 to 1977, it is doubtful that such a discontinuance of government sales will have a negative effect on consumption. In fact, with the decrease in domestic ferrochromium production--a result of factors unrelated to chromite supply--an ore oversupply has been depressing the U.S. chromite market.[6]

---

[4]See the Introduction to this study.

[5]The grade of Soviet and Turkish ores has been declining over recent years, indicating perhaps depleting resources. Turkey also intends to increase ferrochrome production exports, thereby reducing chromite exports.

[6]American Metal Market, December 8, 1978.

Ferrochromium

Declining aggregate consumption of metallurgical-grade chromite is
primarily the result of decreased usage by the metallurgical industry.
This is in turn the result of the decreasing relative role of domestic
production in total ferrochromium supply. The latter decline has been
from approximately 80 to 85 percent of total supply in the 1960s to the
50 percent range or lower in the late 1970s. This trend is matched by
a comparable increase in ferrochrome imports, originating primarily in
South Africa, the largest possessor of chromite appropriate to the production of high-carbon ferrochromium usable in the argon-oxygen decarburization process. Rhodesia has also been a significant exporter of ferrochromium, reflecting the general desire and trend of ore-producing countries to upgrade their production before exportation.

The domestic ferrochrome industry may be given a boost by the imposition, for a three-year period, of an additional 4-cents-per-pound duty on
imported ferrochromium selling at port of origin for less than 38 cents
a pound.[7] U.S. ferrochromium producers have contended that they have been
at a competitive disadvantage in relation not only to ore producers, but
also to ferrochromium exporters who do not produce ores. However, there
has not been any sustained increase in imports of low-carbon ferrochromium,
which is the type characteristic of supplies received from the non-ore-
producing countries, in contrast with persistently much higher levels of
high-carbon ferrochromium, the type principally exported by the ore
producers.

Exports of ferrochromium have never been very large and, given the
domestic competitive position in relation to foreign producers, are unlikely to be so in the future. Approximately 70 percent of domestic ferrochromium consumption is for use in stainless steel production, with the

---

[7] The Union Carbide Corp. responded to the duty by increasing the
price of 50 to 55 percent "charge" chrome produced at its ferrochrome
plant in Tubatse, South Africa from 36.5 to 38 cents a pound, creating a
delivered price of 43 cents a pound f.o.b. East Liverpool, Ohio, 42 cents
a pound, Baltimore, Md. (American Metal Market, December 8, 1978.)

remainder used primarily in other steels (20 percent), cast irons (3 percent), and superalloys (3 percent).

Manganese

Manganese Ore

As with other ferroalloy ores, the United States is resource-poor in manganese. Since 1973, the only manganese mined here has been the so-called ferruginous ore, containing less than 35 percent manganese. Even in 1969, the peak year for U.S. production during the period covered by table 4-4, domestic mines provided less than 6 percent of total supply. Consequently, throughout the period, consumers have been heavily reliant on imports and on stock drawdowns. Since the mid-1960s, government sales have been significant, but unlike the situation with cobalt and chromite, these will probably continue, since physical inventories are greater than stated stockpile goals. Ultimately, however, the United States is nearly totally dependent on foreign sources for its manganese ore.

U.S. imports have historically followed general world patterns in manganese production and exportation. In the 1950s, when India was the primary world exporter of manganese, the United States obtained the majority of its ore from India. Then, with India's self-imposed restriction on exports, the U.S. consumer looked elsewhere. Similarly, Ghana and Zaire were main sources until their production began to fall. In recent years, two countries, Brazil and Gabon, have been the important manganese-ore suppliers; in any given year after 1960, combined imports from these two sources have accounted for 30 to 60 percent of total U.S. supply. While imports from Gabon began only in 1962, they have been a continually important source ever since. Those from Brazil have been important since the mid-1950s, but are declining as the result of increased ferromanganese production within Brazil itself.

Ninety-five percent of the manganese ore consumed in 1976 was used in iron and steel production, with the remainder consumed primarily by the chemical and dry-cell battery industries. Similar percentages describe domestic consumption in 1960.

Table 4-4. Sources and Disposition of U.S. Supply of Manganese Ore

(percentages, except for total supply)

| Year | Sources | | | | | | Total supply (1,000 short tons, Mn Content)[b] | Disposition | | | |
| | Domestic production[a] | Imports | | | Stock drawdown[b] | | | Apparent consumption[b] | Exports | Stock increases[b] | |
		Total	Gabon[c]	Brazil	Industry	Government				Industry	Government
1960	4.0	92.5	--	32.1	3.6	--	1313	70.8	*	--	29.1
1961	3.0	82.8	--	30.3	14.2	--	1191	71.5	.2	--	28.3
1962	3.2	79.4	.8	33.9	17.4	--	1173	71.4	.2	--	28.4
1963	4.9	92.4	10.1	38.4	2.6	--	1072	81.3	.1	--	18.7
1964	3.6	91.4	20.5	24.3	4.9	--	1072	87.5	*	--	12.5
1965	3.8	87.6	20.3	18.5	2.0	6.7	1381	99.9	.1	--	--
1966	3.7	91.1	18.8	24.2	--	5.2	1329	87.7	.2	12.3	--
1967	4.0	82.6	33.4	10.8	--	13.5	1181	97.6	.3	2.2	--
1968	3.6	79.8	24.0	23.3	6.1	10.5	1089	99.7	.3	--	--
1969	5.5	86.3	29.8	30.8	--	8.2	1149	99.5	.3	.2	--
1970	4.8	78.6	27.3	27.1	1.6	15.0	1078	99.7	.3	--	--
1971	2.5	86.4	30.1	30.9	--	11.1	1085	88.3	.7	11.0	--
1972	1.5	72.3	26.1	25.8	8.0	18.3	1293	99.8	.2	--	--
1973	2.4	67.8	18.4	28.0	11.1	18.7	1067	99.3	.5	--	--
1974	3.1	52.4	13.3	19.6	--	44.5	1132	84.7	2.6	12.7	--
1975	1.8	72.1	23.0	28.9	--	26.2	1063	87.5	2.2	10.3	--
1976	2.7	66.2	27.6	16.4	--	31.1	980	88.8	1.6	9.6	--
1977	2.2	40.1	21.6	9.9	26.1	31.5	1132	98.4	1.6	--	--

* --negligible

Source: U.S. Bureau of Mines, Minerals Yearbook and unpublished data.

Note: Detail may not add to 100 percent owing to rounding.

[a] Includes manganese in ores of 10 percent or greater manganese content.

[b] Manganese content estimated by RFF.

[c] Includes imports reported from Western Africa (all years), Congo (Brazzaville)/Zaire (1967-1976), and Angola (1970-1973), since they were known actually to be from Gabon.

Ferromanganese

Table 4-5 details sources and disposition of the U.S. ferromanganese supply from 1960 to 1977. The amounts therein are not totally consistent with those listed in table 1-8, since the latter quantities are in thousand metric tons gross weight, while these are reduced to thousand short tons of manganese content. The Bureau of Mines reports manganese content for both imports and production, while RFF has estimated the content of stocks and of exports. The derived quantities usually reflect the average manganese content of ferromanganese produced, as listed in the table titled "Ferromanganese and silicomanganese produced in the United States...," of the "Manganese" chapter of the Minerals Yearbook.

Domestic production of ferromanganese, as a percentage of total supply, has followed the same general trend as that of ferrochromium. During the 1960s, domestic production generally accounted for 75 to 85 percent of the U.S. ferromanganese supply, but subsequently, a large percentage of domestic production was replaced by imports. The reversal of positions of domestic and foreign production as sources of supply has been so complete that by 1976, ferromanganese imports were actually larger than domestic production.

The bulk of manganese in imported ferromanganese comes from South Africa and France. France has always been a main source of such imports while South Africa's relatively recent entrance into and dominance of the U.S. import market is apparently part of a concerted effort to increase exports to several industrialized countries. These imports from South Africa are an exception to the general proposition that U.S. imports of ferromanganese have tended to come from countries poor in manganese ore which import the ores for refining in order to export the refined metal (table 4-6). Even in recent years, with the increasing trend in ore-rich countries to upgrade their mineral resources before exportation, the proportion of U.S. ferromanganese imports from countries without domestic manganese resources is still above 50 percent.

Table 4- 5. Sources and Disposition of U.S. Supply of Ferromanganese[a]

(percentages, except for total supply)

| | Sources | | | | | | Total supply | Disposition | | | |
| | Domestic | All | Imports | | Stock drawdown[b] | | (1,000 short tons, | Apparent | | Stock increases[b] | |
Year	Production	Sources	South Africa	France	Industry	Government	Mn content)	consumption	Exports[b]	Industry	Government
1960	87.4	12.6	1.2	2.4	–	–	749	91.5	0.1	8.4	–
1961	76.8	23.2	3.0	4.2	–	–	738	99.6	–	0.4	–
1962	86.1	13.9	1.7	5.0	–	–	698	89.0	0.4	5.0	4.7
1963	78.0	15.3	2.0	4.4	6.7	–	744	98.4	0.1	–	1.5
1964	79.7	17.8	1.5	3.3	2.5	–	906	88.3	0.3	–	11.4
1965	81.8	18.2	2.5	4.9	–	–	1,092	91.3	.2	2.5	6.0
1966	75.7	19.8	2.1	4.8	4.5	–	984	99.9	0.1	–	–
1967	82.0	18.0	3.6	3.2	–	–	898	94.9	0.2	4.9	–
1968	80.4	18.8	3.9	4.8	0.8	–	853	86.5	0.4	–	13.1
1969	71.1	25.7	10.2	5.3	2.3	1.0	927	99.8	0.2	–	–
1970	74.3	25.7	10.7	8.8	–	–	882	96.8	0.5	0.3	–
1971	76.1	23.9	9.0	9.0	–	–	785	97.0	0.6	2.5	–
1972	69.6	30.4	13.4	8.6	11.5	–	901	90.6	0.6	8.8	–
1973	53.4	30.0	10.8	10.5	–	5.2	1,008	99.3	0.7	–	–
1974	38.5	29.7	9.1	15.0	–	31.8	1,101	94.6	0.5	4.9	–
1975	56.3	38.3	11.8	13.3	–	5.3	806	90.1	3.1	6.8	–
1976	42.6	46.5	15.2	10.4	10.2	0.7	896	99.3	0.7	–	–
1977	37.5	59.1	16.3	14.2	3.4	–	704	99.3	0.7	–	–

Source: U.S. Bureau of Mines, Minerals Yearbook and unpublished data.

Note: Detail may not add to 100 percent owing to rounding.

[a]Includes high-, low-, and medium-carbon ferromanganese.

[b]Manganese content estimated by RFF.

252

Table 4-6. U.S. Imports of Manganese in Ferromanganese from Ore-producing
and Ore-poor Countries, Respectively

(percentages, except for total column)

Year	From ore-producing countries	From ore-poor countries	Total imports (thousand tons)
1960	44	56	94
1965	39	61	199
1970	63	47	227
1975	35	65	309
1976	37	63	417
1977	42	58	416

Source: U.S. Bureau of Mines, Minerals Yearbook.

The United States exports very little of its total ferromanganese
supply, but, rather, consumes the bulk for its own steel production. In
1976, 97 percent of all ferromanganese consumed went into the steel
industry, with the remaining 3 percent distributed between consumption
in cast irons, superalloys, nonsteel alloys, and various unspecified
industries.

Aluminum

Bauxite

Tables 4-7 and 4-8 present details on the U.S. supply of gibbsitic
and mixed bauxite, respectively. As with refractory and metallurgical
chromite, it is necessary to combine the two types in order to match the
total U.S. apparent consumption listed in table 1-10. Additionally, the

quantities listed in tables 4-7 and 4-8 represent total ore, on a dry-equivalent basis,[8] while those in 1-10 are in terms of estimated aluminum content. Disaggregated stock data are available only for government inventories and not for industry changes.

U.S. gibbsitic bauxite production has remained rather stable since 1965, mine production in 1977 being only 5 percent greater than that in 1965. Thus its relative contribution to total domestic supply has declined approximately 8 percentage points over the same period.

Regarding imports, the most noticeable trends have been the shifts in supply importance of Surinam and Guinea. Prior to 1968, the United States did not import bauxite from Guinea, whereas by 1977 such imports accounted for over 40 percent of the total U.S. supply. This dramatic increase roughly parallels the Guinea mine production increase from about 2,000 long tons in 1968 to over 11,000 tons in 1977. Surinam, on the other hand, has declined in relative importance for U.S. bauxite supplies, by over 30 percentage points in the past twelve years. Apparently this import decrease is the result of Surinam's reduction in mine output, its increased emphasis on domestic upgrading rather than bauxite exportation, and perhaps of consumers' preference for alternative bauxite sources, since Surinam ores cost more than other gibbsitic imports.

In the early 1970s, government stockpile sales also contributed large quantities to supply. However, even though current government inventories are equivalent to over one year's apparent domestic consumption and the current stockpile goal for Surinam-type bauxite rests at zero, future sales are likely to be constricted, since large quantities of the bauxite excess are used to offset a corresponding shortfall from the alumina stockpile goal.

The United States is totally dependent on imports for its mixed bauxite supply, with sources varying little over the preceding twenty-three years. Jamaica accounts for over 80 percent of imports, while Haiti and the Dominican Republic make up the difference. Stock variations have not been important during this period.

---

[8]See footnote 15 in chapter 6 for a brief discussion of the discrepancy between official import data and the quantities listed herein.

Table 4-7. Sources and Disposition of U.S. Supply of Gibbsitic Bauxite

(percentages, except for total supply)

Year	Sources						Total (1,000 long tons, dry equivalent)	Disposition	
	Domestic production	Imports[a]				Stock drawdown[b]		Apparent consumption	Exports[c]
		All sources	Surinam	Guinea	Guyana				
1965	31.3	68.7	58.2	--	1.7	--	5,085	97.1	2.9
1966	30.4	69.6	62.0	--	5.8	--	5,646	98.9	1.1
1967	28.0	72.0	54.8	--	6.8	--	5,601	99.9	neg.
1968	27.1	72.9	49.1	6.7	6.7	--	5,831	99.9	0.1
1969	29.1	70.9	46.7	7.2	5.5	--	6,031	99.9	0.1
1970	29.4	70.6	46.0	8.0	5.0	--	6,357	99.9	neg.
1971	26.5	62.2	42.7	0.7	4.0	11.3	6,728	99.5	0.5
1972	27.1	63.2	42.0	1.1	11.7	9.7	6,037	99.5	0.5
1973	26.5	66.8	41.7	2.0	14.9	6.7	6,362	99.8	0.2
1974	23.5	73.7	39.4	22.7	10.2	2.8	7,371	99.8	0.2
1975	23.7	74.9	28.6	40.0	4.5	1.3	6,499	99.7	0.3
1976	24.1	75.9	22.3	43.6	9.2	--	6,916	99.8	0.2
1977	23.4	73.6	26.0	41.5	4.9	3.0	7,177	99.6	0.4

Source: U.S. Bureau of Mines, Minerals Yearbook and unpublished data.

Note: Detail may not add to 100 percent, owing to rounding.

[a]Includes imports to the Virgin Islands, for all years after 1966.

[b]Includes government stock drawdowns only.

[c]Assumes that all exports are of gibbsitic bauxite.

Table 4-8. Sources and Disposition of U.S. Supply of Mixed Bauxite

(percentages, except for total column)

Year	Sources Imports			Total (1,000 long tons, dry equivalent)	Disposition	
	Jamaica	Haiti	Dominican Republic		Apparent consumption	Stock increase[a]
1965	83.3	4.8	11.9	7,926	93.5	6.5
1966	85.3	4.5	10.2	7,812	100.0	—
1967	83.6	4.3	12.0	8,331	..	—
1968	82.2	5.6	12.2	7,771	..	—
1969	80.0	7.4	12.5	8,910	..	—
1970	81.2	6.9	12.0	9,243	..	—
1971	81.5	6.7	11.8	9,305	..	—
1972	81.2	6.8	11.9	8,567	..	—
1973	80.2	7.7	12.1	9,070	..	—
1974	81.4	6.1	12.5	9,542	..	—
1975	81.4	7.5	11.2	6,633	..	—
1976	84.7	8.3	7.0	7,300	..	—
1977	83.3	7.7	[b]9.0	7,508	..	—

Source: U.S. Bureau of Mines, Minerals Yearbook and unpublished data.

Note: Detail may not add to 100 percent owing to rounding.

[a]Includes government stock increases only.

[b]RFF estimate.

It may be significant that while gibbsitic supplies have grown, albeit slowly, mixed bauxite supplies have no clear trend, despite a 1977 total which was lower by 21 percent than its 1975 high. All refineries which use mixed bauxite as feedstock are located in the continental United States. Those which consume gibbsitic bauxite include one in the Virgin Islands, where import and energy costs are lower than at continental ports and refineries.

Alumina

The obvious trend to be seen in table 4-9 is the decline of domestic alumina, as a proportion of total supply, by more than 35 percentage points from 1965 to 1977. This relative supply shift toward imports is explained, not only by the increasing cost of domestic alumina production, but by the phenomenal growth of domestic aluminum production and the consequent increase in alumina requirements. Even if domestic calcined-alumina[9] capacity had been in total use in 1975, rather than near only 85 percent, it still would have been necessary to import approximately 28 percent of needed supplies. Imports are actually always greater than the aluminum required, in order to offset alumina exports, which since 1968 have fluctuated around 10 percent of total annual supply and to an extent represent smelting abroad on U.S. account. Australia is now the main source of U.S. alumina imports, and considering the Australian desire to expand its share of the alumina world market, that country is likely, at least for a time, to continue to dominate the U.S. import source mix.

Aluminum

Refined aluminum is the first commodity so far discussed in which domestic production totally dominates the U.S. supply picture. For any year in the past twenty-five, domestic primary plus secondary production (see table 4-10) accounts for over 80 percent of total supply—roughly 70 to 75 percent being primary and 13 to 17 percent being secondary. Despite increasing energy costs, which are inhibiting the growth of primary

---

[9]The type used for processing into aluminum metal.

Table 4-9. Sources and Disposition of U.S. Supply of Alumina

(percentages, except for total supply)

| | | Sources | | | | | Disposition | | |
| | | | Imports | | | | | | |
Year	Domestic production[a]	All sources	Australia	Jamaica	Stock drawdown[b]	Total supply (1,000 short tons)	Apparent consumption	Exports[a]	Stock increases
1965	96.1	3.9	–	0.7	N.A.	5,765	94.5	5.5	N.A.
1966	92.3	7.7	0.3	1.4	"	6,341	94.9	5.1	"
1967	86.6	13.4	4.3	1.8	"	7,106	92.3	7.7	"
1968	82.1	17.9	9.5	1.5	"	7,368	88.3	11.7	"
1969	78.4	21.6	14.8	1.2	"	8,832	88.9	11.1	"
1970	72.1	27.9	12.8	9.4	–	9,249	84.5	13.2	2.2
1971	73.1	26.9	13.8	5.1	–	8,955	85.9	13.7	0.4
1972	68.6	31.4	12.9	8.2	–	9,085	87.6	12.3	0.1
1973	66.7	33.3	19.2	8.8	–	10,241	88.5	10.0	1.5
1974	66.1	33.9	20.6	8.4	–	10,686	90.2	8.7	1.1
1975	59.8	40.2	24.7	8.9	–	8,730	87.3	11.5	1.2
1976	61.8	38.0	28.8	6.5	0.2	9,544	88.2	11.8	–
1977	60.1	39.9	27.4	6.6	–	10,230	88.5	9.2	2.3

Source: U.S. Bureau of Mines, Minerals Yearbook and unpublished data.

N.A. – Not available.

Note: Detail may not add to 100 percent, owing to rounding.

[a]Includes production in, and exports from, the Virgin Islands.

[b]See appendix to chapter 6 in the NTIS version of this paper for detailed description of industry stock changes. There are no government stocks of alumina.

Table 4-10. Sources and Disposition of U.S. Supply of Refined Aluminum

(percentages, except for total supply)

| | Sources | | | | Stock drawdown | | | Disposition | | | |
| | Domestic | | Imports | | | | Total supply | Apparent | | Stock increases[c] | |
Year	Primary production	Secondary Recovery[a]	All sources	Canada	Industry[b]	Government[c]	(1,000 short tons)	consumption	Exports	Industry	Government[c]
1952	68.6	21.9	9.4	8.5	0.1	—	1,366	99.9	0.1	—	—
1953	65.4	18.9	15.7	11.7	—	—	1,915	98.2	0.1	1.7	—
1954	73.7	14.5	10.9	9.9	0.9	—	1,981	85.5	0.2	—	14.3
1955	75.2	16.0	8.5	8.2	0.3	—	2,082	99.7	0.3	—	—
1956	75.3	15.0	9.7	9.0	—	—	2,231	94.5	1.2	3.0	—
1957	74.0	16.0	10.0	9.2	—	—	2,226	81.0	1.3	17.6	—
1958	73.5	13.4	12.0	10.0	1.2	—	2,131	82.4	2.5	—	15.2
1959	75.6	13.7	9.3	6.5	1.3	—	2,584	95.1	2.1	—	2.8
1960	80.8	13.0	6.2	4.2	—	—	2,494	87.4	5.1	5.9	1.5
1961	76.4	13.6	8.0	4.8	2.1	—	2,493	92.7	5.2	—	2.1
1962	73.3	13.7	10.6	7.3	2.3	—	2,890	93.4	5.2	—	1.4
1963	70.8	15.1	12.7	8.4	1.3	—	3,264	94.2	5.1	—	0.7
1964	72.2	15.2	11.1	7.3	.1	1.4	3,536	94.1	5.9	—	—
1965	69.8	15.8	13.3	8.7	.8	.2	3,945	94.8	5.2	—	—
1966	66.1	15.1	11.6	8.6	—	7.3	4,491	95.6	4.2	.2	—
1967	73.3	15.3	10.1	8.0	—	1.4	4,463	92.3	4.7	3.0	—
1968	65.7	16.4	13.8	9.8	3.0	1.1	4,956	96.4	3.6	—	—
1969	72.0	15.9	8.9	7.6	.5	2.6	5,269	93.5	6.5	—	—
1970	77.7	15.0	6.8	6.4	—	.5	5,120	90.1	8.0	1.9	—
1971	74.3	15.2	10.5	8.3	—	—	5,285	97.2	2.1	.7	—
1972	71.4	16.1	11.4	8.8	.9	.2	5,774	98.1	1.9	—	—
1973	66.2	14.8	7.4	6.3	.9	10.7	6,837	96.6	3.4	—	—
1974	71.7	13.4	7.4	6.0	—	7.5	6,839	95.8	3.0	1.2	—
1975	74.1	17.6	8.3	6.5	—	.1	5,235	92.0	3.6	4.4	—
1976	69.7	17.7	9.4	6.2	3.0	.2	6,102	97.5	2.5	—	—
1977	70.8	18.8	10.4	7.8	—	—	6,413	97.9	1.5	.6	—

Note: Detail may not add to 100 percent owing to rounding.

Source: U.S. Bureau of Mines, Minerals Yearbook and unpublished data; American Bureau of Metal Statistics, Non-Ferrous Metal Data.

[a] From the table, "Aluminum recovered from purchased scrap processed in the U.S.," as presented in the "Aluminum" chapter of Minerals Yearbook. Confined to secondary aluminum whose form of recovery is as metal and aluminum alloys.

[b] For the years prior to 1976 stock changes are estimated as the difference between production and shipments of primary aluminum. The amounts shown for 1976 and 1977 are based on total reported year-end (producer and consumer) stocks; thus 1976-1977 quantities are not totally consistent with previous listings, but are believed to provide a better estimate of available supply. Data are not available to extend either series throughout the 1952-1977 period.

[c] Quantity indicated for 1952-1957 estimated by subtracting the Bureau of the Mines surveyed consumption from total available supply of primary refined aluminum. This procedure necessitated by the fact that government stock changes for those years were considered unpublishable security information.

aluminum capacity in the United States,[10] imports have not yet reduced domestic producers' share of the U.S. market. Imports as a proportion of total supply are in fact 1 to 3 percentage points below what they were during most of the 1960s. Nevertheless, they have been rising in recent years. Because of lower production costs, the United States is likely to look increasingly toward the Middle East or South America for future imports, although it would take some time for these areas to displace Canada as the principal U.S. supplier.

Although secondary aluminum supply, in the short run, is primarily a function of price and of supply excess or shortage of virgin aluminum ingot, it has been growing faster than primary supply over the past few years. With declining rates of growth in total aluminum consumption, the increase in relative role of secondary aluminum should continue.

The United States exports only small quantities of refined aluminum, and since 1970, exports have never exceeded 4 percent of total supply. Thus, apparent consumption accounts for the bulk of aluminum disposition. Building and construction is for all years the largest end-use industry, generally followed by transportation (the automotive industry). The largest growth in aluminum usage has been by the container and packaging industry, since the mid-1960s.

Aluminum Scrap

The data presented in table 4-11 are for the gross weight of scrap. Consequently, the consumption quantities indicated are not the same as those used in table 1-13. Detail on stocks and international trade in aluminum scrap, as well as on current generation and consumption, are available only on a gross weight basis.

As is the case for all scrap tables in this chapter, a percentage breakdown is provided between old and new scrap[11] (for aluminum, there is

---

[10]The annual rate of growth has dropped from 8 percent a year during the earlier postwar period to 3.5 percent in 1975 and is expected to drop to 1 percent by 1983. (New York Times, January 19, 1979.)

[11]See chapter 10 for a further discussion of the terms old and new scrap.

Table 4-11. Sources and Disposition of U.S. Supply of Aluminum Scrap

(percentages, except for total supply)

Year	Sources — Current generation[a] — New	Old	Sweated pig	Imports	Stock drawdown	Total supply (1,000 short tons, gross weight)	Disposition — Consumption	Exports	Stock increases
1952	74.9	23.1	(b)	2.0	-	355	98.8	0.3	1.7
1953	72.9	20.8	(b)	6.3	-	425	97.2	1.1	1.6
1954	73.8	21.4	(b)	3.8	1.0	390	89.9	10.1	-
1955	68.4	22.4	(b)	.1	-	447	95.5	4.1	0.3
1956	72.3	22.0	(b)	5.6	-	464	94.7	4.2	1.1
1957	N.A.	N.A.	N.A.	N.A.	N.A.	N.A.	N.A.	N.A.	N.A.
1958	73.7	23.7	(b)	2.5	-	397	94.6	4.8	0.5
1959	74.8	23.0	(b)	2.1	-	514	92.6	6.3	1.1
1960	78.1	20.1	(b)	1.0	0.8	521	84.7	15.3	-
1961	66.6	13.7	18.7	1.0	-	591	84.3	13.9	1.8
1962	70.2	14.4	13.8	1.0	0.5	664	90.0	9.9	-
1963	75.2	14.1	9.4	1.3	-	728	88.9	9.8	1.3
1964	76.0	14.5	8.4	1.0	-	781	91.2	8.8	-
1965	71.4	15.5	9.9	3.1	-	865	94.4	4.5	1.1
1966	76.0	11.7	7.6	3.6	1.2	945	94.8	5.2	-
1967	78.0	11.8	7.0	3.2	-	945	93.4	5.8	0.8
1968	76.9	11.7	8.0	3.5	-	1,061	95.3	4.6	0.1
1969	80.1	11.2	6.1	2.5	-	1,197	92.7	7.2	0.1
1970	77.2	13.5	5.8	3.6	-	1,036	93.9	5.5	0.6
1971	73.1	12.9	8.0	5.9	0.1	1,056	95.2	2.9	1.9
1972	74.4	12.6	8.3	4.3	0.5	1,219	94.5	5.4	-
1973	76.0	13.4	6.5	3.4	0.7	1,378	91.6	8.4	-
1974	72.3	15.3	6.8	5.6	-	1,323	91.2	6.1	2.8
1975	69.6	19.2	7.0	4.2	-	1,302	94.6	5.0	0.3
1976	68.1	20.1	6.4	5.4	-	1,586	92.4	6.9	0.7
1977	64.7	23.0	7.0	5.3	-	1,685	93.1	6.0	0.8

Source: U.S. Bureau of Mines, Minerals Yearbook and unpublished data.

N.A.--Not available.

Note: Detail may not add to 100 percent owing to rounding.

[a] Data are actually for domestically generated amounts received by scrap consumers. Information on amounts of scrap going through earlier collection and generation stages is not regularly available. The breakdown between new and old is actually for quantities consumed rather than acquired, but is taken as a reasonable approximation of the latter.

[b] Apparently included in old scrap quantities. Separate data are not available.

also included a separate accounting for "sweated pig," a melted but otherwise unprocessed form of scrap). Although they are presented as a breakdown of sources, the percentages actually refer to consumption; stock data by which to adjust the consumption figures to a more precise supply breakdown are not available.

Current domestic generation provides the great bulk of U.S. aluminum scrap; there are scrap imports but they have been a minor supply factor. Stock variations, which involve industry stocks only since the government does not maintain an aluminum scrap stockpile, have an even less significant impact on supplies. While the United States does export larger quantities of aluminum scrap than it imports, by far the major disposition of scrap supplies is domestic consumption.

What is significant is the relative decline of new scrap in relation to old scrap over the past ten years. This is not surprising since new scrap generation--and, therefore, consumption--should rise in rough proportion to current refined aluminum consumption, while old scrap consumption will lag somewhat behind. Since refined aluminum consumption rose four times as fast in the 1960s as in the 1970s (see figure 1-26), old scrap should, as sixties products are discarded and recycled, start to account for relatively larger proportions of supply. Also, aluminum cans, an important form of old scrap, which are subject to rather immediate disposal and recycling, did not capture large quantities of the container market until the late 1960s. In addition, taking into consideration increasing emphasis on recycling in general, the trend toward greater relative use of "old" aluminum is likely to continue.

Copper

Copper Ore

Even though the United States has been the world's leading copper producing country over the period shown in table 4-12--and, in fact, for many years earlier--with the exception of 1968 and 1970, it has also been a net importer of copper ores. The relative percentages have, however, declined. In the 1950s, imports accounted for 8 to 12 percent

Table 4-12. Sources and Disposition of U.S. Supply of Copper Ore

(percentages, except for total supply)

Year	Sources		Total supply	Disposition	
	Domestic production[a]	Total imports[b]	(1,000 short tons, Cu content)	Apparent consumption	Exports
1952	90.1	9.9	1,027	99.9	0.1
1953	89.1	10.9	1,040	99.9	0.1
1954	88.1	11.9	948	99.8	0.2
1955	89.5	10.5	1,116	98.8	1.2
1956	90.6	9.4	1,219	98.9	1.1
1957	90.2	9.8	1,205	98.7	1.3
1958	91.8	8.2	1,067	98.9	1.1
1959	92.0	8.0	897	99.7	0.3
1960	93.4	6.6	1,156	99.0	1.0
1961	96.2	3.8	1,211	99.6	0.4
1962	96.6	3.4	1,271	99.9	0.1
1963	96.2	3.8	1,261	99.9	0.1
1964	96.1	3.9	1,298	99.6	0.4
1965	97.4	2.6	1,388	98.9	1.1
1966	97.1	2.9	1,471	99.9	0.1
1967	96.7	3.3	987	96.1	3.9
1968	97.8	2.2	1,232	94.7	5.3
1969	97.6	2.4	1,583	99.9	0.1
1970	98.2	1.8	1,752	96.5	3.5
1971	98.0	2.0	1,553	99.5	0.5
1972	96.9	3.1	1,718	99.0	1.0
1973	97.6	2.4	1,761	98.7	1.3
1974	96.8	3.2	1,650	99.2	0.8
1975	95.6	4.4	1,478	99.4	0.6
1976	95.8	4.2	1,676	98.9	1.1
1977	97.3	2.7	1,546	98.4	1.6

Source: U.S. Bureau of Mines, Minerals Yearbook and unpublished data.

[a]Recoverable copper content in ore.

[b]Imports are general imports, used on the assumption that ores were often refined in bonded smelting-warehouses before being entered as imports for consumption.

Table 4-13. Sources and Disposition of U.S. Supply of Blister Copper

(percentages, except for total supply)

Year	Sources Domestic production[a]	Sources All sources	Imports[b] Chile	Sources Stock drawdowns	Total supply (1,000 short tons, copper content)	Disposition Apparent consumption	Disposition Exports	Disposition Stock increases
1953	80.4	19.6	8.4	-	1,394	99.9	N.A.	0.1
1954	80.1	19.9	10.0	-	1,286	99.5	..	0.5
1955	81.8	17.9	9.7	0.3	1,418	100.0	..	-
1956	82.5	17.3	11.0	0.2	1,592	100.0	..	-
1957	80.6	19.4	13.4	-	1,555	98.7	..	1.3
1958	80.4	19.1	13.0	0.5	1,406	100.0	..	-
1959	75.7	24.3	19.2	-	1,184	97.9	..	2.1
1960	81.3	18.5	11.8	0.2	1,609	100.0	..	-
1961	77.8	20.5	13.4	1.6	1,652	100.0	..	-
1962	81.0	19.0	12.9	-	1,741	99.9	..	0.1
1963	79.1	20.9	12.4	-	1,764	100.0	..	-
1964	78.6	21.4	13.8	-	1,816	99.5	-	0.5
1965	81.9	17.8	10.1	0.3	1,866	100.0	-	-
1966	81.4	18.4	9.4	0.1	1,943	100.0	-	-
1967	77.6	22.4	11.8	-	1,202	96.1	1.7	2.2
1968	82.0	16.4	8.3	1.6	1,648	99.0	1.0	-
1969	87.5	12.5	5.3	-	1,901	98.8	0.2	1.0
1970	88.4	11.5	5.0	-	1,945	99.0	0.4	0.6
1971	90.9	9.1	2.4	-	1,723	97.6	1.7	0.7
1972	91.8	8.2	1.7	-	1,917	99.0	0.4	0.6
1973	90.2	7.6	1.5	2.2	2,020	99.6	0.4	-
1974	88.8	11.2	3.5	-	1,857	99.6	0.1	0.3
1975	94.4	5.6	1.7	-	1,586	99.7	0.1	0.2
1976	97.1	2.7	1.9	0.1	1,633	99.8	0.2	-
1977	97.0	3.0	2.1	-	1,531	98.9	0.5	0.6

Source: U.S. Bureau of Mines, Minerals Yearbook and unpublished data; American Bureau of Metal Statistics, Yearbook and Non-Ferrous Metal Data.

N.A. – Not available.

Note: Detail may not add to 100 percent, owing to rounding.

[a] Both primary and secondary production.

[b] Imports are general imports.

of total supplies, while by the mid-1970s the proportion had fallen to less than 5 percent. This is explained not only by increased domestic mine production, but also by the trend, both for U.S. companies with foreign subsidiaries and for nationalized foreign companies, toward processing the ore before exportation. In any event, domestic supplies have always been sufficient for the vast bulk of U.S. smelter feedstock.

Almost all the U.S. supply of copper ore is smelted into blister copper, with exports of ore seldom rising above 2 percent of total availabilities. There are no government stocks of copper ore, and industry stock data are unavailable.

Blister Copper

As is the case for copper ore, imports of blister copper have been declining not only as a percentage of total supply, but also in terms of absolute quantity (see table 4-13). With the increasing production of refined copper in the ore-producing countries, this is not surprising. The blister which the United States does import comes primarily from Chile.

Table 4-14 gives the relative breakdown of domestic blister copper production between primary and secondary production. Although the absolute amounts have varied little over the past twenty-five years, secondary blister copper as a percentage of total production has fallen about 40 percent. The United States consumes nearly 100 percent of its annual available supplies.

Table 4-14. Primary and Secondary Blister Copper as a Percentage of Total U.S. Blister Copper Production

	1955	1960	1965	1970	1975	1977
Primary	94.8	94.3	93.9	95.4	96.7	96.7
Secondary	5.2	5.7	6.1	4.6	3.3	3.3

Source: U.S. Bureau of Mines, Minerals Yearbook and unpublished data.

Refined Copper

The quantities detailed in table 4-15 for the years 1965 to 1977 are consistent with the amounts listed for the United States in table 1-20, "World Apparent Consumption of Refined Copper." For years prior to 1965, the underlying data are slightly different, since table 4-15 details government stock changes for all years, while adjustments for strategic stockpile changes were not made by Metallgesellschaft, the data source for table 1-20, until after 1964.

Combined domestic primary production and secondary recovery have accounted for anywhere between 71 percent[12] and 95 percent of annual U.S. refined copper supplies. The percentages have followed no clear trend, but rather have responded to fluctuating market demand and the timing of world stop-pages. Secondary production, viewed separately, has been more consistent over the past eighteen years, generally supplying 15 to 20 percent of total supplies, depending on the slackness or tightness of total copper demand and the availability of alternative supplies.

Imports of refined copper, which historically have come predominantly from Canada, have made their largest relative contributions to total domestic supplies during years in which the domestic copper industry has been hit hardest by strikes: 1959, 1967 (with 1968 imports apparently having been contracted to a large extent as the result of the preceding year's strikes), and 1974. Increased imports in 1976 and 1977 may have been effected as a guard against anticipated future import restrictions, although it is also possible that some domestic production was being dis-placed by foreign refined copper. Refined copper imports from such ore producers as Chile, Peru, Zambia, and Yugoslavia have been increasing.

Though government stockpiles are not held for economic purposes, releases from them have made significant contributions to total available supplies, especially in or near strike years. The releases have curtailed the need to increase imports during years when domestic supplies were

---

[12]In 1967, a year in which strikes in the copper industry disrupted about 65 percent of refinery capacity.

Table 4-15. Sources and Disposition of U.S. Supply of Refined Copper

(percentages, except for total supply)

Year	Domestic Primary recovery	Domestic Secondary recovery	Imports[a] All sources	Imports[a] Canada	Stock drawdown Industry[b]	Stock drawdown Government	Total supply (1,000 short tons)	Apparent consumption	Exports	Stock increases Industry	Stock increases Government
1956	76.0	13.8	10.1	4.9	—	—	1,897	82.5	11.7	5.7	—
1957	78.5	12.8	8.8	4.7	—	—	1,853	74.5	18.7	2.5	4.3
1958	74.8	13.6	7.1	3.5	4.7	—	1,809	71.8	21.3	—	6.9
1959	65.9	15.0	12.9	6.2	6.2	—	1,666	90.1	9.6	—	0.3
1960	77.8	14.9	7.3	5.2	—	—	1,953	71.1	22.3	6.3	0.3
1961	79.9	14.5	3.4	3.2	1.9	0.3	1,940	77.7	22.3	—	—
1962	80.3	14.4	4.9	3.8	—	0.4	2,008	80.9	16.8	2.2	—
1963	76.8	14.5	5.7	3.5	2.4	0.5	2,079	85.0	15.0	—	—
1964	75.4	16.0	6.3	3.9	1.1	1.2	2,197	85.6	14.4	—	—
1965	70.8	18.4	5.7	3.0	—	5.1	2,417	84.8	13.7	1.5	—
1966	61.3	16.9	5.8	3.1	—	15.9	2,791	85.2	10.0	4.8	—
1967	52.9	18.4	15.3	6.6	5.2	8.3	2,143	92.5	7.5	—	—
1968	63.8	17.8	17.8	6.0	—	0.6	2,253	83.3	11.1	5.6	—
1969	73.7	20.0	5.5	3.6	0.5	0.3	2,365	90.9	9.1	—	—
1970	74.3	20.1	5.6	3.9	—	0.1	2,375	86.4	9.3	4.3	—
1971	72.1	16.8	7.4	5.6	3.6	—	2,209	91.5	8.5	—	—
1972	76.4	15.7	7.8	5.1	—	—	2,451	91.3	7.5	1.2	—
1973	70.7	16.8	7.7	4.9	3.5	1.3	2,642	91.8	7.2	—	—
1974	62.8	18.4	11.9	4.5	—	6.9	2,635	83.8	4.8	11.4	—
1975	74.8	17.1	7.6	3.7	—	0.5	1,929	79.8	9.0	11.2	—
1976	67.4	15.5	16.8	4.1	—	0.3	2,280	86.3	5.0	8.7	—
1977	65.9	16.9	17.2	4.4	—	—	2,271	96.8	2.8	0.4	—

Source: Metallgesellschaft AG, Metal Statistics; Copper Development Association, Annual Data.

Note: Detail may not add to 100 percent, owing to rounding.

[a] Imports are general imports.

[b] Industry stock changes are assumed to be the difference between government stock changes and total apparent change, both as reported by the Copper Development Association.

267

especially restricted. However, as is the situation with most of the commodities already discussed, the current government copper inventory is far below the present stockpile goal and therefore government stocks as a source of supply should not be available as they have been in the recent past.

Refined copper exports as a percentage of total supply distribution are larger than those of any other metal and commodity form discussed in this report. But even then, exports--going primarily to other advanced industrial countries--have not been over 10 percent of total supplies since 1968 and fell to below 3 percent of supplies in 1977.

Domestic consumption accounts generally for 80 to 90 percent of total supplies, the exact proportion depending as much on stock variations as on exports. Wire mills account for approximately 70 percent of total consumption, with brass mills consuming most of the remaining refined copper. According to the Bureau of Mines (<u>Mineral Commodity Summaries 1979</u>), 58 percent of primary and old scrap copper was ultimately consumed in the electrical industry in 1978, 19 percent in construction, 9 percent in industrial machinery, 8 percent in transportation, and 6 percent in other industries.

Copper Scrap

Copper scrap data presented in table 4-16 differ from the data collected for table 1-21 on world apparent consumption, in that the quantities in table 4-16 are in gross weight (and in short tons) while those in the apparent-consumption table are in copper content (and in metric tons). Therefore, direct comparison is not possible.

The United States imports very little of its copper scrap, relying almost exclusively, instead, on domestic generation. Only in recent years have imports reached even 2 percent of annual supply totals. Also, scrap stocks have not been subject to large variations over the years,[13] as have, for example, refined copper stocks.

---

[13]That is, stocks in the hands of consumers. Dealer stocks are not reported.

Table 4-16. Sources and Disposition of U.S. Supply of Copper Scrap

(percentages, except for total supply)

	Sources				Total supply (1,000 short tons lead content)	Disposition		
	Current generation[a]		Imports	Stock drawdown		Consumption	Exports	Stock increases
	New	Old						
1952	54.2	45.0	0.8	-	1,339	96.3	0.7	3.0
1953	53.8	45.5	0.7	-	1,444	96.0	2.4	1.6
1954	48.8	47.1	0.3	3.7	1,314	93.5	5.7	-
1955	47.8	51.3	0.9	-	1,422	95.7	2.2	3.1
1956	48.9	50.1	0.9	0.1	1,368	94.4	5.6	-
1957	45.8	50.8	1.1	2.3	1,282	90.2	9.3	-
1958	46.6	52.3	1.1	-	1,161	95.6	4.3	0.3
1959	49.2	50.4	0.4	-	1,343	94.4	3.0	3.2
1960	49.3	48.6	0.2	1.9	1,401	86.3	13.3	-
1961	49.3	48.4	0.2	2.1	1,321	88.6	11.5	-
1962	53.2	46.4	0.4	-	1,340	94.4	3.6	2.4
1963	53.9	45.2	0.3	0.6	1,400	97.2	3.4	-
1964	54.1	44.9	0.4	0.6	1,644	92.1	7.0	-
1965	56.3	42.6	1.1	-	1,826	95.0	5.3	0.1
1966	56.5	41.9	1.6	-	1,934	96.6	3.2	0.8
1967	56.3	42.5	1.2	-	1,615	95.4	5.1	0.5
1968	54.8	42.3	0.8	2.1	1,810	91.8	8.0	-
1969	56.3	43.6	0.4	-	1,996	94.8	4.3	1.0
1970	55.1	44.7	0.2	-	1,891	92.5	6.7	1.0
1971	58.3	38.9	0.9	1.8	1,765	94.0	5.4	-
1972	61.0	37.2	1.2	0.6	1,867	95.4	4.6	-
1973	62.0	36.4	1.6	-	2,015	92.5	7.5	0.4
1974	60.0	37.6	2.4	-	1,936	91.8	8.2	0.1
1975	60.0	37.8	1.7	0.5	1,396	89.7	10.3	-
1976	60.9	37.0	2.1	-	1,650	91.8	6.9	1.5
1977	59.9	38.2	1.9	-	1,707	92.3	7.0	1.2

Source: U.S. Bureau of Mines, Minerals Yearbook and unpublished data.

Note: Detail may not add to totals, owing both to rounding and to inconsistencies between consumer-reported stock and consumption data.

[a]Data are actually for domestically generated amounts received by scrap consumers. Information on amounts of scrap going through earlier collection and generation stages is not regularly available. The breakdown between new and old is actually for quantities consumed rather than acquired, but is taken as a reasonable approximation of the latter.

269

Of all nonferrous scrap exports, those of copper have generally been
viewed by domestic consumers with the most apprehension. While it is true,
however, that copper scrap exports as a percentage of supply are generally
larger than exports of other nonferrous scrap, the apprehension may not be
too well founded. Of the four years with an unusually high proportion of
exports--1957, 1960, 1961, and 1975--a comparison with the data in tables
1-20 and 6-16 indicates that all except 1961 were years of falling domestic
copper demand and scrap prices, while 1961 demand and price were not much
above the 1960 trough. It is possible, though, that at least the 1960
and 1975 export surges represented a disgorging of inventory that had
been speculatively built up in preceding high-demand years.

The breakdown between old and new scrap consumption shows a leaning
toward new scrap in the early 1950s, a shift toward old in the mid- and
late 1950s, and a subsequent continuing (but ever weakening) emphasis on
new. The shifting trends are probably explainable in part by the varying
rates of growth in copper consumption, higher rates normally predisposing
toward relatively higher proportions of new-scrap availability.

Lead

Lead Ores

Both lead and zinc, unlike other ores, have over the past twenty
years shown a relative reversal of supply sources between imports and
domestic production, in favor of the latter. Whereas in earlier years
lead ore imports had amounted to over one-third of total ore supply, by
the early 1970s they were contributing less than 15 percent of this total
(table 4-17). During the late 1960s and early 1970s, U.S. mine production
increased almost 70 percent, as a result of the opening and full-scale
production of four mines in the Missouri lead belt. It is only in the
past few years that domestic mine production has decreased slightly, and
this is mostly the result of decreased demand.

Lead ore imports have traditionally come from South Africa, Australia,
Canada, and Peru. Since the mid-1970s, however, there have been no imports
from South Africa, but, rather, increasing quantities from Honduras.

Table 4-17. Sources and Disposition of U.S. Supply of Lead Ore

(percentages, except for total supply)

Year	Sources Domestic production	Sources Total imports	Sources Stock drawdown[a]	Total supply (1,000 short tons, lead content)	Disposition Apparent consumption	Disposition Stock increases
1954	60.6	36.8	2.6	532	100.0	–
1955	67.2	32.8	–	478	97.3	2.7
1956	64.6	35.4	–	541	99.6	0.4
1957	59.0	40.9	–	573	99.1	0.9
1958	51.6	45.9	2.5	518	100.0	–
1959	65.2	34.8	–	392	99.4	0.6
1960	64.2	35.8	–	384	93.2	6.8
1961	62.4	32.6	6.1	420	100.0	–
1962	64.1	35.9	–	370	98.9	1.1
1963	65.1	34.9	–	389	98.6	1.4
1964	66.5	29.8	3.7	430	100.0	–
1965	70.0	30.0	–	430	96.7	3.3
1966	83.7	16.3	–	391	92.4	7.6
1967	68.7	31.3	–	461	98.2	1.8
1968	75.1	20.3	4.6	478	100.0	–
1969	81.4	18.6	–	625	100.0	–
1970	93.1	6.9	–	614	96.7	3.3
1971	83.4	12.7	4.0	694	100.0	–
1972	92.2	7.8	–	671	97.9	2.1
1973	84.7	13.2	2.1	712	100.0	–
1974	91.4	8.6	–	727	96.8	3.2
1975	91.9	6.7	1.4	676	100.0	–
1976	87.0	13.0	–	701	99.6	0.4
1977	85.5	14.5	–	689	98.9	1.1

Source: U.S. Bureau of Mines, Minerals Yearbook and unpublished data.

Note: Detail may not add to 100 percent, owing to rounding.

[a] Lead ore exports have been insignificant throughout the listed years.

[b] Lead in ore and matte at primary smelters and refineries.

Still, even in 1977, when the Honduran contribution was almost 42,000 tons (lead content) and the largest single source of imports, it amounted to only 6 percent of total U.S. supply.

The United States consumes domestically the great bulk of its ore supplies. Export data have actually been unavailable since 1965, but such shipments reached their last twenty-five year high point in 1961, at only 1 percent of total supply.

Stock changes listed in table 4-17 are for consumer stocks only, and there is no lead ore in the government stockpile.

Refined Lead

As may be seen in table 4-18, domestic primary and secondary output has accounted for 70 to 90 percent of refined lead supply. Production has usually been fairly evenly distributed between new and recycled, although there have been years in which the differences were as much as 12 percentage points in favor of the recycled. Table 4-19 details, for selected years, the breakdown of the total supply, not only between primary and secondary, but by type. As may be seen, antimonial lead is produced primarily as a form of secondary recovery. An increased turnover of storage batteries can increase such recovery even as primary lead production remains relatively unaffected.

Refined lead imports historically have come from relatively stable sources, the principal ones being Canada, Mexico, Australia, and Peru. It is apparent from table 4-18 that, while imports as a contribution to total supply may on balance be declining, their percentage has fluctuated significantly. It is even possible that, since government stockpile sales, which amounted to more than 10 percent of total supplies in 1973 and 1974, are no longer a viable supply source for U.S. consumers, refined lead imports may once again be on the upswing. It is possible, however, that increases in recycling will offset the need for any major increases in imports. Government inventories, after the large sales in the 1970s, are currently below the stockpile goals.

Regarding the disposition of refined lead supplies, the United States exports little and consumes almost all. As table 4-20 details, the

Table 4-18. Sources and Disposition of U.S. Supply Refined Lead.
(percentages, except for total supply)

Year	Sources Domestic Primary Production	Sources Domestic Secondary Recovery	Imports[a]	Stock drawdown Industry[b]	Stock drawdown Gov't	Total supply (1,000 short tons, lead content)	Apparent consumption	Exports	Stock increases Industry[b]	Stock increases Gov't
1954	39.7	38.3	22.0	–	N.A.	1,257	98.5	–	1.5	N.A.
1955	37.3	37.9	19.9	4.9	"	1,325	100.0	–	–	"
1956	41.9	38.3	19.8	–	–	1,326	93.8	0.3	2.1	e3.8
1957	40.5	35.8	23.7	–	–	1,367	88.7	0.3	3.7	e7.3
1958	38.7	32.0	29.3	–	–	1,257	88.9	0.1	7.7	3.3
1959	31.2	39.9	23.3	5.7	–	1,132	95.8	0.2	–	4.0
1960	36.3	44.3	19.4	–	–	1,061	98.9	0.2	0.9	–
1961	40.0	38.3	21.7	–	–	1,184	94.0	0.2	4.0	1.8
1962	34.4	37.9	21.9	5.7	–	1,172	92.7	0.2	–	7.1
1963	35.1	40.6	18.7	4.9	0.6	1,214	99.9	0.1	–	–
1964	36.0	42.5	16.3	2.0	3.2	1,273	99.2	0.8	–	–
1965	32.8	44.6	17.0	1.5	4.1	1,298	99.4	0.6	–	–
1966	32.6	41.4	20.6	–	3.9	1,385	99.6	0.4	–	–
1967	29.2	41.5	27.3	–	2.0	1,334	98.2	0.5	1.3	–
1968	33.8	38.3	23.5	2.4	2.0	1,439	99.4	0.6	–	–
1969	41.9	38.6	17.8	–	1.7	1,563	96.1	0.2	3.7	–
1970	44.4	39.1	16.0	–	0.5	1,529	94.4	5.3	0.3	–
1971	43.8	39.2	12.9	3.5	0.7	1,522	99.8	0.2	–	–
1972	43.2	38.7	15.2	–	2.8	1,592	99.4	0.3	0.3	–
1973	39.0	37.1	10.1	1.8	12.0	1,764	97.3	2.7	–	–
1974	38.7	39.6	6.7	–	15.0	1,766	94.5	2.6	2.8	–
1975	45.5	46.9	7.2	–	0.5	1,404	97.7	1.2	1.1	–
1976	41.9	46.3	9.0	2.7	–	1,568	99.9	0.1	–	–
1977	37.4	45.5	15.6	1.5	–	1,635	99.9	0.1	–	–

Source: U.S. Bureau of Mines, Minerals Yearbook and unpublished data.

e – estimated.
N.A. – Not available.

Note: Detail may not add to 100 percent, owing to rounding.

[a] Imports are general imports of refined lead.

[b] Consumer stocks and stocks at primary smelters and refineries of refined soft/pig lead and lead in antimonial lead.

273

Table 4-19. Domestic Primary and Secondary Production of Refined Lead, by Type
(thousand short tons, lead content)

| | Primary Production | | Secondary Recovery | | |
	Soft lead	Antimonial lead	Soft lead	Antimonial lead	Other alloys
1955	479	15	128	248	126
1960	382	12	148	206	116
1965	418	7	182	271	123
1970	667	12	159	348	90
1975	636	2	271	315	72
1977	605	8	317	358	67

Source: U.S. Bureau of Mines, Minerals Yearbook and unpublished data.

largest category of lead consumption is in storage batteries, the bulk
of the remainder being used primarily in pigments and chemicals (especially
tetraethyl lead) and in metal products (ammunition, cable coverings, and
other).[14] Lead in antimonial lead accounts for over 40 percent of total
lead consumed for storage batteries.

Table 4-20. U.S. Consumption of Lead, By Product

(percentages, except for total supply)

	1955	1960	1965	1970	1975
Metal products	41.2	33.8	30.6	23.9	20.4
Storage batteries	31.5	36.1	38.3	44.8	53.4
Pigments and chemicals	24.3	27.8	27.8	28.5	22.2
Other	3.0	2.3	3.3	2.8	4.0
Total supply (thousand short tons)	1,203	978	1,190	1,324	1,297

Source: Derived from U.S. Bureau of Mines, Minerals Yearbook.

Lead Scrap

As in the tables for aluminum and copper scrap, the data in table
4-21 on supplies of lead scrap are not totally consistent with those in
the U.S. column in table 1-28, "World Apparent Consumption of Lead (and
Lead Alloy) Scrap." The quantities in table 1-28 are in lead content
(the only kind of data available on a world basis), while those in table
4-21 are in gross weight of scrap, basis for the most complete data concerning U.S. sources of supply.

_____

[14]The table actually refers to lead in all forms, but all, or nearly
all, consumption seems to require the prior production of refined lead or
equivalent secondary alloy.

Table 4-21. Sources and Disposition of U.S. Supply of Lead Scrap

(percentages, except for total supply)

Year	Current generation[a] New	Current generation[a] Old	Imports	Stock drawdown	Total supply (1,000 short tons, gross weight)	Consumption	Exports	Stock increases
1952	12.8	84.7	2.4	0.1	609	100.0	–	–
1953	12.6	86.5	.8	–	627	98.9	0.4	0.7
1954	13.0	85.5	1.5	–	636	99.2	0.6	0.2
1955	11.2	82.9	3.7	2.2	657	99.5	0.5	–
1956	12.1	84.0	3.9	–	664	98.5	0.3	1.2
1957	11.9	85.0	1.6	1.5	613	99.8	0.2	–
1958	14.7	83.2	2.1	–	527	98.8	0.2	1.0
1959	12.8	84.9	1.7	0.6	582	99.8	0.2	–
1960	13.0	84.5	1.2	1.3	613	99.5	0.5	–
1961	13.7	84.5	0.8	1.0	593	99.1	0.9	–
1962	11.1	88.4	0.5	–	586	98.8	0.4	0.8
1963	12.8	84.3	2.9	–	664	96.5	0.4	3.1
1964	12.9	86.8	0.3	–	724	97.4	1.8	0.8
1965	13.2	84.0	0.6	2.2	752	99.5	0.5	–
1966	15.0	84.1	0.6	0.3	747	99.1	0.9	–
1967	13.7	84.8	1.5	–	739	98.3	0.9	0.7
1968	14.2	85.0	0.7	0.1	735	98.7	1.3	–
1969	14.3	84.7	1.0	–	821	97.2	0.9	1.9
1970	15.4	84.1	0.4	0.1	790	99.5	0.5	–
1971	18.2	81.2	0.6	–	797	98.4	1.2	0.4
1972	19.5	80.4	0.1	0.9	850	95.8	4.2	–
1973	17.8	82.2	0.1	–	946	91.7	6.3	1.9
1974	13.9	86.0	0.1	–	1,008	92.2	5.9	1.9
1975	14.8	84.1	0.2	0.9	959	94.8	5.2	–
1976	15.0	84.7	0.3	–	1,056	95.5	4.4	0.6
1977	16.5	83.1	0.4	–	1,256	92.4	6.8	0.8

Source: U.S. Bureau of Mines, Minerals Yearbook and unpublished data.

Note: Detail may not add to 100 percent owing to rounding.

[a]Data are actually for domestically generated amounts received by scrap consumers. Information on amounts of scrap going through earlier collection and generation stages is not regularly available. The breakdown between new and old is actually for quantities consumed rather than acquired, but is taken as a reasonable approximation of the latter.

276

Imports have not been a significant supply source of lead scrap, and there are no government stockpiles. Exports of lead scrap, on the other hand, have been increasing and in 1977 accounted for almost 7 percent of the total scrap disposition. Belgium, the Netherlands, and Canada were the primary recipients of such exports.

Old scrap is the really significant contributor to lead scrap supplies, the bulk of it being battery plates. New scrap, drosses, and residues tend to account for about 15 percent of total scrap supplies, although the proportion has fluctuated between 10 and 20 percent.

Zinc

Zinc Ores

Table 4-22 details the sources of supply for zinc ores. The total quantities do not match those listed for U.S. apparent consumption in table 1-32, inasmuch as the data in table 1-32 utilize "general imports" while table 4-22 is based on "imports for consumption." While in most years the differences are slight, there are several years in which total supply and apparent consumption quantities are affected significantly.[15]

There are no government stocks and our consumption data do not include changes in private inventories; therefore the listed sources of supply are simply imports for consumption and domestic mine production. From a first glance at table 4-22, it might appear that domestic mine production has increased dramatically since 1971, but by applying the source percentages to the total supply figures, one sees that mine production has

---

[15] For example, 1975 zinc ore imports for consumption were 428,544 tons, 47.7 percent of supply, whereas general imports were only 144,987 tons, which would have been 23.6 percent of the total supply.

The reason for using the two different bases--which was done also for lead ores, but in that case entirely without significant effect on the data--was solely one of convenience of sources for the two different purposes. Generally, "imports for consumption" place consumption more nearly in the correct year, although this is not true if there is any significant amount of smelting in bond.

Table 4-22. Sources and Disposition of U.S. Supply of Zinc Ores[a]

(percentages, except for total supply)

| Year | Sources | | | | Total supply (1,000 short tons, zinc content) | Disposition |
| | Domestic production | Imports | | | | Apparent consumption |
		All sources	Canada	Mexico		
1954	49.6	50.4	[b]18.6	17.7	954	100
1955	57.3	42.7	[b]16.9	17.3	899	"
1956	54.0	46.0	[b]14.5	18.6	1005	"
1957	43.9	56.1	18.0	21.6	1211	"
1958	43.3	56.7	17.8	21.9	951	"
1959	50.0	50.0	16.2	17.4	849	"
1960	53.2	46.8	16.3	17.4	818	"
1961	56.5	43.5	13.4	17.0	822	"
1962	56.6	43.4	15.2	15.6	893	"
1963	58.7	41.3	14.6	15.4	901	"
1964	64.9	35.1	13.3	11.9	886	"
1965	60.3	39.7	19.9	10.4	1014	"
1966	59.1	40.9	24.0	9.0	969	"
1967	56.1	43.9	28.0	8.5	981	"
1968	52.2	47.8	29.7	10.0	1014	"
1969	49.4	50.6	29.2	12.7	1118	"
1970	54.2	45.8	26.7	10.3	985	"
1971	51.8	48.2	26.5	12.5	970	"
1972	73.3	26.7	16.8	6.0	652	"
1973	75.7	24.3	14.0	4.9	633	"
1974	78.9	[c]21.1	11.6	4.2	634	"
1975	52.3	47.7	23.3	6.9	898	"
1976	75.7	24.3	19.4	1.5	640	"
1977	79.4	20.6	10.5	.6	577	"

Source: U.S. Bureau of Mines, Minerals Yearbook and unpublished data.

Note: Detail may not add to 100 percent, owing to rounding.

[a]Recoverable zinc content.

[b]Includes Newfoundland and Labrador.

[c]See footnote 14.

actually declined 9 percent. It is thus only as a percentage of total supply that domestic mine production has on balance increased in importance. However, production did increase rather steadily in both absolute and relative terms from the late 1950s through the mid-1960s before beginning to decline. In 1969, imports of ore also began to fall, along with domestic smelter output. The result is that, while 1977 mine production was roughly the same as that in 1954, 1977 imports were but one-fourth of the 1954 import total.

Canada has been, and continues to be, the main exporter to the United States, increasing its proportion of total imports from 14 to 51 percent over the period shown, even though the absolute quantities declined by two-thirds. The next most significant supply source has been Mexico, with Peru and Honduras between them generally supplying most of the balance, but the non-Canadian source mix is in a state of flux and may be changing.

Refined Zinc

One can see in table 4-23 that domestic production, including both primary and secondary zinc, has declined as a contributor to total supplies by around 35 percentage points over the period shown, although since 1973 the decline seems to have been arrested.[16] Since the contribution from scrap has remained relatively unchanged, it is apparent that the decline in domestic production has been confined essentially to primary output.

Concurrent with the decline in domestic refined zinc production has been a compensatory increase in zinc imports, rising from 15 percent of the 1954 supply total to over 50 percent of 1977's. Although foreign supply sources have been rather dispersed, Canada has consistently accounted for 40 to 50 percent of imports.

---

[16]According to an article in American Metal Market, March 30, 1978, the 1977 market share held by U.S. producers would have been 5 percentage points greater had it not been for the 140-day strike at Bunker Hill Company.

Table 4-23. Sources and Disposition of U.S. Supply of Refined Zinc

(percentages, except for total supply)

| | Sources | | | | | | | Disposition | | | |
| | Domestic production[a] | | Imports[b] | | Stock drawdown | | Total supply | Apparent | | Stock increases | |
Year	From ores	From scrap	All sources	Canada	Industry	Gov't	(1,000 short tons)	consumption	Exports	Industry	Gov't
1954	74.3	6.4	14.7	9.9	3.6	—	1,066	83.3	2.3	—	c14.4
1955	74.7	5.1	15.2	8.8	5.0	—	1,290	87.0	1.4	—	c11.6
1956	75.6	5.5	18.8	9.0	—	—	1,301	77.2	0.7	0.6	c21.5
1957	74.8	5.0	20.2	7.8	—	—	1,327	65.6	0.8	5.5	28.1
1958	76.3	4.6	19.1	9.1	1.8	—	1,023	89.2	0.2	3.2	7.3
1959	77.3	5.6	15.2	8.6	0.2	—	1,033	95.9	1.1	—	3.0
1960	80.7	6.9	12.2	7.5	1.8	—	991	92.2	7.6	—	0.2
1961	81.3	5.3	12.2	6.9	1.2	—	1,042	95.2	4.8	—	—
1962	79.9	5.4	12.9	6.6	1.8	—	1,100	96.6	3.3	—	0.1
1963	75.9	5.1	12.3	6.3	6.7	—	1,177	97.1	2.9	—	—
1964	77.9	5.8	9.7	6.2	0.5	6.1	1,225	97.8	2.2	—	—
1965	69.8	5.9	10.7	6.2	—	13.6	1,424	96.8	0.4	2.8	—
1966	69.5	5.7	18.9	7.9	—	5.9	1,474	98.8	0.1	1.0	—
1967	73.8	5.8	17.5	6.3	0.8	2.1	1,271	98.7	1.3	—	—
1968	69.9	5.5	20.9	8.0	1.2	2.6	1,460	97.7	2.3	—	—
1969	71.5	4.9	22.3	10.2	—	1.3	1,454	99.4	0.6	—	—
1970	72.2	6.4	21.4	9.9	—	0.1	1,215	95.9	0.1	4.0	—
1971	61.2	6.5	25.9	12.0	6.1	0.3	1,252	98.9	1.1	—	—
1972	43.4	5.0	35.7	18.5	—	15.9	1,462	98.7	0.3	1.0	—
1973	37.7	5.4	38.3	22.3	1.0	17.6	1,546	99.1	0.9	—	—
1974	38.0	5.4	37.0	18.5	—	19.6	1,459	91.1	1.3	7.6	—
1975	46.1	6.1	40.0	19.1	7.1	0.6	950	99.3	0.7	—	—
1976	39.1	4.9	56.0	24.5	—	—	1,277	97.0	0.3	2.7	—
1977	37.2	7.5	51.1	21.2	4.0	0.2	1,129	99.9	0.1	—	—

Source: U.S. Bureau of Mines, Minerals Yearbook and unpublished data.

Note: Detail may not add to 100 percent, owing to rounding.

[a]Includes electrolytic and distilled primary and secondary slab zinc, but excludes remelted zinc.

[b]Imports are general imports.

[c]Government stock variations not reported; data were estimated by subtracting Bureau of Mines surveyed consumption from total supply.

280

It is worth noting that the Council on Wage and Price Stability (COWPS) concludes that the displacement of domestic supply is a result of the zinc industry's never having recovered from the 1974 recession, partly because of a substitution of lighter materials for zinc, especially in automobiles.[17] Other reasons given by COWPS for the closure of zinc smelting and refining plants are difficulties in meeting environmental standards, obsolescent plants, and lack of sufficient supply of domestic ores and concentrates.

According to Metallgesellschaft, Metal Statistics 1967-1977, the 1978 American car contains on average only 36.5 pounds zinc, compared with 61.7 pounds in 1975 models, as the result of replacement by plastics and aluminum.

In addition to imports and domestic production, inventory variations have also played a significant role in the total supply picture. Historically, industry stocks have been very volatile, owing to the sensitivity of producers and consumers to both real and anticipated price and supply/demand changes. Movements were particularly large in 1974 and 1975 as a consequence of the 1973 economic boom and subsequent bust.

Also, government acquisitions and sales have affected refined zinc supplies more than they have affected those of any of the other nonferrous metals reviewed in this report. The mid-1950s saw large purchases of refined zinc under the aegis of Defense Production Act programs, as well as the barter program of the Commodity Credit Corporation--a flow into government which was reversed starting in 1964. In fact, from 1972 to 1974, government sales amounted to almost 18 percent of the total availability of refined zinc. Now, however, since current federal inventories are far below goals, additional sales of refined zinc are unlikely and the trend toward increasing imports will probably continue. Given this situation, it is not surprising that the United States exports only very small quantities out of its refined zinc supply.

---

[17] Statement of the U.S. Council on Wage and Price Stability before the International Trade Commission, investigation TA-201-31, April 10, 1978.

Summary

U.S. mine production as a source of total ore supplies is negligible or nonexistent for the ferroalloy metals, is of decreasing importance for bauxite, and has provided relatively increasing percentages for the remaining nonferrous metals. However, where domestic ores have accounted for such an increased percentage, the reason has been as much a relinquishment of relative domestic position in smelting and refining as it has been any improved competitiveness of domestic mining.

With regard specifically to the refined metals, there is no commodity studied herein which has not had at least a slight shift in supply sources, between the 1960s and the 1970s, in favor of imports. This shift has been significant enough for refined zinc, ferrochromium, and ferromanganese that actual quantities of domestic production have decreased in addition to the relative percentages.

With the introduction of new, higher stockpile goals in October 1976 for most of the commodities discussed, the availability of government supplies was effectively curtailed. For most of the ores and refined metals, this supply loss will likely be made up by further increases in imports.

What is more significant than imports as such is the generally limited number of foreign suppliers. The number of companies as well as the number of countries is limited, and a steadily increasing proportion of the supplying companies are under other than U.S.--frequently host-government--control.

Nevertheless, the United States is still the world's largest producer of copper, lead, and zinc ores, and the needs for these ores are likely to be met primarily by domestic production for some time to come. The domestic supplies of refined aluminum, copper, and lead metal have also generally held their own, giving way only in relative terms to increasing metal production in ore-producing countries and--especially in the case of aluminum--a reliance primarily on imports to meet increments in demand. The absolute shifts in favor of imports for alumina and for refined zinc are unique. The former results largely from the possibility of meeting expanding alumina needs from less expensive sources, coupled with an increasing insistence of bauxite producers on exporting alumina rather than ores. The increase in refined zinc imports is a symptom of the difficult situation in which the industry finds itself. Though the position of the zinc producers has probably now stabilized, neither shift is likely soon to be reversed.

Supplies of all types of scrap have been and will continue to be almost exclusively a result of domestic generation.

Chapter 5

FUTURE SUPPLY POTENTIAL

Introduction

On a long-term, worldwide basis, there is no logical reason for supply to differ at all from consumption, except for long-run buildup or
drawdown of stocks. Generally it is a buildup, since consumption trends
ordinarily are upward, but the average annual stock accrual tends to be
insignificant over any lengthy period in relation to consumption per se.

Two circumstances render a separate examination of supply in order,
and both are central to this study's purposes. One is location: the geographical distribution of potentially available supplies may not match the
distribution of potential industrial consumption. The other, and more
critical, circumstance is that potentially available global supply may not
come close to matching the predicted global volume of consumption. If
potential supply is projected to be only mildly insufficient or in excess
of needs, there is no practical way to draw any inferences as to supply or
price problems: the uncertainty surrounding the initial consumption projections is compounded by the general ignorance concerning supply potential and the long-run impacts of price on consumption or of supply overages and shortfalls on price. What it is reasonable to assume, however,
is that there is generally a fairly sizable range within which price is
significantly less important as a determinant of consumption than are
economic growth, technology, and institutional factors.

Note the emphasis on supply "potential." It is assumed here that
actual production, on average, will match projected consumption, so long
as the production potential is at least as great and not far in excess.
If we find a prolonged period ahead during which it appears that supply

potential will be less than projected consumption, we have found, by our definition, a supply problem, though not necessarily a significant, let alone a "major," one. If there is a predictable buildup toward potential production well in excess of projected consumption, this also signifies a supply problem, though in this case a problem for producers rather than consumers. Our method thus differs from that sometimes used, namely, making independent tentative predictions of consumption and actual production and then determining how much either or both, as well as price, must change in order to achieve equilibrium.[1] To the extent that more studied forecasts could be made of both consumption and supply than were possible in the present research, the differences in approach could be narrowed, but the utility of projecting supply potential, or capacity, rather than production per se, would remain.

We focus on capacity at two geographical levels: the world as a whole and principal world traders. For some commodities, the "world," as a practical matter, is less than global, since for part of it there are not even crude historical estimates. The "world traders" of interest differ from commodity to commodity and include not only net exporters but net importers, since both have an influence on world prices. Of importance is the fact that, for any particular commodity, the net exporters may be utilizing part of their total supply for domestic consumption, and the net importers may be partly self-supplied. In this chapter, we have explicitly identified the "principal international suppliers" figuring in our capacity projections, but have been less rigorous in identifying the consuming countries taken into account in the trading-world comparisons, which were made only roughly and the results of which are given only on a qualitative basis. In general, however, they are the principal international traders discussed in chapter 2.

As in the case of the consumption projections, supply potential is considered individually for each of the mineral forms for which distinctions have been made and for which the requisite data are available. In fact, in discussing supplies of bauxite and of chromite, this chapter

---

[1]An even greater contrast exists for dynamic modeling methods, which chain together a series of short-term equilibria connected by price feedbacks on production and consumption.

makes further distinctions as to specific type which were not possible on a global basis for the consumption projections.

The potential supply of any given mineral commodity is constrained both by production capacity and by the current supply of the cruder form of the commodity required as feedstock. For the crudest forms—ores and the obsolete component of scrap—supplies are constrained by available resources, "in" or "above" ground. The availability of new scrap is constrained by the current consumption of the particular metal in refined form. Consumption projections at various levels have already been made roughly consistent with one another in the analysis in chapter 2, but the discovery in this chapter of supply overages or shortfalls for any one form of a mineral commodity may turn out to have implications for the supply and consumption of some other form.

Cobalt

Because until recently there was little or no cobalt metal produced in the United States, there seemed to be no need to give attention to the consumption of cobalt ore or other feedstock for such production.[2] Supply of the metal, however, is important to the United States and depends in turn on the world supply of cobalt ore, concentrates, matte, or other feedstock, as well as on metal refining capacity. The cobalt supply system as a whole is unusually complicated by the fact that there are varying routes to metallic cobalt, varying degrees of refining prior to consumption, and an involved geography of metal flow from mine to consumer. The one salient factor about the system, however, is that it is controlled by relatively few refiners—especially by the Belgian firm Union Miniere, its

[2] The situation began to change with the inauguration in 1975 of an Amax Inc. refinery in Louisiana, which is moving toward an output of 1 million pounds of cobalt a year. Another plant of equal size was started up in North Carolina in 1980 by Metallurgie Hoboken Overpelt, part of the Union Miniere cobalt refining and marketing group. Together, however, these plants represent only about 3 percent of current world cobalt consumption and only about 10 percent of U.S. consumption (to which not all of the plants' output is being directed).

affiliates, and its Zairian cooperators, who together account for some
three-fifths of non-Communist-world metallic cobalt production.[3]

As of 1977, the U.S. Bureau of Mines and the U.S. Geological Survey
jointly estimated identified world cobalt resources at about three times
reserves; reserves, in turn, were almost 50 times current production.
These figures do not include the ocean nodules, the exploitation of which
is distinctly possible starting in the late 1980s. Unless restricted by
international agreement or authority, this mining might yield very large
amounts of cobalt at well under current prices. World cobalt reserves are
among the largest, in relation to production, of almost any metal, and,
since cobalt is one of the more common elements in the earth's crust (more
common, for example, than lead), there are undoubtedly large additional
resources that exploration could identify. Physically, therefore, there
is no ultimate resource constraint on meeting the roughly 60 percent increase in cobalt consumption projected for the period 1975-2000.

The important constraints are political and economic. As a practical
matter, just about all cobalt so far has been extracted as a by-product
either of copper or nickel, and especially of the former. Since copper
consumption is being projected nearly to double over the 1975-2000 period,
it is not at all impossible that the required cobalt production will
readily be forthcoming. But it is particularly the African copper that
has substantial quantities of cobalt associated with it, and African output may or may not double. On the other hand, given the considerable
amounts of cobalt, associated usually with nickel, in so-called "later-
itic" ores around the world, including the United States, there is potential for increasing amounts of economic production from this kind of
source.

Essentially, therefore, sufficiency of cobalt supply seems to come
down to timely construction of processing capacity. It is difficult to
predict whether this will in fact occur, since economically sized reduction units are expensive and few, and, owing to the variety of routes
from ore or concentrate to refined metal, it is difficult to achieve the

---

[3] James C. Burrows, Charles River Associates, Cobalt: An Industry
Analysis (Lexington, Mass., D.C. Heath, 1971) pp. 115-116.

matching of the various steps in the process that is necessary for capacity to be fully utilized. For example, full use of refining capacity in
Belgium may mean less than full use in Zaire, or vice versa. Expansion of
output in Zaire depends in part on completion of power transmission facilities. Output of the large Marinduque Mining cobalt "refinery" in the
Philippines (actually a semiprocessing operation) is being finally refined
in Japan. Japan has been increasing its refining operations, but their
effective capacity may depend on a major expansion of the Marinduque operation. Large new mine production of cobalt (from laterite deposits) was
reported being planned for Indonesia, but the report does not mention
processing plans. In general, a great deal of cobalt which is mined in
conjunction with other minerals seems currently to remain unrecovered, so
there is an apparent supply potential that hinges only on processing economics.[4]

Construction time for at least the processing and refining aspects of
cobalt production does not appear to be more than a few years; thus most
of the lead time needed for production expansion has to do, at the one
end, with decision-making and the arranging of financing and, at the other
end, with overcoming startup problems that interfere with rapid attainment
of full production. On balance, it seems a reasonable conclusion that, so
long as there is relative confidence in the persistence of high prices for
cobalt, the needed metal production capacity will be forthcoming. The
very existence of this capacity is likely to become one of the major
blocks to the development of deep-sea cobalt extraction, depending upon
ownership patterns and the extent to which the various land-oriented
plants can be adapted to deep-sea cobalt processing and refining.

In sum, a current best guess is that world cobalt capacity will expand haltingly to meet projected consumption levels, and that controls of
one sort or another, both private and official, will effectively operate
to avert any long-run surplus.

---

[4]Information on existing and prospective plants is from Scott F.
Sibley, "Cobalt" (draft, Mineral Commodity Profiles, 5, May 1978) p. 2;
and Engineering and Mining Journal, January 1979, "Survey of Mine and
Plant Expansion."

Trading World

Normally, the USSR does not draw on the market-oriented economies for cobalt, since it has substantial mine production of its own and access to expanding supplies from Cuba.[5] Principal trading-world consumer-importers are, therefore, the United States, West Germany, France, the United Kingdom, and Japan. Japan is doing a great deal to ensure its own supplies, by establishing ore and intermediate flows, particularly from the Philippines and Australia, and expanding its own refining industry. France has important supply arrangements with Morocco. But essentially, the price of traded metal is a worldwide one, set by the mutual consent of the free-world producers, sustained by the dominant Belgian-Zairian partnership. Should surpluses ever develop, the Zairians would be less likely to sustain prices than to sustain their share of the market against competitors. As of now, however, it also looks as if their influence with other "Third World" countries would permit them to prevent any serious price erosion as the result of the recovery of cobalt from ocean nodules, either by delaying ocean mining or by seeing to the international setting of the marine cobalt price.

Chromium

Chromite

The most important fact about the world's chromite supply is its high concentration; some 40 percent of the world's current production, 60 percent of the non-Communist world's production, and over 99 percent of the whole world's identified resources are in two southern African countries—the Union of South Africa and Zimbabwe (Rhodesia). Yet the small portion of resources which lies outside of southern Africa, even omitting those located within the Soviet Union, is sizable enough to sustain non-Communist world consumption well into the next century. Moreover, the grade distinctions which once were of considerable importance have mostly dis-

---

[5]One exception was in May 1978, when a large quantity was purchased from Zaire.

appeared in respect to metallurgical applications, the largest category of chromium usage and the one in which chromium is least replaceable.

The pertinent questions, therefore, have to do with the timely development of mining and processing capacity, and with the distribution of that capacity. During the period 1973-78, world chromite mining capacity was increasing at about 5 percent per year, compared with only about 4 1/2 percent per year for world consumption, and was comfortably in excess of absolute consumption levels. U.S. Bureau of Mines world chromite mining capacity projections for 1980 remain comfortably in excess of the world chromite demand we have projected as a 1978-82 average (4.9 million metric tons of mining capacity compared with 4.3 million tons of consumption).[6] The implied rate of capacity growth for this current period is not quite 4 percent per annum, but our estimated trend rate of consumption growth for 1975-80 (moving averages) is only about 3 percent.

A first approximation of longer range capacity projections for chromite is given in table 5-1. Specific considerations behind the individual projections follow:

> About a quarter of the world's chromite capacity is currently in South Africa, and the record suggests a tendency for a rate of development there that will more or less maintain this share. Zimbabwe, according to Bureau of Mines estimates, has been losing share by not adding to its capacity over the recent past, but this may be, if not simply a matter of missing information, a function of the embargoes; and, in fact, the Bureau estimates a 20-percent increase between 1978 and 1980. Combined, Zimbabwe and the Union of South Africa probably account for about one-third of world chromite capacity as of 1980. Since the availability of chromite resources in these two countries is far more than ample, their rate of expansion of production capacity beyond 1980 would seem to be primarily a matter of domestic and international politics. Given the record of continuing expansion under unfavorable circumstances, however, it is not unreasonable to assume a rate of future expansion of as much as 4 percent per year.

> Almost another quarter of the world's current chromite capacity is to be found in the Soviet Union. The USSR is facing declining ore grades and location, however: it recent-

---

[6]John L. Morning, "Chromium" (draft, Mineral Commodity Profiles, 1, May 1978) p. 3. The various 1980 country projections given herein are from the same source.

Table 5-1.   Projections of World Chromite Capacity, 1980-2000, Compared with 1975 Capacity and with Estimated and Projected Chromite Consumption

(million metric tons of Cr_2O_3)

	1975[a]	1980[a]	1985	1990	1995	2000
Principal international chromite suppliers:						
South Africa and Rhodesia	1.26	1.59	1.93	2.4	2.9	3.5
USSR	1.08	1.13	1.23	1.3	1.4	1.4
Turkey	.33	.36	.40	.4	.5	.5
India	.24	.24	.26	.3	.3	.4
Philippines	.24	.27	.30	.4	.4	.5
Albania	.34	.40	.46	.5	.6	.6
Total	3.49	3.99	4.58	5.3	6.1	6.9
Brazil	.05	.33	.50	.6	.7	.8
All principal producers	3.54	4.32	5.08	5.9	6.8	7.7
Percent of world capacity	91.9	88.5	86.8	86	86	85
World capacity	3.85	4.88	5.85	6.9	7.9	9.1
Cf. World consumption	3.68	4.29	4.80	5.5	6.1	6.7

[a]Estimates for these years converted from data in chromite content given in John L. Morning, Chromium (Mineral Commodity Profiles, 1, May 1977 and draft, May 1978).

ly opened its first--a very large--concentrating mill and is in the course of going underground for the bulk of its ore. There has been a record of almost continuing decline in mine capacity in relation to domestic consumption, and it is assumed that this trend will continue--at least up to the point of eliminating almost all capability, by the year 2000, to produce an export surplus. Since potential reserves are large enough to support at least self-sufficiency for long into the future, it is assumed that the USSR is not likely to allow itself actually to become import-dependent. Almost all the Russian ore is suitable for metallurgical use; the small amount of refractory grade probably has little or no relevance to world markets.

Well behind the Soviet Union, but still one of the world's principal chromite sources, is Turkey. Turkey was once reported (American Metal Market, May 25, 1977) to be doubling its productive capacity, with most of the increase slated for Japan. However, it has also been reported to be having problems of declining ore grades, making it necessary to stretch the specifications of what is suitable for metallurgical use. The projections given in table 5-1 assume that some significant near-term increase in capacity will be accomplished, but that further increases will be limited by Turkey's inability, for the most part, to meet southern African competition.

Until recently Brazil was not an important factor in world chromite production, but it is coming up so rapidly that its capacity is now almost on a par with that of Turkey. Brazil, too, was reported in May 1977 (American Metal Market) to be doubling its capacity. With estimated chromite resources comparable in size to those of Turkey, it seems likely that Brazil will before long achieve a rather larger output capacity, in part because of momentum and in part because it will be developing more of a domestic demand for this mineral. Because of the domestic requirements, however, Brazil is not likely to be a significant world supplier.

Also comparable with Turkey--and over a longer period-- is Albania. Like Turkey, Albania has high-chromium ores, but its total resource position has been estimated as somewhat lower.[7] Given the lack of any other indications, its mine capacity has been projected to grow at about the same rate (arithmetically) as it has over the past several years.

Philippine capacity had been stationary over a number of years, but the U.S. Bureau of Mines has noted some expansion in progress. The Philippine resource position has been estimated as about on a par with that of Turkey, but only about

[7]Morning, "Chromium."

a fifth of the ore is of metallurgical type, the rest being appropriate for refractory use.

India's chromite resources are believed to be considerably greater than those of Turkey, and of comparable quality, though actually established reserves so far are no larger. Reports of a doubling of productive capacity (American Metal Market, May 25, 1977) were applied to India, as well as to Brazil and Turkey. While, in India's case, the actual pace seems likely to fall even further short of this prediction (at least over any near future), it is reasonable to assume that a combination of its internal requirements for stainless steel and its need for foreign exchange will push it toward continuingly larger chromite output.

Chromite production capacity has been getting progressively more decentralized--undoubtedly in part because of the embargoes that were placed on Rhodesia and concern about the dependability of South Africa. A number of countries beyond the eight leading ones listed are already world suppliers (e.g., Finland, Iran, Mozambique, and Malagasy); and there are a number of others (e.g., Cuba, Canada, and the United States) with chromite resources, if not reserves (identified, economically minable deposits). The projections for world capacity in table 5-1 assume that further decentralization will occur, although at a lessening pace. If so, the amount of capacity that would develop outside of South Africa and Zimbabwe would be enough to meet world consumption outside those two countries within a very few years and would provide progressively larger margins. Whether or not the rest of the world would still remain dependent upon South Africa and Zimbabwe because of their ferrochromium capacity is discussed below.[8] In part however, the capacity projections in table 5-1 take into account the disincentive that chromite capacity in southern Africa has on the development of capacity elsewhere; less secure

---

[8]One reason for the relatively declining net export contribution of chromite by southern Africa is the increasing proportion of that area's chromite which is being converted within the area to ferrochrome.

prospects here would very likely be met by more rapid expansion elsewhere than the table indicates.[9]

In interpreting the chromite capacity figures in relation to U.S. needs, it should be borne in mind that what is relevant is not only the mine capacity of direct suppliers, but that which is available to the producers of the ferrochrome on whose imports the United States is becoming increasingly dependent. So long as South Africa remains open as a source of ferrochromium supply, the latter question becomes of progressively diminishing importance.

The continued adequacy of that portion of the total chromite supply which is suitable for refractory use is also relevant. Since the Philippines are the principal source of refractory chromite, the fact that their chromite capacity in general is projected to increase more slowly than world capacity suggests that there may be a problem. Philippine supplies by themselves, moreover, appear to be insufficient to meet all refractory chromite needs, so that availability from other countries would also be relevant. Without a detailed evaluation of world consumption and capacity for refractory chromite alone (for which there is no statistical base), the question of sufficient supply capacity for this particular grade has to remain somewhat open.

Ferrochromium

Capacity data for ferrochromium are somewhat equivocal, since ferroalloy furnaces may be fairly easily switched among different types of ferroalloys or (especially for blast furnaces) to the making of pig iron. In particular, what has in the past been estimated as ferrochromium capacity may in some instances include capacity for ferrochromium silicon.

---

[9] In interpreting the comparison between projected capacity and consumption--and the apparent surplus--in table 5-1 and other such tables, it is important to bear in mind that the consumption figure is an average value centered on that year, while capacity, conceptually, is the point projection for the end of that year. To be significantly in excess, capacity for a given year has to be substantially more than an amount which is perhaps midway between the consumption figure shown for that same year and projected consumption five years later.

Very few reports are available even on near-future prospects for ferrochrome capacity. Thus, table 5-2 reflects what appear to be trends in the various principal producing countries and reasonable expectations in the light of their chromite capacity, electric power resources, and apparent national plans. In particular, the ferrochromium capacity projections have been made consistent with our projections of chromite consumption.

As will be noted, scattered available data indicate that not only the United States, but Japan and various other of the OECD countries have been reducing, rather than increasing, ferrochromium capacity. In general (Japan being an exception) it is assumed that these trends will continue-- or at least not be reversed. In Japan's case, it is assumed that Japan will tend toward self-sufficiency, but will not regain its former export capacity. The absolute level of USSR capacity is not known: the estimate shown for 1974 is commensurate with unpublished U.S. Bureau of Mines data on Soviet production of ferrochromium. It is evident, however, that major expansion of such capacity has been in progress, and press reports indicate that another 200,000 metric tons (chromium content) of capacity is slated to be brought into production in 1980 (reflected in our projection for 1985). What is not clear is the extent to which this added capacity is intended to meet domestic needs and that of the Comecon countries, rather than being a means of substituting ferrochromium for chromite exports to the West.

If our projections are correct, there will be a continuingly comfortable margin of ferrochrome capacity on a world basis (narrowing somewhat in the mid-1980s), but an increasing proportion of this will be concentrated in southern Africa. Within a decade, in fact, that area would have more than a third of the world's ferrochromium capacity, and the proportion is likely to keep growing, despite considerable expansion in countries like Turkey and Brazil. The only materially large fallback producers would be the USSR and Japan; and the latter country would be requiring the great bulk of its output for home consumption, in addition to being considerably dependent upon southern Africa for its chromite feedstocks.

Table 5-2. Projections of World Ferrochromium Capacity, 1980-2000, Compared with 1974 Capacity and with Estimated and Projected Ferrochromium Consumption

(million metric tons of chromium content)

	1974[a]	1980	1985	1990	1995	2000
Principal international suppliers:						
South Africa and Rhodesia	.34	.57	.71	.94	1.10	1.25
Germany	.11	.14	.14	.14	.12	.12
Turkey	.01[c]	.03	.07	.10	.12	.14
USSR[b]	.16[d]	.32	.44	.52	.59	.66
Brazil	.04[d]	.06	.09	.15	.24	.36
Total	.66	1.12	1.45	1.85	2.17	2.53
Other principal producers:						
Japan	.54	.30	.32	.35	.38	.42
United States	.27[d]	.24	.21	.19	.19	.17
France	.12[d]	.10	.10	.10	.10	.10
Sweden	.07	.07	.07	.07	.07	.07
All principal producers	1.66	1.83	2.15	2.56	2.91	3.29
Percent of world capacity	90	92	94	95	96	97
World capacity	1.84[f]	1.99	2.29	2.69	3.03	3.39
Cf. World consumption[e]	1.33[f]	1.59	1.81	2.21	2.51	2.79

[a]Bundensanstalt fur Geowissenschaften und Rohstoffe and Deutsches Institut fur Wirtschaftsforschung, "Untersuchungen über Angebot und Nachfrage mineralischer Rohstoffe, vol. VII, Chrom (Berlin, 1975), unless otherwise noted.

[b]Estimate based on unpublished U.S. Bureau of Mines ferrochromium production estimates.

[c]Estimate based on unpublished U.S. Bureau of Mines ferrochromium production estimates.

[d]Source as in note a; chromite content estimated by RFF.

[e]For want of historical data, conceptually omits at least part of the consumption in Eastern Europe (other than the USSR), China (P.R.), and the United Kingdom.

[f]Consumption in 1974 only (rather than five-year average).

296

It is hardly necessary to point out, in connection with this and
other such projections, that their fulfillment depends mostly on investment decisions yet to be made--especially over the coming decade. Even
the planning and construction already in progress, which affect particularly the capacity in place during the 1980s, can be altered, delayed, or
accelerated in considerable degree and thus do not give firm indications.
In fact, such a speculative exercise in the implications of current initiatives and trends as is represented in table 5-2 can in itself alter those
trends. Thus, in this particular case, perceptions about both the competitiveness and the security of the southern African supply, as they exist
now and as they evolve over the next five or ten years, will have substantial bearing on the actual size and geographical distribution of world
ferroalloy--if not specifically ferrochrome--production potential. Of
some relevance is a U.S. corporate connection with part of the South
African supply, via a 49-percent interest of Union Carbide in Tubatse
Ferrochrome, Ltd., one of a handful of large South African producers.

Manganese

The geography of manganese deposits has some remarkable similarities
to that of chromite--particularly in respect to the very large proportion
of world resources which is estimated to lie in South Africa. Because of
the close connection of manganese with steel, the geography of its consumption is also similar to that of chromite, though it is somewhat more
dispersed.

Manganese Ore

Though its wealth of resources has made South Africa one of the
leading manganese ore producers, its position is actually overshadowed by
output and capacity in the Soviet Union. Moreover, a number of countries
with much smaller reserves than those of South Africa are also of considerable importance: they include Gabon, Brazil, India, and Australia--
the last of which has been rising rapidly into prominence.

Table 5-3 shows our projections of manganese mining capacity to the
end of the century. Included in the table, as far as possible, is the mining and concentrating not only of manganese ores as such (35 percent or
higher in situ manganese content), but of ores with a naturally occurring
content of 10 to 35 percent. Because of beneficiation, the manganese content of all these ores may be considerably enhanced before shipment. By
the same token, the large and probably growing extent to which manganese
ores are in fact being subjected to beneficiation makes it difficult to
estimate capacity in terms of manganese content, as the table does. To
the extent that trade sources cite concentrating mill capacities (and, as
usual, conflicting citations are common), they generally do so in terms of
ore input; the translation of this into potential output depends very much
on the grade of ore processed and the completeness of recovery. It is
partly on this basis that U.S. Bureau of Mines estimates of output capacity (in contained manganese) have been vigorously questioned within the
steel industry. The Bureau's estimates of reserves, which are relevant to
the length of time that current mines can continue operating, have also
been questioned. Table 5-3 nevertheless accepts the Bureau's capacity
estimates for 1975 and 1980 as a base for further projections. For future
years, it embodies the assumption that declining ore grades will have a
significant impact on capacity measured as manganese content of ores and
concentrates ready for shipment.

On the other hand, little weight is given to the constraining effect
of presently identified reserves (or even presently identified resources).
For most of the producing areas (Australia is a possible exception), it
seems safe to conclude that modest price rises or modest additional exploration would bring substantial new quantities into the reserve (economically producible) classification. Manganese is quite cheap in relation to the value of steel, with the result that costs increases are
likely to have far more impact on supply than on consumption.

Further considerations for the larger producers are as follows:

South Africa: This is where almost half the world's identified
manganese resources are located. The material is becoming progressively harder to get at, however, with underground mining
beginning to replace open-pit on a large scale. Also, naturally occurring grades are on the low side, making concentrating capacity part of the requisite for output expansion. Even

Table 5-3. Projections of World Manganese Mining Capacity,[a] 1980-2000, Compared with 1975 Capacity and with Estimated and Projected Manganese Ore Consumption

(million metric tons of manganese content)

	1975[b]	1980[b]	1985	1990	1995	2000
Principal int'l manganese ore suppliers:						
South Africa	2.36	2.72	3.0	3.3	3.6	4.0
Gabon	1.12	1.29	2.3	2.3	2.3	2.3
Australia	.82	1.45	1.9	1.7	1.4	1.0
Total	4.30	5.46	7.2	7.3	7.3	7.3
Other principal producers:						
USSR	3.81	4.62	4.8	4.8	4.7	4.6
India	.73	.73	.9	1.0	1.2	1.4
Brazil	1.20	1.59	2.0	2.6	3.0	3.5
All principal producers	10.04	12.40	14.9	15.7	16.2	16.8
Percent of world capacity	88.5	90.7	90	88	85	82
World capacity	11.34	13.67	16.6	17.8	19.1	20.5
Cf. World consumption	9.00	10.30	11.6	13.1	15.0	17.1

[a] Or beneficiating capacity, if this is the constraining element.

[b] Source of 1975 estimates and 1980 projections is Gilbert L. DeHuff and Thomas S. Jones, Manganese (U.S. Bureau of Mines, Mineral Commodity Profiles, 7, Oct. 1977 and draft, May 1978).

conservative opinion holds that South African capacity will
continue to increase, however, and our projections reflect
that view.

Gabon: The COMILOG (Cie. Miniere de L'Ogooue) mine in this
country is said to be the world's largest producer of high-
grade manganese ore. There are plans for more than doubling
the current capacity of some million tons of manganese content
in ore, contingent on completion of the Trans-Gabon Railway
and port facilities at Santa Clara; 1981 has been mentioned
as the date, and our capacity estimate for 1985 reflects the
expansion, though recent reports suggest that completion of
the railway may actually be delayed beyond that year.

Australia: Groote Eylandt Mining Company, the one large producer, has been undergoing major expansion and has been reported interested in further substantial expansion if justified by market demand. However, the market will not be very
attractive; ore grades are declining; and there appears to be
an insufficiency of resources for sustained production. Both
an initial expansion and the effects of declining ore grades
are reflected in the projections.

Other principal producers (USSR, India, Brazil): All three
of these countries have been important world suppliers. However, USSR and India have already more or less withdrawn from
such a role and there seems great likelihood that Brazil will
follow. Although USSR manganese resources are estimated by
the U.S. Brueau of Mines to be almost as large as those of
South Africa, doubts have been expressed about the validity
of these estimates. In any case, there is substantial evidence that costs are high and that the USSR output may be
wholly needed to support Soviet and Comecon steelmaking.
India apparently still supplies some manganese ore to Japan,
but is concerned about the extent of its reserves and is
inclined for the most part to preserve them for its own future
needs. Brazil, too, is concerned about the sufficiency of
its reserves for future domestic requirements, especially as
some important deposits have already started to give out. All
three of these countries, nevertheless, have substantial steel
expansion in prospect and are likely to try to increase their
manganese mining capacity to support it. The table reflects
this, except that it also assumes something of a resource constraint.

Manganese mining has had a tendency to become more concentrated in
recent years, but, besides the six countries listed in table 5-3, there
are a rather large number (including the United States) with lower grade
manganese resources, and in at least some of these countries productive
capacity is likely to be significant. Hence, a mild reversal of concen-

tration is assumed, with the results shown. As may be seen, the projections imply a comfortable excess of capacity over requirements, increasing
somewhat during the early 1980s and narrowing thereafter. Morever, most
of the projections shown in the table have been constrained by conservation and market considerations and could easily have been put at a higher
level. Even at their present levels, however, they are contingent on some
amount of dipping into higher cost resources, timely exploration and development (especially India), and development of transportation and other
infrastructure (especially Brazil).

Additional world capacity may be forthcoming as the result of ocean
nodule mining. Greatest interest in these "manganese" nodules, however,
is not for their manganese, but for their values in nickel, and, secondarily, copper and cobalt, which would be recovered as co- or by-products.
Only two of the four North American consortia interested in ocean mining
have reported potential interest in the manganese; of these, the consortium led by International Nickel would apparently recover it as a "syn-
thetic ore," and that led by Deepsea Ventures, Inc. (now a subsidiary of
U.S. Steel and others in a consortium known as Ocean Mining Association)
has indicated recovery of manganese as pure metal. It is not clear that
an ore equivalent would be forthcoming from even the former, however, given
the probable advantages of integrated further processing into ferromanganese. If priced competitively with the manganese in ferromanganese, the
pure manganese would be a partial substitute. Thus, the most probable
impact of ocean mining would be on the capacity to deliver ferromanganese
or its equivalent in pure metal, but it would also render world mining
capacity in the 1990s more ample in relation to world manganese ore demand
than it would otherwise be.

Ferromanganese

As with ferrochromium, capacity indications for ferromanganese cannot
be very precise, since capacity is convertible to other ferroalloys and
to manganese metal. The blast furnace portion of ferromanganese capacity
is particularly convertible to other iron-manganese alloys and to pig
iron. The data and the projections therefore have to be taken as no more
than rough indications.

Thus qualified, the prospects for potential ferromanganese supply are set forth in table 5-4. The projections are heavily conjectural; even current capacity data are not available in some instances (USSR) and are probably erroneous in others (South Africa). It is known, however, that capacity has been closed down very rapidly in the United States, in part because of difficulty in meeting pollution abatement requirements, and it is likely that Japan will follow suit, although not to the extent of forgoing self-sufficiency. French and Norwegian capacities at best are not likely to be expanded, given the increasing competition in the export markets on which those countries' outputs significantly depend. On the other hand, because it controls such a large part of the mineral resource, the likelihood is great that South Africa will be steadily expanding its ferromanganese capacity; in fact, a major expansion, from virtually nil a few years ago, has already taken place. The USSR and Brazil are almost certain to keep expanding in order to meet their domestic steelmaking needs and will probably maintain a modicum of export capacity as well. In addition to the seven countries listed in table 5-4, a number of others, including India, Belgium, and Spain, already have significant ferromanganese capacity, and some of these will likely expand that capacity fast enough that countries not listed will become a slightly larger portion of the world total.

Part of the readjustment in ferromanganese capacity that is currently taking place may be said to have been prompted by an apparent global excess. Net contraction should turn into expansion again during the 1980s and beyond, but our projections suggest an untenable thinning of the capacity margin, particularly near the end of the century.

The rapidity of this later ferromanganese capacity expansion will depend to a degree on developments in ocean nodule mining. As noted earlier, it is possible that such mining may lead to the installation of ferromanganese capacity integrated with the nodule processing, or--alternatively or in addition--may involve the recovery of pure manganese metal that can be substituted (within limits) for ferromanganese. The amount of the latter would probably not be great enough to significantly discourage conventional ferromanganese expansion, judging by the fact that Deepsea Venture's initial plans call for less than 300,000 tons annually of man-

303

Table 5-4. Projections of World Ferromanganese Capacity, 1980–2000, Compared with 1986 Capacity and with Estimated and Projected Ferromanganese Consumption

(million metric tons)

	1976[a]	1980	1985	1990	1995	2000
Principal international suppliers:						
France	.6	.6	.6	.6	.6	.6
Norway	.4[b]	.4	.4	.4	.4	.4
South Africa	.5	.7	.8	.9	1.0	1.1
Japan	1.0	.7	.7	.8	.8	.8
Total	2.5	2.4	2.5	2.7	2.8	2.9
Other principal producers:						
United States	.6[b]	.3	.4	.4	.4	.4
USSR	1.0	1.2	1.4	1.6	1.7	1.8
Brazil	.1	.2	.4	.6	.7	.8
All principal producers	4.2	4.1	4.7	5.3	5.6	5.9
Percent of world capacity	72	72	72	72	71	70
World capacity	5.8[c]	5.7	6.5	7.4	7.9	8.4
Cf. World consumption	4.4	4.9	5.5	6.1	7.0	8.1

[a] Bundesanstalt für Geowissenschaften und Rohstoffe and Deutsches Institut für Wirtschaftsforschung, Untersuchungen über Angebot und Nachfrage mineralischer Rohstoffe, vol. VIII, Mangan (Berlin, 1977) unless otherwise noted includes silicomanganese, which is an appreciable proportion of total capacity in Japan, Norway, and Spain. Several countries adjusted to exclude amounts estimated to be devoted to silicomanganese.

[b] Estimated on the basis of output or other indicators.

[c] Partially estimated.

ganese metal output.[10] If the scale of this operation were expanded or if
additional producers opted for the recovery of manganese, either in ferromanganese or as pure metal, the impact would be more substantial, but in
either case the likely outcome would be a net increase in total capacity
to produce manganese in a form suitable for steelmaking and other metallurgical operations. In other words, ocean mining could make the difference between a rather tight ferromanganese situation near the end of the
century and a comfortable one. Conversely, if the tightness comes to pass
and is evident enough, it could be the factor that stimulates rather more
recovery of manganese from ocean nodules than would otherwise be the case.

Aluminum

Because aluminum grew up as a highly integrated industry, there has
tended to be a continuing matching of capacity for aluminum production at
its ore, intermediate, and refined metal stages. Decentralization of ownership has lately been taking place, however, and such decentralization is
all the greater as one gets back into the earlier stages of mining and
processing. Thus, even though some of the new (sometimes national) enterprises are themselves moving toward either integration or assured feedstock
arrangements, there is a greater possibility than there used to be that
supplies and consumption of ore and intermediates may fall out of balance.

Bauxite

Bauxite supply potential has been particularly affected by the shifting pressures and vacuums of economic cycles, national development im-
pulses and goals, and concerns about supply security. In the middle of
the 1970s, there was a flurry of activity among aluminum makers in the
principal producing countries to ensure themselves of sources of bauxite
supply, along with protection against abruptly raised national levies, at
the same time as producing areas, developing and semideveloped (Australia),

---

[10]The Economic Value of Ocean Resources to the United States (U.S.
Senate Committee on Commerce, Committee Print, December 1974) p. 21.

sought to make the most of their opportunities to exact higher economic rents and move into forward processing. With demand slackening later in the decade, many of the ambitious plans for new mines were being dropped, extended, or put up for new bidders.

The projections in table 5-5 are in considerable measure keyed to actually announced or reported plans, although some of these plans have only vague timetables. The balance of the projections are judgments based on momentum and on the extent of the various countries' estimated bauxite resources. For comparative purposes, the projections have all been stated in terms of estimated aluminum content. Base estimates, as of 1977, are from the U.S. Bureau of Mines.

Australia, which, after Guinea, has the largest reported resources of bauxite of any single country, seems likely to maintain its position during the balance of the century as the world's largest bauxite producer.[11] A current capacity expansion of about 1.7 million tons of bauxite annually (approximately 340,000 tons of contained aluminum) is the basis for the 1980 capacity projection; the 1985 projection is the same as the 1983 projection of the U.S. Bureau of Mines.[12] Long-range plans already publicized, but not yet in the form of firm projects, suggest a further stepping up in pace thereafter; and the momentum is assumed to continue, although at a slackening relative rate, through the balance of the century.[13]

Guinea's expansion of bauxite production seems likely for a while to be more rapid than that of Australia. We have assumed a slowing down toward the end of the century, however, with the result that the net rate of

[11]John W. Stamper and Horace F. Kurtz, Aluminum (U.S. Bureau of Mines, Mineral Commodity Profiles, 14 May 1978) p. 9.

[12]Projection for Oceania, converted from short tons. Source: Stamper and Kurtz, Aluminum, p. 4.

[13]Two projects, initial phases of each of which have been reported under feasibility study, would eventually involve about 3 million tons per year of bauxite each--equivalent to about 600,000 tons each of aluminum. One project, initially planned for 1 1/2 million tons of bauxite per year, is a consortium operation which would evidently provide feedstock for both Australian and Japanese refineries, while the other, initially planned for about a third of its ultimate size, would be part of an integrated mine/ refinery complex.

Table 5-5. Projections of World Bauxite Mining Capacity, 1980-2000, Compared with 1977 Capacity and with Estimated and Projected Bauxite Consumption

(million metric tons of contained aluminum)

	1977[a]	1980	1985	1990	1995	2000
Principal international suppliers:[b]						
Australia (gibbsite)	6.1	6.4	7.3	12.0	16.0	20.0
Guinea (gibbsite)	3.0	3.5	5.4	8.0	9.2	10.0
Jamaica (mixed)	3.4	3.6	3.9	4.3	4.7	5.2
Guyana (gibbsite)	1.0	1.0	1.2	1.5	2.0	2.7
Surinam (gibbsite)	1.8	1.8	2.0	2.2	2.5	3.0
Total	15.3	16.3	19.8	28.0	34.4	40.9
Other principal producers:						
Brazil[c]	.3	1.0	1.7	3.0	3.6	4.2
USSR[d]	.9	.8	1.0	1.2	1.2	1.0
All principal producers	16.5	18.1	22.5	32.2	39.2	46.1
Percent of world capacity	74.7	74	75	77	79	80
World capacity	22.1	24.5	30.0	41.8	49.6	57.6
Cf. World consumption	[e]17.7	22.6	28.1	34.7	41.9	49.0

[a] Source: John W. Stamper and Horace F. Kurtz, Aluminum (U.S. Bureau of Mines, Mineral Commodity Profiles, 14, May 1978), p. 3.

[b] As time goes on, most of these countries are moving toward relatively complete domestic processing of bauxite into alumina and will therefore cease to be principal international suppliers of bauxite.

[c] Although some Brazilian bauxite is likely to be exported, it is assumed that the great bulk will be processed domestically into alumina.

[d] Some of the USSR's requirements for alumina production are being met from nepheline and from alunite--not included in these projections.

[e] Single year only.

306

increase over the projection period as a whole would be roughly the same for the two countries. The 1980 figure reflects an expansion of the Boke operations of the Cie. Bauxite de Guinee. The 1985 figure includes an 8-million-ton-per-year (gross weight) operation of Alusiusse and the Guinea government, reportedly (Engineering and Mining Journal, January 1979) already under construction. The 1990 figure adds a planned operation, including refinery, which is to be owned by the government and a variety of foreign partners. The 1995 figure reflects a planned further expansion of the Alusiusse/government plant.

Jamaica currently has larger bauxite production capacity than Guinea, but because of its smaller resource base and alienation of potential investors in recent years, Jamaica's expansion is projected to be slower. The 1980 figure represents expansion reportedly completed. Further growth depends at least in part on proposed intergovernmental deals with Mexico and Venezuela—arrangements which past delays and cancellations suggest will not be consummated too rapidly, if at all.

By the year 2000, Brazil should be the world's fourth largest producer of bauxite, having undergone by far the most rapid rate of expansion. The 1980 projection represents mostly expansion by Mineracao Rio do Norte at Trombetas, and the 1985 figure is for further construction under way at the same site. A variety of other projects are in various stages of planning or feasibility study, and although there have been postponements because of poor markets over the past several years, a fairly rapid continuing pace of expansion seems likely. A Brazilian government corporation (CVRD) is involved in a number of these projects, sometimes jointly with foreign aluminum companies, and the intent is usually to supply alumina, rather than bauxite, for domestic or foreign smelting. Brazil's strategy is reportedly to develop its bauxite/aluminum capacity rapidly enough to offset all other nonferrous metal imports by the mid-1980s.

Expansion in both Guyana and Surinam is assumed to be slowed by limitations on total resources and, in Guyana, by political problems as well. The USSR is apparently severly constrained by inadequate resources.

Because of the major expansion potential in some of the countries specifically enumerated in table 5-5, they are projected eventually to account for a somewhat larger, rather than smaller, proportion of total world supply. The resultant world capacity projections, compared with consumption, show a rather tight supply situation throughout the 1980s, with some easing thereafter--but far from a large surplus. It should be noted, however, that our projections for 1985 are well below those made in March 1977 by World Bank staff, the difference being essentially explainable by the Bank's more rapid growth assumptions for Australia and Guinea.[14] They are roughly consistent, on the other hand, with the U.S. Bureau of Mines projections for 1983,[15] and our 1980 projection is a shade higher than the Bank's for that year.

Brazil's bauxite expansion is assumed to be so much committed to domestic processing that Brazil is discounted as a world bauxite supplier. The result is that the rate of gain in capacity on the part of those we do list as principal international suppliers is slightly less rapid than that for the world as a whole. At about 4.4 percent per year, over the 1975-2000 period as a whole, it still considerably exceeds the 3.1 percent per year growth rate in consumption on the part of principal international traders, but the shift to domestic processing even among substantial bauxite exporters raises a question as to the potential sufficiency of export surpluses.

There is also the question of bauxite types. The United States has depended essentially on Guinea, Surinam, and domestic resources for its gibbsitic bauxite; and Guinean expansion goes a long way toward meeting this need. There could be more of a problem with regard to mixed bauxite, for which Jamaica, with its limited expansion and continuing insistence on local processing, is the only major source. Any expansion of bauxite consumption (refining), however, carries with it the option to design facilities in accordance with the kind of feedstock that will be available. Moreover, the expected expansion rate of bauxite refining in the United States, only 0.7 percent per annum, is small enough to seem well within the capacity of available world export surpluses to satisfy.

---

[14] Commodity Paper No. 24. The Bank's projections did not go beyond 1985.

[15] Stamper and Kurtz, _Aluminum_.

Alumina

The U.S. Bureau of Mines notes: "In 1977 about one-half of the metallurgical-grade bauxite mined was processed to alumina or aluminum in the
country of origin." The proportion is increasing, especially for alumina.
Nevertheless, alumina capacity continues to be widely spread around the
world, some of it being operated by aluminum producers and not an insignificant amount by third-party processors (or by related processors at
detached locations). Still, at present, some four-fifths of world capacity
is accounted for by ten leading countries, listed in table 5-6.

As of 1977, the United States still had the largest alumina capacity,
barely edging out Australia. Over the past half-dozen years, U.S. capacity
has remained essentially unchanged, except for an addition at the Martin
Marietta plant at St. Croix, Virgin Islands. The latter is reflected in
the projected U.S. capacity for 1980, and a further expected expansion is
reflected in the projection for 1985. The only other initiative reported
for the United States is a proposed 600,000-ton refinery in Utah, which
would produce alumina from alunite, rather than bauxite, mined at the same
site. On the grounds that the relative bauxite stringency we have projected for the early 1980s will tend to move this project forward, despite
its borderline nature, we have included it in the capacity projection for
1990. Subsequent years' figures represent a speculative allowance for
modest further increases in alumina refineries operating on bauxite.

In contrast with the United States, the alumina situation in Australia
is anything but quiescent. For example, a new Alcoa refinery there--which
will bring to three the number of refineries in Australia owned by a 51-
percent subsidiary of Aluminum Company of America--is still under construction (scheduled for opening in 1982), but its target capacity has already
been raised from 200,000 to 500,000 metric tons.[16] Moreover, Alcoa is
said to have environmental clearance for capacity at that site of as much
as 2 million tons. Another company, jointly owned by Reynolds and Anacon-
da, plus Dutch and Japanese interests, is planning a million-ton refinery
for the early 1980s, and there are announced plans, less well advanced, by

---

[16]*American Metal Market*, May 17, 1979.

Table 5-6. Projections of World Alumina Capacity, 1980-2000, Compared with 1977 Capacity and with Estimated and Projected Alumina Consumption

(million metric tons of Al_2O_3)

	1977[a]	1980	1985	1990	1995	2000
Principal international suppliers:						
Australia	6.7	7.2	8.3	10.0	13.0	16.0
Jamaica	3.0	3.0	3.3	3.6	4.0	4.4
Surinam	1.3	1.3	1.5	1.5	1.5	1.5
Brazil	.4	.7	1.5	3.0	5.5	8.0
Total	11.4	12.2	14.6	18.1	24.0	29.9
Other principal producers:						
United States	7.0	7.1	7.2	8.0	8.4	8.6
USSR	3.1	4.3	4.4	5.5	6.0	6.5
Japan	2.6	2.8	2.8	2.8	3.0	3.2
Canada	1.2	1.4	1.4	1.6	1.6	1.8
France	1.3	1.5	1.8	2.0	2.2	2.4
Germany (F.R.)	1.7	2.3	2.5	2.8	3.2	3.8
All principal producers	28.3	31.6	34.7	40.8	48.4	56.2
Percent of world capacity	81.3	83.5	81.0	77.0	73.5	70.0
World capacity	34.8	37.8	42.8	53.0	65.9	80.3
Cf. World consumption	b30.0	39.8	49.6	59.6	70.0	81.1

Source: John W. Stamper and Horace F. Kurtz, Aluminum (U.S. Bureau of Mines, Mineral Commodity Profiles, 14, May 1978), p. 3. Data converted from source data in short tons of contained aluminum.

[a] Single year only.

Alumax (a company owned by Amax, along with Japanese and Dutch interests) for another 1.5 million tons--far more than enough fuel for an Australian aluminum plant it is thinking about for the mid-1980s. Still another firm is contemplating a 600,000- to 1-million ton refinery for the 1980s; this has been delayed by opposition on environmental grounds.

It appears, however, that even all these plans may be insufficient to sustain the growth in alumina capacity in Australia that the rest of the world may be depending upon. Our earlier projections of Australia's contribution to world alumina supply (table 2-12, in chapter 2) called for Australia to process its own bauxite to the extent, for example, of 7.1 million tons (aluminum content) in 1985 and 11.5 million in 2000. Even with a fairly liberal allowance for use of bauxite for other than alumina and for losses in processing, this equates to alumina production (aluminum oxide) of some 12 and 19 million tons, respectively. This contrasts with prospective capacity, projected on rather optimistic assumptions as to the rate of progress in fulfilling plans and completing construction, of only about 8 million tons in 1985 and 16 million in the year 2000. Clearly, some rethinking of Australia's contribution is called for.

Is there a prospect for spare refinery capacity elsewhere in the world? Not in the United States--at least in the near future. If our projections for this country are anywhere near accurate, there would barely be enough capacity throughout the 1980s to handle the bauxite whose consumption in the United States we have already projected. By the year 2000, on the other hand, there might be a margin of perhaps a million tons, and there is more than enough time between now and then for this to be enlarged.

The USSR is another of the world's largest bauxite refiners, and it will be depending increasingly on imported bauxite. The large jump in Soviet capacity projected for 1980 represents mostly the assumed coming on stream of a million-ton plant reported several years ago to be under construction at Nikolayev, on the Black Sea, to supply a smelter under construction in Siberia; recent reports suggest that the project has been delayed. The similar large jump in 1990 is mostly attributable to a new operation planned for the Pacific Coast. Rather than Australian bauxite, however, at least the first of these two Russian installations was to be fed with Guinean bauxite whose extraction was developed with the help of Soviet financing.

It should be noted that there is a considerable discrepancy between base data on USSR alumina capacity and its bauxite consumption. Allowing for the use of alunite and nepheline, it would have taken perhaps 5 million tons of alumina capacity in 1977 to process the bauxite estimated to have been consumed in that year. However, the bauxite consumption data are subject to considerable estimation error, particularly as to aluminum content. If, on the other hand, it were the capacity rather than bauxite consumption data that were at fault, absolute levels of USSR alumina capacity, past and future, would have to be estimated much higher--though not enough to undo the implication of world capacity shortfall shown in table 5-6 and noted further later.

The continuing large importer of Australian bauxite has been Japan, but there has been no report of Japanese plans for refinery expansion. Thus, the projected capacity growth shown in table 5-6 represents essentially that needed to handle the bauxite consumption which we had earlier projected. The projections for West Germany, based partly on announced plans and partly on momentum, suggest that future bauxite consumption may have been slightly overstated for that country. Alumina capacity in lesser producing countries has similarly been projected partly on the basis of announced plans and partly on the basis of the projections of bauxite consumption in chapter 2.

Assumptions for the relative decentralization of alumina capacity have followed those adopted earlier for bauxite consumption, with adjustment for the inclusion in this table of express data for Brazil. As may be seen in the table, implied world capacity shortfalls begin in the near future, reach a peak in the late 1980s or early 1990s, and just about dissipate by the end of the century. The lack of margin implies persistent difficulty even at that point, however, because of the commitment of much of the production to particular buyers.

On the other hand, between the self-supply capability of principal alumina consumers and the total capacity of the principal international suppliers, there should be more than enough supply potential to meet the total requirements of the principal consumers. If, for example, approxi-

mately two-thirds of the output (at capacity) of principal international
suppliers were actually available on the international market, the needs
of principal consumers could be met throughout the projection period,
though only barely so in the mid-1980s. This would constitute a substantial (and probably unachievable) preemption, however, against those countries with aluminum reduction plants or potential, but without domestic
alumina facilities.

Comparisons are possible with projections of alumina capacity made by
the U.S. Bureau of Mines for 1983 and by the World Bank for 1980 and
1985.[17] The latter's projections are slightly higher for 1980 and considerably higher for 1985 (in fact, in excess even of our 1990 projections);
we believe them to have been invalidated by the numerous project cancellations and postponements that have occurred since they were made in 1977.
The Bureau of Mines projection for 1983 was made early in 1978, by which
time some of these expansion postponements were evident. It is slightly
in excess of our 1985 projection (when converted from the aluminum equivalent short tons in which it is stated) and thus tends to reinforce our
nearer term projection when further project postponements are considered.
Ideally, of course, projections such as these should be self-defeating
prophecies, though the room for readjustment between now and 1985 is
rather limited.

Refined Aluminum

Since aluminum reduction capacity is generally planned with specific
sources of alumina in mind (if not actual companion projects), one would
expect to find a similar shortfall in the outlook for aluminum capacity.
There is, in fact, a shortfall, as may be seen in table 5-7, but it is
less severe than that for alumina. Moreover, if consumption develops as

---

[17]Stamper and Kurtz, _Aluminum_, and World Bank Commodity paper No. 24
(March 1977), Annex V.

projected, its effect on expansion plans could easily invalidate the projected shortfall by the final decade of the century.[18]

For the years beyond 1985, the projections in table 5-7 have been taken from a U.S. Bureau of Mines tabulation of announced expansions. Generally, however, the Bureau of Mines 1983 total for each country has been taken as our 1985 projection, and an allowance has been made for secondary aluminum capacity, since the Bureau tabulates primary capacity only. Secondary capacity is particularly important in the United States, where it has been estimated by the Aluminum Recycling Association at some 2.6 billion pounds,[19] but it is also significant (or likely to become significant) in all the other countries listed except Norway.

For years beyond 1985, the projections generally follow the implications of the changes in alumina consumption projected in chapter 2, a partial exception being made for France, which appears to have excess reduction capacity (unless the alumina data are seriously in error). There is assumed to be a continued rapid spread of aluminum smelting in countries not now principal producers. Brazil, Venezuela, Spain, Yugoslavia, Indonesia, and Saudi Arabia are among the countries with prospectively substantial new capacity.

Since much of the proposed new capacity will be oriented toward aluminum for export, it is difficult to determine the extent to which shortfalls in world capacity would affect the availability of aluminum to principal market-economy consumer-importers. Japan will be in an increasingly import-dependent position, and the United States will be particularly import dependent over the next decade. From the looks of things, a substantial proportion of the world's exportable surpluses will be from the Soviet Union--which has some obligation to the Communist bloc, but also appears to have a substantial interest in utilizing aluminum to convert

---

[18] It is likely, of course, that in terms of lead time, planning for aluminum smelters precedes the planning for sources of alumina feed, so that as one looks further in the future, a widening gap between the two kinds of plans is more or less to be expected.

[19] *American Metal Market*, May 26, 1978. (The article erroneously refers to "billion tons," where "billion pounds" is evidently intended.)

Table 5-7.   Projections of World Aluminum Capacity, 1980-2000, Compared with
1977 Capacity and with Estimated and Projected Aluminum Consumption

(million metric tons)

	1977[a]	1980[a]	1985[b]	1990	1995	2000
Principal international suppliers:						
Norway	.7	.8	.9	1.2	1.4	1.6
Canada	1.1	1.2	1.3	1.5	1.6	1.7
USSR[c]	2.6	3.4	3.5	4.2	4.9	5.6
Total	4.4	5.4	5.7	6.9	7.9	8.9
Other principal producers:						
United States	5.9	6.1	6.5	9.0	9.5	'10.0
Japan	2.2	2.2	2.3	2.6	2.9	3.2
France	.6	.7	.9	.9	1.0	1.0
Germany (F.R.)	1.2	1.2	1.4	1.7	1.9	2.1
All principal producers	14.3	15.6	16.8	21.1	23.2	25.2
Percent of world capacity	73.7	71.6	68.6	64.8	60.3	55.2
World capacity	[d]19.4	21.8	24.5	32.6	38.5	45.7
Cf. World consumption	17.2	22.2	27.7	33.3	39.3	46.2

[a]Source: U. S. Bureau of Mines, _Primary Aluminum Plants, Worldwide, Part Two -
Summary_ (listing as of July 31, 1978), plus allowance for aluminum and aluminum-base
alloy recovered from purchased scrap.

[b]As in preceding footnote, with allowance in some cases for additional capacity
starting 1984-85. (Last year of Bureau of Mines tabulation is 1983.)

[c]Although the bulk of USSR exports goes to Comecon countries, a substantial (and
probably growing) amount is destined to market oriented countries.

[d]Single year only; partly estimated.

315

the hydroelectric potential of Siberia into hard-currency earnings. For
much of this aluminum, Japan would be the natural customer.

Aluminum Scrap

Capacity for scrap production is a matter of managing collection and
installing processing equipment. Neither has very long lead times and,
with the heightened importance of recycled containers, an increased proportion of obsolete aluminum scrap will be returned to production channels
semiautomatically. Another portion may require more elaborate separation
equipment than heretofore--particularly that which is potentially recoverable from municipal waste streams and junked motor vehicles.

Copper

If aluminum projects have been cancelled and postponed over the past
half-dozen years, one would have expected even more erratic behavior for
copper, since copper companies, from 1974 to 1978, had a much poorer price
and profits history and went into debt far beyond their historical custom.
The ownership and control of copper facilities are far more dispersed than
those for aluminum, however, so that prevailing consensuses tend to have
less of an impact on the actual rate of world expansion. Moreover, in the
United States at least, energy companies, which are capable of making
substantial financial infusions, have bought into the copper industry and
may be bringing with them a less constrained, longer run, perspective.

Copper Ore

With the gradual historical shift of copper mining into large, open-
pit operations that process large amounts of material of relatively low
copper content, copper ore capacity has more and more tended to be added
in the same sort of large, discontinuous increments as have characterized
aluminum ore (bauxite). There are still many small producers and small
mines, however--enough to have at least negative effects on capacity
through temporary or permanent abandonment. Even if information were
readily and conveniently available about these smaller workings, it would

be difficult to reach conclusions about their meaning for copper ore capacity, since they have varying degrees of susceptibility to rapid expansion and, when inactive, offer varying degrees of practical susceptibility to reentry. The same is true of many of the larger workings as well.

The projections in table 5-8 are mostly impressionistic, therefore, though they are based in large part on an analysis of reported new mines and expansion plans. As is to be expected, slippage in these plans has been common, especially over the past few years, and even seemingly well-advanced projects have sometimes been sent back to the drawing boards. On the other hand, minor, unheralded expansions have a tendency to keep popping up and tend to counterbalance a continuing number of mine closings.

The largest absolute contributions to increased world copper mining capacity, over the 1975-2000 period, seem likely to come from Canada and the Philippines. Other substantial contributions may be expected from Papua New Guinea, the USSR, Mexico, Peru, and Poland. The two largest contributors, plus Papua New Guinea and Mexico, are likely to be among those providing substantial quantities of ore and concentrate for world markets, even if all except possibly Papua New Guinea will be engaged in substantial domestic smelting and refining as well.

A principal contributor to the Canadian expansion (coming in by 1990) is a potential joint venture of Bethlehem Copper Corporation and Valley Copper Mines (both Canadian companies) to exploit copper resources in the Highland Valley of British Columbia. A 50,000-short-ton-per-day (ore) operation is under contemplation, mining 0.45 percent ore. Another large venture, already under development but of unannounced size, is that of Newmont Mines, Ltd., at Copper Mountain, British Columbia; and still another under development is a 500,000-short-ton-per-year (2.9 percent copper content ore) operation of Falconbridge Copper, Ltd., in Quebec Province. Also under development is a major expansion of a Texasgulf mine at Kidd Creek, in Ontario; in addition, a Texasgulf subsidiary has studies under way for a potential zinc-copper-lead mine at Izok Lake, in the Northwest Territories.

Expansion in the Philippines is likely to be supported by a variety of operations, including, between 1977 and 1980, those of Benguet

Table 5-8. Projections of World Copper Mining Capacity,[a] 1980-2000, Compared with 1977 Capacity and with Estimated and Projected Consumption (million metric tons, copper content[b])

	1977[c]	1980	1985	1990	1995	2000
Principal international suppliers:						
Canada	.98	1.0	1.1	1.3	1.5	1.6
Mexico	.13	.3	.4	.4	.5	.5
Philippines	.21	.3	.5	.6	.7	.8
Papua New Guinea	.18	.2	.3	.4	.5	.6
Chile	1.00	1.0	1.0	1.0	1.1	1.2
Total	2.50	2.8	3.3	3.7	4.3	4.7
Other principal producers						
United States	1.92	2.0	2.0	2.1	2.2	2.2
USSR	1.16	1.2	1.3	1.4	1.5	1.6
Zaire	.65	.8	.8	.9	.9	.9
Zambia	.77	.8	.9	1.0	1.1	1.2
Peru	.43	.4	.6	.6	.7	.8
South Africa	.28	.3	.4	.4	.4	.4
Australia	.30	.3	.4	.4	.4	.4
Poland	.37	.4	.5	.6	.7	.8
All principal producers	8.38	9.0	10.2	11.1	12.2	13.0
Percent of world capacity	91	86	81	77	73	69
World capacity	9.19	10.5	12.6	14.4	16.7	18.8
Cf. World consumption	[d]7.79	9.0	10.5	11.9	13.6	15.2

[a]Or concentrating mill capacity, if that is separately known as the constraining factor.

[b]Or recoverable content, in some instances.

[c]Data primarily from H.J. Schroeder, "Copper" (draft, U.S. Bureau of Mines, Mineral Commodity Profiles, 3, June 1978), pp. 4, 5.

[d]Single year only.

318

Consolidated, at Dizon, and CDCP Mining Corp., at Basay. Potential large contributors to further expansion are Marinduque Mining & Industrial Corp., at Sipalay; Membusar Consolidated Mining (Suso-Damutan); Marcopper Mining Corporation (San Antonio); and Apex Exploration (Mapula).

The Mexican expansion has been widely publicized and will result in large new quantities of copper concentrates for export as well as for domestic smelting. The key component is La Caridad mine, near Sonora, which was expected to be producing 164,000 metric tons per year (copper content) when fully operational. Another large contributor, also already partly in operation, is the Cananea mine (Cia. Minera de Cananea) in the same vicinity, which should have a second stage in operation by 1985.

Two new mines in Papua New Guinea--the Ok Tedi and Frieda River--are behind the assumed expansion in that country. A Centromin (government) expansion at Cobriza and a number of new operations of Mineroperu are part of what underlies the projections for Peru. The potential expansion in Poland has been reported in general terms in the trade press.[20] Soviet copper production plans were recently summarized in Mining Magazine.[21]

Since a number of significant producers and potential producers have been omitted from the specific listing (e.g., Indonesia, Panama, Brazil, India, China, Iran,[22] Turkey) and copper resources are rather ubiquitous around the globe, it is assumed that concentration of production will continue to decrease. Thus, though the capacity of the listed producers is projected to increase only by about half over the period covered, world capacity is projected approximately to double.

If the projections are correct, there would be a comfortable, but not excessive, capacity margin, worldwide, throughout the balance of the century. It may well be, however, that the prospect of such a margin

---

[20]For example, American Metal Market, September 15, 1976 and March 29, 1978.

[21]May 1979; see reference 26.

[22]The bulk of Iranian copper mining expansion rests upon the much publicized Sar Cheshmeh mine. How rapidly planned production capacity can be attained has been of questionable certainty, especially in light of 1978-80 political events.

might lead to a somewhat lesser capacity in fact, owing to greater stretching out of plans and a larger amount of mine closures. Our projection for 1980 is very close to that of the U.S. Bureau of Mines, which has not published capacity projections beyond that point. Excluding Poland and the USSR, for the sake of comparability, our projections become progressively higher than those made to 1990 in a United Nations study[23]--and this is before subsequent adjustments made in that study for possible nonfulfillment of announced plans as well as probable closing and diminution of prevailing grades in existing mines. As just noted, there may be insufficient allowance in our projections for mine closure, but it seems likely that there is greater scope for error in ignoring the potential for new mines and expansions which have not as yet been announced or for capacity which may come upon the scene as an aggregate of smaller operations never individually reported. Increasing resort to the leaching of dump ore and old workings may particularly operate to expand the quantities of copper coming from such miscellaneous sources.

If U.S. capacity is added to that of the "principal international suppliers" and compared with the consumption projections for "principal international traders" in chapter 2 (table 2-16), it may be seen that a relatively thin margin persists for the "trading world" until the 1990s, with some easing up in that last decade.

Up to now, U.S. mining capacity for copper has been sufficiently in balance with smelting capacity that imports of copper ore have not been physically necessary. The small amount of net imports (there is also some exportation of copper ore and concentrate) has evidently been responsive to special situations. If our projections of both ore consumption and mine capacity are correct, however, consumption would progressively eat into and, by the 1990s, exceed spare mining capacity, making it necessary either to increase importation of ores to support

---

[23]Wolfgang Gluschke, Joseph Shaw, and Bension Varon, Copper: The Next Fifteen Years (Hingham, Mass., D. Reidel, 1979) pp. 69-73. The projections in this book exclude the centrally planned economies.

smelting activity or to reduce smelting activity and substitute greater
importation of copper in more advanced forms. Implicitly, we may well
have overestimated smelting activity, which may be reduced because of the
impact of environmental and health and safety regulations, on the other
hand, part of the increased amount of ore consumption that has been
projected would be feed for electrowinning rather than for traditional
smelting processes.

Blister Copper

As noted earlier in this report, only a limited amount of blister
copper moves in commerce and even less in world trade, refining generally
taking place in the country of production, if not at the same site as the
smelting. There currently remains only one important supplier of blister
copper--Chile--and even that country is moving progressively into more
domestic refining. In addition, there is a special relationship between
Zaire and Belgium, in which the former supplies the latter not only with
blister copper, but with electrowon cathode copper which Belgium then
subjects to further electrolytic refining (presumably to recover gold,
silver, and other trace elements which are not separated out in the first,
cruder electrolysis).

Immediate prospects for smelter investment in Chile relate more to
maintaining and rebuilding capacity than to expanding it. The increase
projected for 1985 (table 5-9) assumes that a still uncertain joint project of the Chilean government (CODELCO) and Noranda Mines, Ltd. (Canadian
corporation) will be implemented, with a smelter being included. Subsequent increases in capacity are consistent with our earlier (chapter 2)
projections for ore consumption in Chile, some of which may take the form
of leach treatment rather than smelting.

It is difficult to predict U.S. capacity because of the uncertain
impact of environmental and health and safety regulations. A U.S.
Department of Commerce study has made a finding of "probable shutdown of
three major smelters and the preclusion of capacity expansion or production increases at the remaining smelters, or by new greenfield

facilities."[24] Without any attempt to verify the validity of this conclusion, our initial projection of U.S. smelting capacity assumed that such
shutdowns would actually take place by 1985 and that the Commerce study's
other assumption--no increase in secondary smelter capacity--would also
persist to that date. It was further assumed, in the absence of announced
plans for new capacity, that the lower capacity would continue through
1990, but subsequently give way to new capacity installation, both primary
and secondary. The result of such assumptions, however, was clearly
inconsistent with the ore consumption projections in chapter 2 (table 2-6),
and it was also institutionally inconsistent with the mining capacity
projections given in table 5-8. While the latter would include some
proportion of leach liquids not requiring smelting,[25] and while there is
precedent for sending copper concentrates abroad for smelting, there has
to be a strong presumption that domestic smelting capacity would be kept
more in balance with mining capacity if this were at all financially
feasible. Our final projections of U.S. smelting capacity therefore show
a maintenance of present capacity levels through the 1980s, with subsequent increases sufficient to allow for the processing of some amount of
imported ore.

Capacity projections for the Soviet Union are based primarily on
information in articles by V.V. Strishkov, of the U.S. Bureau of Mines.[26]
After a small increase (in part secondary) by 1980, USSR smelting capacity

---

[24]Industry and Trade Administration, The Potential Economic Impact
of U.S. Regulations on the U.S. Copper Industry (April 1979). Based in
part on data and analyses supplied by Arthur D. Little, Inc. See especially chapter IV.

[25]In situ leaching of copper deposits (and dumped ore and mill
tailings), which might otherwise be expected to keep expanding, also
faces restriction because of pollution problems, but it is assumed that
the scale of such activity is not large enough for a significant effect
on total mining capacity.

[26]"Eastern Europe," The Mining Journal Limited, Mining Annual Review
1978 (London, June 1978) pp. 559-591 (reprinted in part by U.S. Bureau
of Mines as Mineral Industries of the U.S.S.R.); "The Copper Industry of
the U.S.S.R.: Part Two, 1946-1980," Mining Magazine, May 1979, pp.
429-441.

is assumed to expand by 1985 by something over 100,000 tons in Kazakhstan and by another 100,000 tons at Norilsk, in Eastern Siberia. The latter represents first-stage completion of a copper-nickel smelter being constructed with technical assistance from the Finnish company, Outokumpu Oy. (Targeted completion date for both expansions is 1980, but some slippage is assumed.) A further expansion at Norilsk is assumed to be in place by 1990; capacity increases thereafter are conjectural, based on trend.

Although some new smelter capacity is in prospect for Japan--possibly by 1985--it is assumed that there will be enough closures, partly for environmental reasons, that total smelting capacity will not increase and will eventually fall off slightly. Zambia is currently without expansion plans, but it is assumed that steps will be taken to enable it to take advantage of increasing blister copper demand. Canada has already had some small expansion since 1977 and there are a number of plans for longer range expansion which are projected to bear fruit by 1990. The Polish expansion is assumed to keep pace with its ore production.

Concentration of smelting capacity in the principal producing countries should decline over time, for various reasons: lessening concentration of mine production, increasing processing among former ore shippers, and industrialized countries' exportation of pollution. If the assumptions in table 5-9 are correct, resultant world capacity will be sufficient throughout the 1975-2000 period to meet world requirements for copper refinery feed, though the situation will become rather tight in the early 1980s, before gradually easing up thereafter.

On the other hand, an examination of total capacity available just to the principal world traders in blister copper (table 2-15) suggests a very tight situation for the balance of the century. The United States would have to start being a significant importer of blister copper (or other refinery feed) by the mid-1980s, even if it does not close down smelter capacity as the Department of Commerce predicts. This importation necessity would continue for a time, but could well disappear by the end of the century.

Table 5-9. Projections of World Copper Smelting (Blister Copper) Capacity, 1980-2000, Compared with 1977 Capacity and with Estimated and Projected Consumption

(million metric tons)

	1977[a]	1980	1985	1990	1995	2000
Principal international suppliers:						
Chile	.94	.9	1.0	1.2	1.3	1.4
Other principal producers:						
United States	[b]1.83	1.8	1.8	1.8	2.1	2.4
USSR	[b]1.06	1.1	1.4	1.5	1.7	2.0
Japan	1.21	1.2	1.2	1.2	1.1	1.1
Zambia[c]	.87	.9	1.0	1.1	1.2	1.3
Zaire[c]	.54	.5	.7	.8	.8	.8
Canada	.64	.7	.7	.8	.9	1.0
Poland	.35	.4	.5	.7	.7	.8
All principal producers	7.44	7.5	8.3	9.1	9.8	10.8
Percent of world capacity	75.9	72	68	65	62	59
World capacity	[d]9.80	10.4	12.2	14.0	15.8	18.3
Cf. World consumption	8.40	9.6	11.1	12.5	14.1	15.6

[a]Data primarily from H.J. Schroeder, "Copper" (draft, U. S. Bureau of Mines, Mineral Commodity Profiles, 3, June 1978), pp. 4, 5.

[b]From data in Mining Journal, Mining Annual Review, 1978, p. 569 (p. 9 of reprint by U. S. Bureau of Mines, titled Mineral Industries of the U.S.S.R.).

[c]For comparability with the world consumption projections, data for Zambia and Zaire include electrowinning capacity, the product of which (leach cathodes) serves as feed for further refining. Zairian blister copper and leach cathodes tend to go exclusively to Belgium.

[d]Single year; partly estimated.

324

Refined Copper

Since the great bulk of copper refining is electrolytic, considerations of electric power cost and availability are relevant to capacity levels--though unlike the case of aluminum, probably not sufficiently so as to cause any copper refineries to be located solely on the basis of power availability, rather than proximity to ore sources or to copper markets.

Outside of a smallish mine-through-refinery project being considered by Exxon Corporation, there appear to be no announced plans for expansion of U.S. refining capacity. It seems likely, however, that there will be at least limited expansion (or improved throughput) at existing facilities, in part to permit the refining of enlarged amounts of secondary copper, as well as of impure leach cathodes and leach liquids directly. The assumed expansion, which is roughly consistent with "baseline" forecasts made by the U.S. Department of Commerce,[27] is shown in table 5-10.

For want of any independent information, USSR prospects for refinery expansion are assumed to be identical with the projections made for smelter expansion. Japan, like the United States, seems to have no current expansion plans, and the considerations behind our projections are similar to those for the United States. Projections for lesser producers (except Poland, for which expansion plans have been publicized[28]) have been made consistent with our earlier projections of blister copper consumption, allowing for varying amounts of secondary copper refining. In Belgium's case, allowance has also been made for the re-refining of Zairian electrowon cathode; even with this allowance, however, Belgian refining capacity appears to be in excess of long-run needs and it is assumed that some of it will be discontinued.

Although increasing amounts of copper refining capacity are likely to be installed in copper producing countries, most of the important producers are already accounted for in table 5-10. Since, moreover,

---

[27]Industry and Trade Administration, Potential Economic Impact p. B-13 (table 9).

[28]American Metal Market, September 15, 1976, and March 29, 1978.

Table 5-10. Projections of World Copper Refining Capacity, 1980-2000, Compared with 1977 Capacity and with Estimated and Projected Consumption

(million metric tons)

	1977[a]	1980	1985	1990	1995	2000
Principal international suppliers:						
Zambia	.77	.8	.9	1.0	1.1	1.2
Chile	.68	.7	.8	.9	1.0	1.1
Canada	.63	.7	.8	.9	.9	1.0
Zaire	.24	.3	.4	.6	.6	.7
Belgium	.82	.8	.7	.7	.7	.7
Total	3.14	3.3	3.6	4.1	4.3	4.7
Other principal producers:						
United States	2.64	2.7	2.9	3.2	3.4	3.6
USSR	1.06	1.1	1.4	1.5	1.7	2.0
Japan	1.24	1.3	1.4	1.5	1.5	1.6
Poland	.31	.4	.5	.7	.7	.8
Germany	.49	.5	.5	.5	.6	.7
All principal producers	8.88	9.3	10.3	11.5	12.2	13.4
Percent of world capacity	83.2	80	77	75	73	71
World capacity	10.67	11.6	13.4	15.3	16.7	18.9
Cf. World consumption	[b]9.01	9.8	11.4	12.8	14.5	16.3

[a] Principal source: H.J. Schroeder, "Copper" (draft, U. S. Bureau of Mines, Mineral Commodity Profiles, 3, June 1978).

[b] Single year.

decentralization in refining is likely to lag behind that in smelting, a lesser rate of increase in such decentralization is assumed. If the resultant world projections are correct, it appears that there will be sufficient capacity throughout the 1975-2000 period, with some tendency toward tightness in the early 1980s and again toward the end of the century. Much of the tightness, however, is the result of the closely coordinated capacity assumed for the centrally planned countries; for the market-oriented trading world, any refinery-capacity constraints on copper consumption seem likely to be progressively--though only mildly--eased. The easing does not apply to the relationship between projected U.S. refinery capacity and refined copper consumption, though so long as there are not feedstock constraints, U.S. refiners could satisfy the entire domestic refined-copper requirement. However, it seems likely that this capacity will be less than fully utilized, owing to competition from imports.

Copper Scrap

As with aluminum, copper scrap capacity is essentially a matter of collection and processing arrangements, with relatively short lead times required for the installation of new processing capacity. In copper, in contrast with aluminum, there is not the element of increasingly institutionalized container recycling, but there have been long-standing arrangements for the recovery both of new scrap generated in current production and old copper from discarded automobiles. In fact, recent methods have tended to increase the amount of automobile copper actually recovered rather than left as a pollutant in the ferrous scrap component. Recovery of copper from demolished buildings has tended to fall victim to the increased costs of hand labor. In any case, obsolete scrap is only the minor portion of total copper scrap potential, though it is the portion which is relatively price elastic and thus tends to respond fairly rapidly to increased requirements. Copper scrap can always be replaced, of course, by new (virgin)copper, but only at a cost penalty which would heavily affect some copper consumers.[29]

---

[29]Background information in part from Fred V. Carrillo et al., Recovery of Secondary Copper and Zinc in the United States (U.S. Bureau Mines Information Circular 8622, 1974).

Lead

Lead Ore

Lead mining capacity is rather difficult to define, since "most of the world's mine production of lead is recovered from complex ores containing zinc, silver, and often copper."[30] In the Missouri lead belt, which is the largest producing area in the United States, mining is primarily for the lead content, but in many other places it is carried on for the joint values in lead and zinc, and in still other places, lead output (usually in the form of separated lead concentrates) is very much a by-product of mining for silver or copper. Table 5-11 uses as a base U.S. Bureau of Mines capacity estimates for 1976 which appear to reflect total lead output at the concentrator level, whatever the principal product of the source mines.[31] Capacity additions shown in the projections, however, are based in part on tabulations as of September 1977 by the International Lead and Zinc Study Group (ILZSG),[32] and these are confined to new mines and expansions which will produce either lead or zinc as a principal product.[33]

Particularly in older producing areas, such as in the United States and Canada, there is a rather significant continuing rate of mine closings; output in metal content terms is also affected by declining ore grades and lead-zinc ratios. Closings may be accelerated for a time by environmental regulations imposed on the disposal of mine waste and concentration tailings. It is possible that the projections in table 5-11 make insufficient allowance for these effects. On the other hand, the effects

---

[30] J. Patrick Ryan and John M. Hague, Lead (U.S. Bureau of Mines, Mineral Commodity Profiles, 9, December 1977) p. 1.

[31] Industry and Trade Administration, Potential Economic Impact, p. 4.

[32] Restricted circulation document made available to member industrial and governmental representatives.

[33] The ILZSG also provides information on recent or current mine closings.

Table 5-11. Projections of World Lead Mining Capacity,[a] 1980-2000, Compared with 1976 Capacity and with Estimated and Projected Lead Ore Consumption

(million metric tons of lead content[b])

	1976[c]	1980	1985	1990	1995	2000
Principal international suppliers:						
Canada	.44	.45	.53	.62	.66	.67
Peru	.24	.26	.27	.27	.28	.28
Total	.68	.71	.80	.89	.94	.95
Other principal producers:						
United States	.62	.59	.57	.60	.62	.64
USSR	.48	.54	.66	.76	.85	.98
Australia	.45	.48	.52	.57	.63	.70
Mexico	.23	.24	.24	.27	.29	.30
Yugoslavia	.16	.20	.22	.23	.24	.24
All principal producers	2.62	2.76	3.01	3.32	3.57	3.81
Percent of world capacity	63.1	62	61	60	59	58
World capacity	[d]4.15	4.45	4.93	5.53	6.05	6.57
Cf. World consumption	3.52	3.85	4.26	4.70	5.16	5.58

[a] Or lead concentrate capacity. Projections based in part on restricted-circulation tabulations of International Lead and Zinc Study Group (ILZSG). Allowance made for closings and lowered ore grades.

[b] Or recoverable content, in some instances.

[c] Data primarily from J. Patrick Ryan and John M. Hague, Lead (U. S. Bureau of Mines, Mineral Commodity Profiles, 9, Dec. 1977), p. 4.

[d] Single year only.

may be offset by near-term projects not yet reported and the accretion of by-product lead flows from other than lead-zinc or zinc-lead mines.

Canada has a great deal of development activity in progress, including several firm projects, as well as some recent small mine closing. The latter amounted to the loss of about 8,000 metric tons of lead in 1977 and 1978, but at the same time, some 24,000 tons of new capacity was added or was due to be added before the end of 1980. Two new projects in the Yukon were expected to bring in around 63,000 tons in the early 1980s and another, 100,000 tons later in the decade. Various smaller projects, after allowance for closing in excess of unreported expansions, account for the 1985 and 1990 projections; those for the balance of the century are conjectural.

The United States lost about 25,000 tons of capacity in 1978, and it is assumed that there will be further losses by 1985. Since the United States has the largest lead reserves of any country, however, and is in a net import position, it is assumed that there will eventually be a turnaround in mine capacity as indicated.

The USSR is likely to have the steepest growth of lead ore production of any country. The projected increase from 1976 to 1980 is consistent with recent output projections, and subsequent growth is on the assumption that the Soviet Union will aim to achieve maximum possible self-sufficiency. Its reported reserves of lead in ore are comparable to those in Australia. Australia's lead reserves, in turn, are not far behind those of the United States, and it is largely on this fact that the projections for Australia are premised. In addition, however, Australia has 23,000 tons of capacity coming on stream (joint Australian/U.S. project in New South Wales) and a half-dozen other projects in various stages of development. Nearer term projections for the lesser producers--Peru, Mexico, and Yugoslavia-- are based on reported plans as evaluated by the International Lead and Zinc Study Group; longer term projections take into account these countries' more limited reserves, compared with the four largest producers.

Since a number of other countries, not specifically listed, have
the potential for enlarging lead mining capacity,[34] as well as plans for
developing such capacity, it is assumed that there will be increasing
decentralization, but only mildly so. The resultant world projections
indicate a comfortable and not excessive margin of lead mining capacity
for the balance of the century. There is only a slight deterioration
over the same period in availability to the principal international traders
(along with ore for domestic processing in Canada and Peru). Unless we
have overestimated the extent of maintenance of domestic smelting capacity,
the United States would become considerably more import-dependent for
its lead concentrate feedstock.

Refined Lead

Refined lead capacity is almost as difficult to define as lead ore
capacity, though for different reasons. Most of the available information
has to do with primary smelting-refining capacity, but, as pointed out
in chapter 2, lead consumption requirements can also be satisfied by lead
reclaimed from scrap--and such reclaimed lead is a rather important portion of total lead consumption. Thus, the base-year estimates and the
projections in table 5-12 attempt to make a reasonable allowance for
secondary lead recovery capacity, whether it is done at secondary "smelters"
or by automobile battery makers (but not including the more specialized
lead in remelt alloy). Even if there were fuller information on secondary
capacity, there would be a problem in determining effective capacity
because much of it is not capable of producing the soft lead that will
apparently be required in increasing proportion in order to meet lead
specifications for the new maintenance-free batteries.

Another difficulty in projecting refined lead capacity is the uncertain extent of shutdowns of existing capacity because of obsolescence
or because of difficulty in meeting health and safety or pollution

---

[34]South Africa, India, and the People's Republic of China seem to
be of particular significance.

Table 5-12. Projections of World Lead Refinery Capacity, 1980-2000, Compared with 1976 Capacity and with Estimated and Projected Refined Lead Consumption[a]

(million metric tons)

	1976[b]	1980	1985	1990	1995	2000
Principal international suppliers:[c]						
Australia	.26	.3	.3	.3	.3	.3
Canada	.30	.3	.3	.3	.3	.3
Mexico	.28	.3	.3	.4	.4	.4
Total	.84	.9	.9	1.0	1.0	1.0
Other principal producers:						
United States	1.63	1.8	1.8	1.9	2.0	2.1
USSR	.71	.8	1.0	1.1	1.2	1.3
Germany (F.R.)	.47	.4	.4	.5	.5	.5
Japan	.34	.3	.3	.3	.4	.4
France	.23	.2	.3	.3	.3	.4
United Kingdom	.32	.3	.3	.4	.4	.4
All principal producers	4.54	4.7	5.0	5.5	5.8	6.0
Percent of world capacity	89.7	85.5	82	79	76	73
World capacity	5.06	5.5	6.1	7.0	7.6	8.2
Cf. World consumption	[d]5.09	5.6	6.2	6.9	7.6	8.3

[a]Includes an allowance for secondary recovery by smelters and battery makers.

[b]Data primarily from J. Patrick Ryan and John M. Hague, Lead (U.S. Bureau of Mines, Mineral Commodity Profiles, 9, Dec., 1977), p. 4. Estimate added for secondary capacity (see footnote a) where it is believed to have been omitted. Also, in some cases, tabulations of ABMS (American Bureau of Metal Statistics) data substituted. For the United States, data from Charles River Associates, Inc., Economic Impact of Proposed OSHA Lead Standards (Executive Summary, March 1977); primary portion essentially same as that estimated by U.S. Bureau of Mines.

[c]Australian refinery capacity is less than its ore consumption, since a great deal of Australian lead is exported as base bullion (smelter product).

[d]Single year only.

abatement requirements or some combination of such problems. Health and safety problems affect secondary as well as primary capacity. In table 5-12, already-reported closings and problem situations have been taken into account, along with conjectural allowances for additional capacity closedowns in the industrialized countries through 1985; it was assumed that any subsequent closings would in most cases be offset by errors in the projections of new capacity.

In general, the primary capacity included in the table refers to integrated smelting and refining. Capacity in the United Kingdom, as an exception, is in large part refinery capacity only, using as its feed-stock imported smelter product (base bullion).

More than half of all lead capacity in the United States is for secondary recovery, and all of the announced new facilities and expansions are of this type. Because of a general "wait-and-see" attitude with regard to the final outcome of environmental and health and safety regu-lations, it is assumed that some of the future capacity will be deferred beyond the original target dates. In addition, a small allowance has been made for closedown of existing secondary facilities, but not for potential closedown of any large primary facilities, even though this has been repeatedly threatened.

Given a lack of information on specific Soviet plans, the projections for the USSR have been made consistent with the lead ore consumption pro-jections in chapter 2, with an allowance for slowly increasing secondary recovery. The projections are also consistent with the chapter 2 assump-tion of a slide in a net import position.

For the lesser producers, too, a similar lack of information (with scattered exceptions) has necessitated projections consistent with pro-jected ore consumption plus some allowance for secondary recovery. For the 1976-80 period, the principal industrial countries (other than the United States and the USSR) are all assumed to have some net losses in secondary capacity.

Estimates of changes in world capacity from 1976 to 1980 benefited from the ILZSG tabulations. These 1976-80 changes, in turn, were used to estimate a rate of change in the concentration of world capacity, which will undoubtedly become considerably more decentralized as both primary

and secondary capacity is developed in countries like Brazil, India,
China, Mexico, Peru, Bolivia, and Morocco.

The resultant world capacity projections bear an impossible relationship to the consumption projections. The estimated base relationship for 1976 suggests that there may be a systematic understatement--
particularly of secondary capacity--although the small excess of consumption over year-end capacity, in an industry where capacity has shown
tendencies to decline, could satisfactorily be explained by consumption
out of stocks. (The world market was slack in 1975, and stocks in the
United States, at least, were in fact heavily drawn upon in 1976.) Even
if some understatement is allowed for, however, the projections suggest
a continuing capacity/consumption relationship so tight that adjustment
either on the supply or the consumption side would be necessary. Given
the relative diminution over time in sources of secondary lead, it would
seem necessary that somewhere in the world a higher level of primary lead
production be provided for.

Further analysis suggests that the "somewhere" would most likely
have to be in the non-market-oriented countries. Between their domestic
capacity and that of principal international suppliers, there does not
seem to be any shortage for the principal countries of the trading world.
A conceivable adjustment to the projected global supply-demand situation
is that the Soviet Union will install more smelting and refining capacity
than has been projected and seek to import lead concentrates to support it.

The United States, if the projections are correct, would have a progressively smaller surplus of capacity in relation to refined lead demand
and, before the close of the century, would be finding itself a confirmed
(rather than economically opportunistic) net importer.

Lead Scrap

For the bulk of lead scrap, the institutional and physical collection
capacity is well established and adaptable to changes in size of supply
potential. This refers to the portion that consists of old betteries,
which are customarily either exchanged for new ones or routinely removed
from scrapped automobiles. Shortages, if any, would arise, not from
scrap handling capacity, but from an insufficiency of underlying supply,

occasioned either by spurts of new car production in relation to old-car
scrappage, or by the transitory effects of the introduction of longer
lived batteries. Cable covering is another form of scrap that may be
assumed to be routinely recovered, but changing technology is causing
the source of the scrap gradually to dry up. The same has already happened
in many countries with regard to lead in building construction (chiefly
plumbing), and what does become available in those countries is no longer
routinely reclaimed.

Zinc

Zinc tends to be closely allied with lead in nature and in the nature
of its supply problems. Most of it comes out of the selfsame ores and
it is subject to the same kinds of environmental problems, though it
does not have the acute health and safety problems of lead. In the United
States, closure of smelting capacity has kept the pressure off of mine
capacity by lowering the domestic demand for ore. The separation of refining from ore reduction (smelting) is even less common for zinc than
for lead, though there seems to be more variety for zinc in modes of
arriving at the finally refined metal. Unlike lead, zinc (or zinc-based)
scrap is relatively unimportant, and is not covered in this study.

Zinc Ore

As with lead, zinc more often than not is extracted from complex ores,
so that in reality zinc "ore" usually means zinc concentrates, separated
out at the beneficiating mill. Lead is the mineral most commonly associated with zinc and has tended, up to now, to be at best a co-product,
but it is not impossible that for a period, at least, lead will become the
more sought after element and zinc a by-product.

Canada is by far the world's leading zinc miner and will continue to
be so, providing zinc both in concentrate and in metallic form. The projections in table 5-13 are derived primarily from announced expansion
plans--both firm and not-so-firm--extending into the mid-1980s, all of
which have been assumed to come to actual fruition by 1990. Most important among these are long-range plans of Cominco, Ltd., in British

Table 5-13. Projections of World Zinc Mining Capacity,[a] 1980-2000, Compared with 1977 Capacity and with Estimated and Projected Zinc Ore Consumption

(million metric tons, zinc content[b])

	1977[c]	1980	1985	1990	1995	2000
Principal international suppliers:						
Canada	1.55	1.6	1.9	2.4	2.8	3.1
Peru	.54	.6	.6	.7	.7	.7
Australia	.55	.6	.7	.8	.9	1.0
Ireland	.28	.5	.6	.6	.7	.7
Total	2.92	3.3	3.8	4.5	5.1	5.5
Other principal producers:						
United States	.49	.6	.7	.8	.9	1.0
USSR	.72	.7	.8	.9	1.0	1.1
Mexico	.34	.4	.4	.5	.5	.6
Japan	.34	.3	.4	.4	.5	.5
Spain	.18	.3	.4	.5	.5	.6
All principal producers	4.99	5.6	6.5	7.6	8.5	9.3
Percent of world capacity	65.6	65	64	63	62	61
World capacity	[d]7.61	8.6	10.2	12.1	13.7	15.2
Cf. World consumption	6.02	6.7	7.6	8.6	9.7	10.8

[a] Or zinc concentrating capacity.

[b] Or recoverable content, in some instances.

[c] Data primarily from V. Anthony Cammarota, Jr., Zinc (U. S. Bureau of Mines, Mineral Commodity Profiles, 12, May 1978), p. 4. Modified according to U. S. and Canada closure information for 1977 reported by International Lead and Zinc Study Group (confidential tabulation), since the Bureau did not appear to take these 1977 closures into account.

[d] Single year only.

Columbia; of Placer Development, Ltd., in the Yukon; and a joint venture
of Kerr Addison Mines and Canadian Natural Resources, also in the Yukon.

The USSR capacity for 1977 includes a recent expansion, and no additional expansion appears in sight by 1980. With respect to the further
future, it is assumed that the Soviet Union's large zinc resources, coupled
with its desire to satisfy as much as possible of its ore needs from domestic sources, will result in continuing enlargement of its zinc mining
and concentrating capability.

The United States, which also has very large unproduced reserves,
should expand just about as rapidly as the USSR. Most of the current
expansion is in Tennessee, in mines owned by New Jersey Zinc Company or
jointly by that company and Union Miniere of Belgium. A large longer
range development, assumed to be producing by 1990, is that of Exxon Corporation in Wisconsin.

Australia, too, has large ore reserves and should rank among the
leaders in mine expansion. Expansion for the immediate future is predicated on the start-up of a large mine in New South Wales, already mentioned under "lead"; the subsequent projections are conjectural. Ireland,
a newcomer among leading zinc producers, has had two mines under development: a very large one, Tara, started up in 1977 and is by now presumably
in full production; the second one, belonging to Bula Ltd., is assumed
to reach full production by 1985. The Peruvian projections for 1980 are
based on reported expansions of existing mines and are conjectural thereafter. The Mexican projections are based on reported plans by Industrial
Minera Mexico S.A. (in which Asarco has a minority interest) to expand
existing mines and by a Rio Tinto subsidiary to open a new mine in the
early 1980s. In total, Industria Minera was reported in early 1978 to
be aiming at enlarging its mine production of zinc by 114,000 metric
tons by 1983, in order to supply feed for a new electrolytic smelter
at San Luis Potosi. Projections for Spain through 1985 are based on
reported plans, mostly for new mines. Zinc mining in Japan is assumed
to remain relatively static on balance, although a smallish new mine
has been announced for the early 1980s.

Because some of the lesser producing areas omitted from specific consideration (e.g., Yugoslavia, India, Iran, Poland) are likely to expand relatively rapidly, the degree of concentration represented by the listed countries is assumed to decline mildly. If the resultant world capacity projections are correct (for 1980 they are slightly in excess of those of the U.S. Bureau of Mines), there would be, on a world basis, a fair excess of capacity over consumption--especially in the latter part of the projection period. For those countries particularly involved in the international market place, either as buyers or as sellers (this excludes the United States and the USSR, among others), the surplus of capacity develops to an extent that it is likely to discourage fulfillment of the projections, but we may have insufficiently allowed for declining ore grades and mine closings.

For the United States, also, the projections suggest a growing excess of mine capacity over requirements for smelter feed. One may expect that in any case some quantity of U.S. ores will be sent abroad for custom (or intracompany) smelting, but this route may be insufficient to account for all of the surplus ore capacity, and it does not appear that the world market will be in a position to absorb it on a competitive basis. Under the circumstances, mine closings may be greater than we have allowed for; already there is reported to be a significant amount of capacity, not quite closed, but on a "care and maintenance" basis.

Refined Zinc

Table 5-14 gives our projections of zinc smelting capacity (capacity for refined zinc production). Such projections are hazardous at best, but are particularly hazardous at present because of the uncertain impact of pollution abatement requirements in the industrialized countries, and disparate and fluctuating industry views regarding the prospect of shortage or surplus.

Projections for Canada through 1985 are based on reported expansion plans--particularly a 100,000 metric-ton-per-year smelter planned for New Brunswick by Brunswick Mining & Smelting Corp., Ltd. Beyond 1985, the expansion of capacity is assumed to be slower, owing to a continuing overhang of excess capacity.[35] Part of the discrepancy between projected capacity and ore consumption, however, may be explained by secondary recovery (see table 2-22).

Belgium, like Canada, has an anomalous relationship between ore consumption and smelter capacity--particularly if the latter is taken to include retort capacity listed by the American Bureau of Metal Statistics (ABMS), rather than just the electrolytic capacity tabulated for Belgium by the U.S. Bureau of Mines. It is presumed that, in addition to some secondary recovery, the apparent excess capacity is in part devoted to further refining of zinc which has already been once smelted. While this may be thought of as capacity double-counting, it is not necessarily so, since the less fully refined zinc does have direct consumption uses. The projection for Belgium for 1980 includes a small expansion, reportedly already in place, of the electrolytic refinery of Metallurgie Hoboken-Overpelt. It is assumed that existing excess capacity, in combination with environmental problems, will tend to restrian further expansion, with some of the older, smaller (retort) capacity being shut down.

The third leading world supplier, Australia, is assumed to be somewhat less constrained in its expansion. No specific plans appear to be outstanding, and the projections are roughly consistent with those previously made for ore consumption (table 2-22).

Among countries which will be producing zinc primarily for domestic consumption, Japan is clearly the most important and is likely to maintain its present lead position. The base capacity figure is derived from ABMS data and seems to include some capacity not in the U.S. Bureau of Mines tabulation (secondary, probably, as well as electrolytic reduction capacity in excess of slab casting capacity), but is reasonable in relation to estimated ore consumption. The projections for Japan, as for Australia, are on the basis of the previously projected ore consumption.

---

[35]There is already an apparent excess of smelting capacity: cf. table 1-32.

Table 5-14. Projections of World Zinc Reduction Capacity, 1980-2000, Compared with 1977 Capacity[a] and with Estimated and Projected Refined Zinc Consumption

(million metric tons)

	1977[b]	1980	1985	1990	1995	2000
Principal international suppliers:						
Canada	c .63	.7	.8	.8	.9	.9
Belgium	c .45	.5	.5	.6	.6	.6
Australia	.32	.4	.5	.5	.5	.6
Total	1.40	1.6	1.8	1.9	2.0	2.1
Other principal producers:						
United States	c .67	.6	.8	.9	.9	1.0
USSR	c .75	.8	1.0	1.2	1.4	1.5
Japan	c 1.17	1.3	1.3	1.4	1.5	1.6
Germany (F.R.)	c .47	.5	.5	.6	.6	.7
France	.29	.3	.4	.5	.5	.6

Italy	.25	.3	.3	.4	.4	.4
Poland	.28	.3	.3	.3	.4	.4
All principal producers	5.28	5.7	6.4	7.2	7.7	8.3
Percent of world capacity	70.8	71	71	71	71	71
World capacity [d]	7.46	8.0	9.0	10.1	10.8	11.7
Cf. World consumption [e]	5.75	6.5	7.4	8.4	9.4	10.7

[a] Refined zinc is used here in the source of reduced, unalloyed zinc metal in general rather than in the special sense of an upgraded form of distilled zinc.

[b] Data primarily from V. Anthony Cammarota, Jr., Zinc (U. S. Bureau of Mines, Mineral Commodity Profiles, 12, May, 1978), pp. 4-5. ABMS tabulations used in some instances, as noted.

[c] From American Bureau of Metal Statistics, Non-Ferrous Metal Data 1977 (ABMS, 1978), pp. 77-78 and 81-82.

[d] Bureau of Mines total, adjusted for additional capacity listed by ABMS.

[e] Single year only.

The U.S. capacity shown in table 5-14 is projected from an ABMS base figure and definitely includes secondary recovery capacity. There has been a considerable closure of U.S. zinc smelting capacity since 1972--attributed largely to problems of meeting environmental standards--but there has also been at least one major new project, a 90,000 short ton refinery in Tennessee jointly owned by New Jersey Zinc and Union Miniere. The figure for 1990 reflects the probable installation of a refinery to process ores from Exxon's contemplated Wisconsin mine.

No immediate plans have been reported for the USSR, but over the longer run that country is likely to want to match its zinc smelting capacity to its rather considerable zinc resources. There is an inconsistency between the USSR capacity estimates of the U.S. Bureau of Mines and the smelter production estimates of Metallgesellschaft, the latter being conspicuously higher (see table 1-32). One may suspect that this is because reported capacity is understated, but the projections nevertheless start from the Bureau of Mines base, and are increased over time by amounts roughly consistent with increases in our projected amounts of ore consumption.[36]

Projections for Germany, France, Italy, and Poland are all conjectural and based essentially on our earlier projections of ore consumption, although some amount of new capacity has been reported under development or under consideration for all of these countries except Germany.

Although significant expansion of zinc smelting is contemplated in some of the countries not specifically listed (e.g., Ireland, Mexico, India, Brazil), it is assumed not to change materially the degree of world concentration. The resultant world capacity projections turn out to be rather reasonable in relation to projected world consumption, although they imply that a progressive tightness develops. Our 1980 projection, adjusted to a common base, is about half a million tons higher

---

[36]
It should be noted that the ore consumption level is probably overstated, since for the historical base it was necessary to substitute estimated smelter production, and the latter would include some secondary. This would not seriously affect the reasonableness of changes over time, however.

than that either of the International Lead and Zinc Study Group or the
U.S. Bureau of Mines. It is thus possible that our figures may embody
some amount of overestimation, at least for the earlier years. It would
not be enough, however, to affect the basic finding of a continuing
sufficiency of world capacity, given relatively high levels of utilization.

Since some of the individual countries, as noted, appear to have a
surplus of capacity, the world conclusion implies a possibly unrealistic
balancing out of trade and consumption. A rough comparison, however,
of capacity and consumption in the principal international suppliers
and their principal customers suggests a reasonable relationship, with
a slight tendency toward easing, in the overall balance among those
countries accustomed to trade with one another.

For the United States, by itself, the projections show little change
in degree of import dependency over the projection period. Generally
speaking, capacity constraints would make it necessary for at least one-
third, more or less, of U.S. refined zinc consumption to be met by imports throughout the projection period. The actual proportion (recently
about one-half) would depend on economics and tend to be a little higher,
but stabilization of the refined zinc-dependency ratio would in itself
represent a signal change from the decline in ratio that has taken place
over the past fifteen years or so.

PART III: PRICES

Chapter 6

HISTORICAL PRICE PATTERNS

Introduction

This study focuses on U.S. supply. More precisely, our attention is directed to those aspects of mineral supply that have to do with the flow and cost of mineral-commodity feedstock to domestic industrial consumers. In the process, we illuminate any competitive problems for those same commodities' domestic producers.

It follows that the most meaningful "prices," for our purposes, are (1) average unit delivered cost to U.S. industrial consumers and (2) average unit sales realization by competitive U.S. producers. At least this is true in an aggregate sense. What should not be overlooked is that, in problem circumstances, some users may bear unit costs distinctly different from other users or some suppliers (if not producers) may realize unit returns distinctly different from other suppliers. Such a situation can arise, for example, in a market which is characterized both by contract and by spot sales or in one which has a "free," "gray," or "black" segment. What may not be a price problem on the average, therefore, may be a problem for some consumers or some producers. Whether or not such a selective impact is a national problem depends on how much importance is attached to the situation of the particular disadvantaged segments and those dependent on them.

As a practical matter, the only systematically available indicator of changing average cost, for some of the commodities under review, is

the average value of U.S. imports.[1] Although published price quotations
are available for other commodities in this study, one would expect on
a priori grounds that even for these the import data provide a better
reading on actual transaction prices.

Until the past few years, imports were valued in the U.S. trade data
only as of their country of origin. This required estimating the additional impact of ocean freight, insurance, and other charges which become
part of delivered cost. The new data on c.i.f.[2] values now permit drawing
more direct conclusions regarding each commodity's delivered cost in the
United States, as well as the relationship of that cost to cost or price
in principal markets of origin or quotation.

The way in which either landed cost in the United States or some
domestic price quotation relates to finally delivered cost or to domestic
producers' return, and the extent to which either of these relationships
is even ascertainable, tends to differ from commodity to commodity. So
also does the particular way in which average U.S. cost relates to domestic
and international supply and demand factors. In preceding chapters, we
made some effort to distinguish, for each mineral commodity, the consumption and supply history and prospects of those countries that are
currently or potentially significant in world trade of those commodities.
Our hypothesis is that, in general, it is the offerings and requirements
of such principal trading countries that determine world mineral prices
and it is world prices that in turn determine the costs of the particular
mineral commodities to U.S. industrial consumers. Delivered costs in
the United States may also be significantly affected, however, by the

---

[1]Even then, the declared value on a tariff-free commodity may be
of questionable accuracy.

[2]"Cost, insurance and freight"--or, essentially, cost at port of
importation before any applicable duties and import taxes. A new import-
data series is also available on an "f.a.s." ("free alongside ship,"
port of origin) basis, but as a practical matter there is only negligible
difference, for most mineral commodities, between f.a.s. values and the
"customs values" which are the basis of the traditional statistical
reporting.

particular, changing country mix of U.S. suppliers. In this chapter we attempt to identify these various elements in price behavior to the extent that they seem especially relevant.

This mode of treatment may appear to be at odds with classical economic conceptions of a market. In part it actually is not, inasmuch as the international market for a mineral commodity typically relates to a given delivery point; it follows from this that there has to be a diversity of f.o.b. prices at supply sources and at delivery points other than that used for international price quotations. In practice, the mix of suppliers is perhaps more significant, however, by virtue of the fact that many transfers of metallic mineral commodities take place at prices that vary considerably from those on the current world market. Many such transfers are among units of the same firm and others are wholly within countries in which national policy considerations dictate prices other than those that are strictly market based. Within the United States, among other countries, price controls have affected transaction prices at times, and for a number of metals there have traditionally been "producers' prices" maintained at more stable levels, for the bulk of domestic demand, than the prices applied to residual offerings or to purchases on the open market.

What is most inconsistent with the classical model is the notion that world prices are affected only by the consumption and production of those countries that are significant international traders. Are not the countries that are in domestic supply-demand balance also part of the price formation mechanism? Were the latter the case, however, in anything more than theoretical terms, countries would be only transitorily out of the world market, coming in either as purchasers or as sellers with each change in world price. The fact is, though, that the few important producers or consumers of metallic mineral commodities that hold themselves aloof from international trade in a particular commodity do so with some consistency. The Soviet bloc, particularly, prefers internal demand-supply balance to a degree that causes them to enter some mineral markets (e.g., manganese) as sellers only when prices are unusually high or as purchasers (e.g., bauxite) only when they face unusual supply problems. There are also other countries, however, whose desire for a secure flow of feedstock or for reaping the value added in further processing leads to regulations, taxes, allocated supply flows, or differential pricing that keeps the country essentially out of the world market for extended periods of time. So far as world demand and supply curves are concerned, these countries represent discontinuities. Our analysis recognizes that because of the potential of such countries to enter the world market, the list of principal trading countries is not static—and that it is all the less static because of constantly changing consumption levels and production capacities over time. We have in fact altered the list of trading countries for future years for some commodities.

Aside from inspection of the available data and an attempt to relate those data to background information on the respective industries, the principal method of analysis here is the mathematical separation of longer term trends from shorter term fluctuations. This is done, crudely, by moving-average analysis. It is unlikely, in view of the irregularity of cyclical movements in the various price (or unit value) series, as well as the important influence of discrete events for many of them, that more sophisticated types of time series analysis would have yielded distinctly superior results.

There has been no attempt at deflation of any of the series. A principal reason for this is that what is basically required for "problem" analysis is an identification of (1) distinct changes in trend, (2) fluctuations around trend, and (3) discrete alterations in trend level, such as might be caused by a cartellike action. A relatively constant trend, of whatever slope and howsoever determined, essentially represents normality. It makes little difference how much of the slope reflects long-term trends in real-cost elements and how much reflects the long-term rate of inflation. Similarly, the kinds of mineral-commodity price fluctuations that occur during booms and recessions may in part represent real shortages and surpluses of those commodities and in part the fluctuations of the country's general price level, but the impact on mineral commodity consumers and, through them, on the economy, is essentially independent of the composition of causes.

There is also a practical problem in price deflation, which has to do with selecting the appropriate deflator. If a reflection of real costs is desired, the most appropriate deflator is that which shows the changing prices of real economic inputs in the countries of a particular commodity's production. In general, there is no ready-made deflator that meets this standard. Labor rates in the countries of origin appear to be the one best criterion, but using this kind of measure would require arriving at weighted average rates, year by year, for each commodity's supply mix. One might then still not have a valid indicator of true economic cost changes, because mineral commodity prices may include changing proportions of economic rent, depending upon sellers' market power and buyers' opportunity costs, as well as on aggregate demand and scarcity.

There is no deflator, either, whose use yields any clearly better measure of "real" costs to the industrial purchaser than do current market values. An industrial consumer whose revenues are inflated by prices that reflect his own increased labor costs, for example, is not thereby rendered any the better able to pay increased prices for his mineral inputs. It would have to be assumed that the end product prices chargeable by the consumers of mineral commodities are fully attributable to demand factors or to money supply, and entirely independent of cost factors, for a general price deflator to provide a measure of the ease with which dollars are obtained to purchase mineral inputs. The international exchange value of the dollar is even less useful a criterion for our purposes, since it only measures the ease with which dollars are obtained by foreign entities.

The various price and average-value discussions that follow, therefore, are all in terms of current dollars. The projections in chapter 7 are in the same terms, although they implicitly assume that any controlling prices of real economic inputs, as well as the dollar equivalencies of given physical demand levels, continue to change in consistency with long-term trend.

Cobalt

Cobalt presents one of the best examples of "administered" pricing among the mineral commodities. For years, cobalt production was a near-monopoly of the Belgian corporation, Union Miniere de Haut-Katanga,[3] which recovered cobalt metal from copper ores mined in the Katanga region of the Belgian Congo--now Zaire's Shaba Province. While most cobalt metal is produced in Zaire itself, a Union Miniere affiliate also processes a cobalt-rich matte from Zaire into metal in Belgium.[4]

Some cobalt metal, apparently, is further processed in Belgium, especially into the more valuable product, cobalt powder. Sozacom (Societe Zairoise de Commercialization) is the government-owned, official marketing agency for Zairian cobalt, but a Union Miniere affiliate, the Societe General des Minerais (SGM) has effectively managed the marketing operations for both Sozacom and Union Miniere. In the United States, moreover, both companies are represented by the same exclusive sales agent, African Metals Corporation. The latter sells only on a spot basis and, to all intents and purposes, sets the U.S. "producer" price of cobalt as a reflection of the world price decided upon by the Belgian-Zairian consortium. The latter currently controls roughly three-fifths of the world and about three-fourths of the U.S. metal supply.

The fact that the Belgian-Zairian group is not quite a monopoly has the practical meaning that there has been price leadership rather than outright monopolistic pricing. Usually that leadership has come from Belgium or Zaire, but on at least one occasion during the steep price rises of 1978, Zambia and Finland took the initiative, with Zaire following.

The ostensible principal reason for cobalt price changes through the early 1970s has been the cost of mining and refining, with world

---

[3]During one period prior to World War II, this company (now known simply as Union Miniere, S.A.) was instrumental in forming a cartel which embraced virtually all world cobalt production.

[4]Metallurgie Hoboken Overpelt, a Belgian corporation in which Union Miniere has a controlling interest.

demand changes and currency revaluations also playing a part.[5] However, as brought out in a 1971 study (published 1977) by Charles River Associates for the General Services Administration,[6] the largest single factor, through the mid-1960s, appears to have been, first, purchases and then, sales under the U.S. stockpiling program.[7] One must conclude that, aside from such transitory events as nationalization in Zaire and repetitive fighting in Shaba, the price of cobalt, both long-term and short, has been primarily determined by fluctuations in demand. This is the kind of response that would be expected of a monopolist aiming at maximization of net revenue. Moreover, it is evident from the postwar record that this particular monopolist has been more attuned to opportunities for exploiting scarcity or the appearance of scarcity than to any possible consumption elasticity. To put it another way, the constraining factor on prices has been more nearly that of possible competitive cobalt offerings (especially in a slack market) than the risk of stimulating substitution.

In fact, most of the time since the mid-1960s the pressure of demand has been enough to permit a persistent rise in cobalt prices even in the face of sales from the U.S. stockpile. This constraint is now totally absent. Aside from some small amounts (probably minor allocations to defense producers), stockpile dispositions ceased late in 1976, and instead a higher goal, calling for new acquisition, was then set.

One of the factors making for upward pressure on U.S. price has been the continuing depreciation of the dollar against the Belgian franc, since it is in terms of the latter currency that the controlling Zairian price is set. This alone would have caused a price increase between 1970 and October 1978 of 70 percent; the implied increase in the one year preceding October 1978 was 22 percent. This is hardly sufficient, however,

---

[5] See Scott F. Sibley, Cobalt (Mineral Commodity Profiles, 5, Bureau of Mines, U.S. Department of the Interior, July 1977) p. 13.

[6] James C. Burrows, Cobalt: An Industry Analysis (Lexington, Mass., Heath Lexington, 1971).

[7] Ibid., p. 129 and chart, p. 128.

to explain the actual ninefold multiplication of price between 1970 and November 1978 or the near-quadrupling in the one year immediately preceding the latter date.[8] The more fundamental explanation, clearly, is the market psychology accompanying a resurgence in industrial demand for cobalt and a dwindling of visible stocks, in a period when replacement of stocks was interrupted both by the insurgency in Shaba and a two-week strike in the Belgian processing plant. Adding to the psychological pressure on consumers was the institution by African Metals, in May 1978, of sales ceilings of 70 percent of each consumer's average 1977 purchases and the emergence of a dealers' "free" market with prices double the already inflated prices being quoted by the producers' agent. News reports that the bulk of Belgian technicians had fled Zaire served further to cloud the supply outlook.

Average delivered prices of cobalt metal at consumers' plants in the United States are not available. Deducing them is particularly difficult in times of supply stringency, because of the free, or gray, market, which may be estimated to have come to as much as 15 percent of consumer purchases, judging by figures on reported total consumption, if the 70 percent African Metals allocation was actually effective. Usually, however, there is a very close correspondence between the reported price of standard metal (cathodes, shot, granules) at New York and the average value of imports, as may be seen in table 6-1. The correspondence is perhaps too close, considering that the imports include significant amounts of the higher grades of cobalt metal (for example, powder)--a factor which should presumably outweigh the fact that the traditional "customs" values shown in the table are net of ocean freight and other delivery costs. Moreover, as shown in table 6-2, there is considerable variation in average import value among the different countries of supply.

Given the normal correspondence of the New York price for cobalt and the average landed cost of cobalt in the United States, the price series is as good an indicator as any of the longer run changes in the cost of cobalt to U.S. industry. There is no more representative world

---

[8]Another 25 percent increase, in February 1979, brought the price to $25 per pound.

Table 6-1. Average Value of Cobalt Metal Imports Into the United States,
1959-1979, Compared With Average Price, f.o.b. New York, for
Standard Grade of Cobalt Metal

(dollars per pound)

Year	Aver. value of imports[a]	Average price[b]	Year	Aver. value of imports[a]	Average price[b]
1959	1.79	1.75	1969	1.80	1.89
1960	1.58	1.50	1970	2.19	2.20
1961	1.48	1.50	1971	2.16	2.20
1962	1.45	1.50	1972	2.34	2.25
1963	1.42	1.50	1973	2.92	2.96
1964	1.46	1.50	1974	3.36	3.46
1965	1.56	1.62	1975	4.20	3.99
1966	1.55	1.65	1976	4.38	4.39
1967	1.81	1.85	1977	5.45	5.60
1968	1.77	1.85	1978	10.17	11.53
			1979	24.16	24.58

[a]Based on customs value for all cobalt metal, as reported in Minerals Yearbook and in published and unpublished tabulations of Foreign Trade Division, U.S. Bureau of the Census. Customs value, for cobalt, is very close to f.a.s. value, foreign port (see table 6-2).

[b]Refers to shot, granules, and cathodes--the basic forms of the metal. Data as reported by Metals Week, American Metal Market, and various publications of U.S. Bureau of Mines.

Table 6-2. Comparison of Average Customs, F.a.s., and C.i.f. Values for Cobalt Metal Imported Into the United States, 1974-1979, by Principal Supplying Country

(dollars per pound)

Country	Basis of valuation	1974	1975	1976	1977	1978	1979
Zaire	Customs	3.25	3.86	4.28	5.23	9.86	23.38
	F.a.s.	3.25	3.86	4.28	5.23	9.86	23.36
	C.i.f.	3.29	3.90	4.35	5.30	9.94	23.48
Belgium	Customs	3.75	5.67	5.32	6.36	12.68	26.54
	F.a.s.	3.75	5.67	5.39	6.36	12.68	26.53
	C.i.f.	3.80	5.75	5.46	6.44	12.77	26.66
Zambia	Customs	3.11	-	4.34	5.22	8.89[a]	23.94
	F.a.s.	3.11	-	4.34	5.21	8.61	23.94
	C.i.f.	3.16	-	4.40	5.52	8.75	24.58
Finland	Customs	3.59	4.04	4.51	5.71	10.58	26.32
	F.a.s.	3.59	4.04	4.52	5.71	10.58	26.32
	C.i.f.	3.60	4.05	4.52	5.72	10.64	26.49
Norway	Customs	3.23	3.89	4.14	5.13	9.85	28.88
	F.a.s.	3.22	3.89	4.14	5.13	9.85	28.88
	C.i.f.	3.22	3.89	4.14	5.18	9.92	29.00
Canada	Customs	3.58	3.47	4.26	5.48	10.59	26.81
	F.a.s.	3.58	3.47	4.27	5.49	10.61	26.84
	C.i.f.	3.58	3.48	4.27	5.49	10.61	26.84
All sources	Customs	3.36	4.20	4.38	5.45	10.17[b]	24.47
	F.a.s.	3.36	4.21	4.39	5.45	10.13	24.47
	C.i.f.	3.39	4.24	4.45	5.52	10.21	24.69

Source: Foreign Trade Division, U.S. Bureau of the Census, published and unpublished tabulations.

Dash (-) indicates no imports.

[a]Anomaly which may be caused by a large reporting error in June 1978 data.

[b]See footnote above relating to Zambia.

price with which to compare it. Owing to its highly administered character, however, and to the explosive 1978 increases, it would be rash
to read into its recent record anything that may reasonably be called
a trend. Projections of the price of cobalt will have to rest entirely
on other factors.

Chromium

We have defined three important forms in which chromium enters as
feedstock to U.S. industry: (1) chromite (chromium ores) suitable for
metallurgical and/or chemical use, (2) chromite suitable for making refractories, and (3) ferroalloys of chromium. The price history of each
of these broad forms is discussed separately.

Chromite for Metallurgical Use

Until rather recently, the cost of chromium ore for conversion into
ferrochrome and other ferroalloys--the bulk of its consumption--or into
chromium metal was significantly influenced by the need, for the most
part, to use a specifically "metallurgical" grade. Owing to the emergence
of the AOD (argon-oxygen decarburization) process in stainless steelmaking
and the consequent greater freedom to use high-carbon ferrochrome, the
derived requirement for chromite can now be met in large measure by the
use of "chemical" grade chromite, which contains a higher proportion
of iron in relation to chromium. It was to be expected that easing of
this constraint would be reflected in a reduction of the differential
formerly paid for the more specifically metallurgical ore. As may be
seen in table 6-3, however, it took a while for this influence to make
itself felt. The AOD process began to show up in the United States in
1970; its introduction was particularly rapid in the early 1970s, accelerated again in 1977, and by now should have attained a saturation of
around 90 percent. Yet the old metallurgical grade, as nearly as can
be determined, carried a widening price premium through 1976. Part of
the explanation for the seeming anomaly may lie in the crudeness of comparisons based on import statistics, which distinguish among ore types

only by ranges of chromic oxide content and country of origin, rather
than by the full assortment of grade-determining specifications. However,
the anomalous movements show up even more strongly in the price quotations.
What is probably the case is that the off-again-on-again embargoes and
political-military uncertainties in southern Africa have given special
importance to the fluctuating procurement of supplies from the USSR and
Turkey, both of which countries have not hesitated to take advantage
of their current position as fill-in and "insurance" sources. In contrast,
South Africa has been modest in its price requirements: the explanation
may perhaps lie in willingness to accept a price penalty in order to
maintain sales in the face of what might appear to its customers to be
uncertainties of contract fulfillment, given both the threat of an international embargo and the danger to transportation routes from potential
insurgents. Possibly some of its pricing reflects the inclusion of
Rhodesian ore, which during the embargo period probably had to accept a
large penalty to be marketable as South African product. It may also
be that some of the South African ore, being mined by organizations in
which U.S. firms have an ownership interest, enters the United States
at less than "arm's length" prices.

The underlying implication, if one is to look to the past as a guide
to the future, is that the cost of metallurgical-use chromite to the U.S.
ferroalloy producer depends more heavily on the current supply mix (a
function, in turn, of current demand pressures) than on any other factor.
This is borne out by the comparative average values, shown in table 6-4,
for the types of ores actually being consumed. The South African ore,
in particular, includes large amounts that would formerly have been considered suitable only for chemical use.

Chromite for refractory use is supplied to the U.S. predominantly
by the Philippines, and there has been a clear steady acceleration in
the climb of Philippine chromite prices. Inasmuch as the costs of
Philippine chromite have continued to rise into 1979, it is not clear
when a downward change in the rate of acceleration, let alone in the
trend price, might possibly occur. Yet neither inflation in the United
States nor the demand for refractory chromite (see chapter 4) is growing
at a rate which would explain this persistent rise. What seems a more

Table 6-3. Comparison of Average Costs of Chromium Ores of Various Types, 1964-1979

Year	Average f.a.s. value of U.S. imports[a] (per long ton of chromite (Cr_2O_3) content)			Representative price[b] (per long ton, gross weight)	
	Metallur-gical	Chemical	Refractory	Metallur-gical[c]	Chemical[d]
1964	41.36	27.83	60.86	31.0	18.50
1965	40.86	30.45	61.53	31.0	19.75
1966	41.56	31.24	59.60	31.5	19.75
1967	45.42	32.69	64.08	34.0	19.75
1968	43.70	26.03	57.56	36.5	20.25
1969	45.92	30.73	54.28	48.0	20.25
1970	61.97	30.88	58.96	48.0	26.00
1971	60.23	30.36	68.49	55.5	26.00
1972	66.43	40.23	66.68	55.5	26.00
1973	64.38	33.25	72.00	58.0	33.50
1974	72.09	34.98	76.75	59.0	47.00
1975	143.17	78.75	124.11	137.0	44.50
1976	217.65	89.07	135.68	137.0	42.00
1977	149.83	115.21	176.07	137.0	58.50
1978	143.20	123.85	169.15	105.0	58.00
1979	148.12	129.86	167.17	110.0	58.00

Source: Published and unpublished data of U.S. Bureau of Mines and Foreign Trade Division, U.S. Bureau of the Census; Metals Week.

[a]Actually refers to "customs" value, which is usually close to, if not identical with, f.a.s. value.

[b]1964-73: f.o.b. cars, East Coast, U.S.; 1974-78: f.o.b., supplying country port. Arithmetic average, for years when a price range was reported.

[c]Turkish ore, 48 percent Cr_2O_3, 3:1 Cr:Fe.

[d]South African (Transvaal) ore, 44 percent Cr_2O_3, Cr:Fe ratio not specified. Ratio is actually about 1.6:1, per Bureau of Mines commodity specialists.

Table 6-4. Average Values, for Various Countries of Origin, 1970-1979, of Chromium Ores Imported Into the United States for Metallurgical Use[a]

(dollars per long ton of Cr_2O_3)

Year	South Africa[b]	Rhodesia	USSR[c]	Turkey[d]	Finland[d]	All sources
1970	30	e	64	71	–	60
1971	31	72	77	77	–	62
1972	32	72	73	62	–	62
1973	34	79	58	80	–	53
1974	46	83	69	86	–	59
1975	52	122	155	161	165	125
1976	81	104	291	239	93	150
1977	105	e	283	234	139	141
1978	119	e	220	190	152	132
1979	116	e	–	204	132	135

Source: U.S. Bureau of Mines, Minerals Yearbook and Mineral Industry Surveys.

[a]Selection of sources and grades based in part on trade reports as to application of different countries' ores. The figures relate to "customs" values--that is, values in countries of origin.

[b]May include Rhodesian ore shipped as ostensibly South African.

[c]Ore of 46 percent or greater Cr_2O_3 content only.

[d]All U.S. imports, much of which are below theoretical minimum percentage (46 percent) for metallurgical ore, but which trade reports indicate are shipped essentially for metallurgical consumption.

[e]Embargo year; no imports recorded.

plausible explanation is that the Philippine producers have been feeling
their way to an economic rent equilibrium that recognizes both their
semimonopoly in refractory-type ore and the technical disadvantages to
consumers of introducing other types of refractory materials in the
furnace-lining uses to which chromite is now applied.[9] In part, the price
of refractory-grade ore has probably been pulled up by the rise in price
of metallurgical-grade ore, which the Philippines also exports (principally
to Japan); in fact, some presumably refractory ore may possibly have
been put to metallurgical use.

The relatively few years of data on U.S. foreign trade on a c.i.f.
basis provide the only ready indication for refractory-grade chromite,
as they do for metallurgical chromite, of the additional cost imposed
by ocean shipping charges. Per long ton of chromic oxide content, these
charges seem to be hovering around $45. Presumably this is higher than
the roughly $25 to $30 per ton of Cr_2O_3 for the metallurgical ore because
of the length of haul from the Philippines and the lower chromic oxide
content in a gross ton of shipped material.

Ferrochromium

Unlike chromite, ferrochromium price quotations are available on
a delivered basis. A consistent long-term series is difficult to construct, however, since the specifications for material quoted have been
subject to frequent change, and, in the case of domestically produced
material, it is not clear whether the quotations are f.o.b. producer or
at some other point. Generally speaking, however, domestic producers
have maintained a "producers'" price, with greater stability, in the
face of import prices which have undercut the domestic quotations in
slack times and risen well beyond them when domestic producers were having
trouble satisfying the market. The differences between such producers'
and import prices have tended to exceed the price differences owing to

---

[9]There is actually a technical disadvantage with respect to basic
oxygen furnaces, and chromite refractories have lost ground because of
this, but the switch from open-hearth to basic oxygen furnaces is coming
near to having run its course.

grade of ferrochromium, as measured by chromium and other content. In part, this is because the quotations are per unit of chromium content.[10]

Table 6-5 contrasts the average annual values, since 1972, of low-carbon and high-carbon ferrochrome, both domestic and imported. As in the case of chromite, one would have expected the increased use of the AOD process to have narrowed the price differences between the two grades. That something more nearly opposite has been the case appears to be mainly the result of the diminishing total consumption of low-carbon ferrochrome, the residual demand for which (mostly in uses in which the AOD process is not applicable) is the least dispensable.

There has been a diminished supply as well as diminished consumption of low-carbon ferrochrome, which is consistent with the declining grade of the input chromite. In these circumstances, added (long-run) resilience has been given to the low-carbon price by the reinforcing role of imports. Low-carbon ferrochromium was roughly three-fourths the imported chromium supply in 1964 (measured in terms of chromium content). By 1975, it was only about a fifth of imports, which were eleven times as large, and in 1979 it was a little less than an eighth of imports, which had declined two-fifths from their 1975 peak.

A small part of the premium for low-carbon ferrochrome is maintained by a 4-percent _ad valorem_ duty on this product, now much larger in its effect than the 5/8 cents per pound duty on the high-carbon product. By a presidential decision on November 2, 1978, the latter was raised to 4 5/8 cents, effective for a three-year period, whenever import prices are below 38 cents per pound. In response, the price of South African low-carbon ferrochromium was raised to the 38-cent level.

Table 6-6 provides composite average values for all imported ferro-chromium for 1960 through 1977. In recent years freight costs have added 2 to 3 cents per pound of chromium content to the values in country of origin; customs duties have added roughly another penny. In earlier years,

---

[10]There has been a distinct lowering, over the years, of the average grade of ferrochromium utilized—caused by advancing AOD technology. However, domestic output remains relatively heavy in the higher grades, while imported ferrochromium has tended toward lower chromium content.

Table 6-5. Average Values of Domestic and Imported Ferrochrome,[a]
Low-Carbon and High-Carbon, 1972-1979

(cents per pound of contained chromium)

	1972	1973	1974	1975	1976	1977	1978	1979
Domestic								
Low-carbon	34.4	31.8	52.7	93.1	91.6	76.4	76.3	87.5
High-carbon	18.8	20.9	30.4	50.3	38.8	32.4	34.2	44.4
Ratio, high to low	.55	.66	.58	.54	.42	.42	.45	.51
Imported								
(f.a.s.)								
Low-carbon	25.2	28.0	36.0	69.6	63.8	62.8	63.7	75.7
High-carbon	12.8	13.1	23.2	42.7	32.6	31.7	29.0	39.4
Ratio, high to low	.51	.47	.64	.61	.51	.50	.46	.52
(c.i.f.)								
Low-carbon	N.A.	N.A.	38.6	73.0	66.5	65.5	67.0	80.0
High-carbon	N.A.	N.A.	25.7	45.4	34.4	33.7	31.1	42.6
Ratio, high to low	–	–	.67	.62	.52	.51	.46	.53

Source: U.S. Bureau of Mines, Minerals Yearbook, "Ferroalloys" chapter, and prepublication data; Foreign Trade Division, U.S. Bureau of the Census, published and unpublished data.

N.A. - Not available.

[a]Shipments, for domestic; imports for consumption, in case of imports. Import values are before payment of duties.

Table 6-6. Composite Average Value of Chromium in Imported and Domestic
Ferrochromium,[a] 1960-1979

(cents per pound)

Year	Imported			Domestic[d] (f.o.b.)	Total supplies
	Value in country of origin	C.i.f. value[b]	C.i.f. + duties[c]		
1960	20.9	21.9	23.2	31.2	29.5
1961	20.3	21.3	22.9	28.0	27.5
1962	19.8	20.7	22.3	27.9	26.9
1963	17.1	18.1	19.4	20.6	20.4
1964	16.3	17.3	18.6	19.2	19.1
1965	17.9	19.1	20.6	20.9	20.8
1966	16.7	17.7	19.0	20.7	20.3
1967	17.9	19.0	20.4	20.3	20.3
1968	17.3	18.4	19.6	19.1	19.2
1969	15.6	16.6	17.6	19.9	19.5
1970	18.5	19.9	20.9	25.2	24.7
1971	21.0	21.9	22.9	29.2	27.7
1972	19.2	20.1	20.9	24.2	23.0
1973	17.6	19.5	20.3	24.1	23.0
1974	27.2	29.6	30.4	37.3	35.2
1975	48.1	51.0	52.0	62.3	55.7
1976	41.5	43.6	44.8	47.6	46.0
1977	37.5	39.6	40.6	[e]37.2	38.8
1978	31.2	33.4	34.1	39.0	36.2
1979	44.3	47.2	48.2	51.8	50.2

[a]All grades.

[b]Freight and insurance estimated, 1960-73. C.i.f. values for 1974-79 are as
reported by the U.S. Bureau of Census.

[c]Duties calculated on basis of applicable rates for low-carbon and high-
carbon, respectively.

[d]Based on shipments as reported in Minerals Yearbook, "Ferroalloys " chapter.
Percentage content used for calculation is that reported for production in the
corresponding years.

[e]Price may be slightly understated. Would be roughly 1/2 cent higher were
it not for a jump in reported average chromium content. Quoted prices in 1977
were at least 4 cents per pound higher.

the freight component was lower and duties higher. Table 6-6 also gives averages for domestic output and composite average costs for the total supply at first U.S. shipping point.

Chromium supply over the past seventeen years has been too highly affected by political risks and constraints for trend analysis to have much utility. Together with the relative levels of industrial-country demand, such political considerations promise to determine the relative mix of U.S. suppliers for some time. This mix, in turn, together with demand pressures, is a principal determinant of the relative cost of both chromite and derived ferrochromium to the U.S. consumer.

The relationship of overall average cost in the United States to relative demand levels is explored in figure 6-1. The latter seems to confirm a rough tendency of price to respond, with some lag, to demand changes. The "step" increase in consumption which occurred in the early 1960s, however, was only mildly reflected in price until the UN embargo on Rhodesia (agreed on in 1967) began to take hold and supply stringency was strengthened by the world demand surge of 1973. The lag is probably due to some extent to the relative general price stability in the United States in the early 1960s.

Manganese

Manganese Ore

The consumption of manganese-bearing ore in the United States is mostly confined to the higher grades, used overwhelmingly in the manufacture of ferromanganese. For most of the analytical purposes of this report, therefore, including much of the price analysis, we either single out these higher grade ores or ignore grade differences and deal with the manganese content of all manganese-containing ores combined.

Although close to half of all the manganese ore consumed in the world first moves from a supplying to a separate consuming country, it

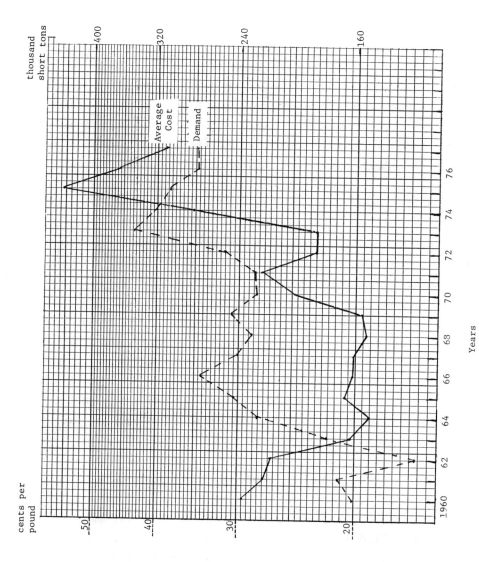

Figure 6-1. Average Cost of Ferrochromium to U.S. Industrial
Consumers, 1960-1977, Compared With Total Demand
for Ferrochromium in the United States

363

is not traded on any commodity exchange and there is no explicit world market.[11] Generally, supplies move on an annual contract basis, with prices being negotiated between sellers and buyers late in the preceding year. Recently, however, market uncertainties have been such that contracting has slipped behind--well into the spring of the year of actual delivery--and there have also been some midyear price adjustments. Reported price quotations are merely indicative of the range of contract prices, which appear to be negotiated on a c.i.f. basis by dealers in the principal consuming countries. The U.S. Bureau of Mines "representative" 1979 price c.i.f. East Coast for 46-48 percent ore is 140 cents per long ton unit (22.4 lb of contained manganese); this is consistent with the average value of imports as recorded in the trade statistics.

Figure 6-2 compares price and cost indicators, including a constructed landed value derived from the average customs (country-of-origin) values by adding estimated freight and duty (the latter in the years applicable). Unlike such commodities as ferrochromium, where ocean freight is a relatively small fraction of landed cost, freight costs for manganese ore are both difficult to estimate and a sizable component of the eventual cost to U.S. consumers. Despite this, the constructed duty-paid landed value is probably the single most reliable cost indicator. For most years, however, it is tracked closely enough by the "representative" price quotations that the latter can be considered a reasonable alternative.

The dip in prices during the 1960s has been attributed to the opening up of new, low-cost ore deposits, and the subsequent increases to "high demand; increased freight, environmental, and energy costs; and inflation."[12] The failure of prices to drop in the past several years, despite the slackening of demand, is probably due to the shift in strategic stockpile stance from disposition to a contemplated higher target. The record of the period graphed is clearly inappropriate for trend analysis.

---

[11]There does, however, appear to be some informal exchange of information on price intentions before annual contracts are formalized. Industry sources indicate that, in fact, suppliers are kept informed of the direction of each other's negotiations both before and during contract discussions.

[12]Gilbert L. DeHuff and Thomas S. Jones, Manganese (Mineral Commodity Profiles, 7, October 1977) p. 12.

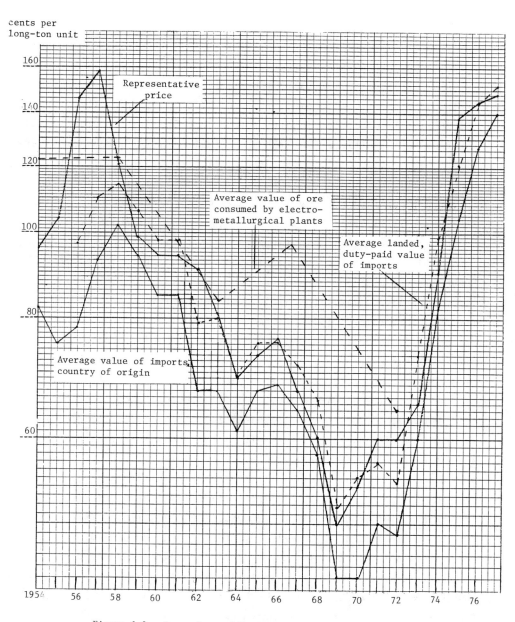

Figure 6-2. Comparison of Various Cost Indicators for Manganese
Ore in the United States, 1954-1977

365

Ferromanganese

As noted in the Introduction, there is currently sufficient inter-changeability among the various grades of ferromanganese that, for the most part, all of these may be considered as a single commodity. Direct readings on the cost of this product to U.S. industrial consumers (steel producers) are available from Censuses of Manufactures; the average values in dollars per long ton are: 1954, 237; 1958, 287, 1963, 191; 1967, 180; and 1972, 204.

A more continuous series may be arrived at, as in the case of the materials discussed earlier, by combining the data for quantity and value of domestic shipments of ferromanganese with a constructed duty-paid landed value of imports. This series, shown in table 6-7, runs rather lower than the Census averages, as might be expected of evaluation of inland delivery costs. There is a closer correspondence between the constructed average-value series and one of the more indicative price series for ferromanganese--that for domestic "standard"--which is also shown in table 6-7.[13] Over most of the period covered, domestic ferromanganese constituted the large bulk of the total supply. In 1977, for the first time, imported ferromanganese became the major supply ele-ment. Its price quotations, designated as delivered to Pittsburgh or Chicago, are also shown in table 6-7, for the years for which they are available; it will be noted that they generally run well under those of the domestic product. References in Metal Statistics suggest that the domestic price quotations (if not also the imported) are not "posted," but are supplied by producers on request, and even then at times are subject to discounting. At best they are only crudely indicative.

Figure 6-3 compares the average cost of ferromanganese (at first U.S. shipping point) with the level of demand. The price trend and price-consumption relationships, as may be seen, are roughly similar to those for ferrochrome, though the price responses to demand are less sharp in this case, and there is a more muted step function. The world demand

---

[13]From American Metal Market. The series pertains, in the earlier years, to 74-76 percent Mn content; in the later years, to 78 percent content. The date of transition is not clear.

Table 6-7. Comparison of Various Indicators of Ferromanganese Cost in the
United States, 1958-1979

(dollars per long ton)

Year	Average values			Average price quotations	
	Domestic, f.o.b. plant	Imports, U.S. ports, incl. duties[a]	Combined domestic & imports	Domestic standard	Imported standard[b]
1958	268	213	263	245	N.A.
1959	267	196	259	245	N.A.
1960	238	197	232	225	N.A.
1961	235	194	226	219.5	N.A.
1962	207	168	201	190	158
1963	175	152	171	172	158
1964	161	152	159	168	N.A.
1965	164	159	163	175	N.A.
1966	166	164	165	167.5	N.A.
1967	165	157	163	166	151
1968	172	136	165	164.5	149.5
1969	160	134	153	164.5	146
1970	187	142	175	188	169
1971	189	168	184	190	182
1972	195	174	188	190	178
1973	197	175	189	200	187
1974	316	263	294	[c]298	355
1975	448	391	424	440	432
1976	470	369	418	431	388
1977	469	352	397	404	334
1978	512	316	378	416	332
1979	613	377	444	479	434

Source: For average-value data--U.S. Bureau of Mines, Minerals Yearbook and updating publications; Foreign Trade Division, U.S. Bureau of the Census, published and unpublished tabulations. For price quotations, American Metal Market, Metal Statistics; U.S. Bureau of Mines, Minerals Yearbook; Metals Week.

N.A. - Not available.

[a]Ocean freight and insurance component estimated, 1957-73. C.i.f. values for 1974-79 reported directly by U.S. Bureau of the Census.

[b]Rough average of quotations reported quarterly in Metals Week.

[c]Price was 200 dollars per long ton until removal of price controls in March 1974. Dual pricing existed during at least a part of this period, at 200 and 250 dollars. The producer price then became 270 dollars per ton, progressively rising thereafter to 400 dollars per ton by November 1.

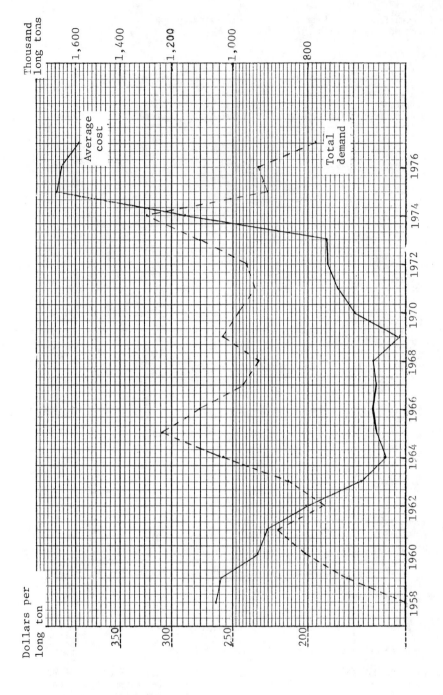

Figure 6-3. Average Cost of Ferromanganese to U.S. Industrial Consumers, 1958–1977, Compared With Total Demand for Ferromanganese in the United States

surge of 1973 is a clear influence (the graph shows U.S. demand only), as, probably, is the uncertainty connected with the fact that a significant part of the U.S. supply of ferromanganese now comes from South Africa. As with ferrochromium, the relative general U.S. price stability of the early 1960s was another likely factor at work during that particular period.

Aluminum

Bauxite

About the only continuing indication of the cost of bauxite to U.S. industrial consumers (alumina plants) is that provided by the average values of domestic production and imports. These seem most useful if expressed on a dry-equivalent basis, which means dependence on quantity data, obtained or estimated by the U.S. Bureau of Mines, which have been subjected to occasional serious revision. The averages given herein thus have to be considered far from precise, but should more nearly represent the quantities being paid for than do the gross weights.[14]

Table 6-8 summarizes the data that can be readily compiled or estimated. Values are shown separately for each of the two general types of bauxite consumed in the United States (including, for recent years, an alumina plant in the Virgin Islands), as determined by the origin of the material.[15] In addition to the overall average values of each type, the table provides separate values for domestic bauxite (which

---

[14]Not all the originally reported data require adjustment. "Dry equivalent" actually allows for a standard amount of "free" moisture (around 5 percent, by weight), and a number of countries dry their bauxite, before shipment, to that standard. It should also be noted that some of the Bureau of Mines figures (perhaps yet to be revised) are badly inconsistent with the values given in the foreign trade statistics, and in those cases (limited in number) either the gross weight shipped has been used in our calculations or a substitute estimate is based on the apparent usual average amount of moisture in shipments from the country in question.

[15]See the Introduction for a discussion of distinguishable bauxite commodities.

Table 6-8. Average Values of Bauxite Consumed in the United States, 1963-1979, by Type[a]

(dollars per long ton, dry equivalent)

		Gibbsite			Mixed (all imported)	
	Domestic (f.o.b. mine)	Imported		Total[d] (U.S. port or plant)		
		F.a.s.	C.i.f.[c]		F.a.s.	C.i.f.[c]
1963	11.30	10.13	12.72	12.25	13.38	14.63
1964	11.16	9.73	12.32	11.95	13.74	14.99
1965	11.28	9.46	12.35	11.99	13.60	15.00
1966	11.31	9.75	12.26	11.97	13.96	15.17
1967	11.63	9.35	12.04	11.92	14.07	15.37
1968	14.58	8.76	11.40	12.26	13.93	13.20
1969	14.08	8.91	11.46	12.22	24.85	16.03
1970	14.07	9.63	13.04	13.34	12.88	14.53
1971	14.03	10.44	12.82	13.17	12.62	13.74
1972	12.86	10.75	13.00	12.96	13.43	14.47
1973	14.17	10.88	15.79	15.33	11.66	13.85
1974	13.63	11.36	17.58	16.63	11.52	14.53
1975	14.88	16.20	23.38	21.34	26.26	28.90
1976	14.69	19.19	26.99	24.02	29.38	36.63
1977	14.83	20.01	28.51	25.24	32.32	36.02
1978	14.84	20.82	28.94	26.27	35.83	39.12
1979	14.60	21.61	29.78	26.93	34.46	34.48

Source: U.S. Bureau of Mines, Minerals Yearbook and Foreign Trade Division, U.S. Bureau of the Census, published and unpublished tabulations.

[a]Includes imports into the Virgin Islands, where bauxite has been converted into alumina since 1967. Cost of these imports estimated by RFF for years prior to 1972.

[b]Arkansas production only, since that mined in Alabama and Georgia is used for refractory, rather than aluminum extraction, purposes.

[c]For 1963-73, ocean freight and insurance estimated by RFF, on basis of Norwegian Shipping Cost Index, as reported by Charles River Associates. No U.S. duty was applicable.

[d]Weighted average, calculated by RFF.

consists of gibbsite only) and f.a.s. as well as c.i.f. values of the
imported material. The persistence of stable domestic costs in the face
of doubled costs for imported ore at first view seems to reflect known
bauxite-supply circumstances.[16]

For the period as a whole which is covered by table 6-8, the principal
explanation for cost changes appears to be the mix of supplying areas,
which affects both the original costs and the fairly significant element
of ocean freight. Starting in 1974, however, increases in ocean freight
began to be dwarfed by large increases in taxation imposed by the members
of the newly formed International Bauxite Association, led by Jamaica.
Jamaica's export tax on bauxite went from around $1.60 per long dry ton
to $11 and subsequently to $18. Surinam, Haiti, and the Dominican
Republic imposed similar increases, while Guinea made less of an
increase.[17] Late in 1978, the International Bauxite Association decided
to tie its members' price cooperation to the device of an average floor
price, to be based on the American Metal Market quotations for aluminum
ingot. For 1979, the floor price was to be 2 percent of the ingot price,
or about $24 per metric ton of bauxite, but the IBA looked forward to
the institution of ratios of 2 1/2 to 3 percent in times of stronger
markets. However, Guinea, Guyana, Surinam, and Haiti have been exporting
bauxite to the United States at below the $24 figure, while bauxite from
Jamaica and the Dominican Republic runs well above it.[18] Jamaica's higher
f.a.s. prices are partly offset by lower ocean freight costs. Also,
Guinea, Guyana, and Surinam sell in an essentially separate market. Like
the f.a.s. prices, the ocean freight charges are to some extent arbitrary,

---

[16] According to the U.S. Bureau of Mines, domestic ores are more
expensive to process; this could also contribute to the lower domestic
values.

[17] Charles River Associates, Maritime Transport of Dry Bulk Materials
(prepared for Bureau of Mines, U.S. Department of the Interior, May 1978)
p. 58.

[18] U.S. Bureau of Census, series IM 146.

since the shorter hauls particularly tend to be in vessels owned by the aluminum companies.[19] The Surinam rates are affected by a need for trans-shipment at Trinidad.

Alumina

Even more than for bauxite, the cost of alumina to the U.S. aluminum smelting industry is a matter of transfer pricing among units of the same company. Also, until about 1958, the supply of calcined alumina (the kind used in aluminum production) was totally domestic; but Australia, particularly, has now become an important supplier, accounting for about a third of the total consumption. Imports in general account for about two-fifths of total calcined alumina consumption.

Domestic price quotations for calcined alumina appear to refer to material of chemical grade, in small lots, rather than to the bulk material used in aluminum production, and there is no international price series. Again, therefore, the presumably best indication of average cost to alumi-num plants is a constructed series of the sort given in table 6-9.[20] The relative stability prior to 1974 and the sharp cost escalation there-after is plain.

With imported alumina becoming a progressively larger proportion of total supply, the source mix of supply is beginning to have some impact on average delivered cost. As yet, however, it is the transfer price between domestic plants that mostly determines the "cost" of alumina to aluminum producers, with imports from Australia having a minor temporiz-ing effect. Australia's interest in expanding its alumina market should be of growing importance in holding down U.S. prices since only a portion of Australia's production appears to be under U.S. control or ownership. In a sense, both countries are now benefiting from the better than 50 percent freight saving which derives from shipping alumina rather than bauxite. That benefit is small, however, compared with the extra income

---

[19]Charles River Associates, *Maritime Transport*, p. 33.

[20]Also listed in table 6-9 is the cost of imported alumina, f.a.s. Australia, the series being utilized in the chapter 7 price projections.

Table 6-9. Average Values of Alumina Consumed in the United States, 1967–1979

(dollars per short ton)

	Domestic shipments (f.o.b. plant)	Imports		Total (U.S. port or plant)	Imports from Australia (f.a.s.)
		F.a.s.	C.i.f.		
1967	66.60	52.65	56.58	65.26	50.10
1968	67.80	55.65	59.50	66.32	53.84
1969	67.80	55.61	59.16	65.93	53.46
1970	67.60	60.75	65.73	66.79	55.93
1971	67.04	58.88	62.27	65.76	53.74
1972	65.60	60.85	63.96	65.08	57.94
1973	66.85	62.02	68.76	67.48	60.17
1974	88.59	74.83	83.92	87.01	70.11
1975	116.35	105.01	113.81	115.34	93.66
1976	128.00	111.50	118.98	124.57	103.19
1977[b]	139.00	123.74	131.65	136.05	111.49
1978[b]	181.00	133.94	141.90	164.94	119.64
1979[b]	191.00	146.60	155.41	177.23	133.26

Source: U.S. Bureau of Mines, Minerals Yearbook and unpublished data; Foreign Trade Division, U.S. Bureau of the Census, published and unpublished tabulation.

[a]For years prior to 1974, ocean freight and insurance estimated by RFF.

[b]Domestic price estimates are based on a limited sample.

that Australia has gained from the upward valuation of bauxite as such and compared with the increase in processing costs for both countries, due mostly to the multiplication in the price of fuel. The margin in the costing of U.S. domestic alumina, over and above the cost of the bauxite, has risen from a range of about $35 to $39, which held through 1973, to $73 in 1977. The original amount was pretty well accounted for by about $6 per ton for fuel,[21] $3 for caustic soda, $3 in maintenance costs, and $19 to $27 in liberally estimated capital charges; unit labor costs were very small.[22] While a possible $30 for fuel and $10 for other variable costs still leaves an unexplained margin within the $73 per ton markup over bauxite value in 1977, it would not have taken much escalation in capital costs to fill the gap. Still, it seems reasonable to conclude that the figures chosen by domestic aluminum companies to reflect their alumina costs embody profit and provide an umbrella for similar profit on the Australian side.

Aluminum Metal

Although the bulk of aluminum metal flows to affiliated fabricators, the proportions are not nearly as great as in the case of bauxite or alumina, and there is a situation more nearly approaching arm's length pricing. The independent fabricator (aluminum roller, extruder, caster, etc.) has the option of choosing from among a number of primary suppliers; and, more important, he can also turn to suppliers of secondary ingot and to dealers in imported aluminum. Though the extent of his option is limited by the extent of the market share held by primary producers, coupled with price leadership and a large hold even on the secondary metal flow, the price quotations (and even more so, the effective trans-

---

[21]By 1973, a substantial increase had already occurred in industrial fuel oil prices, compared with the 1960s, but appears not yet to have been incorporated into alumina pricing.

[22]This cost picture was summarized in Sterling Brubaker, Trends in the World Aluminum Industry (Baltimore, Md., Johns Hopkins University Press for Resources for the Future, 1967) p. 152. Some of Brubaker's data are from the U.S. Bureau of Mines, Report of Investigations 6730 (1966).

action prices) offered by the primary producers must respond at least in limited degree to the relative existence of shortage and surplus in the secondary and imported supplies needed to fill out total demand.

Determining the effective cost of refined aluminum to aluminum users, however, is not easy. The published, or list, price is not necessarily a good indication, since there have been periods of significant discounting. The average value calculable from U.S. Bureau of Mines production data is not any better an indicator, since aggregate value is arrived at, according to the Bureau, by multiplying each month's prevailing list price by the month's reported production.[23] A "market price" is estimated by Metals Week, but this refers only to dealer offerings and thus to a rather minor portion of the total supply.[24] The Bureau of Labor Statistics in 1971 started to calculate its price index for aluminum ingot on the basis of a combination of the Metals Week index with independent reports from four or more aluminum buyers. Though the average values per pound are not published as such, a benchmark reading (for December 1978) obtained from the BLS permits the average-value approximations shown in table 6-10. Comparison with the averaged monthly Engineering and Mining Journal quotations for producer prices, as well as with the Bureau of Mines weighted average producer prices (both of which are included in table 6-10 for convenience), confirms the tendency of producers' and transaction prices to fluctuate around one another.

---

[23] Telephone communication from John W. Stamper, January 24, 1979. The average value calculable from the Bureau of Mines data almost always runs slightly below that of the annual (unweighted) average of list prices, though the two results are quite close.

[24] Metals Week Price Handbook, 1976 (New York, McGraw-Hill, 1977) and telephone information from Marie Z. Harris, Office of Business Research and Analysis, U.S. Department of Commerce.

Table 6-10. Average Buyers' Prices for Primary Aluminum Ingot,
            Billet, and Hot Metal, 1971-79, Compared With
            Average Producers' List Prices

(cents per pound)

| | | Producers list prices | |
Year	Buyers' average[a]	Time average[b]	Weighted average[c]
1971	25.2	29.0	27.4
1972	24.1	26.4	25.3
1973	25.2	25.0	24.4
1974	37.5	34.1	30.7
1975	39.8	39.8	38.4
1976	44.0	44.3	44.5
1977	51.2	51.3	51.6
1978	54.2	53.1	54.6
1979	61.1	59.4	59.4

[a]Derived from Bureau of Labor Statistics index values, applied to
unpublished benchmark value for December 1978.

[b]Annual averages of monthly prices.

[c]Implicit average of monthly prices weighted by monthly production.

The utility of the BLS series is limited by questions as to its
representativeness,[25] the limited period for which it is available,[26]
and the lack of explicit average-value quotations. Over a longer time
span, the average price for secondary ingot seems to be a somewhat better
indicator of the current state of the aluminum market. Best of all,
probably, is the average value of imports, since this represents the
product most nearly comparable to that provided by primary producers
and may be guessed to come closest to producers' current transaction

----

[25]In reviewing the 1974-75 rise in aluminum prices, the Council on
Wage and Price Stability staff (Aluminum Prices, 1974-75, Staff Report,
September 1976) chose to adjust the new BLS series by eliminating the
influence of the Metals Week market index (p. 118).

[26]An ostensibly unbroken index series considerably predates 1971,
but it earlier conformed only to producer list prices.

prices. There being no really firm basis for adjusting producers' list prices, however, the composite values for both domestic and total supply shown in table 6-11 have started with the Bureau of Mines average for domestic primary productions as the key element.[27]

Aluminum Scrap

The role of aluminum scrap in the U.S. economy is a complicated one and is in a current state of considerable flux. The value of scrap to some consumers--e.g., secondary smelters--is a matter of the current value of the recovered secondary aluminum, which in turn largely reflects the preemptive value of its purchase in terms of diluting potential competition from independent aluminum suppliers.[29] Much scrap aluminum--at least of the obsolete scrap variety--now merits an additional premium from primary producers as a means of disarming governmental and other efforts toward curtailment of the use of aluminum containers. The value of scrap in relation to virgin aluminum has also been enhanced by the tremendous escalation, in recent years, of the cost of energy. It is required in much greater quantities for primary than for secondary smelting.

---

[27] It is presumed that some amount of secondary aluminum, processed by primary producers, also gets sold at producers' primary prices, and that primary producer pricing may be underweighted in the composites. The price for the secondary portion of aluminum, supply, conversely, may be overweighted. It may also be slightly overstated, owing to the generally higher unit value of the small amounts of alloying elements in the producer (ingot No. 380) used as the unit value indicator.

[28] Secondary smelters play a dominant role in the supply of ingot for casting, according to the Council on Wage and Price Stability (Aluminum Prices, p. 30). The price of secondary ingot is nonetheless tied to that of primary aluminum, differing by a discount or a premium, depending on the slackness or tightness of the market (see table 6-11).

[29] Ibid., p. 226.

Table 6-11. Comparative Costs of Aluminum Metal
Consumed in the United States, 1952-1979,
According to Various Indicators

(cents per pound)

	Weighted average producers' list price[a]	Dealers' price, New York[b]	Average price of secondary ingot[c]	Average value of domestic aluminum[d]	Average value of imports[e]	Average value of total consumption[f]	Canadian ingot C.i.f. U.K.[g]
1952	18.4		20.5	18.9	N.A.	—	—
1953	19.8		22.2	20.4	"	—	—
1954	20.3		20.6	20.3	"	—	—
1955	21.8		28.3	23.0	"	—	20.9
1956	24.0		27.0	24.5	25.1	24.6	23.8
1957	25.4		22.7	24.9	25.8	25.0	24.6
1958	24.7		22.1	24.3	24.5	24.3	23.0
1959	24.4		23.4	24.3	24.7	24.3	22.5
1960	25.6		24.7	25.5	26.1	25.5	23.3
1961	24.9		22.6	24.6	24.5	24.6	23.3
1962	23.6		21.2	23.2	22.5	23.1	22.6
1963	22.5		21.1	22.2	21.3	22.1	22.6
1964	23.4		22.1	23.2	22.3	23.1	23.9
1965	24.3		24.2	24.3	22.3	24.0	24.5
1966	24.4		24.3	24.4	22.4	24.2	24.5
1967	24.7		24.8	24.7	23.3	24.6	24.5
1968	25.2		25.0	25.1	23.3	24.9	25.1
1969	26.5		26.8	26.6	24.4	26.5	26.7
1970	27.5	24.9	27.7	27.6	24.9	27.4	27.9
1971	23.4	22.5	22.9	27.5	24.5	27.2	28.4
1972	25.3	20.9	27.7	25.7	24.1	25.5	26.3
1973	24.4	27.6	30.6	25.5	23.8	25.4	27.2
1974	30.7	42.9	50.2	33.7	32.9	33.7	34.7
1975	38.4	34.6	43.9	39.4	38.4	39.3	39.5
1976	44.5	41.2	47.8	35.5	40.2	36.0	40.4

1977	51.6	N.A.	54.6	52.2	48.8	51.9	51.9
1978	54.6	N.A.	54.5	54.5	48.8	54.2	60.1
1979	59.4	N.A.	(h)	N.A.	56.8	N.A.	72.7

Source: See notes below.

N.A. - Not readily available.

[a]Average value of primary aluminum production as reported by the U.S. Bureau of Mines (Minerals Yearbook). The Bureau arrives at the value by multiplying quantities produced by the concurrently prevailing producers' list price.

[b]Averages of Metals Week monthly estimates. Since systematic data on actual transaction prices of aluminum producers are not available, this is the only available direct indicator of current market prices, though said to represent a very thin market. Source: Council on Wage and Price Stability, Aluminum Prices 1974-75 (Staff Report, September 1976), p. 133, and Metals Week Price Handbook, 1976. Data for omitted years not readily available.

[c]New York price of remelt aluminum ingots, No. 380 (1% Zn, 97 1/2%+ Al). Source: American Metal Market, Metal Statistics.

[d]Composite of primary supply at producers' prices and secondary supply (refined) at prices for secondary ingot.

[e]Duty paid. Except for 1974-79, freight and insurance component estimated.

[f]Composite of domestic and imported supply at average values in two preceding columns.

[g]Source: For 1952-77, UNCTAD Consideration of International Measures on Bauxite (TD/B/IPC/BAUXITE/2/Add. 1, 6 March 1978). For 1978-79, American Bureau of Metal Statistics, Non-Ferrous Metal Data 1979.

[h]Metal Statistics series discontinued.

In general, moreover, declining rates of aluminum growth promise an increasing relative role for obsolete scrap in the total aluminum economy.[30]

In general, with frequently as much as half of the "purchased" scrap
flow[31] coming back into the hands of the integrated producers, and with
all of it having a value closely geared to that of primary aluminum, there
is somewhat more stability in the cost of aluminum scrap to its users
than in the cost of its acquisition by dealers. The impact that the
integrated producers have on the average cost of aluminum scrap is visible
in part in the figures in table 6-12 for the three census years for which
separate data are available for interplant transfers. In 1967, when the
prices for the two kinds of flows were closest, interplant transfers
were slightly over half the "purchased" scrap supply, compared with about
25 percent and 42 percent in 1972 and 1963, respectively.

A small amount of imported aluminum scrap--from Canada, Germany,
Great Britain, and the USSR--tends to come in at a small premium over the
average delivered price within the United States, possibly because of
its particular mix. There appears to be nothing resembling a competitive
international market.

General Price Factors for Aluminum

The price of primary aluminum metal has been said to reflect essentially its cost of production.[32] Since the alternative forms of metallic
aluminum (secondary ingot and aluminum scrap) are clearly related in
their price to the primary ingot price, the reliability (and permanence)

---

[30]This is the case at least in the United States and in one or two
other industrialized countries. Worldwide, the situation is mixed (see
chapter 2).

[31]"Purchased" scrap data omit only "home" scrap (that reused in the
plants in which generated) and actually include large amounts of scrap
(sometimes as much as half the total) which are transferred among plants
of the same company.

[32]See, for example, Council on Wage and Price Stability, Aluminum
Prices, p. 116. The Council cites both industry testimony and a study by
Charles River Associates for the General Services Administration (Charles
River Associates, An Economic Analysis of the Aluminum Market, March 1971,
pp. 5-16).

of this proposition is a question of considerable importance. There is
reason to doubt, however, that production costs are any more than one
of several price-determining factors. And since the usual reference is
to total costs, including capital charges, rather than to the marginal
costs of added units of output, there is reason to question how precise
a standard the proposition might provide, even if true. In a capital-
intensive industry like that of aluminum, the unit allocation of capital
costs can vary over a wide range, depending upon the assumptions (or
choices) made as to rate of capacity utilization. Even more important
perhaps in arriving at total average cost is the wide latitude for selection of rates of depreciation and of target return on investment.

Most important, the obvious recognition by bauxite-producing countries
of an opportunity to reap economic rent, and the linking of that economic
rent to the price of aluminum, suggest that whatever may once have governed
the pricing of aluminum, the line of causation now runs at least partly
from demand to price to costs, rather than costs to price. The economic
rent sought by bauxite producers is in only minor degree a reflection
of their natural advantages in relation to other bauxite producers. Much
more important is that part of economic rent which aluminum metal is in
a position to garner in relation to other metals and industrial materials.

Table 6-12. Average Value of Aluminum and Aluminum-base Alloy Scrap
            Consumed by Secondary Smelters and Aluminum Processors,
            Census Years, 1954-1972

(cents per pound)

Year	Intracompany transfers	Other sources	Total
1954	N.A.	N.A.	15.4
1958	N.A.	N.A.	17.7
1963	13.5	24.0	13.8
1967	16.7	16.3	16.4
1972	17.1	14.5	15.4

N.A. - Not available.

Source: U.S. Bureau of the Census, Census of Manufactures.

Aluminum prices may be expected always to cover the marginal costs of mining bauxite and of processing into aluminum in the short run, and that plus some amount of capital recovery and earnings return if output is to expand over the longer run. The apparent floor which the Council on Wage and Price Stability found to have been supporting aluminum prices in 1974-75, however,[33] was considerably above the short-run minimum and— were the in situ value of bauxite to be omitted—well above the long-run minimum as well. The fact that it could be sustained was clearly the result of market power and the distance still remaining between costs and an effective price constraint. Whatever the degree of accounting justification and of institutionalization of bauxite taxes, the price of aluminum appears to be as closely appended to a substitution-elasticity ceiling above as it is sustained by a floor below. The demand for aluminum depends on much more, of course, than the immediate price of substitutes, but where aluminum pricing policy might once have given large weight to penetrating markets and achieving lower costs through scale, it appears now to be more concerned with upper limits.

Figure 6-4, which compares producer prices for aluminum with those for two of its closest competitors—copper and zinc—lends support to these price-behavior assumptions. While it is difficult to interpret the meaning of costs in a situation where each increase in the price of aluminum presumably carries with it an automatic increase in the price of one of its principal ingredients (bauxite), one may guess that between 1973 and 1977, the cost of making aluminum increased by a little more than half. Producer prices, however, more than doubled, and there were further increases in 1978 and 1979. Prior to 1973, and at least back to 1958, aluminum pricing had been increasingly more favorable to industrial consumers in relation to the prices of both copper and zinc,[34] and considerable substitution for both of these metals was taking place. Since 1973, in the case of

---

[33]Ibid.

[34]There has actually been a rather steady decline in the price of aluminum relative to copper over most of the period since the mid-1920s, when aluminum sold at 27 cents per pound and copper at 14 cents. Aluminum has cost less per pound than copper since 1947.

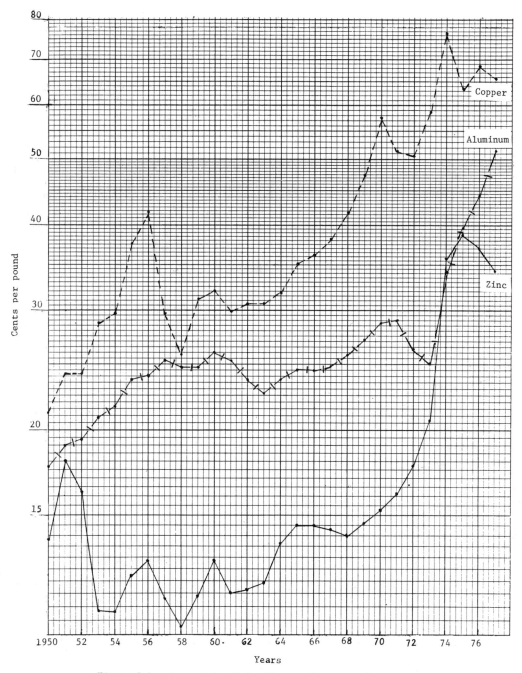

Figure 6-4. Comparative Price History (Producers' Prices, U.S.)
of Aluminum, Copper, and Zinc, 1950-1977

383

copper, and since 1975, in the case of zinc, aluminum producers have, on the face of things, been dissipating this competitive advantage. If recent aluminum price history is compared, however, with expectations as to the longer run prices of copper and zinc rather than their actual prices,[35] aluminum producers may be interpreted as now making the most of their accumulated advantage. Their security in testing the limits of substitution elasticity is no doubt strengthened by the external circumstance of a governmentally imposed premium on weight reduction in what is perhaps the largest remaining application for aluminum to conquer-- the passenger automobile.

Copper

Copper pricing to U.S. consumers has for some time exhibited the pattern toward which aluminum is now tending: refined metal prices which are heavily influenced by current market tightness or slackness, and ore and intermediate-form prices (or unit values) which are determined by refined metal prices. In copper, as in aluminum, a good deal of the intermediate "pricing" involves transfers among units of the same company, so that accounting practices and considerations of tax and other governmental relationships may be important. But the copper industry has been contending much longer with the intervention of foreign governments that have not only sought to influence the degree of processing and the terms of sale, but have nationalized many operations. It has also sought, and sometimes obtained, domestic price support from the federal government, and at other times has been constrained (as has aluminum) by price controls. Most important, there has long been an institutionalized procedure whereby the producer of ore, even if organizationally independent, receives payment according to the current price of refined copper (and of any other constituents in his ore or concentrate). This is true regardless of whether the independent mining operation sells its ore or concentrate to

---

[35]Prices of both these metals, as well as the prices of finished steel, another aluminum competitor, were tending upward late in 1978. So was the dealers' price of aluminum ingot, a more direct competitor.

the smelter or has it smelted on "toll" and sells the blister copper[36]
(or has it sold) for its own account.

In recent years, the system has tended to move even closer to one
of market-based pricing, transmitted from the metal to the blister and ore.
U.S. producer pricing of copper, while seeking to avoid the grosser fluctuations of New York Commodity Exchange (Comex) and London Metal Exchange
(LME) fluctuations, had long tended to follow the market far more closely
than had aluminum producer pricing, but several copper companies have
now (though not necessarily permanently) given up on producer pricing
altogether, keying their sales prices directly to the Comex quotations.
Concurrently, foreign shipments for the U.S. market are by now almost
wholly keyed to LME copper prices, though CIPEC[37] has for several years
been toying with the idea of an internationally agreed-upon producer
price system that would at least dampen the fluctuations transmitted
by the LME.

Despite this obvious impact of current demand conditions on copper
pricing, analysts appear to consider the longer run price of copper to
be determined, instead, by full incremental costs of production. The
argument is that new investment does not provide the capacity needed to
balance demand except at a prospective price which will cover all costs
and a reasonable return on the capital employed. The validity of this
proposition must be qualified, however, at least by (1) the lack of
perfect foresight as to how much copper will be absorbed at any given
price, and (2) the well-recognized cycles of over- and underinvestment
that are propagated by market conditions at the time that investment
decisions are made. In the event, rather than in the planning, the marginal producer will at some times not be able to recover a desired rate
of return and amortization on his sunk costs and at other times reap
economic rent out of the delays in getting new facilities into operation.
The average is probably more closely related to long-run demand schedules
(elasticities of demand at various prices) than it is to underlying costs,

---

[36]Or refined copper, if the toll processing includes that stage.

[37]These are the initials of the French name for the International
Council of Copper Exporting Countries.

despite the relative competitiveness of the industry. In any case, given
the elusiveness of information on costs, long-run relationships between
cost and price are almost impossible to deduce. Even were they deducible,
they would probably have little relevance to an emerging world copper
picture that shows a growing number of independent decision makers, as
multinational companies yield to the regulatory and takeover initiatives
of multiple nations and as some of those nations, in turn, engage in
cooperative efforts to exert control over the international market.

Copper Ore

Since the bulk of copper smelter feed in the United States is domestic
ore and concentrate,[38] and a substantial portion of this material is
transferred between units of the same company, it would be particularly
valuable in this instance to know year-by-year costs of production. Not
only is this impossible from any practical standpoint, there is not even
any continuing series on the "price" of domestic ore or concentrate. The
value of production series of the Bureau of Mines are no more than the
quantities of mine output valued at refined copper prices. Only the
economic censuses give an inkling as to the values of the minerals as
such. And there is a problem even here, so far as smelter consumption
is concerned, since the quantities consumed are reported in gross rather
than content weight. The only direct reading on value per unit of contained copper is that given in the Census of Mineral Industries.[39] This
refers to production rather than consumption, but a rough approximation
of the average copper content of ores and concentrates may be calculated
from other data in the Census of Mineral Industries and used to derive
an average value per pound of contained copper in the ores, etc., consumed

----

[38]"Ore," where used in this report, should generally be read as "ore
and concentrate." Direct shipping ores have become progressively less
important since World War II and have by now almost wholly been replaced
by concentrated ores. A modest quantity of copper precipitated from
leach liquid is also shipped, but is beginning to give way to direct
shipment of leach liquid to refineries.

[39]Ostensibly reported as total, rather than recoverable, content--but
possibly not strictly so, considering conventional reporting to the U.S.
Bureau of Mines.

by the smelting and refining industry, as reported in the Census of
Manufactures. In both cases, the reported values appear to include credits
for metals other than copper (especially gold and silver) and are therefore
presumably overstated as to copper value alone--by about 3 1/2 percent
in 1972, more in earlier years.

The results of these calculations are given in table 6-13. The
values calculable from the minerals census, for the years available, are
consistently higher than those estimated from the manufactures census--an
anomaly which is all the greater in view of presumed transportation costs
from mine to smelter and the consumption by the latter of some imported,
higher priced ores. The only piece of relevant independent intelligence
which came to our attention suggests that the manufactures census may
be the closer of the two to being correct.[40]

Price quotations for imported ores are no more available than for
domestic ores. The various average-value series calculable from the
foreign trade statistics (table 6-14), rather than throwing any light
on the costs of smelter feed in general, may be relevant only to the
marginal role played by imported supplies. The volatility of import
prices (which in turn reflect the volatility of LME prices) is evident
from fluctuations in the average value of U.S. ore/concentrate imports
for consumption: 36.9 cents per pound of gross copper content in 1971,
50.2 in 1972, 40.9 in 1973, 76.6 in 1974, 60.8 in 1975, 72.7 in 1976,
and 55.1 in 1977.[41] Given the speculation that manifests itself in frequent substantial accumulation or de-accumulation of customs bonded stocks,

---

[40]Estimate by an industry spokesman that there was an average 15-cent
smelting and refining cost in North American operations in 1971. Quoted
by Raymond F. Mikesell, in The World Copper Industry (Baltimore, Md., Johns
Hopkins University Press for Resources for the Future, 1979) p. 121.

There would be reason, in view of the profits limit on percentage
depletion, for integrated companies to account for as much profit as
possible in the mining operation. This does not, however, explain why
the smelter valuations should differ.

[41]From U.S. Bureau of Mines, Minerals Yearbook; Foreign Trade Division, U.S. Bureau of the Census, FT 246.

Table 6-13. Average Values of U.S. Copper Smelter Feeds,[a]
From Reports of Mines and Smelters, Respectively,
Compared With Imported Ore Average and Average
Producer Prices,[b] for Census Years, 1954-1972

(cents per pound of gross copper content[c])

	1954	1958	1963	1967	1972
Mine reports[c]	N.A.	18.8	22.0	28.6	38.7
Smelter/refinery reports[c,d]	20.3	16.6	17.4	26.4	37.4
Imported ores and concentrates[e]	N.A.	24.2	30.0	41.8	51.7
Producers' prices, copper metal[b]	29.7	25.8	30.6	38.2	50.6

Source: U.S. Bureau of the Census, Census of Mineral
Industries; Census of Manufactures; FT 246.

N.A. - Not available.

[a]Includes ore, concentrates, and precipitates. The great bulk
of the material is concentrates.

[b]F.o.b. refinery. From Engineering and Mining Journal
(averaged from Metals Week).

[c]The calculations unavoidably attribute to copper the
by-product values of other contained metals, especially gold and
silver. For 1972, the overstatement is estimated at 3 1/2 percent.

[d]Original data are in gross weight. Copper content estimated
by using average content of mine shipments, as reported in
Census of Mineral Industries in corresponding years. An additional
adjustment was made in the 1967 estimate to deal with a dispropor-
tionate amount of copper precipiates included in the smelter
consumption, but not mine production, data.

[e]Duty-paid, landed value of "imports for consumption." The
freight component was estimated by RFF.

Table 6-14.   Average Values of Blister Copper in the United
States, as Produced, Consumed, and Imported, for
Census Years, 1954-1967

(cents per pound)

	1954	1958	1963	1967
Census of Manufactures				
Blister or anode shipped from smelters:				
To other plants of same company	31.5	27.3	28.2	N.A.
To different companies	28.7	25.6	29.5	"
Total	30.6	27.0	28.7	37.5
Blister or anode consumed by refineries	32.0	25.0	27.5	N.A.
Reports to U.S. Bureau of Mines				
Smelter output from domestic ores	29.5	26.3	N.A.	N.A.
Imports for Consumption[a]	29.3	23.9	30.0	40.2
Cf. Producers' price, copper metal	29.7	25.8	30.6	38.2

Source: U.S. Bureau of the Census, Census of Manufactures and FT246; U.S. Bureau of Mines, Minerals Yearbook.

N.A. - Not available.

[a] "Customs value," which tends to be close to f.a.s. International freight and insurance add roughly another 2 cents per pound. Duty on blister copper was suspended during the period covered.

it should be noted that average values for the year of entry for consumption may for some years be significantly affected by prices in the prior years in which much of the material may actually have been purchased from abroad.

Blister Copper

Only a small percentage of the blister copper consumed by refineries in the United States comes from other than domestic smelters operated by the same company (about two-thirds of this small amount is supplied from abroad).[42] Pricing is therefore essentially an intracompany affair, but, as with ore, it appears to be closely tied to the current producer price for copper. Again, there are no published price quotations, so that the only indications of the prices assigned are those calculable from the Census of Manufactures and from U.S. foreign trade statistics, as well as from a Bureau of Mines series that was terminated in 1960. The Manufactures data on blister, moreover, have either been combined with data on refined copper or suppressed altogether in recent years--presumably for reasons of confidentiality--so that no separate data on blister copper, either as produced or as consumed, are available for 1972, and there are gaps in the earlier censuses. Available average-value comparisons, including those derivable from imports for consumption, are shown in table 6-14. Because blister is about 99 percent copper, the averages are for gross weight.

As with ores and concentrates, the comparisons present some anomalies. In this case not only are producers' prices generally lower than the landed value (see table footnote) of imported blister, but they imply either a negative or seemingly insufficient refining margin with regard to domestic blister. The figures are generally closer to each other, however, than those for ores and concentrates, so that, save for years of exceptional shortage or surplus, the imported blister values appear to provide a reasonable indicator of year-to-year changes in the overall

---

[42]Harold J. Schroeder, Copper (U.S. Bureau of Mines, Mineral Commodity Profiles, 3, June 1977) figure 1. Earlier Census of Manufactures data show somewhat larger, but still minor, proportions moving between plants of unrelated companies.

cost of refinery feed. The average f.a.s. values of such imports are shown in table 6-15. To these values may be added roughly 2 cents per pound for international and inland freight. As in the case of ores, the price fluctuations for blister reflect evident inventory speculation.

Refined Copper

Series on U.S. refined copper prices come in a number of variants and have been altered in exact specification over the years. The most useful series are those that show the course of producer prices, since these apply to the bulk of the copper consumed.

It is difficult to assemble a dealers' price series for copper, though this would be desirable to reflect, particularly, the premiums paid in times when producer supplies are rationed. New York Commodity Exchange prices are quoted in ranges and there is no way of systematically weighting or correcting for that part of the trading which is purely speculative and involves no actual delivery; moreover, a long-term series is not readily available. As a free-market indicator, the London Metal Exchange cash-settlement price, which is shown in table 6-16, is almost equivalent to the Comex price,[43] and annual averages in terms of U.S. currency do happen to be readily available.

About the only nonproducer sales it is possible systematically to account for as part of domestic consumption are those of imported copper, data on the average value of which[44] are also shown in table 6-16, both on as f.a.s. (or approximate f.a.s.) and on a landed, duty-paid basis.[45]

---

[43]Arbitrage keeps the two markets in fairly close correspondence.

[44]Since some of the imports are subject to additional transportation (and possibly processing) charges and to dealers' markups, there is probably a somewhat higher average value actually paid by consumers.

[45]The estimates for 1974-79 were derived from actually reported c.i.f. values, with the addition of the 0.8 cents per pound specific duty; for earlier years ocean shipping costs were estimated by RFF. The duty on refined copper was reduced by 0.1 cent per year from 2.0 cents in 1955 to 1.7 cents in 1958, and again, by 0.2 cent per year, from 1.7 cents in 1967 to 0.8 cent in 1972.

Table 6-15. Average Values of U.S. Imports for Consumption of
             Blister Copper, 1952-1977, Compared With Corres-
             ponding Values for Ores and Concentrates[a]

(cents per pound)

Year	Blister Copper	Ores, etc. Copper content
1952	30.7	27.2
1953	32.1	27.5
1954	29.3	27.4
1955	35.9	32.6
1956	40.9	36.3
1957	29.8	27.9
1958	23.9	22.2
1959	31.0	29.5
1960	32.0	29.5
1961	29.6	28.7
1962	29.9	30.4
1963	30.0	28.7
1964	30.2	26.1
1965	30.1	27.0
1966	40.4	30.1
1967	40.2	40.4
1968	40.9	46.1
1969	48.3	45.6
1970	54.8	59.9
1971	47.0	36.9
1972	47.0	50.2
1973	62.4	40.9
1974	95.6	76.6
1975	57.5	60.8
1976	57.5	72.7
1977	66.2	55.1

Source: U.S. Bureau of Mines, Minerals Yearbook; Foreign
Trade Division, U.S. Bureau of the Census, FT 246.

[a] Data are based on reported customs (essentially f.a.s.)
values.

A composite average unit value has also been calculated and is shown in
the table. Since this value is based on the partly unrealistic assumptions
that all of domestic refined copper supply (including secondary) is delivered at producer wirebar prices and that all of imported supply is
delivered at average duty-paid value, it very likely understates the
actual unit price paid by industrial consumers in times of tight supply
and overstates it for periods of surplus. It seems, however, a reasonable
indicator both of long-term price changes and much of the intermediate
fluctuation. As noted earlier in this section, producers' prices for
copper have all along tended to adjust, albeit incompletely, to commodity-
market price trends, and a number of important producers are now directly
tying their quotations to Comex prices.[46]

To explore the relationship between U.S. and world prices, figure 6-5
compares a five-year moving-average trend in the LME settlement price
with a similar moving average in our U.S. constructed-cost series.[47] As
a further preliminary clue to what may govern price trends, world refined
copper consumption is similarly charted. The series are graphed on a
ratio scale, so that they may be compared on a comparative rate-of-change
basis. In trend it appears that the cost of copper to U.S. consumers
responds--sluggishly and fairly evenly--to changes in world price levels,
and the latter show considerable sensitivity to accelerations and decelerations in the growth of world demand--particularly that of the principal trading countries (see table 1-20 for the original data). The
apparently contrary behavior during the latter 1950s is explained by a
surge in capacity which was brought on by previous shortages and what
at that time were historically high price peaks.

Copper Scrap

There are a number of regularly published domestic price quotations
for copper scrap: a key series currently is that of the American Metal

---

[46]This development is too recent to be reflected in the table 6-16
series.

[47]To provide a slightly longer trend line, values for 1952-55 were
roughly estimated.

Table 6-16. Domestic Producer Prices for Copper Wirebar, 1952-1979, Compared With Other Price and Average Value Series

(cents per pound)

Year	Producer prices, wirebar		LME wire-bar (cash)[b]	Average value of imported refined[c]		Overall average cost, f.o.b. port or plant[d]
	E&MJ[a]	Bureau of Mines		Customs or f.a.s.[c]	C.i.f., duty paid[a]	
1952	24.2	24.2	32.4	32.7	N.A.	N.A.
1953	28.8	28.7	30.1	33.2	N.A.	N.A.
1954	29.7	29.5	31.1	29.5	N.A.	N.A.
1955	37.5	37.3	43.9	38.1	N.A.	N.A.
1956	41.8	42.5	41.1	41.2	43.8	42.7
1957	29.6	30.1	27.4	29.9	32.1	30.3
1958	25.8	26.3	24.7	24.5	26.6	26.3
1959	31.2	30.7	29.7	30.9	33.8	31.2
1960	32.1	32.1	30.8	32.0	35.1	32.3
1961	29.9	30.0	28.7	29.8	32.9	30.1
1962	30.6	30.8	29.3	29.6	32.5	30.9
1963	30.6	30.8	29.3	29.0	32.1	30.9
1964	32.0	32.6	43.9	29.9	33.0	32.6
1965	35.0	35.4	58.5	34.3	37.6	35.5
1966	36.2	36.6	69.4	40.9	42.3	36.8
1967	38.2	38.6	51.6	46.9	48.3	40.4
1968	41.8	42.2	56.3	54.3	55.8	44.7
1969	47.5	47.9	66.5	50.5	51.8	48.1

Year						
1970	57.7	58.2	64.1	55.3	57.1	58.1
1971	51.4	52.0	49.0	50.4	51.6	52.0
1972	50.6	51.2	48.6	49.6	50.7	51.2
1973	58.9	59.5	80.9	63.8	66.7	60.0
1974	76.6	77.3	93.4	86.4	89.8	78.9
1975	63.5	64.2	56.1	58.4	60.1	63.9
1976	68.8	69.6	63.5	59.6	62.5	68.4
1977	65.8	66.8	59.4	61.1	63.5	66.2
1978	65.5	66.5	59.2	58.0	59.9	64.5
1979	92.2	93.3	86.9	86.7	88.5	92.9

N.A. - Not readily available or calculable.

[a] Originally from Metals Week quotations. Information on specifications is contradictory, but the E&MJ series appears to be on a delivered-New York basis through 1963 and on an f.o.b. refinery basis thereafter. From 1970, it is indicated as being a production-weighted average. The Bureau of Mines series is production-weighted throughout and on a delivered (U.S. destinations) basis from 1955 (f.o.b. New York, 1952-54).

[b] Calculated from data in dollars per metric ton assembled by the World Bank (Report No. EC-166/79, Commodity Trade and Price Trends (1979 Edition), p. 100.

[c] Foreign Trade Division, U.S. Bureau of the Census, FT 246 (1974-77); U.S. Bureau of Mines, Minerals Yearbook (earlier years). C.i.f. component, 1974-79, calculated from U.S. Bureau of the Census reports of quantity and value. For earlier years, ocean shipping costs, estimated by RFF, were added to "customs" unit value calculated from the trade data. Duty additions are given in text footnote 48.

[d] Weighted average of domestic supply at Bureau of Mines producer prices and imported supply at estimated average duty-paid values.

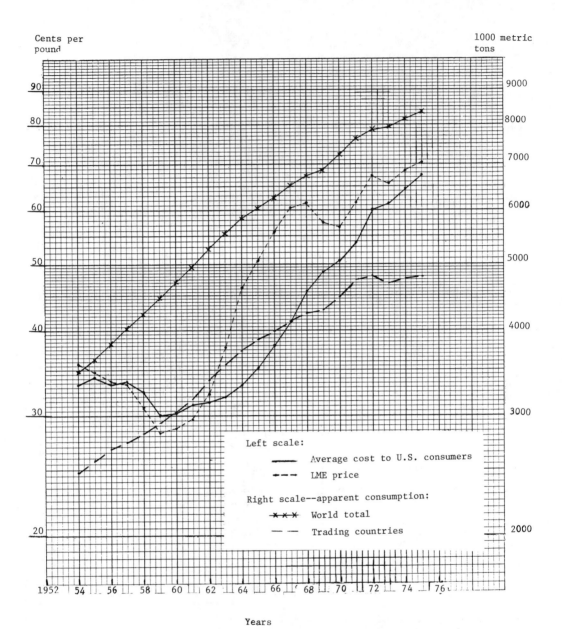

Figure 6-5. Trends in Cost of Refined Copper to U.S. Industrial
Consumers, Compared With LME Cash Price and World
Refined Copper Consumption (Five-Year Moving Averages)

Market (AMM) on dealers' buying prices, New York, for No. 2 scrap (heavy).
Monthly and yearly averages are given for this series in AMM Metal Statistics, which also shows a companion series (many entries being estimated
rather than based on actual quotations) for refinery buying prices. Both
price series refer to relatively pure, unalloyed scrap, both new and old.
What is less clear is how much of purchased scrap each series represents.
For one thing, unalloyed scrap is frequently a less important part of
the supply than "composition" scrap, recovery from which is directly as
alloy ingot. Prices for this material maintain a far less than constant
ratio to the prices of No. 2 heavy scrap. The same may be said of scrap
purchased by refineries, which may be a mixture of light and heavy and,
on the whole, tends to have a higher price. It is not clear, furthermore,
how much of the total copper scrap supply passes through dealers' hands;
how much from fabricators back to brass mills, etc. and smelters/refin-
eries; and how much of both home and purchased scrap is smelted and refined
on toll. That the amount of toll refining may be quite significant is
suggested by a comparison of "purchased" scrap quantities reported, respectively, by the Bureau of Mines and the Bureau of the Census in Census
of Manufactures years.

The three buying-price series shown in table 6-17, therefore, may
be considered only indicative of changes in actual consumer costs.
Dealers' buying prices, in particular, tend to reflect market expectations
as much as they do current costs, since scrap dealers have traditionally
been interested in speculative as well as in assembling and processing
margins. Theoretically, the best general indicator--especially as it
combines all kinds of copper scrap--should be the average value of exported
scrap copper, as shown in the table. This material is normally sold by
dealers and in a sense represents the marginal opportunity cost for domestic purchasers.

The overall scrap acquisition costs given on the third line of table
6-18 are costs for all of the significant consuming industries identifiable
in the Census. These include primary refineries and copper alloy foundries, but neither of these categories is comparable in magnitude with

Table 6-17. Four Indicator Series of the Cost of Copper Scrap to U.S. Industrial Consumers, 1952-1979

(cents per pound)

| Year | Buying prices, New York | | | Average value of copper-base scrap exports |
| | No. 2 Scrap[a] | | Composition,[b] dealers | |
	Dealers	Refiners		
1952	19.0	N.A.	18.0	20.7
1953	22.4	N.A.	17.1	22.2
1954	24.5	N.A.	18.8	23.2
1955	33.6	N.A.	26.8	29.5
1956	31.6	N.A.	27.1	32.7
1957	20.1	22.9	19.1	25.8
1958	17.6	20.3	15.8	19.7
1959	22.6	25.4	18.7	22.2
1960	21.2	24.6	17.7	22.8
1961	21.8	25.0	19.7	23.1
1962	21.6	24.9	20.1	22.8
1963	22.2	25.1	20.8	22.5
1964	26.0	30.5	24.9	27.1
1965	34.5	38.9	27.9	30.6
1966	44.7	50.1	33.1	35.7
1967	33.2	37.3	30.0	32.9
1968	32.8	38.7	27.3	37.8

1969	42.9	49.1	37.0	41.5
1970	30.5	49.2	36.3	41.4
1971	27.6	38.4	29.9	38.7
1972	39.0	39.0[c]	29.5	38.0
1973	50.2	60.2	40.9	37.2
1974	54.9	67.8	43.8	54.3
1975	33.9	41.1	32.5	43.3
1976	40.7	47.7	34.1	44.3
1977	34.2	44.4	34.2	42.4
1978	40.5	50.7	39.7	43.4
1979	60.9	71.0	57.4	55.8

Source: American Metal Market, Metal Statistics; U.S. Bureau of Mines, Minerals Yearbook; Foreign Trade Division, U.S. Bureau of the Census, FT 410.

N.A. - Not readily available.

[a] In the case of dealers, "heavy" scrap.

[b] Also referred to as "red brass" scrap.

[c] Re-averaged from monthly averages in Metal Statistics, whose annual-average calculation appeared to be in error.

Table 6-18.   Average Value of Purchased Copper Scrap Consumed
in U.S. Industry, Compared with Various Price
Indicators, for Census Years, 1954-1972

(cents per pound)

	1954	1958	1963	1967	1972
Census of Manufactures					
Secondary smelters/ refiners	18.8	17.8	22.2	30.7	39.3
Copper rolling and drawing (brass and wire mills)	23.6	19.8	24.9	35.3	39.8
All significant consumers[a]	21.4	19.0	23.7	33.3	39.5
Buying prices, New York					
Dealers: No.2 Scrap	24.5	17.6	22.2	33.2	39.0
Composition scrap	18.8	15.8	20.8	30.0	29.5
Refiners	N.A.	20.3	25.1	37.3	39.0
Average value of exports	23.2	19.7	27.1	32.9	38.0

Source: U.S. Bureau of the Census, Census of Manufactures:
table 6-17.

[a]Includes also primary smelters/refiners and brass/bronze/
copper foundries.

the two industries specifically shown.[48]   Partly, as suggested earlier,
this is because copper scrap processed on toll is not included in the
Census data for consumption by refineries, though such toll processing
apparently accounts for the better part of their scrap throughout.

Lead

Lead Ores

Although concentrates, rather than ores as such, are the bulk of
material referred to as "ore" in the case of most of the minerals considered in this report, an emphasis on this specification is especially
important in the case of lead. The reason is that a particularly large
portion of the mine production of lead is derived from ores classified
as zinc or other metals; and many lead ores themselves contain substantial
proportions of zinc, silver, or other metals. The lead and zinc are
substantially separated from one another at the concentrating stage;
other metals may remain part of the essential product--lead concentrates,
howsoever derived--whose price is discussed here.[49]

As was the case with copper, no annual series is available on the
value of output of lead ore and concentrates; the U.S. Bureau of Mines
values copper, lead, and zinc all at their refined metal equivalent. Some
indication of cost may be derived, however, from the record on imports
of lead ore and concentrates, which have recently fluctuated around a
tenth of the total ore/concentrate supply. For the years 1974-79, when
actual f.a.s. as well as c.i.f. values are reported, table 6-19 provides
a comparison of various unit value calculations, both on an imports-for-
consumption and a general-imports basis. For further comparison, the
average U.S. price of lead metal is also shown. Since general imports
come closer to the timing of the actual import transactions than do
imports for consumption, it is not surprising that the former maintain

---

[48]Moreover, within the second category shown, wire mill consumption
is insignificant.

[49]Small amounts may still be directly smelted as ore.

Table 6-19. Comparison of Various Measures of the Average Value of Lead
            Ore and Concentrates Imported Into the United States,
            1974-1979

(cents per pound, gross lead content)

	1974	1975	1976	1977	1978	1979
General imports:						
Customs value	17.6	15.5	16.7	23.6	22.8	42.6
F.a.s. value	18.5	16.4	17.4	24.3	23.7	43.4
C.i.f. value	12.1	13.7	16.2	20.6	18.5	33.3
Imports for consumption:						
Customs value	12.1	13.7	16.2	20.6	18.5	33.3
F.a.s. value	12.8	14.5	16.6	21.3	19.1	33.9
C.i.f. value	13.8	15.4	17.8	22.6	20.7	35.6
Duty-paid value[a]	14.5	16.2	18.6	23.4	21.5	36.4
Cf. price of lead metal	22.5	21.5	23.1	30.7	33.7	52.6

Source: Foreign Trade Division, U.S. Bureau of the Census, FT 135 and
246; Engineering and Mining Journal, March 1980.

[a]Includes duty of 0.75 cents per pound.

a more consistent relationship to average lead prices in the same year, although there was an increase between 1974 and 1979 from roughly a 3-cent to an 8-cent differential.

Unlike copper, it is not possible to derive, from the Census of Manufactures, a usable unit value for lead ores and concentrates consumed by smelters: the lead and zinc data are combined, with no indication of the individual metal content. The only check on import values as a cost indicator, therefore, is production data from the Census of Mineral Industries. Even here, a small adjustment was required to apportion between lead and zinc the value of combined ores shipped without prior concentration. For a comparison of the import values, moreover, it was necessary, as with other metals, to estimate international shipping charges and to assume an identity between average customs and average f.a.s. values. The results of the comparison are shown in table 6-20. The average values shown therein for mine production include those assigned to transfers to plants of the same company--the situation which in fact characterizes the bulk of domestic lead production.[50] From the comparison, it is hard to draw a clear conclusion as to the utility of the series on average value of lead in imported ore and concentrates as a continuing cost indicator. The differences between the import and domestic values are not great, however, and the former appear to provide something of a working ceiling.

Lead Metal

Prices are regularly quoted for "common corroding" pig lead (originally on a New York, and now on a delivered, basis); American Metal Market and Engineering and Mining Journal annual averages differ not at all or only slightly in virtually all years. The E&MJ averages are shown in table 6-21 for comparison with prices for the same commodity on the London Metal Exchange,[51] as well as with the average customs (country-of-origin) value of U.S. imports of refined lead. As may be seen, the last

---

[50]See J. Patrick Ryan and John M. Hague, Lead (U.S. Bureau of Mines, Mineral Commodity Profiles, 9, December 1977) p. 3.

[51]Converted by source into U.S. currency.

Table 6-20. Average Value of Lead Ores and Concentrates Produced in the
            United States, Compared With Estimated Average Duty-Paid
            Value of Imports, for Census Years, 1958-1972[a]

(cents per pound of gross lead content)

	1958	1963	1967	1972
Production (shipments), per Census of Mineral Industries[b]	10.3	9.8	9.3	11.0
Imports for consumption, duty-paid[c]	12.3	9.5	11.8	11.8
Cf. Price of refined metal[d]	12.1	11.1	14.0	15.0

Source: U.S. Bureau of the Census, Census of Mineral Industries;
U.S. Bureau of Mines, Minerals Yearbook.

[a]1954 data not available.

[b]For 1958-67, includes an adjustment to allocate between lead and
zinc the total value of a small proportion of combined lead-zinc ores.
Data for 1972 are for concentrates only.

[c]International shipping costs estimated by RFF. The duty was 0.75
cents per pound in all of the years listed.

[d]Common lead, Engineering and Mining Journal.

Table 6-21. Comparison of Average Annual Prices for Pig Lead in the United
States (New York or Delivered) and on London Metal Exchange,
1952-1979, With Average Value (in Country of Origin) of U.S.
Refined Lead Imports

(cents per pound)

Year	U.S.[a]	LME[b]	Average value of imports[c]	Year	U.S.[a]	LME[b]	Average value of imports[c]
1952	16.5	17.0	16.2	1966	15.1	11.9	13.2
1953	13.5	11.5	12.6	1967	14.0	10.3	12.2
1954	14.1	12.1	12.5	1968	13.2	10.9	12.0
1955	15.1	13.2	13.8	1969	14.9	13.1	12.9
1956	16.0	14.5	14.8	1970	15.6	13.7	15.0
1957	14.7	12.1	13.2	1971	13.8	11.5	12.5
1958	12.1	9.1	10.1	1972	15.0	13.7	13.0
1959	12.2	8.9	10.4	1973	16.3	19.4	14.9
1960	11.9	9.3	10.6	1974	22.5	26.8	24.4
1961	10.9	8.0	9.3	1975	21.5	18.7	23.6
1962	9.6	7.1	8.1	1976	23.1	20.5	21.2
1963	11.1	7.9	9.1	1977	30.7	28.0	29.5
1964	13.6	12.6	10.8	1978	33.7	29.8	34.2
1965	16.0	14.4	13.6	1979	52.6	54.5	51.9

Source: Engineering and Mining Journal, March 1980; Metal Bulletin;
U.S. Bureau of Mines, Minerals Yearbook: Foreign Trade Division, U.S.
Bureau of the Census, FT 246.

[a]New York basis through 1971; delivered price thereafter.

[b]Settlement price.

[c]Imports for consumption, customs value.

value runs higher than the LME average price and lower than the U.S. average price in most years, though exceptions recently have become more frequent. The LME price is normally separated from the U.S. price by an average transportation differential plus a duty differential (1 1/16 cents per pound, for the period shown), but this basic relationship between the two series is also obviously influenced by the lesser fluctuations of what in the United States is a producer price.[52] Similarly, the difference between U.S. price and average customs value of imported lead metal represents, at various times, something more or less than the costs of transportation and duty payment. More specifically, given their rising role in U.S. supply, imports have usually arrived at a cost which reflects the volatility of world pricing as represented by the LME, but approaches the U.S. producer price in years of relatively slack demand. The relatively high cost of imported lead in 1975 may be presumed to be a hangover from the scarcities that manifested themselves in the boom years 1973-74.

Though the contribution of imported refined lead to total supply may on balance be declining, it fluctuates considerably and has been significant enough at times (as much as one-fourth the supply) that one would expect it to influence the average cost of lead to the U.S. industrial consumer. However, as may be seen in table 6-22, the domestic delivered price series as an indicator of the consumption cost of unalloyed lead is not particularly improved by the introduction of an adjustment for the duty-paid cost of imports. Neither an unadjusted or adjusted series, moreover, is fully representative of the total average cost of lead to the industrial consumer, since, as may be seen in table 6-22, antimonial lead is significantly higher priced. This is a reflection of the much higher price of antimony than of lead; the roughly 7 to 12 percent of antimonial content would probably imply a much greater differential between the two products were it not for the fact that the bulk of antimonial lead is repetitively recycled as such.

---

[52] In 1951/52 and 1973, the U.S. price was also held down by government controls.

Table 6-22. Comparison of Estimated Average Cost of U.S. Refined Lead
Supply (Including Secondary and Antimonial) With Reported
Average Costs of Domestic Production (Shipments) and
Consumption, for Census Years, 1954-1972

(cents per pound)

	1954	1958	1963	1967	1972
Census of Manufactures: Production:[a]					
Refined, unalloyed lead[b]	13.9	11.5	11.1	13.1	14.9
Antimonial lead[c]	15.5	12.7	11.9	15.4	16.9
Combined	14.5	11.9	11.4	14.0	15.4
Consumption:[d]					
Refined, unalloyed lead	14.0	12.5	10.9	13.9	15.0
Antimonial lead	15.1	14.9	12.8	14.4	16.2
Combined	14.7	14.1	12.1	14.2	15.7
Domestic price, unalloyed lead[e]	14.1	12.1	11.1	14.0	15.0
Imports, duty-paid[f]	N.A.	11.8	11.8	13.9	14.7
Total supply[g]	N.A.	12.0	11.0	14.0	15.0

Source: U.S. Bureau of the Census, Census of Manufactures;
U.S. Bureau of Mines, Minerals Yearbook.

N.A. - not readily available or calculable.

[a] Calculations actually based on shipments.

[b] Primary and secondary.

[c] Essentially secondary.

[d] Data consistently available for storage battery industry only.

[e] New York basis except for 1972, when quoted delivered.

[f] Average customs value, plus inland and ocean shipping
costs as estimated by RFF, plus 1 1/16 cent duty.

[g] Combines domestic supply of refined and antimonial lead
(lead content only), at unalloyed lead price, and lead content
of all lead metal imports, at estimated duty-paid value.

Lead Scrap

For a large secondary lead smelting industry and its principal customers, battery manufacturers, the price of lead scrap is probably more
important than that of refined lead. Because this is almost wholly a
domestic market, one would expect it to be influenced more by the supply
of discarded storage batteries and the current demand for new ones than
by the price of lead in New York and London. The supply of battery lead
in large measure is balanced off by the demand for replacement batteries,
but will tend to be in short supply at times of rapid increase in the
motor vehicle stock and relatively plentiful when new car sales are slack.

Unfortunately, only indirect evidence is readily available on year-
by-year cost changes in the kind of scrap that constitutes the better part
of the secondary lead supply. The readily available series--that shown
in figure 6-6--is for soft lead scrap, rather than battery plates and
other antimonial (hard) lead. This does not necessarily invalidate the
comparison between lead scrap and refined lead, since the refined lead
price series is also for soft lead, but it does diminish the utility
of the available series as an overall cost indicator.

Table 6-23 compares the scrap price series with reported average
amounts refineries have paid for lead scrap in economic census years.
The comparison shows an apparently growing dealer's margin. One cannot
be certain, however, whether there was such a trend or not, since dealer
buying rates tend to be speculatively related to expectations as to future
demand and supply of scrap, whereas refinery acquisition costs should
be more closely related to refined lead prices at the time of their scrap
purchases. All the recent census years appear to have been years of
relatively slack markets.

In addition, there remains the fact that the average acquisition
prices shown in the census are for all kinds of lead scrap, whereas the
dealer's price quotations are for soft lead only. Too recent to be
reflected in table 6-23 is a growing relative demand for soft lead, accompanying the introduction of maintenance-free batteries. According to
the Bureau of Mines, these require little or no antimony, and their
production has significantly decreased the proportion of secondary lead
recovered in antominial form in recent years, to where it now only slightly

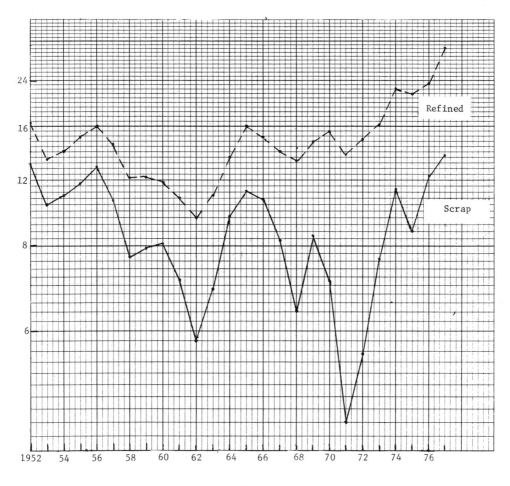

Figure 6-6. U.S. Dealer Buying Prices for Soft Lead Scrap,
1952-1977, Compared With New York/Delivered
Prices for Refined Lead

409

Table 6-23. Average Value of Lead and Lead-Alloy Scrap Consumed by
            Secondary Smelters, Compared With Dealers' Buying Prices
            and Prices of Refined Metal, for Census Years, 1954-1972

(cents per pound)

	1954	1958	1963	1967	1972
Average value of scrap consumed by secondary smelters	10.2	9.4	7.4	10.3	10.6
Average dealers' buying price for soft lead scrap	11.0	7.7	5.8	8.3	5.7
Average New York or delivered price for common lead	14.1	12.1	11.1	14.0	15.0

Source: U.S. Bureau of the Census, Census of Manufactures; American
Metal Market, Metal Statistics.

exceeds the amount recovered as soft lead.[53] For the census years shown,
all one can say is that the difference in specification probably accounts
for part of the gap between dealers' price quotations and consumers' costs
in four of the census years and suggests a greater anomaly for 1954 than
appears on the surface.

                                    Zinc

    Because zinc scrap is relatively unimportant in the total zinc con-
sumption picture, zinc pricing occurs in a somewhat different context
from that of lead. Like both lead and copper, however, zinc is traded
on the London Metal Exchange, and the fairly substantial contribution
of imports to U.S. total supply ensures the influence of the LME price
on domestic producer pricing. Zinc futures are also now traded on the
New York Commodity Exchange, but this is too recent a development to
provide any usable record.

Zinc Ores

    Again, like both lead and copper, there is no compilation of annual
value data on zinc mine output; and like lead, the frequent occurrence
of zinc in combination with important quantities of lead as well as other
metallic minerals means that the "mine" production of zinc really refers
in substantial measure to its initial separation as a zinc concentrate.
Since concentration is the rule even for more purely zinc ores, "ore"
has to be read as concentrate for all practical purposes.

    The one type of annual data that does exist on the cost of zinc ore
to U.S. consumers is that for the average value of imports. This is a
less important overall indicator than it used to be because, where imported
ore has been half or more of the total ore supply even within the past
decade, the decline in domestic zinc smelting activity has by now reduced
the needed amount of imported ore supplementation down to one-fifth or
less. Long-term import series are available on a customs (country-of-

---

[53]Ryan and Hague, Lead, p. 13.

origin) valuation basis only; such a series is shown in table 6-24, along with zinc metal prices for comparison. The "prime western" zinc quoted domestically is the same as the "common ordinary grade" or "good ordinary brands" quoted on the London market.

The customs value of imports is useful primarily as a crude indicator of historical year-to-year changes. More recent trade data, which are available also on an f.a.s. and a c.i.f. basis, are better for judging actual cost to U.S. smelters, especially if the customs duty (when applicable[54]) is also added. Table 6-25 compares these new series, both on an imports-for-consumption and a general-imports basis. The crude data behind the average values suggest a large excess of general imports in 1973-74 which were either put into storage or into processing in bonded smelters (it is not possible to tell which) and subsequently drawn upon as imports for consumption. These and subsequent speculative imports may explain the consistently higher average values registered for general imports until 1979.

As with lead, the only even approximate check on the unit values which may be estimated for imports is for the years in which there was a Census of Mineral Industries. That the values do not consistently match is evident from table 6-26. It would have been useful to have had corresponding values for consumption of zinc ores and concentrates by zinc smelters, but the data shown in the Census of Manufactures are only in gross weight of ores and concentrates, and owing to the variety of material processed, it seemed impractical to attempt any estimation of the contained metal. The large bulk of domestic ore is shipped to smelters of the same company, so that valuations are largely on an intra-company basis; there is also considerable integration with foreign sources of ore supply, but there could be reasons connected with each of the several principal supplying countries (Canada, Honduras, and Mexico) why the valuations are different. Part of the explanation may also lie in the timing of shipments, since some of the imports for consumption in any one year may have been shipped (or at least priced) in an earlier year, in some cases having been held for an extended period in bonded

---

[54]The 0.67-cent-per-pound duty was suspended from August 9, 1975 through June 30, 1978.

Table 6-24. Average Customs Value of U.S. Imports for Consumption of
             Zinc Ores and Concentrates, 1952-1979, Compared With
             Average U.S. and London Prices for Zinc Metal

(cents per pound)

Year	U.S. ore imports (zinc content)	Zinc metal, producers' prices	LME price, in equiv. U.S. currency[b]
1952	9.7	16.2	18.6
1953	5.3	10.9	9.4
1954	5.5	10.7	9.8
1955	4.8	12.3	11.3
1956	5.3	13.5	12.2
1957	6.5	11.4	10.2
1958	4.8	10.3	8.3
1959	4.4	11.4	10.3
1960	5.1	12.9	11.2
1961	4.5	11.5	9.7
1962	4.1	11.6	8.5
1963	4.1	12.0	9.6
1964	5.8	13.6	14.7
1965	6.7	14.5	14.1
1966	6.5	14.5	12.6
1967	6.7	13.8	12.3
1968	7.1	13.5	11.9
1969	7.0	14.6	12.9
1970	7.4	15.3	13.4
1971	6.7	16.1	14.1
1972	7.0	17.8	17.1
1973	8.0	20.7	38.3
1974	11.8	35.9	56.0
1975	12.7	39.0	33.8
1976	16.2	37.0	32.3
1977	15.7	34.4	26.7
1978	15.9	31.0	26.9
1979	19.2	37.3	33.6

Source: U.S. Bureau of Mines, Minerals Yearbook; Foreign Trade
Division, U.S. Bureau of the Census, FT 246; Engineering and Mining Journal,
March 1980; American Bureau of Metal Statistics, Non-Ferrous Metal Data
(formerly Yearbook).

[a] Prime Western Zinc. East St. Louis basis through 1970, delivered
thereafter.

[b] Cash settlement price, common ordinary grade.

Table 6-25.   Comparison of Average Values of Imports of Zinc Ores and
             Concentrates, 1974–1979, on Various Valuation Bases

(cents per pound of zinc content)

	1974	1975	1976	1977	1978	1979
General imports						
Customs value	15.4	18.0	19.6	16.1	16.2	18.6
F.a.s. value	15.8	18.3	20.0	16.3	16.7	19.1
C.i.f. value	16.3	19.1	20.7	17.3	17.3	19.9
Imports for consumption						
Customs value	11.8	12.7	16.2	15.7	15.9	19.2
F.a.s. value	11.9	13.1	16.7	15.9	16.3	19.2
C.i.f. value	12.2	13.8	17.1	16.8	17.2	20.8
Duty-paid value[a]	12.9	14.2	17.1	16.8	17.5	21.1
Cf. Delivered price, prime Western zinc	35.9	39.0	37.0	34.4	31.0	37.3

Source: Foreign Trade Division, U.S. Bureau of the Census, FT 135 and
246; Engineering and Mining Journal, March 1980.

[a]Calculated by RFF.

Table 6-26.   Comparison of Estimated Average Duty-Paid Value of Zinc Ores
             and Concentrates With Reported Average Value of Zinc Ores
             and Concentrates Produced, for Census Years, 1958–1972

(cents per pound of gross zinc content)

Year	Domestic production (shipments)	Imports for consumption[a]
1958	4.9	5.8
1963	5.6	5.3
1967	9.2	9.3
1972	9.5	8.2

Source: U.S. Bureau of the Census, Census of Mineral Industries;
U.S. Bureau of Mines, Minerals Yearbook.

[a]Includes transportation costs and duty (when applicable), as estimated
or calculated by RFF.

storage or in smelting warehouses. Whatever the explanations, the annual
fluctuations shown by the import values have to be considered as only
approximate indications.

Refined Zinc

The basis for checking on the validity of various indicators of the
cost of refined zinc is somewhat better. Here it is possible to compare
with census average values for zinc metal both as produced and as consumed:
the data are shown in table 6-27. The record seems rather clear that
producers' prices apply fairly exclusively to steel mills (which use
zinc in galvanizing). Brass mills, which use the zinc to make up brass
and bronze ingot, have a higher cost, paying something approximating
the average cost of imports. Zinc foundries (mostly diecasting) pay the
highest prices of all. These differences may or may not reflect producer
discrimination, since steel mills do use the lowest grades of zinc, brass
mills an intermediate grade, and diecasting a high grade. It is likely,
however, that the sometimes higher cost of imported zinc also reflects
premiums for making up needed supplies in times of heightened demand.

A year-by-year set of estimates for the duty-paid cost of imported
zinc metal is given in table 6-28, along with the producers' price series
and the LME price series, repeated for ease of comparison. As may be
seen, the domestic producers' price has generally tended to follow the
LME price, with a premium for transportation and the very small duty,
but to ignore its more extreme fluctuations. Since 1956, imported zinc
has generally commanded a small premium over domestic, except when the
London price is too far below the domestic quotation, in which case it
may sell at a discount, or when the London price is well above the domestic
quotation, in which case the imported-zinc premium may widen.

Figure 6-7, by means of five-year moving averages, compares longer
term movements in LME and U.S. producer prices, and both of them with
world consumption of refined zinc and the consumption of principal trading
countries. The general, swing-flattening response of the U.S. price to
the LME price is fairly clear. The persistent rise in the LME price in
the face of evident softness of demand in the trading world is harder
to explain. It could be the result of either matching supply problems

or the decline in value of both the pound and the dollar, or a combination
of the two. The decline in currency value is probably the more cogent
influence, but supply difficulties, originating in part in obsolescent
facilities and pollution-control requirements in the United States, have
also been present.

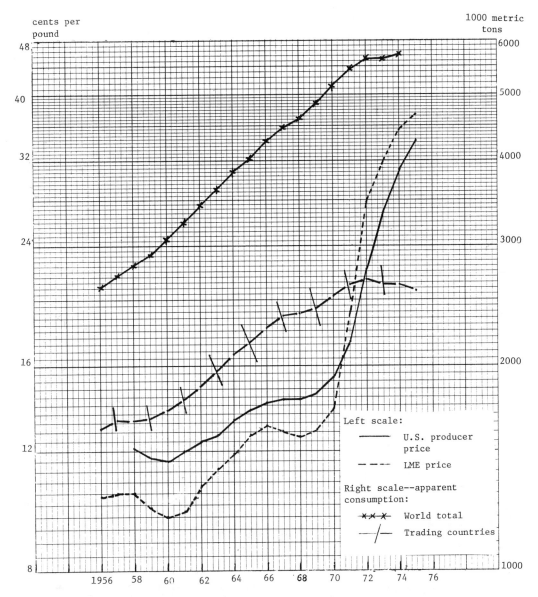

cents per
pound

1000 metric
tons

Figure 6-7. Trends in Cost of Refined Zinc to U.S. Industrial
Consumers, Compared With LME Cash Price and World
Refined Zinc Consumption (Five-Year Moving Averages)

417

Table 6-27. Average Value of Zinc Metal Produced and Consumed in the
United States, According to Various Indicators, for Census
Years, 1954-1972

(cents per pound)

	1954	1958	1963	1967	1972
Census of Manufactures					
Production (shipments):					
Unalloyed:					
Primary refineries	11.2	10.2	11.7	13.7	17.6
Total[a]	11.3	10.2	11.7	13.8	18.0
Zinc-base alloys:					
Primary refineries	15.4	N.A.	12.4	9.2	N.A.
Secondary refineries	15.0	N.A.	14.2	17.3	N.A.
Total	15.3	15.7	13.3	12.5	20.7
Consumption:					
Steel mills	N.A.	10.2	12.0	14.5	18.0
Brass and wire mills	11.8	11.2	12.3	14.8	18.4
Nonferrous foundries					
(except aluminum and					
copper)[b]	N.A.	12.6	13.2	16.1	20.7
Total[c]	12.3	11.0	12.4	15.0	18.9
Imported zinc metal[d]	N.A.	11.1	12.2	14.6	18.7
Producers' price, domestic,					
East St. Louis or	10.7	10.3	12.0	13.8	17.8
delivered					
Constructed unit value, total					
supply[e]	N.A.	10.5	12.0	14.0	18.1

Source: U.S. Bureau of the Census, Census of Manufactures;
U.S. Bureau of Mines, Minerals Yearbook; Engineering and
Mining Journal, March 1978.

N.A. - Not available, not separately available, or not readily
available.

[a]Production of unalloyed refined zinc by secondary refineries is small in
relation to the total.

[b]Zinc diecasting is the bulk of this category.

[c]Total identified, including, besides categories shown, other nonferrous
(including zinc) rolling mills, secondary smelters, and aluminum foundries. All
of these consume smaller amounts of zinc than the categories specifically shown.
For 1954, total excludes steel mills.

[d]Inland and ocean transportation costs estimated by RFF; duty of .07 cents
per pound added.

[e]Weighted average, calculated by RFF, of domestic metal at producers'
delivered prices and imported metal at estimated duty-paid cost.

Table 6-28.   Estimated Duty-Paid Cost of Imported Zinc Metal, 1956-1979,
              Compared With Producers' and LME Prices of Prime Western
              (or Equivalent) Zinc

(cents per pound)

Year	Imported zinc[a]	Domestic, producer price[b]	LME price[c]
1956	15.3	13.5	12.2
1957	13.8	11.4	10.2
1958	11.1	10.3	8.3
1959	11.9	11.4	10.3
1960	13.8	12.9	11.2
1961	12.6	11.5	9.7
1962	12.0	11.6	8.5
1963	12.2	12.0	9.6
1964	13.5	13.6	14.7
1965	15.5	14.5	14.1
1966	15.1	14.5	12.6
1967	14.6	13.8	12.3
1968	14.0	13.5	11.9
1969	14.6	14.6	12.9
1970	15.9	15.3	13.4
1971	16.0	16.1	14.1
1972	18.7	17.8	17.1
1973	25.2	20.7	38.3
1974	42.0	35.9	56.0
1975	38.8	39.0	33.8
1976	36.6	37.0	32.3
1977	34.6	34.4	26.7
1978	30.1	31.0	26.9
1979	35.4	37.3	33.6

Source: U.S. Bureau of Mines, Minerals Yearbook, Foreign Trade
Division, U.S. Bureau of the Census, FT 246; Engineering and Mining Journal,
March 1978. American Bureau of Metal Statistics, Non-Ferrous Metal Data
(formerly Yearbook).

[a] Imports for consumption. Transportation costs, except for 1974-1979,
estimated by RFF; .07 cents per pound duty added by RFF.

[b] Prime Western. East St. Louis through 1970, delivered thereafter.

[c] Cash settlement price, ordinary grades.

Chapter 7

PROJECTED PRICES

Introduction

There is probably no better way of summarizing the long-term prospects for a mineral commodity shortage or surplus than by predicting the long-term behavior of prices. It is not done here with any illusion that such predictions can be anywhere near accurate, but as a way of clarifying the meaning of qualitative judgments.

What is of particular interest in this study, as was pointed out in chapter 6, is the delivered cost of mineral commodities to U.S. industrial consumers. In many cases there is also interest in the ultimate sales realization by U.S. domestic producers. In each case, such unit cost or sales realization is directly or indirectly, more or less, determined by the prices of reference mineral commodities figuring in international trade. For the ferroalloying minerals, there may be a separate international standard for each form of the mineral. In the case of the non-ferrous metals, the international price of the mineral in refined form tends to determine its price in other forms as well. The degree to which U.S. unit costs and sales realizations relate to such international indicators depends upon the degree of import dependence, the sources of imports, and the institutional arrangements (including degree of buyer-seller independence) applicable to U.S. marketing and supply.

Our projections are made directly in terms of current prices, rather than following the procedure sometimes used of ascribing a constant-currency character to long-term price projections and then inflating them by some projected general price series. It may be objected that we are implicitly building inflation into our series and that it would be better

to indicate to what extent our projected price changes are ascribable to
general price levels and to what extent they are "real." However, there
is a considerable choice of deflators, and, even assuming that the requisite ones could be meaningfully projected, what is "real" to one party in
a mineral commodity transaction may differ considerably from what is real
to the other party or what is real to the national economies involved.

It deserves to be added that, on a trend basis, it is difficult to
perceive more meaningful cause-effect relationships between long-term
supply/demand circumstances and deflated commodity prices than between such
circumstances and current commodity prices. Introducing the abstraction
of relative prices is not so patently helpful, therefore. Alternatively,
projecting in terms of current prices and then applying a general deflator
not only enlarges the room for error, but ignores the need, just noted, for
different reference standards for different kinds of questions.[1]

Except for one mineral commodity, the uniform analytical procedure
behind this chapter was to examine projected trends in consumption and in
supply potential (established, respectively, in chapters 2 and 5), comparing them, to the extent possible, with similar trends of the past and with
past price responses to such trends. To this end, shorter term fluctuations in historical prices were eliminated from consideration by the calculation of moving averages, and judgments as to future prices were made on
the basis of graphic analysis of the various trends. The graphs are not
reproduced, but important characteristics are noted in the text. Once the
reference price projections are established, further judgments are given
as to their implications for unit cost and sales realization in the United
States for each of the specific forms of the metal in question.

---

[1]The latter drawback does not necessarily exist if there is a narrow-
ly defined analytical purpose. From the standpoint of development economics, for example, there is a certain amount of justification for the World
Bank practice of deflating the prices of commodities that developing countries sell by the prices of those (internationally traded manufactured
goods) they are deemed to buy.

Cobalt

The exceptional commodity, of course, is cobalt. The essentially monopolistic basis on which this price is set was pointed out in chapter 6, as was the evident desire of the price-setters to make the most of a period of strong demand facing a constrained supply. The deteriorating exchange rate of the U.S. dollar against the Belgian franc was also mentioned, but in the final analysis must be considered a secondary element, since so much of the world's demand is in the United States that the price will be implicitly set in dollars.

Whatever the future stability or instability of producing areas in Zaire, it seems evident that future supply will remain constrained. The degree of constraint, however, is likely to ease from what it is at present. At the same time, there has been enough of a reaction to recent high prices that some of the cobalt demand that would otherwise have developed will be switched into substitutes. One must therefore draw the judgmental conclusion that, on a trend basis (if the word, "trend" can be applied at all to a commodity price so patently administered), the price of cobalt is somewhere near a peak. Some time soon a downtrend should set in, though stockpile acquisition and increasing wage rates in the ore-producing areas will probably keep the downtrend from being very sharp. In the unlikely event that recovery of cobalt from ocean nodules should be allowed to develop without undue constraint, the price downtrend would be accelerated, and in any case, the ultimate prospect of ocean mining will tend to put a ceiling on any renewed long-term upward price movement.

The average price of cobalt to U.S. industrial consumers in 1979 was close to $25 per pound. In 1978, it averaged around $12, and this figure is about three times the average for 1973-77. A similar five-year average centered on 1980 might be upwards of $20, followed by decline down to $15 or so by the end of the century. The changing mix of U.S. supply sources, including delivery of metal from refineries in the United States, is likely to have less to do with this outcome than an improved balance between cobalt demand and the amounts currently mined.

Chromium

Though there obviously has to be some relationship between the price of chromite and that of ferrochromium, it is not clear that either one very effectively determines the other. Since there is no international auction market for ferrochromium, there is no basis for looking at the chromite price as a derivative one. If there is causation at all, it more likely runs from the ore to the ferroalloy.

As was done in chapter 6, we distinguish between the cost of chromite for metallurgical use and that for refractory use and ignore a no longer very pertinent distinction between chemical grade and metallurgical grade.

Chromite for Metallurgical Use

Barring any long-term embargoes, it is fairly evidently the price of South African chromite that will determine future trends in the cost of ore to the U.S. ferroalloy maker. While Turkey, Finland, or the Soviet Union may take advantage of intermittent shortages to push prices up temporarily, it is South Africa, along with Zimbabwe, that has the resources to maintain itself as the leading U.S. supplier.

South African Transvaal ore, in fact, though earlier denominated as being of "chemical" grade, has taken over from Turkish ores of "metallurgical" grade as the normal pacesetter for the pricing of world metallurgical chromite supply. At the same time, however, owing to the much higher prices of Turkish ore (the differences are greater than is justified by their higher chromium/iron ratio) and their big jump in price in 1975, it has been possible for the price of Transvaal ores to move up very rapidly and yet gain South Africa an increasing share of the market. As shown in table 7-1, we have assumed that the future rate of increase will become progressively less rapid, owing to a widening gap between world production capacity for metallurgical chromite and world consumption (see table 5-1).

Table 7-1 goes on to convert the projections for Transvaal ore into average price per unit of chromic oxide. The unit value of U.S. imports from Africa in any one year has tended to lag the quoted prices, but as price rises slow down, the discrepancy between the two measures should

Table 7-1. Trends in Chromium Prices and Costs, 1975-2000

	Historical	Projected				
	1975[a]	1980	1985	1990	1995	2000
Chromite for metallurgical use ($ per long ton)						
Transvaal ore, f.o.b. South African port:						
As quoted (gross weight)	44.5	66	81	94	105	113
Per long ton of Cr_2O_3 content[b]	101	150	185	214	239	257
Average value of U.S. imports (Cr_2O_3 content):						
At country of origin						
South African ore	64	120	166	203	233	254
All sources	[c]105	172	203	225	247	262
Delivered U.S. from all sources	134	205	239	265	291	310
Chromite for refractory use[d] ($/L.T. Cr_2O_3):						
At country of origin	116	191	227	254	282	301
Delivered to United States	163	243	284	317	351	377
Ferrochromium (all types)						
Average cost to U.S. consumer (cents per lb. of Cr content)	39.7	47	53	55	56	56

[a]1973-77 average, except for Transvaal ore quotations, for which 1974-76 average. Prior to 1974, quotations for Transvaal ore were on a delivered basis.

[b]Based on specification of 44 percent Cr_2O_3.

[c]Includes an estimate of delivery costs in 1973, which are not directly available.

[d]Philippine chromite. Data are for average value of imports into the United States.

424

narrow. There should also be a narrowing between the average value of South African ore and that of all metallurgical-use chromite imported into the United States, as the South African and Rhodesian ores become a greater proportion of the total and as they become more and more the price determinant for chromite from all sources.

The final entry under metallurgical chromite allows for a slowly increasing average transportation cost, to arrive at projected total average cost of chromite (Cr_2O_3) to the U.S. ferroalloy producer. The projected cost more than doubles over the twenty-five-year period shown, although slowing from a rise at the rate of nearly 8 percent per year in the early part of the period to less than 1 1/2 percent per year by century's end.

Chromite for Refractory Use

Since the bulk of chromite consumed in the United States for refractory purposes has its source in the Philippines, and since there is no obvious reason to believe that this situation will change, it is essentially the cost of Philippine ore that should determine the cost of refractory-grade chromite to the U.S. industrial consumer.[2] There seems to be no regular price quotation for this material, and we have therefore taken as our guide the average value of Philippine chromite imported. In recent years this has lost its price premium over metallurgical ore as such and in some years has even sold at a price penalty (table 6-1), but on average has retained a small margin over at least the "new" metallurgical ore. For projection purposes it is assumed that there will be at least modest reversion to wider margins, in part because the "new" metallurgical ore will continue to be somewhat constrained in its price rise by the further admixture of chemical ore and in part because a recent price-depressing factor—decreasing relative demand for chromite refractories owing to their unsuitability for use in basic oxygen furnaces—is

---

[2]Principal consumers are steel plants, copper smelters, and cement plants.

near to having run its course. Furthermore, Philippine refractory ore, which is used as the basis for estimating cost to U.S. users, may fall increasingly short of meeting world refractory chromite needs (see chapter 5).

Delivery costs for refractory ore are also assumed to rise gradually over the projection period, as in the case of ore for metallurgical use. Owing to the larger importance of such delivery costs for Philippine than for South African ore, the end result for ore delivered to U.S. consumers is just about the same rate of increase for refractory as for metallurgical -use ore over the projection period.

Ferrochromium

There appears to be nothing resembling a world price for ferro-chromium. In chapter 6, we provided series on U.S. domestic quotations for both domestic and imported "charge chrome"--a grade of ferrochromium which seems to have become the most commonly used. The series are rather variable in their specifications, however, and there is no evident advan-tage to projecting them as an initial step, rather than making direct projections, of the composite cost of all ferrochromium to the U.S. indus-trial consumer as is done in table 7-1. This composite cost is already very close (on the average roughly a cent or so lower per pound of con-tained chromium) to the quoted price of imported charge chrome, delivered, and is not likely to stray much from that price, as imports become a greater proportion of total consumption. (Because of this proportion, imports not only have increasingly greater weight in the average, but more effectively set a ceiling on what domestic producers can charge.) Customs duties, particularly the recent Tokyo Round reductions in the tariff on low-carbon ferrochrome, due to become fully effective by 1988, will not provide much more than a penny a pound of protection, in contrast with freight costs of at least twice that magnitude.

The resultant average-cost outlook for ferrochromium is considerably more favorable for the U.S. consumer than for the U.S. producer. With production capacity in the world's principal international suppliers (table 5-2) increasing much more rapidly than demand by principal inter-national purchasers (table 2-6), the recent steeply rising trend in

ferrochromium costs is likely to progressively give way to near stability;
a slowdown in the rate of increase is, in fact, already evident. South
African and Zimbabwean ferrochromium will come increasingly to dominate
the market, and the price of their ores will leave little or no margin
for conversion costs at the receiving end. Shipment of ferrochromium
instead of ore is also protected by perhaps a two-cent-per-pound saving in
freight costs. Under the circumstances, it may well be that the decline
in U.S. capacity projected in table 5-2 is an understatement, although
it is likely that some proportion of U.S. capacity will remain competitive
on the basis of delivery capabilities, inland freight costs, and ferroalloy specifications. Also, unless there are substantial changes in the
apparent political security of supplies from southern Africa, U.S. consumers, as well as producers (e.g., Union Carbide) with a foot on both conti-
nents, are likely to support a certain amount of redundant U.S. capacity
as a form of supply insurance.

Manganese

There are four principal differences, among the many similarities,
between manganese and chromium: (1) manganese is cheaper; (2) it is more
likely to have significant downward as well as upward fluctuations; (3) it
is a significant input into almost all, rather than just some, steel
production; and (4) it is available in quantity from more different places.
The principal similarities include (1) the importance of South Africa and
(2) the decline of ferroalloy production in the United States, with replacement by imports.

Manganese Ore

As noted in chapter 6, reported price quotations for manganese ore
are merely indicative of the range of contract prices, which appear to be
negotiated on a c.i.f. basis by dealers in the principal consuming
countries. There is apparently enough informal exchange of information or
price intentions that these quotations represent something of a world
price, and there is also apparent consensus in using the delivered price

to U.S. ports as a standard quotation basis. Since this last, for which
the U.S. Bureau of Mines compiles an estimated annual average based on
trade reports, is closely matched by the actual average c.i.f. cost of
imported ore, we have used the series as our indicator for projection
purposes. The projections are given in table 7-2 in the same terms as
the usual quotation, namely, dollars per long-ton unit (22.4 pounds of
contained manganese). The series applies to metallurgical ore, currently
specified as containing 46-48 percent manganese.

It may be seen that we expect the recent steep rate of increase
(trend basis) to taper off considerably before a renewed mild acceleration
in the 1990s. The reason is that, until about 1985, the rate of capacity
expansion in the leading supplier countries (table 5-3) is projected to
outstrip the rate of increase in consumption by the principal trader-
importers; after that the reverse would be true. The quoted price actually
reached a peak of about $1.48 in 1977, since declining to $1.40 in 1979;
a trend value of $1.45 for 1980 thus implies a renewal of mild increase.

As may be seen in table 7-2, the World Bank staff, which has projected
manganese ore prices on the basis of Indian ore, which used to be an
international standard but has ceased to be a significant item of trade,
looks for somewhat higher prices than we do. Though we believe the 1990
projection, particularly, to be a little too much on the high side, there
is too much improvisation in this kind of projection not to regard the
IBRD projection as representing an alternative line of development lying
within the bound of reasonable possibility. When adjusted for the difference in quotation basis, the 1980 projection is about identical.

Information is scarce on how the delivered cost of manganese ore at
metallurgical plants relates to c.i.f. values or prices. Rough estimates
of average historical differentials have been derived by comparison with
the economic-census data and extrapolated as shown. It needs to be borne
in mind that there is not an exact correspondence between metallurgical
ore and the ore consumed by metallurgical plants (let alone electrometallurgical plants specifically), and that other kinds of manganese (mostly
higher value) are consumed for other purposes (especially for dry-cell

Table 7-2. Trends in Manganese Prices and Costs, 1970–2000

	Historical[a]		Projected				
	1970	1975	1980	1985	1990	1995	2000
Manganese Ore ($ per long ton unit)							
Average price, metallurgical ore, delivered U.S. ports	.57	1.17	1.45	1.60	1.65	1.75	1.90
C.f. IBRD projection[b]	.60	1.26	1.53	1.98	2.41	–	–
Average cost to U.S. electro-metallurgical plants	[c].70	[c]1.38	1.70	1.85	1.95	2.05	2.20
Ferromanganese, Standard ($/L.T.)							
Aver. price delivered Pittsburgh or Chicago:							
Imported	164	339	445	475	470	465	475
Composite, imported and domestic	173	344	450	485	475	475	480

[a]Five-year averages, centered on year shown.

[b]Unofficial staff document, May 1979. The Bank's projection is said to be for Indian ore, which is actually no longer shipped to the United States, but its series nevertheless serves as an indicator of how Bank staff view the manganese price outlook. The figure shown for 1980 is the average of the Bank's figures for 1978–79 actual and 1980–82 projections.

[c]Estimated on the basis of relationship to average value of imports in economic-census years.

battery manufacture). The cost series, therefore, is only indicative of relative changes.

It should also be borne in mind that the possibility of manganese recovery from ocean nodules is real enough for the 1990s, that the price projection for that period needs to be qualified. If such recovery does take place, a downturn in price past 1990, rather than a renewed upturn, is the likelier development--barring some internationally agreed-upon forms of price maintenance.

Ferromanganese

Given the apparent contraction in ferromanganese capacity going on in both the United States and Japan, it is almost inevitable that the trend of world ferromanganese prices will continue sharply upward in the immediate future, despite an appearance of softness over the past couple of years. (The upturn was already evident in 1979.) The rate of price increase should then decelerate rather abruptly and even give way to a slight decline, as ferroalloy capacity available to the trading world rebounds to more suitable levels. Past 1990, the relevant countries' rates of capacity gain should be more nearly in step with rates of consumption gain, thereby replacing price declines with renewed increases, since capacity will probably remain tight.

The world price indicator we use here is the dealer's price of imported "standard" ferromanganese (78 percent manganese content, among other specifications), delivered to Pittsburgh or Chicago; the projections are shown in table 7-2. Since 1976, imported ferromanganese has been the major portion of the total supply, and the outlook is that this will be increasingly the case, with South Africa taking over as the principal supplier. Domestic supply will remain important enough for a period to pull the average cost to the U.S. consumer (f.o.b. Pittsburgh or Chicago) somewhat above the price of imports in the stronger market immediately ahead; increasingly, however, domestic offerings will have to forgo, on the average, anything but a small premium, stemming from greater supply security and ability to respond to emergency needs. (It is to be remembered that the domestic differential will actually fluctuate significantly around a trend average, occasionally even turning negative.)

Actual average cost of ferromanganese to steel mills may be expected to be somewhat higher than the composite of domestic and imported price quotations, because of variations in ferromanganese specifications and because of delivery costs from the two basing points.

One implication of the projections in table 7-2 is that the ore would become a progressively larger portion of total ferromanganese cost. This is to be expected in a situation where ore-producing countries wish to do more domestic processing. The smelting margin for ferromanganese is quite large, however, and its projected narrowing seems moderate on a relative basis. In absolute size, moreover, it would be rather larger than it has been historically, though much of this increase is presumably needed to cover higher fuel costs.

Extraction of manganese metal from ocean nodules could affect the price of ferromanganese and severely depress it--barring, once again, effective international counteraction.

Aluminum

As is typical for the nonferrous metals, the prices of the forerunners of aluminum--bauxite and alumina--are largely determined by the price of the metal. Aluminum is atypical in that only recently has it had a world auction-market price, and this has yet to be demonstrated to have much practical importance in comparison with the "producers'" prices that are set by a small number of aluminum companies. It differs in degree from the other leading nonferrous metals in that, owing to more pervasive vertical integration, pricing of the ore and the intermediate form of the metal continues to depend relatively more on intracompany decision than on institutional practice. As with the other leading nonferrous metals, there is an international producing - country organization (in this case the International Bauxite Association), which, even if it is not successful in enforcing control of production or price fixing, seems to have strengthened the joint resolve to secure as much as possible of the available economic rent for the governments of those countries and to have set common standards toward that end. Led originally by Jamaica, most of the producing countries have levied taxes and royalty requirements that, whatever the effect on the nominal price of bauxite, have certainly increased its cost to alumina producers. They have also employed differential taxation (e.g., Australia) to create a higher price for bauxite shipped as such than for bauxite refined locally into alumina.

Aluminum Metal

Only since October 1978 has there been trading in aluminum on the London Metal Exchange, and only since the start of 1979 have there been transactions on a spot basis. A close surrogate of longer standing for a world price, however, has been that of Canadian ingot, delivered in London. As the result of something more than coincidence, this runs close to the U.S. producers' price; and the latter, also by something more than coincidence, runs close to what may be calculated as the average actual cost of aluminum—domestic and imported, primary and secondary—to U.S. consumers. It makes little practical difference, therefore, which of these prices one chooses as a future indicator. Of the longer-standing series, however, the Canadian quotations should in theory best reflect the world market. Nominally, it is therefore the series projected in table 7-3. But it can also be read as average cost to U.S. consumers—with which, in recent years, it has been almost identical.

However specified, the price of refined aluminum has been rising quite rapidly and, given the tightening supply situation up until about 1985, promises to continue doing so. Thereafter, the increase should be slower, in response to a somewhat improved adjustment in the relationship between growth of capacity and of demand in principal trading countries. Because supply promises to remain relatively tight, however, "slower" will be significantly faster than "slow."

Actually, there has been some recent hesitation in aluminum price increases, with completion of readjustment to the lifting of price controls and a temporarily softer market. The higher trend levels to come, however, have been presaged by a renewal of the upward trend starting in mid-1978.

Table 7-3. Trends in Aluminum Prices and Costs, 1970-2000

	Historical[a]		Projected				
	1970	1975	1980	1985	1990	1995	2000
Refined Aluminum (cents per lb.)							
Canadian ingot, delivered in London[b]	26.9	37.4	58	80	92	100	110
Cf. IBRD projection, N.Y. dealers' price[c]	27.4	38.9	68	100	129	–	–
Alumina ($ per short ton)							
Aver. customs value[d] of U.S. imports from Australia	55	88	145	211	258	296	341
Aver. cost to U.S. consumer	66	106	173	249	302	343	392
Imported Bauxite							
Aver. customs value[d] ($ per long dry ton):							
Guinean (gibbsite)	4.77	14.43	24.5	34.5	39.0	40.0	41.0
Jamaican (mixed)	13.81	22.95	34.5	38.0	40.5	41.0	42.0
Cost of bauxite to U.S. consumer ($ per short ton, U.S. mine or port):							
Gibbsite (trihydrate)	12.79	20.51	31.0	42.0	47.0	50.0	52.0
Mixed	14.39	25.99	38.5	43.0	46.5	48.0	49.5
Cf. IBRD projection[e]	12.00	23.80	40.9	57.8	74.5	–	–

[a]Five-year averages, centered on year shown.

[b]Projections may also be read as average cost to U.S. industrial consumers, and, probably, as spot price on London Metal Exchange. With a cent or two added, may be read as U.S. producers' price.

[c]Unofficial staff document, May 1979. 1980 figure shown here is 1978-82 average.

[d]Customs values are usually the same as, or close to, f.a.s., foreign port. Include royalties and production levies in countries of origin.

[e]Refers to "U.S. import reference price based on imports from Jamaica," in dollars per metric ton. Source as in footnote c.

World Bank staff have projected the New York dealers' price of aluminum ingot through 1982 and to 1985 and 1990.[3] The latter two points may
be considered trend projections, and on such a trend basis, this normally
very volatile series should be similar in its relative movements to the
Canadian aluminum series we have chosen as our own indicator. It may be
seen from the comparison in table 7-3 that, while the general shape of
the projected trend is similar, the World Bank expects much higher absolute price levels. Except for 1990, which seems to us unduly overestimated, it is difficult to say that these IBRD projections are not also reasonable; they may thus be regarded as an upper limit.

Alumina

Since Australia is expected to retain its lead position in supplying
the world's alumina needs, it may also be considered the world's alumina
price setter. The runner-up world supplier, Brazil, is not likely to
undercut Australian initiatives, and the Australian position will be rein-
forced by a rather tight alumina supply situation for the balance of the
century (see chapter 5).

The most convenient reading on Australian alumina prices is provided
by the average customs value--essentially f.a.s.--of U.S. imports from that
country. The projections given in table 7-3 for this series assume that
Australia will be able to demand for its alumina a mildly increasing proportion of the world market price of aluminum metal (Canadian ingot,
delivered to the United Kingdom). This leaves room for an increasing
absolute margin for smelting, which grows particularly rapidly over the
1970-80 trend period, consistently with the steep increase in the cost
of energy.[4] Later increases in energy costs, particularly in view of
steps taken for greater efficiency, are assumed to be at a slower rate.

---

[3] Commodity Price Forecasts (staff document, May 1979).

[4] Since the ratio of alumina to aluminum is approximately two to one,
the two sets of costs may be roughly compared, in table 7-3, by dividing
the alumina values by 1,000.

The smelting margin is more precisely ascertained by looking at the implications of Australian pricing for the average delivered cost of alumina to U.S. smelters. The latter cost is assumed to exhibit a slowly declining ratio to Australian export prices, on the assumption that delivery charges will not rise quite as rapidly as the cost of the alumina per se. With imported alumina becoming an increasing proportion of total U.S. supply, domestic prices are assumed more or less to conform to the import yardstick.

Bauxite

As was pointed out in chapter 6, not only is there no price series as such for bauxite, but it is not even clear what its cost might be to the U.S. consumer. For example, in 1972, the average cost reported in the Census of Manufactures was about $19 a long ton, while the combined average cost of ore (dry-equivalent basis) reported by domestic mines and by importers was around $12. The average f.a.s. cost of Jamaican bauxite in that year, as well as in 1973, was something over $13, on a dry-equivalent basis. World Bank estimates of the cost of Jamaican bauxite, prior to the imposition of the large tax levy in May 1974, come to about $8 per long ton, when converted to a comparable basis.[5]

It seems clear that the cost of bauxite to the U.S. refinery is regarded as something more than the cost of production (in other words, there is some allocation of profit), and there are apparent differences between the valuations placed on the material by the filers of import declarations and the filers of reports for the U.S. Census of Manufactures --differences which seem to go beyond what might be explained by any discrepancies in basis of measurement.

---

[5]R. Vedavalli, Market Structure of Bauxite/Alumina/Aluminum: and Prospects for Developing Countries (Commodity Paper No. 24, March 1977) p. 10. Conversion based on relative bauxite requirement per ton of alumina.

Under the circumstances, it seems as reasonable a choice as any to
project, for purposes of future cost indication, the constructed series
(table 7-3) for overall cost, f.o.b. U.S. mine or port, of gibbsite (trihydrate) and mixed bauxite, respectively. Though in recent years the
source mix has had an important bearing on this overall cost, especially
for gibbsite, it is reasonable to expect future costs to conform increasingly closely to the delivered cost of Guinean bauxite in the case of
gibbsite, and Jamaican bauxite in the case of mixed. To derive these
delivered values, the values in country of origin of these two types of
bauxite are first projected in the light of the earlier world demand
and supply projections.

As may be seen in table 7-3, we expect gibbsitic bauxite, which
is the major part of world supply, to continue its rapid price rise,
but only until about 1985, after which there is reason to expect a sharp
slowing down. The explanation is that the prospective increase in international bauxite supply capacity in the near future looks as if it will
be considerably outrun by increases in bauxite demand, but starting in
the late 1980s, more or less the reverse should be true. Because of
the commitment of mine output to domestic processing in countries such
as Australia, near-future export surpluses of bauxite as such will be
somewhat limited, but the prospect is that before long inadequate refining
facilities will cause relatively more bauxite to be thrown on the world
market and will even lead to a reduction in the proportion of the proceeds
sought to be retained as export levies.

Jamaican bauxite has already given evidence of being overpriced in
terms of its competitive position, and there is talk of a reduction in
the percentage amount of Jamaica's export levy. It is our assumption
that the bulk of new refining capacity outside of Jamaica itself will
be designed for gibbsitic rather than mixed bauxite and that as a result
the Jamaican f.o.b. price premium (which is partly a matter of transportation cost advantage) will progressively narrow. On a delivered
basis, Jamaican bauxite may well be underselling gibbsitic bauxite by
the last decade of the century, owing to its more constrained market and
competition from other Caribbean areas.

The conversion of f.a.s. costs to average costs at U.S. port or mine is done on the assumption of a moderately expanding cost for delivery. In these U.S. cost terms, the net result of early rapid price rises and later slowdown is a twenty-five-year increase for bauxite which is much less than that either for aluminum or for alumina. In fact, it appears that even including the near years, a slowly declining portion of the alumina dollar will be going to bauxite feed and progressively larger portions, presumably, to processing costs and/or refining profit. At least for the earlier part of the projection period, increased fuel costs should more than account for the shift.

It needs to be noted that World Bank projections of the delivered value of Jamaican bauxite (last line of table 7-3) are conspicuously higher than ours, especially for points beyond 1980.[6] (The IBRD also takes a considerably more expansive view of prospective Jamaican output.) We believe that these projections are implicitly too optimistic as to the future amount of consumer-country refining capacity that will be based on Jamaican bauxite, barring substantial realignments in the perceived reliability of various bauxite-producing areas--realignments which would have to take place in a relatively nearby future to affect the projections as much as the differences indicate. In part, however, the differences in regard to bauxite reflect the similar differences in viewpoint with regard to future prices of aluminum; there is only minor divergence in perception of the share of bauxite in total aluminum revenues.

Aluminum Scrap

As was pointed out in chapter 6, the price of aluminum scrap is affected by the fact that such scrap is in large measure, though not entirely, an alternative to the consumption of alumina. Scrap prices should therefore follow approximately the same relative trend as alumina

---

[6]Vedavalli, _Market Structure._

prices--modified slightly downward by virtue of the fact that, for direct users of scrap, the alternative is the more slowly changing price of refined aluminum.

Scrap prices, especially in the United States, will likely also depend to some degree on the nature of activity undertaken to promote recycling. Mandatory deposit laws, for example, should make scrap a little cheaper. Preemptive collection, such as has occurred in the past both to ward off regulation and to divert supplies from secondary smelters, would tend to raise scrap costs.

Because there is no really good indicator series--even for the United States, let alone the international market--we do not attempt to convert the foregoing qualitative projections into specific numbers.

Copper

Chapter 6 detailed the presumption that, for reasons both of tradition and of competitive economics, long-run (as well as short-run) prices for copper in all of its (unfabricated) forms, are, like the prices of aluminum, transmitted from underlying demand and supply factors via the price of the refined metal. More than in the case of aluminum, however, prices are affected by the foreign-exchange and domestic-employment imperatives of the governments that own or effectively regulate important components of copper supply. Much longer than in the case of aluminum, ore-producing countries have been banded together in a consultative organization,[7] but so far with less effective influence over prices, for the reason, among others, that nonmember countries, including the United States, account for a rather large proportion of the trading-world supply. There has been serious discussion of using CIPEC to establish a "world producers' price" for copper, similar to the U.S. producers' price, but it seems safe to say that, like the U.S. producers' price, any international price would

---

[7]CIPEC--French initials for Intergovernmental Council of Copper Exporting Countries.

have to adapt, over the longer run, to the shifting balance between trends in growth of consumption and those in the growth of productive capacity.[8] It is postulated, therefore, that, whatever may develop in terms of shorter term price stabilization, longer run price changes for copper will respond to determinants similar to those for the other metals.

Refined Copper

It seems safe to assume that in the future, as in the past, the best expressions of the world price of copper are the quotations on the London Metal Exchange. Although the LME deals both on a spot and a future basis, it is the cash settlement (spot) price that is usually regarded as the standard long-term price indicator, and this is the price projected in table 7-4. As quoted, it refers to wirebars.

Comparing the refinery capacity projections in chapter 5 with the refined copper consumption projections in chapter 2, for the combined group of countries identified either as principal world traders or as principal international suppliers, it may be seen that refinery capacity is now and is likely to remain relatively ample, with only minor fluctuations in the differential rate of growth in capacity compared with consumption. If there were no other considerations, this would suggest rather weak rates of gain, on a trend basis, in world refined copper prices. The controlling factor, however, seems likely to be, not refinery capacity, but smelting capacity, and our projections suggest that this will remain rather tight among trading countries for the balance of the century (chapter 5). Moreover, even if it were other than tight, there would be constraints on the amount of ore available, at least until the decade of the 1990s. Although scrap is a potential substitute for part of the virgin copper requirement, both via direct use and via re-refining, its ratio to total refined copper consumption is more likely to decline (mildly) than to increase (chapter 2); furthermore, some of it requires resmelting. It would seem, therefore, that the outlook is for a rather

[8]The potential for CIPEC price control is discussed in Raymond F. Mikesell, The World Copper Industry (Baltimore, Md., Johns Hopkins University Press for Resources for the Future, 1979) pp. 204 ff.

Table 7-4. Trends in Copper Prices and Costs, 1970-2000

(cents per pound)

	Historical[a]		1980	Projected			
	1970	1975	1980	1985	1990	1995	2000
Refined Copper							
LME wirebar (cash price)	56.9	70.7	83	93	101	110	122
Cf. IBRD projection[b]	"	"	92	172	230	–	–
Aver. cost to U.S. consumer (f.o.b. U.S. port or consuming plant[c])	50.8	67.5	79	88	96	104	116
Blister Copper							
Aver. customs valued of U.S. imports for consumption	47.6	67.8	80	89	97	105	117
Copper Ore (Cu content)							
Aver. customs valued of U.S. imports for consumption	47.7	61.2	77	88	97	105	116
Copper Scrap							
Aver. value of U.S. exports	39.5	44.3	62	74	84	90	97

[a] Five-year averages, centered on year shown.

[b] Unofficial staff document, May 1979. 1980 figure shown here is 1978-82 average.

[c] F.o.b. port for imports; delivered U. S. destinations, for domestic production.

[d] Essentially, f.a.s., supplying country.

firm continuing upward trend in refined copper prices over the 1975-2000 period--a little stronger during the early and late portions (owing to varying rates of capacity addition) and a little weaker in-between.

In respect to these copper prices, even more than in respect to aluminum, we find ourselves at odds with the World Bank. As may be seen in the table, IBRD staff expect more than twice as high a current-dollar price for copper by 1990 as that which we have projected. About the only area of agreement is that there will be a slight downturn from current levels before renewed rise, but this fluctuation is lost in the 1978-82 average given here as the Bank's 1980 trend value. While our projections could easily be on the low side, it seems to us that the IBRD staff projections--at least for 1985 and 1990--are too far outside any reasonable range to serve as a high. There is a general tendency for expansiveness in the Bank in estimating prospects for the developing countries and for particular projects therein (including copper), and it seems likely that the copper projections have been especially affected by this tendency.

Because of the large year-to-year fluctuations characteristic of copper prices and the varying degree of resort, depending on relative supply stringency, to other than the U.S. producer-priced market, the average cost of refined copper to the U.S. industrial consumer has varied on both sides of the LME quotations; but on a trend basis, it has run consistently lower. In recent years, the average gap has narrowed because of the closer coupling, in part now formal, of U.S. producers' prices to New York Commodity Exchange (Comex) prices, which are in turn tied by arbitrage to prices on the London exchange.[9] The arbitrage range, in turn, is defined by the physical cost of moving copper between New York and London. Because of this, and because the bulk of the world's future

---

[9] These are transactions that take advantage of the price differentials for a particular commodity in two different markets. Such transactions tend to eliminate the differentials.

refined copper supply will continue to be either closer to U.S. delivery points than to London or at least as close, it is assumed that the narrowed average gap of 1973-78, measured as a relative, will persist for the balance of the century.

Our refined-copper cost projections thus end up as an average annual trend rate of increase of about 2.2 percent per year for the last quarter of the century. This is low enough that it would, at most, yield a stationary "real" price in relation to a rather conservative general price deflator and would mean declining relative copper prices according to more generally accepted views as to long-term inflationary outlook. It thus represents a change from the increasing real price trend for copper that seems to have obtained since the early 1930s.[10] It also runs counter to the current conventional wisdom, which focuses on investment delays, declining resources, and supposedly dwindling ore grades. It is a reversion, on the other hand, to the stable or declining real copper prices of earlier years and is a plausible outcome of the relative shift of production and high technology into areas with generally lower wage rates and richer deposits. On a current-price basis, it represents an upwardly biased extension of LME price trends of the past ten years or so.

Blister Copper

As was pointed out in chapter 6, so little blister copper currently moves in commercial trade (most of it being consumed by refineries of the same company) that it is difficult to identify an appropriate price series. However, it is possible to construct a long-term series (table 6-15) of the customs values (essentially f.a.s. foreign country) of U.S.

---

[10] See Robert S. Manthy, Natural Resource Commodities--A Century of Statistics (Baltimore, Md., Johns Hopkins University Press for Resources for the Future, 1978) fig. 12, p. 12.

imports, and this makes a reasonable world-price indicator. Since delivery costs to the United States appear to be no more than a few cents and thus smaller than the fluctuating differentials between imported blister and domestic blister, there is little point in trying to adjust the level of the series for transportation differentials. Given the different valuations of blister shipped within companies, outside of companies, and reported as consumed, it also seems futile to try to adjust for the lower or higher f.o.b. prices of the much more important U.S. supply component, domestic blister. Moreover, there is some reason to suspect, as noted in chapter 5, that imported blister or some intermediate smelter product may return to being a slightly more important portion of the total U.S. supply mix, with consequent increases in its influence on overall average costs.

Since in our refined copper prices we have already taken into account the relative tightness in world smelting capacity, we may assume that the future course of blister copper prices will follow the refined. This outcome is in a sense also assured by the convention of pricing ores in relation to domestic or LME copper quotations. It is not unusual for blister copper to command a small price premium over refined because of its recoverable values in gold and other higher priced metals; and we have assumed that, on a trend basis, such a differential will persist. The comparison with our refined copper projections should not be taken too literally, however, because of the discrepancies among the various blister copper cost indicators.

Copper Ore

If it is difficult to identify a reliable price series for blister copper, it is even more difficult, as detailed in chapter 6, to do so for copper ore--despite the fact that the latter is much more important as an arm's-length article of commerce. Under the circumstances, even if there were not the probability that imported ore (concentrate) will be of increasing importance to U.S. smelters (though still a rather minor portion of supply), there seems little choice but to make do with the only conveniently available continuous series--average value of U.S. imports. The value series used here is in terms of copper content and

is on a "customs value" basis, thus serving also as a world price indicator. Since the blister copper series is on the same basis, there is
an implication, between the two, for smelting margin. Because actual
differentials are very uneven, however, and because pricing of ores for
export may be presumed to be intermittently higher than pricing for processing in the country of origin, the projected changes in the differential
between the two prices should be taken as nothing more than an expression
of our feeling that the supplementary character and tightness of imported
ore supplies available to the United States--at least up to about 1990--
will result in a contraction of the smelting margin which such ores allow.
Were it not for the prospect of being able to continue to operate substantially on domestic ores, the U.S. smelting and refining industry could
very well face a significant squeeze between ore costs and refined copper
prices. It also follows, if our assumptions are correct, that the 1 percent ad valorem tariff on both blister and refined copper that has
replaced formerly specific duties as the result of the Tokyo Round trade
negotiations is more significant protection than might appear at first
blush.

Copper-base Scrap

Copper (including copper alloy) scrap is a significant input, not
only into smelting and refining, but also directly into the operations of
ingot makers, foundries, and brass mills. There are thus competitive
aspects to its availability, which should become keener as ore and blister
supplies become tighter and dearer.

One may conclude that, particularly over the next decade, scrap
prices are likely to rise somewhat more steeply than those of ore, since,
on average, it is a lower cost substitute. The indicator price used
in table 7-4 is the average value of copper scrap exported from the United
States, which represents a sort of "opportunity cost" for U.S. purchasers.
Since the United States is usually the principal supplier to the world
copper scrap market, it is also an indicator of international copper scrap
prices. The relationship between this and other series is treated in
chapter 6.

Lead

It is difficult to say which form of lead is the pacesetter for lead
prices. Over the projection period, as has been the case in the recent
past, the course of world lead prices seems likely to be determined by a
combination of decreasing excess capacity for refined lead, relative
stringency in ore supply, and relatively declining scrap availabilities.
The probable result is a rather steep continuing rate of rise in lead
prices for the balance of the century.

For lead, the distinction between world traders and nontraders is
especially important from a price standpoint, yet somewhat elusive. Specifically, the Soviet Union has exhibited some of the fastest rates of
growth in lead consumption and, though it does not now draw significantly
on the non-Communist world for its supplies, the choice was made to include
it as a trading country in our consumption analysis. So far it has been
only a modest importer of lead ore from any source and a net exporter of
refined lead. At some point in the future, however, it will probably
become a net importer of both, with the world price impact of this development more likely being transmitted via ore than via refined metal markets.

Refined Lead

The only recent pause in the steeply rising trend in refined lead
prices came during a brief period in the late 1960s in response to a
burgeoning of world smelting capacity. With a subsequent near-cessation
of capacity growth, which has decreased but seems as yet to have come
nowhere near eliminating excess smelting capacity, prices resumed their
rapid ascent.

About the only break that is visible in a continuing narrowing of
the capacity gap is in the latter part of the 1980s. We have assumed
that this will be accompanied by a slowdown (rather than cessation) in
the rate of price rise, to be followed in the 1990s by higher rates once
again, though a little less rapid than previously. Aside from narrowing
capacity, a difficulty in making use of existing capacity owing to changing
market requirements (changing lead specifications) and to environmental

and health and safety regulations is part of the underlying scenario, and it is assumed that those problems will have been largely resolved by the 1990s, although feedstock stringency will remain.

The benchmark projections (table 7-5) are of the LME spot price for pig lead, which, with slightly lesser volatility, is followed closely by the U.S. producers' price (see chapter 6). Once again, despite the steepness of our projections, the IBRD projections are higher, and it is possible that for nearer years at least they may be closer to being correct, since the LME price in 1979 averaged 54 1/2 cents. The volatility of the LME price is such, however, that a 1980 trend value (1978-82 average) could still be at the level of either of the two projections. The Bank's projection for 1985 is also well within range. While its 1990 projection, too, is plausible enough to serve as a high, it seemingly fails to take into account the pause in excess capacity contraction mentioned above.

Given a new 4 percent ad valorem duty on refined lead as of January 1, 1980, and given the additional transportation protection favoring U.S. producers, as well as the "insurance" value of domestic sources, it is assumed that domestic pig (soft) lead prices will bring the indicated premiums over LME averages. Those premiums would be higher for the later years were it not for the assumption that, if it did not happen sooner, the price increases of the 1990s would bring a reduction in the duty or possibly periods of suspension. Since industrial consumption involves a combination of soft lead and the higher priced antimonial lead, the actual average cost to users has usually run a cent or two higher than the pig lead quotations; this premium is assumed to disappear as antimonial lead is substantially phased out.

Lead Ore

Since, as has been pointed out, the basic sustaining factor in the rate of rise of lead prices is the cost of ore, most of the future behavior of ore costs is already subsumed in the lead price projections. Moreover, as in the case of copper, ore prices--especially domestic ore prices--are customarily largely a derivative of the value of lead metal; in fact, much of the consumption involves arbitrary, intracompany value setting.

Table 7-5. Trends in Lead Prices and Costs, 1970-2000

(cents per pound)

	Historical[a]			Projected			
	1970	1975	1980	1985	1990	1995	2000
Refined Lead							
LME pig lead (cash price)	12.6	22.7	35	48	53	67	86
Cf. IBRD projection[b]	"	"	39	55	71	–	–
U.S. pig lead, delivered	14.5	22.8	37	51	56	70	89
Average cost to U.S. consumer[c]	15	24	38	52	56	70	89
Lead Ore (Pb content)							
Average customs value of ore imports	10.1	14.4	28	41	45	58	76

[a] Five-year averages, centered on year shown.

[b] Unofficial staff document, May 1979. 1980 figure shown here is 1978-82 average.

[c] Allows for decreasing use of (higher-priced) antimonial lead. 1968-72 and 1973-77 costs estimated.

448

Once again, the only indicator of imported ore costs which has been
continuously available for an extended period is that of the average
customs value of imports. Accordingly, and since it also serves as a
world price indicator, this is the kind of series projected in table 7-5.
Since it is stated in terms of lead in ore, it implies a smelting/refining
margin, and is in fact derived by assuming an arithmetically increasing,
but proportionally narrowing, margin for the rest of the century. The
presumption is that there will be a certain amount of competition among
smelters for ore supplies, but it should also be borne in mind that the
margin needs to allow for transportation costs and for the duty of three
fourths of a cent per pound which is being continued under the Tokyo Round
agreements.

Because of the inconclusive record, it is difficult to relate overall
ore cost to U.S. smelters to the average value of imports. It should be
noted, however, that imports have been projected to become progressively
more important in the total supply mix, especially in the near future,
and will thus become increasingly the determinant of what domestic ore
can sell for. Probably the combined duty and transportation protection,
as well as established intracompany and other institutionalized relationships, will permit domestic ore to bring a premium of three to five cents
a pound of lead content, and the average cost to smelters of domestic and
imported ore combined will run a penny or two under the domestic price.

Lead Scrap

As suggested in chapter 6, there is no really satisfactory continuing
indicator of the cost of lead scrap. About the most that it seems possible
to say of its long-term trend is that it will run close behind the average
cost of refined lead. The margin between the two forms of metal will
tend to widen as a result of the stronger purchasing position of a reduced
number of secondary smelters, as well as increased smelting costs; the
relative stringency of the virgin lead supply will tend to narrow it.

The asymmetry that now seems to exist between the kind of lead found
in batteries being scrapped and that required for newer batteries (more
soft lead) will presumably disappear within a relatively short period,
with the result, on the whole, of a strengthening of scrap prices. Matura-

tion of the trend toward longer lived batteries should have an opposite effect. A movement out of lead and into other types of batteries could result in surpluses of scrap, but any substantial development along these lines seems unlikely within the projection period.

Zinc

Zinc appears in one respect to be the inverse of lead, in that the more constraining element in supply is likely to be smelting capacity, prospective ore supplies, in comparison, being apparently ample. However, the constraint is less than binding, so that, despite a past price trend as steep as that for lead, future rates of price change for zinc promise to be considerably less rapid.

Refined Zinc

As with copper and lead, the controlling international price for zinc appears to be that for cash trades on the London Metal Exchange; the series is projected in table 7-6. On a trend basis, this price has been slowing in its rate of rise, and, because of our finding that zinc smelting capacity in the trading world is currently increasing much more rapidly on average than is demand in the trading world (currently rather flat), we expect the near-future rate of price gain to further decelerate. Subsequently, with some diminution of the capacity excess after 1990, a slight pick-up in the rate of gain is assumed.

If our projections are correct, lead will have changed places with zinc, for the balance of the century, as the more valuable (per pound) of the two metals. This is not so, however, according to World Bank staff projections, which foresee an even abrupter current flattening out in zinc price trends than we do, but then a resumption of steep rates of rise. The former is not an implausible projection, but the latter seems to us well beyond likelihood in view of the continuing substantial gap we foresee between capacity and consumption both in the world as a whole and among trading nations. Accuracy of either set of projections with respect to the relative values of lead and zinc tends to be self-reinforcing, for

Table 7-6. Trends in Zinc Prices and Costs, 1970-2000

(cents per pound)

	Historical[a]			Projected			
	1970	1975	1980	1985	1990	1995	2000
Refined Zinc							
LME ordinary grades (cash price)	13.9	37.4	41	44	48	53	59
Cf. IBRD projections[b]	"	"	37	64	87	-	-
U. S. producers' prices[c]	15.5	33.4	38	42	47	53	60
Zinc Ore							
Average customs value of ore imports	7.0	12.9	14	15	16	17	18

[a] Five-year averages, centerd on year shown.

[b] Unofficial staff document, May 1979. 1980 figure shown here is 1978-82 average.

[c] Assumed to be so set as to balance foreign offerings and be approximately the same as average cost to U. S. consumers.

whichever of the two metals has the tendency to become the by-product is likely further to be depressed in price by being produced, at the mine level, in excess quantities.

Given the probable desire of domestic smelters to maximize use of capacity, yet not depress prices, it is likely that their pricing will on average be equal to the LME price plus U.S. duty and plus transportation costs for the better situated foreign producers, thus cutting out excess imports. Despite the new, higher duty on slab zinc (1 1/2 percent ad valorem) that went into effect at the start of 1980, such a policy would keep the domestic producers' price for zinc below the LME level (where it now is) in the proximate future, but allow it to rise slightly above the LME level as the market improves somewhat toward the end of the century. Limiting the increase in relation to LME is the likelihood that much of the transportation is only from Canada, which probably will retain its lead position as world supplier, though possibly losing some relative ground to Australia.

Zinc Ore

As goes the price of zinc metal, so, it is to be expected, will go the price of ore--but with a downward bias. If zinc does become the by-product metal, it will be at the mining (concentrator) stage, and it is thus logical to expect ore prices to bear the brunt of the relatively lower demand for zinc than for lead. Moreover, to the extent that supplies are from arm's-length sources, there will be competitiveness for a limited smelter market. In fact, however, the ores of zinc, like those of the other nonferrous metals discussed, are largely transferred within companies, and pricing is therefore more or less arbitrary. This will become even truer as the United States moves into a situation where it does not really require zinc ore imports, but probably continues to bring them in for company and institutional reasons.

For want of a better series, that projected in table 7-6 is for the average customs value of U.S. imports. The series serves also as a world price indicator and may be assumed to be within a few cents of the average cost to U.S. smelters. The tariff on zinc ore is unimportant and has been reduced further pursuant to the Tokyo Round agreements. Transportation protection will be limited by Canada's being a principal source of imports.

PART IV: PROBLEMS

Chapter 8

LONG-TERM SUPPLY OR PRICE PROBLEMS

This chapter deals with the kinds of problems associated with trends in consumption, supply, and price of the minerals discussed in this volume. It considers the nearby as well as the farther off future, up until the end of the century (which, at this point, is more accurately regarded as medium than long term). It also considers only "probable" events, even though it allows for a broad range of confidence (more strictly, "nonconfidence") regarding what is probable. The next chapter, by contrast, focuses on the more or less improbable events--"contingencies"--that have the potential for producing problems should the events actually occur. Because it is relatively futile to try to estimate the probability of such contingencies very far ahead, the horizon for chapter 9 is "short-term"-- to approximately 1985.

In the discussion that follows, we maintain this report's distinction between a metallic mineral in general and a metallic mineral in each of its commercially significant commodity forms, on the assumption that problems are most meaningful with respect to the specific commodity forms even though some problems may also affect particular minerals across the board.

Cobalt

If there are any long-term problems connected with cobalt, we have probably already experienced them. The difficulty is that, as of the moment, little may be said about cobalt with any high degree of confidence. In short, the supply of this metal is a "possible" long-term problem, but not a probable one. In view of the short-term problems discussed in the next chapter, the long-term question may not be important.

So far as the United States is concerned, any problem connected with cobalt has to do with the refined form of this mineral, which is a feed-stock for the metallic materials industries and other manufacturers. Cobalt refining is new in the United States, and such refineries as have been or are being established seem to have their feedstock guaranteed for them.

The possible long-term problem is that a high degree of concentration in the ownership and control of the world's refining capacity, coupled with a scarcity of economic sources of virgin cobalt, provides a framework for a continuing sharp upward pressure on prices. Such a problem cannot be attacked at the refining stage alone, for any truly competitive refining facilities would have difficulty in securing feedstock (cobalt in matte or concentrates). Our judgment, however, is that ore will tend over time to become more freely and widely available in relation to demand for metal. In addition, an improved supply/demand balance will result as some users adjust to the recent steep increases in cobalt prices; in other words, except for contingencies, the cobalt problem may have been already encountered and largely resolved.

We deem it likely that the long-term trend of metallic cobalt prices is now downward rather than upward, but even if current price levels are sustained or even moderately increased, the adaptability of consumers would prevent any problem from becoming a major one. Generally speaking, in some of its most critical uses (such as jet engines) the cost of cobalt, even at present elevated prices, is not nearly great enough to have a major impact on costs of the final product. Nevertheless, the steepness of the price increase has spurred conservation and substitution in such uses, thereby easing the pressure on those applications--for example, electronic goods containing permanent magnets--where substitution may be more diffi-cult and the cost of cobalt may be moderately more important.

Chromium

The only long-term problem for the metallurgical consumer of chromium (ferrochromium)--but it is a major one--is that the sources of supply are increasingly concentrated in southern Africa. Among the principal international marketers of ferrochrome, the proportion of capacity located in South Africa and Zimbabwe should remain essentially unchanged, at about one-half the total, but in terms of U.S. supply, the proportion will increase. The reason is that domestic supply capacity will decrease, according to our projections, from around 90 percent of consumption currently, to little more than 40 percent by the year 2000. However, there has been excess capacity, with the result that in actuality, 55 percent of U.S. supply has come from abroad in recent years. Of the imports, some 60 percent has come from southern Africa.

While ferrochromium consumers will be increasingly less protected against contingencies, ferrochromium producers have been beset by serious problems of import competition. We have assumed that it is this competition that will result in progressive net diminution of U.S. productive capacity, though eventually at a lesser rate of decline than currently obtains. Not all of this diminution will necessarily mean complete plant closedowns, since there seems to be a fair chance that some capacity will be switched to other ferroalloys, to metal refining, or to the production of special kinds of pig iron. The facilities in question are not particularly large employers, moreover, so that the direct impact of even complete closedowns is fairly limited.[1]

Because of the decline of ferrochromium manufacture, supplies of metallurgical chromite[2] to U.S. plants are of decreasing importance. World supplies look as if they will become increasingly more ample, moreover,

_____

[1] In 1972, all electrometallurgical plants combined reported some 9,500 employees, with a payroll of $94 million.

[2] "Metallurgical" is used in this paragraph in the sense of ore suitable for metallurgical use, thus including chemical grade, as well as metallurgical grade in the narrower sense.

with price rises becoming progressively more muted. The principal problem is, once again, continuing exposure to political contingencies that affect supplies from southern Africa. We expect these supplies to account for an increasing proportion of metallurgical chromite mining capacity, ending at about half the total for principal international suppliers by the year 2000. This phenomenon is due in large measure to the increasing acceptability of the former "chemical grade" chromite for metallurgical use; this is a grade with which South Africa, for one, is particularly well endowed.

Something more than a contingency problem, on the other hand, attends prospective supply circumstances for refractory-grade chromite. The United States has depended essentially upon the Philippines for this type of chromite, and it appears that there may not be enough mine capacity in that country to meet all international needs. Without more information than we have gathered, it is difficult to conclude whether or not this is a serious problem, since chromite from other sources (e.g., South Africa, USSR, Turkey) can be substituted and since some amount of other types of refractories is also substitutable in meeting a total requirement which, because of changing modes of steelmaking, is not increasing very rapidly (if at all) in its overall dimensions.

The United States has an interest, of course, not only in the chromite it consumes directly, but in that which supports its expected ferrochromium imports. So long as the supply lines from southern Africa are open, however, this indirect requirement does not seem to be a problem.

Manganese

Large proportions of manganese ore and ferroalloy supply are also located in politically dubious parts of Africa and thus are exposed to significant contingency risks. The ore is seemingly more of a problem than is the ferromanganese, with South Africa and Gabon most likely supplying some 85 percent of the world's ore by century's end, while the ferromanganese capacity in South Africa (Gabon is not significant) rises only from about a quarter to about a third of that available for U.S. supply. In actuality, however, ferromanganese is at least as serious a concern as the ore since the principal alternative suppliers of ferromanganese, such as Japan, Norway, and the United States itself, all depend heavily on African ore.

There is another and even more acute problem connected with ferro-manganese, moreover, which is a "trend" problem only in the sense that it represents a persistent situation rather than a temporary fluctuation. This is the contraction of ferromanganese production capacity, particularly in the United States and Japan, to the extent that the total capacity in these and other trading countries looks to be less than commensurate with average demand over the next five years or so. The impact of trend plus short-term fluctuation is already visible in price levels that exceed those indicated in our projections as being the 1985 trend value (see table 7-2). Undoubtedly this situation will be met by entry into the market of impermanent suppliers (perhaps the USSR among them), as well as by intermittent conversion of blast furnace capacity to ferroalloy production, but only after steep price rises. Though the situation will ease considerably during the 1980s--enough in all probability to halt and even temporarily reverse the upward price trend--it will remain tight through the balance of the century.

The current decline in U.S. ferromanganese capacity presents, of course, a special problem for those connected with the ferroalloy industry. Basically, however, given the strong price trend, the worst seems to be about over. The Tokyo Round negotiations have effected what amounts to a reduction of tariff protection in the course of changing from specific (or compound) duties to straight ad valorem, but it seems unlikely that this will be of much significance for the industry's competitiveness. Except for the contingency problem, the supply of ore, despite some indus-try misgivings, also does not seem to us to be a major problem. Neither do ore prices, despite some greater rates of gain in such prices relative to ferromanganese prices, since costs other than ore seem to be more consequential.

Aluminum

If our projections are correct, we may expect tight supplies in
aluminum at all phases, with the largest expected capacity shortfalls
occurring at the refining stage--that is, the production of metallurgical,
or "calcined," alumina. There will be a corresponding impact on prices,
particularly over the next five years or so, after which capacity shortfalls should be largely eliminated, but not to the extent of curbing price
rises altogether.

The principal reason for this situation is the reluctance of major
alumimum companies, faced with the uncertain market conditions of recent
years, to proceed with all of the bauxite, alumina, and aluminum expansion
that looked attractive during the 1973-74 boom (and is now beginning to
look attractive again). World expansion, wherever it takes place, is particularly dependent on the investment decisions of U.S. and Japanese companies, and their decision-making process has been decidedly stretched out.
Contributing to the near-future capacity/consumption imbalance have been
the steps taken by bauxite-producing countries--particularly Australia--to
divert bauxite into domestic processing, yet not expand refining capacity
rapidly enough to meet prospective demand. The other side of the balance
is the still steeply rising level of world aluminum consumption; were it
not for this, expansion of aluminum capacity would seem anything but slow.
In fact, an important new international supplier, the Soviet Union, seems
to be coming onto the aluminum scene.

Little of the sharp rise now taking place in aluminum prices seems
properly ascribable to the initiatives taken by Jamaica and the International Bauxite Association (IBA) to increase the proceeds from their
bauxite production. In fact, those actions have on balance been salutary
since they prompted steps to diversify sources of bauxite; this is now the
one aspect of aluminum production for which there is minimal risk of prolonged shortage. Rather than stemming from increased payments to bauxite
producers, rising aluminum prices seem to be due mostly to the industry's
altered pricing policy, which is designed to take advantage of strong
demand for already established aluminum uses instead of employing relative
price advantage to capture new territory. Without the extra taxes imposed

by bauxite-producing countries and without those countries' movement into refining, aluminum companies might have had somewhat greater gross profit margins, but aluminum prices are not likely to have been much lower. The standard followed by the IBA, in fact, is to obtain what they consider a fair share of the ultimate aluminum price, rather than some independently fixed absolute level of proceeds.

If any cost element has had a major bearing on pricing, it is most likely the cost of energy. This has already led to important research and development toward energy conversation, as well as shifts in the geographical distribution of aluminum smelting, and there will be much more of the same in the future. Still, the outlook for the United States is that there will be only a moderate relative movement into import dependence for aluminum metal, the relative shift toward foreign sources of supply for alumina being far more significant. The sources of alumina are reasonably diversified geographically, however, and many of them are at least partially controlled by U.S. companies or by consortia in which U.S. companies participate. On balance, economic costs have been lowered by the reduction in bulk that is achieved by converting bauxite into alumina before long-distance shipment, and some of this saving is likely to be passed through rather than being completely preempted by bauxite producers. The degree of exposure to contingencies that results from the heavy concentration of alumina supply in Australia is already a fact and is not likely to change much in the future in relation to total consumption.

A possible new kind of problem is introduced with the recent addition of aluminum on the London Metal Exchange, since such trading has tended to exacerbate short-term price fluctuations in other metals, notably copper. LME trading will no doubt also introduce greater short-term fluctuation in aluminum prices than would otherwise have been the case; but the greater concentration of control that exists in the aluminum industry, coupled with the lesser likelihood of intermittent supply surpluses (the two factors being in part interrelated), suggests that instability will not become a major concern. Since so little of the world aluminum supply is likely to be contracted on the LME, even extreme price fluctuations there would have little effect on the average cost of aluminum to fabricators and other users. The latter, in any case, are frequently within the same private or national corporate structures as aluminum smelters and thus can make compensating input-output price adjustments.

Do any of the foregoing possibilities qualify as a major problem? Steeply rising prices and possible supply shortfalls (allocated supply) in the near-term future come closest to qualifying, if they are a correct projection. For two reasons, however, the answer seems to be negative. One reason is that for most of the important products using aluminum, the value of the aluminum metal, even at elevated prices, is likely to be a rather small part of the value of the finished item. The other reason is that, just as aluminum has been able to substitute for other materials, so many other materials substitute for aluminum--and by this time new materials (and new ways of utilizing old ones) have come along. Unless, as discussed in chapter 9, all materials become in short supply at once, aluminum supply shortages would not be critical. Such a generalized supply shortage has happened in the past, and recurrence may or may not be a continuing long-run risk.

Copper

Preoccupation with CIPEC--the Intergovernmental Council of Copper Exporting Countries--has faded to the extent that few people still perceive this organization as posing the risk of lasting price escalation. Nothing on the horizon suggests that long-term price levels for copper will be determined by anything other than trends in supply and demand. There is continuing possibility of greater institutional limitation of short-term price fluctuations, but most observers would consider such a development, not a problem, but the elimination of one. As the discussion in chapter 7 pointed out, we expect a certain amount of supply tightness in copper, particularly in the nearby future, with consequent upward pressure on prices. This is a problem in that it gives particular impetus to short-term upward fluctuations, but the trend rate of increase, it seems to us, will be relatively modest and therefore absorbable without much difficulty by copper consumers.

Also pointed out was the likelihood that, with ore supplies being tight, there would be something of a squeeze on world copper smelting margins. However, because of the large portion of U.S. smelter feed which is domestic, and the fact that the price of such ores tends to be a residual, such a problem would be minimal for U.S. smelters. In many cases the price of ore is simply a matter of intracompany allocation. U.S. companies also control much foreign ore, but in this respect remain subject to the actions of host governments.

The division of refined copper proceeds between smelter and refinery is even more a matter of intracompany allocation than such division between mine and smelter; thus the relative tightness of smelting capacity has its principal impact on the price of refined copper. It seems a likely possibility that domestic companies will step up the importation of copper matte or blister in order to piece out the total requirement for refinery feed and at the same time avoid the more acute pollution-control problems connected with smelting ores and concentrates. There is also likely to be a continuing growth of electrowinning processes which permit bypassing smelting operations while at the same time making it possible to stretch the potential for domestic copper production.

In short, both consumers and producers of copper may need to make many significant readjustments, but none of these problems looks severe enough, on a trend basis, to qualify as major. Most of the problems connected with copper have to do with its unusually high vulnerability to cyclical influences. This includes the sometimes acute problem that occurs for consumers of copper scrap when foreign purchasers bid away domestic supplies. It also includes the problem of financing new facilities, since this is a difficulty that tends to subside when prices are headed upward. It includes, too, the mine closures that are brought on by exhaustion of deposits--or at least of higher-grade ore in deposits; there is enough employment involved that this can be a major problem at particular times in particular localities, but it is unlikely to involve any significant net curtailment of ore supplies or any significant net replacement of domestic ores by foreign. Such closures are therefore not so much a supply problem as the result of a supply problem, in the sense that they come about through competition from foreign sources that generally have higher grade resources left.

Lead

If we are correct in our projection that lead prices are headed steeply upward, lead certainly presents a supply problem and there is a good possibility that the problem will be a major one. Concern about the sufficiency of markets for lead is relatively recent, owing in part to the phase-out of leaded gasoline in the United States and possibly other countries as well, but what promises to swamp this and other consumption reducing factors is the continued rapid increase in demand for lead for storage batteries, with an extra fillip being imparted by a decreased relative contribution (at least in the world as a whole) from recycling. Probably because of the recent concern over markets, coupled with additional uncertainty as to the ultimate full impact of environmental, health and safety regulations, there has been delay in the expansion of lead refining facilities, talk of closedown, and some actual closedown of secondary recovery operations. Thus a capacity squeeze of sorts is in prospect (see chapter 5) and it looks as if it will be relatively persistent over the balance of the century.

This prospective squeeze in lead refining capacity is not so great, however, that it can be defined as a shortage. What is likely to propel lead prices upward is not outright capacity shortfalls, either at the mine or the refinery (or the secondary recovery) level, but a series of imbalances, each of which will take time to be corrected. Relatively decreasing usability of antimonial lead, for example, stemming from changes in battery specifications, will impose a greater need for secondary smelting which can produce soft (pure) lead, yet new capacity of this sort is delayed by regulatory procedures. Demand for lead which increases faster than the demand for zinc has to be met out of ores whose recovery economics depend upon zinc as well as lead proceeds; to make matters worse, it looks as if the ores may be tending toward lower lead ratios. The USSR will probably be increasing its lead consumption at a very rapid rate and will probably succeed in increasing its refining capacity to match, but there is a good chance it will be coming on the market for the first time as a substantial purchaser of lead concentrates.

What looks like a problem for lead could in part turn out to be a problem for zinc instead. If combined ore production is pushed to the extent needed to meet lead consumption levels, there is a good chance that zinc concentrates will be in comparative surplus, thus adversely affecting producers that depend primarily on zinc mines.

There seems little chance that rapidly rising prices will materially reduce lead consumption below what it would have been at lower price levels. There will obviously be some acceleration of the phase-out of lead from gasoline, paints, and some other uses, but most of this would have occurred anyway. There will also be some acceleration in the development of new types of storage batteries, but these are, for the most part, unlikely to be cheaper than lead batteries even at elevated prices for lead, and will be making their market instead in terms of capacity/weight ratio, length of life, and other technical characteristics.

Basically, even a tripling of battery prices between 1975 and the year 2000--which is about the most effect that can be expected from the lead price increases--would have relatively small impact on the total purchase cost of a vehicle and its continued operation. It is in vehicles (and other internal combustion equipment) that nearly all storage batteries end up. Under the circumstances, the projected increase in lead prices cannot be counted as a major problem.

Zinc

As already suggested in connection with lead, there is unlikely to be a significant supply problem for zinc consumers in the United States. Problems, if any, would affect zinc miners and smelters--particularly the former, since the U.S. smelting industry has already gone through a shakeout, while excess mining capacity lies mostly in the future. On a trend basis, however, any such problem looks to be considerably less than "major." Despite market slackness, prices seem likely to continue an

upward trend, and as of mid-1979 had already recovered from their depressed
state in 1977-78.

The United States will remain considerably dependent on imported
refined zinc, but this does not seem to be a significant supply problem,
in view of prospectively ample refining capacity in the trading world as
a whole and the fact that a large share of the imported supply will probably come from Canada. Moreover, since domestic ores promise to be more
than ample, it is possible that they will come to be smelted abroad under
intracompany or toll arrangements, thus effectively increasing the proportion of refined zinc supply that is actually of domestic origin.

Types of Problems

From the foregoing discussion, a number of problem types emerge.
Our recapitulation is not necessarily exhaustive, in part because all
the significant problems connected with the minerals studied here may
not have been identified, but, more important, because there may be significant problems of different types that are associated with other minerals. However, supply problems for the seven minerals are sufficiently
representative of the situations characterizing U.S. metallic minerals
consumption that omissions are not too likely.

Monopolistic Circumstances

A clear kind of long-term problem, exemplified by cobalt, is the
situation in which a rather critical mineral remains persistently under
monopoly control, thus exposing consumers to the risk of sharp upward
price movements, as well as price levels that are much more onerous than
those that might lie closer to production costs. Cobalt is probably
typical of the metals subject to this kind of risk, in that its sources
are geographically concentrated, it is used in relatively small quantities,
and it is relatively price inelastic, owing to a combination of high utility in its applications and small cost in relation to the end products in
which it is used. Even a commodity like this has a certain amount of
long-term elasticity, however, and it appears that recent cobalt price

increases were large enough and abrupt enough to have stimulated a significant amount of movement toward conservation and substitution. For
this reason, and because there is a certain amount of underlying pressure
on supplying areas to maintain revenue flows, it is likely that the price
has been pushed to levels that cannot be sustained. Thus, though cobalt
may have been by now permanently revalued at higher levels, there seem to
be built-in constraints on continuing price escalation. In fact, the easing
of threats to production and transportation in the Shaba (Zaire) region in
which much of the world's cobalt is recovered, as well as increasing prospects of recovering cobalt from ocean nodules, may add to the constraining
factors sufficiently to cause some price weakening.

It is probably safe to say that similarly unique conditions apply to
the other minerals (e.g., industrial diamonds) that lend themselves to
monopoly price setting, except for conservation and substitution, which
would tend to place a price lid (in trend terms) on almost any commodity.

Contingency Risks

A second type of problem, best exemplified by chromium (and by platinum, among minerals not investigated in this report) is the long-term exposure to short-term supply contingencies, owing to physical concentration
of supply in areas (in this case South Africa) particularly subject to
politically precipitated supply interruptions. The power of price manipu-
lation frequently accompanies such physical concentration, but it has been
utilized more sparingly for chromium than it has for cobalt. Chromium is
subject to the same kind of ultimate consumption elasticity constraints
as is cobalt, although in the case of chromium, the significant alternatives more clearly have to do with conservation and with the substitution
of other materials for stainless and alloy steel, rather than with the
(essentially impossible) substitution of other alloying elements to impart
equivalent material characteristics. In both cases, the kind of constraint
referred to relates to business reaction to market circumstances, which,
rather than any other kind of conscious planning, qualifies the size and
impact of any potential problem.

Among the minerals studied, manganese is affected to some extent by the same sort of problem as chromium, since it also is substantially concentrated in politically uncertain parts of Africa. The concentration is so much less than that of chromite, however, that the problem does not seem to be a major one. It may be more nearly major in the case of the platinum-related metals.

The long-term problem here, it should be reiterated, is exposure to contingency risks. Details of the risks are discussed in chapter 9.

Processing Facilities

Processing is really not one type of problem, but several, all having to do with the absolute or relative diminution of U.S. domestic processing of metallic ores into refined metal. It may be a long-term problem because of increasing vulnerability, because of loss of employment and income in the processing industries, because of loss of an outlet for domestic ores, or because of some combination of these consequences. Decreased processing may also entail a benefit--the "export" of pollution--but this in turn may have its own problems.

There has been an absolute decrease in domestic processing of ferro-alloys generally, as well as in zinc refining. There has been a relative decrease in refining bauxite into alumina and smelting lead and copper. These are past occurrences, but they are likely to continue into the future, with the qualification that future losses with regard to ferro-manganese and zinc are more likely to be losses relative to total consumption rather than losses in absolute levels of capacity and output; absolute losses are likely to continue in the case of ferrochrome.

Of the possible problems mentioned above, which are connected with either relative or absolute declines in domestic processing, none appears to qualify as an actual problem of major importance. This is because their consequences are limited, or because they are not really the essential problem, or--most usually--because of both these qualifications. In the case of the ferroalloys, for example, the real problem is one of control of the ultimate sources of chromite: no amount of processing capacity is useful to us without the chromite to feed it. On the other hand, extra processing capacity could be part of a solution to the problem if we had reserve sources of chromite—stockpiled or currently produced—that could be called upon in an emergency.

Conversely, if much of the processing capacity along with relevant ore supply is in relatively safe sources (as in the case of zinc and aluminum), the fact that the mineral material has to be imported in refined rather than in crude form should not be of major concern from a supply security standpoint. Not even domestic sources are wholly secure—being subject to strikes, for example, and transportation interruptions—and it is not always justifiable, in order to gain small increments of security, to incur the disbenefits that caused a shift to imports in the first place.

Refining facilities, unlike some kinds of mining, rarely have a major local impact on employment and never have a significant impact nationally. There were about 20,000 production workers engaged in primary aluminum processing in 1972 (the latest available Census statistic), 14,000 in primary copper, and 21,000 in all other branches of nonferrous metals smelting and refining (including secondary).[3] Even if these figures were larger, the real problem would not be the absolute or relative loss of refining employment, but the inability of national and local administrators to engineer full employment at the tasks for which the U.S. or the local economy has the greatest comparative advantage.

There are times, of course, when maladministration results in the closing or nonexpansion of metals processing facilities even though there would, in fact, be economic advantage in retaining such facilities. The culprit most frequently pointed to is government regulation, and it is likely that regulatory excesses have on occasion caused the sacrifice of processing capacity that it would have made long-run economic sense to have retained. In making an assessment, however, it is not defensible to write off the avoidance of environmental pollution as not being a legitimate type of economic output. Alternatively, the sacrifice of health, safety, and other environmental values must be considered as much a cost of producing metals as the direct expenditures for mining and processing,

---

[3]1975 data for total employment, given in County Business Patterns, suggest essentially no change from 1972.

and such a cost should not be ignored in considering comparative advantage merely because it is difficult to put a monetary value on it.

If the lack of processing facilities is to be considered a problem because it reduces market outlets for domestic mining, such a character- ization can be valid only if there is independent reason for wanting a higher level of domestic mining. There is little virtue (probably more of the opposite, considering environmental damage) in mining as such; its utility comes from the employment and income it provides, the resulting economic stimulus, and the added security it may provide for a continuing flow of the products made out of minerals. Shortfalls in achieving these underlying objectives are what are more accurately described as problems, even if there are circumstances where maintaining higher levels of domestic processing in order to support higher levels of domestic mining may be one kind of solution. It is doubtful that the lack of such a contribution can under any interpretation be considered a major problem. For example, copper mining, which is the largest single category of nonferrous metal mining in the United States, in 1972 employed 28,000 production workers and had 36,000 employees overall.[4] Any future expansion of domestic smelt- ing and refining facilities would increase the number only slightly. More- over, there is no evidence that copper mining is held back for lack of smelting facilities; if it were, we would presumably not be importing copper ores. Only in zinc does it appear possible that such a situation might develop, and, since the 1972 Census shows only some 6,000 production workers involved in lead and zinc mining combined,[5] the number of addi- tional jobs that might have been available but for lack of smelting facil- ities would have to be small indeed. Moreover, as suggested earlier, there is no necessary reason why all domestic ores must be smelted domestically, even if they are ultimately destined for U.S. consumption. Transportation costs to and from foreign smelters are not always higher than such costs within the United States and, where they are, may well be more than made up by other savings. It is nothing unusual for large volumes of U.S.

---

[4] Total employment declined slightly (to 33,000) by 1975 (County Business Patterns).

[5] Total employment was about 8,000 in both 1972 and 1975.

commodities of various sorts to be sent abroad for further processing or manufacture, then returned for domestic consumption--all for sound business reasons.

Steep Price Rises

Among the metals studied, prospective price trends for aluminum and lead look to be rather steep. Such trends (already apparently under way in both cases) all the more suggest a possible problem because they represent a considerable departure from historical tendencies toward flatness or decline. Projected price trends for the other metals studied are more modest in their rise, generally represent a deceleration from past trend rates of rise, and at times are projected to turn flat.

Long-term upward price trends--particularly if they exceed the general rate of inflation--are often considered to be a symptom of an underlying problem, resource scarcity. However, while the fact of progressive depletion cannot be denied, neither for aluminum nor for lead has this been the basis for our projections. In fact, ultimate resource constraints in both cases seem too far off to have any material effect on prices within this century; but the rate of growth of capacity for exploiting and processing such resources, in relation to the rate of increase of demand for aluminum and lead, will have a material effect.

Continuing price rises of such magnitude do have to be considered something of a problem, for they are clearly sufficient to stir up appreciable defensive activity in the form of efforts at conservation and substitution. It is doubtful, however, that these or any other of the long-term price rises projected in this study can be considered a major problem. To qualify as such they would have to have enough ultimate impact on final consumer price levels to significantly curtail real income. Yet the nonferrous metals generally (as well as the ferroalloying elements) are for the most part too small a component of the total cost of what ultimately reaches consumers to have much effect on the prices of finished items; and where they do, it is for items that are too small in cost to have much impact on the expenditure of total income.

High prices can also qualify as a major problem if they are sufficiently associated with imports to indicate significant draining off of
national income. (In other cases, they connote mostly domestic redistribution of income.) For aluminum, particularly, the increasing importation
of bauxite and alumina implies such a drain. But if the total cost of
aluminum metal, say, is not enough to make much of a dent in total consumer
income, then the portion that goes to pay for imports must necessarily
make a smaller dent. The fact is that metallic and nonmetallic minerals
combined, completely processed into industrial raw materials, amount to
only about 20 percent of the U.S. gross national product,[6] and the import
component, in turn, is little more than 10 percent of the processed minerals total. Moreover, the price rises we are talking about, since they
occur over time in the context of other rising prices, represent only a
minor fraction of the foregoing proportions. It takes exceedingly large
rates of price gain, for a commodity as important in the import bill as
petroleum, to approach any significant percentage of U.S. gross income
and output.

It may be objected that increased mineral costs are not just passed
through; they are normally passed along with a percentage markup. This
may be true, but the problem in this case is a markup, not a mineral,
problem. Only to the extent that inventory financing and perhaps sales
commissions are increased is there any kind of an actual percentage cost
increase to subsequent manufacturers and distributors.

It may also be objected that the domestic redistribution of income
that accompanies rapid increases in mineral prices is itself a problem.
The small proportion of total national product which even processed minerals constitute makes this dubious. But in any event, whether the transfer
of income from consumers generally to the portion of the population dependent on mining and minerals processing is a problem or a desideratum is a
matter of normative or political judgment; it is unlikely to have significant economic consequences.

---

[6]See U.S. Bureau of Mines, _Minerals in the U.S. Economy_ (May 1979)
p. 3.

Low Prices

For the two ferroalloys studied, ferrochromium and ferromanganese, price trends look as if they will turn flat before long (in the ferromanganese case, for a time they may even slightly sag). This is a conceivable problem for U.S. ferroalloy producers, especially as the costs of the relevant ores will probably continue to rise. Yet in both cases, as noted above, much more of the production cost appears to be in the smelting than in the raw material, so that energy, particularly, is likely to be the more critical problem, along with South African and other foreign competition. We have no basis for predicting how severely the ferroalloy industry will be affected, although we have assumed that U.S. ferrochrome capacity will be further reduced and that ferromanganese capacity will be no more than maintained at a level slightly higher than that to which it is currently falling (see tables 5-2 and 5-4). From the standpoint of the country as a whole, however, this cannot be termed a major problem, since (1) employment in the ferroalloy industries is fairly low, (2) some of the capacity previously used for ferrochromium and ferromanganese will probably be turned over to other ferroalloys, and (3) the weak price trends benefit ferroalloy consumers. Implications for supply security are limited, as discussed above.

Price Instability

Persistent price instability has been a characteristic of three of the nonferrous metals studied (copper, lead, and zinc) and, as noted above, may in the future also come to characterize aluminum. This is a problem related to, but different from, that of exposure to abrupt price jumps under unusual circumstances, which is discussed in chapter 9. It is a problem because instability has economic costs attached to it, which include those associated with ill-timed decisions to expand capacity and frequent startup and closedown of operations or parts of operations. The second effect is particularly costly for mining operations and may lead to the permanent or protracted loss of what would have been economically minable material if production had been carried on at more constant levels. Fluctuation in output also entails maintenance costs for shutdown facilities which would not otherwise have been incurred and which, again, can be particularly onerous for mining operations. The size of such costs is the factor that frequently leads owners to abandon unused workings to caving and flooding. Severe fluctuation also involves recurrent loss of skilled labor and added costs for training new labor.

Whether price instability is a major problem depends upon an assessment of the economic damage done. We have not made such an assessment, but have the feeling that the economic costs are substantial enough for some minerals to warrant the adjective.

Physical Supply Stringency

For a number of the mineral commodities studied, we suggested that there might be periods of supply stringency—even outright shortage. For the most part, this translated into a problem of rapidly rising prices, but short supplies can also be allocated by selling firms and by governmental authorities. There are two kinds of problems that may accompany the various modes of allocation: (1) nonmarket allocation may lead to less than maximum economic efficiency; market allocation may lead to undue departure from nonmarket objectives, (2) there may be a curtailment of total economic output. It seems unlikely, however, that any persistent (trend) shortages in the minerals under review are likely to be large enough to cause serious effects of either variety. Short-term shortages, discussed in the next chapter, are another matter.

Chapter 9

SHORT-TERM CONTINGENCIES

Introduction

This chapter evaluates the probability and implications of contingencies that might significantly affect the flow of nonfuel mineral supplies to U.S. industrial consumers over the nearer term future. Specifically, it attempts to assess (1) the likelihood that significant shortages
or abrupt price changes could occur for a number of important mineral
commodities through approximately 1985 and (2) the seriousness of any such
occurrence. It addresses itself, not to those mineral supply developments
that are expected to occur within the next decade, but to those which
might occur.

The various kinds of events--or causes--that could produce supply
contingencies fall into four general categories:

1. Foreign governments or other entities may take deliberate action
to disrupt or restrict the normal flow of a particular mineral to the
United States or its allies. Among other possible objectives, the purpose
of such actions may be to raise the prices a country receives for its
exports or to influence the policies of the importing country. Such moves
by members of the OPEC cartel in 1973-74 stirred public apprehension about
similar interruptions in the supplies of other minerals that the U.S.
imports in relatively large quantities.

There is little evidence of significant interruption in U.S. receipts
of nonfuel minerals as a result of such actions by foreign governments
in the past. However, the rhetoric of the New International Economic
Order, UN resolutions, and unilateral acts in the form of expropriation

and levies on mineral investments created in the 1970s a new climate which suggests that supply disruptions of this sort are likely to occur with greater frequency in the future. On the other hand, if growth in demand slows for the rest of this century (as is expected), the demand/supply balance on world markets will be less propitious for attempts to force economic and political concessions by disrupting supplies. The Group of 77 represents in general only about one-third of world production and known reserves of nonfuel minerals; its membership has found it easier to reach unanimity on UN resolutions than on collective actions that could prove costly to many of its members.

2. Mineral supplies may be interrupted as a side effect of civil or military disturbances. In the broadest sense, this includes labor troubles, which can occur in U.S. as well as foreign processing facilities and which are normally directed against the owners of the facilities, not the users of the material. Military actions and political upheavals may be directed against the government of the country in which the mine or processing facility is located or of the country through which the mineral must be transported to markets.

This form of interruption differs from the first in that the governments of producing countries are likely to try to minimize the supply interruption and to resume a normal flow as soon as possible. While disruptions resulting from political instability in the less developed world have been frequent over the past thirty years, they have seldom been significant and, on the whole, have been short-lived. Production and exports at normal levels have been resumed quickly in most cases.

Such disruption may be minimized by expanding the utilization of capacity at other mines and processing centers and by drawing on inventories. If the end of the disruption can be foreseen with some confidence, there will be minimal loss to mineral consumers. Only if such a disruption occurs when mining (or processing) capacity is near full utilization and demand is near a cyclical peak, with inventories in pipeline already depleted, is it likely to have significant market impact.

3. The third potential cause of shortages consists of an abrupt surge in demand. To be significant, such a surge must be beyond previous excess capacity (mining or primary processing). Such surges created

widespread shortages of nonfuel mineral commodities in the early 1950s, as a result of the Korean War, and again, twenty years later   during the 1973-74 period, when there was simultaneous peaking of cyclical demand in almost all Western industrialized countries.

A relative shift of gross domestic product (GDP) from the industrial to the services sector in OECD countries, combined with rising energy costs and decreasing rates of GDP growth, is reducing the likelihood of a generalized surge in demand for metallic minerals in these countries in the near future. Nevertheless, the possibility of demand surges that would outdistance available capacity--particularly as we get nearer 1985--cannot be discounted entirely. An economic recovery that occurred at about the same time in North America, Western Europe, and Japan could cause a strong surge in demand for most mineral commodities. In view of the recent low level of investment in new mines and processing facilities, this could lead to shortages. Final demand for these commodities tends to be highly concentrated in those economic sectors--construction, capital equipment, transportation, and consumer durables--whose output fluctuates with, and considerably more sharply than, the general level of economic activity. Should a general economic upturn nurture the fear of shortages, fabricators and other consumers are likely to build up their inventories, or at least try to, thereby accentuating the increase in demand. Independent speculators who are neither producers nor consumers are also likely to enter the market during such occasions.

4. The final possible cause of mineral commodity shortages is natural disasters. Fire and other mine accidents can interrupt mineral supplies. A typhoon can destroy processing facilities located near deepwater ports or the port facilities needed for transloading. Lack of rainfall can curtail hydroelectric power needed for aluminum smelting. Such disasters are most likely to pose a problem where capacity is highly concentrated in a few plants and geographic regions.

An assessment of the probability of a supply contingency is at best a highly judgmental exercise that relies upon the forecaster's intuitive understanding of the processes that may shape future events, as well as the historical record. Factors that must be taken into account include the probable origin of the contingency; its extent, duration, and location; the availability of alternative supplies and substitutes; the amount of excess capacity for producing and processing the mineral; and the speed with which this capacity can be utilized or expanded. The role of the U.S. government in forestalling or minimizing supply interruptions must also be considered. Although for the sake of clarity, we couch our appraisals in quantitative terms, they should not be taken as other than subjective judgments.

Mode of Appraisal

Since most supply contingencies take the form of shortfalls and since for most people this is an easily understood concept, we use the concept of demand-supply gap as a common denominator. In reality, there will always be some additional supplies available at higher prices, and thus the actual adjustment to any shortage is likely to be partly in prices and partly in curtailment of consumption. However, by expressing the size of the contingency in terms of gross shortage (initial shortfall), we can abstract from the variability in actual shortage that results from price adjustments.

Shortages that constitute less than 5 percent of the total rate of consumption are ignored. Presumably, these are the most marginal units consumed and are therefore not significant. Moreover, for this degree of shortage, inventory withdrawals and other modest adjustment measures can almost always prevent serious problems.

Shortages of 5-20 percent are considered small; 20-50 percent, medium; and 50-100 percent large. The duration period is subdivided into three categories: less than 2 months, 2 to 6 months, and over 6 months. The probability factors themselves are viewed as being either high, moderate, low, or nil. The approximate arithmetic equivalents are, respectively, over 25 percent, 10-25 percent, 2-10 percent, and less than 2 percent.

Cobalt

Vulnerability

As noted earlier in this study, cobalt is used primarily in high technology production processes, in relatively small amounts. Unlike the major metals, statistics are usually reported in pounds rather than tons. World demand in the 1970s (cobalt metal) fluctuated around an average 55 million pounds per year, with over 80 percent reflecting the needs of industries in the United States and its allies in Western Europe and Japan. Demand is based on highly specialized applications--magnets, superalloys for jet engines, and very high strength cutting tools. The cost of the cobalt is usually a tiny fraction of the cost of the final goods that it is used to produce.

Neither Western Europe nor Japan now produces cobalt from domestic mines. The United States recovered relatively small quantities from domestic ores prior to the 1970s; it has additional cobalt resources that could be mined at higher cost than that of imported supplies, though perhaps not much higher than the extraordinary prices prevailing in 1978 and 1979. So-called manganese nodules found in the seabed contain enough cobalt to represent a possible doubling of world reserves, depending on the extent to which legal and economic barriers to their recovery are overcome. Reported secondary recovery of old cobalt accounts for very little of recent supplies, though the reporting appears to underestimate significantly the volume of scrap consumption.

Ores mined in Zaire have been the basis for three-fourths of U.S. imports, the rest being supplied almost entirely from mines in three other countries--Zambia, Finland, and Canada. The cobalt is produced essentially as a by-product of copper or nikel mining. Some of the Zairian ores and smelter product (matte) are refined in Belgium for export to the United States and some of the Canadian ore is refined in Norway and then exported to the United States. Secondary recovery for the U.S. market also takes place in Western Europe and was scheduled to begin in 1979 at a new U.S. plant, built by GTE Sylvania. East-West trade in cobalt is negligible.

Zairian mines, almost entirely concentrated in the southern part of
the country, recently yielded about three-fifths of world cobalt production
outside the communist countries, and there are plans for expanding output
further. A government company, Societe Generale des Carrieres et des
Mines (Gecamines), mines and refines the ore and another government agency,
Societe Zairoise de Commercialization (SOZACOM), markets it. The Societe
General des Minerais (SGM), a subsidiary of Union Miniere (Belgian private
enterprise that owned Zaire's mines until 1967), provides technical advice.
The Zairian marketing subsidiary SOZACOM sets the world price, also with
the help of SGM expertise. Cobalt from both Zaire and Belgium is marketed
in the United States through the same exclusive agent (African Metals
Corporation of New York). As a matter of policy, the agent refuses to
enter into long-term contracts.

In addition to Zairian mines, supplies for the Western developed
countries originate in mines in Zambia (United Kingdom and Japan), Morocco
(France), Philippines (Japan), Australia (Japan), Canada (United Kingdom),
Finland (West Germany), and Botswana (United States). The USSR, Cuba,
and New Caledonia account for the rest of world cobalt mine production.

France, West Germany, Norway, and Finland produce metallic cobalt,
as do Zaire, Belgium, and Zambia. Japan is substantially expanding its
refining capacity, which will satisfy 50 percent of its cobalt requirements
when completed. The United States is providing some exports from a new
refinery opened in 1975, whose output has been contracted for primarily
by European customers. It uses copper-nickel and nickel matte from
Botswana, New Caledonia, and the Republic of South Africa.

At the end of May 1980, the government stockpile (40.8 million
pounds) was equal to some two years of consumption at the 1977 rate.
Estimated industry stocks normally tend to average another 4 months of
consumption.[1] Over the decade ending in 1976, the U.S. government sold
off about 60 percent of its stockpile, supplying a significant fraction
of each year's demand and exerting some depressing effect on prices.
Nevertheless, the price fixing monopoly was able to raise prices steadily

---

[1]*Mineral Commodity Profiles*, 1978, Cobalt, p. 11.

over the same period and at an accelerated pace between 1973 and 1977
(averaging over 20 percent per year). The increases have occurred
regularly, with little relation to the volume of U.S. imports, which
have fluctuated considerably.

The possibility of a significant supply contingency has to be judged
in the context of an annual rate of growth in demand, between now and
1985, of around 3 percent (see chapter 2). This does not include acquisitions to meet the new stockpile target (85,415,000 pounds), which
would require the procurement of an additional two and one-half years of
consumption needs. For the rest of the world, growth in demand is estimated at around 1 1/2 percent per year.

Probability of Supply Contingencies

Deliberate Disruptions. The probability of a supply contingency initiated by a foreign government depends primarily on the behavior of the
dominant supplier--the government of Zaire. For no other commodity does
a single country hold so large a share of the world market. The United
States has no current domestic mine production, and demand for cobalt
has so far not been very responsive to price changes.

In fact, however, Zaire's dependence on the United States and its
allies is at least as great as the latter's dependence on Zaire. Thus,
the probability that the government of Zaire will purposely cut off cobalt
supplies, or even threaten to do so, is rather low. On the other hand,
U.S. users were put on a 70 percent allocation[2] as of May 1978 by the
Zairian-Belgian selling agent; subsequently, producer prices almost
quadrupled, rising from approximately $7 in May 1978 to $20 per pound
by the beginning of November and $25 in February 1979. In addition, a
gray market developed in which small amounts of cobalt sold at around
twice the producer price quotations. In short, the cobalt market came
to be characterized by considerable disorder. However, the causes and
nature are far from self-evident. The problem may well have been only
temporary and highly unusual, and it appeared to have no significant

---

[2]Seventy percent of average monthly purchases in 1977. The allocation system was ended in July 1980.

effect on the actual level of U.S. cobalt consumption. A careful review
of the evidence (some of which has yet to become public) must precede
any firm conclusions as to what these events forebode for future supply
contingencies of either the price or the shortage variety.

The Zairian-Belgian syndicate clearly controls the world price, even
if other producers have initiated some of the recent price increases.
It does so partly because it is the dominant producer and supplier and
partly because it maintains sufficient stocks of both ore and metal in
Belgium (as well as inventories in Zaire) to discourage attempts by other
producers to undercut it. It is difficult to document whether actual
market-sharing agreements of any sort exist in the industry. It may be
significant in this connection that the syndicate's share of the U.S.
market declined somewhat in the 1970s.

Reliable data on stocks of ore and metal are difficult to come by;
and Belgian data on inventories, foreign trade, and production of cobalt
have not been available for a number of years. It is known that consumers
and dealers were attempting to increase inventories in the first half
of 1978, but information is lacking about the extent to which the monopoly
was actually able to satisfy that demand by stepping up production and
depleting its inventories. Production in Zaire in August 1978 was reported
to be 50 percent higher than in an average month of 1977, but still well
below the 1974 peak. If production continues to increase, both in Zaire
and elsewhere, the market could become quite competitive and the present
high prices would eventually come under significant pressure. In other
words, what we have been witnessing may have been a true short-term
contingency.

Considerable substitution of other materials (especially nickel)
is technically possible, and other sources of cobalt can expand their
production capacity. In 1978 Zambia and Finland increased their share
of the U.S. market. Japan and the Western European countries have substantially reduced their dependence on the Zaire-Union Miniere cobalt
monopoly by developing alternative resources and building domestic refineries. The United States has relied on political influence and a large
government stockpile to minimize its vulnerability. Though the stockpile

is no longer considered sufficient for strategic purposes and disposals
have therefore ceased, further releases could conceivably occur in the
event of an emergency.

As alternative sources expand and as production in Zaire increases,
that country's ability to raise prices without losing revenue will be
diminished. Even at current prices, Zaire could well find itself with a
shrinking share of a static or shrinking world market. On the other
hand, the replacement of Zaire's price-setting role by a formal cartel
(including Zaire, Belgium, Canada, Zambia, Finland, Morocco, and Australia)
is possible. Besides high-cost, mostly by-product recovery of cobalt
from North American sources, as well as substitution of other materials
in some uses, about the only constraint in sight on such a cartel would
be the prospect of deep-sea mining. Despite attempts by the Third World
bloc to continue to delay such a development, the possibility that significant amounts of cobalt may be forthcoming from deep-sea nodules by
the late 1980s seems real enough to exert a restraining influence on
monopoly price-making decisions. In fact, such restraint may be essential
to the success of any delaying tactics.

Other Disruptions. The most serious threat of direct supply disruption (rather than price actions) appears to be associated with such
military initiatives as the 1978 invasion of Shaba from Angola. A brief
supply shortage actually did occur in mid-1976 when the Benguela railroad
could no longer be used to export Zairian cobalt as the result of political
strife in Angola, but alternative transportation was quickly arranged.
The 1978 price multiplication was attributed to the invasion from Angolan
bases. It was only later than consumers learned that very little production was actually lost. Even then, skeptical consumers continued to doubt
the reported production level and to question whether it could be maintained wihtout substantial return of expatriate technicians. A subsequent
diplomatic initiative appeared to have produced Angolan agreement to
disarm the returning dissident Katangans and to restore the long-disrupted
transportation of Shaba's production of metals via the Benguela railroad,
though Angola's ability to keep the railroad open in the face of sabotage
by that country's own UNITA rebels is at least problematical. Both Zaire
and Angola are now committed to preventing the use of their territory as

a base for armed attack on the other. On balance, new political and
military disruptions seem less probable than they have for a number of
years past.

Nevertheless, the central government's popularity and its ability to
control metal-producing Shaba province remain sufficiently tenuous to
provide a significant probability of future disruptive actions. The
present regime in Angola is also far from secure. Further political
turmoil in Shaba province between now and 1985 cannot be discounted. The
withdrawal of Cuban troops from Angola and a more complete discouragement
of the Katangan dissidents may be necessary conditions for minimizing the
risk of military and political disruption of the flow of cobalt from
Zaire to Western markets.

If further attempts were made to establish a state in Shaba independent of the government of Zaire, physical destruction and the loss
of technical personnel could conceivably disrupt the production of metal at
the Kolwezi and Luilu refineries and at the Panda-Likasi smelter, unlike
the 1976 and 1978 experiences. Whether in those circumstances the total
flow of imported supplies to the United States would be significantly curtailed would depend on the speed with which production and export could
be resumed, the availability of refined metal stocks at the Belgian
cobalt refinery, and the availability of raw material stocks and excess
capacity at that refinery. An expansion of the refinery was scheduled
for completion in 1980. Given the high concentration of cobalt processing
facilities, a natural disaster of substantial proportions could conceivably eliminate a significant portion of the cobalt supply as effectively, if not more so, than military action or civil upheavals. Since,
however, there is no reason to believe that these facilities are particularly vulnerable to "acts of God," the risk of supply interruption
from this cause would be eclipsed by the causes already discussed.

Any future demand surges for cobalt are more likely to counteract
downward price pressures than to create physical shortages.

Summary. The probability of a significant supply contingency appears
to depend largely on whether there is a prolonged renewal of civil strife
in Zaire. There is both some probability of a physical interruption of

cobalt supplies to U.S. consumers and some probability of a future re-
petition of the recent abrupt price hikes. Except briefly and at the
margin, however, the degree of probability, as indicated in table 9-1,
seems less than 25 percent.

It is easy to confuse the price and the supply phenomena, especially
since a physical interruption could provide either the reason or the
excuse for a price hike. It is unwarranted, however, to conclude that
the present allocation system and recent price multiplications confirm
a large possibility of future price hikes and shortages. The very fact
of the recent large price increases—well beyond the preceding and probably
sustainable rate of trend adjustment—actually tends to reduce the probability of such increases in the future.

Table 9-1. Estimated Probabilities of Shortages in Cobalt Metal Supplies
for U.S. Industrial Consumption Through 1985[a]

Size[b]	Less than 2 months	2-6 months	Over 6 months
Small (5-20%)	High	Moderate	Moderate
Medium (20-50%)	Moderate	Small	Nil
Large (50-100%)	Small	Small	Nil

[a]Approximate arithmetic equivalent of the probabilities: nil - less
than 2%, small - 2-10%; moderate - 10-25%; high - over 25%.

[b]The size or magnitude of a shortage is measured in terms of gross
shortfalls from the consumption rate that would otherwise have prevailed,
at the price that would otherwise have prevailed, before allowance for
that part of any substitute supply that responds to a price rise. Shortages of less than 5 percent of consumption rate were considered a priori
to be insignificant.

Chromium

Vulnerability

Throughout this century, chromite has been the quintessential strategic material. It has been the object of strategic stockpiling, national security subsidies, preclusive buying, political embargoes, and even rationalizations for invading other countries. It provides resistance to corrosion and oxidation over a wide range of temperatures, it is an indispensable ingredient of stainless steel and is also used in other specialty steels. However, because chrome deposits are relatively ample, in concentrations yielding 20 percent or more chromium, prices are relatively low.

Apart from metallurgy, 20 to 25 percent of U.S. annual use is for the chemical and refractory industries. Until recently, the three major grades of chromite (metallurgical, chemical, and refractory) needed to be considered separately in evaluating U.S. vulnerability to foreign suppliers, since the major sources were different. The USSR, Turkey, and Rhodesia (now Zimbabwe) supplied metallurgical grade; South African production dominated chemical grade imports; and the Philippines supplied most of the refractory grade. Now, with the new argon-oxygen decarburization (AOD) process, which utilizes high-carbon ferrochrome rather than low-carbon ferrochrome (which is richer in chromium content), what used to be called chemical grade can be used to make stainless steel, and as a result, the potential sources of ore are more varied.

The strategic significance of chromium stems from the fact that a relatively few sources have tended to dominate the global export trade at any one time, though over time the identity of the dominant supplier has varied. Moreover, of the major powers involved in international confrontations, only the Soviet Union can produce enough chromite to meet its needs. Recently, the struggle for majority rule in Africa centered on the two largest non-Communist producers of chromite--Rhodesia and South Africa.

Nevertheless, chromium has not been a particularly effective instru-
ment of economic warfare in this century. The defensive measures taken
by modern powers to assure chromium supplies appear to have represented
substantial overkill. In neither World War I and II nor in the Korean
conflict was any participant's war effort significantly hampered for lack
of chrome; production incentive programs were cut back well before the
end of World War II was in sight.

While large chrome-bearing deposits exist in the United States, they
cannot be exploited at prices competitive with foreign ore bodies because
of their low grade and high transportation costs. Throughout this century,
the domestic production of chromite in significant quantity has required
heavy government subsidies. The last period of subsidies came to an end
in the early 1960s, and since that time no significant domestic mining of
chromite has taken place. Peak U.S. production was reached in 1943 at
160,000 short tons, with an estimated 48,000 short tons of chromium con-
tent--a level that would satisfy about 10 percent of current U.S. demand.

By 1975, the adoption of the AOD process had proceeded to the point
that South Africa, with its high-iron "chemical" grade ore, was becoming
the principal supplier of chromite to the United States, replacing the
USSR, Rhodesia, and Turkey. At the time the United States reimposed its
embargo in 1977, Rhodesia had only a minor share of the U.S. market.
By 1976, Finland had become a significant supplier (10 percent) and South
Africa was the source of two-fifths of U.S. imports (chrome content).
The South African share ran to 54 percent in 1977 but was back down to
40 percent in 1978. The Philippines continues to supply virtually all
of the U.S. requirements for refractory grade ore.

At least under recent market conditions, the USSR seems to prefer
to channel its output to Eastern Europe and its domestic market, both of
which are sharply expanding stainless steel production.

South Africa and Rhodesia together have 95 percent of the world's
reported reserves of chromite and about 97 percent of the additional
known resources. However, they account for only a third of global production. Despite the United Nations embargo, Rhodesia continued to
produce and export both chromite and ferrochrome. The embargo resulted

in a shifting of trade channels, and the reliability of statistics reporting the source of world chrome imports left much to be desired. Available
data indicate that South Africa and Rhodesia accounted for a fourth of
world chromite exports in 1975. (See chapter 3.) The USSR is a large
producer, and smaller quantities are reported by India, Brazil, Albania,
Malagasy, Iran, Sudan, Mozambique, and Finland. While both the reserves
and chromite resources of the latter countries are small relative to those
of South Africa and Rhodesia, their production increased during the 1970s
and the export capabilities of some of them can be enlarged significantly
through investment in mining, inland transportation, and port facilities.

Brazil is the only Western Hemisphere country that currently mines
significant quantities of chromite. Its output is exported to Japan or
converted into ferrochrome within Brazil and exported in that form. Greenland has large deposits of low quality ore that could be mined in an
emergency but would not be economical at current market prices.

For a decade after the mid-1960s, the United States steadily made
disposals from the strategic stockpile it had accumulated during the Korean
War. By 1977, the stockpile had been reduced to about a three-year supply
at current rates of industrial demand and remains at that level, which
is roughly equivalent to the current strategic stockpile goal.

Industrial stocks vary with market conditions, running in the aggregate between 6 and 12 months of industrial demand. At the end of 1978,
all private stocks reported to the Bureau of Mines were approximately
equal to industrial demand over the preceding 12 months. With uncertainties about events in southern Africa, U.S. industrial users appear to
have decided to maintain inventories sufficient to carry them over a
complete supply interruption for a full year. The two principal U.S.
producers of ferrochrome respectively maintain a one-year and a two-year
supply of chromite on hand as a matter of policy.

Probability of Supply Contingencies

Deliberate Disruptions. The possibility of a supply contingency
stemming from the policies of the producing governments may be greater
in the case of chromium than for any nonfuel mineral other than cobalt,

platinum, and industrial diamonds. However, the government policies of
concern are not of the type that have worried major powers throughout the
first two-thirds of this century. The higher probability of a supply
interruption concerns U.S. cooperation in a possible UN embargo on its
principal chrome supplier--the present government of South Africa.

As noted, global production capacity for the ores needed to produce
ferrochrome is heavily concentrated in the USSR, South Africa, Zimbabwe,
and Turkey. Tensions do exist between each of these countries and the
United States and/or its allies. Nevertheless, the probability that any
of them will embargo chromite shipments for the purpose of registering
political displeasure or of forcing changes in U.S. foreign policy cannot
be rated very high.

The USSR used this technique on two occasions without significant
effect. Its recent withdrawal of its high-chromium ores from the U.S.
market gave no evidence of political purpose, nor was it accompanied by
any shortage of supply in the United States. It appears to have been
motivated more by strong demand within the COMECON bloc and a declining
U.S. market for premium (the old metallurgical grade) ores. In fact,
1979 U.S. imports of low-chromium ores from the USSR reached an historical
high.

Despite disagreement with the United States over Cyprus, Turkey
remains a member of NATO and depends on the United States for a substantial
flow of military assistance. Even during the crisis over congressional
reluctance to authorize a resumption of military aid, Turkey did not
attempt to use its chromite as a bargaining tool. Turkey's economy is
heavily strained, deeply in debt, and dependent on a continuing flow of
economic assistance from Europe and the World Bank family.

Rhodesia successfully evaded UN sanctions and earned foreign exchange
by continuing to export chromite in the form of both ore and ferroalloy.
The new government of Zimbabwe is not likely to initiate a cutoff.

The present South African regime is not likely to resort to an
embargo of its chrome exports in order to gain support for its policies.
Indeed, it is currently threatened by a UN embargo if it fails to honor
its pledges concerning the granting of independence to Namibia. Hitherto,

the United States has resisted demands for such an embargo from Communist and developing nation members of the United Nations on the ground that it would be more likely to retard than advance Namibian independence. Should agreement fail and the United States cooperate in the imposition of sanctions, it would be faced with a significant interruption in its imported chromium supply.

In such an event, the price of chromite and ferrochrome may be expected to soar in the face of hedge buying and speculation. Sanctions could be maintained for many months, however, without interrupting industrial production, partly because of the large inventories of chromite in the hands of U.S. ferrochrome producers. High prices would probably stimulate both conservation and secondary recovery, and deliveries from other suppliers would undoubtedly be expanded. The combination of high prices and political advantage from supporing sanctions against South Africa might well induce the USSR to increase its exports once again.

Even if Namibian independence is achieved without sanctions, a UN call for an embargo on South Africa looks like a recurring possibility until the question of majority rule in South Africa is resolved. The present regime is likely to remain intransigent and the United States may well feel at some point that its interests in the rest of Africa--and elsewhere--would be best served by enforcing UN-sponsored sanctions. The probability of such an event before 1985 must be rated high.

While the political character of future regimes in South Africa and Zimbabwe may be unpredictable and their economic policies even more so, they are likely to need foreign exchange to pay for imports and finance economic development. They are unlikely to feel threatened by industrialized countries that want to import their chrome even if political relations should become strained. Should relations deteriorate, they would probably realize that an embargo on chrome exports would be unlikely to change the policies of importing nations and would certainly damage their own economies.

Nor is there a large probability of significant disruption through cartel action in the period through 1985. It may have made economic sense for the USSR and Turkey to raise prices while they could for their

high-chromium ores, but their position is now weakened by increasing use
of the AOD process. South Africa, the dominant producer of high-iron
chromite and thus the principal beneficiary of the new process, cannot
exercise monopoly power unless the USSR and Turkey cooperate or stay out
of the market. Also, given very much of a price rise, less richly endowed
suppliers of chromite would find it profitable to expand their exports.
Rather than looking to high prices and supply restrictions, South Africa
seems to be encouraging private investment in expanded capacity, with a
view to increasing exports. South Africa's large mineral reserve position
seems to be best exploited by sufficient price restraint so as not to stimulate conservation and substitution on the part of consumers and increased
production on the part of higher cost suppliers.

Other Disruptions. While political, labor, or military disruptions
are conceivable in any of the exporting countries, the probabilities of
a significant supply interruption on that account are rather low except
in the case of South Africa. Some amount of supply disruption from South
Africa, as the result of persistent political turmoil, does seem probable
between now and 1985 and could on occasion touch off a sharp price rise.
A more difficult question is how protracted the actual loss of chromite
or ferrochromium supply would be and, particularly, whether it could be
great enough and long enough to exhaust U.S. private inventories. An
interruption of chromite supply would probably be offset by high inventories and the U.S. stockpile, but in the case of ferrochromium, an interruption could be great enough to have significant impact.

Past demand surges for ferrochromium have been strong, and the next
peak in U.S. industrial output is likely to involve another such surge.
However, both mine and ferrochrome facilities are today operating worldwide
at levels well below capacity. U.S. ferrochrome producers were reported
as of mid-1978 to be operating at only 60 percent. Thus, expansion of
output to meet the next peak demand should be readily possible, even if
the peaks are once again synchronized in the United States and other
developed countries--so long as the surge is not coincident with disturbances in the principal supplying countries.

Summary. Some amount of supply disruption from South Africa, as the result of political turmoil, seems probable between now and 1985. Should there be a violent transition to a new political regime, both chromite and ferrochromium supplies from South Africa would probably be interrupted for a period even if facilities were not directly damaged. The impact of this on U.S. industrial consumers would differ between the ore and the ferroalloy and would depend a great deal on whether or not the events in question took place at a time of high levels of steelmaking in the United States. As there is only a moderate possibility of such a juxtaposition, there is only a comparable probability that supplies of ferrochromium would be significantly interrupted, and this only for a limited period. The bottleneck, in such circumstances, would be U.S. and other Western ferroalloy capacity; so long as the situation in southern Africa looks precarious, it may be assumed that ferroalloy makers will continue to hold large stocks of chromite. In addition, there is the likelihood, in a protracted emergency, of releases of chromite from the U.S. stockpile.

In one sense, chrome markets have already experienced a supply interruption, resulting from UN sanctions on Rhodesia. However, inventories are high, excess capacity is prevalent among ferrochrome producers, and prices are below the peak levels experienced several years ago. A significant supply interruption manifestly has not come about. Moreover, a variety of sources outside of southern Africa are expanding mining capacity and could increase deliveries above current levels. Nevertheless, the possibility of an embargo against South Africa has serious enough implications to warrant concern. Such an embargo would represent a significant supply interruption, and substantial price increases would probably result. The higher prices would stimulate increased deliveries from other suppliers, probably including the Soviet Union, and thus mitigate the effects of a supply contingency, but would not erase it. Because of the indispensability of chromium for stainless steel, such a contingency could have major economic impact.

Table 9-2 summarizes our estimate of the combined probabilities of a U.S. supply shortage in chromium from any or all causes. It is to be borne in mind that the quantification is gross, before allowance for new supplies stimulated by higher prices.

Table 9-2. Estimated Probabilities of Shortages in Chromite and Ferro-chromium for Industrial Consumption Through 1985[a]

Size[b]	Less than 2 months	2-6 months	Over 6 months
Small (5-20%)			
Chromite	High	Moderate	Moderate
Ferrochromium	High	Moderate	Moderate
Medium (20-50%)			
Chromite	Moderate	Moderate	Moderate
Ferrochromium	Moderate	Moderate	Moderate
Large (50-100%)			
Chromite	Moderate	Small	Small
Ferrochromium	Small	Small	Nil

[a]Approximate arithmetic equivalent of the probabilities: nil - less than 2%; small - 2-10%; moderate - 20-25%; high - over 25%.

[b]The size or magnitude of a shortage is measured in terms of gross shortfalls from the consumption rate that would otherwise have prevailed, at the price that would otherwise have prevailed, before allowance for that part of any substitute supply that responds to a price rise. Short-ages of less than 5 percent of consumption rate were considered a priori to be insignificant.

Manganese

Vulnerability

Manganese, mostly in the form of ferromanganese or silicomanganese, is a key ingredient in steelmaking, which accounts for about 90 percent of world manganese consumption. Other uses are for dry cell batteries and chemicals. The amounts of new manganese used in steelmaking vary significantly (unusually high in the USSR).[3] In the United States it is around 1 percent of the weight of steel and in allied countries no more than 2 percent.

In recent years, estimated U.S. industrial demand has varied between 1.1 and 1.6 million short tons per year (manganese content).[4] Only infrequently, however, has it exceeded 1.4 million tons. Given the very slow rate of growth of U.S. steel production, U.S. demand for manganese has also shown little or no recent growth.

The United States currently recovers only minimal quantities of manganese, equivalent to about 2 percent of domestic demand, from relatively low grade domestic ores.[5] It has no reserves of manganese ore as such, but significant lower grade resources. They were exploited to produce 14 percent of U.S. consumption in 1943, but only with the help of a highly subsidized wartime government purchase program. In the 1950s, a government subsidy program induced further mining of these ores, though the prices paid were 70 to 130 percent over the 1959 market. Increases in U.S. mining costs suggest that such percentages would now have to be significantly higher to induce output.

---

[3] In addition to new (virgin) manganese, secondary manganese is introduced into steel furnaces via steel scrap and via recycling of some steelmaking slag into blast furnaces (source of pig iron).

[4] U.S. Bureau of Mines, Minerals in the U.S. Economy (1966-75 and 1968-77).

[5] Ferruginous ores.

European allies of the United States have neither reserves nor known resources, with the sole exception of Greece, which has some reserves of battery-grade ore, a special grade commanding a relatively high price. However, Australia began producing in the late 1950s, became a major world supplier in the 1970s, and has large new projects under way that should at least double its capacity in the 1980s (see chapter 5). Manganese is one of the few minerals for which Japan can look to its own production, but domestic mines meet only about 5 percent of the country's needs and the grade of the ores is dropping. Once legal and technical obstacles are overcome, manganese nodules from the ocean seabed may add significantly to reserves. A significant flow from this source seems unlikely until well after 1985, and even then depends upon uncertain prospects as to the extent that manganese will actually be recovered; but the very prospect must affect the marketing strategies of important producing countries.

Known world reserves are very large relative to prospective demand and have been expanding faster than demand. Though most of these reserves are located in a relatively few countries, the economic and political structures of the producing countries are diverse, and they are scattered geographically. Global production is heavily concentrated in the Soviet Union and South Africa, with the former accounting for approximately a third and the latter a fourth of aggregate manganese output in 1977. Prior to World War II and for a decade thereafter, the USSR was the dominant producer and supplier of world markets, accounting for about three-fifths of global production. Subsequently, the USSR retreated from the world market, cutting off supplies to Western markets completely just before the Korean War. Currently, it supplies less than 10 percent of the requirements of any single U.S. ally.

South African production expanded sharply in the late 1930s and thereafter. Currently, it supplies about 30 percent of Western consumption, but a smaller proportion of U.S. needs. Brazil and Gabon now account for three-fourths of U.S. imports of manganese ore, with South Africa and France providing about half of U.S. ferromanganese imports.

Formerly, virtually all U.S. imports were in the form of ore, but increasingly imports have taken the form of alloys and metal (approximately 30 percent of total imports of contained manganese in the 1970s). For the industrialized countries as a group, however, aggregate ferromanganese capacity is more than ample. High energy and pollution control costs elsewhere have encouraged South Africa, Brazil, and India to move more quickly toward their goal of processing more of their manganese ores into ferromanganese rather than exporting the ores as such. France and Japan have substantial capacity, and Australia recently expanded its capacity. In such circumstances, the competitiveness of U.S. processing is becoming increasingly doubtful.

The same blast furnaces can be used to make either pig iron or high carbon ferromanganese, and furnaces are often converted from one use to the other, though such switching is difficult during periods of high demand. Electric furnaces can be used to make various grades of ferro-manganese and silicomanganese; these furnaces are the same as those used to make other ferroalloys, and some shifting occurs.

The United States accumulated a large strategic stockpile of manganese ore over the quarter century after the enactment of the Strategic Materials Act of 1939. Systematic net disposal began in the second half of the 1960s and was accelerated in the 1970s. Since 1975, stockpile sales have been confined to deliveries against existing contracts. The current stockpile is equivalent to about 27 months of industrial demand at the average level of the 1970s. U.S. industry stocks of ore tend to fluctuate upwards of 8 months' supply; ferromanganese stocks are more meager.

Probability of Supply Contingencies

Deliberate Disruptions. Despite the fact that more than four-fifths of world exports come from South Africa, Australia, Gabon, and Brazil, a major supply disruption seems most unlikely, particularly one caused by the governments of those countries acting singly or in concert.

The government of South Africa is isolated politically by almost universal condemnation of its apartheid policies. Nevertheless, its economy remains very dependent on Western industrialized countries and

it is unlikely to increase antagonism in those countries by embargoing
exports of manganese. Little short of a last-ditch siege mentality would
suffice for resort to so crude and ineffective a weapon for sustaining
the present government. It is also difficult to imagine why a successor
government, if there were such a change, would wish to embargo manganese
exports.

A political embargo on manganese exports imposed by an Australian
government must rate close to zero probability. Without South African
and Australian export, a political embargo by all the other producers
acting in concert would not be very effective. Nor is it easy to conceive
of political circumstances within the next decade that would lead Brazil
and Gabon to unite together with India, Indonesia, Upper Volta (a prospective new producer in the 1980s), and Morocco in imposing a political
embargo on manganese exports to the world's steel producing countries.

A more likely contingency is the imposition of UN sanctions against
South Africa (see discussion of chromium). An effective embargo would
deprive non-Communist countries of 30 percent of their manganese ore and
20 percent of their imports of ferromanganese. South Africa now supplies
less than 5 percent of U.S. imports of manganese ore, but up to 40 percent
of U.S. imports of ferromanganese. Excess mining capacity in less developed countries could easily replace the balance of South Africa's ore
shipments to the United States, and Australian production could also be
increased significantly within a fairly brief period. The remaining
shortfall for the Western countries in general might well be met by the
Soviet Union, which has been offering the West in recent years only its
low to medium grade Nicopol ores. Private inventories and, in a crisis,
releases from the U.S. strategic stockpile would suffice to provide
sufficient time for these adjustments in the pattern of world trade to
take place without significant interruption of ore supplies and only
limited interruption of the ferromanganese needed for steelmaking.

It is possible at least to imagine a manganese ore producers' cartel,
given the dominant role of four exporting countries. However, the probability of such a cartel within the next decade must be rated very low.
The political complexion of the four countries and their economic and

strategic interests could not be more diverse. Their principal customers
are large steel companies and the ferroalloy producers that have long-term
contracts with, or financial positions in, one or more ore producers.
(Prices and tonnages to be delivered are negotiated annually.) Recently,
more than in the past, some firms have used their ore positions to contract
with underemployed ferroalloy producers for ore conversion, apparently at
lower cost than using their own furnaces.

To be sure, all manganese producers would find common ground in the
desire to get larger receipts from their manganese exports, but all have
broader interests that would be damaged by antagonizing the major steel
producing countries.

South Africa's participation in a cartel would be critical, not only
because of its dominant share of the global export market, but also because
its reserves (estimated at 790 million short tons of contained manganese,
or approximately 45 percent of world reserves) and production potential
are so large. However, its plans for substantial increases in production
in the early 1980s are hardly consistent with supply restriction. Nor is
it apt to risk whatever international understanding its government still
commands by participating in a cartel arrangement with respect to a commodity that accounts for only a small percentage of the total value of its
exports. A cartel without South Africa might well see its restrictions
operate primarily to the advantage of South African producers.

When the Labour Party was in power, the Australian government was
much concerned with maintaining national control over its resources and
with discouraging foreign private investment. However, Australia has very
strong political and strategic ties with the United States. It has benefited considerably from its status as a stable and fair source of minerals.
Moreover, its economy is heavily tied to that of Japan, the United States,
and Western Europe, in a tangle of trade and financial interdependencies.
Japan is the major market, absorbing most of Australia's output of cok-
ing coal, copper, and zinc and much of its bauxite and iron ore. For
these reasons Australia would hardly find it worthwhile to join a re-
trictive manganese cartel, an act that could encourage its principal
minerals customers to seek to reduce their dependence on Australia for

other products. With mineral exports booming and considerable expansion
in prospect, Australia is thus an unlikely prospect for participation
in a cartel arrangement involving market sharing or export restrictions.
While it has joined the intergovernmental associations on iron ore and
bauxite, it has resisted discussion of price-fixing and export restrictions
within these groups.

As for the other non-Communist exporting countries, they all belong
to the Group of 77 bloc of less developed countries. Even though manganese
was one of the 18 commodities placed in the Integrated Programme for
Commodities at the 1977 Nairobi meeting, it is doubtful, given the
expanding role of South Africa and Australia as well as the USSR potential,
that manganese will be deemed an attractive commodity for agreements to
enlarge Third World income from commodity exports. The principal less
developed exporters--Brazil and Gabon--are not particularly aggressive
members of the bloc and their interests are very divergent.

Brazil has become heavily overloaded with debt in the aftermath of
OPEC and urgently needs open markets in the industrialized world for its
exports of manufactures if it is to service that debt. Its manganese
is being used increasingly in its own rapidly expanding steel industry;
manganese accounts for less than 1 percent of its commodity exports and
that proportion is likely to decline.

Upon completion of planned transportation facilities, Gabon may well
be the world's lowest cost supplier of manganese ore, and it has ambitious
plans for expanding production. It is an unlikely leader or participant in
a manganese cartel, since it might well find its expansion plans hindered
thereby. Indeed, the value of its heavy transportation investment program
could be seriously undermined and service of the related debt could be
complicated if Gabon were unable to use the new facilities for exporting
much larger quantities of manganese than at present.

Incidental Disruptions. Political or military disruptions could
occur in South Africa, Brazil, or Gabon over the next decade. However,
there is every reason to believe that any such disruptions would not have
significant supply consequences. Disruptions are unlikely to be simultaneous, nor should losses in deliveries of manganese be long continued.

Such losses as do occur are apt to be manageable by depleting private inventories in consuming countries, making fuller use of production capacity elsewhere, and possibly resorting to the U.S. strategic stockpile in the event of a real emergency.

The likelihood of disruption is probably greater in South Africa than in the other countries. The mines are 600 miles from port, and deliveries are vulnerable to disruption of transportation facilities. In the past, railroad limitations and port congestion have impeded the smooth delivery of ores to overseas consumers. However, with completion of the St. Croix port, the length of the rail haul and port congestion should be eased considerably. Guerrilla-type activity would be disruptive, but such damage can usually be repaired rapidly and traffic can be diverted over other routes to avoid a major percentage reduction in annual shipments. Moreover, South Africa's military and internal security forces seem capable of protecting both the mining and the transportation facilities against extended interruption.

Brazil has experienced political coups in the past without major disruption in its economic life and there is no particular reason to expect extensive destruction of transportation facilities or mining installations if another change in government occurs.

To date Gabon has been relatively tranquil. Only one military coup has been attempted (1964) since independence was achieved in 1960 and it was quickly put down. The government has been an authoritarian one-party state along fairly typical African lines since the early months after independence. Few other African governments can claim that their first president died a natural death in office and was replaced peaceably by the present one (Albert Bongo). Thus, there is no particular reason to expect a revolutionary attempt in Gabon, though it is not impossible. In some other African countries, coups have occurred after years of apparent stability, but they have ended quickly, with minimal disruption to economic activities.

Other Disruptions. Demand for manganese varies with the level of steel production, so that it has long fluctuated considerably in response to the general business cycle. A global surge of steel production to

levels as much as 20 percent above 1974 (783 million short tons) is conceivable at some point between now and 1985, but not probable. If it
occurs independently of any other contingency, it can be accommodated
within the spare mine and ferroalloy capacity.

The high dependence of some of the manganese supplies on critical
transportation facilities (such as a ropeway in Gabon) suggests a certain
amount of vulnerability to natural disasters, but there is no reason to
consider that the location of any of these facilities makes them particularly prone to natural disasters. Moreover, the ropeway is to be
replaced by rail connection, and other transportation facilities, such
as those in South Africa, are not without alternatives.

Summary. The highest probability of interruption in the supply of
manganese ores or of ferromanganese would result from the imposition, and
enforcement by all developed countries, of sanctions on South Africa.
The impact in the United States would be felt at both the ore and the
ferroalloy stage. Given the current world excess capacity for manganese
ore production, which is expected to grow during the first half of the
1980s, part of the ore shortage could be made up by other manganese mining
countries. But the same supplies would be sought by non-U.S. ferroalloy
producers, including those, like France, which now depend heavily on
South African ore and are also principal ferroalloy suppliers to the
United States. Thus, despite excess world capacity for alloy production,
it would be difficult quickly to replace all South African ferromanganese
supplies. The adjustment would be less acute given continuing releases
from the U.S. strategic stockpile.

Given probable continuing slack in world steel production, existing
blast-furnace capacity could in part be turned over to ferroalloy production and some retired capacity could probably be reactivated, but only
with some delay and increase in manganese costs.

The probability is rather low of a synchronized boom in the demand
for steel in all industrialized countries, at least until well into the
1980s. The possibility becomes somewhat greater as one looks further
ahead, but it seems more likely that the United States, Western Europe,
and Japan will continue to experience peak demands for steel at different

times, so that global demand for manganese should not surge again to the extent that it did in 1973-74. Barring effective sanctions against South Africa, both ore and ferromanganese should be sufficient to cope with such a surge, if it does occur. With sanctions in effect, capacity in the rest of the world would probably be expanded, but probably not in time to cope fully with a demand surge. An especially significant supply interruption would occur if a synchronized boom occurred on the heels of sanctions imposed on South Africa and a prolonged strike then interrupted the flow of manganese from Australia, but such a combination of events seems quite improbable.

Table 9-3 summarizes estimates as to a shortfall in manganese supplies, after private stock utilization, but before allowance for any increased supplies called forth by higher prices. The "high" rating assigned to the possibility of a short-term shortfall of a small portion of the ferromanganese supply is predicated on an assumed imposition of UN sanctions in the midst of a period of at least average levels of economic activity. There is a moderate possibility (if ore ran short or if sanctions were imposed during a period of high economic activity) that the shortfall could exceed 20 percent of the desired supply. The direct impact of any such contingency on the U.S. supply of manganese ores for smelting would probably be quite limited, since little U.S. ore now comes from South Africa.

Table 9-3. Estimated Probabilities of Shortages in Manganese and Ferromanganese Ore Supply for U.S. Industrial Consumption Through
1985[a]

Size[b]	Less than 2 months	2-6 months	Over 6 months
Small (5-20%)			
Manganese	Small	Small	Nil
Ferromanganese	High	Moderate	Small
Medium (20-50%)			
Manganese	Small	Nil	Nil
Ferromanganese	Moderate	Small	Nil
Large (50-100%)			
Manganese	Nil	Nil	Nil
Ferromanganese	Small	Nil	Nil

[a]Approximate arithmetic equivalent of the probabilities:
nil - less than 2%; small - 2-10%; moderate - 10-25%; high - over 25%.

[b]The size or magnitude of a shortage is measured in terms of gross
shortfalls from the consumption rate that would otherwise have prevailed,
at the price that would otherwise have prevailed, before allowance for
that part of any substitute supply that responds to a price rise. Shortages of less than 5 percent of consumption rate considered a priori to
be insignificant.

Aluminum

Vulnerability

The United States, Canada, Japan, and Western Europe are the major producers and consumers of aluminum outside the centrally planned economies. All depend heavily on bauxite and alumina imports. The United States does some domestic mining, primarily in Arkansas, but its production in recent years has satisfied less than 15 percent of total bauxite requirements. (See chapter 4). Moreover, the country's dependence on foreign bauxite has been rising. In Western Europe, France and Greece are also significant bauxite producers. While Greece exports a substantial portion of its output, France consumes most of its bauxite domestically, and in addition it imports an amount roughly equal to its own production. The other major aluminum-producing countries of Western Europe, as well as Canada and Japan, are completely dependent on bauxite imports.

The principal exporting countries are Guinea, Australia, Jamaica, Surinam, and Guyana. (See chapter 3.) In recent years the percentages of total world exports coming from Guinea and Australia have risen while those from Jamaica, Surinam, and Guyana have declined. This trend is likely to continue in the future, and Brazil will become a major exporter as well.

Exporting countries generally ship their bauxite to particular importing countries. Australia, for example, sends almost all of the bauxite that it exports to Japan and Western Europe. Guinea concentrates on markets in North America, Western Europe, and the Soviet Union. Jamaica and Surinam export predominantly to the United States, and Guyana to the United States and Canada. These trade flows tend to persist over time, in part because the major aluminum firms have developed most of the bauxite mines to secure a source of raw materials for their alumina plants and in part because different types of bauxite require different refining practices. Thus, modifications would be costly.

The United States need not be directly concerned about monohydrate bauxite, which is supplied principally by Greece and Yugoslavia and used primarily in Europe. Should exporting countries cut off supplies of this type of bauxite, it would have little effect on the United States. This simplifies the analysis somewhat, though the differentiated nature of bauxite ores still requires a separate examination for each of the two types of bauxite--mixed and trihydrate (gibbsitic)--used heavily in the United States. An interruption in the supplies of trihydrate bauxite would pose difficulties for alumina facilities designed for this type of ore, even assuming that supplies of mixed bauxite could easily be increased.

In recent years, the United States has obtained about 80 percent of its mixed bauxite from Jamaica, with the remainder coming from Haiti and the Dominican Republic. Between 80 and 90 percent of its imported trihydrate bauxite (60-70 percent of total supplies) comes from Guinea and Surinam, with Guyana providing most of the rest.

Like production, bauxite reserves are also highly concentrated outside of North America, Western Europe, and Japan. Indeed, roughly one-third of total world reserves are found in Guinea, while nearly another third are located in Australia and Brazil. Technically, aluminum can also be produced from aluminum clays, anorthosite, alunite, and other nonbauxitic ores. The Soviet Union, for example, has reportedly produced a portion of its alumina requirements from domestic deposits of nepheline and alunite, in order to minimize its dependence on foreign bauxite. However, it is significantly more expensive to process such ores, and they therefore do not generally qualify as "reserves."

The United States and a number of its allies rely on alumina imports to supplement their domestic processing of bauxite. Roughly a third of U.S. alumina is imported. The same is true for Japan. Canada and Britain produce most of their aluminum using foreign alumina and are thus even more heavily dependent on alumina imports.

Australia is by far the largest exporter of alumina, accounting for half of all that commodity entering international trade. The second largest exporter is Jamaica, with between 10 and 15 percent of world trade. Unlike bauxite, alumina is a relatively homogeneous commodity, and supplies from one country can easily be substituted for those from another.

Using imported bauxite or alumina, the major industrial countries have in recent years produced most of their primary aluminum needs domestically.

Still, there have been significant flows of aluminum from Canada to the United States, and from Norway to Great Britain, Germany, Belgium, and the Netherlands. In the past, Canada and Norway have been the only major producers of primary aluminum that exported most of their output.[6] Both of these countries have benefited from abundant hydroelectric power and close proximity to major aluminum markets in the United States and Western Europe. More aluminum smelting, however, is likely to take place in other countries in the future, as higher energy and environmental costs increasingly favor a shift of production to the Middle East and other areas where energy resources are relatively abundant and environmental regulations less severe. Much of the spread will involve increased smelting of aluminum by developing and semideveloped countries for home consumption.

Aluminum scrap, the only other aluminum material considered in this section, is generated largely in the industrial countries. While these countries do trade aluminum scrap, largely among each other, imports and exports typically constitute only a small portion of the available domestic supplies of scrap.

Probability of Supply Contingencies

Deliberate Disruptions. This section assesses the likelihood that foreign governments will deliberately disrupt or raise the cost of U.S. supplies of bauxite, alumina, aluminum ingot, or scrap. Such actions might be undertaken to raise the returns producing countries receive for their commodities, or, as in the case of the Arab oil embargo against the United States and the Netherlands in 1973, to pressure importing countries to change their foreign policies.

In 1974, Jamaica raised its taxes on bauxite production from under $2 to around $14 per dried ton. In addition, it tied its future production levies to the price of aluminum, so that the country's returns from bauxite mining would increase automatically as the price of aluminum rose. The Dominican Republic, Guyana, Haiti, and Surinam introduced similar

---

[6]Among lesser export-oriented producers, Ghana is an important supplier to the United States and Bahrain to Japan.

changes in their tax structure as well. Guinea, Sierre Leone, and Indonesia also raised bauxite taxes, though in these countries the level of
the tax was not tied to the price of aluminum.

Also in 1974, Australia, Guinea, Guyana, Jamaica, Sierra Leone,
Surinam, and Yugoslavia agreed to establish a producers' association, the
International Bauxite Association. The Dominican Republic, Haiti, Ghana,
and Indonesia have since joined. One of the principal objectives of this
association is "to secure for member countries fair and reasonable returns
from the exploitation, processing and marketing of bauxite and its products for the economic and social development of their peoples..."

In light of these recent developments, the possibility of future
attempts by producing governments to raise appreciably the returns they
receive from their bauxite operations, particularly during periods of
strong economic activity when aluminum and bauxite are in short supply,
cannot be ruled out. For several reasons, however, the probability that
this will actually occur over the next five years or so appears low.
First, past confrontation between Jamaica and other producing governments,
on the one hand, and the multinational aluminum companies and their home
governments, on the other, has had some adverse consequences for the
producing countries. In Jamaica, for example, little new investment
in bauxite has occurred in recent years, as companies there have tried
to diversify their sources of supply and reduce their dependence on that
country. One company, Revere, has even closed down its Jamaican alumina
plant operations. Jamaica and other producing governments now appear to
be trying to consolidate their earlier gains. Confrontation is being replaced by reconciliation, in an effort to alleviate the fears and concerns
of multinational firms and their home governments.

Second, the bauxite industry is going through a period of severe
structural change. Over most of the postwar period, Jamaica has been
the world's largest producer. However, in recent years Australia and
Guinea have expanded their output rapidly. Both these countries now
produce more bauxite than Jamaica. Ambitious expansion plans are also
being carried out in Brazil. (See chapter 5.)

While Australia and Guinea have joined the International Bauxite
Association, their behavior there and in other international forums

appears rather restrained. Nor have they been willing to go as far as Jamaica and certain other producers in raising bauxite taxes. The Brazilian government has been actively trying to attract foreign companies to help develop its bauxite and other mineral resources. For this reason, it has refused to join the International Bauxite Association or to follow Jamaica's lead in raising the level and changing the nature of taxes on mineral production. It has also been cool to the demands of many less developed countries for a New International Economic Order and has provided little support to the Group of 77 who have tried under the auspices of the United Nations Conference on Trade and Development (UNCTAD) to implement the Integrated Commodities Program. This last envisages a "common fund" of several billion dollars, contributed largely by the developed countries, that would be used primarily to support a number of commodity agreements for individual mineral and agricultural products produced by developing countries.

Without the active support and cooperation of Australia, Guinea, and Brazil, it would be difficult for Jamaica or any other bauxite producing country to effect further substantial increases in taxes. This would simply accelerate the efforts of the multinational aluminum firms to find new sources of supplies elsewhere. It would also likely stimulate research on the use of nonbauxitic ores. For these reasons, a second abrupt increase in bauxite prices, like that imposed by producing countries in 1974, seems improbable.

The possibility that foreign governments might deliberately restrict supplies for purely political reasons appears even more remote. The dominant producing countries--Australia, Guinea, Jamaica, Surinam, and, in the near future, Brazil--have different political interests and are not likely to act together for a common political cause. An embargo by one country could be offset, at least in part, by an increase in output elsewhere (unless the industry were operating at full capacity). Certain aluminum refineries would operate at lower efficiencies and might have to be modified at some expense if the embargo were to continue for a long period of time. The U.S. government stockpile could also conceivably be used to mitigate shortage effects. Thus, embargoes of bauxite shipments for political reasons would likely fail in their objective, even as they encouraged pursuit of alternative bauxite supplies. With little to gain and much to lose, exporting countries must be judged not likely to engage in this type of behavior.

Unlike bauxite, alumina is a homogeneous product. Moreover, transportation costs are not a serious constraint on the worldwide movement of this material. Australia ships large tonnages of alumina to Japan, Western Europe, and North America. This suggests that an interruption in supply anywhere could cause sharp increases in price and a shortage in the United States regardless of the ultimate destination of the shipments interrupted. In practice, however, the United States obtains nearly all its alumina either from subsidiaries of U.S. firms (or joint ventures in which U.S. firms have an interest) or under long-term contracts. Consequently, an interruption in alumina shipments destined for Europe or Japan would not greatly disrupt the U.S. industry. Conversely, an interruption in the traditional channels of U.S. supplies could not easily be offset by bidding alumina away from other countries.

Australia is by far the most important exporter of alumina to the United States, providing between 20 and 30 percent of domestic requirements in recent years. The second largest exporter, Jamaica, accounts for less than 10 percent of U.S. requirements. The dominance of Australia, coupled with the fact that between 60 and 75 percent of U.S. alumina needs are met from domestic production, suggests that there is little possibility of alumina shortages in the near future as a result of deliberate actions by foreign governments.

The same is also true for aluminum ingot. Here, however, the dominant exporter to the U.S. market is Canada, which in recent years has accounted for over two-thirds of U.S. imports. While Canada is dependent on foreign sources of bauxite and alumina, it is unlikely that these sources would be interrupted by deliberate government actions in producing countries, for reasons already discussed. Moreover, while Canada accounts for most U.S. imports, net imports from Canada and elsewhere have in recent years accounted for less than 10 percent of U.S. consumption. Consequently, unless the domestic industry were operating at full capacity, any cutback in imports could probably be offset by an increase in U.S. production.

Finally, there is little or no possibility that foreign governments would provoke shortages of aluminum scrap in the United States within the foreseeable future. The United States, as mentioned earlier, is a major generator of new and old scrap, and it exports more of this mineral commodity than its imports.

Incidental Disruptions. Jamaica, Guinea, Surinam, and Guyana are the most important countries exporting bauxite to the United States. In 1977, for example, these four countries accounted for 48, 23, 15, and 3 percent of total U.S. imports respectively. All these countries are confronted with serious internal problems that could cause civil disorders over the next five years or so. In addition, two of these countries could become embroiled in military conflict with neighboring states.

Jamaica is a racially tense society. While the population is composed largely of blacks and mulattoes, most of the country's wealth and economic power is still enjoyed by whites. In addition, recent governments have pursued policies that have discouraged foreign investment in a country that traditionally has depended heavily on such investment. This, coupled with a falloff in tourism, has complicated the nation's already difficult economic situation. Unemployment is high, and ghettos of unemployed and underemployed surround Kingston, the capital. Crime is a serious problem.

Guinea was the only country in the French community to vote for complete independence during the 1958 referendum. The break was abrupt, and the political life of the country has been turbulent ever since. Although top political figures, including President Ahmed Sekou Toure, have remained in power, lower echelons of essential technical people have been replaced several times. The government professes to be socialist, not Communist, but for years the Russians have provided essential aid and services. (In recent years, however, ties with the Soviet Union appear to have been weakening.) The government claims to be struggling to export its "revolution" to neighboring countries and throughout Africa. Outside the bauxite sector, it has banned private enterprise. These political and economic policies have driven roughly 20 percent of the country's population, primarily the better educated and trained, into exile, and seriously strained its relations with neighboring states, such as the Ivory Coast.

Surinam, like Jamaica, has a racial problem. While most of the population is black, control over the economy rests largely with whites of Dutch origin. Moreover, a large number of Brazilians have emigrated to the southern regions of the country. In some areas they constitute a majority of the population. The potential for political upheaval is illustrated by a rebellion in March 1980 that led to a change in government, but the likelihood of physical disruption does not appear as great as in the other three countries.

Perhaps the most unstable of all is Guyana. It, too, has a racial problem. As in Jamaica and Surinam, a white minority enjoys much of the wealth and economic power. The rest of the population is composed of East Indians and blacks, and relations between these two groups are strained as well. Recent governments have pushed Marxist or radical policies, which has discouraged investment in the country and helped depress the local economy. Finally, large portions of Guyana are claimed by Venezuela, Brazil, and Surinam. Indeed, in Venezuela it is illegal to publish a map that does not show nearly half of Guyana as a part of Venezuela waiting to be reclaimed.

The potential over the near term for disruption in alumina, aluminum ingot, and aluminum scrap supplies appears far less than for bauxite. It is possible that strikes could disrupt shipments of alumina and aluminum ingot coming from Australia, Canada, and domestic plants, but the historical record suggests that labor difficulties are not likely to create significant shortages. Strikes are usually anticipated, and inventories built up. In addition, a loss of production in one country can often be made up by an increase in imports from other areas. Strikes can, however, aggravate shortages that arise for other reasons. For example, the 1968 strike in the U.S. aluminum industry reduced output for that year by 4 to 5 percent below what had been anticipated. Had this strike occurred during the tight market of 1973-74, the shortages experienced then would have been considerably more serious.

Demand Surges. Aluminum consumption in the United States has grown at an average annual rate of 6.3 percent since 1950. This average rate, however, hides the substantial differences in growth that occur from year to year. Aluminum demand is highly concentrated in a few economic sectors, namely, construction, transportation equipment, and cans and containers. With the exception of the last, the output of these end-using industries tends to be highly sensitive to fluctuations in the business cycle. In addition, during periods of economic expansion, fabricators and other users of aluminum products attempt to build up their inventories. This is partly because their sales are up, but also because they fear supplies may become difficult to obtain.

The shortages of primary aluminum experienced during 1973 and 1974 were caused in large part by a surge in demand. The simultaneous peaking of the business cycle in the United States, Western Europe, and Japan was largely responsible for this surge in demand, though it was accentuated by speculative activity.

Despite their poor performance in recent years, a strong recovery of the economies of the major industrialized nations is possible between now and 1985. Given the relatively high levels at which the aluminum industry is currently using its existing capacity, such a resurgence in demand would likely cause significant shortages of primary aluminum. (See chapters 5 and 7.) A similar capacity shortage exists for alumina and, as detailed in chapter 5, may actually be more severe than that for aluminum.

Since aluminum scrap can substitute for primary aluminum in casting and other uses, a shortage of primary aluminum would almost certainly spill over into the scrap market. A surge in metal demand could also result in shortages of alumina, if the latter is, in fact, more constrained in its capacity, but is not likely to produce shortages of bauxite, where output is less constrained. Moreover, while the output of some mines may be constrained by port capacity or other facilities, some open-pit bauxite mines can increase output relatively easily and quickly.

Natural Disasters. A historical review suggests that inadequate snow cover and rainfall in the Pacific Northwest, where some 30 percent of U.S. smelter capacity is located, is the principal natural threat to aluminum supplies. Insufficient precipitation reduces the amount of hydroelectric power that can be produced. The Bonneville Power Administration has more than once been forced to cut back power to aluminum producers in recent years; this reduced U.S. aluminum production in 1973 and again in 1977. Losses during the 1977 drought were significant--300,000 to 500,000 tons-- which is equivalent to between 5 and 10 percent of U.S. consumption. A similar, though somewhat smaller, problem occurred in the winter of 1979-80.

Demand for power in the Pacific Northwest has been growing rapidly. Since aluminum producers purchase power on interruptible contract, it is possible that additional cutbacks in power supplies will be necessary between now and 1985 in this area and perhaps other areas as well. The significance of such interruptions, like those for strikes, will depend greatly on market conditions at the time. Should they occur when demand is weak and idle capacity is available elsewhere, they will create few, if any, supply problems. On the other hand, should they occur when a surge in demand or other factors have laid the basis for a shortage, they could either tip the situation into one of significant shortages or enlarge the magnitude of a shortage that already exists.

Summary. The principal threat, in our judgment, to U.S. supplies of both trihydrate and mixed bauxite is the possibility that production in Jamaica, Guinea, Surinam, or Guyana will be disrupted by internal strife or military conflict with neighboring states. Mining operations are likely to be a prime target for sabotage, given their economic importance to those states. If equipment and facilities are damaged, it would likely require several weeks, and perhaps several months, to return to normal operations. For this reason, table 9-4 assesses as "moderate" the probability of a shortage in trihydrate bauxite lasting up to 2 months and cutting off up to 50 percent of U.S. requirements. Since no one country accounts for 50 percent of U.S. consumption of trihydrate bauxite, and since it is unlikely that this type of disruption would occur in two countries simultaneously, the probability of a shortage that exceeds 50 percent of U.S. requirements is judged to be nil. A small probability is assigned to an interruption of up to 50 percent of U.S. requirements for 2-6 months, since in some instances it could take that long for damaged facilities to be repaired.

The probabilities for shortages of mixed bauxite are similar to those for trihydrate bauxite, with the exception that a moderate probability had to be assigned to a large interruption of U.S. supplies lasting up to 2 months and a small probability of such an interruption for longer periods. This is because Jamaica supplies some 80 percent of U.S. requirements of mixed bauxite, and so an interruption of supplies from that country would constitute a large shortage.

For alumina, the probabilities of an interruption in supply of up to 20 percent of U.S. requirements are assessed as high for 2 months or less, and as moderate for a period of from 2-6 months. This assessment is based on two possible situations: (1) alumina imports from Jamaica could be cut off by internal strife within that country, (2) bauxite imports into the United States could be restricted, thus forcing some domestic alumina plants to cut back their production.

For aluminum ingot and scrap, the most likely cause of shortages in our judgment is a surge in demand between now and 1985. Should there be a strong concurrent economic recovery in the industrialized countries some time over the next six years, demand for aluminum products would increase sharply, and owing to capacity limitations, may well exceed available supplies by over 20 percent. Although the probability is lower, demand could conceivably exceed supply under such circumstance by over 50 percent. For this reason, along with the fact that an economic recovery is likely to last more than 6 months, it is judged moderately possible that the United States will experience a period lasting at least 6 months when available U.S. supplies will be insufficient to satisfy 20 percent or more of U.S. demand (not considering any limitation of demand by consequent higher prices). A smaller probability is assigned to a shortage so severe that demand would exceed supply by 50 percent for a period of over 6 months, and a higher probability to a shortage of a smaller magnitude generated by a near-synchronization of business cycle peaks in industrial countries. Since a shortage of aluminum ingot would spill over into the scrap market, comparable probabilities are assigned to aluminum scrap.

The probabilities that the United States will encounter, between now and 1985, shortages of aluminum in its various forms are shown in table 9-4.

Table 9-4. Estimated Probabilities of Shortages of Aluminum Mineral Commodities for U.S. Industrial Consumption Through 1985[a]

Size[b]	Less than 2 months	2-6 months	Over 6 months
Small (5-20%)			
Trihydrate bauxite	Moderate	Small	Nil
Mixed bauxite	Moderate	Small	Nil
Alumina	High	Moderate	Small
Aluminum ingot	High	High	High
Aluminum scrap	High	High	High
Medium (20-50%)			
Trihydrate bauxite	Moderate	Small	Nil
Mixed bauxite	Moderate	Small	Nil
Alumina	Moderate	Small	Nil
Aluminum ingot	Moderate	Moderate	Moderate
Aluminum scrap	Moderate	Moderate	Moderate
Large (50-100%)			
Trihydrate bauxite	Nil	Nil	Nil
Mixed bauxite	Moderate	Small	Nil
Alumina	Nil	Nil	Nil
Aluminum ingot	Small	Small	Small
Aluminum scrap	Small	Small	Small

[a]Approximate arithmetic equivalent of the probabilities: Nil - less than 2%; small - 2-10%; moderate - 10-25%; high - over 25%.

[b]The size or magnitude of a shortage is measured in terms of gross shortfalls from the consumption rate that would otherwise have prevailed at the price that would otherwise have prevailed, before allowance for that part of any substitute supply that responds to a price rise.

Shortages of less than 5 percent of consumption rate were considered a priori to be insignificant.

Copper

Vulnerability

The United States, Japan, and Western Europe are the major consumers
of copper, accounting for nearly 90 percent of world usage outside the
centrally planned countries. Consumption in Brazil, Mexico, and certain
other developing countries has been growing rapidly, though, and is likely
to become more important in the future.

Of the major consuming countries in market-economy countries, only
the United States comes close to enjoying self-sufficiency in copper production. It is the world's largest producing country, and in recent years
has mined 80 percent or more of its requirements. While Japan and Western
Europe mine small amounts of copper, they must import over 80 percent of
their needs. They depend primarily on Chile, Canada, Indonesia, Zambia,
Zaire, the Philippines, Peru, Papua New Guinea, and Australia. (See
chapter 3.)

Unlike aluminum, the major mining countries tend to process their
copper ores domestically and export mostly refined metal. However, in
recent years, the share of ore and concentrate in copper trade has steadily
grown, while that of blister has declined. This change can be attributed
largely to the economic recovery of Japan and that country's preference
to import copper concentrate and process it domestically. In 1976, for
example, some 60 percent of all copper ore and concentrate entering trade
was destined for Japan. Most of these shipments came from Canada, the
Philippines, and Papua New Guinea. The United States, Germany, and Norway
also import some copper ore and concentrate, though their imports, unlike
those of Japan, represent a small portion of their total domestic copper
requirements.

Trade in blister, which now accounts for less than 20 percent of
copper trade, is also largely confined to a few importing and exporting
countries. The largest importer, Belgium, is responsible for over 40
percent of this trade. Two other countries, Germany and Britain, account
for an additional 30 percent. Shipments to Belgium come largely from
Zaire, a former Belgian colony, while those going to Germany and Britain
are mostly from Chile and South Africa (including Namibia).

The principal importers of refined copper are Germany, Britain, France, Italy, the United States, and Japan. The major exporting countries providing these countries with needed imports are Zambia, Chile, and Canada. Belgium is also a major exporter of refined copper, produced largely from blister imported from Zaire. Almost all its exports are purchased by other European countries.

World copper reserves correspond roughly with mine production. The United States and Chile each have slightly under 20 percent of the total. The USSR, Canada, Peru, Zambia, and Zaire possess between 5 and 10 percent. The Philippines, Papua New Guinea, Poland, and Australia, though their share of total reserves is under 5 percent, also have identified significant quantities.

Most copper scrap is generated in the industrialized countries and is used internally by those countries, though the United States and Western European countries do some exporting, largely to each other, as well as to Japan and Korea. U.S. exports of copper scrap have been recently in a range of around 5 to 10 percent of total U.S. secondary copper production, but reached 14 percent in 1975.

Probability of Supply Contingencies

Deliberate Disruptions. It is probable that foreign governments, through cartel efforts, embargoes, or other deliberate actions, could significantly disrupt U.S. imports of either copper ore and concentrate or blister copper. As noted, however, the United States is largely self-sufficient in copper production and its imports account for only a small fraction of the consumption of ore and concentrate (around 2 percent in 1978) and of blister (5 percent). An interruption in supplies to Western Europe or Japan would probably not cause much diversion of domestic supplies to those areas. Since the major firms producing copper in the United States are vertically integrated, they would continue to ship their ores and concentrates to their own smelters, and their blister to their own refineries.

At the refined metal stage, the United States is slightly more vulnerable. In recent years, imports of refined metal have varied between 5 and 17 percent of consumption. While this is not a large

percentage, if supplies to other major consuming countries were interrupted, it is possible that some copper normally shipped to the United
States would be delivered to other countries. In addition, since the
U.S. market for refined copper is closely integrated with the world market,
a disruption of supplies abroad would likely cause a significant increase
in the U.S. price of copper. It is true that in the past, at least, most
copper has been sold in the United States at a domestic producers' price,
while prevailing prices elsewhere are tied to the London Metal Exchange
(LME) price. For a long time, however, the U.S. producers' price has
tended to follow the LME price, albeit with some lag and with lesser
amplitude of fluctuation. Moreover, several major producers have recently
abandoned the producers' price and are now selling copper on the basis of
the price set by the Commodity Exchange (Comex) in New York. Since the
Comex and LME prices are both free market prices, they tend to parallel
one another quite closely. (See chapter 6.)

This suggests that restrictions on supplies imposed by the major
copper exporting countries, if they were sufficient to disrupt the world
market, could affect the United States as well, even if domestic producers
did not participate in such actions. This raises the question of how
likely the major exporting countries are to engage in such efforts, either
individually or as a group.

The probability of a country's acting alone appears quite low. Even
the largest exporter, Chile, accounts for less than 25 percent of world
exports. Consequently, any country that acted unilaterally could cut off
only a minor part of world supplies. If excess stocks or capacity were
available in other producing countries, as is presently the case, its
action would have even less of an impact. Moreover, the cost to the
country would be high in terms of lost foreign exchange and government
revenues. In addition, new investment would likely be diverted to other
producing countries, as consuming countries tried to increase imports
from more secure sources. In some cases, the consuming countries might
also engage in economic or political retaliation.

The prospects for collective action by the major exporting countries
are not much more favorable. In 1967, Chile, Peru, Zambia, and Zaire
established the Intergovernmental Council of Copper Exporting Countries

(CIPEC, after its name in French). In 1975 Indonesia joined CIPEC, and Australia and Papua New Guinea became associate (nonvoting) members. A year later Mauritania became a full member. Despite the considerable concern over depressed copper prices expressed by all members in recent years, CIPEC has not been successful in raising prices. Following the collapse of the copper market in 1974, CIPEC tried to implement a scheme whereby all its members would cut back exports by 15 percent. A number of members apparently did not honor this commitment, and so the effort had little or no price effect.

Dismayed by their inability to cooperate effectively, CIPEC members turned in 1976 to the UNCTAD Integrated Programme for Commodities (IPC), in the hope that within IPC an international commodity agreement for copper that included both producers and consumers would be able to deal effectively with the instability of the copper market, and particularly with the depressed price. So far, little progress has been made.

The record of these past attempts by major exporting countries to cooperate within UNCTAD suggests that within the near future there is little likelihood that foreign governments, acting together, will succeed in restricting copper exports for either political or economic reasons. In addition to the historical evidence, there are other reasons for suspecting that at least certain of the major exporting countries would hesitate to participate in any such effort. Chile, for example, under its present government, is anxious to expand its share of the world copper market. It is trying to attract foreign capital back into that important sector of its economy and therefore has little interest in arrangements that require cutbacks in production. Canada, another major exporter, has close political and economic ties not only with the United States, but with Western Europe and Japan as well. These other interests are likely to discourage its participation in any joint attempt to restrict world supplies or to push copper prices up sharply. Finally, all except the most developed copper producing countries must to some extent be concerned about the impact that a deliberate attempt to disrupt copper supplies would have on the efforts of the major consuming countries to move ahead with deep-sea nodule mining.

Turning to secondary copper, one finds little or no probability that foreign governments would disrupt U.S. supplies. The United States is on balance an exporter of copper scrap. It is possible that U.S. scrap would be diverted overseas if a severe shortage occurred in Western Europe or Japan, but such a shortage would not arise as the result of a deliberate intent by governments of the other major scrap generating countries, which are the selfsame consuming countries, to withhold supplies.

Incidental Disruptions. For some of the same reasons just discussed, there is little likelihood that U.S. supplies of copper ore and concentrate, blister, or scrap will be disrupted between now and 1985 as the incidental result of political or military actions. U.S. supplies of these three copper materials come for the most part from domestic sources. In the case of scrap, where dealers are not vertically integrated and thus free to sell abroad, an interruption in supplies overseas caused by a political or military disruption could create higher prices and shortages in the United States. However, the disruption would have to occur in either Western Europe or Japan, and again the likelihood of this seems low.

Refined copper, however, presents a different situation. The United States depends for its imports of refined copper principally on Zambia, Canada, and Chile; for two of these countries, between now and 1985, there is a significant possibility of political or military actions that might disrupt supplies. The dependence of Belgium, another important supplier of refined copper to the world, on Zairian ore, puts that part of the world supply also at risk, with the attendant possibility of derived price rises in the United States. The impact of any of these events would fall essentially on the consumers of refined copper, since any induced increases in domestic ore prices would be passed through.

Over the past decade Chile has gone through a period of political turmoil. The banning of political parties and elections leaves those opposing the Pinochet government few alternatives for legally expressing their opposition. When, in 1977, workers at the El Teniente copper mine went on strike, it was the first strike since the military junta had taken control. In general, antigovernment demonstrations and protests have become more widespread in recent years.

The Shaba province of Zaire, with its rich copper and cobalt operations, suffered through a serious civil war following the country's independence from Belgium in 1960, and more recently from invasions launched
by rebels exiled in Angola. These actions disrupted mining operations and
encouraged non-nationals with needed technical skills to flee the country.
Given the weak central government in Kinshasa, political developments
could again adversely affect copper production and exports, as they have
in the past.

Very few strikes have much of an effect on the world output of copper.
A major exception was the 1967 strike of the United Steelworkers against
almost the entire U.S. copper industry, which lasted nearly a year. Estimates of the amount of copper lost range from 0.8 to 1.5 million tons.
At the time, U.S. production was running about 1.5 million tons of refined
copper a year, and world production outside the centrally planned countries
about 5.5 million tons. Since then, a strike lasting several months in
1971 caused the loss of between 0.2 and 0.3 million tons; in 1977 another
strike curtailed U.S. output by 0.1 to 0.2 million tons; and a major
strike was under way in 1980.

Demand Surges. Copper, like many other mineral commodities, is
largely used in the construction, capital equipment, transportation, and
consumer durable sectors. Since the output of these sectors tends to
fluctuate sharply with changes in the business cycle, the demand for
copper is highly sensitive over the short term to changes in national
income.

This raises the possibility that a resurgence in the business cycle
within the next five years or so might be a cause of copper shortages.
There is now widespread recognition that the simultaneous peaking of
the business cycle in the United States, Western Europe, and Japan during
1973 and early 1974 was in large part responsible for the severe copper
shortages encountered at that time. Still, there are those who argue
that the situation is different today, and that the likelihood of copper
shortages between now and 1985 as the result of demand surges is small.

Those that adhere to the latter position maintain that the 1973-74
economic boom was unusual, that in the past the business cycles of the

United States, Europe, and Japan have typically been out of phase. If so, an increase in demand generated by a boom in the United States could be met by diverting copper from other areas. Those who hold this view point out, moreover, that the idle capacity and large stocks of copper lately depressing the market could be drawn upon to meet any surge in demand that might arise over the next few years. They also anticipate that the average growth in copper demand will be slower in the future, in part because the Japanese economy will not continue to expand at the brisk rate experienced over the past decade.

While these points are generally valid, one should not rule out entirely the possibility of copper shortages induced by demand surges between now and 1985. Since the mid-1960s there has been tendency for the business cycles of the United States, Europe, and Japan to move increasingly together—which is not at all surprising given the growing economic interdependence of these areas. Thus a simultaneous peaking of the business cycles in the industrial countries, such as occurred in 1973-74, may be less unusual in the future than it has been in the past.

Moreover, if copper demand is to grow more slowly in the future, the same is true for capacity. The depressed market conditions that have plagued the copper industry since mid-1974 have discouraged new investment. Only one new project has been under development—La Caridad in Mexico. While many known deposits exist that could be developed should the need arise, it takes five years or longer to bring such deposits into production. In the meanwhile, only a group of smaller projects will be providing additions to world copper capacity (see chapter 5). However, present capacity, including the 5 to 20 percent that is idle in the major producing countries, along with the new capacity being built, is sufficient to meet our projected demand.

Copper stocks that overhang the industry appear large, but their importance in fending off shortages, should a surge in demand occur, can easily be exaggerated. The excess would quickly evaporate if the world were to experience an economic boom similar to that of 1973-74.

Moreover, a significant turnaround in the economy would increase the level of stocks that copper consumers would want to hold. Copper fabricators generally keep their inventories at a minimum to reduce their carrying costs. Should these firms anticipate difficulties in obtaining copper, they would want to build up inventories. It is also likely that speculators who are neither copper producers nor consumers would try to increase their holdings in anticipation of a rise in the price of this commodity.[7]

These considerations suggest that between now and 1985 the world may in fact face a significant shortage of copper due to a surge in demand. The most immediate capacity bottlenecks would be encountered at the mining and smelting stages, but the lack of feedstock would in turn also cause shortages of refined copper. Since secondary copper is a substitute for virgin metal, a shortage of ore and blister would also lead to shortages of copper scrap.

Natural Disasters. From time to time natural disasters interrupt copper production. Mine disasters, water shortages caused by droughts, landslides, washed-out bridges, earthquakes, flooding, and avalanches have all taken their toll. Most of these disasters, however, have affected only one facility and only for a limited period of time. Probably the most serious incident was the cave-in at the Mufulira underground mine in Zambia during 1970. Eighty-nine miners were killed in this accident, and an estimated 150,000 tons of copper lost. Even so, this loss represented less than 3 percent of all the copper produced that year outside the centrally planned countries.

Summary. Of the various factors reviewed in the preceding sections that might give rise to copper shortages between now and 1985, the most serious, in our view, is the possibility of a surge in demand. It is possible that strikes, political or military actions in certain producing countries, and other factors could interrupt the flow of copper from a particular country for a time. However, until the demand for copper recovers and is pushing on available capacity, the impact of such interruptions, should they occur, would be modest at most.

---

[7]In addition, some of the inflation-related speculation in gold and silver is believed to have spilled over into copper.

A surge in demand for copper in the United States, Western Europe, or Japan that is not offset by a countervailing decline in demand elsewhere seems relatively probable between now and 1985. For this reason, the likelihood of a small shortage, equivalent to 5 to 20 percent of U.S. consumption sometime during this period, is rated as high in table 9-5. Moreover, since cyclical swings in demand tend to last for a number of months, such a shortage would likely persist for more than 6 months.

The probability of a medium or large shortage, one that is equivalent to 20 percent or more of U.S. copper consumption, would likely require a simultaneous surge in demand in several industrial countries. The probability that a shortage might occur some time before the end of 1985 we believe to be above 10 percent and probably closer to 25 percent. As a result, the likelihood of a medium-sized shortage is indicated in table 9-5 as "moderate." A shortage of half or more of what would otherwise have been the rate of industrial consumption, save for scrap, seems generally of lesser probability.

While the United States will probably have spare refining capacity, there is unlikely to be enough blister copper, in such a contingency situation, to feed it. U.S. demand for ore, on the other hand, will probably be constrained by the insufficiency of smelting capacity.

Though the United States is normally self-sufficient in copper scrap, this is a commodity which, because of the nature of its collection and marketing, is readily siphoned off in large proportion by foreign purchasers (or ultimately could be retained domestically only at the cost of sharp price rises). Thus, scrap would participate in the shortages.

It should be emphasized that all these estimates are conditional upon the probably unrealistic assumption of no federal export control actions. They do allow for private rationing of all items save scrap, to the disadvantage of would-be foreign purchasers.

Table 9-5. Estimated Probabilities of Shortages in Copper Mineral Commodities for U.S. Industrial Consumption Through 1985[a]

Size[b]	Less than 2 months	2-6 months	Over 6 months
Small (5-20%)			
Copper ore	Moderate	Moderate	Moderate
Blister copper	High	High	High
Refined copper	High	High	High
Copper scrap	High	High	High
Medium (20-50%)			
Copper ore	Small	Small	Small
Blister copper	Moderate	Moderate	Moderate
Refined copper	Moderate	Moderate	Moderate
Copper scrap	Moderate	Moderate	Moderate
Large (50-100%)			
Copper ore	Nil	Nil	Nil
Blister copper	Small	Small	Small
Refined copper	Small	Small	Small
Copper scrap	Small	Small	Small

[a]Approximate arithmetic equivalent of the probabilities: nil - less than 2%, small - 2-10%; moderate - 10-25%; high - over 25%.

[b]The size or magnitude of a shortage is measured in terms of gross shortfalls from the consumption rate that would otherwise have prevailed, at the price that would otherwise have prevailed, before allowance for that part of any substitute supply that responds to a price rise.

Shortages of less than 5 percent of consumption rate were considered a priori to be insignificant.

Lead

Vulnerability

The production of primary lead involves three major steps: (1) the mining of ore and its milling into concentrate, (2) the smelting of concentrate into bullion, (3) the conversion of bullion into refined metal. In the United States, however, steps 2 and 3 are normally integrated and bullion is thus a minor article of commerce. Secondary lead is derived from used batteries, drosses, residues, and other forms of new and old scrap, and is a major factor in world supplies. In 1977, for example, lead produced from scrap accounted for 46 percent of gross U.S. industrial consumption at the refined lead level.

The United States is the largest user of lead, and is responsible for somewhat more than a third of the lead consumed outside the centrally planned countries. Other large users are Japan, Britain, Germany, France, and Italy. Along with the United States, these countries account for about 70 percent of free world consumption.

The United States is also the world's largest producer of lead. As a result, imports of ore and concentrate and of refined metal have so far accounted for only a minor portion of domestic consumption. Most of these imports have been refined metal, though the share of ore and concentrate has ranged recently from 29 to 46 percent, depending on the year. It is likely that in the future (see chapter 5), imports will gradually regain some of their former greater importance as a proportion of the U.S. lead supply.

Except for Britain, the other major consuming countries also produce significant quantities of lead ore. Their mine production, however, is appreciably less than their imports of ore and concentrate plus refined lead. There are also differences among these countries in the composition of their lead imports. Britain and Italy, like the United States, import mostly refined metal, while Japan, Germany, and France import primarily ore and concentrate. The dependence of these countries on imports is reduced by the fact that, with the exception of Italy, they all satisfy between a fourth and a half of their lead requirements from secondary production. Moreover, most of the recycled scrap they use in producing secondary lead is generated domestically.

After the United States, the major producers of lead ore, in order of their importance, are Australia, Canada, Mexico, Peru, and Yugoslavia. These countries plus the United States accounted for 70 percent of world mine production outside the centrally planned countries in 1976.

World trade patterns for both ore and concentrate and for refined metal tend to be diversified, with each of the major importing and exporting countries trading with a number of partners. (See chapter 3.) The largest exporter of ore and concentrate is Canada, which ships about half its exports to Japan. The second largest exporter, Peru, trades principally with Belgium and Japan. Germany, which after Japan is the largest importer of ore and concentrate, obtains its supplies principally from Sweden, with smaller amounts coming from a variety of sources, including the United States.

The largest importers of refined metal are the United States, Britain, and Italy. The United States relies primarily on Canada and Mexico and secondarily on Peru and Yugoslavia. The first two countries each accounted for nearly a third of U.S. refined lead imports in 1976, and Peru and Yugoslavia each for about a sixth. The United Kingdom acquires almost all its imports in approximately equal amounts from Australia and Canada, both Commonwealth members. Italy obtains the largest share of its imports, as much as 25 percent in recent years, from Germany. It also depends significantly on Australia, Peru, and Mexico.

Although the scrap used to produce secondary lead is largely generated internally by principal consuming countries, some trade in this commodity does occur. Destinations tend to vary from year to year. The largest exporter is the United States, with important shipments at times to Canada, Western Europe, Japan, and Korea. The United Kingdom and Germany are also important exporters; they market their scrap primarily in Europe.

Probability of Supply Contingencies

Deliberate Disruptions. The probability that U.S. supplies of lead ore and concentrate will be interrupted or restricted between now and 1985

by the deliberate actions of foreign governments must be rated as extremely low for two reasons. First, the United States currently imports less
than 15 percent of its lead ore and concentrate requirements. Since
domestic mine production is carried out principally by large, vertically
integrated firms, an interruption of supplies to Europe or Japan would
probably not cause a diversion of domestic ore and concentrate abroad.
Second, a large number of countries export lead ore and concentrate. The
largest exporter, Canada, accounts for only slightly more than 20 percent
of the total entering international trade, and the share of most other
exporters is much smaller. This makes it impossible for any one country
to restrict supplies effectively without the cooperation of other exporting countries. Among the major exporting countries, moreover, are Canada,
Australia, Sweden, Ireland, Greenland, and Greece, which have close economic and political ties with the major consuming countries. For this
and other reasons, they are not likely to participate in a cooperative
effort to restrict ore and concentrate supplies.

Similarly for refined lead, an interruption in U.S. supplies caused
by the deliberate actions of exporting countries seems unlikely. Imports
of refined lead, like those of ore, have lately tended to run less than
15 percent of total refined lead (including secondary) consumption. Just
how much importance should be attached to this high level of self-sufficiency, however, is less clear in the case of refined lead than of ore
and concentrate, since the U.S. market is at least partially integrated
with the world market. As detailed in chapter 6 there is, for example,
a tendency for the domestic producers' price of lead to follow the London
Metal Exchange (LME) price. Consequently, an interruption in supplies to
Europe and Japan would probably have price repercussions in the U.S.
market. Still, the likelihood that foreign producers will restrict their
exports seems very low. As with ore and concentrate, no one producer is
important enough to contemplate acting alone. Collective action would
require the support of Australia, the largest exporting country, and
Canada, the second largest exporting country. In addition, Belgium,
Germany, and the United Kingdom are important exporters. It is improbable
that these countries would participate in a collective effort to restrict
supplies.

Nor are U.S. supplies of lead scrap vulnerable to the actions of foreign governments. The United States generates nearly all the scrap it consumes and is the world's principal exporter as well. Canada, Britain, Germany, the Netherlands, and other European countries are also important exporters. These countries are not likely to withhold their scrap to push up prices or to pressure importing countries into changing their policies.

Incidental Disruptions. The United States imports nearly all of its lead ore and concentrate from four countries--Canada, Honduras, Australia, and Peru. Both Canada and Australia are politically stable countries. The one political issue that could still cause serious dissension in Canada in the near future concerns the Quebec separatist movement, led by Rene Levesque and the Parti Quebecois. Canada's long history of resolving its problems peacefully, however, suggests that this issue will not cause serious disruption of lead supplies. The prospects for political stability are less favorable in Honduras and Peru. Honduras has been under military rule since December 1972, and Peru suffered from internal turmoil over the last decade.

Despite these conditions, however, the likelihood that political or military developments would significantly interupt U.S. ore and concentrate supplies is low, since imports from any one country constitute no more than 7 percent of U.S. requirements. There seems little probability that political or military actions would interrupt supplies from two or more countries at the same time. While an interruption in supplies to Europe or Japan might cause the diversion of some ore and concentrate that otherwise would be sent to the United States, the impact on total domestic supplies would be small, given the minor portion of U.S. requirements that is imported. The exposure is likely to grow, over time, as the import percentage increases, but would still be small.

At the refined metal stage, the major exporters are, with the possible exception of Peru, relatively stable countries. Australia and Canada are the largest exporters, followed by Mexico, Peru, and Belgium. However, given the ties between the United States and world lead markets, the relative U.S. self-sufficiency does not provide complete insulation from

world developments. Thus, there could be some scrambling for supplies
in the event of an interruption, with a consequent sharp impact on prices.

Lead scrap is generated and processed largely in the major consuming
countries. Consequently, its supply is not vulnerable to political or
military disruptions abroad.

The lead industry has been subjected to a fairly large number of
strikes in the United States, Canada, Australia, Peru, and other producing
countries. However, most strikes interrupt production at only one or
a few facilities, for a limited time. The major exception occurred in
1967 and early 1968 when a United Steelworkers strike idled 42 percent
of lead refining capacity in the United States for 8 months.

Other Disruptions. Lead is used primarily in the manufacture of
storage batteries. In the United States, about 50 percent of all the
lead consumed currently goes into automobile batteries. Its second
largest (though a relatively declining) use is in additives to gasolines.
In addition, sizable quantities of lead are consumed in the electrical
and construction sectors to protect underground and underwater cables
from corrosion and moisture, to dampen the transmission of sound, and for
many other purposes. Lead is also needed in significant amounts to produce paints and ammunition.

The demand for some of these uses remains relatively stable over the
business cycle. The output of replacement batteries, gasoline additives,
and ammunition is little affected by swings in the economy. This is not
the case, however, for other uses--the batteries in new automobiles,
electrical uses, and applications in the construction sector. As a result,
the demand for lead does respond to changes in the overall level of economic activity. Moreover, lead demand is likely to become more sensitive
to changes in the business cycles as the relative importance of several
end uses whose output is little affected by overall business conditions
declines.

For these reasons, an economic recovery in the United States, particularly if it coincided with a similar development in Western Europe
or Japan, could appreciably increase lead demand at some point in the
future. If this happened, bottlenecks would most likely occur in both

the mining and refining sectors. As detailed in chapter 5, the world capacity/consumption ratio for refined lead is becoming tighter. Given a demand surge, there might not be enough facilities available to meet added world requirements. In the United States specifically, there does appear to be some excess capacity, but this would probably not be enough to counter both the increase in domestic demand and the decline in lead imports that would accompany a world demand surge. Ore supplies would also fall short, but not to the same extent as refined metal, since demand would be limited by the bottleneck in smelting capacity.

It is unlikely that such a problem could be significantly offset by an increase in secondary production. This would require excess stocks of scrap that could be drawn upon. Most lead scrap comes from the re-cycling of batteries; since this is a relatively cheap source of lead, most batteries are recycled rather promptly, and large, standby inventories that could be drawn on during shortages are not normally maintained.[8] Much metallic lead (and its alloys) is locked up in structures and objects whose scrappage does not respond to the business cycle. In any case, an increase in secondary lead to compensate for insufficient mine capacity would require that the secondary industry maintain capacity appreciably above normal requirements, and there is little likelihood that this will be the case.

The probability of natural disasters that could curtail lead production is small, and their past impact on world lead supplies has been negligible. This is not surprising given the wide geographic dispersion of lead mines and refining facilities.

Summary. The most likely threat to lead supplies comes from a surge in demand caused by a strong upturn in the business cycle. Given the sensitivity of lead demand to changes in overall level of economic activity, and the likelihood that this sensitivity will increase in the future, a strong economic recovery in the United States, Western Europe,

---

[8] During the current period of readjustment of secondary capacity for greater recovery of soft rather than antimonial, lead, one might expect some used battery inventory build-up.

or Japan that is not offset by a recession elsewhere could easily produce
a shortage in the United States within the range of 5 to 20 percent of
U.S. consumption. On the assumption that the probability of such a recovery over the next five years or so is in excess of 25 percent, table
9-6 rates the likelihood of a small shortage of refined lead as "high."
Since economic booms typically last longer than 6 months, such a shortage
would last over 6 months.

Since capacity at the refined lead level (including capacity for battery lead reprocessing and other secondary recovery) is likely to be
tight, there is even a "moderate" (20-25 percent) chance that a lead shortage could exceed 20 percent of the otherwise achievable consumption level.

Because of the capacity constraints on both primary smelting and
secondary lead recovery (soft and antimonial), consumption of ore or
scrap could not respond fully to any demand surge. Thus, there would be
lesser shortfalls at the ore and scrap levels. Since the two original
lead sources are in large measure substitutable for one another (assuming
sufficiency of both pig lead and secondary recovery capacity), any given
degree of feedstock shortfall would have to be equally attributed to both.

Zinc

Vulnerability

The production of primary zinc involves two principal steps: first,
the mining and concentrating of ore; second, the smelting of concentrate
into refined metal. Zinc metal is then used for galvanizing, brass and
bronze products, castings, and rolled zinc products. A considerable
amount of zinc is recovered from scrap, both new and old, but much of
this is copper-base scrap (brass and bronze). Zinc-base scrap as such
fluctuates at around 10 percent of total industrial zinc supply and is
thus of only limited importance. This section therefore omits any consideration of shortages of zinc-base scrap, but instead focuses on possible shortages of ore and concentrate and of refined metal.

Table 9-6. Estimated Probabilities of Shortages of Lead Mineral
Commodities for U.S. Industrial Consumption
Through 1985[a]

Size[b]	Less than 2 months	2-6 months	Over 6 months
Small (5-20%)			
Lead ore	Moderate	Moderate	Moderate
Refined lead (including antimonial)	High	High	High
Lead scrap	Moderate	Moderate	Moderate
Medium (20-50%)			
Lead ore	Small	Small	Small
Refined lead	Moderate	Moderate	Moderate
Lead scrap	Small	Small	Small
Large (50-100%)			
Lead ore	Nil	Nil	Nil
Refined lead	Small	Small	Small
Lead scrap	Nil	Nil	Nil

[a]Approximate arithmetic equivalent of the probabilities: nil - less
than 2%, small - 2-10%; moderate - 10-25%; high - over 25%.

[b]The size or magnitude of a shortage is measured in terms of gross
shortfalls from the consumption rate that would otherwise have prevailed,
at the price that would otherwise have prevailed, before allowance for
that part of any substitute supply that responds to a price rise. Shortages of less than 5 percent of consumption rate were considered a priori
to be insignificant.

The United States is the world's largest consumer of zinc. Excluding the centrally planned countries, the second largest consumer is Japan, which is followed by the major industrialized countries of Western Europe—Germany, France, Britain, Italy, Belgium—and Canada. These countries use some 70 percent of all zinc consumed in the market economy countries. (See chapter 1.)

The largest free-world producers of zinc ore and concentrate are, in order of 1977 importance, Canada, Australia, Peru, the United States, Japan, Mexico, Germany, Sweden, and Yugoslavia.[9] These countries are responsible for somewhat more than 70 percent of the zinc ore mined outside the centrally planned countries.

Although the United States is a major producer of zinc, it buys abroad more than half of its requirements, mostly as refined metal. The two other major consuming countries that also produce substantial quantities of zinc ore are Japan and Germany. Like the United States, they supplement domestic production with foreign zinc, importing more than half of their needs. However, these countries import primarily ore and concentrate, which they then process domestically.

World trade patterns for zinc, like those for lead, tend to be diversified. (See chapter 3.) The three principal exporters of ore and concentrate are Canada, Peru, and Australia, which together accounted for some 60 percent of the ore and concentrate entering international trade in 1976. Canada sells most of its exports to Belgium, Germany, and Japan. Peru roughly divides its shipments between Japan and a number of European countries. Australia's largest customer is Japan, followed by the Netherlands and Belgium.

The principal exporters of refined zinc are Canada, Belgium (which depends mostly on Canada for ore and concentrate), Australia, Mexico, the Netherlands (which processes mostly Australian ore and concentrate), and Finland. These six countries produced over 60 percent of the zinc metal traded in 1976. Canada exports primarily to the United States, with smaller quantities to Great Britain; Belgium to Germany, France,

---

[9]V. Anthony Cammarota, Jr., _Zinc_ (U.S. Bureau of Mines, Mineral Commodity Profiles, 12, May 1978) p. 4.

and other European countries; Australia to the United States, Iran, New
Zealand, Thailand, Taiwan, and Indonesia; Mexico to the United States
and Brazil; the Netherlands to Britain and other European countries; and
Finland to Britain, the United States, and Switzerland.

Probability of Supply Contingencies

Deliberate Disruptions. No one country is in a position to restrict
its zinc exports unilaterally without running the risk that other countries would soon replace its share of the market. This suggests that a
collective effort among the major exporters would be necessary for any
deliberate supply restriction, but the likelihood of this is low, since
Canada, Australia, and other developed countries are major exporters.
Consequently, there appears to be little possibility that world supplies
either of ore and concentrate or of refined metal will be restricted
between now and 1985 by the deliberate actions of exporting countries.

Moreover, the U.S. ore and concentrate market is to a large extent
insulated from the world market. The United States no longer imports
much ore and concentrate, and domestic production is largely carried out
by vertically integrated firms that are likely to continue shipping concentrate production to their own smelters even if a shortage should arise
abroad.

Incidental Disruptions. U.S. supplies of ore and concentrate are
not likely to be significantly affected even incidentally by political
or military actions abroad, for the reason just discussed: vertically
integrated firms produce most of the ore and concentrate consumed in
the country.

This is not true for refined zinc. Still, the prospects for political or military actions causing shortages of this material also appear
small, since the major producing countries are stable politically. An
exception of sorts is Peru. While Peru is not itself a significant exporter of refined zinc, its shipments of ore and concentrate are utilized
by smelters in Japan and Western Europe, whose production might thereby
be affected. However, Peru accounts for only about 10 percent of the
zinc ore mined outside the centrally planned countries, and an interruption

in its ore shipments, particularly if it did not last more than several
months, could probably be offset by expanded output elsewhere, so long as
demand was not for other reasons already straining available capacity.

Strikes pose another potential threat to U.S. and world zinc supplies.
However, most of the strikes in the zinc industry, like those in the lead
industry, affect the output of only one or a few plants, and rarely last
for more than a few weeks.

Demand Surges. Zinc ends up mostly in the construction, transportation, electrical, and machinery sectors, which in 1976, were responsible
for three-quarters of the zinc consumed in the United States.[10] Moreover,
the U.S. Bureau of Mines anticipates that the share of U.S. consumption
going to these four sectors will increase over the next quarter century.
Since the output of these sectors tends to fluctuate with, and more strongly than, the overall level of economic activity, this raises the possibility that a strong recovery of the business cycle, particularly if this were
to occur in a number of the major industrial countries at the same time,
could cause zinc shortages between now and 1985.

It is true that considerable capacity at both the mining and smelting
stages is now idle and could be activated to meet a surge in demand. For
example, smelter production in 1977 was only 65 percent of capacity for
the United States and 75 percent of capacity for all market economy countries combined. Mine production was 82 percent of capacity for the United
States and 75 percent of capacity for all market economy countries.[11]

By the 1980s, however, some of this capacity will have been needed to
meet the growth in demand. If one accepts our projection of a trend demand
level for refined zinc of 7.4 million tons worldwide in 1985, and 1980
world smelter capacity of 8.3 million tons, the smelter-refinery margin may
not be large enough to handle strong demand surges. Projected 1980 world
mine capacity of 8.6 million tons would constitute less of a constraint.

Natural Disasters. The number of past natural disasters that have
interrupted zinc production have been small and their impact on world

---

[10]Cammarota, Zinc, p. 15.

[11]Ibid., p. 4 (as corrected by errata sheet).

Table 9-7. Estimated Probabilities of Shortages of Zinc Mineral Commodities for U.S. Industrial Consumption Through 1985[a]

Size[b]	Less than 2 months	2-6 months	Over 6 months
Small (5-20%)			
Refined zinc	Moderate	Moderate	Moderate
Zinc ore	Nil	Nil	Nil
Medium (20-50%)			
Refined zinc	Nil	Nil	Nil
Zinc ore	Nil	Nil	Nil
Large (50-100%)			
Refined zinc	Nil	Nil	Nil
Zinc ore	Nil	Nil	Nil

[a]Approximate arithmetic equivalent of the probabilities: nil - less than 2%, small - 2-10%; moderate - 10-25%; high - over 25%.

[b]The size or magnitude of a shortage is measured in terms of gross shortfalls from the consumption rate that would otherwise have prevailed, at the price that would otherwise have prevailed, before allowance for that part of any substitute supply that responds to a price rise.

Shortages of less than 5 percent of consumption rate were considered a priori to be insignificant.

production limited. Thus, if the past is a reliable guide to the future, natural disasters do not pose a serious threat to U.S. or world zinc supplies in the near future. The wide geographic distribution of zinc mining and smelting reinforces this conclusion.

Summary. The preceding discussion suggests that a surge in demand is the most likely causative agent, if any, of a zinc shortage between now and 1985. Natural disasters, strikes, military or political upheavals, and deliberate restrictions on supplies by exporting countries either are not likely to have much impact on zinc supplies or are not likely to occur.

A strong concurrent upswing in the business cycle in the United States, Europe, and Japan seems a sufficient possibility between now and 1985 to warrant consideration. Should it occur, it would significantly stimulate the construction, transportation, electrical, and machinery sectors, which in turn would sharply increase zinc demand. Under such conditions, a small shortage of zinc metal, equivalent to between 5 and 20 percent of U.S. consumption, seems moderately possible, as indicated in table 9-7. The shortage would presumably be felt to some degree as long as strong economic conditions prevailed, which on the basis of past experience is likely to be more than 6 months.

Even if world mine capacity, contrary to our assumption, were a bottleneck which caused a world shortage of ore and concentrate, this would not necessarily mean a shortage for the United States. As pointed out earlier, most U.S. zinc mining is conducted by vertically integrated firms. Moreover, the fraction produced by independent mining firms is not likely to be exported, since to do so would in most cases entail a long and expensive overland shipment before the ore and concentrate even reached an ocean port. While imports from Canada and elsewhere might be diverted to other countries, in recent years less than 20 percent of the feed used by the country's smelters has come from abroad. Thus, a surge in demand for zinc metal could not cause much of a shortage of zinc ore and concentrate in the United States. For this reason, the probabilities of such shortages are assessed in table 9-7 as nil.